THE LATIN AMERICA READERS

Series edited by Robin Kirk and Orin Starn

THE ARGENTINA READER
Edited by Gabriela Nouzeilles and Graciela Montaldo

THE BRAZIL READER
Edited by Robert M. Levine and John J. Crocitti

THE CHILE READER
Edited by Elizabeth Quay Hutchison, Thomas Miller Klubock,
Nara Milanich, and Peter Winn

THE COLOMBIA READER
Edited by Ann Farnsworth-Alvear, Marco Palacios,
and Ana María Gómez López

THE COSTA RICA READER
Edited by Steven Palmer and Iván Molina

THE CUBA READER
Edited by Aviva Chomsky, Barry Carr, and Pamela Maria Smorkaloff

THE DOMINICAN REPUBLIC READER
Edited by Paul Roorda, Lauren Derby, and Raymundo González

THE ECUADOR READER
Edited by Carlos de la Torre and Steve Striffler

THE GUATEMALA READER
Edited by Greg Grandin, Deborah T. Levenson, and Elizabeth Oglesby

THE MEXICO READER
Edited by Gilbert M. Joseph and Timothy J. Henderson

THE PARAGUAY READER
Edited by Peter Lambert and Andrew Nickson

THE PERU READER, 2ND EDITION
Edited by Orin Starn, Iván Degregori, and Robin Kirk

THE RIO DE JANEIRO READER
Edited by Daryle Williams, Amy Chazkel, and Paulo Knauss

The Colombia Reader

THE

COLOMBIA

READER

HISTORY, CULTURE, POLITICS

Ann Farnsworth-Alvear, Marco Palacios,
and Ana María Gómez López, editors

DUKE UNIVERSITY PRESS   *Durham and London*   2017

© 2017 Duke University Press
All rights reserved
Printed in the United States of America on acid-free paper ∞
Typeset in Monotype Dante by BW&A Books, Inc.

Library of Congress Cataloging-in-Publication Data
Names: Farnsworth-Alvear, Ann, [date] editor. | Palacios, Marco, editor. |
Gómez López, Ana María, [date] editor.
Title: The Colombia reader : history, culture, politics / edited by
Ann Farnsworth-Alvear, Marco Palacios, and Ana María Gómez López.
Other titles: Latin America readers.
Description: Durham : Duke University Press, 2016. | Series: The Latin America
readers | Includes bibliographical references and index.
Identifiers:
LCCN 2016023569 (print)
LCCN 2016024534 (ebook)
ISBN 9780822362074 (hardcover : alk. paper)
ISBN 9780822362289 (pbk. : alk. paper)
ISBN 9780822373865 (e-book)
Subjects: LCSH: Colombia—History. | Colombia—Civilization. |
Colombia—Politics and government.
Classification: LCC F2258.C677 2016 (print) | LCC F2258 (ebook) |
DDC 986.1—dc 3
LC record available at https://lccn.loc.gov/2016023569

Cover art: "Fish-seller." Tumaco, Colombia, May 2016.
Photograph by Carolina Navas.

Contents

III   *City and Country*   173

IV   *Lived Inequalities*   243

V   *Violence*   323

Acknowledgments

Putting this anthology together has taken years, and it is by now impossible to accurately thank the many students, colleagues, friends, and family members who have helped us think about what to include or, more difficult, what to exclude. We owe debts beyond what we can enumerate here. Anonymous helpers lurking in translation chat-rooms, neighbors who happen to be bilingual, casual acquaintances, and sometimes passersby were all roped into the project in one way or another. More directly, the federal work-study program allowed several students at the University of Pennsylvania to be pressed into service. Special thanks go to Seth Amos, Tivan Amour, Bernardo Aparicio, Christa Avampato, Claudia Henriquez, Marco Herndon, Karla Molina, Camille Reyes, Mariantonia Rojas Cabal, Alexia Temme, and Brandi Waters. At the University of Pennsylvania, the Latin American and Latino Studies Program and the History Department provided critical support. Our greatest debt is to Valerie Millholland and Miriam Angress at Duke University Press. We also thank Heather Hensley, Isabel Rios-Torres, Silvia Serrano, Liz Smith, and Christi Stanforth, who worked to produce this volume.

Numerous professionals gave unstintingly of their expertise. We are grateful for help offered by José Alvear Sanín, Juan Pablo Ardila, Tulio Aristizábal, SJ, Andrés Castro Samoya, Migdalia Carrasquillo, Andrea Cote Botero, May Summer Farnsworth, Nancy Farriss, Luz Mary Giraldo, Viviana Goelkel, Diana Marcela Gómez, Beatríz González, Nelson González, Joseph Holub, Lina Martínez Hernández, Ricardo López, Catalina Muñoz, Juan Guillermo Múnera, Diana Milena Murcia, Eric Perramond, Javier Revelo Rebolledo, Amanda Romero Medina, Guillermo Saldarriaga, Libia Tattay Bolaños, and Luis van Isschot. Mauricio Tovar at the Archivo General de la Nación provided valuable assistance throughout the course of the project. Alexander Montoya Prada advised us with respect to the inclusion of texts by Manuel Quintín Lame. José Roca gave early constructive suggestions regarding images of contemporary Colombian artists to be included, both as a Whitney-Lauder Curatorial Fellow at the Institute of Contemporary Art in Philadelphia and as curator at the Banco de la República in Bogotá. We extend our gratitude also to Adolfo Aristizábal Taylor and Maritza Jinete Manjarres for helping us include the stamp featuring Vanessa Mendoza Bustos. A special mention is due to Harry Mantilla Vivas and Mariana Vásquez Cortes for their assistance with "photocopy runs" to the Biblioteca Luis Angel Arango and the National University of Colombia in Bogotá. Cristina Espinel and Charlie Roberts were key touchstones for consultations regarding human rights in Colombia and translation inquiries alike.

Ana María expresses her deepest gratitude to Angela and Phillip Berryman, whose warm home and enormous generosity made much of her work on this anthology possible. Ana María also thanks the entire Gómez López family, William, Dorys, and Mauricio, as well as Dorys Davidson Manning and Ruth Camacho de Gómez, for their continued help with odd translation inquiries, from outmoded cultural references to Colombian youth slang. Finally, Pamela Jordan remained an unflagging source of encouragement, patience, and humor, all of which proved vital throughout the duration of this project.

Ann thanks Jimena Alviar, Josh Block, Julie Cristol, Evelyne Laurent Perrault, Jessi Roemer, and, in Colombia, Jairo Alviar Restrepo and family, Alejandro Múnera, Fabio Andrés Saldarriaga, Lucrecia Sanín Bernal, and José Fernando Velasquéz. María Helena Saldarriaga and María Ester Sanín Bernal deserve a special *mil gracias*. Huge gratitude is due also to Salvador, Lola, and María Cristina. That Ann was able to see the project through to the end was made possible by the love and support she receives from Rui DaSilva and from our much-loved children, Kiamesso, Jorge, and Matondo.

Introduction

Colombians struggle to describe their nation in ways that will be true to a kaleidoscopic reality. Multiple generations have despaired of fratricidal cycles of violence. Criminal impunity and corruption are endemic. Deep divisions persist. Yet the country is modern, with a well-functioning financial sector, a good urban infrastructure, and a sophisticated, if unequal, health system. Colombian jurists have a reputation for thoughtfulness and innovation. The nation's libraries and museums are beacons of culture and of optimism about the nation's future. Through recent decades marked by war, Colombian artists, musicians, and writers have produced enduring works and gained an international audience.

This emphasis on multiplicity and contradiction will be familiar to many who know Colombia. The country is very regionally distinct, and our aim in part I is to introduce readers to the mental map Colombians have in their minds when they project their own lives onto the canvas of nationhood. Just as educated New Yorkers imagine themselves as living within a nation that includes the history of New England's fisheries, Mark Twain's stories about the Mississippi River, and Wyoming's wide expanses, so residents of Bogotá look eastward and know that on the other side of the mountains lie broad plains, home to a tradition analogous to that of the Argentine pampa, or the ranching land of northern Mexico, and similarly described in song and story. Bogotanos also think themselves westward, across Andean peaks sometimes visible from the city itself, still snow-topped in the present but likely to lose their snow in coming generations. Their "West" extends first toward the ports of the Magdalena River, the country's transport artery and a symbol of layered cultural forms in music and dance, and second to the Cauca River Valley and the rainforest regions of the country's Pacific lowlands. Well-read city dwellers have in their minds images created by famous writers such as José Eustacio Rivera, Jorge Isaacs, and Candelario Obeso. Similarly, families in cities such as Medellín and Cali understand their nation as including Caribbean traditions that they might experience by taking a long bus trip northward, or perhaps by reading a novel by Gabriel García Márquez, as well as an Amazonian expanse that they are more likely to see

Map of Colombia

on television or in the 2015 Oscar-nominated film by Ciro Guerra, *Embrace of the Serpent*, than to visit by flying to Colombia's southernmost region. Conversely, the geographic awareness that teachers communicate to schoolchildren in Buenaventura, a port city on the Pacific Coast, or Leticia, the regional capital of Amazonas department, is one that involves a view from the periphery toward the cities of the nation's interior—vastly different in their built environment than what people in faraway provinces or departments would find familiar.[1] Nevertheless, in the present a palpable sense of nation links Colombians to one another. Knit together by a thriving media industry and by mandated school curricula, people know that they live in a large and diverse nation.

Colombians also know that their country boasts stunning natural beauty and a system of national parks. The diversity of climates produced by the country's wide range of altitudes yields rich terrestrial, aquatic, and marine ecosystems: jungles, savannas, deserts, wetlands, and beaches, sometimes a few miles from each other, hold abundant natural resources and thousands of unique animal and plant species. Yet many of these areas have long been largely off-limits for Colombians—remote areas of the country have been sites of gruesome violence, where unmarked graves mark the extent of the country's bloodshed.

Generations of Colombians have lived with this sense that their country holds terrible dangers. For some, that has meant restrictions on their mobility; for others, it has meant that the direct threat of violence has made staying in their homes impossible. At present, more than 5.7 million Colombians—over 15 percent of the country—have been internally displaced by the country's long-standing violence, and almost four hundred thousand have been made refugees beyond the country's borders. The nation has perhaps only recently begun to recognize itself in talk of reparations for victims and for refugees, but conflict in Colombia extends far back into the country's shared memory. Like the United States and Mexico, Colombia experienced devastating mid-nineteenth-century wars, with political consequences that stretched into the twentieth century. Of these, the War of the Thousand Days (La Guerra de los Mil Días), fought between Liberals and Conservatives from 1899 to 1903, was by far the bloodiest. Twenty-five years later, a terrible labor massacre in 1928, in which soldiers sent from the interior opened fire on striking banana workers, generated long years of recriminations. The Masacre de las Bananeras serves as a symbolic historical milestone for many Colombians, and, as with the War of the Thousand Days, diverging interpretations of 1928 colored political life for decades afterward.

The 1940s and 1950s are known by the term "La Violencia," which is used to describe what amounted to an undeclared war between Liberals and Conservatives. The human cost of La Violencia was enormous, with over 250,000 dead and scores of displaced families. Scholars tend to take the assassination of Liberal presidential candidate Jorge Eliécer Gaitán on April 9, 1948, as the event that triggered twenty years of extreme bipartisan carnage. The two political parties were heterogeneous in their makeup: Conservatives included Catholics sympathetic to a Falangist view of the world as well as those closer to a nineteenth-century kind of aristocratic authoritarianism, while Liberals ranged from anticommunist anglophiles and admirers of the United States' New Deal to socialists of various stripes.

In the 1960s and 1970s, Colombian politics were thoroughly permeated by the divisions of the Cold War, although the country avoided the outright dictatorship seen in Argentina, Brazil, and Chile. Colombia remained formally democratic, with Liberals and Conservatives trading power in a famous pact called the National Front (el Frente Nacional). La Violencia did not so much end as transform itself. Large sectors of the Colombian population found themselves excluded from formal politics. For some historians, that exclusion is part of why the National Front years saw the formation of the FARC (Fuerzas Armadas Revolucionarias de Colombia) and the smaller ELN (Ejército de Liberación Nacional), along with a set of still-smaller leftist armies, such as the M-19 (Movimiento 19 de Abril) and the EPL (Ejército Popular de Liberación), who together became what Colombians raised in the 1980s and 1990s simply called *la guerrilla*.

But by the beginning of the twenty-first century, the ideological divisions of earlier generations no longer provided much ground for understanding why so much blood was being spilled in Colombia. During the 1980s, it became clear that the violence Colombians lived with was about the drug trade as much as anything else. Paramilitary groups proliferated; later, a set of these right-wing groups joined to become the United Self-Defense Forces of Colombia or Autodefensas Unidas de Colombia (AUC). Financed by mafia leaders and often working in concert with the Colombian military, the *paras*, as they came to be known, declared war on guerrilla groups and their perceived supporters. By the end of the twentieth century, all sides were getting their war chests from the United States, whether as "dirty money" earned in the drug trade or as direct military and police aid, which added up to nearly $7 billion from the US government between 2000 and 2010. Reformists hailing from many different political positions often agreed with an idea expressed by García Márquez: "The Colombian drama is such that, to be exact, it is not possible to imagine that an end will be put to drug-trafficking, without consumption being legalized." Yet international politics meant that decriminalizing drugs was not something the country could attempt on its own. Only after 2000 did a coalition of Latin American governments emerge to challenge the so-called war on drugs, with Colombian policy makers (and peace negotiators) taking a leading role.

Today, Colombians from different political backgrounds tend to agree that the high profits generated by illegal drugs made the violence of the last three decades exponentially worse. The flow of cocaine northward was met by a flow of arms southward, including pistols and assault rifles made in the United States and smuggled illegally into Colombia. Through the worst years, homicides averaged nine per day, giving Colombia the highest per capita murder rate in the world, in a context where murders were underreported. As evidence has emerged of clandestine cemeteries, especially in rural areas, the scale of such atrocities has become clearer. In Colombia, killings that occurred within the frame of guerrilla and counterinsurgency warfare have included scores of civilians, murdered by military, paramilitary, and guerrilla forces alike. In one egregious set of scandals, signaled by the phrase "false positives," hundreds of young men were killed and their corpses presented by military commanders as evidence that guerrillas had been killed in combat. Yet many deaths continue to be linked in some way to the ongoing competition among drug trafficking organizations—all of them with ties to criminal networks in the cocaine-importing economies of the United States, Europe, and Brazil.

As was true in the nineteenth century and through the 1960s, the conflicts of recent memory have hit the rural poor hardest. Most displaced Colombians are poor, as are most of those conscripted into military service—and the national army depends very heavily on conscription. Paramilitary and guerrilla organizations, too, have long depended on forced recruitment, often of minors. Families in the countryside have been torn apart by paramilitary, military, and guerrilla violence. They have supplied a disproportionate share of the rank-and-file soldiers on all sides of the war—there are few educational opportunities and few jobs in the Colombian countryside. Nor was going to the cities an option that would necessarily benefit campesinos: those who fled to urban areas often lost effective title to their land in the process—decades of war have meant decades of dispossession. And hidden within the statistics on dispossession and displacement are estimates of destruction wrought by land mines: close to ten thousand wounded and two thousand killed over the past twenty-five years. Colombian smallholders who plant and harvest still exist, and wage labor remains a possibility on large ranches and farms that produce food (as well as coffee and flowers) both for the domestic market and for export. But rural earnings are low.

Even the minority of Colombian farmers who have planted coca have failed to find a path out of poverty. Producers of leaf garner none of the high profits that smugglers of the finished product can expect from cocaine.

Like people in the countryside, those in city neighborhoods have suffered from the long decades of violence. Apart from the criminal use of "false positives," people in city neighborhoods have long been familiar with gang violence and the horrible Orwellian language of "social cleansing," used to describe death squads' attacks on homeless individuals, drug users, homosexuals, and prostitutes living in marginal neighborhoods. Colombian cities have also been the site of mafia-led violence: car bombs, explosions, and assassinations of public figures in broad daylight during the 1980s and 1990s have left memories that linger for those who live in Bogotá, Cali, and Medellín. Wealthy people and middling landowners living in these and smaller cities have also lived with the risk of kidnapping: for the better part of the last few decades, the country's kidnapping rates have remained the highest in the world.

Colombia has seen multiple attempts at peace talks and judicial mechanisms for amnesty that have generally yielded disappointing results. In 1999–2002, Colombian president Andrés Pastrana Arango attempted formal negotiations with the FARC. The failure of that process created a high level of disillusion, which helped give Pastrana's successor, Álvaro Uribe Vélez, an electoral mandate for the hardline approach that became his trademark. Praising the sacrifices made by military personnel and their families, Uribe convinced a majority of voters that an uncompromising approach toward defeating the FARC would improve their lives. The army went on the offensive, and several FARC leaders were killed in military raids that severely weakened the guerrillas. Parallel to that military push, and embracing slogans such as "Colombia Es Pasión" (Colombia Is Passion), Uribe and his government worked to increase domestic vacationing, international tourism, and foreign investment. Winning the war was conceived as a package that included state services, productivity, and leisure. Uribe's supporters praise his passion and his emphasis on security, and they credit him with "retaking" large swaths of the country.

Uribe remained popular even as evidence mounted that the Colombian Army was colluding with death squads and that he had authorized illegal surveillance and wiretapping by Colombia's DAS, or Departamento Administrativo de Seguridad (then Colombia's counterpart to the FBI). Scandals involving politicians from his administration and from political parties that supported Uribe pointed to paramilitary influence in local, regional, and national political offices. Because Uribe's opponents alleged that the presi-

Manuel María Paz, *Piedra del Aipe*, 1857. Watercolor. In the 1850s, Colombia's first geographic commission, the Comisión Corográfica, was charged with describing the nation's natural history, geography, and regional culture. Led initially by Italian cartographer Agustín Codazzi (see part VI), this group of military officers, engineers, scientists, artists, and researchers covered twelve thousand kilometers of difficult terrain, largely aided by anonymous assistants and local guides. Manuel María Paz produced this sketch of petroglyphs in southwestern Colombia, near the headwaters of the Magdalena River. These watercolors represent some of the first efforts to document pre-Columbian petroglyphs. Many such petroglyphs are visible in the present; others have been defaced or are severely deteriorated. In Agustín Codazzi, *Obras completas de la Comisión Corográfica*, vol. 2 (COAMA-Unión Europea, 2005), 218.

dent and those close to him benefited from tight links to paramilitary commanders, the way his administration managed what Colombians called the Law of Justice and Peace (Ley de Justicia y Paz)—a demobilization process that disbanded paramilitary units and allowed their "reinsertion" into Colombian society—was deeply divisive. A legal struggle ensued over whether or not paramilitary actors who had participated in massacres and crimes against humanity would face prosecution in Colombian courts.

Uribe's successor, Juan Manuel Santos Calderón, who had been Uribe's defense minister, took attempts at peace in a new direction. Breaking with his former boss, Santos put political capital into negotiating with the FARC and thus pushed Colombia toward the path traced by those countries that have produced truth commissions, official human rights reports, and systems by which those victimized by all armed groups receive reparations. One important by-product of the negotiations undertaken by the Santos administration was that Colombians as a whole were reminded of the human cost produced by generations of war. Victims' families gained a platform from which to address perpetrators of violence, although what they have come forward to say still tends to fall along the political fault lines that separate Colombians from one another. There is more recognition extended and more participation by victims in public debates, yet assassinations, forced displacement, and death threats against activists pushing for social change remain frequent.

Just how deep the political divide remains was clear in 2016. On September 26, in the port city of Cartagena, the Santos administration and the FARC signed a peace accord, rooted in the 2012 text excerpted in part VII. It had taken six years to negotiate, and the final text was almost three hundred pages long. To go forward, the 2016 accord had to be approved by Colombia's 34 million voters in a historic plebiscite. On October 2 the "yes" option lost by a very slim margin, with former president Uribe positioning himself as a leader for the "no" option. Nevertheless, President Santos was awarded the Nobel Peace Prize only days afterward. What remained unclear after the vote, however, was what the 63 percent of voters who simply did not cast ballots thought about the peace process, the accords, or the plebiscite.

But the Colombian story is not only one of war or of failed attempts at peace. As in past generations, Colombians often insist on this and demand that outsiders focus on the good. Nineteenth-century travelers who wrote about trips to Colombia emphasized the country's backwardness and its supposed lack of entrepreneurial spirit. They bemoaned the discomforts of the river steamers and mule trains that connected Colombian cities. Nevertheless, their writings also demonstrate that local people took them to see colorful markets, beautiful waterfalls, town plazas, and valuable colonial paintings. At the turn of the twentieth century, local boosters were taking better-off travelers to see carefully designed villas, new coffee plantings, perhaps a recently built electrical plant. "Don't show only the bad" became an injunction that would result in a visiting scientist, student, investor, or family member being escorted to view the good. By the 1950s, a well-connected guest might be taken to a fully outfitted country club or an efficient new factory employing thousands of neatly clad workers. In the present, local landscapes of modernity—experienced in terms of "the good"—include gleaming new supermarkets and malls, as well as city-specific markers. Medellín's centrally located Barefoot Park, for example, served by the city's above-ground Metro, symbolizes the city's comeback, allowing a wide cross-section of rich and poor to splash together in carefully policed abandon. When rich families host travelers, they have recourse to the pricey, landscaped *fincas* that ring Colombia's biggest cities. Those with less money may take visitors along on bus trips to water-based family theme parks or to provincial music festivals. Across the lines that divide them (lines of class, rural vs. urban experience, or whether or not recent violence has resulted in family tragedy), Colombians cherish whatever opportunities they have to enjoy the country's beauty and their own capacity for wholesome fun—both unequivocally components of "the good."

Thus Colombians recognize themselves in images of violence and narratives of victimization, but they also recognize themselves in the modern, consumer-centered world of the nation's cities—a world of art galleries, entertainment events, and well-stocked department stores. Representing Colombia effectively means pushing past the drug-fueled conflicts that have dominated international media reports in recent decades. In assembling a volume that traces five centuries, we have attempted to offer both breadth and depth. Each thematic part includes texts that provide a glimpse of the social structures that shaped the colonial period and the nineteenth and early twentieth centuries. Readers have the opportunity to hear voices from different generations describe culture and politics in the spaces they recognized as Colombia. These include the mule paths of the Andean highlands, the platinum-rich tributaries of the San Juan, the lowlands of the Pacific Coast, the rubber-producing Amazon, and soccer stadiums all over the world. We have included conquistadors, friars, and ex-slaves who freed themselves by running away—and who revealed little about themselves when recaptured—as well as politicians, entrepreneurs, trade unionists, soldiers, poets, and activists for indigenous rights. Throughout, we have tried to pay tribute to the creativity with which Colombians have endeavored to describe what they see before them in the layered human world of a beautiful country.

Note

1. What were at different times called "provinces" and sometimes "states" in Colombia are now departments. Designations such as "territories," "intendancies," or *comisarías* have also been used at different times for subregions that did not have the political level of departments. Additionally, the city now known as Bogotá was originally called Santa Fe, then Santafé. Because this anthology includes texts from across the centuries, readers can expect to see a variety of terms.

I

Human Geography

Boasting Andean peaks, a port on the Amazon River, and coasts along both the Atlantic and Pacific Oceans, Colombia's unique interrelation of climate, elevation, and topography creates sharply distinct regional and cultural differentiation. One way to sketch a simplified map of regions and subregions is to trace five broad areas:

1. Colombia's Caribbean: This is bisected by the Magdalena River; it extends westward to Panama and eastward to the Guajira peninsula and Venezuela.

2. The Eastern Cordillera: Known in the colonial period as El Reino (The Kingdom), this refers to a large region that coheres in cultural terms and includes Cundinamarca, Boyacá, the Santanderes, Huila, and Tolima—even though the last two are not part of the eastern mountains.

3. Oriente: The eastern grasslands, known as los Llanos, transition to the South into the Colombian Amazon. The grasslands and Amazonia are very different, but together they form a borderlands region that connects Colombia to Venezuela and the Orinoco watershed, as well as to northwestern Brazil.

4. Occidente: This complex area must be understood as a set of subregions: first, what Colombians will refer to as Greater Cauca, which includes the political departments of Cauca and Valle de Cauca and is often understood in reference to the cities of Popayán and Cali; second, a broad zone culturally bound by its having been an agricultural frontier in the late nineteenth century, including most of what are now the political departments of Antioquia, Caldas, Risaralda, and Quindío; third, the southernmost mountains, culturally rooted in an Andean indigenous experience that cuts across Colombia's borders with Ecuador and Peru.

5. The Pacific Lowlands: Colombia's long Pacific coast, from Panama to the Ecuadorian border and from the westernmost foothills of the Andes down to the sea, is associated with riches, in the form of enormous biodiversity and huge quantities of exported gold and platinum, as well as with immense poverty.

Texts in this introductory part provide glimpses of the historical, cultural, and political patterns that tie Colombian regions to a shared idea of "nation." We include extracts of well-known pieces, such as Jiménez de Quesada's chronicle of his conquest of what he named "New Granada," and José Eustasio Rivera's famous descriptions of the Colombian Amazon. Yet our geographic overview cuts in unusual directions as well—toward a cultural imaginary that stretches from attempts to recover pre-Columbian mythic spaces to New York City and the World Cup, myths in themselves.

Ahpikondiá

Gerardo Reichel-Dolmatoff

Indigenous peoples' knowledge of the rich biodiversity of Colombia's ecosystems has long enabled their cultural survival. Communities survived against violent colonial systems of control and then against development projects and natural resource exploitation in the national period. Today, eighty-five indigenous communities make up approximately 1.5 percent of the population and live in arid deserts, littoral mangrove swamps, tropical rainforests, and high-altitude grasslands. Their survival has depended on organized projects of self-affirmation and resistance, such as the political struggle that resulted in Colombia's 1991 Constitution, which officially recognizes cultural and ethnic diversity and cedes 25 percent of the country's national territory to indigenous and Afro-Colombian communities. Although its implementation is riddled with complications, this legal achievement provided official acknowledgment of land as a foundational principle for indigenous and Afro-Colombian worldviews—something activists insisted on as the Constitution was drafted.

The compilation, transcription, and publication of indigenous oral tradition began as a colonial project and has been continued by local and foreign anthropologists since the early twentieth century, and Austro-Colombian Gerardo Reichel-Dolmatoff (1912–94) has been a key figure. He became a Colombian citizen in 1942 and with his wife, Alicia Dussán, conducted pioneering ethnographic fieldwork among several indigenous groups, as well as archaeological excavations of pre-Columbian artifacts nationwide. Later generations of anthropologists have debated his legacy and his understandings. For example, his version of a Tukano narration about Ahpikondiá, which some take as an underworld paradise and others understand as the Milky Way, may reflect the interest Reichel-Dolmatoff and his generation took in creation myths more than it describes a deep cosmovision for indigenous people living along the Vaupés River. Reichel-Dolmatoff often worked in contexts where indigenous people exercised little power, as in the Vaupés, and the narrations he collected reflect cultural influences that were more diverse than he let on, given that he wrote about indigenous communities that had been targeted by missionaries and military recruiters. Ahpikondiá and other invisible geographies are by now products of modern Colombia—a nation that has an anthropological *sense of itself and that increasingly recognizes an inheritance that includes multiple creation stories.*

The Sun had created the earth with its animals and plants, but there were still no people. Now he decided to people the earth, and for this he made a man of each tribe of the Vaupés; he made a Desana and a Pira-Tapuya, a Uanano, a Tuyuka, and others, one from each tribe. Then, to send the people to the earth, the Sun made use of a being called *Pamuri-mahsë*. He was a man, a creator of people, whom the Sun sent to people the earth. *Pamuri-mahsë* was in *Ahpikondiá*, and he set forth from there in a large canoe. It was a live canoe, in reality a large snake that swam on the bottom of the river. This Snake-Canoe was called *pamuri-gahsíru*, and its skin was painted yellow and had stripes with black diamonds. On the inside, which was red, sat the people: a Desana, a Pira-Tapuya, a Uanano, one from each tribe. Together with the Snake-Canoe came the fish; but they were not in the inside but outside, in the gills; the crabs also came, attached to the rear. It was a very long journey, and the Snake-Canoe was going up the river because *Pamuri-mahsë* was going to establish mankind at the headwaters. Whenever they arrived at a large rapids, the Snake-Canoe made the waters rise in order to pass by and caused the torrent to be calm. Thus they went on for a long time, and the people became very tired.

At that time night did not yet exist, and so they traveled in the light, always under the yellow light of the Sun. When the first men set forth, the Sun had given each one something, some object, for him to carry carefully. To one of them he had given a small, black purse, closed tightly, and now, with the journey being so long, the man looked inside the purse. He did not know what was inside. He opened it, and suddenly a multitude of black ants came out of the purse, so many that they covered the light, making everything dark. This was the First Night. *Pamuri-mahsë* gave to each man a firefly in order to light his way, but the light was very weak. The ants multiplied, and the men tried to invoke them to return to the purse, but at that time they did not know about invocations. Then the Sun Father himself descended and with a stick beat the purse and made the ants enter it again. But those which did not obey remained in the forest and made their anthills. From that time on there have been ants. Once the ants were inside the purse, the light returned; but since then night has come into existence. This was the First Night, *nyamí mengá*, the Night of the Ant, and the man who had opened the purse was called *nyamíri mahsë*, Man of Night.

So they continued on in the Snake-Canoe, but when they arrived at *Ipanoré*, on the Vaupés River, they struck against a large rock near the bank.

The people went ashore because they were tired of the long journey and thought that they had already reached their destination. They left by way of an opening at the prow of the canoe. *Pamurí-mahsë* did not want them to disembark there because he was thinking of taking them to the headwaters of the rivers, and therefore he stopped up the opening with his foot. But the people had already got out, having rushed from the Snake-Canoe; they were dispersing throughout the rivers and the forests. But before they got away, *Pamurí-mahsë* gave each one of them the objects they had brought from *Ahpikondiá* and that, from then on, were going to indicate the future activities of each tribe. He gave a bow and arrow to the Desana; to the Tukano, the Pira-Tapuya, Vaiyára, and the Neéroa he gave a fishing rod; to the Kuripáko he gave the manioc grater; he gave a blowgun and a basket to the Makú and a mask of barkcloth to the Cubeo. He gave a loincloth to each one, but to the Desana he gave only a piece of string. He pointed out the places where each tribe should live, but when he was about to indicate the future home of the Desana, this one had fled to seek refuge at the headwaters. The Uanano had also gone and went up to the clouds in the sky. Then *Pamurí-mahsë* entered the Snake-Canoe again and returned to *Ahpikondiá*.

The Sun created the various beings so that they would represent him and serve as intermediaries between him and the earth. To these beings he gave the duty of caring for and protecting his Creation and of promoting the fertility of life.

First the Sun created *Emëkóri-mahsë* and *Diroá-mahsë* and put them in the sky and in the rivers so that, from there, they could protect the world. *Emëkóri-mahsë* is the Being of Day, and his job is to set down all the norms, the rules, and the laws according to which the spiritual life of human beings should develop. *Diroá-mahsë*, who is the Being of Blood, is in charge of all that is corporeal, all that is connected with health and the good life. Then he created *Vihó-mahsë*, the Being of *Vihó*, the hallucinogenic powder, and ordered him to serve as an intermediary so that through hallucinations people could put themselves in contact with all the other supernatural beings. The powder of *vihó* itself had belonged to the Sun who had kept it hidden in his navel, but the Daughter of the Sun had scratched his navel and had found the powder. While *Emëkóri-mahsë* and *Diroá-mahsë* always represent the principle of good, the Sun gave *Vihó-mahsë* the power of being good and evil and put him in the Milky Way as the owner of sickness and witchcraft.

Then the Sun created *Vaí-mahsë*, the Master of Animals. There are two beings called *Vaí-mahsë*, one for the animals of the forest and the other for the fish. The Sun assigned to each one the places where he ought to live; one was given a large maloca inside the rocky hills of the forest, and the other a large maloca at the bottom of the waters of the rapids. He put them there so that they could watch over the animals and their multiplication. Together with the *Vaí-mahsë* of the waters, the Sun put *Vaí-bogó*, the Mother of Fish. The Sun also created *Wuá*, the Owner of Thatch, the owner of the palm leaves that are used to make the roofs of the malocas.

Then the Sun created *Nyamikëri-mahsë*, the Night People, and put them in the Dark Region to the west of *Ahpikondiá*. To them he gave the job of serving as intermediaries for witchcraft and sorcery, because the Sun did not create only the principle of good but also of evil, to punish mankind when it did not follow the customs of tradition.

Then the Sun created the jaguar so that he would represent him in this world. He gave him the color of his power and gave him the voice of thunder that is the voice of the Sun; he entrusted him to watch over his Creation and to protect it and take care of it, especially of the malocas. The Sun created all these beings so that there would be life in this world.

Photographs of Indigenous People

Gerardo Reichel-Dolmatoff

An important part of Reichel-Dolmatoff's legacy is found in his published photographs of indigenous people. For communities in the present, grandparents or great-grandparents are sometimes recognizable in such images, and activists today have a complicated relationship with the visual record left by anthropologists. On the one hand, a beautiful and enduring image may be one way to document the skills and autonomy of previous generations. On the other, these are photographs that testify to the power of the outsider. An indigenous person might or might not have given permission for an image to be circulated, and they might or might not have been credited by name in any given publication.

In the current generation, indigenous activists in Colombia are sophisticated about the political implications of self-representation. They mobilize resources to produce photography, television segments, and documentaries that would have been impossible to create a generation ago. A minority group of professionally trained indigenous people work as anthropologists, writers, photographers, videographers, and documentary filmmakers. They struggle to create representations that respond to a community's sense of itself, but they are aware that heterogeneous viewpoints within their own communities make that a complex project. One example among various is the work of the Zigoneshi Communications Collective in the region of the Sierra Nevada de Santa Marta, which has produced work addressing political autonomy, guerrilla violence, and the threat that global warming poses to the snowy peaks of their home region, the Sierra Nevada de Santa Marta—some of it available via the Internet. Much has changed since Reichel-Dolmatoff took the pictures reproduced here, but much has not. Finding ways to convey the political urgency of indigenous people's struggles to retain autonomy remains a challenge, even if it is now taken up in new ways.

Reichel-Dolmatoff's photographs can be taken as tokens both of anthropological understanding and of misunderstanding, especially in the way that images he published alongside his written descriptions of indigenous life have circulated to a broad international audience. People around the world know more about indigenous cultures because of his anthropological work, but sometimes the way a scrap of knowl-

edge is framed means that outsiders feel they understand more than perhaps they do. For example, when urbanites read a description of the use an indigenous group makes of a psychoactive plant, whether Erythroxylum novogranatense *(a species of coca) or* Banisteriopsis caapi *(used to prepare the hallucinogenic tea known as* ayahuasca *or* yagé*), they may jump to unwarranted conclusions. Similarly, when a photograph's caption describes a person as "Tukano," the viewer may imagine that as a clearly demarcated ethnicity within the geographic space of the Colombian Amazon, which would be an error. In this region, language exogamy structured traditional social life: that is, for generations people took marriage partners from communities that spoke a language different from their paternal one (and children grew up in multilingual family contexts). Tukano was thus a language spoken in contexts where multilingualism was more the norm than an ethnic label as such. In Reichel-Dolmatoff's photograph of women he identifies as "Guajiro," and for whom others would use the term "Wayúu," there is also a slipperiness as to what viewers learn from the image and from his caption. The anthropologist was on the Guajira peninsula, part of Colombia's northernmost coastline, in the context of research done not only by him but also by his wife, Alicia Dussán de Reichel, a researcher in her own right, and by Virginia Gutiérrez de Pineda. Reichel's inclusion of a gender perspective in his caption for the image included here may owe a lot to the work done by Dussán, Gutiérrez, and a select group of other women researchers who traveled to the peninsula in the 1940s and 1950s and carefully collected data to demonstrate the relative egalitarianism of Wayúu groups. Did the presence of women fieldworkers shape the way the seated women appear in the photograph? Scholars and cultural critics are only beginning to understand the complexity involved in mid-twentieth-century representations of indigenous life.*

Tukano artisan from Vaupés, in the Colombian Amazon, ca. 1968. Photograph by
Gerardo Reichel-Dolmatoff. Available at ICANH, Biblioteca Luis Ángel Arango.
Courtesy of Banco de la República.

Women from Wayúu communities (northeastern Colombia, Atlantic Coast region),
ca. 1953. Photograph by Gerardo Reichel-Dolmatoff. Reichel-Dolmatoff included
this photograph in a 1991 collection with a caption that identified these communities
as matrilineal groups of herders and described the "Guajiros," a term used for the
Wayúu, as among the most numerous and dynamic indigenous groups in Colombia.
Available at ICANH, Biblioteca Luis Ángel Arango. Courtesy of Banco de la República.

A Kogi man in the Sierra Nevada de Santa Marta (northwestern Colombia, Atlantic Coast region), ca. 1977. Photograph by Gerardo Reichel-Dolmatoff. With this image, Reichel-Dolmatoff included the explanation that the man is chewing coca leaves and is placing in his mouth a small quantity of powdered lime to extract stimulant from the leaf. This way of consuming coca stretches back millennia. It produces a mild effect, reducing hunger and fatigue. It is not cocaine (see part VI). Available at ICANH, Biblioteca Luis Ángel Arango. Courtesy of Banco de la República.

"One after the Other, They All Fell under Your Majesty's Rule": Lands Loyal to the Bogotá Become New Granada

Gonzalo Jiménez de Quesada and Anonymous

In 1536 Colombia's most important river, the Magdalena, may have been known as the Yuma, Guacahayo, Manúkaka, or Kariguañá, among other names, by people living at different points along its banks. But for the conquistador Jiménez de Quesada, setting off upriver in search of treasure and the chance to claim land for the Spanish Crown, the region's massive artery was the Río Grande, as it was called by Spanish soldiers living in the garrison town of Santa Marta, a precarious coastal settlement founded eleven years previously as a stopping-off place for Spanish ships.

Jiménez arrived as part of an expedition, organized by Pedro Fernández de Lugo, that included at least ten ships and more than a thousand people (including European men, some European women, a small number of enslaved African men, and perhaps a few enslaved African women as well). After some initial excursions near Santa Marta itself brought back gold—often obtained by pillaging and burning Indian settlements and then sorting through the ashes—and after Lugo's son had departed for Spain with an initial cargo of loot, Jiménez was sent on a military expedition that resulted in the subjugation of the Muisca people and spectacular gains for the Europeans involved. Historians' estimates suggest that the gold and emeralds Jiménez's troops looted from the highland areas of central Colombia made this perhaps the second most profitable expedition of the sixteenth century, after Francisco Pizarro's exploits in Peru.

The documents translated here include some of the best descriptions historians have of these highland towns—which owed allegiance to the caciques of Tunja, Sogamoso, Chía, and, principally, Bogotá. The man Jiménez encountered as "the Bogotá" was killed under mysterious circumstances—perhaps by Spaniards unaware of his status. The Europeans thought his successor, identified in the documents as Sagipa, was holding back gold: Jiménez had him tortured and killed.

Excerpts from the "Epítome del Nuevo Reino de Granada"

Between the provinces of Santa Marta and Cartagena flows a river that divides the two provinces; they call it the Magdalena River. However, it is more commonly referred to as the Río Grande, because in truth, this river is very grand indeed. The fury and violence with which it crashes into the sea is so great that it pushes fresh water one league into the sea. . . .

In the month of April of the year 1536, Gonzalo Jiménez de Quesada, who at present is Mariscal [Marshall] of this New Kingdom, departed from the coastal city of Santa Marta to explore the Río Grande. He took with him six hundred soldiers, divided into eight infantry companies, as well as one hundred horsemen. Furthermore, certain brigs were dispatched to pursue Jiménez and his men upriver, and to offer assistance to those traveling overland along the river's edge. . . . The brigs returned to the sea. However, most of the crew, and the brigs' captains remained with Jiménez, as partial replacements for the large numbers of Jiménez's men who had died on the expedition. Jiménez spent many days in the discovery of the Opón Mountains, which extend fifty leagues, across rough, mountainous terrain, sparsely populated by Indians. It was with enormous difficulty that Jiménez crossed them. . . .

One might say with some certainty that this New Kingdom of Granada, which begins just beyond the Opón Mountains, is completely flat and densely populated. Its inhabitants are settled in valleys, with each valley supporting its own population. These plains and the entire New Kingdom are surrounded and enclosed by mountains and hills, which are inhabited by a certain group of Indians, called Panches. These Panches consume human flesh, and they are different from those in the New Kingdom, who do not. The climate in Panche territory also is different; it is a torrid zone, whereas the New Kingdom boasts a frigid climate, or at least a temperate one. And just as that group of Indians carries the name Panches, the Indians from the New Kingdom are a different people and thus have a different name; they are called Moxcas [Muiscas]. This New Kingdom is 130 leagues in length more or less, and perhaps 30 wide; however, in some places it narrows to just 20 or even less. Most of the region is found five degrees from the Equinoctial line, although some of it falls at four, and still other parts are at three. This New Kingdom is divided into two parts, or rather, two

nator,quod ille,qui nouo Granatæ regno deprædabatur, eum
deprædationum,& cædium focium admittere nollet,inquifiti-
ones & probationes,multis teftibus confirmatas confecit, quibus probat cædes,& homicidia,quæ ille commifit,& in quibus
committendis vfq; in præfentem diem perfeuerat,quæ in Con-
filio Indiæ lectæ funt,& hodie adhuc afferuantur.
    In dicta inquifitione teftes deponunt,cum omnia hæc re-

Theodor de Bry, *Torture of Bogotá*, from a drawing by Joost van de Wighe. Engraving to
accompany a 1598 edition of Bartolomé de las Casas's *Short Description of the Destruction
of the Indies*. Courtesy of the John Carter Brown Library.

provinces. One is called Bogotá, while the other is called Tunja; and the lords of [these respective provinces] adopt these titles as their surnames. Both lords are extremely powerful, and each one rules over other great lords and caciques. The province of Bogotá is larger, and its lord more powerful than Tunja; in my opinion, the lord of Bogotá is capable of sending sixty thousand men, more or less, into battle. And here I offer a conservative estimate; others would suggest a much higher number. The lord Tunja is able to send forty thousand; but again, this figure likely is conservative and it does not conform to the opinion of others. These lords and the people of both provinces always have had their differences. Thus, from time immemorial the Indians from Bogotá and those from Tunja have been engaged in constant warfare, especially those from Bogotá. The reason for that is because they also fight against the Panches, who are much closer to Bogotá than they are to Tunja. As we already have mentioned, the Panches have the province of Bogotá surrounded.

The soil in Tunja is richer than the land in Bogotá, although the latter also is highly productive. And the best gold and precious emerald stones are always found in Tunja. . . . As far as emeralds are concerned, far greater quantities were found in this New Kingdom than were discovered during the conquest of Peru; not only that, but it has been said that never, since the creation of the world, have so many been found in one place. When it came time to divide the shares among the soldiers after the Conquest was completed, they distributed among themselves more than seven thousand emeralds, including some very rich stones of great value. And this is one of the reasons why the discovery of this New Kingdom must be considered the greatest thing to have happened in all the Indies; we know of no other Christian Prince, nor infidel, who possesses what has been discovered in this New Kingdom, and this in spite of the fact that for so long the Indians tried to keep the location of the mines a secret. . . .

As far as the conquest itself is concerned, when the Christians entered that New Kingdom, the native people received them with great fear; in fact, so great was their fear that they believed that the Christians were children of the sun and the moon whom these Indians worshipped. The Indians claim that, as man and wife, the sun and the moon have sexual relations and that the Christians were their offspring, whom the sun and moon sent from the sky in order to punish the Indians for their sins. For that reason, they called the Spaniards *uchies,* a term composed from the word *usa,* which in their language means "sun," and the word *chia,* which means "moon." Put together, the term means "children of the sun and moon." Thus, when the Christians entered into the first towns of the New Kingdom, the inhabitants abandoned their settlements, and climbed to the top of the nearby mountains. From there, they cast their newborn children over the edge for the Spaniards to eat, thinking that this act would appease the anger of the men whom they believed had come from the sky.

But more than anything else, the Indians feared horses; so great was this fear that it is difficult even to imagine. Nevertheless, as best they possibly could, the Spaniards behaved in a most friendly manner, trying to make the Indians understand their peaceful intentions; and thus, little by little their fears began to subside. And when the Indians realized that the Christians were just men, like them, they decided to test their fortune against them, which they did when the Christians were in the province of Bogotá, deep inside the New Kingdom. There, the Indians came out to meet them in battle, marching forward with great order and discipline. However, despite their numbers, which we mentioned above, they were easily defeated. When they saw the horses galloping toward them, so great was their fright that they all turned their backs and ran. The same thing occurred in the province of Tunja. For that reason, it is not necessary to provide specific accounts of each military encounter or skirmish that the Christians have had with those barbarians. Suffice it to say that most of the year 1537 and part of 1538 was spent in subjugating them, some through peaceful methods, and others through necessary force. In the end, the two provinces of Tunja and Bogotá were left well subjugated, and the Indians firmly under the just obedience that is owed to Your Majesty.

The nation and province of the Panches was left equally subjugated, in spite of the fact that the Panches are a more indomitable and tougher people than the Moxcas. And not only are they more valiant, but they also are aided by the difficult terrain in which they reside, which consists of densely forested and rough mountains, where it was not possible take advantage of the horses. For those reasons, the Panches believed that they would not suffer the same fate as that which had befallen their neighbors; however, they thought wrong. What happened to them was precisely the same; and one after the other, they all fell under Your Majesty's rule. . . .

As previously mentioned, this territory boasts a frigid climate; however, it is such a mild cold that it is not a great bother or discomfort; nor does it take anything away from the marvelous splendor of this land when one first enters into it. . . .

In spite of the fact that their houses and buildings are made from wood and are covered in the long thatch that is native to that region, they still reflect the most marvelous workmanship and design ever seen. This is especially true of the private residences of the caciques and principal men, which are like palaces, encircled by many walls. These palaces look similar to the manner in which the Labyrinth of Troy is portrayed in paintings here in Spain. The houses boast great patios, with very tall relief figurative carvings throughout; and they are also filled with paintings. . . .

These Indians divide time into months and years, and do so with very specific intent. During the first ten days of each month they consume a certain herb, which the Indians along the northern coast call *hayo* [coca leaf]. They devote the following ten days to their crops and to domestic tasks. The final ten days that remain in each month are spent inside their houses, where they converse with their wives and take their pleasure with them. Men and women do not share the same room; rather, the women all share one room while the man sleeps in the other. The manner in which the months are divided is done differently in some parts of the New Kingdom, where the Indians increase the time and the number of days they dedicate to each one [of the above-mentioned activities]. . . .

In terms of the religion of these Indians, I say that in their false and mistaken ways, they are deeply religious. In addition to each town having its own temples, which the Spaniards there call sanctuaries, they also have a great many temples outside their towns; and they have built numerous roads and paths that extend from their towns and lead directly to those very temples. Furthermore, they have an infinite number of hermitages in the mountains, along the roads and in different parts of the kingdom. And all of these houses of worship contain great quantities of gold and emeralds. . . .

In their false religion, they have many consecrated forests and lakes, where they would not dare to cut a tree or take a drop of water for anything in the world. They go into these forests to perform their sacrifices, and they bury gold and emeralds in them. And they are most certain that no person would touch their offerings because they all believe that anyone who tampers with such offerings would then fall dead. The same can be said of the lakes that they have dedicated for their sacrifices: they go and toss in great quantities of gold and precious stones, which remain lost forever. These Indians consider the sun and the moon as the creators of all things, and they believe that the two united as husband and wife, and that they engage in sexual relations. In addition to that belief, they also possess a great number of idols, which they worship in the same way that we worship our saints here [in Spain]. They pray to these idols, asking them to intercede on their behalf before the sun and the moon. And thus, each one of their sanctuaries or temples is dedicated to the name of one of these idols. In addition to the idols in the temples, every Indian, no matter how poor, has his own idol, or two, or three, or more. These idols are exactly the same as the ones possessed by the Gentiles in their time, which were called lares. These house-hold idols are made from very fine gold; and in a hole in the idol's belly they place many emeralds, in accordance with the wealth of the idol's owner. If the Indian is too poor to have a gold idol in his house, he has one made out of wood; he also places as much gold and as many emeralds as he is able into the hole in the idol's belly. These domestic idols are small in size; the largest ones are roughly the same length as the distance between the hand and the elbow. And their devotion to these idols is so strong that they do not go anywhere, whether it is to work their fields, or to any other place, at any time, without them. They carry their idols in a small basket, which hangs from their arms. And what is most alarming is that they even carry them to war as well; with one arm they fight and with the other they hold their idol. This is especially true in the province of Tunja, where the Indians are deeply religious.

In terms of burial practices, the Indians inter the dead in two different ways. They bind the corpses tightly in cloth, having first removed the intes-tines and the rest of their insides. Then they fill the empty stomachs with gold and emeralds. They also place much gold around the corpse and on top of it, before tightly wrapping the entire corpse in cloth. They build a type of large bed, which sits just above the ground inside certain sanctuaries, which are used only for that purpose, and are dedicated to the deceased. They then place the corpses there and leave them on top of those beds, without ever burying them; this practice later proved to be of no small benefit to the Spaniards. . . .

In the land and nation of the Panche, which surrounds this New King-dom, there is very little about their religion and moral life that is worth relating because they are such a bestial people that they do not worship or believe in anything but their own wicked acts and vices. Nor do they respect any rules or norms whatsoever. The Panches are a people who re-fuse to exchange their gold, or anything else for that matter, unless it is for something they can eat and from which they can take pleasure; they are especially willing to trade if it allows them to acquire human flesh to eat, which is their greatest vice. . . .

Excerpt from the Anonymous "Relación de Santa Marta" (ca. 1545)

From the emerald mines, Captain Valenzuela returned to camp bringing with him three or four valuable stones that the Indians had presented him. The camp was located at Turmequé, and while there, Jiménez sent some captains, led by Captain Cardoso, to launch an assault. They captured a number of Indians, two of whom promised Cardoso that they would take him to the great cacique Tunja. They claimed that Tunja possessed three houses filled with gold, and that the support posts on the houses were all made of gold. Therefore, the Christians decided to go there. The Indian guides led them through many towns, and a journey that should have taken no more than one day turned into a fourteen-day expedition. When they approached Tunja, they marched forward at great speed. At sunset, they arrived to where the lord Tunja lived, and they took the cacique captive. The lieutenant Jiménez dismounted, followed by Captain Céspedes and several other captains. Captain Cardoso remained on horseback, apprehensive of all the people they saw gathering. Those who dismounted from their horses rushed the cacique, and all the gold and emerald stones they found, out of harm's way. In the meantime, Captain Cardoso and his men patrolled around the lord Tunja's fenced houses. It took until the early hours of the morning to gather all the gold, emerald stones, beads, and fine mantas. The Christians seized a great quantity of everything, especially clothing, which was of very fine quality. During the entire night, they heard great murmurs and mutterings that the Indians were about to riot. A scuffle ensued shortly before daybreak, and some Indian allies perished while defending lord Tunja and Captain Cardoso. Exhausted, and frightened by the sight of the Indians they had killed, the Spaniards stopped fighting. Captain Cardoso dismounted, and placed guards on sentry duty in order to prevent the Indians from attacking again.

That night the Christians seized close to 180,000 pesos of fine and low-grade gold, as well as a great number of emeralds. The sun had not been up for three hours when another group of Indians attacked; however, having placed sentries on duty, and being well rested from the night before, the Christians quickly mounted their horses and rode against the Indians, forcing their retreat. With the fighting ended, the Christians began to negotiate with the cacique Tunja, informing him that they had heard reports that he possessed a great quantity of gold. And the Christians promised that they would release him and be his friend and ally if the cacique gave them the gold. Tunja promised to deliver it, but he brought only false promises. At times he would say that certain Indians had taken the gold and had hidden it in the mountains. At other times, he claimed that he had buried it himself, making the Christians dig holes around many of his residences; but they never found a thing. Seeing this, the Christians decided to move against another cacique, who resided eight or nine leagues away from Tunja. His name was Sogamoso, and it was rumored that he possessed a great quantity of gold. However, Sogamoso did not await their arrival and instead fled. In

Sogamoso's sanctuaries, the Christians discovered upward of thirty thousand pesos of gold in precious objects, fashioned in the shapes of eagles and crowns which Sogamoso had offered to his *tunxos*, or gods. They found other jewels of various kinds, gold *texuelos*, and some gold leaf worth about ten marcs. And they found some emeralds, some beads, and some fine mantas. At a nearby mountain, they had a brief skirmish with some Indians. From there the Christians returned to Tunja, where they remained for several days. While in Tunja, a neighboring cacique, himself a great lord and valiant warrior, sent some of his Indians to warn the Christians that he intended to kill them all, and make shields from the skins of their horses, and use their teeth to make necklaces for his women. And when the Christians least expected it, a large number of his Indians launched a surprise attack. A battle ensued, and the Indians were routed; a great number of Indians died there.

For weapons, the Indians carried very strong palm spears, some thirty and thirty-five hands in length. And they wielded *macanas*, which are like swords. They also used arrows from the same palm, and some carried shields. With great order and discipline they arrived and waited in the open battlefield; but they all fled at the first sight of the carnage inflicted upon them by the Christians.

Several days after the battle occurred, and in order to convince the Christians to leave their territory, the Indians told stories of a land called Neiva, located toward Quito, in which there was a great quantity of gold. The Indians spoke of a house that was filled with gold trinkets, and the same house had support posts made entirely from gold. The reports filled the Christians with a great desire to go there. Jiménez thus appointed Captain San Martín, Captain Céspedes, Captain Cardoso, Captain Lebrija, Captain Albarrazín, Captain Suárez, and several other Spaniards to accompany him to Neiva.

Jiménez left his brother Hernán Pérez de Quesada, as well as Captain Juan del Junco, in charge to guard the camp and all the gold, and he departed with the abovementioned people toward Neiva. They arrived in the land of Bogotá and from there they made their way to the town of Pasca. There the Indians from Pasca showed them which path to take, which they knew well because they carry salt to Neiva, which they exchange for gold. The Christians also learned in Pasca that the road to Neiva crossed through vast, uninhabited lands, and that there would be no place to procure foodstuffs except for one small village, which stored nothing but potatoes. Therefore, the Christians gathered their provisions in Pasca, with supplies of bread, dried meat, and maize; they also brought four hundred Indian men and women carriers, each loaded with food and provisions. They endured many hardships on this expedition. At long last they arrived in Neiva, where they found absolutely nothing of which the Indians had spoken. . . .

This land is very unhealthy; in the little time that the Christians roamed around in its heat, not a single man remained who had not fallen ill. One soldier died, and many others would have if they had lingered any longer. Thus they all returned to Bogotá, and from there they journeyed to Tunja, where they remained for several days, trying to make peace with the local caciques. From there, the entire camp returned to Bogotá, where they began to establish friendships with certain caciques.

The cacique Suba Usaque came to the Christians as a great friend and ally, and his loyalty never wavered. The reason for this friendship was: Suba Usaque's son-in-law, the cacique Bogotá, learned that Suba Usaque earlier had gone to see the Christians and had given them food and other things. And because Bogotá was a more powerful lord than his father-in-law, he had Suba Usaque arrested, many of his houses burned, and large numbers of his Indians executed. He also stole some of his gold. For that reason, Suba Usaque later became a close ally to the Christians, and he has remained a loyal friend.

With matters thus, the Christians learned where Bogotá was hiding, which was high in a mountain where the cacique had built some houses, protected by surrounding walls. The Christians decided one night to go out to capture him. They left the camp where it was, and they approached to within three leagues of Bogotá's location. From there, the Christians dispatched messengers in order to assure Bogotá that they did not want to wage war against him; rather, they wanted to make peace. And they requested that the cacique issue a response by the following day because they could wait no longer. Bogotá sent neither messenger nor message of any kind. Thus, on the following day, the Christians seized all of the Indian men and women who served Bogotá. They left these Indians in their lodgings, with their hands and feet tied. There they remained until past nightfall, tightly bound so that none of them could escape to warn Bogotá or anyone else for that matter. The Christians departed at 10:00 in the evening, silently, so as not to be heard. One or two hours before sunrise they arrived at Bogotá's enclosure. There they placed soldiers and horsemen around the outside walls so that no one could escape without being captured. Lieutenant Jiménez and many others rushed inside and seized some Indians. Many others escaped. It was learned later that Bogotá managed to flee through a trap door. As fortune would have it, two horsemen and two foot soldiers happened to be guarding Bogotá's escape route. In their great lust to steal the rich manta that Bogotá was wearing, the soldiers stabbed the cacique with a knife. And after taking his manta, they let the injured Bogotá go free; later, the soldiers falsely claimed that not a single Indian had passed through the area where they had stood guard.

And that was how the cacique was injured, there on the mountain, very close to where he died. No one knew until his body was discovered by some birds, called *gallinas* [presumably *gallinazos*, or turkey vultures], which eat human flesh. The Indians watched as those birds gathered in that place to feast; and because they could not locate Bogotá, they followed the birds, suspecting what they would find. There they discovered his corpse. However, the Christians did not learn of his death for another year, and they thought he was still alive.

From there, the Christians returned to where they had left the Indians bound, but they had all escaped, having been untied by other Indians from the area. From there, they sent a message back to camp to have the others join them. After several months, they learned of Bogotá's death. They also discovered that one of Bogotá's great captains, called Sagipa, had risen up and usurped control of the land. With all kinds of flattery and affection, the Christians endeavored to lure Sagipa to come forward and make peace; and after a few months he came to them. He told them that he was at war with the Panches, a fierce people who eat human flesh, and he requested Jiménez's assistance to go to Panche territory to kill them. If the Christians agreed to help, then he would be their friend, and he would accompany them. Lieutenant Jiménez accepted, and the Christians joined Sagipa. Together, they engaged the Panches in battle and killed many of them. They all then returned to where they had camped. Sagipa proceeded to flee from the Christians, moving stealthily about the region. The Christians therefore decided to take matters into their own hands, and they had Sagipa arrested. They marched over to where he was and, somewhat against his will, they brought the cacique back to camp. On his arrival, Lieutenant Jiménez spoke to him on behalf of the entire camp, telling him that Bogotá was an enemy of the Christians, and as their enemy he had died. Therefore, all of Bogotá's gold, as it was enemy property, belonged to the king and to the Christians. Jiménez ordered Sagipa to hand the gold over, because they knew for certain that he had it. The lieutenant added that he was not asking Sagipa to relinquish any of his own possessions; instead, the Christians only wanted what had belonged to Bogotá. Sagipa responded that he would, with great pleasure, give them the gold. He asked them to extend him a reasonable deadline in order to do so, promising that he would fill a small house with Bogotá's gold; but he needed a few days in order to gather all the gold. They granted the time that Sagipa had requested; and they kept him under guard in order to prevent him from escaping. During that time, Indian messengers came and went, but when the deadline expired Sagipa had not complied. He handed over three or four thousand pesos of fine and low-grade gold, and nothing more. Seeing this, the Christians began to plead with Lieutenant Jiménez to place Sagipa in irons and have him tortured. The lieutenant chose not to do that, which sparked many grumblings that Jiménez had reached some accord with the cacique. Thus, the Christians all came together and renewed their pleas, granting legal authority to Jerónimo de Ayusa to argue their case. Seeing this, Jiménez appointed his brother, Hernán Pérez de Quesada, who was administered the oath as Sagipa's defender. Both Ayusa and Pérez de Quesada argued their cases as best they possibly could, after which point the Christians proceeded to torture Sagipa in order to compel him to hand over Bogotá's gold and confess where he had hidden it; in the end, Sagipa died.

A City in the African Diaspora

Anonymous and Álvaro José Arroyo

For centuries, enslaved Africans were sold at auction in the port city of Cartagena. Some arrived there directly, having been taken on board at slaving ports along the African coast after sale or capture near Senegambia or the Bight of Benin or Luanda. Others entered Cartagena as survivors of a second slaver voyage: having been sold in one port, they were now "pieces" to be resold to Colombian buyers.

The following two texts present strikingly different perspectives on the colonial history of Cartagena. The first is a document recording the sale of a thirteen-year-old girl on January 26, 1736. Its power lies in the banality it evinces. By 1736, notaries in Cartagena were using preprinted forms, with spaces left blank for buyers' and sellers' names to be written in, and with a large space in the left margin for the notary to sketch the shape of the brands that appeared on a given person's body—even the locations of the brands applied, the right breast and left shoulder, were preprinted to save a notary time. The second text is a 1983 hit by salsa great Álvaro José "Joe" Arroyo (1955–2011), iconic in Colombia for his musicianship and for his politicized lyrics. The lyrics to "Rebelión" conjured history in Arroyo's present—Africans arrive in Cartagena to "perpetual slavery." The song's chorus, "No le pegue a la negra," "Don't hit that black woman," became a touchstone of racial identity for Colombians.

Arroyo's lyrics reference local oral tradition, something that a girl sold at auction even as far back as 1736 would have encountered for herself as she became a part of colonial Cartagena's multiple black communities. By the time of her arrival, Africans and their descendants in Cartagena already told stories about the Spanish Jesuits Alonso de Sandoval, who baptized slaves in the early 1600s, and Pedro Claver, trained by Sandoval, who would be declared a Catholic saint in 1888. Enslaved people likely described Claver's famous slave-ship baptisms to one another (see part II). Other stories, or many conflicting stories, would have circulated about a man known as Benkos Biohó, who led the longest-lived of the many palenques, or communities of escaped slaves, near Cartagena (see part IV).

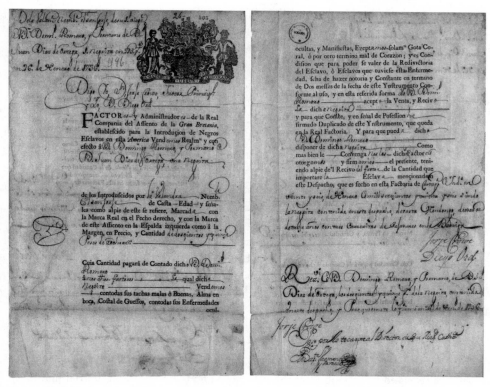

Facsimile, Bill of Sale, 1736. Tomo 8, Folio 505R, Colonial Folio, Archivo General de la Nación.
http://negrosyesclavos.archivogeneral.gov.co/portal/resources/files/archivos/f505r.jpg. Courtesy
of Archivo General de la Nación de Colombia.

The Principal *Factor* of the Royal Company of the *Asiento* of Great Britain
sells a black girl, fifteen years old, for 215 pesos to Don Domingo Romero.[1]

From the vessel named the Saint George, on its first voyage, Don Domingo Romero received from the hand of Juan Diaz de Ortega, 1 black girl
for 215 pesos.

On January 26, 1736, I, Jorge Crove, Principal *Factor*, and I, Don Diego
Ord, *Factors* and Administrators of the Royal Company of the *Asiento* of
Great Britain, established to introduce Black Slaves to this America, do
Lawfully and with immediate effect Sell to Don Domingo Romero, from
the hand of Don Juan Díaz de Ortega, a black girl Brought by the vessel
called the Saint George, of Caste _____, Age _____, and markings referred
to below: bearing the Royal Mark on her right breast and the Mark of this
Asiento on the left side of her back, as shown in the Margin; for the price and
quantity of two hundred and fifteen pesos of eight reales.

Said sum will be paid in full by the aforesaid Don Domingo Romero, to us, Aforesaid *factores* _____, who sell the aforesaid black girl with all of her qualities, bad or good, Soul in mouth, Bag of bones; with all her Illnesses, hidden and Manifest, with the sole exception of *Gota Coral*, or by another name heart disease.[2] In order to validate a Slave Warranty for slaves that have this illness, it is a Condition that official notice and documentation be Provided within two months from the date agreed in this instrument, and it is in this stated manner that I, Don Domingo Romero, accept the sale, and receive the aforementioned black girl, and in proof and confirmation of this possession I have signed a duplicate of this instrument, which will remain in the Royal *Factoría*. And in order for the aforesaid Don Domingo Romero to dispose of said black girl as he sees fit, we the aforesaid *factores* concede to and sign this document, the *Factor* having received the amount for the import of the slave mentioned herein, held in this *Factoría* of Cartagena of Indies on January 26, 1736, being the black girl included in this deed of sale, of Mondongo caste, thirteen years of age,[3] with three incisions running parallel along the skin on her stomach,

[Signed]
Jorge Crove
Diego Ord

I received from Don Domingo Romero and from the hand of Don Juan Díaz de Ortega two hundred and fifteen pesos for the little black girl, and have signed in confirmation of this on January 26, 1736.

[Signed]
Jorge Crove

Translated by Ana María Gómez López

Joe Arroyo's "Rebelión"

Brother, I want to sing you a little piece of black history,
Of our history,
Sir, it goes like this:
In the 1600s, when the tyrant ruled,
Cartagena's streets lived this history.
When the slave-ships arrived,
Africans in chains,
They kissed my land—perpetual slavery

Perpetual slavery
Perpetual slavery
Salomé can tell you,
She can . . .

An African husband and wife, slaves of a Spaniard,
Who treated them, so badly
And hit his black woman
And it was there he rebelled, the brave and handsome black man
He avenged his love,
And you can still hear him at the gates,
Don't hit my black woman!
Don't you hit her!
¡No le pegue a la negra!
You heard me, man.

Don't hit that black woman!
Don't you hit her!
¡No le pegue a la negra!
Oh no, no, no, no, no, no, no, no . . .

Don't hit that black woman,
You're gonna respect her!
¡No le pegue a la negra!
Yeah, you can hear him at the gates
Don't hit that black woman . . .
No, no, no, no, no
   No, no, no, no, no
Black woman who says to me . . .
Dark-souled Spaniard,
¡No le pegue a la negra!
Don't hit her, don't hit her, don't hit her, don't hit another's
Don't hit that black woman!
Listen, my black is coming,
¡No le pegue a la negra!
Chapetón [Spaniard] with your dark soul,
Chapetón with your perverse mind,
¡No le pegue a la negra!
No, no, no, no, don't hit her . . .

Don't you hit her!

Don't hit that black woman.
You're gonna respect her . . .
Abuser who hits another's,
Don't hit that black woman.
'Cause, 'cause, 'cause, my soul it explodes inside me,
Don't hit my black woman.
¡No le pegue a la negra! . . .
No, no, no,

Don't hit that black woman.
Because my soul, it throbs within me, my woman,
¡No le pegue a la negra!
You saw it on the beach, girl—
On the beach at Cartagena . . .

No, no, no, no, no, no, no,
Don't hit that black woman.

The beaches of Marbella . . .
The black soul that sings and that weeps,
Don't hit that black woman, don't, don't . . .
Because my soul throbs, girl,

¡No le pegue a la negra!

Chombo knows it,
And you do too![4]

Translated by Ann Farnsworth-Alvear and Ana María Gómez López

Notes

Personal and place names have been reproduced from the original document, with omitted accent marks and inconsistencies.
1. *Factors* were appointed by the Spanish Crown as part of royal involvement in the slave trade. The *asiento* was a concession granted by the Spanish Crown allowing the monopoly privilege of supplying African slaves to Spanish colonies in the Americas.
2. *Gota Coral* was used to refer to epilepsy, yet the printed text on this document links it to heart disease.

3. The inconsistency in ages is reproduced from the original document.

4. Several clarifications are in order. First: multiple versions of the song circulate, as video recordings of Arroyo's performances include lyrics that vary. We have not attempted to identify a definitive version; rather, we have used some of the phrases Arroyo added during live performances, viewable on the Internet (see https://www.youtube.com/watch?v=RXXI8xqHvXU and https://www.youtube.com/watch?v=1TwEHIiSEpA, among others) and have drawn on websites that host lyrics, particularly http://planetadeletras.com/index.php?m=s&lid=196419, with a transcription attributed to Oscar Campuzano, and http://lyricstranslate.com/en/rebeli%C3%B3n-no-le-pegue-la-negra-rebellion-dont-hit-black-woman.html, with a translation attributed to "Bellavoz," both accessed July 1, 2015. Second: the song may have first been recorded not by Joe Arroyo but by Roberto Urquijo Fonseca, with authorship attributed to Adela Martelo de Arroyo. This seems to have been a legal nicety, given that Arroyo was under contract with a competing label when his friend recorded the song. Third: translating "No le pegue a la negra" is a complex undertaking. In the context of this song, which makes references to distinctly black Cartagenero slang, a reader of Harlem Renaissance playwrights or African American writing through the 1980s might plausibly render Arroyo's phrasing as "Don't hit mah 'oman!" or that of his backup singers as "Don't hit dat sistah!" We have opted to leave the ambiguity of the Spanish alongside a more literal translation. Liliana Angulo, Jakia Bell, Rui DaSilva, Evelyne Laurent-Perrault, and Tukufu Zuberi offered advice on the translation; errors are our own.

Crossing to Nationhood across a *Cabuya*
Bridge in the Eastern Andes

Manuel Ancízar

Manuel Esteban Ancízar (1812–82) called himself "el Alpha," or "the Beginning."
In 1853 he published a two-volume travel narrative, Alpha's Pilgrimage, *which*
undertook to familiarize Colombians with their new republic. With other members
of a state-appointed Chorographic Commission, he had traversed the Eastern Andes
mountains, from Bogotá to Pamplona, in what is now the department of Norte de
Santander. Educated men and women (such as Ancízar's wife, Agripina Acosta,
also a writer) now had a mass of new information about the country: its rivers and
mountains, climate zones, trails, and available or potentially available resources—
beginning with human resources. The commission's statistical overview included
data on population density, transport networks, ethnic groupings, and agricultural
production.

In contrast to the rigorous empiricism of Chorographic Commission scientists,
Alpha's Pilgrimage *borders on fiction and journalism. The extract below takes*
us to the town of Socorro, site of the legendary Comunero revolt of 1781 (see part III)
and thus a symbol of nationhood. In the extract included here Ancízar described the
precariousness of transport in an adverse topography. Modernity, he hoped, would
bring a bridge to Simacota. In fact, within a generation, Geo von Lengerke, a Ger-
man immigrant and entrepreneur (see part VII), contracted with an engineering
firm in Bremen to build a suspension bridge there. Quite another kind of modernity
is also part of Simacota's legacy, as the ELN or Ejército de Liberación Nacional,
one of Colombia's twentieth-century rebel armies, used the town for its own initial
proclamation of "revolutionary struggle" (see part V).

Ancizar's note on the river's name is fascinating in what it communicates about
his relationship not only to the Comuneros and the symbolism of nationhood but
also to the memory of the sixteenth century: "When Gonzalo Jiménez de Quesada
invaded the country of the Muiscas in 1537, the march from Chipatá to Moniquirá
required crossing the swift waters of the Sarabita River. Captain Gonzalo Suárez's
horse came close to drowning, for which the Sarabita came to be known as the Suárez

Carmelo Fernández, *Cabuya de Simacota sobre el rio Saravita*, 1850. Simacota is a town in Santander, located on Colombia's Eastern Cordillera. The Saravita drains to the Magdalena River. This watercolor was produced for the Chorographic Commission by Carmelo Fernández, a soldier, draftsman, and artist who worked with Agustín Codazzi. In Gonzalo Hernández de Alba, ed., *En busca de un país: La Comisión Corográfica* (Bogotá: Carlos Valencia Editores, 1984). Prints from the Comisión Corográfica (Cabuya de Simacota sobre el Sarabita). Courtesy of Biblioteca Nacional, Bogotá.

River, and we insist on this reference despite its ridiculous origins and the beauty of the indigenous name."

The Suárez River measures 100 yards in width at the pass to Simacota, bellowing as it runs impetuously over the rough and broken rocks scattered on its bed. There is no bridge, yet native industry has overcome this obstacle by placing there a thick rope that they call *cabuya* [made from *fique*, a type of hemp], as has also been done in other similar passages. A robust tree from the river's edge is paired with another found on the opposite side of the riverbank; if this is not possible, thick forked poles are anchored in the ravine 20 or more yards above the river waters. These trees or upright columns are called *morones*, and are surrounded by a platform with a light thatched roof. One *morón* is attached to another by a thick cable made up of 24 strips of twisted leather, that when crossing the river sags naturally at its middle, eight or ten yards over the current. This is the line of trajectory. Two sturdy and sliding wooden clamp rings are placed above each cable. There are two ropes tied with solid knots to the bottom of each ring, which fasten a seat made up of a square of leather hide stitched to a fibrous stick frame. This contraption in the form of a flat-bottomed basket is called a *puerta*. Two long *cabuyas* are tied to each side of the *puerta*, for the purpose of pulling the machine from one side of the river to another by sliding the rings to which the seat is tied. A holdfast secures the *puerta* as it approaches each *morón*, without which it would slide back to the middle of the river given that the cable forms the aforementioned curve, where one half offers a rapid descent, and the other a slippery climb. Four passengers can be seated back to back, holding their balance with their legs in the air, or one passenger with two trunks of luggage and their horse trappings. Once the load is ready and secured, the *cabuyeros* on this side of the river signal to those on the other with a whistle: they release the holdfast that restrains the *puerta*, which sets off downward at high-speed due to its own weight, and quickly reaches the lowest point of the bowed rope. From there, the *cabuyeros* on the other side begin to pull on the rope to bring the *puerta* upward until it is firmly fixed to the *morón*, where passengers and their luggage disembark. When the person riding is a day-laboring *peón* or a miser, he requests not a *puerta* but a hook. This hook is even more of an indigenous invention than the *puerta*. Imagine a pothook made from wood of a guava-tree, with grooves or notches on each end: four lengthy rope bands are attached to the notch of the longer end, while a short band is affixed to the lesser. Our fellowman takes the pothook that best suits him and climbs up the tree until he reaches the cable, to which he fastens the pothook, harnessing its ends with the shorter band. He then fits his legs through two of the hoops and his arms through the remaining pair, so that he is hanging from the cable in the manner of a spider, his head facing the opposite end of the river. Once his hat is securely fastened, he lets go of the cable, and shoots head-forward like a rocket, oscillating over the ravine with rocks rugged by the turbulent river. But the involuntary momentum ends past the middle of the cable, and thus begins a series of grotesque maneuvers using all four limbs to climb the rope up to the high *morón*, a task done swiftly by veterans but not without much sweat and toil by recruits and novices.

It is not impossible for the cable's leather straps to break after being soaked by a storm, due to the intense friction of the pothooks or the *puerta*'s clamp rings. One can imagine the fate of those passengers who fall precipitously into the river. Thus the provincial courts have decreed special ordinances determining the number of straps that must make up each cable, which can be no less than 24, specifying precautions and safety measures regarding the *puerta* and related devices that must be followed. Even in the best possible conditions, one will inevitably waste a great amount of time passing through the *cabuyas*, given that each round trip for one load takes 10 minutes. Livestock must swim across, guided by swimmers, with the evident risk of perishing when the river water is high, dragging them far out and pelting them against the jagged rocks. Greater knowledge and awareness about these dangers regarding the construction of suspension bridges will hopefully consign *cabuyas* to the archive of memories of our past industrial and social backwardness.

Translated by Ana María Gómez López

A Gaping Mouth Swallowing Men

José Eustasio Rivera

La Vorágine, *a novel by José Eustasio Rivera (1888–1928), has been translated as* The Vortex. *It is largely autobiographical; an introductory letter from Rivera represents the work as a memoir by Arturo Cova, a foil he reinforces by using pictures of himself for Cova. Allegedly, Cova is a poet who impulsively travels to the eastern plains with his pregnant wife Alicia to make his fortune. The memorable line "Jugué mi corazón al azar y me lo ganó la violencia"—"I gambled my heart in a game of chance and lost it to violence"—summarizes Cova's ill luck. After his wife deserts him and he is accused of murder, Cova must skirt corrupt local bureaucrats, leave the plains, and escape to the rubber region of Yaguanarí. There, after being driven progressively insane, he is, in Rivera's words, "devoured by the jungle."*

La Vorágine *is divided into two sections: the plains and the jungle. Rivera's novel is rich in describing both landscapes: he catalogs rivers and their tributaries, provides names for flora and fauna, and traces folkways. His knowledge was rooted in the months he spent as a member of an official commission sent to trace the 1,375-mile border shared by Colombia and Venezuela. Along with other Colombian, Venezuelan, and Swiss officials, engineers, and experts, Rivera had traveled to San Fernando de Atabapo, a Venezuelan town at the convergence of the Orinoco and Guaviare Rivers, in what is now the meeting point between the Colombian departments of Vichada and Guainía, and the Venezuelan department of Amazonas. From there the group's experiences crossing rivers, swamps, and jungle areas were so overwhelmingly difficult that every member of the official commission resigned before the process of delineating the border had been completed. In writing, Rivera also drew on Walter Ernest Hardenburg's* The Putumayo, the Devil's Paradise *(1909), which described atrocities perpetrated against indigenous rubber-gatherers and was part of an international outcry against Casa Arana, a Peruvian rubber company. After* La Vorágine's *publication, Rivera continued to denounce crimes committed against indigenous communities, and he undertook new excursions to little-known areas of the country, such as Caquetá. He also went to New York City, seeking to publish his novel in English and have it made into a film—plans that were cut short. He died in New York after suffering seizures and complications related to*

hemiplagia and possibly malaria. By the mid-1930s, La Vorágine had been trans-
lated into English, French, German, Italian, Portuguese, and Russian.

Oh, jungle, wedded to silence, mother of solitude and mists! What malignant fate imprisoned me within your green walls? Your foliage, like an immense vault, is between my hopes and the clear skies, of which I see only
glimpses, when the twilight breeze stirs your lofty tops. Where is the loved
star that walks the hills at evening? Where are those cloud-sweeps of gold
and purple? . . .

You are a cathedral of sorrows. Unknown gods speak in hushed voices,
whispering promises of long life to your majestic trees, trees that were the
contemporaries of paradise, old when the first tribes appeared on the face of
the earth, and which impassively await the sinking of future centuries. Your
vegetation is a family that never betrays itself. The embrace your boughs
cannot give is tarried by creepers and lianas. You share even in the pain of
the leaf that falls. Your multisonous voices rise like a chorus bewailing the
giants that crash to earth; and in, every breach that is made new germ cells
hasten their gestation. . . .

Let me flee, oh jungle, from your sickly shadows, formed by the breath
of beings who have died in the abandonment of your majesty. You yourself
seem but an enormous cemetery, where you decay and are reborn. I want to
return to the places where there are no secrets to frighten, where slavery is
impossible, where the eye can reach out into the distance, where the spirit
rises in light that is free! I want the heat of the sand dunes, the sparkle of
stars, the vibrating air of the open pampas. Let me return to the land from
which I came. Let me unwalk that path of tears and blood, which I entered
on an evil day, when, on the trail of a woman, I plunged into jungle and wilderness, seeking Vengeance, the implacable goddess who smiles only over
tombs! . . .

I have been a rubber worker, I am a rubber worker. I live in the miry
swamps, in the solitude of the jungles, with my malarial squad of men, scor-
ing the bark of trees, which, like gods, have white blood.

A thousand leagues from where I was born, I curse memory, because
memories are all sad ones: of my parents, who grew old in poverty, hoping
for help from the absent son; of my sisters, young and beautiful, who smile
at disappointments without the brother to ease their cares, to take them the
saving gold that transforms life. . . .

I have three hundred trees to take care of, and it takes me nine days to
lacerate them. I have cleaned them of creepers and lianas. I have opened a
path toward each of them. On trudging through this army of giants, to fell

the ones that don't shed latex, I often find tappers stealing my rubber. We tear each other with fists and machetes; and the disputed latex is splashed with red. But what does it matter if our veins increase the supply of sap? The overseer demands ten liters a day, and the lash is a usurer that never forgives.

And what if my neighbor dies of fever? I see him stretched out on the leafy mold, shaking himself, trying to rid himself of flies that will not let him die in peace. Tomorrow I shall move away, driven elsewhere by the stench. But I shall steal the latex he gathered. My work will be so much lighter. They'll do the same with me when I die. I who have never stolen, not even to help my parents, will steal when I can for my oppressors.

I have been a rubber worker, I am a rubber worker. And what my hand has done to trees, it can also do to men. . . .

For the first time I saw the inhuman jungle in all its horror, saw the pitiless struggle for existence. Deformed trees were held imprisoned by creepers. Lianas bound them together in a death grip. Stretched from tree to palm in long elastic curves, like carelessly hung nets, they caught falling leaves, branches, and fruits, held them for years until they sagged and burst like rotten bags, scattering blind reptiles, rusty salamanders, hairy spiders and decayed vegetable matter over the underbrush.

Everywhere the *matapalo*—the pulpy creeper of the forests—sticks its tentacles on the tree trunks, twisting and strangling them, injecting itself into them, and fusing with them in a painful metempsychosis. . . . The *comején* grub gnaws at the trees like quick-spreading syphilis, boring unseen from within, rotting tissue and pulverizing bark, until the weight of branches that are still living brings the giant crashing to the ground.

Meanwhile the earth continues its successive renovations: at the foot of the colossus that falls, new germs are budding; pollen is flying in the midst of miasmas; everywhere is the reek of fermentation, steaming shadows, the sopor of death, the enervating process of procreation. Where is that solitude poets sing of? Where are those butterflies like translucent flowers, the magic birds, those singing streams? Poor phantasies of those who know only domesticated retreats!

No cooing nightingales here, no Versaillian gardens or sentimental vistas! Instead the croaking of dropsical frogs, the tangled misanthropic undergrowth, the stagnant backwaters and swamps. Here the aphrodisiac parasite that covers the ground with dead insects; the disgusting blooms that throb with sensual palpitations, their sticky smell intoxicating as a drug; the malignant liana, the hairs of which blind animals; the *pringamosa* that irritates the skin; the berry of the *curujú*, a rainbow-hued globe that holds only a caustic ash; the purging grape; the bitter nut of the *corojo* palm. . . .

And yet it is civilized man who is the champion of destruction. There is something magnificent in the story of these pirates who enslave their peons, exploit the environment, and struggle with the jungle. Buffeted by misfortune, they leave the anonymity of cities to plunge into the wilderness, seeking a purpose for their sterile life. Delirious from malaria, they loose themselves of their conscience, and adapt themselves to the environment; and with no arms but the rifle and the machete, they suffer the most atrocious needs, while longing for pleasures and plenty. They live exposed to the elements, always ravenous, even naked, for here clothes rot on one's body.

Then some day, on the rock of some river, they build their thatched hut and appoint themselves "masters of the enterprise." Although the jungle is their enemy, they don't know whom to fight; so they fall upon one another and kill and subdue their own kind during intervals in their onslaught on the forests; and at times their trail is like that left by an avalanche. Every year the rubber workers in Colombia destroy millions of trees, while in Venezuela the balata rubber tree has disappeared. In this way they defraud the coming generations.

The story of El Cayeno symbolizes the fierce urge of these men. He escaped from a celebrated prison that has the ocean as its moat. Although he knew that the guards feed the sharks in order to keep them swimming near the walls, he threw himself into the water without removing his irons. He reached the banks of the Papunagua, attacked a settlement, and subdued the fugitive rubber tappers. He established a monopoly on the exploitation of rubber, and lived with his henchmen and his slaves on the Guaracú. The distant lights of his settlement twinkled through the heavy foliage one night when we finally drew close to it, and then waited till daybreak before advancing any further.

Who could have told us that we were to follow the same path of cruelty!

On the trip over this trail to the Guaracú, I had made a humiliating discovery: my physical well-being was only apparent. My body, wasted by fevers, tired very easily. On the other hand, my companions seemed immune to fatigue; and even old man Silva, despite his years and scars, was more vigorous on the marches. Every now and again they had to stop to wait for me; and even though they lightened me of my load, relieving me of my knapsack and carbine, I had to continue forcing myself on, my pride keeping me from falling to the ground and confessing my weakness. . . .

This physical inferiority of mine made me distrustful, irritable, testy. Old man Silva, of course, was practically in charge of us during the trip, and I began to feel jealous of him. I began to suspect that he had chosen this route purposely, so that he could convince me of my physical inability to handle El Cayeno. Don Clemente, too, lost no opportunity to make me conscious of the horrors of life in that settlement, and how remote was the possibility of escaping from there. Escape—that perennial dream of all rubber tappers, who see it always before their eyes and yet never attempt it, because they know that death closes all the exits of the jungle. . . .

As they seldom penetrated the jungle very far from the river banks, their sense of direction was not well-developed. This helped Don Clemente to acquire a reputation as guide. He would plunge deep into the jungle, sink his machete into a tree, and, days afterwards, guide them back to it, starting from any point the workers selected.

One morning at sunrise came unexpected disaster. The sick workers who had remained in the main hut to doctor their livers suddenly heard shouts from the river. They hastily gathered on the rocky ledge. Floating down the middle of the stream, like enormous black ducks, were the balls of rubber; and behind them came a peon in a small dugout, pushing with his pole the spheres that tarried in the eddies and backwaters. As he herded his black flock into the inlet of the little bay, he raised a cry more frightful than any war cry:

"*Tambochas! Tambochas!* And the men are isolated!"

Tambochas! That meant suspending work, leaving shelter, throwing barriers of fire across the trail, and seeking refuge elsewhere. An invasion of carnivorous ants, born who knows where, emigrating to die as winter comes, sweeping the hills for leagues and leagues with the rustle and crackle of a distant forest fire. Wingless wasps, with red heads and lemon-colored bodies, scattering terror in their path because of their venomous bite and swarming multitudes. Every cave, every crevice, every hole—trees, shrubs, nests, beehives—everything suffers from the overpowering flow of that heavy and fetid wave that devours young birds, rodents, reptiles, and puts to flight whole villages of men and beasts.

The news spread consternation. The peons of the camp scurried around madly, gathering tools and equipment.

"On which side is the swarm coming?" asked Manuel Cardoso.

"On both banks, it seems. The tapirs and peccaries are plunging into the river from this side, but the bees are swarming on the other side."

"Who are the workers who are isolated?"

"Five in El Silencio swamp—they don't even have a boat."

"What can we do? They'll have to shift for themselves! We can't help. Who'd risk losing himself in these swamps?"

"I," replied old man Clemente Silva.

And a young Brazilian youth named Lauro Coutinho joined him.

"I'll go too," he said. "My brother's there!"

Gathering together what provisions they could, and supplied with arms and matches, the two set out along a trail that plunged into the jungle toward the Marié River.

They traveled hastily over oozing mud and through tangled underbrush, eyes and ears on the alert. Of a sudden, as the old man was clearing a path before him, forcing a trail toward El Silencio marsh, Lauro Coutinho stopped him.

"Now's the time to escape!"

The same thought had already crossed Don Clemente's mind, but he gave no sign of his pleasure at the suggestion.

"We should consult the others . . ."

"I can assure you they'll agree—without hesitation."

And he was right. They found the five men the following day, in a rude shelter, shooting craps on a handkerchief spread on the earth, drunk from the *palmachonta* wine they were imbibing from a gourd that went its ceaseless rounds.

"Ants? to hell with the ants! We laugh at *tambochas*! To escape, escape! With a guide like you—even from hell you could lead us!"

And there they go through the jungles with the illusion of freedom before them, laughing, full of plans, praising their guide, promising him their friendship, their remembrance, their gratitude. Lauro Coutinho has cut a palm-leaf and carries it aloft like a banner. Souza Machado will not abandon his ball of crude rubber. It weighs ten pounds, but with its price he hopes to enjoy two nights of a woman's caresses, a white and fair woman, fragrant of roses and brandy. The Italian Peggi babbles of going to a city and getting a job as cook in a hotel where there is an abundance of leftovers and tips are generous. Coutinho, the elder, wants to marry a wench who boasts an income. The Indian Venancio wants to spend the rest of his days making dugouts. Pedro Fajardo aspires to buying a cottage that will shelter his old blind mother. Don Clemente dreams of finding the grave. It is a procession of unfortunates, a march from misery to death.

And which the route they sought? The Curí-curiarí River. From there they would go up the Río Negro, seventy leagues above Naranjal, passing to Umarituba to seek shelter. Señor Castanheira Fontes was a good man. He would help them. There a broad horizon would spread itself before them. In case of capture, the explanation was obvious: they were fleeing before the *tambochas*. Let them ask the foreman.

On the fourth day through the jungles the crisis began; food was scarce and the swamps interminable. They stopped to rest. They took off their shirts, and tore them into strips to wrap around their legs, tortured by the leeches that lurked in the muddy waters. Souza Machado, made generous by fatigue, slashed his ball of rubber with a knife, and shared it with his companions. Fajardo would not receive his portion. Souza took it. It was black gold, and not to be despised.

A thoughtless one asked:

"Where now?"

And all replied, reproachful:

"Forward! of course."

But the guide was lost. He advanced doubtfully, feeling his way, yet without stopping or saying anything in order not to alarm the others. Three times within an hour he found himself back at the same swamp, but fortunately his companions did not recognize it. . . .

They grew nervous. Forebodings of misfortune pressed heavily upon them. A careless word and the repressed emotions might be released—in panic, rage, madness. Each struggled to resist. Forward!

Lauro Coutinho made a sorry effort to appear carefree. He bantered with Souza Machado, who had stopped to throw away the remains of his rubber ball. Machado attempted hilarity. They talked a while. Then someone, I don't know who, asked Don Clemente some questions.

"Silence!" growled the Italian. "Remember that pilots and guides must not be spoken to!"

But old man Silva, stopping short, raised his arms as one who surrenders to captors, and, facing his friends, sobbed: "We are lost!"

Instantly the unhappy group, with their eyes lifted to the lofty branches, howled like dogs, raising a chorus of blasphemy and prayer:

"Inhuman God! Save us, oh God! We are lost!"

"We are lost!" Simple and common words,—yet uttered in the jungles they strike terror in the heart. To the mind of the person who hears them comes the vision of a man-consuming hell, a gaping mouth swallowing men whom hunger and disappointment place in the jaws.

Neither vows, nor warnings, nor the tears of the guide, who promised to find his way again, could serve to calm the men's panic.

"This old fellow is to blame! He lost his way because he wanted to go to the Vaupés!"

"Wretch! Bandit! You were deceiving us. You were taking us to sell us, God knows where!"

"Yes, you criminal! But God blasted your schemes!"

Seeing that his crazed companions might kill him, old man Silva started to run, but the treacherous lianas of a tree caught his legs and tripped him. There they tied him up, while Peggi urged they rip him to shreds. Then it was that Don Clemente spoke the words that saved him.

"You want to kill me?" he said, "How can you do anything without me? I'm your only hope!"

The men stopped mechanically.

"Yes, yes, it's necessary that he live in order to save us."

"But without letting him loose, or he'll escape!"

And although they would not unfasten him, they knelt before him to beg him that he save them.

"Don't desert us!"

"Let's return to the hut!"

"If you abandon us, we'll starve!" . . .

Don Clemente, his head in his hands, searched his memory for some clarifying hint. Only the sky could help him. Let it only tell him where the light of dawn came. That would be enough to plan another route.

Through a clear space in the lofty ceiling of foil a skylight in the forest, he saw a fragment of blue, fractured by the riblike branches of a withered bough. He recalled his map again. To see the sun, to see the sun! That was the key. If those tall cones of green, which every day saw it pass over them, could only speak! Why should silent trees refuse to tell a man what to do that he might not die? And, thinking again on God, he began to pray to the jungle, a prayer that begged forgiveness for the injury done the forests through bantering talk.

To climb one of those giants was next to impossible: the enormous trunks, the remote branches, dizziness lurking in the foliage to overtake the one who dared. If Lauro Coutinho, dozing nervously, were to try. . . .

Silva was about to call him, when a noise, as of gnawing on fine wood, scratched across the stillness. It was the teeth of his companions, chewing on the hard seeds of the vegetable ivory tree.

Don Clemente felt a surge of compassion. He would console them, even though by lying.

"What is it?" they whispered, bringing their shadowed faces near.

And anxious hands felt the knots of the cords that bound him.

"We are saved!"

Dulled with joy, they repeated the words, "Saved! Saved!" They knelt down and pressed the mud with their knees for suffering had left them contrite. Without even asking what it was that offered them salvation, they gave vent to a hoarse prayer of thanks. It was enough that another promised it.

Don Clemente received embraces, entreaties of forgiveness, apologies to amend wrong they had done him. Some took all the credit for the miracle:

"The prayers of my little mother!" "The masses that I offered!"

"The blessed amulet I carry!"

And meanwhile, in the shadows, death must have laughed!

Dawn broke.

The hope that sustained them accentuated the tragedy on their faces. Emaciated, feverish, with bloodshot eyes and fluttering pulses they waited for the sun to rise. Their actions inspired fear. They had forgotten how to smile, or if they thought of smiling only a frightful grimace moved their lips.

Vainly they searched for a place where they might see the sun. Then softly it began to rain. No one said a word. They understood. The sun was not to be theirs.

They decided to return, traveling over the trails traversed the previous day, skirting a swamp where footprints left tiny pools into which the waters gurgled and wiped away the traces. Yet the guide stuck to the route. Silently they kept on until about nine in the morning, when they entered a heavy growth of coarse and matted bamboo. There they encountered a singular phenomenon: troops of rabbits and agoutis that hid under their legs seeking refuge, whether because they were docile or because they were suddenly stupefied.[1] A few moments later and a sound as of swirling rapids was heard reverberating through the wilderness.

"Good God! The *tambochas!*"

Flight was the only thought then. Turning they stumbled back, and then plunged into the swamp until the stagnant waters swept over their shoulders. Better the leeches than the ants.

From there they watched the first swarm pass by. Like ashes thrown from a distant conflagration, clouds of fugitive roaches and coleoptera swept down to the waters, while the edges of the marsh grew dense with arachnids and reptiles, forcing the men to splash the foul waters so that the insects would not come towards them. A continual tremor agitated the ground, as if the vegetation of the jungles were boiling. From under trunks and roots came the tumultuous invaders; over the trees spread a dark stain, sheathing the trunks like a flowing shell that crept upward implacably to torture the branches, plunder the nests, swarm the apertures and cracks. A blind weasel, a tardy lizard, a newborn rat—these were coveted prey for the avaricious army which, grating shrilly, stripped the bones of flesh like some fast-dissolving acid.

How long did the martyrdom of those men last? Buried to the chin in the slimy liquid, with terror-stricken eyes, they watched the swarms of the enemy passing, passing, and again passing. Nerve-racking hours, during which they sipped and sipped the bitter depths of slow torture. When at length the last swarm was sweeping into the distance, they tried to emerge; but their limbs were numb, too weak to wrench themselves from the hungry mud that gripped them.

Yet they must not die there. They must struggle out. The Indian Venancio managed to grasp some plants, and began to pull. Then he caught hold of a clump of reeds. Several stray *tambochas* gnawed the flesh of his hands, eating deeply. Little by little he felt the clammy mold that gripped him loosening its hold. His legs, as they tore from the bottom, cracked loudly. "Up! Once more, and don't faint! Courage! Courage!"

He's out. The waters gurgled and bubbled in the hole he left.

Panting, on his back, he heard his despairing comrades calling on him for help. "Let me rest, let me rest!"

An hour later, by means of branches and lianas, he had managed to get them all out.

This was the last time they suffered together. Which way had they been going? They felt their heads in flames, their bodies stiff. Pedro Fajardo began to cough convulsively. Of a sudden he fell bathed in frothy blood that he vomited in an attack of haemoptysis.

But they could feel no pity for the dying man. Coutinho, the elder, advised them to lose no time. "Take his knife from his belt, and leave him there. Why did he come if he was ill? He mustn't hamper us." So saying, he forced his brother to climb a *copaiba* to seek the sun.

The unfortunate youth bound his ankles with strips of shirt. Vainly he tried to grip the tree trunk. They raised him on their shoulders so that he might catch hold higher up. He continued his efforts, but the bark peeled off. He would slide down to start anew. They held him up, propping him with long, forked branches, and feeling their height tripled in their effort to help him. Finally he grasped the first branch. Stomach, arms, chest, and knees shed blood. "Do you see anything? Do you see anything?" they asked. And with his head he answered, "No!"

They no longer remembered to be silent in order not to provoke the jungle. An absurd violence filled them, and the fury of drowning people surged through them, the fury that knows neither friend nor relative, fighting off those who would clamber into a boat that can hold no more. With their hands they gesticulated heavenwards, as they called to Lauro Coutinho.

"You see nothing? Climb higher—and look well!"

Lauro, on a branch, clutching the trunk, panted without replying. At such a height he seemed a wounded monkey, trying to squirm into frantic hiding from the hunter. "Coward! You must climb higher!" And those below, mad with rage, threatened him.

Suddenly, however, the youth started to descend. A roar of hate rose from the ground. Lauro, terrified, tried to explain: "More *tambochas*—coming—com . . ." The last syllable died in his throat. The elder Coutinho, with a shot from his rifle, had pierced his chest. The youth fell like a plummet.

The fratricide stood still, his eyes on the crumpled, bleeding body.

"My God!" he broke out suddenly, "I've killed my brother—killed my brother!" Then, throwing away his gun, he fled. The others ran too, not knowing where. And they scattered, never to meet again.

Many nights later Don Clemente heard them shouting, but he was afraid they would kill him. He, too, had lost all pity. The jungle possessed him. Then remorse set him weeping, although the need of saving his own life justified his act before his conscience. Eventually he went back to look for them. He found the skulls and a few femurs.

Without fire or gun, he wandered two months, reduced almost to imbecility, deprived of his senses, animalized by the jungle, despised even by death, chewing roots, husks, mushrooms like a herbivorous animal, with the sole difference that he had to watch what kind of fruit or berries the monkeys ate, in order to avoid the poisonous ones.

But one morning he had a sudden revelation. He stopped before a *cananguche* palm, and to his mind came the tradition that tells how this species follows the sun, like a sunflower. Never had he given the matter any thought before. He spent anxious moments watching, and he thought he saw the lofty foliage slowly bending, with the rhythm of a head that took exactly twelve hours to move from the right shoulder over to the left. The secret voice filled his soul. Was it possible that this palm, planted in the wilderness like an index pointing to the blue, was showing him his route? True or false, he heard it speak. And he believed! That was all he needed—belief. And from the course the palm tree followed, he plotted his own.

So it was that he reached the banks of the Tiquié. That river, narrow and curving, seemed more like a stagnant pond in the marshes than a stream. He began throwing leaves into the waters to see if they moved. The Albuquerque brothers found him thus occupied, and almost dragging him, took him to the shelter.

"Who's that scarecrow you've found?" the rubber gatherers asked.

"A fugitive who can only say: 'Coutinho! . . . Peggi! . . . Souza Machado! . . .'"

Then after working there a year, he escaped in a dugout to the Vaupés.

Now he's sitting here in my company, waiting for dawn to break before going down to the shacks of Guaracú. Perhaps he's thinking of Yaguanarí, of Yavaraté, of his lost companions. "Don't go to Yaguanarí," he's always telling me. But I, remembering Alicia and my enemy, cry angrily:

"I'll go, I'll go, I'll go!"

Note

1. Because of an error in the 1935 translation this sentence has been retranslated by the editors of this volume.

Frontier "Incidents" Trouble Bogotá

Jane M. Rausch and Alfredo Villamil Fajardo

In 1917 and again in 1932, two of Colombia's international frontier zones saw the kind of violent political action that can make a mockery of centralized states. None of the national governments involved were able to police their boundaries. Indeed, it remains true that Peruvians, Ecuadorians, Venezuelans, Brazilians, and Colombians share space in borderland zones where none of these national governments act as final arbiters.

Of the two incidents, the takeover of Leticia, on September 1, 1932, is the better-known, given that it resulted in a so-called War with Peru. A diplomatic settlement ended the conflict, and Colombia was able to retain its status as a country with a claim on the Amazon. In the extract included here the Colombian official assigned to Leticia writes from the Brazilian river town of Benjamin Constant to inform President Olaya Herrera that a group of Peruvians has easily subdued his poorly outfitted force of "settler police" and has occupied Leticia. From the relatively wealthy Peruvian town of Iquitos, an export oligarchy sought to overthrow the terms of a 1922 treaty, the better to expand their power in the rubber-trade world described in La Vorágine.

The conflict with Peru was a turning point for Colombian national identity. It strengthened a recently elected Liberal administration and generated displays of patriotism across Colombia. Yet the lesser-known case of the Humbertera revolt of 1917 unfolded in ways similar to the Leticia incident. All of Colombia's remote border towns were marked by porous forms of local authority, and all were vulnerable to attack.

Author of four densely researched books about the history of the Llanos, Jane Rausch is uniquely able to describe the human geography of the vast, low-lying savannahs of the Colombian-Venezuelan borderlands region. Through the 1910s, the Llanos economy depended on a low-profit cattle industry that had changed very little since the eighteenth century, on the one hand, and on a massive illegal trade in heron (garza) and egret feathers, on the other. Along with other contrabandistas, the men who joined Humberto Gómez's rebellion killed birds in huge quantities, *hauling out their plumage in huge bales that fetched fantastic prices in the millinery shops of London and Paris.*

Whether for survival or for cashing in on the feather trade, llaneros *depended on their skill with canoes and horses and on close familiarity with the topography. Especially in the Arauca floodplain bordering Venezuela, low-density settlement, enormous distances between towns, governmental neglect, and intense seasonal rains fed an "every man for himself" kind of sensibility. By Humberto Gómez's time the centaurlike image of the undefeatable* llanero *was thus stuff of nationalist myth and had been since Simon Bolívar had ridden with his* llaneros *to surprise and defeat Royalist forces at the battles of Pantano de Vargas and Boyacá, in July and August 1819.*

La Humbertera fed on discontent after Colombia's War of the Thousand Days (1899–1902), with Liberals and Conservatives arrayed against one another, and Liberals still smarting from their military defeat. The Llanos region, traditionally Liberal, chafed under Conservative rule. What it meant to Gómez that he proclaimed himself a Liberal is perhaps unclear. What is clear is that in the volatile mix of border smuggling, constant rumors of plots against the Conservatives, and an ongoing personal feud against the local commissioner, Gómez and forty armed llaneros *attacked the town of Arauca on December 30, 1916, killing the commissioner and thirteen guards. The rebels burned the local government archive; took a few Conservatives prisoner, including members of the commissioner's family; and emptied the town treasury. Gómez insisted that his action was part of a generalized Liberal campaign against the Conservative government, and he declared an "Independent Republic of Arauca." Colombia's president, José Vicente Concha, learned of the event after four days had passed, because there was no direct telegraph line in Arauca City and a telegram from the Colombian consul in the Venezuelan town of El Amparo had to be relayed through San Cristóbal (also in Venezuela) and across the border back to Colombia via Cúcuta.*

Humberto Gómez, blond, blue-eyed, and deeply tanned, was twenty-nine years old in 1916. Born in Santander, he lived as a child in Sogamoso and Cúcuta, where he learned rudimentary pharmacy and carpentry from his foster father. An intelligent, audacious young man, he moved to Guárico, Venezuela, where he won the patronage of the local caudillos, the Gabaldón brothers. Sometime after 1911 he settled in Arauca, married, and worked as *mayordomo* on the *hato* Las Delicias. Some of his neighbors regarded Gómez as nothing more than an honest cattleman. Others alleged that he and the Gabaldón brothers were trafficking illegally in *garza* feathers. In the opinion of a former comisario, Eduardo Carvajal, who knew him personally, Gómez

Cattle-wrangling, ca. 1915. From a richly produced bilingual guide, the *Blue Book of Colombia* (1918), published in New York as part of a series representing countries of the Americas. In Jorge Posada Callejas, *Libro azul de Colombia—Blue Book of Colombia* (New York: J. J. Little & Ives Company, 1918), 476.

was "one of many vicious products of the Colombian and Venezuelan interior who flee to the frontier to avoid jail and who take advantage of the freedom there to commit new crimes." Evidently, Comisario Escallón shared this view, for all accounts agree that it was Escallón's tireless persecution of Gómez that drove him into Venezuela in September 1916.

While in exile, Humberto plotted his move against Escallón. His plan to capture Arauca City and sack the government treasury won the allegiance of former followers of Pérez Delgado who were still at liberty. Later, other malcontents, including some soldiers discharged by Captain Santos for insubordination, joined the conspiracy. Humberto armed his men from a cache of Mausers and Winchesters hidden by Pérez Delgado, and by mid-December he was ready. . . .

Before dawn on December 30, Humberto and thirty-seven companions crossed the Arauca River, where they were joined by Eloy Sánchez and twelve others. Proceeding stealthily to the plaza, they killed the sentinel. Then, shouting "Viva la República de Arauca!," they attacked the barracks. . . . Commandeering the town arsenal, he seized 5,000 pesos from the treasury and 150 pesos from the aduana [customs office]. Gómez burned the archives of the *comisaría* and the circuit court. He imprisoned all those who opposed him and demanded ransom for Marco Torres Elicechea, General Luis Nieto, Colonel Alejandro Díaz, Colonel Manuel Molano Briceño, and Alfonso and Zoilo Escallón, sons of the slain *comisario*. Later, he sent a posse to trap Captain Santos. Finding him in the Llanos south of Arauca City on January 1, the rebels forced Santos to retreat to Pore. With no other Colombian force to challenge him, the former *contrabandista* was "Master of Arauca." . . .

His ample supplies of horses, *aguardiente*, and guns attracted new recruits, who swelled his army to three hundred men. Throughout January they roamed the Llanos, attacking *hatos* and carrying off cattle and horses. As accounts of unprovoked atrocities circulated, peaceful settlers fled to the forests or to safety in El Amparo. Especially notorious was the cruelty of one of Humberto's lieutenants, Monte de Oca, who beheaded children with his machete. It was said that Humberto himself was afraid of this bloodthirsty Venezuelan and one evening ordered his men to tie him up. The next day, he delivered Monte de Oca to the Venezuelan army, who obligingly executed him.

Gómez planned to hold Arauca City until he had collected enough booty to make a profitable retreat into Venezuela or Brazil, before the Colombian army might arrive. Despite reports that he was marching with a thousand men on Tame, Orocué, and even Tunja, the only town he occupied besides Arauca City was Cravo Norte. By the end of January his army was already beginning to dwindle. Gómez released his prisoners through the mediation of the president of Apure, Pérez Soro. His last attack fell on El Viento, where he burned and sacked the business district. Then, on February 3, along with most of his officers, a large quantity of hides, merchandise, and horses, he crossed the border and was captured by the Venezuelan army. The "Republic of Arauca" dissolved five days before the first Colombian soldier appeared on the scene.

Leticia
Benjamin Constant, Boca del Yavarí, September 7, 1932
His Excellency the President of the Republic
Bogotá

I confirm to Your Excellency (henceforth Y.E.), all the radiograms and cables I addressed to Y.E., sent from the first day of this month to the present, some directly and others through the Colombian Consulate General in Manaos, through which I have brought to Y.E.'s attention the serious events that took place in Leticia on the first day of the present month at five thirty five in the morning, which I will proceed to describe to Y.E.

Finding myself on the specified date and aforementioned time in my pajamas, walking through the halls of the Intendent's house located on the town plaza of Leticia, I saw a group of 14 to 16 individuals whom, carrying assault rifles, were heading towards the Intendent's office. I immediately called out, "Stop right there! Who are you?" Without delay, the man who seemed to command this group aimed his rifle and said "You are now a prisoner," as he shot in my direction. Immediately I went around to another corridor of the house that stands 80 meters apart from the public school building, and throwing myself onto the patio I shouted loudly at the *colono* police who have their barracks there, "Police! Police! The Peruvians are here!" Thereupon I leaped over the fence surrounding the house, and as I landed on the other side, I came upon four men amid the grass pointing their carbines, and was shot point-blank by those laying closest to me. . . .

I expressed to Engineer Ordóñez that, in the name of the Government of Colombia, I resoundly protested this sudden violation that had just taken place in Leticia, an exposed town, defenseless and without garrison, which Colombia had not appropriated by assault, but through a solemn Border Treaty. I asked him to inform me immediately of his opinion regarding those of us being held captive, and I allowed myself to bring to his attention the need to avoid at all costs the possibility of his subordinates becoming inebriated, as he could not control the excesses they might commit in that state. I also demanded that Mr. Ordóñez allow me to go home in order to change my clothes. . . .

. . . As I put on my clothes, he addressed me by saying, Look, Mr. Villamil: these unfortunate events are the result of that debasing treaty signed by Leguía [President Augusto B. Leguía y Salcedo] "which has not been abided to by Colombia." . . .

Naturally, I brought to Ordóñez's attention that we had claimed our right to the Amazonian region for one hundred and ten years, and that it had only been due to its great Americanist spirit that Colombia had decided to settle. . . .

Colombian Population in Leticia. Men: On September 1, there were 33 Colombian men in Leticia: 14 *colono* police (there are 17 police on the payroll, but 3 were on leave), the rest being public administration officials and a few civilians. Women and children: The number of women and children on the day of Leticia's assault was 44. The rest of the population, which amounted more or less for 450 souls, were Peruvian elements. Eleven Colombians had left to Manaos two days earlier aboard the Brazilian steamboat "Delio," dispatched by the Intendent's office to serve as crew for the steamboat "Nariño." The attackers were aware of this departure, as several of the Nariño crewmen resided in the Ronda island, located in front of the Hacienda La Victoria, which as mentioned earlier served as the attackers' gathering place. . . .

I have reached the end of this report, Your Excellency, and only have left to address the mistaken opinion which I firmly held until the last moment: that the treaty with Colombia considered in Loreto was a settled matter. I did not believe there would be a group of sufficiently irresponsible individuals bold enough to attempt such a venture . . .

I am, with the greatest respect, Y.E.'s attentive server,

> *[Signed and sealed]*
> *Alfredo Villamil Fajardo*
> *Intendent*

Translated by Ana María Gómez López

Crab Antics on San Andrés and Providencia

Peter Wilson

Especially after the passage of the 1991 Constitution, Colombian intellectuals and activists generally have used plural terms to describe Afro-Colombian communities. Palenquero and raizal are included as ethnic identities within the umbrella category of "black communities." A palenquera would be a woman from one of the Colombian communities that traces its history to those enslaved Africans who escaped to create new lives on the outskirts of colonial-era towns. A mujer raizal would be a woman descended from the English and Creole-speaking families that lived for generations on the Caribbean islands of San Andrés and Providencia, or on one of a set of smaller islets nearby. Colombians also use the term isleña or isleño, meaning simply islander.

The meanings of all such terms are shaped by the geographic and cultural distance between marginalized black communities and the government in Bogotá—something that is true for residents of faraway towns but perhaps even more true for islanders. Writing in the early 1970s, anthropologist Peter Wilson described the problem succinctly. For people in Providencia, he explained, the national government was simply alien: "[Their] isolation and the difference in language and culture between Providencia and Colombia have created an antipathy toward government resembling that felt by colonized peoples toward their alien colonial governments." Nevertheless, locals tended not to blame all of their problems on Bogotá. Wilson found people on Providencia to be self-reliant and often perceptive in their self-criticism. "Crab antics," for example, was an expression islanders used to capture the fact that local social relationships included "contentiousness" and "covetousness," as they put it. People, they told Wilson, behave like crabs in a barrel—they all try to climb up at once, and when one succeeds in pulling itself up, the others pull it back down.[1]

Wilson's thoroughness as an ethnographer is evident in the short extract below, which manages to convey a sense of religious life, health care options, and residential patterns, even as Wilson traces the subtleties of the economic connections between San Andrés, Providencia, and Panama. His book includes a thorough overview of island history, and Wilson was careful to describe the way islanders' cultural and political relationship to Bogotá was complicated by international politics. His astute observations are still relevant. From the 1910s through the 2010s, there have periodically been tensions between the governments of Colombia and Nicaragua, both of which claim territorial and maritime rights in the archipelago area of barrier reefs around San Andrés and Providencia. Local residents have their own ties to the Central American coastline or to the Canal Zone, a longtime source of wages and goods, as well as to mainland Colombia, which has much stronger links to the islands now than it did during Wilson's fieldwork.

Increasingly, formal international organizations have had a role on the islands as well. In 2000 the archipelago was declared part of a UNESCO-designated network of marine protected areas. Nongovernmental organizations based abroad are recruited by locals in their efforts to address both long-standing problems, such as access to health care or islanders' desire to promote bilingualism, and newer ones, such as the challenge of disposing waste produced by tourists.

From Cartagena to San Andrés is a flight of an hour and a half over four hundred miles of empty sea. From the air San Andrés looks like a hundred thousand palms growing straight out of the sea. It used to be just a coconut island until the government "developed" it. Now it is the "pearl of the Caribbean," a free port for weekend shoppers. North-end sands became concrete, palms gave way to steel and concrete pillars that became the Hotel Miami, or Broadway. Thatch bars, shanty shops, and boutiques sprang up where once stood jacaranda and frangipani. Electric blenders, radios, phonographs, lamps, typewriters, cameras, wristwatches, Parker pens, Johnny Walker, Vat 69, Coca-Cola, spaghetti, Del Monte, Nestlé's, Newports and Salems, plastic bowls, aluminum pans, Jantzen, Chanel No. 5, and Wrigley's gum. Flora of San Andrés.

From San Andrés to Providencia is only forty-eight miles, but you have to wait for a boat that intends to go there. Not many boats do, because Providencia is not "developed" and not much money is to be made by calling there. . . . The first time I went from San Andrés to Providencia I sailed on the M.V. *Victoria*, skipper, Captain Jamesie Howard, red faced, blustery, no nonsense. He invited me to dine with him since we had set sail at about 7 P.M. We sat in the gallery at sea level, and dinner was a lump of pork fat, some fried plantain, and boiled manioc. Out beyond the reef the sea rose and fell carrying the little boat with it. In the steadiest voice I could muster I told Captain Jamesie I had already eaten supper (which was true) and that since I was not too good a sailor I ought to get to my bunk. He didn't believe an Englishman could be a bad sailor. I apologized for any disillusionment I had brought him and left to spend the night in abject, pathetic, vomiting misery.

Much to my astonishment I was still alive at dawn when we dropped anchor. A mug of hot coffee encouraged the blood to go through my veins again and now I could walk around the boat and, much more to the point, take my first look at Providencia. . . .

In spite of its rugged hills and massive bulk, the island is small, measuring only five miles by three at its broadest points. The even smaller island of Santa Catalina provides a third side for the symmetrical bay where we were anchored. Two thousand people live on Providencia. They dwell in fourteen villages connected by a path that encircles the island keeping as close as possible to the flat shoreline. At two places, however, one on the east and the other on the west coast, the path has to traverse high and precipitous bluffs. During the rainy season the path is washed out here and the island cut in two. Canoe is the only way to get around. In 1960 the government built a road around the island and the first vehicles made their appearance. For a while the to-ing and fro-ing was quite hectic; but the old cars were no match for the rocks and holes, spare parts were hard to come by and expensive, gasoline was scarce, and after one boat blew up with a cargo of gasoline, no one was willing to ship it. In a very short while horses and Shanks' Pony regained their eminence. . . .

Providencia is indeed a green and pleasant island, and its people are certainly not insensitive to this, for most of them have experienced the outside world and have a good base for comparison. There are, however, certain unavoidable disadvantages to life there. Illness is one—not that Providencia is prone to more diseases than other Caribbean islands, but its isolation and limited medical facilities make treatment difficult. Malaria, tuberculosis, hepatitis, cancer, cirrhosis of the liver, high and low pressure, and anemia present constant threats to people's equanimity. Although there are two doctors and two nurses, they rarely have more than aspirin to treat their patients. Those who become really ill must go to San Andrés and from there they may be transferred to Cartagena, Barranquilla, or Panama. Emergencies are beyond hope. In addition to the doctors there are a number of "bush doctors," each with his own specialty and reputation.

Government is also an unpleasant part of life. The history of the island's isolation from Colombia . . . and the difference in language and culture between Providencia and Colombia have created an antipathy toward government resembling that felt by colonized peoples toward their alien colonial governments. This sense of alienation has been aggravated by the religious difficulties that have beset Protestants in Colombia. Since the middle of the last century, both San Andrés and Providencia have been overwhelmingly Baptist. But as Colombian government has become more aware of some of the possibilities of the islands, there has been a concerted attempt by both government and the officially recognized Catholic Church to convert the islanders. Throughout Colombia there has been, from time to time, persecution of Protestants, and the islands have had to face this. As a result, and in response to such blandishments as school scholarships and guaranteed jobs, an increasing number of islanders have converted to Catholicism. Many of these say they don't really "mean" their Catholicism but are simply exploiting the situation. Those who remain Protestant term the renegades "job" Catholics. By the time I arrived on the island, overt enmity between Protestants and Catholics had pretty well disappeared, though each enjoyed any opportunity to malign and sneer at the others. . . .

The vagaries of Providencia's political standing are indicative of the more than physical isolation and neglect imposed by the mainland. Politically, socially, culturally, and even economically it has been left to find its own way. Consequently it has staunchly, one might almost say defiantly, upheld its Jamaican English language and culture while asserting disdain for Spaniards (*panyas* or *pays*) and matters Spanish. Only since the early 1960s, when Colombia's own political situation seemed at last to be settling in an upright position, has there been any sign of mutual recognition between island and mainland—accompanied by promises to Hispanicize in return for promises to allot funds to modernize. . . .

Isaac and Lena

Isaac and Lena live in Bottom House, the island's "poorest" and "blackest" community. Isaac is about thirty-four years old, and what strikes one immediately about him is an idea of precision. His speech is fast and clipped, his walk brisk, his appearance neat. His hair is close shaved, his moustache meticulously trimmed, and his steel-rimmed eyeglasses so clean that sometimes I used to wonder whether there were lenses. This whole impression was completed, for me, by his mannerism of slowly drawing his lips over his teeth to a final close whenever he finished a sentence. He had had a few years of schooling and was able to read English fluently, but his writing was hesitant and he avoided it whenever he could. He loved to read—adventure novels if they were available, otherwise comics.

Lena, about twenty-eight years old, is soft, quiet, and flowing in her presence. She never raises her voice, her smile, ever present, is never too extensive, and even when she laughs she laughs quietly, so that her laughter is most evident in the cocking of her head to one side. Laughter is a keynote for this family, because Isaac is a great joker, delighting in puns (a delight he shares with most islanders). . . .

Isaac had built their home before they had begun to live together. It was a small, two-room house made out of wood that he had imported, using money he had earned when working in Panama. There was also a small thatched kitchen standing separate from the house, and this is where Lena spends most of her day. The house stands on about an acre of land that Isaac inherited from his father. Only a small part of this is level, the rest being a steep, rocky slope. Still, Isaac planted yucca on the slope and also tethers a goat on the grass. Lena cultivates a garden around the house—squash, melons, cucumbers, beans, peas, and yams grow healthily, while in one corner of the property are a couple of banana and plantain trees. She uses all she grows and doesn't remember ever having sold produce. Isaac bought a cow and pastured it on land he rented. He reckons on using the milk, possibly even selling some, but eventually making some money by slaughtering it when it is fat enough.

Isaac loves to fish and he goes out to the reef at least twice a week in his homemade canoe with its floursack sail. He uses nets that he has woven himself, and he weaves nets for sale—if somebody asks him to. He sells most of what he catches straight from the boat, keeping aside enough for his household and always making sure they have some dried fish, which he not only enjoys for its own sake but which stands them in good stead when the weather prevents him from going fishing and which Lena can use when he is away on one of his "trips." . . .

These take place on an average of every eight months or so, when he goes to San Andrés or Panama to work. He likes to sign on as crew for one or two voyages with one of the small boats that ply the waters of the southern Caribbean. This provides him with some cash, perhaps a hundred pesos, which, though useful, is not much. More to the point, it gives him the opportunity to do a little trading of his own. Isaac enjoys a good reputation among his neighbors in Bottom House as being trustworthy and intelligent, so before leaving for a trip he solicits orders from his friends and neighbors for any goods they might want that he can buy for them. When he comes back it is usually with an assortment of goods: a bolt of cloth, a sewing machine, a bedstead, a chest, tinned foods, tools, spectacles, and so forth. For each item he receives a small commission. The most lucrative source of cash on these trips, however, is smuggling. While abroad he will procure a few thousand American cigarettes or a case of whisky. Sometimes he gets these from San Andrés, the free port, but most often they come from a "friend" in Panama, an agent for stolen goods. He sells them either in Cartagena, or, if he has procured them cheaply enough, to tourists in San Andrés. . . .

Isaac works hard to provide for his household and Lena backs him up. They respect each other and have great affection for one another and for their children. Consequently they appear quite happy. But were it not for Isaac's trips abroad and their hard work, the family would be in dire straits. As I was leaving after my last visit, a possible crisis was looming. Lena was pregnant, but she was anemic and had kidney trouble. There was fear of complications and expense ahead. . . .

Cayetano and Rosalia

Cayetano is about thirty-eight years old, a short, squat, powerful man. . . . His chief interest and occupations . . . are woodworking and fishing. He is not considered as being among the best carpenters on the island, but he is adequate for relatively minor house repairs and boat mending. At fishing he excels. His specialty is crab fishing, which is done at night by torchlight. He also makes his own lobster pots and often sets as many as twenty at a time—more than anyone else on the island. He sells most of what he hauls, and whenever he can he sends a catch down to San Andrés, where the price is far above that on Providence. . . .

Cayetano is an agent for Mr. Ling, who runs the main "numbers" game on the island and also sells tickets for the national lottery. Cayetano gets his supply of tickets each week to sell around Rocky Point, and every Sunday makes his way to Mr. Ling's store to get the results, hand over his takings, and collect his commission. Mr. Ling, or his son, gets the results via the radio receptor at the telegraph office.

When Cayetano is away on trip Rosalia in her effortless way takes over everything—except the fishing. She collects produce and has it taken around to St. Isabel for sale. On one occasion she collected nearly 2,500 coconuts from all around, far more than Cayetano had ever managed. . . .

Cayetano was a little reticent about divulging his income from all his activities, and the fact is that he had probably never totaled it. I reckoned he made about five thousand pesos a year (about seven hundred dollars U.S. in 1960). Given a general island tendency to underestimate one's income and plead poverty, this figure should be regarded as a very conservative estimate.

Most of the cash comes to Cayetano, but he gives Rosalia money whenever she asks for it. He stores the cash in various hiding places around the house and in secret places elsewhere on the island. Rosalia also hides money. Sometimes their ingenuity gets the better of them, as when Cayetano hid a hundred pesos in a lamp and Rosalia filled and lit it!

Note

1. Peter J. Wilson, *Crab Antics: The Social Anthropology of English-Speaking Negro Societies of the Caribbean* (New Haven, CT: Yale University Press, 1973), 9, 22, 58.

Pacific Coast Communities and Law 70 of 1993

Senate of the Republic of Colombia

What Colombians mean by the term el Pacífico, *no less than* los llanos *or* el Caribe, *can be vague in its boundaries, but wherever these are drawn, the Pacific Coast region is huge—perhaps thirteen hundred kilometers long. It stretches from Panama to Ecuador and extends from the coast into the foothills of Colombia's Western cordillera. For centuries, Pacific Coast land was almost wholly untitled—families and communities lived in places without their "ownership" being registered anywhere in Bogotá. The old colonial cities of Popayán and Cali had a deep historical connection to the Pacific region, as the gold panned there by slave gangs created enormous family fortunes for slave owners. Nevertheless, Colombians whose lives centered on highland cities or who were connected to the Magdalena River and the Caribbean ports have for centuries understood the western lowlands primarily in terms of racial stereotypes: it is a region defined by the presence of black and indigenous people.*

In the present, when communities from the Pacific Coast make political claims, they often identify themselves by reference to specific rivers: the Atrato, the Río San Juan, the Patía, the Güelmambí, the Yurumanguí. These rivers, and the communities tied to them, became more fully part of Colombians' sense of their nation after 1991, when activists in the constitutional convention pushed for an article that then, in 1993, became Law 70, the "Law of the Black Communities," extracted below. Law 70 established the possibility of collective land title for rural Afro-Colombian communities and focused on the Pacific region, although some communities in the Caribbean region have also claimed land under its provisions, including the successful claim made in the Palenque of San Basilio (see part IV). Beyond land title, Law 70 charged the state with supporting the cultural identity of black communities and reforming existing curricula to include more about the history and culture of Afro-Colombians. This push was joined to the larger current of the 1991 Constitution, which defined Colombia as a pluri-ethnic nation and provided a legal framework for claims to territory, curricular reforms, and linguistic and cultural rights—whether made on behalf of indigenous or black communities.

Since 1991, a large part of indigenous and black activism in Colombia has been directed toward making constitutional guarantees a reality on the ground. In addi-

*tion to the general problem of ongoing armed conflict in regions with resident black
and indigenous communities, activists began to be attacked explicitly because of
their actions to defend their territorial rights. Those with access to the means to sow
terror locally use displacement and paramilitary violence to gain physical control of
land—a control that later can be used to undermine attempts to claim collective titles, as an ethnically defined collective title requires that claimants demonstrate that
traditional subsistence practices are in use on the land. And black activists, in particular, are often divided about what priority to assign to the struggle for collective
land title. Some argue that focusing on the racial politics of urban areas is equally
or more important, given the growing population of Afro-Colombians coming of age
in the cities—in part as a direct result of the violent displacement. Numbers of those
displaced by the conflict in rural zones over the last two decades vary by source, but
the United Nations High Commissioner for Refugees has repeatedly ranked Colombia as having one of the largest internally displaced populations in the world.*

Article 1. The object of the present Law is to recognize the right of the Black
Communities that have been living on *tierras baldías* [untitled lands] in rural areas along the rivers of the Pacific Basin, in accordance with their traditional production practices, to their collective property as specified and
instructed in the articles that follow. Similarly, the purpose of the Law is
to establish mechanisms for protecting the cultural identity and rights of
the Black Communities of Colombia as an ethnic group and to foster their
economic and social development, in order to guarantee that these communities have real equal opportunities compared to the rest of Colombian
society. . . .

Rivers of the Pacific Basin. Are the rivers of the Pacific region, which
comprise:

a) the Pacific flow made up of superficial waters of rivers and creeks
   that drain directly into the Pacific Ocean and its subsidiaries, the
   basins of the rivers Mira, Rosario, Chajul, Patía, Curay, Sanquianga,
   Tola, Tapaje, Iscuandé, Guapi, Timbiquí, Buey, Saija, Micay, Naya,
   Yurumanguí, Tumba Grande, Tumbita, Cajambre, Mallorquín, Ra-
   poso, Anchicayá, Dagua, Bongo, San Juan, Ijua, Docampadó, Capiro,
   Ordó, Sivirú, Dotendó, Usaraga, Baudó, Piliza, Catripre, Virudo,
   Coquí, Nuquí, Tribugá, Chori, El Valle, Huaca, Abega, Cupica,
   Changuera, Borojó, Curiche, Putumia, Juradó, and other smaller
   tributaries which drain directly into the Pacific Ocean;

Woman in Tadó, Chocó (Pacific Coast), ca. 1953. Photograph by Robert West. 3/17 (R25, N27), Archivo Fotográfico Robert West, Las Tierras Bajas del Pacífico Colombiano, Biblioteca Luis Ángel Arango, Bogotá. http://robertwest.uniandes.edu.co/.

Municipal Pier, Buenaventura (Pacific Coast), ca. 1953. Photograph by Robert West. This and the other West photograph included here are part of an online exhibition organized by Claudia Leal and hosted by Universidad de los Andes. 5/15 (18B), Archivo Fotográfico Robert West, Las Tierras Bajas del Pacífico Colombiano, Biblioteca Luis Ángel Arango, Bogotá. http://robertwest.uniandes.edu.co/.

   b) the basins of the Atrato, Acandí, and Toló Rivers, that flow into the Caribbean.

Rural Riparian Lands. Are the lands bordering the banks of the rivers mentioned in the preceding paragraph that are outside urban perimeters as defined by the Municipal Councils of the area municipalities in question in accordance with the provisions of Municipal Regulation Code (Decree 1333 of 1986), and any subsequent added laws that develop or amend it and in which the respective community is settled.

Tierras baldías. Are the lands situated within the borders of the national territory belonging to the State and no other owner, and that, having been categorized as such, shall return to the domain of the State in accordance with article 56 of Law 110 of 1913, and any other regulations that augment, develop, or reform it.

Black Community. Is the group of families of Afro-Colombian descent who possesses its own culture, shares a common history and has its own traditions and customs within a rural-urban setting and which reveals and preserves a consciousness of identity that distinguishes it from other ethnic groups.

Collective Settlement. Is the historic and ancestral settling of Black Communities in lands for their collective use, lands that constitute their habitat, and where they currently develop their traditional practices of production.

Traditional Practices of Production. Are the technical, agricultural, mining, forestal extractions, grazing, hunting, fishing, and general harvesting activities of natural resources, customarily used by the Black Communities to guarantee the conservation of their lives and their self-sustaining development. . . .

Article 4. The State will grant collective property to the Black Communities referred to in this Law, in areas that, according to the definitions in Article II, comprise unclaimed lands located along the riverbanks in rural riparian areas of the Pacific Basin as well as those in areas specified in the second clause of Article 1 of the present Law: lands that they have been occupying in accordance with their traditional practices of production.

For all legal purposes the lands, for which collective property rights are established, will be called: The Lands of the Black Communities. . . .

Article 39. In order to offer fair and equitable information about the society and culture of the Black Communities, the State shall be vigilant so that within the National Educational system the Black Communities' own cultural practices and contributions to the history and culture of Colombia are known and promoted.

In the social sciences area at all educational levels, the subject of Afro-Colombian Studies that conforms to the corresponding curricula should be included. . . .

Article 41. The State will support, by providing the necessary resources, the organizational processes of the Black Communities, in order to recover, preserve, and develop their cultural identity.

Article 42. The Ministry of Education will formulate and execute a policy of Ethno-education for the Black Communities, and will create a pedagogical commission to assess said policy with representation of the communities.

Translated by Norma Jackson and Peter Jackson

Toward a History of Colombian Musics

Egberto Bermúdez

For all its regionalism, Colombian culture has an undeniably national aspect. The following three texts highlight spaces in which a "Colombian" sensibility is often readily apparent: music, soccer and emigration. The first of the three is a scholarly overview provided by musicologist Egberto Bermúdez. Ranging across five centuries, he contextualizes both the music Colombians hear at a wide array of festivals (Festival Nacional del Bambuco in Huila, Festival de la Leyenda Vallenata in Valledupar, Cesar, and Festival de Música del Pacífico Petronio Álvarez in Cali, Valle del Cauca, to name just a few), as well as what is produced by the country's mass media and recording industry. Colombian artists today increasingly reach beyond the country's borders, combining traditional rhythms with hip-hop, zouk, reggaeton, and electronic music. In the 2000s, groups that have become international headliners include ChocQuibTown, Bomba Estéreo, and Systema Solar. They followed paths blazed by Colombian artists who looked to international audiences, such as Toto la Momposina, among many others.

The demonization of Amerindian culture and music—or as Tomlinson prefers to call it, the positioning of Amerindian beliefs under the aegis of the Christian supernatural—permeates early reports of aboriginal music.[1] In his *Sumario* (1526) and *Historia* (1547), recalling his days in the Colombian Darién in the mid-1510s, Gonzalo Fernández de Oviedo (1478–1557) describes local history recorded in chants, thus confirming the Amerindian preeminence of song. Performances included dancing, he adds, and involved musical instruments—aerophones, xylophonic logs, shakers, and other idiophones. (This classification is based on the agent producing sound: in aerophones, a vibrating column of air; in membranophones, a membrane in tension; in chordophones, a string in tension; and in idiophones, the vibrating body of the instrument itself.) Fernández de Oviedo also strives to compare this genre to dance songs from Flanders and Spain and reckons that Spanish narrative romances serve the same purpose. However, he associates Indian ritual specialists (priests, shamans) with the devil, identifying it with their

Matilde Díaz and Lucho Bermúdez surrounded by their records, 1974. The Orquesta
Lucho Bermúdez was famous to local and international audiences for bringing a
Big Band sound to musical genres from the Colombian Atlantic coast, such as *porro*,
cumbia, and *merecumbé*. Photographer unknown. *Revista Cromos*, no. 2928, March 4,
1974. Used by permission of *Revista Cromos*.

highest deity. His prestigious view became official and was strictly followed
by later writers but departed from earlier tolerant views such as that of Co-
lumbus himself, who asserted that Indians had "no idolatry" and equated
their ceremonial houses to Christian churches. Alas, in the following years
the former view offered ample justification for the systematic destruction of
Amerindian musical systems.

Official narratives—some of them ethnomusicological avant la lettre—
furnish additional details about Colombian Indian musical culture. In 1580
we find (in Tenerife on the Magdalena River) paired duct-flutes (one of them
played with a maraca) that survive today both among the Indian communities (Kogi, Wiwa and I'ka) of the Sierra Nevada de Santa Marta and as part

of peasant musical style (named *gaitas*) in the northern coastal area. Earlier, in 1563, the cacique of Ubaqué (southeast of Bogotá)—with permission from his *encomendero*—celebrated the winter solstice (Christmas time for the Spaniards) with vocal and instrumental music, dance, and pantomime. Judicial proceedings ordered by the authorities emphasized the mournful tone of the celebration was intended as an anticipated funerary service for the cacique. Eduardo Londoño suggests that it may also have been a metaphorical funeral for Muisca culture itself, broken to pieces by almost three decades of Spanish conquest.

Beginning in the 1550s, the establishment in Santafé of the Real Audiencia and a cathedral allowed for the beginning of the development of European musical traditions. The first chapel master, Gonzalo García Zorro (ca. 1548–1617), was a mestizo priest, the son of an illiterate Spanish captain and an Indian woman, later barred from obtaining a Church sinecure on grounds of his racial status. In 1584 the new Fiscal of the Audiencia brought with him, as part of his hometown retinue, Gutierre Fernández Hidalgo (ca. 1547–1622/23), a composer and former chapel master at Talavera de la Reina, propitiating the ousting of García Zorro. The authorities installed Fernández Hidalgo as chapel master and rector of the recently founded San Luis Seminary, which provided music instruction only to Spanish pupils. After two years, and finding his professional horizon too narrow, Fernández Hidalgo decided to move south (Quito, Lima, Cuzco, La Plata) and for more than three decades his pupil Alonso Garzón de Tahuste (ca. 1558–ca. 1651), also a son of a minor conquistador, remained in charge of the music at the Cathedral. Those years marked the introduction of polyphonic international church music, and the early seventeenth-century manuscripts held today at the Cathedral Archive—as testimony to local musical and cultural conservatism—are said to be the oldest examples in South America and have traces of having been used until the 1830s.

For Colombia the Amerindian demographic catastrophe followed the pattern of most of America and by 1600 approximately 80 percent of the indigenous population had disappeared. Africans (slaves and freemen) were present in small numbers since the early 1500s but a century later had become almost 4 percent of the total population, highly significant in comparison to the 1.3 percent of Spaniards. In 1546 and again in 1573, blacks were forbidden to sing, dance and play drums publicly in Cartagena and fifty years later—as they kept doing so, especially for their funerals—Jesuit Pedro Claver (see part II) ordered their drums seized, held and returned only in exchange for a cash ransom. His order and the Franciscans began to employ black slaves and freemen as musicians (*ministriles*) during these same years. Colmenares distinguishes two economic cycles of gold mining dependent on enslaved Africans. The first (1550–1640) was mainly located in Antioquia, Tolima, and Pamplona and the second (1680–1800) centered in the Pacific areas of Chocó, Cauca, and Nariño. All the African ethnic groups arriving during these periods left their musical mark in a syncretic process where new cultural layers (eighteenth-century English and French trade of Ewe, Fanti, Akan, Calabar, Kru, Temne, Mende) superimposed old ones (sixteenth-century Portuguese trade of Biafara, Zape, Balanta, Wolof) but allowing continuity to other cultural horizons—present in the first period and reinforced in the second—as the Mande, Angola, and Congo.

The dual scheme of a *república de indios* segregated from the *república de españoles* allowed the reproduction of organized cathedral music in small *pueblos de indios* (especially around Bogotá and Tunja). Through the seventeenth century—according to royal ordinances—four Indians (named *cantores*) were exempted from tributes and taxes to perform musical duties (especially as instrumentalists) at the local churches. The Jesuits took this scheme to the extreme in their missions and *reducciones* along the Colombo-Venezuelan frontier and—as in the province of Paraguay—excelled in using Western music as an ideal means of acculturation.[2] The Indians however, secretly kept using their songs, instruments, and dances, as was revealed in Santafé in 1591 when one night the authorities surprised many Indians from both sexes in a private home drinking *chicha*,[3] singing with flutes, dancing in circle and stamping their feet on the floor "as is the custom of the gentile Indians." In their houses—according to archival records—the Spaniards sang *coplas*, *romances*, and *decimas* and played *adufes*, *vihuelas*, guitars, *bandolas*, harps, harpsichords, and later violin and flutes for their private entertainment. On the other hand, the fife and drum and the trumpet and timpani were the military ensembles traditional in infantry and cavalry troops, with the fife and drum being used also by civil militias.

Three chapel masters (two from the same family) controlled the music at Santafé cathedral from approximately 1650 to 1740, long years marked by musical stagnation and aversion to new trends. . . . Church music sank into mediocrity, and by the 1770s there were no composers attached to the cathedral.

A new Crown Regiment arrived in 1784, and change was in the air: new musical instruments (clarinets and horns), new dances, and the establishment of public theaters (*coliseos*) in Cartagena in 1772 and in Santafé in 1793. Already in 1804 local dances (*torbellino* and *manta*) alternated in Santafé elite balls with French minuet and passepied and Spanish fandango and *jota*. Professional musicians worked at church, the military regiments, and the

theater, and apparently also the elite participated actively in public enter-
tainments. Rafaela Isasi (1759–1834), known as "La Jerezana"—a Spanish amateur actress and singer married to the second marquis of San Jorge—sang
tonadillas at the local Coliseo, celebrating the Spanish victory over the Royal
Navy in Buenos Aires in 1808.

In 1768, the Crown had instructed authorities in Cartagena to collect
information on the dances and fandangos locally called *bundes* (danced in
circles of men and women with drums and *coplas*) that were suspected to be
"dishonest" and prone to sinful excesses. The local authorities replied that
they complied with established rules and were "universal and very ancient"
in the whole province banning them only on nights before major religious
feasts. However, in 1781 the bishop remarked that "no means have been effective to prevent" those dances where "indians, mulatos, mestizos, blacks,
zambos and other inferior castes" of both sexes danced, played drums, sang
lascivious verses and drank *aguardiente, guarapo,* and *chicha*[4] not only in distant localities but in the cities themselves. And precisely, those castes were
the slaves and freemen so-called *de todos los colores* (of all colors)—including
the Indians—that in those years amounted to the vast majority of the population of the coastal provinces (88 percent in Riohacha, 70 percent in Santa
Marta, and 60 percent in Cartagena). Along with *costeño porros* and *chandés,*
today *bundes* represent survivals of a West African song and dance ritual
complex marginally present in other Latin American and Caribbean countries. Moreover the African musical presence had wide coverage: from the
Pacific lowlands where the African-derived marimba is reported in 1760 to
El Socorro (northeast of Bogotá) where for the festivities for newly ascended
King Charles IV in 1791, local black slaves and freemen along with some
whites took part in a ritual battle with music "in the manner of Tangos or
black Cabildos of Havana, Cartagena or Panama," perhaps one of the earliest appearances of this term. Thus, the profile of Colombian regional music
traditions started to consolidate.

On the other hand, the colonial elite rhetorically incorporated Indian
identity to the apparatus of public festivities. In 1747 in Popayán, giants, pyg-
mies, Turks, Armenians, and Greek gods and deities—dancing and playing
musical instruments such as violins, guitars, flutes and *tiples*—alternated
with Amerindians (real and fake), all symbolically representing the four
continents at the feet of Ferdinand VI, Spain's new monarch. Allegories
to Indian America (with flags, hieroglyphs, disguises, speeches, poetry,
music and dance) would become a standard means of displaying new national pride during the independence period. Indian realities however, went
separate ways, and from the mid-seventeenth century Colombian Indian

communities—pushed by military campaigns—fled to the periphery and maintained their culture and language until they were "rediscovered" in the second half of the nineteenth century. Their musical instruments and dances, for instance, reappear in the drawings and reports of the Comisión Corográfica, a government project inventorying the land and searching for national identity. An isolated aerophone product of those pioneering ethnographic efforts is still held today at the National Museum. Music and dance were also frequent protagonists of *costumbrista* literature beginning in the late 1840s. Later such fictions eventually became "history," helping to consolidate regional stereotypes of carefree, "joyous" blacks, devious mestizos, sexy and licentious mulattas, and defeated, "sad" Indians.

During the nineteenth and twentieth centuries, the relationship between music and politics played a major role in the processes of definition of "Colombian-ness." Independence only relocated our economic dependency, and by the 1820s state-of-the-art European musical items (pianos, organs, violins, flutes, and harps) were included as part of the ideal cargo described in the foreign investment prospectus for Colombia published in London in 1822. Patriotic songs appeared soon as part of the military and cultural influences that came from Venezuela during the independence wars, represented by composer and violin player Nicolás Quevedo (1803–74). Thus a national repertoire was inaugurated and later complemented through the work of some musically educated adventurers and foreign clerks—such as amateur musician and painter Henry Price (1819–63)—an Englishman who very soon spotted the essence of local colonial musical traditions. In 1850–60, Price worked with local musicians, such as pianist and composer Manuel María Párraga (1835–1906), to create the first paradigm of Colombian "national music." Their means was the piano, the bourgeois instrument par excellence, with a repertoire—coming in the bags of entrepreneurs and merchants from Paris or New York—of mass-produced dances, opera selections, *morceaux brillants*, and bravura pieces. In Europe public performances changed slowly from this repertoire to classic concert pieces (Bach, Beethoven, Mozart), but in our case no such change happened in the nineteenth century. Zarzuela and opera companies—often combining both—and very few visiting artists completed the scarce local musical offer until the close of the century.

Colombian insertion in the capitalist world severely affected, and keeps affecting, local Indian communities—from the Jesuit-sponsored expansion of the cattle frontier in the early eighteenth century (along the border with Venezuela) to the Amazonian rubber boom in the late nineteenth-century Amazon and into our present. In the twenty-first century, plans developed to favor the extraction of oil and coal are a threat, as are the creation of new river dams that will transform ancestral territories (Putumayo, Los Llanos, Sierra Nevada de Santa Marta, northern coastal plains, and Guajira).

From the 1890s government-sponsored Catholic and Christian missionaries started their work among Indian communities barring their traditional culture and music. Foreign and Colombian archaeologists and anthropologists provided ethnographic reports of Atlantic coastal Indian groups and also the first recordings (aural and visual) of their music and dances (Konrad Th. Preuss, 1914–15, and John A. Mason, 1923). Understanding archaeological remains that may have had a musical function is a tricky thing and assuming that present day Amerindian music seriously represents the pre-1492 situation can lead to misrepresentations. Nevertheless, careful cross-examination of both archeological and ethnomusicological evidence (living traditions) is a good way to understand continuity and change. Over time, the consolidation of Indian organizations and legislation incorporated into the 1991 Constitution helped to neutralize the effect of racist policies and is allowing Indian music to insert itself in local music networks and markets.

In the twentieth century, Colombian art music oscillated between nationalism and universalism and the same options still seem to be the dilemma for contemporary composers. After his return from Paris in 1909, Guillermo Uribe Holguín (1880–1972)—a member of the Bogotá elite—introduced contemporary repertoires and tried to transform the old music academy into a conservatory. His universal stance led to a clash with local "nationalist" musicians, creating a divide based on prejudice and ignorance more than on musical arguments. To a minor extent popular music bore the same limitations and the first version of Colombian "national music," consolidated in the 1880s and based on *bambuco*, *pasillo*, and *danza* lasted—enriched and modified—until around 1940. Then as a result of pressure from international recording companies and the changing cultural climate during López Pumarejo's "Revolución en marcha," this paradigm began to be replaced by another consisting of dance music, *música caliente o bailable*, championed by Luis Eduardo "Lucho" Bermúdez (1912–94) and modeled on international and Caribbean trends but still based in local Costeño peasant traditions. From the mid-1970s, international vogues from salsa to disco challenged the supremacy of *cumbia* and other *bailable* genres (*porro*, *gaita*), but the local media and record industry soon found in *vallenato* an appropriate means of resurging. This genre, associated stylistically with *cumbia* and *porro*, helped the industry to regain lost terrain—in the midst of dramatic social changes brought along by the first period of generalization of the drug trade in Colombian society.

In the mid-1960s, rock culture was slowly assimilated but never gained

An artist-made poster promoting a punk festival in Bogotá, along with traditional *carranga* music. Punk as a musical import has a multigenerational history in Colombia, while *carranga* is a folk music genre from Boyacá, made famous by Jorge Velosa. Image by Henry Güiza Cepeda. http://movimientoalzadoenartes.blogspot.com/2011_07_01_archive.html. Courtesy of the artist.

momentum—losing the battle with international Spanish pop and locally produced youth-oriented *costeño* dance music (Los Graduados and Los Hispanos). Through these years this music was "made in Medellín," the unchallenged epicenter of the Colombian phonographic industry. Revolutionary ideology stimulated local *música de protesta* (Pablus Gallinazus, Ana y Jaime, Nelson Osorio), some of it too near foreign models and obviously too intellectual for guerrillas themselves, who listened to *rancheras* and *corridos* and modeled themselves on the heroes of Mexican films (Mariachi, Charro Negro). *El barcino* by Jorge Villamil (1929) aired peasant social conflicts but Hernando Marín (1944), who was hailed as champion of the *vallenato de protesta*, ended up in the late 1970s eulogizing drug lords (*El gavilán mayor*, recorded by Diomedes Díaz).

Colombia's persistent and strong aesthetic nationalism, along with the cultural hopes opened by the Constitution of 1991, provided a fertile ground for the adoption and recycling of ethnic and traditional local musics through the record industry and the mass media which resulted in varying degrees of "fusions" and "revivals." Since the late 1980s, these have been the most commonly accepted formats for "Colombian" national music. Nowadays, as with most fusions around the world, young professional musicians consider them the ideal meeting place of traditional and modern styles but—not far from that creative arena—fusions and their artists are also used by the government and private enterprises to promote their agendas of "Colombian-ness."

Notes

1. Gary Tomlinson, *The Singing of the New World: Indigenous Voice in the Era of European Contact* (Cambridge: Cambridge University Press, 2007), 48.
2. *Reducciones* were colonial settlements of forced relocation for indigenous people.
3. *Chicha* is primarily a corn beer consumed in Andean communities, but the term has a history that extends throughout the circum-Caribbean region and in some contexts can refer to brews made from other products.
4. *Aguardiente* is a distilled liquor made from sugarcane, often flavored with anise. *Guarapo* is juiced sugarcane, and has for centuries been consumed both fresh and fermented; here the reference is to its fermented form, which would have been produced by adding a yeast starter.

Colombian Soccer Is Transformed:

The Selección Nacional in the 1990s

Andrés Dávila Ladrón de Guevara

The popular culture phenomenon of spectator sports is relatively recent in Colombia. A fan base for professional cycling and professional soccer (fútbol) emerged only in the 1950s, as team owners began to connect with a public hungry for the emotional world of sports. Cycling and its high-profile race, La Vuelta a Colombia (Tour of Colombia), led in popularity through the mid-1960s, when football began to take off. Both sports emerged during the years of diffuse, ubiquitous fear that marked Colombians' collective psyche after Jorge Eliécer Gaitán's assassination on April 9, 1948.

In their relationship to the fan base, politicians, and those who put up money, cycling and football sometimes overlapped and sometimes diverged. Fans bonded and developed locally based affinities fueled by radio stations, visual emblems (colors and crests), and the patronage of industrialists promoting brand names. During the 1950s the military government of Rojas Pinilla even used La Vuelta a Colombia to promote the "Government of the Armed Forces" (1953–58) as a brand, mounting its own team. The rules of professional football prevented the Colombian military from fielding a team, but the government built stadiums that soccer clubs rented, and over the years Colombian football teams became profit-generating enterprises. With the rise of narco-trafficking, teams began to have more or less obvious links to drug money, and the mafia's ways became the soccer clubs' ways.

Football stars belong, simultaneously, to a club and to a national team, the Selección Nacional. World Cup record scorer James Rodríguez and other players who have succeeded abroad, such as Radamel Falcao, are national and international celebrities. However, for many Colombians, the Selección Colombia of 1990 and 1994 remains the country's most famous: it included Carlos Alberto "El Pibe" Valderrama, an incredibly shrewd midfielder whose afro-style mane of blond ringlets became an icon; René Higuita, known for his breakneck acrobatic saves; and marvelous scorers—Freddy Rincón, Faustino Asprilla, and Adolfo "El Tren" ("The Train") Valencia.

The troubles of the narco-terror years of the 1990s carved themselves into the landscape of Colombian football. Andrés Dávila, a faculty member at Bogotá's Pontificia Universidad Javeriana, explains that Colombia's historic 1993 win against Argentina, with a score of 5–0, happened in the context of scandal. Goalkeeper René Higuita had just gone to prison, despite fans' hopes for a last-minute judicial pardon. He had acted as a go-between for a man whose daughter had been kidnapped as part of an internal feud within the Medellín Cartel, and he was also kept out of the 1994 World Cup, in which the team lost to the United States and which resulted in tragedy. Forward Andrés Escobar (who had accidentally scored an own goal and ensured his team's defeat by the United States) was murdered in a Medellín parking lot, fueling renewed rumors that despite the killing of Pablo Escobar months previously, the traffickers' links to the world of football ran deep. But the realities of narco-traffickers' power was only part of the story of the 1994 Selección. Given a new constitution that emphasized the country's ethnic and cultural pluralism, the constant, visual presence of a multiracial national team, with Afro-Colombians among the star players, was part of a sea change in the way Colombians thought about their mixed identity as a nation.

First Half

It is 1990, June 19. There are two minutes remaining in the game and Colombia loses 1–0, after having played as an equal against the powerful German team, about to be world champions. Suddenly, without anyone understanding exactly how they do it, the team recovers its identity, its form, its style of play, all of which two minutes ago had seemed rubbed out by that goal against them. In overtime [injury time], the team retakes the ball and executes a perfect, unhurried play that culminates in a game-tying goal. Everyone immediately starts celebrating: the players, the reporters (one of whom yells at the top of his lungs, "God is Colombian"), the few Colombians present in the stadium, and, in Colombia, the whole country.

That celebrated goal proved something not only to Colombia but also to the world of football: that something was happening, something that later would be called "the process." It was marked by continuity and success in the labor of sport, but what was more important was its deeper meaning, which went beyond the spatio-temporal boundaries of the game and its rituals. This was a process anchored by an appealing idea about what Colombian football could be—both modern and lyrical, both scientific and ludic. In real life, this was an unexpected but convincing synthesis: To win, but by playing well. To get results, but without giving up on fun and entertainment. To gain triumphs, titles, epic wins, but without losing a certain style, an identity, an image of what the game could be, of what Colombian football could be, as aesthetic expression.

For some in the world of football and in the world-world, this was a set of values, ideas, and expressive possibilities that did not fit either the time or the country. Colombia at the end of the 1980s was marked by an unusual rise in violence that owed, in large part, to the phenomenon of drug trafficking (which also had a lot to do with the improvement of the level of play in Colombian football). Because of this, what was unexpected was that the football played by the national team had nothing to do with the laws of winning at any price. . . .

In the Colombia of that moment—without collective points of reference beyond the lack of collective points of reference, increasingly consumed by violence, corruption, and easy money, submerged in a crisis of values, and having lost its traditional mechanisms of legitimation (the Church, the two-party system)—in that Colombia, football became the only thing that brought people together in a constructive way. As a Colombian social scientist put it, "Maturana [Francisco Antonio Maturana, known as "Pacho"] (the ideological [Colombian] coach) connected a Black-Antioqueño-Costeño Colombia to its *barrio* sense of itself. He framed the game within spatial and temporal coordinates and gave it local markers." And: "With the national team, the Colombian people came into an existence, not because they went into the streets to celebrate but because they were now a real category of people, present in the way the national team played the game."

Second Half

The scene now is Monumental Stadium, of [the soccer club] River Plate, in Buenos Aires. Colombia and Argentina compete in a World Cup qualifying match. In Argentina's favor is the local venue and, as [Diego Armando] Maradona said, "history." In Colombia's favor is the classification table and its game: a tie will get them into the longed-for World Cup. Ninety minutes later and after a magnificent display of footballing, Colombia was going to the United States [host of the World Cup]. They had beaten history five goals to zero. Once again, the process and commitment to a certain style had paid off. For the Argentines, it was *shame*, as one famous sports magazine headlined it (and for Maradona it was "zero in history," as an ad in a Colombian newspaper emphasized).

For the Colombians, there was the obvious satisfaction of defeating the powerful, of humiliating the arrogant, of winning everything thanks to "faith in ourselves" . . . but this victory had something new in it also: its forcefulness, the goals, the novel experience of having achieved it without so much suffering. As if the country, finally, would really find its way out of purgatory.

From then on it was celebration, an unending party for the whole country, the president receiving the team in a packed stadium . . . and a unanimous request made in the stadium, for the freedom of the team's former goalkeeper, in prison for helping negotiate a kidnapping.

The whole country was represented there, with all its contradictions. Excessive, absurd, opportunistic. Surely all of that and more. Yet there was something else there also, something more than unproductive collective madness or using what had happened for political or economic gain. That *historic triumph* unfurled something new and it began to strengthen—an intangible process of constructing a nationality and consolidating an identity.

Translated by Ann Farnsworth-Alvear

Colombian Queens

Jaime Manrique

Whether for music or soccer, Colombian audiences are regional, national, and in-
ternational. The largest emigrant populations are in the United States, Venezuela,
and Spain, although estimates of how many Colombians live in these countries are
not always reliable. In 2010, the US census found just over nine hundred thousand
Colombians residing in the United States, with the highest concentration in the
Miami-Dade area. Yet the nickname "Little Colombia" is most often used in refer-
ence to Jackson Heights, in Queens, New York. In the following excerpt from his
novel Latin Moon in Manhattan *(1995), Jaime Manrique describes Jackson Heights*
using references to foods immediately recognizable to Colombians and many of their
US-born children: arepas, chicharrón, tostones, *and so on.*

Manrique himself immigrated not to New York but to Lakeland, Florida. He
arrived there from Barraquilla in 1967, and in recounting what it was like to be
the new kid in a US high school, he emphasizes how unprepared he was for the
racial confrontations he witnessed. "I knew right away I had arrived in a society
where racial conflict was a matter of life and death, not a submerged issue, the
way it was in Colombia, where blacks were invisible and voiceless."[1] Manrique
remembers identifying with the black students and describes himself as racially
mixed, but he was wedged into the segregated world of public high school as an
outsider—as were most of the Colombians who arrived as teenagers in the 1960s,
1970s, and 1980s.

Latin Moon in Manhattan was not his first novel—he had published in Span-
ish for a Colombian audience—but it was his first important work in English and
the first novel he wrote as an openly gay man. As in much of his other work, Man-
rique combines high-culture references and subtle erudition, on the one hand, with
a determinedly low-brow, ironic voice, on the other.

A gentle breeze blew through the white lace curtains and through them I
caught a glimpse of a sunny day and a cloudless sky. After many months
in Manhattan where I had only seen concrete and glass, the deep green
branches of the tree by my window had a soothing effect on me. . . .

Watching a 2014 World Cup game between Colombia and Ivory Coast at Leños Bar in Queens, New York. Photograph by Ruth Fremson. This image captures not only fans' identification with the national team (either yellow shirts or reproductions of the team's shirts), but also the community space of the bar, where photographs of entertainers and of family-hosted events hang side by side. Expatriate Colombians who gather to watch national teams play *fútbol* share an experience different from that of fans who come together in venues within the country. At a viewing party held abroad, those present sometimes have little in common aside from their sense of connection to Colombia. Used by permission of Ruth Fremson / The New York Times / Redux.

In the kitchen, a Spanish radio station was playing a Gardel program. I could hear my mother, singing along with Gardel, the lyrics of *"Yira, Yira"*:

When luck is rotten
Laughing and laughing
While you lie in the streets

. . .

"Sammy," Mother cried, stopping her singing. "Did you sleep well?" she added in Spanish, rushing over to kiss me. "I've been making your breakfast."

There was enough food on the table for a baseball team. "How are you, Mother?" I asked, sitting at the table and pouring myself a cup of chocolate. The pile of *arepas* in a straw basket was warm and tender.

"I'm as good as could be expected, considering everything. How's Mr. MacDonald?" she asked.

It was nice of her to inquire after my cat, but it mortified me that after many years she hadn't taken the trouble to get his name correctly. "His name is Mr. O'Donnell. He's the same, I guess."

"No wonder he's sick, cooped up in that apartment all the time. Look at my cats, they've lived all their lives outside and they're as healthy as can be."

"Mother," I said calmly, concentrating on my breathing, trying to muster a serenity I never had when we conversed. "First, I cannot let him out in Manhattan; he'd be killed in a minute. Second, he has an enlarged heart, and that's a congenital condition." As I finished saying this, I realized the absurdity of trying to explain anything rationally to a Colombian.

"Anyway, it's unnatural to love a cat that way," Mother said, baiting me. "That's what happens to men when they don't get married and have a family."

I felt like saying, Oh yeah? And why is it more *natural* to love a stupid parrot? But I held back. I didn't want to get upset before breakfast. Besides, I had been in her presence barely five minutes and had the rest of the week-end to fight. . . .

She placed a tray of pork *chicharrones* on the table. "It's been fifty years since Gardel died," she said dreamily, changing the subject, "but for my money he sings better every day."

I cut open an *arepa* and buttered it. "Ummm, it's delicious," I commented, since I didn't feel like discussing Gardel. Half-closing her eyes, Mother hummed to herself the last bars of *"Yira, Yira."*

Waiting for the song to end, I picked up one of the *chicharrones* and bit off a juicy piece of pork meat. As I chewed, I studied my mother who was sitting next to me, her legs crossed. Even this early in the morning she wore a ton of jewelry, Colombian style: her wedding band, her heart-shaped emerald ring, gold bracelets, a gold chain with an emerald and diamond crucifix, plus her diamond earrings. I wondered if she ever took these things off. As usual, her auburn hair was made up and lacquered, her fingernails manicured and painted a transparent pink. She wore a Mexican cotton blouse with short sleeves, khaki bermudas, and open-toed blue cotton slippers. She had turned seventy in the spring, but with the years she had grown svelte. It bothers me that I got a kick out of how nice she still looked.

Mother selected a *chicharrón* and took a dainty bite. Her wonderfully lustrous maple sugar skin was smooth, unwrinkled, and the only places her age showed were on the back of her hands, and her neck and thighs, where her flesh sagged a bit. When she married Victor, over ten years ago, mother had the bags under her eyes removed and this procedure had considerably enlarged her marvelous hazel eyes so that at first she looked spooked, as if she had just seen a ghost. But with the passage of time, the eyes became more natural-looking and attractive. The Gardel program came to an end and Mother got up to turn off the radio. Then she got a pitcher of *guanabana* juice out of the refrigerator and poured me a glassful. I realized these gargantuan breakfasts Mother subjected me to were a continuation of my grandparents' breakfast table, where meat, fish, wild game, *suero*, butter and cheese, breads, *arepas*, and *empanadas*, fried plantains and *yucca*, papaya, mango, pineapple juice, coffee, chocolate, and *kumis* were the fare.

I was finishing my first cup of deliciously brewed Colombian coffee, when the phone rang.

"You'd better get it; it's for you," Mother informed me.

"*Lorito real, lorito real,*" Simón Bolívar twaddled, excited by the phone.

"It's Carmen Elvira," Mother went on. "I told her you'd be up by eleven and to call you then."

"Why is Carmen Elvira calling me?"

"She wants to invite you to become a member of their literary society, The Colombian Parnassus. Please, Santiago, don't humiliate me. She's one of my best friends. So please accept her invitation. It's a great honor."

The phone kept ringing and Simón Bolívar continued screaming his nonsense and flapping his wings.

"Please, Santiago, it will be the last thing I'll ever ask of you. She knows you're here. If you don't pick up, she'll come over."

"This is blackmail," I protested, picking up the receiver. "Hello," I said with great trepidation.

"*Hola, Sammy. Es Carmen Elvira.*"

"Hello, Carmen Elvira. How are you?"

"Fine, thank you, honey, and you?" she said in her polite *cachaco* manner. "I'm calling to give you great news; you're being invited to become a member of The Colombian Parnassus. *Enhorabuena!* Congratulations," she added in English.

I couldn't feign surprise, or happiness for that matter. But I saw Mother getting up and approaching me, so I said, "Thank you very much; I'm honored." Mother smiled at me.

"I thought you'd be. Anyway, we plan to induct you this afternoon. We're meeting at Olga's home around 12:30, American time. You know where she lives, don't you?"

"Yes," I said grimly.

"Well, *cariño*, it's been a real pleasure talking to you. Say hello to Lucy," she said, referring to my mother. . . .

I was about to ring the bell of Olga's home when the door opened and the hostess greeted me with kisses on both cheeks. The pleasant smell of burnt eucalyptus hit my nostrils. Walking down the wide-planked hall carpeted with cowhides, I experienced déjà vu: I felt as if I were in a house in Bogotá. Every detail was Colombian—the furniture, the pictures on the walls, even the plastic flowers.

I greeted Carmen Elvira and Irma, who were sitting on a couch drinking *tinto*, the espresso-like demitasse that Colombians swill nonstop. The air-conditioning was on and the curtains drawn, so that the room was in semidarkness, giving the scene a vaguely conspiratorial atmosphere. The three women, who ranged in age from their late forties to midfifties, differed sharply in appearance: Carmen Elvira, who was from the Cauca Valley, was tall and her complexion and features Mediterranean in color and shape; Irma, who was from Pasto, was on the short side, stocky, and her features were Incan. She wore her hair in a crew cut and was dressed in bermudas and sandals.

Olga, who was from Bogotá, was extremely petite and a natural blond. She was dressed in a sleeveless white cotton dress and wore high heels. It was spooky how, because of their close association, they seemed, at least in spirit, three weird sisters.

I was offered, and accepted, a *tinto*. Without asking for my preference, the hostess put two heaping spoonfuls of sugar in the inch-and-a-half cup. I decided to be gracious and drink it this way for fear of being labeled a gringo. The three women looked at me with curious but benign expressions. . . .

For the next five minutes we inquired about each other's parents, husbands, brothers and sisters, children, and even pets. By then I had finished my cigarette and the sickeningly sweet *tinto*. It occurred to me that good manners required that I acknowledge the dubious honor of being elected a member of The Colombian Parnassus.

"Don't mention it," beamed Carmen Elvira as the unacknowledged spokesperson of the group. "We have to move with the times, and welcome the new generation."

"Personally, I'm not very fond of modern poetry. I prefer the old poets like Carranza. Ah, those sonnets. Do you love Carranza?" Irma asked me.

"Yes, I do." Like all Colombian children I had learned Carranza's poems in school, and did, indeed, favor his exuberant romanticism.

"The 'Sonnet to Teresa,'" Olga sighed, full of nostalgia for the poetry of the past.

Olga and Carmen Elvira looked at Irma beseechingly. Her expression becoming devout, Irma began reciting the sonnet:

Teresa, en cuya frente el cielo empieza,
como el aroma en la sien de la flor.
Teresa, la del suave desamor
y el arroyuelo azul en la cabeza.

Her eyes closed, her hands resting on her considerable breasts, Irma finished reciting the famous sonnet, which I will not endeavor to translate for you because its beautiful rhymes and music demand a greater translator than I could ever hope to be. When she finished, the women sighed and burst into applause. I joined them.

"That's poetry," Olga pronounced.

Carmen Elvira pontificated, "That's what I call great poetry."

"That's what I call love," elaborated Olga. "It's not enough to be a great poet. Oh, no. That's too easy. To write poetry like that, one must love very deeply and be a great lover. Like . . . like . . . Petrarch. I hope some day you'll write a sonnet like that to your girlfriend, Sammy."

Unsure of how to respond, I said, "I hope so too."

"By the way," Irma interjected, "do you have a girlfriend?"

I assumed a blank expression and said nothing. It was one thing to join the Parnassus, but to have my life scrutinized by these ladies was out of the question.

"Yes, he does," Carmen Elvira said, to my astonishment. "Lucy told me all about it, Sammy."

"All about what?" I said.

Carmen Elvira flashed a maternal, approving smile. "About you and Claudia."

"Claudia!" I exclaimed, for the second time that day.

"Claudia Urrutia?" asked Irma in disbelief, giving me a long, searching look. "She's so . . ."

"So wealthy," said Carmen Elvira to settle the issue.

"Hey, look," I said to no one in particular. "I—"

"I hope you don't mind my mentioning it," Carmen Elvira interrupted me, "but Lucy told me you're practically engaged, that you're proposing tonight at the Saigon Rose."

"Congratulations, honey!" exclaimed Olga, leaping from the couch. This calls for a celebration. I have an *aguardiente* bottle I've been saving for a special occasion. Excuse me, I'll be right back."

"I'll help you with the glasses," Carmen Elvira offered, getting up too.

"We might as well have our lunch after the toast," Irma threw in. "I'll serve the *pasteles*. You do like *pasteles*, don't you?" And without waiting for confirmation, she followed the rest of the Parnassus into the kitchen.

I could have killed my mother. I reached for the telephone, but in the middle of dialing her number, I changed my mind. "Maybe I'm dreaming," I blurted out. I shook my head in an effort to wake myself up. But dreams are odorless and I could smell the *pasteles*. The situation reminded me of something; I couldn't, though, tell quite what. *Rosemary's Baby*, *Macbeth*, and *The Trial* all came to mind. I wondered if Claudia had been let into this plot, or whether we were both just random bystanders snarled in the machinations of a bunch of crazed Queens matrons.

Toasting my induction to the Parnassus, we drank the *aguardiente* Colombian style—a small glass filled to the top, followed by a quarter of a lime soaked in salt, which I chewed until my teeth felt as if they would fall out. Tears choked my vision. Carmen Elvira proposed another toast to my imminent engagement. I figured it would be better to play along than to go into long explanations about my and Claudia's sexuality. We drank to love and happiness. I had never seen Colombian women drink *aguardiente*: it is essentially a man's drink, but then, I reasoned, I was among intellectuals, not conventional housewives. . . .

I made small talk, asking, "Who made the *pasteles?*"

"I did," Irma said proudly.

"I never thought it would be possible to make a *pastel* taste like they do in Colombia. But they taste just as if you had cooked them in banana leaves," Carmen Elvira said.

"This is the best *pastel* I've had in a long time," I complimented the cook.

"Thank you, *su merced*. Have another."

"I will, when I finish this one. It's so big."

"Yes, Irma makes the most generous portions," Carmen Elvira said. "I follow your recipe, my dear, but they just don't taste the same."

"There must be something you're leaving out."

"Obviously. But I wonder what it is. I cook the pork with the chicken in the scallions and tomato sauce."

"Do you use fresh or dry coriander? That makes a big difference."

"Fresh. And I sprinkle the coriander on the meat just before I wrap the pastel in the aluminum foil."

"Maybe you don't use enough *guascas*."

"That's it. The *guascas*! Why didn't I think of it before? But it's impossible to get *guascas* in Jackson Heights."

"I bring it from Colombia. But you know they don't allow fruits or vegetables or spices into the country. I have to hide it in my panties. Once, I had to eat an *anón* at JFK because they were going to confiscate it. So, I said, 'Please, let me eat it.' And I did."

"I remember you told me. It was an *anón* from your mother's yard. I wish I had the guts to do something like that. Nerves of steel, that's what you have."

"In your panties?" I asked.

"Sure, sweetie. It was thrilling; I felt like a drug smuggler."

"Well lucky you," Carmen Elvira complained. "The last time I went to Colombia, when I came back they made me take off my panties. I was furious."

"That's right. You wrote that marvelous column about it. It created an international uproar, Sammy. It was reprinted in two Colombian newspapers."

"That's the power of the press for you," Carmen Elvira said solemnly, looking at me.

"What's *guascas*?" I asked. It seemed to me that I was at least two steps behind in the conversation, but since I had never heard of this herb or spice or whatever it was, I had to ask.

Olga had returned from the kitchen, and was setting a tray with drinks on the table. "What's what, honey?" she asked, handing me my Coke.

"*Guascas*," said Carmen Elvira.

I realized that as the culinary expert of the group, it was up to Olga to explain the mystery. "*Guascas*," she repeated, as she distributed the drinks. With an air of authority, she sat down and smoothed her dress. "In pre-Columbian times, the Indians used it as an aphrodisiac. It's rare because it only grows in the *páramo*. I, for one, think that if we could cultivate and export it commercially, Western cuisine as we know it would be revolutionized overnight."

"I'll be damned," I said.

Note

1. George De Stephano, "Living La Vida 'Loca,'" *The Nation*, August 19, 1999.

II

Religious Pluralities: Faith, Intolerance, Politics, and Accommodation

Christianity arrived in Colombia as the religion of the Spaniards. The association was juridical and explicit—papal bulls issued in Rome conceded to the Spanish and Portuguese monarchs a *patronato*, the right to exercise ecclesiastical authority in the New World. For indigenous people, Christianity was part of a wave of armed assault, death, and disease. From the perspective of enslaved Africans, too, evangelization accompanied violence: some baptisms took place on slave ships.

Evangelizers were often at odds with secular authorities. Readers familiar with the biography of Bartolomé de las Casas, the famous Dominican reformer, will find echoes of his writings in the words of a sixteenth-century Franciscan friar in Bogotá, Fray Jerónimo de San Miguel, who wrote: "My calling is to preach the Gospel and resist the cruelties inflicted upon these sad Indians." Specifically, Fray Jerónimo found himself in a confrontation with the *encomenderos* of Bogotá (an *encomienda* was a grant made by the crown, in which a Spaniard received the right to collect tribute, paid in labor and in goods, from a specific group of Indians). Yet priests received goods and labor from Indians too, and also meted out punishments, meaning that when a voice from the pulpit called for better treatment of Indians, it may have seemed like a mixed message. That same complexity can be seen in the relationship of Catholicism to slavery in the Americas. In this part, for example, the beatification documents for Jesuit priest Pedro Claver are layered with different levels of meaning. Claver expressed his call to evangelize enslaved Africans without denouncing slavery. Tensions nevertheless arose between the Jesuit and local Spaniards, who objected that he seated his black translators prominently and lavished gifts upon them. Reformers such as Claver and Fray Jerónimo often lost out when debates were settled in Europe, however. Vatican and Court authorities repeatedly upheld the *encomienda* system and slavery, institutions of colonial violence.

That official *patronato* continued into the early nineteenth century, when a local-born white elite attempted to argue that the newly independent Republic of New Granada should inherit the ecclesiastical authority the Crown had exercised in Colombia. The Vatican rejected their claim, which in turn fueled the anticlericalism of multiple generations of Liberal state builders, such as Tomás Cipriano de Mosquera, whose letter to Pope Pius IX sets out his reasons for waging a multifronted political attack on the Church. The face-off between Liberals and the Catholic hierarchy continued well into the twentieth century. Colombians generally assume an alliance between the Conservative Party and the right wing of the Catholic Church, just as they often take for granted the ubiquity of Catholicism in schools, hospitals, and workplaces.

The texts collected in this part track the intensity of Colombia's relationship to Catholicism, as well as some of its plasticity and internal contradictions. For most of the twentieth century the country was officially consecrated to the Sacred Heart, and children were exhorted to understand themselves as "Catholic, Apostolic, and Roman," even as they were raised in a culture that was often robustly irreverent. In 1991, a new Constitution drew a sharp boundary between Church and state and formally recognized the nation as multicultural. Indigenous and Afro-Colombian practices gained new possibilities for public respect. By the late twentieth century, Protestant congregations had grown and were holding services without obstacle, after a long history of intimidation. Jewish families, too, faced less of the obvious anti-Semitism they had encountered in earlier decades. And enormous changes had taken place within Catholicism itself—especially in its political role, which had become decidedly plural.

Idolators and *Encomenderos*

Fray Jerónimo de San Miguel

In 1550, Bartolomé las Casas debated Juan Ginés de Sepúlveda, laying out a theological defense of Indian communities that reverberated across Europe and the Americas. Las Casas's arguments grew out of the experiences of a generation of evangelizers who understood their charge as a double one—to Christianize Indians, on the one hand, and to defend even non-Christian Indians against the rapaciousness of conquistadors and their heirs, on the other. Writing to the Spanish king from the highlands of Santa Fe de Bogotá in the same year as the Las Casas/Sepúlveda debate, Fray Jerónimo attempts an even-handed tone. He asks the king to punish those Indians who return to "idolatry" after accepting baptism, but he also criticizes encomenderos for their "cruelties."[1]

His descriptions of the Indians themselves are foreshortened. Fray Jerónimo leaves out specific information: Where did Indians worship? Were their idols shaped in wood, stone, or clay? Were they in human or animal form? He is silent, too, about the form of the rituals and about the panoply of priests or soothsayers who participated. Yet a reader gains the impression that the "return to idolatry" he describes for 1550 is a return realized in secrecy, at risk of discovery, rather than the sort of return that later became common across the Americas—in which Christianity was laced with syncretism and indigenous people simply worshipped the old gods in new, Christian form. What is clear is that Fray Jerónimo, one of the founders of the Franciscan order in Colombia, understands his own world as shaped by power struggles. He knows himself to be a man caught in the middle. He beseeches the Court not to believe the calumnies other Spaniards will write about his ministry. And, indeed, he was later imprisoned by Spaniards angered by his self-appointed role as a protector of Indians.

I would not have done my duty nor what is right by my conscience if I did not make known to Your Royal Highness insofar as concerns the treatment on the natives. And first I wish to say that in this kingdom, although it is of a small amount of land, such vast and profound cruelty has been committed that if I did not know it to be unmistakably true, I would never believe that a

Figurines found in a *huaca* (indigenous burial site) near Quetame (central Colombia, between Bogotá and Villavicencio), as depicted in an engraving by Eustacio Barreto, published in 1882 in Bogotá's most ambitious nineteenth-century newsmagazine, the *Papel Periódico Ilustrado*. Photograph by Julio Racínes. *Papel Periódico Ilustrado*, vol. 21, July 10, 1882, 336, http://www.banrepcultural.org/sites/default/files/lablaa/historia/paperi/vi/vi_21.pdf. Courtesy of Banco de la República.

Altar with a Chibcha [Muisca] Sun Motif. Santo Domingo Church, Tunja (central Colombia, in the Eastern Cordillera). Photographer unknown. Pál and Elisabeth Kelemen Collection, from the exhibition *A Journey through El Dorado*, organized by the Latin American Library at Tulane University in 2000, Philip S. MacLeod, Curator. Used by permission of Tulane University.

Carved and Painted Ceiling over the Apse. Church of Santa Clara el Real, Tunja (central Colombia, in the Eastern Cordillera). Photographer unknown. Pál and Elisabeth Kelemen Collection, from the exhibition *A Journey through El Dorado*, organized by the Latin American Library at Tulane University in 2000, Philip S. MacLeod, Curator. Used by permission of Tulane University.

Christian heart could conceive of such cruel and fierce inhumanity. There is no torment or cruel treatment that has not been inflicted onto these sad and miserable natives by those who pride themselves on being Your Highness's faithful subjects. They have burnt some natives alive, and cut off hands, nose, tongue and other members of others, with great cruelty. Many others, they have hanged, both men and women. They have thrown natives to the dogs, cut off breasts of women and committed cruelties such that the very thought of these acts would make anyone who is a little bit Christian tremble. This is the way they serve Your Highness here, and these are the acts for which they expect to be remunerated. . . .

Treatment [of the Indians by the *encomenderos*] is now more moderate than at first. Yet because they have gone unpunished for their past cruelties, they have not stopped the bloodshed and other torments that I now hear are being carried out in villages, especially during the time of the *Demoras* [the eight months Indians are supposed to work in the mines]. During this time, the Indians' labor is not demanded according to what they can give, but according to the *encomenderos'* greed. . . . My job will be to travel from village to village visiting the Indians. Upon my return, for the sake of these poor Indians, I will tell Your Royal Highness what I see and discover, so that you may remedy the many and serious offenses committed against these natives. . . .

There is a great malady in this Kingdom, which is that many Indians, especially *ladinos*,[2] come to receive our Holy Faith and the sacrament of baptism; but after having lived many years as Christians and having participated in our sacrifices and the mysteries of the Faith, if they are given the occasion, however small, they quit their conversation with Christians and go to their villages, returning to the nepharious rites of their idolatries; and they scorn what they saw among us, betraying what is done in Church and applying it to the veneration of their sanctuaries and idols. And, this being a disparagement of our Holy Faith, a great disgrace to the name of Christ and a condemnation of these Indians, and even an obstacle such that the other [Indians] might not come to know the truth, I humbly plead to Your Royal Highness, honoring Our Lord, that the name of Christ not suffer such great impropriety nor that the other mysteries of our Faith be spread among people so inured in their idolatries, but rather that you fix this by ordering this high court not to allow that these Indians, who professed their faith in God's law in their baptism, return to their sects and customs of idolatry, but instead that they be made to live as Christians. And so that this great malady and grave offense to God might be fixed, it is necessary that Your Royal Highness appoint a person or declare that the high court appoint a person who, looking only to God and leaving behind all pretension for worldly gain or sinister purpose, would go about the Indian villages to see if those who embraced our Faith live correctly, and to prevent them from returning to their idolatries.

Just the same, it seems to me that, as Your Royal Highness has mandated that we come here to ensure the conversion of the natives, something which would come easily with the help of Our God according to what I have seen in the many caciques and principal Indians to whom I have spoken many times through interpreters, it would be beneficial that Your Highness declare that all those who voluntarily came to the sacrament of baptism be made to live as Christians and be reprimanded and even punished for deviation, under the understanding that their idolatries and diabolic rites are only but new weeds. Because to think that they do not keep to that which they promised in their baptism, or that they are not to be reprimanded for their faults with respect to the Faith, makes us ill at ease admitting them to the family of the Church, as provided by Your Royal Highness.

I presently consider it important to notify Your Highness of this matter so that you may issue the appropriate remedy. Of all that would be done here, I will always render a very truthful report to Your Highness, in hopes that by knowing the truth you might provide protection for these natives and so that my conscience might be alleviated. Being that Your Highness sent me here, it is my duty to carry out my mandate even though I know with certainty that many would write hatefully about me, as my calling is to preach the Gospel and resist the cruelties inflicted upon these sad Indians and enforce compliance and respect for the New Laws that Your Highness issued on behalf of the natives' liberty.[3] Yet, I believe that Your Highness will not accept reports from those who lie and only aspire to their own interests and from all those who celebrate the thefts committed against the natives. Those people will work as hard as possible to diminish your opinion of me so that Your Highness might give little credit to my letters, to which I plead that not less be given than the truth with which they were written. If any untruth be found in my letters, I plead that Your Highness would have me punished as a liar because it would be treason to falsely inform on matters of such import to Your Royal Highness. Yet, I hope that the strength of the truth has more power over Your Highness than the malice of those ruled by their passions. Harboring this hope, I shall not refrain from speaking and writing the truth.

May the Lord allow that your Royal Highness's glory and honor continue to grow in the name of God. In the city of Santa Fe of the New Kingdom of Granada, 20 August 1550. Signed by Your Holy Majesty's most humble servant,

Fray Jerónimo de San Miguel

Translated by Larissa Brewer García

Notes

1. The *encomendero* was an individual who received from the Spanish Crown rights to labor and tribute from a specified Indian community or a set of communities. The *encomendero* had a theoretical responsibility to provide protection and the conditions necessary for the Indians' evangelization (often ignored in practice). *Encomiendas* were in many instances inheritable, although the Crown generally sought to place limits on individuals' ability to bequeath their grants.

2. In this context, *ladino* refers to an indigenous person who had been converted to Christianity.

3. The "New Laws" were issued by the Crown in 1542 and were influenced in part by the writings of Bartolomé de las Casas. Because these were reforms that sought to curtail conquistadors' rights over Indian communities, Crown officials found them difficult to enforce, and royal efforts to protect Indians were indeed limited.

Miracles Made Possible
by African Interpreters

Anna María Splendiani and Tulio Aristizábal, SJ

Saint Peter Claver (1581–1654) is perhaps Colombia's most famous religious figure. A Jesuit who was canonized in 1888, he symbolizes black Christians' faith that even if their ancestors first heard of Jesus Christ through white evangelizers and were baptized in racist contexts, their faith could still be redemptive. Taken as "the slave of the slaves," Claver's biography has become central to the way the slave port of Cartagena figures in the Colombian national imagination—understandings that focus on branding and the auction block exist alongside understandings that center on the succor provided first by Alonso de Sandoval, SJ (1576–1652), and then by Claver, Sandoval's disciple. Significantly, neither is understood as having opposed slavery; rather, they are seen as having focused on ministry and baptism. The following narrations were collected in Cartagena between 1658 and 1670 as part of what eventually became the successful effort to canonize Claver. Reading them, part of what stands out is the language the Vatican used to understand holiness; in that sense they are narratives produced with a particular aim. Yet much else is communicated besides. Witnesses to Claver's holiness were also witnesses to his dependence on African translators, to whom he showed deference, and to the material culture that was a part of his ministry, including tobacco, handkerchiefs, medallions, and "high chairs with arms for the interpreters."

Witness, the Reverend Father Nicolás González, temporal coadjutator of the Society of Jesus, forty-six years old.

. . . This witness knows well that Father Claver would feel so much inner joy and happiness upon learning that a slave ship was arriving to this city that he would offer to give masses as a reward to the first person to bring him news of a ship's arrival. . . .

To administer the baptism, he would stand in the middle of the ship surrounded by the slaves, and through the interpreters he would say that he had come there to be everyone's father so that they would be welcomed to the land of the whites where they had arrived. He would do this while giving them many reasons and loving and passionate words to assuage the fear that these poor people always have that whites take them to their lands to kill them and turn them into lard. The devil convinces them of this in their lands. They believe this so firmly that if the Jesuit priests did not disabuse them of this notion, they would be left to die of anguish upon arriving in this city. For this reason, the care that the Father would take to rid them of this falsity was very important, showing himself to be benign and sweet with all of them, giving them many caresses and signs of friendship. Often it would happen that God would immediately reward him for this kindness and effort because, before the Father would leave the ships, some of the many sick slaves who had just been baptized would often die; and the same thing would happen with some of the babies born on the ocean who he had baptized. Claver would take such great joy from this, that his pale and gaunt face would grow red, burning like fire, and he would give infinite thanks to God to have been used as an instrument to save these souls. . . .

If Claver had not been completely possessed by God, it would have been impossible for him to show such holy and extreme signs of kindness. For the first thing he would do was to remove his cloak and place it on the first moribund slave he could find strewn naked on the hard floor. Claver would use it to cover the slave and protect his decency during the entire time needed to attend to him to examine if he was baptized. When the slave was not baptized, Claver would instruct and prepare him to receive the baptism, without concerning himself over the slave's illness, no matter how contagious or nauseating it was. Often, their sickly abscesses would leave stains on the cloak. Other times, the cloak would adhere to the skin of the sick, due to the many putrid discharges with which they tend to arrive. These abscesses produce greater and more nauseating, pestilent stenches than do the most infected wounds. It is customary for every priest to be given two simple handkerchiefs every week so that he can use them to clean the sweat from his face, due to the great heat of this city. Father Claver would never clean his face with them, but would rather only use the back of his cloak. Instead, he would use the handkerchiefs to clean the faces of the sick that were often so full of dirt they seemed to be made of pure mud. . . .

Witness Andrés Sacabuche, black man from Angola, interpreter of the Venerable Servant of God, forty-five years old.

The way Father Peter Claver would catechize blacks was to first teach them, through this witness and the other interpreters, to make the sign of the cross perfectly with the thumb and index fingers of their right hand. He would usually spend one hour doing this because he would examine them one at a time, checking to see if they were doing it well and were correctly making a cross. Sometimes there would be a great number of them, for there could be more than three hundred and sometimes four hundred. Then he would ask them all together to lift up their right hands, showing the perfectly formed sign of the cross. Next, he would teach them to cross themselves. He would give a gift of tobacco to the person who was the best at this and who had learned most quickly, and he would hit the person who was slowest in learning this on the head with the staff of the cross that he held in his hands or he would have one of the witness's fellow interpreters hit this person on the head as punishment for paying little attention and showing little diligence. Next, he would teach them Our Father, Mary Full of Grace, and the Credo. He would command them to believe in only one God, that was the Holy Trinity: God the Father, God the Son and God the Holy Spirit, that even though these seemed to be three people, they were really only one God. To help them better understand this, he would fold his handkerchief into three folds, showing them and making it apparent to them that there were three of them, and then he would say to them that it was only really one piece of cloth. With this, they easily believed that mystery. . . .

He would then ask each one again out loud three times through the interpreters if they wanted to be Christian and if they wanted to be baptized. When they answered "yes," he would baptize them with a pitcher that was sometimes made of silver and other times of clay, spilling the water over their heads and telling them, "Johnny—here he would say the Christian name they were supposed to assume—I baptize you in the name of the Father, the Son, and the Holy Spirit." If Claver had a doubt about whether they had already been baptized, he would baptize them "sub conditione," saying, "If you are not baptized, I baptize you . . ." Upon finishing this, the Father's assistant or one of the interpreters would tie a lead medal on a string, or something similar, around the neck of the recently baptized person, which was a sign that they had been baptized by the hands of the Father. This witness remembers that these medals were engraved on one side with the image of Jesus and on the other with the image of Mary. . . .

Witness Francisco Yolofo, slave, fifty years old.

He would give them loving speeches so that they would feel happy to have come to the land of the Spanish, where they would know the true God and receive the holy baptism. Then he would distribute many presents that he would bring with him after having asked for alms for them among the devout. Then he would kneel among them, and the slaves would imitate him by doing the same. In a soft and devout voice, he would teach them to make a cross with their fingers, to cross themselves, and to say Our Father and the Credo. After, we would say good-bye to them and return to the Jesuit School.[1] The next day he would visit them again, gathering them in the same way as the day before, and through the interpreters he would teach them the mysteries of Our Holy Faith. To do this, he would place blankets, boards, and mats in the corridor for the slaves to sit on. He would send for high chairs with arms for the interpreters to sit in, and he would sit on an empty pot or on some small bench or piece of wood.

Often, when important people . . . would walk in, seeing the Father so badly accommodated and poorly seated, they would grow very upset, asking how it was possible that the interpreters be seated with so much authority and the Father without any. Claver would stand up, defending this witness and all the other interpreters, and say that they were the most important people in this work and that he figured very little in it, and that for this reason they should be seated with the utmost authority so that the slaves would respect them and give credit to what they would say to them. In particular, on one such occasion, the Spanish Captain Don Antonio de Subiza who loved the Father very much for being his good friend became very angry at the witness and the other interpreters, saying to Claver: "How, my friend, can you consent to having these black dogs seated in high backed chairs with armrests, while you, Father, are seated so uncomfortably, without any authority?" The Father responded in defense of this witness and the rest of the interpreters what he had said to others who had also complained. With this, the Captain was left amazed and edified by the Father's humility and mortification. If ever there were insufficient seats of authority for the interpreters, Claver would ask the owners of the house for them. He would not want to begin the instruction and teaching of the slaves until they had brought the chairs and he saw that every interpreter was seated in them. If any black person could not find a seat on the blankets, boards, or mats that he had laid out, Claver would spread out his cloak on the floor and command that they sit on it. Often, he would have men who were sick to their stomachs sit on it, and they would dirty it such that it was necessary to wash them. Yet he would not want it washed until they had returned to the Jesuit school. Even though the slaves would relieve themselves on the cloak, as it has been said, and many sick blacks with repugnant sores would sit on it and stain it with the fluids that secreted from their bodies, it never smelled bad. This was observed by the witness and the rest of his fellow interpreters.

Translated by Larissa Brewer García

Note

1. This is a rare occasion when the scribe forgets to use the third person to transcribe the witness's testimony.

My Soul, Impoverished and Unclothed . . .

Francisca Josefa Castillo

The cloistered nun Francisca Josefa de la Concepción del Castillo y Guevara (1671–1742), known to generations of Colombian students as "la Madre Castillo," wrote poetry and prose marked by intensity and mysticism. The relatively wealthy daughter of a criollo family in Tunja, she was well educated and as an adult read Latin and even ventured into theological writing. Her poetry and autobiographical writing fits within a tradition of nuns' writings in colonial Spanish America, from Mexico's erudite and scientifically inclined Sor Juana Inés de la Cruz (1648–95) to a range of lesser-known women writers who used convent life to follow the example of Saint Teresa (1515–82). Like other nuns whose writings are preserved, la Madre Castillo presents herself as writing to better obey her male confessors and not as an act of interiority or artistic desire. Nevertheless, her language turns on powerful imagery and her authorial voice is compelling; she writes as a thinking, dreaming, doubting "I." Strikingly, this "I" is one of self-abnegation. Readers may find Madre Castillo's descriptions of self-flagellation strange, but it's worth remembering that the practices she describes were an accepted part of colonial Catholicism. The following excerpt provides a glimpse of the emotional way Madre Castillo brings readers into her inner world.

God gave me a great desire for this Holy Spirit and true God, the third person of the Most Blessed Trinity, and I contemplated the joy (never fully understood by all creatures) of the soul, which holds and has It within itself, how rich the soul is, how blessed, and how filled with wealth.

How shall I describe, my God, the evils and depths in which I found myself, surrounded by horrible temptations of this kind, or the things which the enemy moved both within me and without, or the war I had inside myself? Human strength can do little or nothing against this damned vice, if God distances himself, so close is it to us in this most vile flesh, which is no more than a sack of decay. That highest gift of chastity and purity, which makes of the soul the spouse of the Most High God, descends from above, from the Father of Light. I tore open my flesh with iron chains: I had myself beaten at the hands of a servant; I spent the nights in tears; I wore nettles and cilices for relief; I wounded my face with blows; and it was then that I thought I had been defeated at the hands of my enemies. I went around filled with dread and horror, not daring to raise my eyes toward God, nor toward his Holiest Mother, in whom I could not find comfort and life. I consulted my confessor continuously, and I struggled to use the means he provided me; yet I knew that the Most High and Most Pure God wished to humble my pride, and make me hate myself, as if I were a sack of excrement; and so it was that I could not take a step without finding a trap. I do not know if it was for this purpose that, some time before I began to experience this, Our Father had shown me my own soul in the form of a traveler climbing a hill, impoverished and unclothed, and so wasted that he seemed to hold himself up and walk on legs so thin they seemed like blades of straw, hunched over, because he carried a sack of excrement on his back, which also held many foul creatures; arrows were shot at him from one side of that hill and the other, which, hitting those animals, caused them to grunt and cry out in such an ruckus that the poor laborer became greatly burdened and fatigued; I do not know if in order to avoid such irritating noise, he plunged the arrows into himself, or if I was only aware that this could happen; what I do remember is that those wounds made the animals weak and thin, and though still screaming, they gave him less trouble; I then understood the psalm that says *In Domino confido: quomodo dicitis animae meae: Transmigra in montem sicut passer?*[1] This happened a while before this time of tribulation, and now I recall it here.

When Our Father, taking pity on me, wished to mitigate my torment, I would search for Him continuously in solitude, and keep a closer watch over my senses. One day, as I was in prayer, I felt my soul come undone and burn, and later I thought I felt next to me the kindest person, dressed all in white, whose face I could not see; yet that person, throwing arms onto my shoulders, placed upon them a load that, although considerable, was so sweet, so soft, so strong, so calm, that the soul only wished to die and to reach its end within it and with it: yet it could do no more than to receive it and burn within itself.

Even though, given the advice of my confessors and because of my ever-present fears, I looked away as much as I could at the beginning, they would leave the soul with strength to endure these labors, and with an inclination toward virtue. Yet I can see, with the passage of so much time, as can everyone, how far I am from all virtue and its exercise; and it is for this reason that every day my fear increases, and I am consoled only by God's infinite mercy, and that resting on this alone, on the blood that He shed for me, and on the intercession of his Most Holy Mother, will He be willing to safely remove me from this prolonged and arduous path and exile.

Translated by Ana María Gómez López, with assistance from Katherine McKnight

Note

1. The quotation is from Psalms 10:2: "In the Lord I put my trust: how then do you say to my soul: Get thee away from hence to the mountain like a sparrow?" It is worth noting that the psalm continues in a way that would work to vindicate Madre Castillo's claims to voice: "For, lo, the wicked have bent their bow; they have prepared their arrows in the quiver; to shoot in the dark the upright of heart. For they have destroyed the things which thou hast made" (King James Version).

A King of Cups

Gregorio José Rodríguez Carrillo, Bishop of Cartagena

In November 1819, after the battles of Vargas' Swamp and Boyacá (in July and August 1819), and just before the constitution of the Republic of Colombia (at Angostura in 1819), the bishop of Cartagena issued a political message. He did so from the relative safety of a Royalist stronghold, as Cartagena did not fall to the patriots until October 1821, more than a year after Bolívar, in his August 1820 siege of the city, had attempted to gain a bloodless surrender of the plaza. His message is a clear example of the rhetoric of the high clergy loyal to the Crown, as churchmen in the Americas were split over the question of republicanism. In general, the ecclesiastical hierarchy sided with the Crown, while parish priests and the orders adopted a variety of positions, from Royalist to neutral to fiercely pro-independence; some even wrote out catechisms to demonstrate biblical supports for Republican ideals. In this same year, 1819, for example, Bolívar's then vice president, Francisco de Paula Santander (who managed the business of governing while Bolívar managed the war), issued a decree demanding that priests explain to their parishioners that supporting the patriots was not a heresy. Some priests were so fervent in their republicanism that they went so far as to describe the Spanish Conquest itself, three hundred years previous, as an illegitimate usurpation of "natural rights" given by God.

Writing more than ten years after Napoleon forced Charles IV and his son Ferdinand to formally cede their claims to the Spanish throne—a move they insisted was illegitimate—the bishop understood the nature of the crisis: Whom to obey in the absence of the king? In 1814 Ferdinand had returned to the throne and had repudiated the Liberal (but promonarchy) Constitution of 1812. For local elites living in theaters of war such as New Granada and Venezuela—or, to the south, Buenos Aires and the captaincy of Chile—that repudiation became a point of no return. The patriot armies were now seeking independence, and they were republicans. For the bishop, on the other hand, Ferdinand's return is to be celebrated by all Spaniards—he is a father to all, "whatsoever one's education, condition, or class." Those who disagreed were "Robespierres of Venezuela," "traitors," "insatiable monsters." Bolívar, above all, he excoriates as an upstart who cannot feed even a single battalion for one month yet puts himself up as a lord and treats his followers as "slaves." Again, the date of Bishop José Gregorio's message is significant. Bolívar's 1813 decree of "war to the death," his declaration of terror, is in full force (see part V). The war will not end until Bolívar signs a treaty with the Liberal Spanish general Pablo Murillo in 1820.

Spaniards of the Kingdom:

. . . I see torn and in pieces the most sacred bonds of religion, of society, of politics, which should bind us eternally with an unalterable cordiality, due to the harmful influence that the enemy has thrown among you. The principles of the sacred religion we profess should identify us more and more as the greatest of all alliances, even if you were not as you are a great family under the direction of the common father and Lord of all the Spains, Ferdinand VII, great, high, powerful, virtuous and loved by all peoples and protected by God. Each of us should not want for himself more than he should want for others; nor should he do unto others more than that which he would wish done unto him. It was on this principle that in creation God established all the harmony and accord of civilized humankind, later sanctified by the human blood of the Redeemer. The Divine Master imbued with this principle all the spirit of Christianity. You will love God above everything else, and your neighbor as yourself. See here, brothers, the sum of all the prophets and the gospels. And is there anything else that conforms more to the innate desires of the human heart? Who, despite their roughness and boorishness, cannot know the weight of this truth? Who among you would want to be murdered and have taken the fruit of your efforts, your sweat, and your toil, while being in peace, within the holiness of your home, and the arms of your family? Who among you wishes for such an insult, regardless of your studies, your condition, your class? And if no one wishes it for themselves, why is it that so many engage and practice this disgrace of reason with fellow Spaniards, with fellow servants of King Ferdinand, with fellow Christians and sons of God, under the vain and frivolous pretext that they were not born in their parish? What is the delirium of these inhumane men? What insanity? What barbarity? What fury out of the abyss and out of hell? Who has inspired such blasphemous and sacrilegious moralities, so contrary to the glory of your character, of your religion, and of your laws? The traitors? Oh, monsters insatiable for human blood! Oh, new Robespierres from Venezuela! Oh, Neros a thousand times more barbaric than Agrippina the murderer! Hypocrites! What centaurs could cause as much harm to their nation as has been caused by your cruel envy and insatiable ambition? Brothers and companions, let us move aside the veil of this mystery of inequity that has enveloped you in its shadows, and begin to see things as they are and in their true image. The treacherous traitors, transformed into evil and lying foxes, have fooled your docility, telling you that they need nothing from you; that it is only America's freedom that has compelled them to take up arms; that it is only toward this sacred ideal that they sacrifice their fortune, their calm, their peace, and their amenities; that war against tyrants must be eternal; and that they will willingly perish for the independence of their country. And you believe them? And you ascertain that they speak to you in good faith and what they say is a clear truth? Oh! How you fool yourselves! Oh! And how you innocently run toward sacrifice! Those who want nothing of you want it all; they want your property, however limited it might be, they want your liberty, they want your obedience, they want your respect, they want your peace, they want your life, your blood, your ruin, and your eternal damnation. This is all these measly uninterested men want. Look at their ventures, to see if this is not true: some want to be demagogues, others to share power among three, while others want to be dictators; this one, Landaman; the other, King; and yet this other, Caesar. And what resources do these shirtless men have to aspire to such power, however meagerly rich they may be? To leave such a position of penury for one of such splendor? To maintain a civil war that pits one against the other, and destroys towns and provinces like wild beasts? Then it is that this is a lie, it is falseness, it is deceit, and it is a hypocrisy of the highest kind to claim that they want nothing from you, that what they aspire to is independence in your territory, freedom and equality for all citizens, and the downfall of tyranny and despotism. And in order for you to better understand the evidence of this truth I lay out before you, which of these traitors can equip and maintain just one battalion for even a month, using their own possessions, their own revenue, their own savings, their own home? None, not even Bolívar when he owned the goods of a virtuous Spaniard, diligent and hard working, which he acquired with his own sweat and blood. And if, being the wealthiest of all traitors, even he could not equip a battalion and maintain it for one month, how will he be able to maintain a division, no matter how small? So it is that to do so they will need to ransack towns, destroy families, plunder homes, and not leave anything in the country or towns that they can pillage. Add to this that, not having any possessions of his own, given that he squandered them going to Paris to turn from Christian to atheist, from man to beast, from American Spaniard sweet in his customs to an awful and barbaric Robespierre, without you he is a true beggar, a rogue and a hustler, that has nothing with which to eat or dress or live. And if this is as clear as sunlight in a bright and serene day, how much will he need you to play the part of King, Caesar, Sovereign, which is the only role he wants to play in this comedy. And if this is not so, tell me:

when has he taken up a rifle and fought amid you in the ranks? When has he fought head-on in battle? When has he striven to perish with you who only fight for his cause, and not fled cowardly, trading a general's hat and military jacket for a peasant's nightdress to escape from danger? Your King Bolívar is a spider lord that throws you to the storm while remaining on the banks, to the flames as he blows from afar. You fall, your children die, your towns burn, your fields are destroyed, and that king of cups claims that he needs nothing from you, that all he does is for your own good, your liberty, your equality, and your independence? Oh, tremendous liar! Oh, unabashed deceiver! Oh, unblushing and shameless contortionist! So you want nothing from the Americans and already you are their king? And you treat them as your slaves? Oh, innocent children! Oh, lost young children! And you die physically, morally, and eternally to prolong for two more weeks, two more months, this fabulous comedy by King Bolívar? Oh, deplorable disgrace for you! Oh, cruel condemnation! Oh, everlasting ignominy! Illustrious men: what can be made of a swindling King, without house or home? And this is for whom you rebel against the great Ferdinand? And it is for him you slander your name and that of future generations? And it is for him that you put out the flame of your ancestors? . . .

Bolívar, vain, arrogant, brazen, conceited, impious, without religion, wants to deprive King Ferdinand of the crown inherited from his ancestors, and which God has preserved in the midst of great dangers through a series of miracles. I, an elder Christian, am pleased that His Majesty holds it, possesses it, and rules it for many years, and to sustain this order I will do as much as my strengths will allow, and I am so pleased by this divine disposition that it brings me more happiness that His Majesty be king than if I were to be in his place. And I will tell you a hyperbole: that if it were my will and I were free to do so, I would donate [the crown] to His Majesty, convinced as I am that he is like Saul, better than the rest of his people. Bolívar, hypocrite, liar, has cheated you by saying that he wants nothing more from you than equality, independence, the essential rights of all men. And when he saw you in this troublesome situation, he did not think of you but only of himself, of his kingdom and his crown. I tell you that never, not even for one instant, have there ever been free men, equal men, independent men. Adam obeyed God, his sons obeyed Adam, his grandchildren and descendants their primitive parents. There were kings, there were republics, the first were rulers, while the second, chiefs of the latter. People obeyed constantly one and others without that chimerical liberty. There were classes, there were orders, there were distinctions that not everyone could attain. And in your republic, who is in charge? Schemers, liars, contortionists. Are you the same as them? And do you sit together at the same table? And do you wear the same brocade? And do you attend their councils? And have they married your daughters or have your sons married theirs? So it is they do not recognize you as equal, so it is that they aspire to certain superiority, so it is that they want power, and if anyone disputes this, thus they will kill them as he [Bolívar] killed Piar.

. . . Issued in Cartagena of Indies, on November 29, 1819.

Gregorio José, Bishop.

Translated by Ana María Gómez López and Ann Farnsworth-Alvear

Courting Papal Anger: The "Scandal" of Mortmain Property

Tomás Cipriano de Mosquera

On January 15, 1862, still one generation into Independence, Colombia's best-known politician was the Popayán-born caudillo, aristocrat, and hero of the war against Spain, Tomás Cipriano de Mosquera y Arboleda (1798–1878). Mosquera wrote to Pope Pius IX a letter we include below in a partial transcription. As he wrote, a civil war (1860–62) raged—although it was settled by February 1863; three months later, delegates to a convention in Rionegro, Antioquia, produced a new constitution, markedly Liberal and Federalist, and designated him Colombia's president.

Mosquera's letter captures the full intensity of the deep-rooted political and religious conflict that shaped the institutional relations between Church and state in Colombia—from the Independence period through the late nineteenth century. Since the "discovery" of América, altar and throne had governed jointly, as the papacy conceded to the Spanish Crown extraordinary rights over the Church in the New World. The terms of the patronato, as this set of regulatory concessions was known, included the right to name bishops and ecclesiastical beneficiaries at every level of the Church hierarchy; intervene in ecclesiastical tribunals; receive tithes in the name of the Church; found missions; and, in general, exercise administrative control over the functioning of the regular and secular clergy. By the late eighteenth century, with the expulsion of the Jesuits and the expropriation of their assets, and with the beginning of a series of fiscal and financial measures undertaken by Spain's Bourbon monarchs—more politically and fiscally than religiously motivated—the regime of cooperation between Church and Crown evinced serious fissures.

The majority of New Granadans did not involve themselves in the debate over the relationship between Church and state. These were questions that involved what we might call the political sociability of elites. Mosquera addresses the pope with familiarity, even impudence. He came from one of the viceroyalty's most socially prominent families, had been educated within the canon of the Spanish Enlightenment, and came of age during the war for independence, imbibing the Liberalism of Bolívar's inner circle. For Mosquera, the new Liberal government should inherit *the Church-granted right of patronato. If that authority had for centuries been the king's, it should now be wielded by the new states. Addressing himself to the first pope to have visited the Americas in person, Mosquera wrote as a man of the Enlightenment, as a Freemason, as a Bolivarian military officer, as a man of "progress," but also as a patrician with familial links to systems of authority both civil and religious. His brother Manuel José de Mosquera y Arboleda had been archbishop of Bogotá and had gone into exile after a fierce conflict in 1852 with the Liberal regime of José Hilario López over Church rights. A year later Manuel José died in Marseille while traveling to Rome to meet Pope Pius IX.*

And how did Pius IX respond? Within a few years he had formally denounced Liberalism as an error and described Spanish America as a place of "ferocious war" against the Church. Mosquera's letter allows readers the beginnings of a sense of the way political rhetoric was conjoined with prosaic confrontations over resources and power. Mosquera is intent on defending the Liberals' attempts to expropriate mortmain property, understood as property that could not be sold and that would perpetually remain in the hands of the Church. From Mosquera's perspective, expropriating Church land was within the government's prerogative and would enable better use of an underused resource; from the Vatican's perspective, such action was an attack. He is also explicit that the government has the right to exercise legal and police authority over the clergy. The decree of tuition Mosquera makes reference to in his letter, for example, required priests to swear obedience to Colombia's new national constitution and, in Mosquera's view, allowed for the arrest of priests who opposed his administration.

T. C. Mosquera, president of the United States of Colombia
To His Holiness Pius IX, Supreme Pontiff.

Most Holy Father,

It is not the first time that I must address Your Holiness in my role as first Magistrate of a Nation; and thus, I have no doubt that my official letter will be received by Your Holiness with the same trust and benevolence as my previous ones; and that in it you will find the same loyalty with which I have always spoken to the Holy See and the candor and sincerity required by the Supreme Magistrate of a Nation. . . .

Your Holiness knows well the events that took place in this Nation when complications arose in the relationship between the civil interim Government and the Episcopate of Granada in 1852. To bring this complication to an end, the Government of New Granada decided to satisfy the wishes of Catholics by leaving the Church independent from the Interim Authority. . . .

Emiliano Villa, *Death of a Reprobate*, ca. 1893. Oil on canvas, 140 × 205 cm. Courtesy of Banco de la República.

This withholding of public Authority from strictly spiritual matters was not adequately appreciated by a sector of the Episcopate of Granada nor by the Papal Delegate, both of whom became involved in political questions and hoping to identify religious matters with public questions that unfortunately have divided our Nation. . . .

The Bishops of Pasto and Pamplona, along with members of the clergy, have become involved in supporting one party so that religion may serve as an electoral instrument for political Magistrates. A Canon from Bogotá, Father Sucre, joined an electoral club and, disregarding his Prelate the Bishop, addressed a handbill to all the priests of the Archbishopric, so that the candidacy of General Herrán be substituted for that of Julio Arboleda, who was the candidate of the party that destroyed the federal Constitution. Many clergymen have engaged themselves in the revolution, abusing of their pastoral ministry, in order to agitate the masses to rebel against the constitutional State Governments; some of them have even taken up arms, and there is the scandal of a priest who died in combat while heading a guerrilla [band]. I will not describe to your Holiness other such events, as what is stated is enough to make my point.

For some time we Catholics have had to regret, after the intervention of the civil Government to present to Your Holiness ideal priests for the

Episcopates, that vacancies have instead in some cases been filled with people who are not fit to honorably represent the Episcopate, lacking in character and rightness, such as the Bishop of Cartagena, Father Medina, whose reference is no other than having fought in the civil war of 1851, spear in hand, at Garrapata; Father Arbeláez, who before being ordained as a Bishop required three months of previous study in order to make him suitable for consecration; and the Bishop of Pamplona, a priest of little schooling concerned solely with a party's victory; all this despite that there is no shortage of priests of science and virtue in Granada's Clergy.

We must generally regret the lack of Seminaries in our Nation where youth can be educated for the priesthood; and the ecclesiastical career has become a lucrative profession, practiced by men without science, and in which many individuals have been ordained without even knowing Latin; so that the priestly ministry is exercised without an understanding of the sacred Scripture nor the prayers said in mass.

It with great feeling that I must tell Your Holiness that a growing number of priests live scandalously with concubines, and they are thus unable to preach morality. It is apparent that their preaching recommends the payment of ecclesiastical contributions, in order to use these goods for their families and not for Worship. . . .

There is more, Most Holy Father: the Catholic devotion in this nation had provided great riches to Worship, and since public authority has not intervened in their conservation, many of these properties have disappeared, unlawfully disposed; and, with few exceptions, Bishops have contributed with condemnable condescension to the destruction of these assets. Thus, it was necessary to order the disentitlement of these assets as mortmain property, and thus be introduced into national commerce, consolidating their value in the national Treasury, so that their interests may be faithfully invested in the purpose for which they were donated. This has been verified, and Churches receive what is needed to cover the expenses of Worship, as the Government recognizes the maxim that in a free and independent Nation the Church must also be equally free and independent. The degree of Tuition has been wrongfully understood, and it has been stated that the government is attempting to intervene in strictly ecclesiastical business, and provide authority to priests and Bishops to exercise their ministry. No doubt Your Holiness has been misinformed by the Papal Delegate, whom I had to exile from the country, for having supported the political party that is no longer in power. . . .

Several Bishops, among them the Metropolitan, an old personal friend of mine, have opposed the Government by disobeying the Decrees of Tuition and Disentitlement of Mortmain Property; and I have found myself obliged to confine them to other residences or exile them for rebelling against the interim authority, as they should, in accordance to Papal precepts, submit to those in power, and not forget the precepts of the Holy Bishop of Pospona, Doctor of the Church, Saint Augustine, who counseled obedience even to tyrants. . . .

After abandoning the metropolitan Church, several virtuous priests have held Catholic Worship in their churches, and the faithful take pride in attending these religious functions; they address God, in Colombia's capital, giving thanks for the aid they receive, while those of the likes of Bishop Arbeláez order disobedience of public authority, thus establishing a division among Catholics that only Your Holiness can resolve, by calling upon Colombian Prelates to avoid this division among the faithful, as they have been ordained Bishops to guide the happiness of the Christian people, and in compliance with the interim authority, to remain in their Dioceses so that they may be of use to Christian peoples, as their main duty is to ensure harmony among the faithful. . . .

I know well, Most Holy Father, that in exercising the Supreme Power of this Nation as I do, it is my duty to respect the independence of the Catholic Church, as it is required by law of me; but I also know that civil Power cannot waver in the face of functions that are not ecclesiastic as is practiced by Bishops and priests.

In order for clergy to exercise their ministry with absolute independence, we have provided them with personal exemptions from military service, local offices, and personal contributions from all revenues obtained as alms from the faithful, as well as compensation for all the services they provide in their ministry.

In conclusion, I must express to Your Holiness that the Government of Colombia is willing to allow the return of Bishops to their particular dioceses, as soon as they recognize the Decrees known as Tuition and Disentitlement of Mortmain Property. . . .

With sentiments of filial respect, I reassert myself as a devoted son of Your Holiness,

T. C. DE MOSQUERA
Facatativá, January 15, 1862

Translated by Ana María Gómez López

Liberalism and Sin

Anonymous, Rafael Uribe Uribe, and Andrés Botero

Colombia swung from the fierce anticlericalism of the Liberal decades of the mid-nineteenth century to an unbridled, ultramontane clericalism that announced itself in three portents: the Liberals' defeat in the civil war of 1885, a new pro-Catholic Constitution in 1886, and the Concordat of 1887. The clergy exacted revenge: they rebuilt a presence with immigrant priests who had experienced the realities of secularization in Europe, Mexico, Central America, and Ecuador and who brought their resentments with them. Through the first decades of the twentieth century the Colombian hierarchy formally rejected Liberalism. And they insisted on declarations of faith: by signing an oath such as the first of the three texts included below, individual Liberals might redeem themselves.

If eighty years previously the dictum had been that Independence was a sin, now Liberalism was a sin, and this equation would persist in Colombia—overtly or covertly—until the early 1960s. By then, of course, the Church itself was changing. Slowly, the ecclesiastic mood moved away from scrutiny, vigilance, and stigmatization. The Conservatives, too, began to change by the 1960s, and open Hispanophilia decreased to a point of invisibility. Part of that change traced back to Liberals' self-defense against the charge of irreligiosity. Rafael Uribe Uribe (1859–1914) emphatically insisted that "liberalism is not a sin." The phrase was a primary part of his leadership years in the Liberal Party, prior to his brutal murder on the streets of Bogotá. In the second extract below, Uribe warns against minimally educated, unimaginative priests caught up in their own pomposity. He uses as a foil Friar Gerundios de Campazas, a preacher so carried away by his own high-sounding language that he never realizes his own ridiculousness. This was a fictional character created by the Jesuit satirist José Francisco de Isla (1703–82). Pulling together official Church publications and writings by Catholic theologians, Uribe undertakes to refute one of the Friar Gerundios, the Spanish priest D. Félix Sardá y Salvany, who, within Spain, supported the anti-Republican claims of followers of Carlos VII, who unsuccessfully claimed himself heir to the Spanish throne. Uribe also dedicates several pages to Pope Pius IX's Syllabus and denominates various types of Liberalism, connecting them to ideas about progress. Colombian Liberalism, he maintains, *is political only. What he was up against is especially clear in a third extract, a "catechism" that Conservative Catholics circulated in the city of Medellín. Taken together, these three texts sketch the back-and-forth politics of Liberalism and Conservatism in Colombia. It was a dynamic that extended backward toward the late eighteenth century even as its legacy reached into the 1960s.*

I _____, Catholic and a member of _____ parish, united in love to our infallible Holy Father, through whose mouth Jesus Christ my lord and savior speaks, condemn with the Holy Father without any qualms all types of Liberalism—religious or political. I condemn with all my heart all those false freedoms which threaten and damage our Catholic faith. Such freedoms lead us away from God and his only son, Jesus Christ.

I openly adhere to all the teaching of the Latin American Council of Bishops, especially those relating to Liberalism.

I humbly ask God's and the Church's forgiveness.

———————————

The word *liberalism*, used by the Church to name a collection of political and religious mistakes and mainly condemned by Pius IX in the *Syllabus* . . . is invoked by some with pride and loathed by others as a standard of ignominy, carried and presented on pulpits, confessionals, platforms, and newspapers, at the mercy of all ignorance and all passion; unfailing and vulgar commonplace for preachers more fiery than discreet, to speak their mind when lacking in ability or knowledge to take on matters of greater importance. They have managed to shroud the Word with such confusion and defend it or reject it with such fierceness that it is difficult to hear the serene voice of reason, particularly over those interested in maintaining this confusion, from which they benefit, like fishermen who trouble the waters.

Inspired and supported in the doctrine of this opus in the Encyclicals of several Popes and the authority of various Cardinals, Bishops, priests and other orthodox commentators, I judge the following conclusions to be sufficiently established and demonstrated:

- Proposition 80 of the Syllabus condemns the idea that the Roman Pontiff can or should reconcile with progress, with liberalism and modern civilization; but just as there is a need to distinguish what progress and what civilization are admitted as licit and which are considered incompatible with Catholic doctrine, there is also the need to distinguish between the several classes of liberalism, to know which are condemned and which are not;

Calle real – Cinco mil niñas de primera comunion.

A procession in Bogotá of five thousand girls celebrating their First Communion, ca. 1917. Photographer unknown. Biblioteca Luis Ángel Arango. Sala de Libros Raros y Manuscritos, TP011, Postales, 1917, TP: 8. Courtesy of Banco de la República.

Girls from a Kuna indigenous community dressed for their First Communion.
Photograph by Francisco Mejía, 1935. *Congreso Eucarístico (Primeras comuniones)* [1935],
Francisco Mejía (1899–1979). Biblioteca Pública Piloto de Medellín / Archivo Fotográ-
fico. Courtesy of Biblioteca Pública Piloto de Medellín.

- There are meanings of the word *liberal* that the Church accepts as ad-
  missible, and among those is the word used by Liberal Colombians;
- The usage of the term *liberal* in Colombian politics dates prior to the
  Syllabus' condemnation;
- The words *liberty, liberal, liberalism* and their derivatives have experienced variations throughout time and do not hold the same meaning
  in every country;
- The strongest advantage the Liberal Party holds over the Conservative
  Party is manifest in the fact that if the Church were to withdraw its
  support of the latter, it would be defeated ipso facto in the elections by
  the former; . . .
- In matters of liberalism, as with all matters that require delicate analysis, there prevails a true ignorance, not only amid the masses but also
  in educated people, an ignorance that stems from the lack of study of
  these matters as well as impassioned politics that has sown obscurity
  and confusion. At the mercy of this, I am sure that there will be many
  honorable and sincere adversaries (who have been made to believe that

whomever is Liberal cannot be Catholic, and vice versa, and who have become imbued with a brutal and savage implacableness) whom upon coming to know the simple doctrine that liberalism presents, might exclaim in surprise, "Is it not more than this? But this is how I have always believed it to be! How is it that no one told me this before?"

Translated by Ana María Gómez López

Q. *Which party in Colombia stands for good politics?*

A. The Conservative party.

Q. *Why?*

A. Because the Conservative party does not have in its political creed a single principle condemned by the Church; because by repressing the press it protects the honour and religious beliefs of the citizens, and does not allow Religion to be insulted. . . .

Q. *Which party in Colombia stands for bad politics?*

A. The Liberal party.

Q. *Why?*

A. Because the Liberal party has in its political creed several canons or principles that are reproved and condemned by the Church, that is, by the Pope who is the head of the Church, teacher and guide of all Catholics.

Sabina, Bring Some Candles
to Light to the Virgin

Albalucía Ángel

Through the nineteenth and twentieth centuries, Colombians often understood themselves as Catholic not because they subscribed to formal doctrine but because they participated in a panoply of daily devotional practices: praying the Rosary, keeping a saint's image nearby, reciting novenas at home, or giving themselves or others dear to them la bendición *or the sign of the cross. Novelist Albalucía Ángel captures the fervor and enveloping, quotidian feel of home Catholicism in her acclaimed novel* Estaba la pájara pinta sentada en el verde limón.[1] *The novel itself ranges well past the religious upbringing of the protagonist, Ana. Yet Ana's memories ground Ángel's narrative in a world of Catholicism very familiar to her readers.*

Ana is a child in 1948, when Gaitán is killed, but by 1967, when Che Guevara dies in Bolivia, she is a young woman who can no longer believe in her parents' middleclass provincialism. Ángel's style mixes collage and a layering of voices with stream of consciousness to communicate the subjective worlds of Ana, her friends, the nuns at her school, a family that is politically Liberal but deeply conservative, the maid Sabina, and, later in Ana's life, a group of young revolutionaries who inspire her. In the extract below, the family listens to radio broadcasts informing the nation that Gaitán has been shot and that a riot rages in Bogotá. They are in a provincial city, but an aunt, Lucrecia (described as mean to children), is in Bogotá, and Ana's mother wonders aloud about Lucrecia's middle-class neighborhood, Chapinero. Part of what is sketched is the relationship between Ana's mother and the family's maid, Sabina, who does both household work and the work of reassuring Ana's mother. Here, as elsewhere in the novel, the dialogue is interspersed with both voices from the radio and the unheard voices of witnesses. Readers thus have a triple access—to Ana's interior voice, to dialogue in the home, and to voices from "history" placed in the text by the writer. Ángel challenges her readers by not marking the voices off from one another. History is jumbled.

Rioters, April 9, 1948. This photograph by Sady González, one of the main visual chroniclers of "El Bogotazo," became a reference point for Colombians' understandings of the destruction that exploded in the capital after Gaitán's death. The title of this photograph, *Machetes*, refers to the cleaverlike knives held by the men in the picture—an everyday tool in rural Colombia for clearing brush and other agricultural uses, yet also a weapon for lethal violence. Archivo Fotográfico de Sady González, Biblioteca Luis Ángel Arango. http://admin.banrepcultural.org/prensa/boletin-de-prensa/foto-sady-recuerdos-de-la-realidad. Courtesy of Banco de la República.

Sabina went back and forth like an old hen, crossing herself every couple of minutes: sainted mother, holy virgin, pray for us . . . Her father's face was getting paler and paler and he became more and more silent as he listened to the news. Her mother came into the room crying and lit another oil lamp to the Virgin Mary: mommy do you think Freckles' father died? And she said no there was no reason for him to be dead a lot of people escaped from the fires. But the newscaster was saying there weren't enough firemen. And that there were snipers in San Diego Church and in Las Nieves Church. That Jiménez de Quesada Avenue was completely blocked by a group of armed men that were threatening to break down the doors of El Tiempo newspaper. That's all we need, that's it. See what the Conservatives are up to? Attention! Within a few seconds Dr. Ospina Pérez will address the country. She took advantage of the pause, what are snipers? Hush. Do you think he'll announce his resignation? No chance!, her father answered, that one won't be gotten out of there unless it's feet first. The only solution is Echandía. Or Dr. Santos, suggested her mother, too bad he's in New York—militias, how scary. God won't permit that, nor the Virgin Mary. Saint Jude of Thaddeus protect us. . . .

What was she doing standing there? Why hadn't she gone to change out of her uniform?

"We tried to proceed to the presidential palace along Carrera 7, but the crown began to surround us and our efforts were in vain. Dr. Echandía, who said to me, we have to calm the people Dr. Lleras, and so we tried to harangue the crowds so that everyone would stay calm—he from the gates of the old Santo Domingo Church and I from a balcony right on the corner of Calle 12 and Carrera 7. We implored them to let us go alone to the presidential palace to discuss the national situation, but it was absolutely impossible to make oneself heard in the midst of such indescribable confusion.

"Meanwhile, as we were struggling to speak to the people, Dr. Araujo, Dr. Gómez Valderrama, and others had begun to come down the Carrera 7. As they were reaching Calle 11, troops from the Plaza de Bolívar opened fire. A lady who was on the arm of Dr. Araujo was shot dead."

Ana felt an emptiness in her stomach, and she remembered that no one had given her hot chocolate and cookies. She went to the kitchen, but Sabina seemed in a really bad mood and said that it was no time for snacks. Ospina is the president, right? But it also was no time for that kind of question; this girl is an atheist, go back in there—Why don't you pray the Nicene Creed instead of wandering around like a fool? Can't you see I'm busy? It was because she was pounding corn that had already been pounded, and so Ana went back to the living room and back to stay curled up next to the rocking chair.

"The mob advances with shotguns and pistols, machetes, and clubs. The liquor stores have been looted and many of the rioters are by now under the influence. With one blow they break off the neck of the bottle . . . and chug down the rest of the bottle. The threat is joined by shameful news: the police have defected. Their arms are now in the hands of the people, and a number of police officers in civilian clothes are heading the mob. There are at least ten thousand men. The revolutionaries' fire is intense everywhere. They shoot from the street and from the balconies and rooftops of nearby buildings they've taken over. Risking his life, Major Iván Berrío directs the operation from the balcony of the presidential palace and gives the order to fire."

Holymarymotherofgod! What is going to happen? What do you think? What will happen to poor Lucrecia, at least in Chapinero nothing will happen, since it's far from the city center or what do you think? Who's going to hold back a bunch of raggedy bums gone crazy on drink? So much *chicha* and *guarapo* and they're even drinking champagne, that's worse: they've never seen it before! They'll be as drunk as skunks because ragamuffins like that, to get drunk on Armangac, in their whole lives they never even dreamed of it and of course they're feeling brave now, that's for sure. Stealing from better-off people, from he who has, by God and by the Virgin Mary I am going to go crazy, what are we going to do? And to think that Carlos Julio Ramírez was singing at the Colón theater tonight and Lucrecia told me she was going to go with one of the Restrepos. Holy sainted Lord by now they've surely burned the Colón too, the dogs.

"Armed with long-range rifles, the mob concentrates its anger with an almost uncontainable fury. The defending forces give back vigorous fire. I move to look out of the Palace window: the fearlessness of the attackers is such that they grab those in front who have been shot and pull them back by their hair, by their arms, to be able to get in front of the corpses and move toward the machine guns. Scenes of fear and bravery, scenes of suicide. Revolutionary projectiles whistle over the presidential office. The president says to the minister of the interior and to the postal inspector: Why are the radio stations in the hands of the revolutionaries? Send columns to take them at whatever cost. At his feet, every bit as brave as him is his wife, vivacious, alert to the danger, with a pistol at her belt, under a flowered shawl, without any hesitation or vacillation or nervousness, as strong in her resolve as the bravest of all possible men. I tell her, 'If you weren't that you are a lady I would call you doña Manuelita,[2] for your calm and bravery.' She smiles and reholsters her pistol."

Bless me soul of Christ save me body of Christ wash me holy water from Christ's side comfort me passion of Christ oh my good Jesus hear me and hide me within your wounds do not allow me to leave your side defend me from the evil of the enemy call me to you at the hour of my death and send me to you so that with the saints I can praise you for ever and ever amen. I can't take it anymore; I can't take it anymore. Sabina, go get some candles to light to the Virgin, and also two or three bigger votive lights, these ones won't be enough, yes ma'am I'll go over to Don Tobías's right now, holysoulsofpurgatory. And she finally came back with the votive lights and rice and meat and two bags of wheat flour and oil and four packets of salt and a kilo of beans and two bunches of plantains, the big ones, and Luker chocolate and navel oranges and one tub of La Fina margarine and she unpacked and unpacked and put things in the refrigerator and in the boxes from the big pantry and on the shelves, Saint Michael Archangel defend us in the battle and be our refuge against the devil's snares detain him oh lord

Group portrait celebrating a First Communion, 1971. Photograph by Martha Arévalo. *Familia en la Primera Comunión, Bogotá*, 1971 (MdB 1659), Álbum Familiar / Museo de Bogotá. Courtesy of Museo de Bogotá.

as we rightfully beg of you, put the lard in the back pantry, let's see that meat, yes it's loin, good quality, how much did Don Tobías charge you, do you think this will last us?, and Ana thought probably not. At the end they'd probably have to eat rats and even the soles of their shoes like during the siege of Cartagena, when the Spaniards blockaded it in 1815, and everyone chose to die of hunger or disease or of whatever so that they wouldn't give in to the *gachupines*, who knows . . . Everyone including the children will have to fight, like in the time of the crusades. Wrapped in the tricolor flag, at the base of the city wall. Facing the machine guns and they'll have to put a plaque in the Plaza de Bolívar: here her blood was offered up for the homeland and it's the third and final time I'm telling you to change out of your uniform: Ana!, yes ma'am and she was exiled from the kitchen while Sabina and her mother continued and you Prince of the celestial militia armed with Divine Power plunge into hell Satan and all of his evil spirits who wander the earth seeking the damnation of souls, amen. . . .

The Commander of the Armed Forces and the Minister of the Interior have declared that the perturbations of public order that are currently disturbing the country will be resolved within twenty-four hours . . .

—Didn't I tell you?

—My head's going to explode, not even with the aspirins . . .

Ana asked her father what was *la chusma* [the rabble] and her mother, my God! This girl! How many hours has it been since I sent her to change out of her uniform?

From her room she heard her father commenting that this was all lies. That who would know which of the news reports were true. That now was when alarmists and professional agitators would take advantage of everything and launch the country into disorder, you needn't be so alarmed he said, but her mother kept crying and uttering invocations to Saint Jude and Mary Help of Christians, imploring them to save us from all evil and danger, until Sabina came in and said that at least it had started to rain. That way the rabble would disperse and everyone would have to go home.

What will they do out in all that rain? Don't think about it too much, Sabina consoled Ana's mother, and in a calming tone said: tomorrow they'll be tired of making war, you'll see. Have some herb tea.

Translated by Ann Farnsworth-Alvear, with help from Patricia Duncan and Patrick O'Brien

Notes

1. The title is a reference to a well-known nursery rhyme about a speckled bird sitting in a green-leaved lemon tree.
2. *Manuelita* is a reference to Colombian Independence-era heroine Manuelita Sáenz, who would not have been taken as a "lady."

Processions and Festivities

Nereo López, Richard Cross, and Nina Sánchez de Friedemann

In many parts of Colombia the year is marked by holidays celebrated in public space, collective events that for generations have shaped different cities' and regions' sense of identity and been magnets for local talent. Musicians, dancers, and artists of all kinds focus their creative energy to contribute to specific festivals: Pasto's Carnaval de Negros y Blancos (Blacks and Whites Carnival) in January; Barranquilla's huge Lenten carnival in February; the Holy Week festivities celebrated in Popayán, Mompox, and other colonial-era cities; Quibdó's Fiestas de San Pacho (Feast of Saint Francis of Assis) in September and October. In the present, such celebrations also attract the attention of investors hoping to profit from tourism, and of arts and culture professionals linked to the Colombian Ministry of Culture, UNESCO, or academia.

Dance and decorative display are integral to the largest street celebrations. The brightly colored floats and flamboyant costumes of Barranquilla's Carnival, for example, evoke those of its Caribbean counterparts in Kingston, New Orleans, or even, years ago, Havana. Tourist posters for such events can seem glitzy and staged. Nevertheless, most Colombian street festivals have a homespun feel. Revelers go out to the streets with friends and in family groups. Their costumes will in some cases be no more elaborate than coal dust or talcum power rubbed on their faces, or a hastily donned mask, as in Nereo López's 1962 photograph of the Blacks and Whites celebration in Pasto. Or they wear their Sunday best, the better to respect a religious rite. Sometimes the street is an extension of church; sometimes it is an upside-down world of irreverence.

Significantly, the boundary between formally recognized festivals and street celebrations of all types is very porous in Colombia. Bogotá's wide avenues, for example, regularly feature performers of all types, from clowns and stilt-walkers to mimes (in one attempt to teach traffic safety in Colombia's capital, Antanas Mockus Šivickas,

Carnival of Blacks and Whites, Pasto, 1962. Photograph by Nereo López. Used by permission of the artist.

Wedding Procession in the Palenque of San Basilio, ca. 1978. This town in the Montes de María region southeast of Cartagena is Colombia's longest-lived *palenque*, or community founded by Africans who escaped enslavement. It has long been noted for its creolized language (which incorporates Bantu grammatical structures and Spanish) and its sociopolitical organization, as well as for the religious rituals, musical expressions, and daily customs that set the town apart. Photograph by Richard Cross, as part of the anthropological work done in San Basilio by Nina Sánchez de Friedemann. In Nina Sánchez de Friedemann and Carlos Patiño Rosselli, *Lengua y sociedad en el palenque de San Basilio* (Bogotá: Instituto Caro y Cuervo, 1983), plate 19 after p. 191. Courtesy of the Institute for Arts & Media, California State University, Northridge.

Procession ca. 1980 in Mompox, a colonial-era town on the Magda-
lena River famous for its Easter celebrations. Photograph by Nina
Sánchez de Friedemann. In Benjamín Villegas, Nina Sánchez de
Friedemann, and Jeremy Horner, *Fiestas: Celebrations and Rituals of
Colombia* (Bogotá: Villegas Editores, 1995), 107. Courtesy of Villegas
Editores.

*of Lithuanian descent and a two-term mayor of Bogotá, generated attention by hir-
ing hundreds of mimes to create a street dialogue with pedestrians). And in small
towns, street celebrations will often accompany a wedding entourage or a religious
procession, turning outdoor space into a venue for praying, partying, drinking,
dancing, making music—collective life in a wide variety of forms.*

We Were Not Able to Say
That We Were Jewish

Paul Hané

From the colonial period, marked by explicit exclusions and by the presence of the Inquisition, through the twentieth century and into the present, anti-Semitism has shaped Jewish life in Colombia. Jewish families who sought a communal life faced particular obstacles as they founded organizations, businesses, and synagogues. Re-membering the middle decades of the twentieth century, Paul Hané emphasizes the community's resilience and practicality: if the place they had for a synagogue has previously been a garage, so be it. His is a thoroughly modern and optimistic voice, one that echoes forward to the official religious tolerance of twenty-first-century Colombia. It's also a Bogotano voice. Jewish families from other cities would nar-rate other histories. Barranquilla, in particular, had an acknowledged Jewish com-munity that thrived for generations and helped make for a markedly cosmopolitan city. Writing about the Caribbean region of Colombia, including Barranquilla, his-torians Louise Fawcett and Eduardo Posada-Carbó describe three waves of Jewish migration: a stream of Sephardic families who arrived from the Dutch Antilles in the late eighteenth century; one of Syrians, Lebanese, and Palestinians who arrived between 1880 and 1930; and one of European Jews who came as refugees in the 1930s and 1940s. Hané situates his family's particular experience very clearly, telling a young interviewer, Paula Douer, herself a product of the Bogotá community he had for decades helped lead, that his father and uncle came to Colombia not to escape persecution but, rather, as immigrants seeking a better life.

I do believe that my uncle Salomón, my father's brother, was one of the first Jewish people to arrive to Colombia. That was during World War I. He was not fleeing from persecution towards Jews, for truly those of us who came from Greece were not persecuted, but mostly wanted to escape the war between the Greeks, the Turks, and the Bulgarians, and above all, to search for a better life. . . .

My father had tried to escape this dangerous environment, and followed his brother Salomón. . . . In the beginning they had no money, not even to buy or rent a store. What he would do then was carry a pack of cloth trimmings on his back, and travel on horseback to visit towns. They would sell there, sell quite well, as well as buy, and would later make another round with more merchandise, and send us back money to Greece. . . .

There were people from the Ashkenazi community, from Central Europe and Poland; I don't think there were Germans. And toward 1920, it was very difficult to find a *minyan*. On the days of Rosh Hashanah and Yom Kippur we gathered at my home, and said the prayers, yet there were no more than ten or twelve Jewish people at that time, at least who practiced the religion. I am referring to a time when Bogotá had 300,000 inhabitants. . . .

What we needed first was to have a cemetery. This was most urgent, because a young man had already passed away, the brother of Mark Motto who had died of appendicitis, and there was nowhere to bury him. They buried him in the German cemetery. It was then that Moisés Esquenazi took leadership of the organization, and along with others took the initiative of collecting funds to purchase a piece of land located between Carrera 26 and Calle 26. Because of lack of resources, this cemetery was located next to the Catholic cemetery, with no walls separating them. . . .

In 1944, the young men at the time were the Haimes, the Pichottos, and the Haims, who decided to pursue a formal status for the organization, with a legally recognized board of directors. They came to my office one day and asked if I would be willing to lead the board. And I said, "Me? I will do it gladly, but I am not religious. They will not accept me." And indeed, there was a tremendous argument between those who were religious, and those who were not—the Shaios, Miguel Haime, the Pichottos, the Hamris, all of them fought an aggressive campaign, and I believe I was elected coming out only one or two votes ahead (laughter).

At the time of the election, each person placed ballots in a hat that was passed around. They placed their votes inside the hat. And of course, one had to be careful that they did not slip in more than one vote. This was in a house we had rented. . . .

I created the first board of directors. And in order to be fair, I named six people who held me in favor, and six who did not, all while Victor Shaio was present. This way, we had a very agreeable board. . . .

The house had a garage, a very large one, but which was not used for cars. Everyone had a garage in their home, and so I decided to close off the door that faced the street, and transform this space into a small synagogue where we gathered every Friday and Saturday. That led to another never-ending argument. Those who were religious did not accept that a synagogue would be put in a garage (laughter).

Naturally I told them, "Show me where it says in the book of the Torah or any commentary that one cannot build a synagogue in the garage, and I will consider your claims." They searched in the books, but of course none of them specified anything on the matter. We finally created the small synagogue there, and it was very successful. . . .

Outside of business matters, we met to celebrate Rosh Hashanah and Yom Kippur. We did so at first in my father's home, located in the Carrera 5 between Calles 16 and 17. . . . After those first meetings, we moved to the Avenida Caracas and Calle 39. That house still exists, a house with two floors, much more modern. And the meetings had more attendance than the first. Many of these men were already present at the time. I am talking about 1937. Of course, the community was more aware of its identity, and it rented a house in the Teusaquillo neighborhood that was used exclusively for religious celebrations. We did not gather for any other reason. A very modern house, which did not have anything; I remember the windows did not have curtains to pull during the celebrations. During these festivities, we would use soap to make the glass opaque, so that we could pray without being seen. Interesting stories. . . .

We were a very isolated group. I studied at the La Salle School with my cousins. There, we were not able to say that we were Jewish. We had been accepted on that condition, and we had to go to mass in the morning and at night. For a Catholic it is a great victory to convert a Jewish person, or someone who is not Catholic; the brothers at La Salle tried to have us enter their religion. One day, the principal, a Frenchman called brother Francisco, told me, "Paul, you have everything. That is all you are missing." As soon as my father learned this, he immediately took us out of the school and sent us to France. These were the relationships in an extremely Catholic environment, such as in school. . . .

In other environments, particularly among the lower classes, there is anti-Semitism, which is much less than before, but it still exists. Much less than before, for now people of higher social position do not scorn visiting Jewish environments, Jewish homes, and on the contrary are honored to be invited. Politicians often share good words, for Jewish people are generous. They will make themselves present in any disaster that takes place, as well as in political campaigns. And once a person has received help from a Jewish person, they cannot say anything against them. This is why current politicians seek contact with Jewish people, not only during election time, but also in business, as lawyers and directors of companies. I do not consider we can complain about the current situation. I do not know what others might think to themselves, but what they express is positive. There are only some homes in which they believe what the Church has taught them, that a Jewish person is the devil.

Translated by Ana María Gómez López and Ann Farnsworth-Alvear

As a Colombian, as a Sociologist, as a Christian, and as a Priest, I Am a Revolutionary

Camilo Torres Restrepo

Camilo Torres Restrepo (1929–66) embodies the fusion of Christian radicalism and revolutionary fervor that marked the decade of the 1960s in Latin America. His life story inspired a generation of young Colombians on the political Left. Here was a well-educated, handsome, upper-class man who renounced worldly vanities and traveled a path of no return—to seminary, to the priesthood, and, in the end, to a guerrilla encampment. Along the way, Torres did graduate coursework in sociology at the Catholic University of Louvain and worked professionally at the Colombian Institute for Agrarian Reform and the National University of Colombia, where Torres was both a chaplain and cofounder of the faculty of sociology. It was a moment of intense activism, with students criticizing obsolete curricula and the bookish elitism of university courses they described as "lots of teaching, not much learning." Torres did not oppose them, but he did reproach student "revolutionaries" for being unconscious of their own privileges. The texts we include below were issued in 1965, after the Colombian cardinal Luis Concha Córdoba expelled Torres from the priesthood and before Torres left Bogotá to join guerrilla commander Fabio Vásquez, one of the founders of the Ejército de Liberación Nacional (Army of National Liberation), at a jungle camp near Opón, Santander. The expelled priest died in combat only a few months later.

Message to the Christians (excerpts)

What is essential in Catholicism is love of neighbor. "He who loves his neighbor has fulfilled the law" (Romans 13:8). For this love to be real it must seek to be effective. If kindness, alms, the few free schools, the few housing plans, so-called charity does not feed the majority of the hungry, or clothe

the majority of the naked, or teach the majority of the uneducated, we must seek effective means for achieving the well-being of the majorities.

The privileged minorities who hold power are not going to seek them, for generally the means would demand that the minorities sacrifice their privileges. For example, to create more jobs in Colombia capital should not be withdrawn in dollar form, but should be invested in the country. However, since the Colombian peso is devaluing every day, those who have money and power will never prohibit the exportation of money, because in exporting it they escape the effects of devaluation. It is necessary, then, to take the power from the privileged minority and give it to the poor majority. This, if done quickly, is the essential element of a revolution. The Revolution can be peaceful if the minorities put up no violent resistance.

The Revolution is the means of obtaining a government that will feed the hungry, clothe the naked, teach the uneducated, perform works of charity, love their neighbors not only in a transitory and occasional way, not just a few but the majority of their neighbors. For this reason the Revolution is not only permissible but obligatory for Christians who see in it the one effective and complete way to create love for all. . . .

I have given up the duties and privileges of the clergy but I have not ceased to be a priest. I believe that I joined the Revolution out of love of my neighbor. I have stopped saying Mass in order to fulfill this love of neighbor in the temporal, economic, and social world. When my neighbor no longer holds anything against me, when the Revolution has been completed, I will return to offering Mass, God permitting.

Message to Communists

. . . I have said that, as a Colombian, as a sociologist, as a Christian, and as a priest, I am a revolutionary. I feel that the Communist Party has elements that are authentically revolutionary and because of that I cannot, either as a Colombian, or as a sociologist, or as a Christian, or as a priest, be anti-Communist. I am not anti-Communist as a Colombian because anti-Communism is oriented towards persecuting non-conformist compatriots, Communist or not, of whom the majority are the poor. I am not anti-Communist as a sociologist because in the Communist plan of fighting poverty, hunger, illiteracy, lack of housing and services for the people, effective and scientific solutions are to be found. I am not anti-Communist as a Christian because I believe that anti-Communism makes a blanket condemnation of everything Communists defend, and there are both just and unjust things in what they defend. In condemning them all we are condemning the just and the unjust equally, and this is anti-Christian. I am not anti-Communist as a priest because even though the Communists themselves do not know it, there are many among them who are truly Christian. If they are of good faith, they can have sanctifying grace; and if they have sanctifying grace and love their neighbor, they will be saved. My role as a priest, even though I do not exercise the external rite, is to try to lead men to God, and the most effective way to do this is to lead men to serve their neighbors according to their consciences.

I have no intention of proselytizing my Communist brothers, trying to get them to accept the dogma and to practice the cult of the Church. But this I am certainly working towards, that all men act according to their conscience, sincerely seek the truth, and love their neighbor in an effective way. The Communists must well know that I will not join their ranks, that I am not, nor will I be a Communist, either as a Colombian, or as a sociologist, or as a Christian, or as a priest. However, I am ready to fight alongside them for common goals: opposing the oligarchy and the domination of the United States, in order to take power for the popular class.

I do not want the public to identify me with the Communists, and for this reason I have always made it a point to appear in the company not only of the Communists but of all the other revolutionaries. . . .

Message to the Military

After having seen the power of forty armed and disciplined men over a crowd of four thousand in the city of Girardot, I decided to make a fervent call to the armed forces of Colombia to become aware of the historic moment in which we are living, and to decide for themselves now how they will participate in the revolutionary struggle.

On various occasions I have seen uniformed men—farmers and workers, never elements of the ruling class—fighting and persecuting farmers, workers, and students who represent the majority of Colombians. And it is with rare exception that I have found members of the oligarchy among the officials and subofficials. Anyone who considers the contrast between the Colombian majorities clamoring for revolution and the small military minorities repressing the people in order to protect a few small privileged families must ask himself what reasons induce these elements of the people to persecute their fellows.

It could not be for the economic advantages. All military personnel are poorly paid. The military are generally not permitted to study for a life outside the army. When they reach higher rank, they try to buy a corner house to open a store to support them in their retirement. I have seen generals and colonels apply for posts as teachers of physical education in high schools and as insurance salesmen. The salary for personnel on active duty is low, but it is even lower for retired personnel. They receive no medical attention or any other economic benefits. However, we know that a third of our national budget goes to the armed forces. As is obvious, the war budget is not used to pay the Colombian military but to buy the scrap metal the United States sells us, to maintain the material elements, and to support internal repression in which Colombians kill their own brothers.

It may be that the motive behind what the military does is devotion to the fatherland [*patria*, might also be "motherland" or "homeland"], the Constitution, and the laws. But the Colombian Fatherland consists mainly of its men, and the majority of those are suffering and cut off from power. The Constitution is constantly violated in that jobs, property, freedom, and participation in power are not given to the people who ought to be, according to the Constitution, the ones to decide public policy in the country. The Constitution is violated when martial law is maintained after the causes that were the pretext for its declaration have ceased. The laws are violated when citizens are detained without a warrant for arrest, when the mail is withheld, when curfews are imposed, when the telephones are tapped, and lies and tricks are used to persecute the revolutionaries.

Perhaps it is necessary to better inform the military about the Fatherland, the Constitution, and the laws, so that they do not think that the Fatherland consists in the twenty-four families whom they actually protect, for whom they spill their blood, and from whom they receive such poor remuneration. Perhaps the principal reason that the military continues to be the armed extension of the oligarchy is the lack of opportunity in other fields of human activity which exists in Colombia. . . .

Message to Students

Students are a privileged group in any underdeveloped country. Poor nations pay a very high price for their few college and university graduates. In Colombia in particular, given the large number of private colleges and universities, the economic factor has been a determining factor in education. In a country where sixty percent are illiterate, eight percent have a bachelor's degree, and one percent are professionals, the students are one of the few groups equipped to analyze the Colombian situation in comparison to other situations and with regard to possible solutions.

Moreover, the university student—in the university where it is not a crime to hold an opinion and in the college where there is freedom of expression—has simultaneously two privileges: the power to ascend the social scale by means of academic grades, and the power to be non-conformist and rebellious without impeding this ascent. These advantages make the students a decisive element in the Latin American Revolution. During the agitational phase of the Revolution, student efforts were very effective. During the organizational phase, their efforts were secondary in Colombia. In the direct struggle, notwithstanding the honorable exceptions which have arisen in our revolutionary history, their role has not been a determining one either.

We know that agitation is important, but its true effect is lost if it is not followed by organization and the struggle for the power take-over. One of the main reasons why the involvement of the students in the Revolution is transitory and superficial is the lack of student involvement in the personal, family, and economic struggle.

The students' non-conformity tends to be emotional (sentimentalism or frustration) or purely intellectual. This also explains the fact that at the end of a university career the non-conformity disappears or at least is concealed, and the rebel students cease to be non-conformist in order to convert into bourgeois professionals who, to buy the status symbols of the middle class, have to sell their consciences in exchange for a higher salary.

These circumstances can threaten the possibility for a mature and responsible reply by the students to the historic moment that Colombia is now going through. The economic and political crisis is making itself felt most on the workers and farmers.

The student, generally isolated from these problems, could think that purely speculative or superficial revolutionary activity is enough. Their lack of awareness of the problems could make the students betray their historical vocation: that when the country needs their total involvement the students continue with words and good intentions but nothing more; that when the movement of the masses calls for daily and continuous work, the students comply with shouts, stone-throwing, and sporadic demonstrations; that when the popular class needs an effective, disciplined, and responsible presence in its ranks, the students reply with vain promises or excuses.

The revolutionary conviction of the students must carry them through to the very end. Poverty and persecution ought not to be sought out. But under the present system, they are the logical consequences of a fight against the prevailing structures. Under the present system they are the signs which attest to a revolutionary life. Their conviction must bring the students to participate in the economic penury and social persecution of the workers and farmers. Then their involvement with the Revolution passes from theory into practice. If it is complete, it is irreversible; the professional cannot take a step backwards without a flagrant betrayal of his conscience, his people, and his historic calling. . . .

Who Stole the Chalice from Badillo's Church?

Rafael Escalona

Vallenato *songwriter Rafael Calixto Escalona Martínez (1927–2009) was from the outskirts of Valledupar, department of Cesar.* Vallenato, *a word that literally means "born in the valley," refers both to people from his home region and to a genre of Caribbean folk music that originated there.* Vallenato *music became instantly recognizable to inland Colombians mainly because of Escalona. Conjuring characters from García Márquez's novels, Escalona's father was a colonel who had served on the losing Liberal side in Colombia's Thousand Days' War. His uncle was bishop of Santa Marta, the city in which he began composing* vallenatos *as a high school student. Throughout his life, Escalona cultivated connections to Colombian political figures. He gained particular renown in 1953, when Atlantic Coast politicians arranged a widely publicized visit to Bogotá. During his stay, Escalona composed a* vallenato *for dictator Rojas Pinilla, which was played by Colombia's National Symphony Orchestra and was broadcast over public radio. In 1968, he cofounded the Festival de la Leyenda Vallenata (Vallenato Legend Festival) with former president Alfonso López Michelsen and journalist Consuelo Araujo Noguera. Shortly thereafter, he was appointed Colombian consul to Panama. His songs narrated personal experiences, ranging from the death of friends to affairs and unrequited love, but Escalona also wrote about historical events, local figures, and everyday happenings along Colombia's Atlantic Coast, such as the incident narrated in the song translated below, which evokes the down-to-earth culture of small-town Catholicism.*

The Vallenato Legend Festival continues to take place in Valledupar every April. Musicians battle for five days to see who will be crowned the next vallenato *king on the stage named for Francisco "The Man"—a legendary musician who reputedly won an accordion duel with the devil. Rafael Escalona died on May 13, 2009. His public funeral was held on the Francisco "The Man" stage after his body was publicly viewed in Colombia's National Capitol, headquarters of Colombia's Congress.*

It seems that the town of Badillo has had a run of bad luck;
bad luck because one of its relics may have been swapped.

Before it was a statue of Saint Anthony; Enrique Maya was to blame.
But what has happened now is out of the ordinary, as I will explain.

The town's religious relic, one from colonial times
in Gregorio's house was very safely kept.
It was a lovely chalice, very large and heavy,
which for a lightweight one they now want to replace.
It was taken, it was taken
it was taken, now it is lost.
It was taken, it was taken
it was taken, now it is lost.

What is gone is now in the hands of an honorable thief
What happened was thievery by a man of honor.
Although some might accuse the town of Badillo of libel,
the residents have very plainly laid out their evidence.
It lacks the same color, or the same weight,
it is not the right size, so it cannot be the one.

It seems the police inspector was afraid
too afraid to proceed with the case
as no one has come out to say who the thief is,
although everyone knows what might be their name.

Surely it was not I, nor Alfonso López nor Pedro Castro
This time Enrique Maya did not steal it
now they cannot declare a *vallenato* is to blame.

Poor Enrique Maya was arrested
for only taking Saint Anthony out on loan!
Yet there has been no punishment for whoever stole the chalice:
this theft is a wholly buried affair.

Now I am convinced that fame
always brings trouble for those who have it.
The sky was going to come down on Enrique Maya.
What has happened now is more serious, and no one makes a move.

It was taken, it was taken
it was taken, now it is lost.
What is gone is now in the hands of an honorable thief
what happened was thievery by a man of honor.

Oh compadre Colás [Nicolás] Guerra
whenever you have a party
man, keep your eyes wide open and be on steady watch
with a .45 at the church door
so that no one wearing a cassock can get past

And when the mass is over, have them search everyone
from the priest on down!

Translated by Ana María Gómez López

Life Is a Birimbí

Rodrigo Parra Sandoval

In 1902, President José Manuel Marroquín officially consecrated Colombia to the Sacred Heart of Jesus. His supporters saw an opportunity to heal the wounds of the War of the Thousand Days, while opponents feared that such a consecration would deepen the power of the victorious Conservative Party. Decree 820 would be explicitly revalidated in 1927 and again in 1952, with Colombia's statesmen holding yearly commemorations until 1994, when Colombia's Constitutional Court ruled such actions incompatible with the 1991 Constitution. For many Colombians, the Sacred Heart continues to embody a specifically national piety, and it is evident in public observances of religious holidays and televised liturgies, as well as in people's homes.

Rodrigo Parra Sandoval plays on the Sacred Heart as an emblem of Colombia's public and private religiosity in his novel The Secret Album of the Sacred Heart. *Published in 1976 to wide acclaim, it is an experimental narrative presented as a print collage, where brief snapshots of life in Dagua and Cali are vertiginously intermingled with fragments from prayer books, comic strips, letters, news articles, Bible passages, screenplays, song lyrics, and religious certificates. All of this is a backdrop for a critical exposition of the dynamics of race, class, and gender in the author's home region of Valle del Cauca. In the extract below a would-be seminarian receives from his father a kind of indoctrination lesson about machismo—with a connection drawn between "priests" and "fags."*

Herding cattle into the corral to calculate their weight, eyes sizing up the bulk of the whole lot, fifteen head of cattle, for each mistake is a loss and afterward the three-peso hotel at the corner of the market, the Shelter for the Lonely Traveler Hotel and below, shielded by timber piles, the Samarcanda Café, with its furious bright-colored jukebox, the *rancheras*, the swimming fish, the one-eyed *Visión* staring straight as a steel rod, behind his Poker beer, "La Media Vuelta" and "El Peor de los Caminos" by Javier Solís and Miguel Aveces Mugía and toward the end, after many a cold Costeña beer, and several utterances of "Well then, son," the tepid and hoarse misgivings:

Son,
why do you go around with those priests,
crooks with robes,
shadowy traders of dirty, old-fashioned lies
I don't mean to pry
BUT I WANT TO KNOW THAT THERE ARE TWO THINGS YOU ARE NOT:
A CONSERVATIVE AND A FAG,
simple as that,
completely *macho*,
I LIKE MEN WHO YOU CAN'T SEE THROUGH
wholesome,
no loose ends,
no peepholes,
as straight as a die
men who never bend over, and if a storm strikes them
they will come down loudly for everyone to hear
and even if they are screwed they will clench up but never beg because
begging is what women do,
I would rather have you put a serpent around your neck
and sell snake oil and miracle ointments like I did in
those hard times,
but working up a sweat,
hustling,
LIFE IS A BIRIMBÍ
working your fingers to the bone,
it might not help your neighbor but
neither does it hurt you,
that is why I can't figure out those priests,
because they live off handouts,
off the sweat of others,
those skirt-wearing beggars,
but now son,
it is time to give you my only inheritance,
listen closely to
the only laws of man I have obeyed in my life,
so that you too may be an upright man.
I can't give you anything else
but this I give to you from the deepest and darkest part of my fatherly
    heart,
don't forget this,

do not throw it into memory's ripped sack,

this is the dried-up sap that remains after surviving half a century amid
  violent men,

the three commandments of man's law:

FIRST: DO NOT MESS WITH A VIRGIN WOMAN,

THERE IS MORE PAIN AND TEARS AND BACKSTABBING THAN PLEA-
  SURE.

SECOND: DO NOT MESS WITH YOUR FRIEND'S WOMAN BECAUSE

IT IS HARDER TO FIND A FRIEND THAN A HUNDRED WOMEN.

THIRD: FROM THERE ON,

IF IT HAS A SLIT IT'S FAIR GAME

EVEN IF IT'S A LIZARD.

And now let's sing to this chorus-line

because you know that these tears I am crying are not crocodile tears,

they are from feeling anger

over how little I am able to give you

despite how much I love you

but treasure this

as this is all that I have that will remain with you,

son,

ASIDE FROM THE BLOOD THAT GIVES YOU YOUR HONORABLE NAME.

Translated by Ana María Gómez López

Our Lady of the Assassins

Fernando Vallejo

In Los días azules (Blue Days), novelist Fernando Vallejo remembers, "I spent my childhood and youth attending mass or reading novels, and I heard and read so many that I lost faith: in God, which for the purposes of literature is unimportant, and in the third person novelist." Using the first person and the voice of an exiled writer who returns to Medellín in the mid-nineties, when the city was Latin America's homicide capital and stronghold to drug lords, Vallejo explores Colombian Catholicism from the standpoint of teenage sicarios, translated as "hitmen" in the excerpt we include here. The narrator falls in love with Alexis, who, like other sicarios, combines a belief in popular Colombian religious traditions with the life of a paid killer.

. . . On my return to Colombia I came back to Sabaneta with Alexis, accompanying him on a pilgrimage. Alexis, yeah, that's what he calls himself. The name is nice but I didn't give it him, his ma did. According to the habit poor people have of giving their kids the names of rich, extravagant, foreign types: Tayson Alexander, for example, or Faber or Eder or Wílfer or Rommel or Yeison or what have you. I don't know where they dig these names up from or how they invent them. It's the only thing they can give their kids to provide them with a bit of a head start in this miserable life, a vain, stupid, foreign or invented name, showy and ridiculous. Well, ridiculous I thought, when I first heard them, but now I don't think that way. They're the names of bloodstained hitmen. More forthright than a bullet and its charge of hate.

You don't need me, of course, to tell you what a hitman is. My grandpa, sure, he'd need me to, but then my grandpa died years and years ago. He died, my poor grandpa, knowing nothing of the overhead railway or hitmen, smoking Victoria cigarettes, something you've never even heard of, I bet. Victorias were the old folk's *basuco*, and *basuco* is the impure cocaine kids smoke today to see a twisted world more twisted. Or not? Correct me if I'm wrong. Dear Grandfather, if by chance you can hear me from the other

Francisco Flores and Irene Gaviria, ca. 1984. The couple were among the first to receive a home of their own in a neighborhood funded by Pablo Escobar in Medellín. Photograph by James Mollison, from a family snapshot. In James Mollison, *The Memory of Pablo Escobar: Archive of 350 Found Photographs* (London: Chris Boot, 2007), 347. Used by permission of the photographer.

end of eternity I'm going to tell you what a hitman is: it's a young guy, sometimes a kid, who kills to order. And the men? In general, they're not men;
here, the hitmen are kids or young guys, twelve, fifteen, seventeen years
old, like Alexis, my one true love: he had bottomless, clear, green eyes, of a
green as beautiful as any out on the grassy plains. But if Alexis had purity in
his eyes his heart was stricken. And one day, when he most wanted it, when
he least expected it, they killed him, just as they're going to kill us all. Our
ashes are all headed to the same cemetery, the same Elysian Fields.

Today the Virgin of Sabaneta is María Auxiliadora, but she wasn't in my
childhood: it used to be Our Lady of the Carmelites, and the parish was
Santa Ana. As far as I understand these things (which isn't that far), María
Auxiliadora is now the property of the Salesian Fathers, while the parish
of Sabaneta itself is under the influence of the lay preachers. So how did
María Auxiliadora fetch up there? Well, I don't know. When I returned to
Colombia I found her there, enthroned, presiding over the church from the
altar on the left, working miracles. On Tuesdays, a vast crowd used to arrive in Sabaneta from all parts of Medellín to pray to the Virgin, to beg, beg,
beg, which is all poor people know how to do, along with having kids. And
among that heaving throng, the young guys from the slums, the hitmen.
Sabaneta had long ceased to be a village and become just another Medellín *barrio*, the city had overtaken it, swallowed it up; and, in the meantime,
Colombia had slipped from our hands too. We were, from afar, the most
criminal country on earth, and Medellín the capital of hate. But such things
aren't said, they're known, if you'll pardon me. . . .

The taxi passed in front of the Bombay, avoided one pothole, then another, then another, and arrived in Sabaneta. In amongst all the traffic a
throng filled the village. It was the Tuesday pilgrimage, devout, cloying, de-
ceitful. They were coming to beg for favours. Why this begging and more
begging? I'm not from around here. I'm ashamed of this beggarly race. In
the surge of the crowd, in among the spluttering of candles and whispering
of prayers, we entered the church. The muttering of orations was rising up
to heaven like the buzzing of a beehive. The light from outside filtered in
through the stained-glass windows, offering us, in gaudy images, the perverse spectacle of the Passion: Christ scourged, Christ fallen, Christ crucified. Among the bland mass of old men and old women I sought out the
youngsters, the hitmen, and there they were, swarming all over the place.
I must say, the sudden devotion of these young men astonished me. And
there was I thinking that the Church was more bankrupt than Communism
. . . No way! It's alive and kicking. Humanity needs myths and falsehoods
in order to go on living. If someone sees the naked truth, he shoots himself.

For that reason, Alexis, I didn't pick up the revolver that you dropped as you were getting undressed, as you took off your pants. If I pick it up, I will point it at my heart and pull the trigger. And I'm not going to extinguish the spark of hope you've lit in me. Let's offer this candle to the Virgin and pray, let's start pleading since that's what we came for: "O infant Virgin, María Auxiliadora, thou whom I have known since my childhood, since the Salesian Fathers' school where I studied; thou who art more than this novelty-seeking crowd's, grant me one favour: that this boy who thou seest praying to thee, on his knees before thee, by my side, be my last, my one and only true love, that I betray him not and that he betrays me not. Amen." What was Alexis going to ask the Virgin for? Sociologists say that the hitmen ask María Auxiliadora to make sure they don't miss, that she guide their aim when they shoot and that the deal works out well for them. And how do they know this? Are they Dostoyevsky or God the Father maybe when it comes to getting inside other people's minds? A person doesn't know what he's thinking himself so how's he going to know what other people are thinking! In the little church in Sabaneta there's a Fallen Christ in the entrance; on the little altar is Santa Ana with San Joaquín and the Virgin as a child; and on the right-hand side Our Lady of the Carmelites, the former queen of the parish. But all the flowers, all the prayers, all the candles, all the supplications, all the fixed stares, all the beating hearts are directed towards the altar on the left, that of María Auxiliadora, who replaced her. Through her work and grace this little church in Sabaneta that used to be so drab is today joyful, blooming with flowers and miracles. María Auxiliadora, Virgin of mine, of my childhood, the one I love most, is performing them. "Virgin child, thou who hast known me for so long, may my life end as it began, in untold happiness." In among the whispering of disparate voices my soul went up and up like a lighted balloon, without moorings, rising, rising up towards God's infinity way above this miserable earth.

I took off his shirt, he took off his shoes, I took off his pants, he took off his socks and his jocks. He stood naked with three scapulars, the ones the hitmen wear, one at the neck, another on the forearm, another at the ankle: they're for business to come their way, for them to shoot straight and for them to get paid. According to the sociologists, that is, who go around finding out these things. Me, I don't ask. I know what I see and then I forget it. What I can't forget are his eyes, the green of his eyes behind which I tried to divine his soul.

One Woman's Path to Pentecostal Conversion

Elizabeth Brusco

When compared to Brazil or Guatemala, two Latin American countries in which
25 percent of the population identifies with evangelical Protestantism, Colombia
looks to outsiders like a holdout for Catholicism—most estimates are that evangelical Christians amount to less than 15 percent. Nevertheless, Colombians now
take for granted the presence of evangelical churches and, in particular, the growth
of Pentecostalism. Not only is religious pluralism now a commonplace in educational policy and a feature of the nation's Constitution, but urban churches, television broadcasts, and Internet media sites have also become platforms on which new
forms of worship are widely visible. Colombians pass by large Pentecostal congregations such as Cali's Centro Misionero Bethesda, which can hold twenty-five thousand people. They hear radio and other broadcasts aimed at evangelical Christians,
and, increasingly, they have neighbors and acquaintances whose religious faith dif-
fers from their own.

Given the country's history of religious intolerance, these things amount to big
change. Protestants who lived in Colombia in the early and middle decades of the
twentieth century remember intense persecution. Pastors were murdered, services
broken up, and converts found themselves ostracized, dismissed from their jobs,
driven off their land. In the new atmosphere marked by the official 1991 recognition
of libertad de culto [freedom of religion] and an international context in which
ecumenism is valued, the country's Catholic hierarchy disavows earlier intolerance
and employs a language of interfaith dialogue. Yet non-Catholics still understand
themselves as being in the minority and are likely to feel a need to defend their religious choices, whether they join a group with an international presence, such as the
Foursquare Gospel, the Seventh-Day Adventists, or the Church of Latter-Day Saints,
or affiliate with an evangelical group more specific to Colombia, such as Ricardo and
Patricia Rodríguez's Centro de Avivamiento para las Naciones, founded in Bogotá
in the 1990s.

Elizabeth Brusco is an anthropologist who has sought to understand the appeal
of evangelical Christianity in Colombia by focusing on women's conversion expe-

riences. In the excerpt below she profiles an atypical convert—a woman who is relatively well-off.

Hers is not a success story; Rosalinda has not experienced the changes in her life that she would like to have had as the result of her conversion. Although she is comparatively well off, many elements of her story are representative of the kind of response I received from women in a range of economic situations whose husbands had not converted with them. . . .

Rosalinda is fifty-one years old. She is an active member of the Iglesia Cristiana Carismática (Charismatic Christian Church), more commonly known as "Los Juanitos," after the missionary couple, John and Jean Firth, who began the church. The Juanitos are at present missionaries of the Four-Square Gospel church, and have been for many years, since their charismatic "conversion" drove them out of the more theologically conservative Inter-American Mission, a branch of the Oriental Missionary Society.

The Juanitos church is one of the few charismatic or Pentecostal churches that has been established among "professional"-class people in Colombia and is located in the prestigious northern sector of Bogotá. For the bulk of the forty-four years that the Firths have been in Colombia they, like other foreign missionaries, have directed their efforts toward the lower classes. According to the Reverend Firth, it was at the invitation of a cousin of former president Alfonso López that he and his wife moved to the north and began their work with the professional classes. He recounts how López's cousin and his wife converted after a visit from the Firths, and then challenged them, saying, "Why don't you do something for the professional people, too? Why do all you missionaries confine yourselves to the working-class people?" A Major Leal, who was the secretary of the DAS (Departmento Administrativo de Seguridad, Colombia's main governmental intelligence agency) at the time, said the same thing and promised to attend meetings and help if the Firths would come to the north. Starting with eight people in 1979, the church realized an annual growth rate of 100 percent to 130 percent each year, and in 1982 had five hundred members, with over six hundred people attending services on Sunday. In order not to discourage people from attending, the Four-Square Gospel affiliation is kept out of the name of this church because of its lower-class connotations.

The Juanitos have started holding special services devoted to the family, with the objective of pulling more men into the church. John Firth said, "One of the problems amongst the charismatics is we're getting a lot more women than men, and the men are coming along more slowly. The women seem to come first, in most cases. And then, the men sometimes they have another woman, they've got plenty of money, there's a lot of what we call machismo."

Rosalinda's story aptly illustrates the point that the problems that drive women to religion are not unique to the lower class. Rosalinda was born in Barranquilla, on Colombia's Caribbean coast. In terms of the regional stereotypes commonly applied in Colombia, *costeños* are livelier and more open than people from the highlands. In fact, as Rosalinda recounts her story, she is clearly saddened, but she does not have the usual somber reticence of highland women. Although we have met only once before, briefly, at the church, she talks very openly about the problems she has experienced in her marriage. She has five children, three boys and two girls, ranging in age from twenty-nine to sixteen, all of whom still live at home with her. Rosalinda and her husband, an executive, are separated. Her husband lives only a few blocks away, with another woman, with whom he also has children. Rosalinda is an attractive, well-groomed woman with short salt-and-pepper hair. She has a good figure for a Colombian woman of her age (or for any woman who has borne five children) and wears makeup and perfume. She lives in the far north of Bogotá, not far from Unicentro, the shopping mall that is the pride of modern Bogotá. Her house is a large, one-storey white structure of simple cinder block and cement construction, occupying a whole corner in the upper-middle-class neighborhood.

"I was very much in love with my husband when we got married. I adored him, but now I realize that my adoration should be for God. My married life was a disaster—he was always drinking, he always had other women. Like all *costeños*, he liked to enjoy life. I was very proud and I fought with him a lot. There was no peace in the family. His other women would call me on the phone and insult me. I wanted to kill the woman who was going with my husband. If I had had a revolver I would have killed her. My husband was my God. I went to a psychiatrist, and he prescribed sleeping pills for me. Finally, a female dentist gave me a book by Norman Vincent Peale, as a present. I read it, and looked things up in the Bible. I was trying so hard to understand what the book said, but at first I didn't understand. I asked God to help me. I wanted to study the Bible even if I had to pay for it. I had taken courses in glamour, cooking, everything to please my husband, and at that point I thought I might as well pay for a course in Bible study. I told another friend of mine that I wanted to understand the Bible, and my friend, who is also a *costeña*, told me to go to this place, Alpha and Omega. I went there for five years, although all during that time I continued to go to the Catholic church. They do that at Alpha and Omega—they encourage you to continue going to your old church. . . .

My parents were Catholic, but they didn't practice their religion. They were inconstant. My father didn't like priests. My mother used to go to mass every day before she got married. From the time I was little I loved God, but there is a lot of idolatry and error in the Catholic church. The Catholic church doesn't really lead one to God. They don't have the power of the Holy Spirit, so people don't change in that church. There's no love in the Catholic church. The Juanitos church is full of love—they are like Corinthians 13. When you know the Holy Spirit, hate, pride, and jealousy fall away. Because I know the Holy Spirit, I'm able to ask for forgiveness from my children, and from my husband, and even from the woman who lives with my husband. I used to be violent with jealousy over my husband. I am by nature melancholy and sensitive—that's just my personality.

I wouldn't change the Christian life for anything. God is a god of every minute. I live in constant prayer, and I know that I'm not alone. When my husband finally left me for good, I experienced much loneliness, but God was my company. I felt *acompañada*. My husband didn't turn out to be the kind of company I wanted.

There is work for everybody to do within the Christian life. God has helped me so much, I must do as much as I can to help others. I see people who are alone, and I feel drawn to help them, to make them feel less alone. Unfortunately I don't have a *muchacha de servicio* [a maid]. If I could take more time off from the family, that's what I would do, spend my time helping others to feel less alone. Even after I have done a lot of housework, if I am able to help someone in the Lord I feel new—refreshed and full of energy. The Lord gives me strength to do it. . . .

The Juanitos are trying to win souls for Christ among the wealthier people. Their new church, which just opened, is in Chicó, which is the most elegant barrio in Bogotá. They are trying to make headway among people of that social level, but it's always been easier with the poor folk. The Juanitos started their church in Barranquilla in the Barrio del Chino, where the lowest people, the prostitutes, lived. The wealthier people are afraid of the tithing. The Catholic church doesn't ask for the 10 percent—they just ask for alms and for payments for marriages and burials. It's run like a business, so they don't have the power.

The Juanitos also have prayer meetings in people's houses. If you want to have a service in your home, they put your name on a list and it's announced in church. Sometimes it's just more convenient and comfortable to have the meeting in someone's house. The format for the service is basically the same as the *cultos* in church. At the moment there's no special instruction for the leaders of these home prayer groups, but that is something that is needed.

I preached in church once. In order to prepare a sermon you start by praying. Then you go to the Bible. You don't sit and write it all at once, the inspiration comes to you bit by bit, as you're cooking, doing things around the house and all. The Holy Spirit guides you in terms of what to write down. You have to have love and discipline. When I prepared the sermon for the service at the Juanitos I spent all week in prayer, and the Holy Spirit gave me the message little by little. Some people have a real calling to preach, like Rubi, who gave the sermon yesterday. At Alpha and Omega they teach you how to preach. You start in front of small groups. The Holy Spirit helps you get over your nervousness, helps you to forget the people in front of you. People from all different churches come to the Juanitos for the Liberation services, and from all different social classes. The Juanitos have started having services on Thursday nights, special services of intercession, to pray for the family. On Thursdays one of the things we have to do is to pray for more men, to pray that people's husbands will come to church. Men are very cold.

Religion is different from Christianity. Christianity is not a religion, it's an entire change in one's life. In religion, one gets all hung up on the rites of the church, but if you're not fulfilling all of the things in the Bible, it's not Christianity. You have to experience the gifts of God. If there's not a change in your life, Christ hasn't entered.

God is always looking for man. It's not that man is looking for God.

La Ombligada

Sergio Antonio Mosquera

Historian and folklorist Sergio Mosquera was born in Istmina, a mining outpost in the Chocó and one of many towns that trace their history to the slave gangs that dug mines and panned for gold along the rivers of the Pacific Coast region. Mosquera looks to the past, and to rural traditions in the present, to understand not only Africans' experience of enslavement but also the way they remade cultural worlds and sustained those worlds over centuries. With other Colombian scholars, he has worked to document black communities' religious practices and healing arts— rescuing scattered notarial archives to protect the textual record of slavery, inter- viewing elderly men and women to record oral histories, and using ethnography to gain a textured sense of local practices. In the following excerpt, Mosquera collects practitioners' descriptions of la ombligada, *a tradition that welcomes newborns into the human community by bestowing a talent upon them. We have translated* ombligar *as "navel," using the word as a verb. To navel a child and thus bestow a talent, a person trained in the procedure reduces a given substance to a symbolic essence, usually by burning it to ash, and then introduces a minimal speck of the substance into the newborn's body when tying the umbilical cord. To ensure that a grandchild will always elude attackers, a person might navel the baby with the underbelly of an eel; to ensure attractiveness to the opposite sex, other substances would be used; to ensure talent in school, still others. Mosquera includes a chart, not as a user's guide but as a way of explaining to his readers that* la ombligada *emerged from practitioners' understandings of the connections between natural and social worlds. He recognizes that scholars do not understand whether* la ombligada *originated with indigenous peoples in the Pacific lowlands or enslaved Africans brought the practice with them. But he insists on a more concrete point: that the different ethnic groups shared the space of the forest and learned from one another and that* la ombligada *was part of a set of practices that connected the natural and social worlds.*

Ms. María Refa Perea, fifty-three years old, describes the process following the umbilical cord's detachment: "After the umbilical cord falls three, four, or five days after birth, the midwife caring for the mother and the child announces this to the closest relatives, who later meet in order to decide who will navel the baby, based on their previous experience, and what will be used for the boy or girl."

Once the naveling element has been chosen, it will then be reduced to liquid or ashes through heat, and "what can fit between the fingernails of the thumb and index finger will be introduced into the navel." Afterward, once it is enclosed, several precautions must be followed until the navel is healed completely, such as avoiding that the child cries so strongly as to dislodge the amulet, goes hungry, or uncovers their navel when bathing. . . .

Ms. Aura Sánchez Mosquera, fifty-seven years old, told us, "I learned to navel from my mother, Regina Murillo. I naveled my daughter Gertrudis with gold, Fabio with the underside of an eel, and Nohelia with a burnt one-hundred-peso bill so that she would always have enough money."

In turn, Ms. María Agueda Pino, who is currently seventy years old, stated: "I learned to navel from my mother María Bernardina Mosquera, and I naveled all of my children, some with gold, others with fish bone, and others with *guayacán* wood. Naveling has never failed me."

Finally, Ms. Juana Petrona Cossio, seventy-five years old, related the following: "I naveled my daughter María Cossio with gold, so that she would be fortunate in the mines. I used the beak of the *tominejo* [a small, bright-plumaged hummingbird] for my son Juan so that he would attract women, and women all favored him. I learned to navel with my mother: it used to be a mystery, you naveled your children and grandchildren."

From the other side, some people who had been naveled did not refuse to offer their testimony about the effects of the practice. Thus, Oscar Natalio Mosquera Perea, fifty-five years old, commented that "my mother Sara Mosquera naveled me with an armadillo claw, so that I would be extraordinarily good at digging holes and trenches in the mines. That is why I am sought after when opening *hoyaderos* [holes excavated by hand, up to eighteen meters deep or until bedrock is reached], *guaches* [tunnels], *minas de alta*, or *socavones* [shafts]. I swear to you, by God and my mother, that wherever I put my hands nothing crumbles down. I am not a liar: ask Cancharejo, Rafael Bejuco, Efraín Sacapique, or any owner of a large, well-known mine. They often call me to the mines: Tapón, Boca de Soledad . . . truly, any mine owner worth their name has to come and find me so that they can begin work." . . .

Mapping the Ombligada: Substances and effects

MINERAL ELEMENTS

Gold:	Attracts good fortune, luck, and money. A person's navel will ache in the presence of this metal.

ANIMALS

Conga ant:	A regional ant variety intensely black in color, whose bite produces fever and swelling. Provides immunity to the bite's effects. The person's saliva can also soothe the pain of whoever has been bitten.
Bear claw:	Strength in holding onto any object, in order to be a good climber.
Eel slime:	Agility and elusiveness in fights, as his sweat makes the person hard to catch, like this water animal covered in slime.
"Great beast" claw:	Unknown animal, whose claws can be obtained from the Putumayo Indians. It is believed to be of great strength and size. The person naveled with this claw will be a strong, vigorous, and unbeatable fighter.
Deer hoof:	Those naveled with hoof scrapings will be fast in racing.
Arriera ant:	Tireless and hardworking laborer.
Tominejo feather and beak:	Only used to navel men, so that women will favor them.
Fish bone:	A good fisherman who will also be able to help those with bones stuck in their throats.
Armadillo claw:	This animal is an excellent digger, and whoever is [naveled] with its claw will be an expert at making holes, tunnels, and shafts that will not collapse.
Babilla [crocodile] liver:	Prevents asthma.

PLANTS

Quereme:	Plant with an exquisite smell. Endows individuals with amiability, as well as good fortune in love and attracting the opposite sex.

Guayacán:	Tree that is similar to oaks in strength. Those naveled with its trunk will be strong and with good health.
Hierba de Adán:	Avoids curses, especially evil eye.
Seven basils:	Provides amiability and congeniality with people.
Hearth wood ashes:	Will not suffer aches, especially rheumatism.

OTHERS

Mother's saliva:	Will not keep secrets from their mother, and will tell her all that happens.
Human molar:	Cures all toothaches.
Mother's fingernail:	Will share all products from their labor with their mother.
Ashes from printed paper:	Will have pleasing and legible handwriting, and will enjoy studying.
Paper money ashes:	Attracts wealth and money.

Note: This information was obtained in the area of Monte Carmelo, in the municipality of Tadó, on April 18 and May 2, 1998.

Translated by Ann Farnsworth-Alvear

A Witness to Impunity

Javier Giraldo, SJ

*Repeatedly, rural dwellers in Colombia have attempted to declare themselves neutral
—supporters of neither guerrillas nor paramilitaries. They have often turned to the
Catholic Church for support, and in many parts of the country parish priests, members of the religious orders, and both female and male lay workers have transformed
themselves into advocates for human rights. Father Javier Giraldo, a Jesuit priest
with a long history of human rights activism in Colombia, writes movingly about
his attempts to document and denounce the atrocities of the country's dirty war.*

It is difficult for people to really understand the reality in Colombia, so
different from their own, unless it is translated into concrete individuals,
places, dates and incidents they can identify with on a personal level. Perhaps that is why global analyses, even when they refer to dramatic human
situations, tend to be distant and cold. For this reason, I have chosen the
following cases—from among several thousand—to talk about. . . .

I was deeply moved as I listened to Florentino, a young campesino who
had miraculously escaped from his own grave. At 9 P.M. on December 6,
1981, a group of soldiers dragged Florentino and his elderly father from their
home, tied their hands together and gagged them and took them to a nearby
military base where they were holding four other campesinos. At midnight,
the men were taken into the mountains and forced to lie face down before
an open grave that had been dug for them. Then, using knives and rifles,
the soldiers began to kill them. Although seriously wounded in the neck,
Florentino managed to feign death. One by one the bodies were thrown
into the grave and each was covered up with dirt shoveled in by the soldiers.
Suddenly, the killers were momentarily distracted by shouts from other soldiers standing beside a nearby river. Florentino took advantage of their dis-
traction, and, after reaching out to his father's now cold body and realizing
he was dead, fled into the nearby forest alone. Although the soldiers soon
realized that "one of the dead men had escaped," they couldn't make him
out among the trees in the darkness. Florentino made his way cautiously

On May 2, 2002, the church of Bojayá (Chocó department, Pacific Coast region) was destroyed by a pipe bomb launched by FARC soldiers during a period of fighting between the FARC and AUC for control of the Atrato River. Approximately 120 people, including dozens of children, were killed. Photograph by Jesús Abad Colorado. Courtesy of the photographer.

into the river and, swimming as best he could, finally reached a campesino's dwelling down the shore whose occupants helped stop his bleeding and assisted him in making his way to the city of Florencia (capital of the department [of Caquetá]).

I will also never forget the sobs of the young catechism student as she told me of the martyrdom of Ernesto, a young member of a Christian base community. For having gone, or having been forced to go, to a M-19 meeting of the guerrillas, Ernesto and a number of other young residents of his village, San José del Fragua, were tortured for five days on a military base. After the torture, Ernesto was freed on the condition that he report back to the army once a week. On these occasions, the base commander told him he had three alternatives: he could join the guerrilla in which case the army would sooner or later kill him; he could join a counterinsurgency unit and work as an auxiliary to the army; or, lastly, the commander told him, the army would not be responsible for his life and what might befall him. Although his friends insisted he flee the area, Ernesto's mother and family were financially dependent on him and he decided not to abandon them. He categorically refused to join the army, however, saying that would make him nothing more than a murderer, using the words that are so very common among our campesinos: "I don't want to do any harm to anyone."

It had been one of the days that Ernesto was to report to the army base, but that day he was afraid to. Before he left, he told his mother, "Bless me, Mother, I think they are going to kill me." He was right. Members of the counterinsurgency group were waiting for him outside his house and that same day Ernesto disappeared. His body, showing signs of more torture, was found five days later. . . .

Álvaro [Álvaro Ulcué Chocué] was an Indian priest. When he was ordained in 1973, the ceremony made the national news because it was so very rare that an Indian entered the priesthood. A theology student at the time, I felt especially happy for him as I had always been particularly sympathetic to the struggles of the Indians of the Cauca department, heroic survivors of five centuries of oppression. I subsequently met Álvaro at different national meetings of Christian groups. Humble and soft-spoken, he was nevertheless totally committed to the liberation of his people. He took part in different Indian organizations, visiting the territories of other ethnic groups and was considered a leader by his people.

It was not long, however, before Álvaro's decision to work and struggle alongside his own people put him directly into conflict with the region's large landowners whose interests were in opposition to those of the Indians. After he suggested that his Indian parishioners stop choosing wealthy white people as godparents for their children, because landowners subsequently felt they had the right to demand their godchildren work for free on their haciendas, Álvaro became the target of the landowners. The army, too, had him in its sights, accusing him of leading Indian protests and marches in the region and inciting Indians to kill landowners.

By 1981, Álvaro was in the center of the storm. Landowners continued reporting him to the army, and even to the Archbishop, claiming he was inciting the Indians to violence. Soldiers continued abusing the Indians in order to provoke them, and, when they responded by protesting, increased their harassment. During one of these "incidents," Álvaro's sister Gloria was killed and his parents were injured after members of an army patrol attacked them as they were returning from a communal work project.

A communique made public in late 1982 by Christian groups in Cauca announced that "Landowners have placed a bounty on Álvaro's head and only the love shown by those who surround him has so far prevented him from being 'disappeared.'"

Two days before he was murdered, Álvaro met with three army generals to denounce the constant abuses the Indians were suffering and insist the army present evidence to back up their accusations against him. After listening to him in silence, the generals told him they were as convinced as ever that he was provoking the Indians into illegally occupying lands they had no right to.

On November 10, 1984, as he was preparing to officiate a baptism in the small town of Santander de Quilichao, Álvaro was shot and killed by two *sicarios* dressed in civilian clothes.

A witness who later identified both killers as members of the F-2, the intelligence service of the police, was subsequently harassed and received death threats. Soon after that, the case file of the investigation "disappeared" from the prosecutor's office. A mourner at Álvaro's funeral painstakingly copied the dozens of messages that mourners had written on placards and banners. One of these, echoing a thought he expressed on numerous occasions, said, "If I must die, I would like my body to be mixed in with the clay of the forts like a living mortar, spread by God between the stones of the new city." . . .

It was February 21, 1990. A number of campesinos had arrived in Barrancabermeja after fleeing a rural zone near San Vincent de Chucurí that had been bombed by army helicopters and planes. I was in Barranca that day and, together with several members of the local Human Rights Committee, decided to go to the zone where, according to some of the campesinos, there were a number of wounded who needed medical attention and dead bodies which hadn't been identified.

The scenery as we traveled was breathtaking but then, as we made our way up the hill known as the Cerro de la Aurora, we began to notice pools of dried blood by the roadside, and craters that had been opened up by the bombs and rifle shells. The stories we were told by some of the campesinos who had stayed behind during the bombardment were chilling: the soldiers had grabbed one boy, they said, in the presence of many witnesses. Although the witnesses were subsequently forced into a farmhouse, all of them saw the army helicopter arrive and take the boy away.

The discovery a week later of a mound of fresh earth in a nearby hamlet alerted the campesinos. There, they found what was left of his body; it had been ripped into small pieces and they had to use two plastic bags to pick it up.

Near that same spot, two elderly deaf mutes, perhaps they didn't hear the bombs and for that reason didn't flee the area, were savagely tortured and murdered in their humble dwelling. When we entered we saw a puddle of wet blood amidst the disarray of their meager belongings.

One campesina woman in particular impressed me with her strength and acute powers of observation: "Father," she said, "I have lived in these mountains for fifty years and even from far away I know the difference between the smell of a dead animal and a human being." We went down with her about sixty meters, walking off and away from the path through a grove of trees. As we walked, the smell of death became more and more acute. As a few rays of the early afternoon sun filtered through the trees, we saw provisions scattered on the ground, evidence of a recently vacated army camp. Suddenly, we were confronted with a macabre spectacle, a man lay on the ground with his arms and hands extended and opened wide, his mutilated body looked as if it had been crucified. We stood silently, holding our breaths as emotions welled up within each one of us. I could think only of the "Requiem aeternam" and the verses from Job 19 that the Christian tradition has intoned over so many millions of coffins over the centuries, "I know that my Redeemer lives, and that in the end he will stand upon the earth. And after my skin has been destroyed, yet in my flesh I will see God, I myself will see him with my own eyes, I, and not another. How my heart yearns within me!"

The skin had been ripped away from his skull and it had several bullet holes in it, His hands, however, had enough skin on them to see that they had been burned in a bonfire; we found the ashes nearby. Ropes were tied around his feet and we guessed he had been dragged to this spot. The campesina woman who had guided us here pointed out something else, these were not the calloused hands and feet of a campesino, she said. She was right. That same night an investigative commission from the Prosecutor's office arrived, and, after taking skin samples from his fingers in order to identify him, ordered him buried.

Two years later, I learned that the man's identity had been positively established, Juan Fernando Porras, a doctor who had been "disappeared" by members of the B-2 (the army's intelligence unit) several days earlier in Bucaramanga.

He had been accused of collaborating with the guerrillas. Witnesses who were being held at the same cells of the army's Fifth Brigade later told of having seen him there under heavy guard.

City and Country

Today, three of four Colombians live in cities, mirroring the general Latin American trend toward urbanization. About half of the population defined as urban lives in cities of less than five hundred thousand inhabitants, and about a fifth lives in the largest city, Bogotá. Between 1950 and 2000, "pull" factors drew Colombians to urban areas. They came in search of higher wages, immediate access to goods (clothes, shoes, consumer durables, cultural products like music and film, more and more varied food, etc.), and education for their children. They were also "pushed" out of the countryside by poverty, unequal social relations, and atrocious violence. Into the current century, Colombian cities are still receiving tens of thousands of people fleeing death threats, assassinations, and massacres. It is worth noting, however, that today's context is different. In the twentieth century, the nation as a whole went from being majority-rural to being majority-urban, and new arrivals understood themselves as part of a mass experience of migration. In the twenty-first century, however, Colombian cities are large enough that the urban population is growing more from natural increase than from new arrivals. Thus the large numbers of poor people displaced by violence in the countryside who continue to make their way to Colombian cities are arriving to densely populated urban spaces where relatively few people have recent memories of rural life.

Beneath these patterns of change lie long-term continuities in the relationship between country and city. Since the conquest, the wealthy have exercised control over rural districts from positions of relative comfort and security in Colombia's cities. Bureaucratic power sustained by political and clerical authority has been urban in shape, as has the cultural power that inheres in understandings of style and "good taste." Young people with economic, political, or artistic ambition have taken themselves off to the city. The literary greats included in this part—Jorge Isaacs, Candelario Obeso, and Gabriel García Márquez—did exactly that, moving to regional cities or to the country's capital. Nevertheless, those vested with power in the urban centers have not fully controlled the terms of the relationship between city and country in Colombia. Isaacs, Obeso, and García Márquez are all writers who succeeded in representing rurality in ways that trumped the arrogance of city dwellers.

Although the distance between city and country can seem enormous in Colombia, the two are fully interdependent. Culturally, some city residents retain a rural sensibility tied to regional identity, cuisine, and music genres that evoke *las provincias*. And if the cities have changed over recent decades, so has the countryside. Significantly, the skyrocketing profits of cocaine smugglers at the end of the twentieth century redrew the map of rural landholding, as an economist's report included in this chapter reminds us. The nation's exports (especially minerals and agricultural goods) come from rural regions, and in some areas of the countryside midsize landholdings anchor a rural middle class. Now, as in centuries past, Colombia's cities depend on the countryside for food, export products, and a national sense of identity.

Emptying the "Storehouse" of Indian Labor and Goods

Anonymous: "Encomiendas, encomenderos e indígenas tributarios del Nuevo Reino de Granada"

In the early Conquest era, an encomendero *was a Crown appointee who received a grant of Indian labor and collected tribute from a specified Indian community (see part II). The term is associated with Hernán Cortés, as thousands of Indian vassals were assigned to him and his captains. Some of Jiménez de Quesada's soldiers were similarly rewarded with very large* encomiendas. *Within a generation or two, however, the encomenderos of New Granada included many who collected tribute from fewer than ten Indians. In the 1960s, pioneering ethnohistorian Juan Friede (1902–90) was among the first generation of scholars in Colombia to read colonial manuscripts "against the grain" and to use them to write ethnohistory. Born to a Jewish German family living on the Russian-Prussian border, Friede emigrated to Colombia in the 1920s. His activism and institution-building, as well as his high-quality scholarship, changed Colombians' understandings of indigenous and national history; he was also a friend of Quintín Lame (see part VI). Friede described the* encomienda *system in colonial Colombia as a "storehouse" of Indian labor, from which Spaniards needing laborers (he was writing about the emerald mines at Muzo) could "fill in the gaps left by death." Friede used the metaphor to conclude that "the continued decline of the Indian population in the seventeenth century eventually emptied that storehouse."[1]*

However much Spaniards valued gold and emeralds, the storehouse of the encomiendas *also yielded prosaic but essential forms of treasure: food and clothing. Through the early colonial period, Indian communities served as the Europeans' only source for food staples, especially potatoes, corn, and yucca (see part VI). Conquistadors and their heirs also pushed Indian communities to produce new goods, such as chickens, which Indians were required to raise, and to produce old goods in new ways—they enacted rules about what sort of cloth and of what measurements would be accepted as tribute. In providing these goods Indians were understood to be discharging their "debts" not only to their* encomenderos *but also to the Spanish king. They paid twice yearly, at the feasts of Saint John (in June) and at Christmas, by delivering to the* encomendero *whatever quantity of gold, chickens, blankets, corn, honey, or other items they were taken to owe.*

The text below is taken from an inventory produced for the Crown in 1653 by the Spanish official Rodrigo Zapata. In 1964, Colombian historian Jaime Jaramillo Uribe and one of his students, Álvaro González, painstakingly transcribed it for publication, explaining that many folios or parchment pages were ripped and illegible at the bottom and that Nariño and Cauca, regions with important encomiendas, *were for some reason omitted from Zapata's listing. Despite such lacunae, it remains a rich text. Readers sense the span that separates* encomiendas *with hundreds of Indians from those with fewer than ten. We glimpse Spanish women who controlled* encomiendas *in their own name, such as doña Ana de Ordoñez de Valdelomar, widow of captain don Rodrigo Suárez de Vargas, through whom "thirty eight able-bodied Indians" were required to pay their tribute to the Crown. The minutiae of Zapata's reporting attests to his knowledge as a tax collector in the king's service, and, significantly, he flags what he does not know. He has not assessed taxes on the Coyaymas of the river Saldaña, the Natagaymas of the Magdalena, or the Crown's own* encomiendas *in San Juan de los Llanos and el Caguán. For these places, he writes, he has no information.*

In the city of Santa Fe, on the seventh of this month of February, in the year one thousand six hundred and fifty-three. Señor Don Francisco de Bustamante, the *contador* [Royal Keeper of Accounts] for the *corregidores* [provincial authorities],[2] and for quicksilver and tribute, has stated that henceforth, all that pertains to and concerns the exercise of his office will be carried out by Rodrigo Çapata, scribe to his majesty . . . with all that is necessary for his majesty's service, and which is within the *Audiencia*'s power, being done in the keeping of these acts. The above order and disposition shall be carried out within the aforesaid period, without omission or delay, under penalty of fifty silver pieces, half of which shall be for His Majesty's treasury. . . .

In fulfillment of said document, I Rodrigo Çapata de Lobera, scribe for his majesty and for *visitas generales* [visits made by crown-appointed officials] to this New Kingdom of Granada and District of the *Real Audiencia* of Santa Fe, having seen the decrees, general royal inspections, and other documents of my office, as well as the tax lists for tribute made in the district of Tunja by Señor Licenciado don Juan de Valcarzel, *visitador* [official visitor] appointed by the *Real Audiencia* between the years of 1635 and 1636, as well as the tribute lists and numbers of Indians in the remaining provinces visited by Judges, have made the following report. . . .

Environs of Bogotá, ca. 1850. Drawing by C. F. T. Austin, engraving by J. Harris, origi-nally published by Ackermann & Co. in London, ca. 1840. In *Mutis y la Real Expedición Botánica del Nuevo Reyno de Granada,* vol. 1 (Bogotá: Villegas Editores, 1992), 27.

The *repartimiento* of Chita, given in *encomienda* to Captain don Martin de Mendoza y Berrio with one hundred and eighty one able-bodied Indians, subject to tribute, are taxed such that each one of them shall, with addi-tional charges for lateness, give in tax payment one good quality cotton tex-tile each, measured at two *varas* and six in width [roughly six feet six inches] and the same amount in length due on the first *tercio* [feast day of Saint John, in late June], and due on the other *tercio* [Christmas] will be another textile with said measurements, as well as two chickens, one paid each at the *tercios* of San Juan and Christmas. Indians who are not able to make a payment in textiles because they are occupied in neighboring ranches with tasks of care and breeding of cattle for sustenance and the public good, and who do no have time to weave textiles in accordance with the decree issued by the *Real Audiencia* must pay three pesos, each in the amount of eight reales, for each textile that is not paid in-kind, the price regularly charged by this new tax with the charges beginning on the Christmas *tercio* of the year 1635. . . .

In the town of Garagoa of don Bartolome de Veloza, with thirty eight able-bodied Indians, is taxed such that each one shall, with additional charges for lateness, give in tax payment to their *encomendero* one good qual-ity textile due on the *tercio,* and on the other, another cotton textile with said measurements, in addition to two chickens per Indian one paid on each of the two *tercios*, San Juan and Christmas. Indians who are occupied in rural tasks of care and breeding of cattle belonging to farmers must each pay three silver coins and one chicken each *tercio*, a charge that will be collected beginning on the first of January of 1636, and will roll forward remaining payments from the *tercio* of San Juan thereafter, given that the records of the aforesaid *visita* show that the Indians of Garagoa are from hot climates and as such had not paid *requinto* to their majesty for two years, and were relieved. [End of folio torn.]

This tax was appealed by the Indians and is subject to a verdict from the *Real Audiencia*. This town of Garagoa is given in *encomienda* to Andres Baptista de los Reyes. . . .

The towns of Cabita and Cupiagua of doña Ana de Ordoñez de Valdelomar, widow of captain don Rodrigo Suarez de Vargas, with thirty eight able-bodied Indians, is taxed such that each of them shall pay for lateness to their *encomendero* with six pesos, each in the amount of eight reales, and two chickens, paid each year during the two *tercios* of San Juan and Christmas; if these are not provided, payment must be made in agricultural produce in the amount equivalent in price to the aforesaid tax, and where the *corregidor* does not agree to the choice said Indians have made in payment he shall not object but rather will proceed to collect payment in produce and fish and any other goods, at the price these are regularly sold, in the towns where they receive payment, without forcing Indians to bring these out to be sold elsewhere. The *requinto* [a tax linked to the *quinto real*, or royal fifth] and payment of personal service is withdrawn given that they live in warm climate, and the first payment will be collected on the Christmas *tercio* of 1636. [End of folio torn.] . . .

The towns of Cusiana with twenty three able-bodied Indians and Chameza with twenty eight in the hot climate of the *encomienda* of captain Pedro Daza, are each taxed a payment subject to interest to their *encomendero* each year of two white cotton textiles of good quality and finely woven, of the quality in circulation, one each for the two *tercios* of San Juan and Christmas; and the Indian who does not pay the textile because of farm tasks must pay three pesos, each in the amount of eight reales, for each *tercio*, in addition to a chicken. If they wish to pay with honey, black wax and agricultural produce, these can be accepted at the price they are regularly sold, in the amount equivalent to three pesos, in addition to a chicken every *tercio*. Payment of personal service and the *requinto* is withdrawn given that they are Indians living in hot climates, and the first payment subject to interest begins on the Christmas [tercio] of 1636, with all other payments made thereafter. . . .

It is recorded in the decrees carried out by Hernando de Angulo, scribe to the royal treasury, which I have seen, that an increase in taxes was appealed by the Indians of Chiquinquira and their protector on his behalf. These decrees having been seen by the señores President and the Judges of this kingdom's *Real Audiencia*, don Sancho Giron Marques del Sofraga, *President*, and *Licenciado* don Gabriel de Carvajal y Robles de Salcedo, and don Sancho de Torres, Judges, who issued a degree endorsed with their signatures on the first of September of the year sixteen hundred thirty-six, which reads as follows:

Revoking the tax recently collected by Señor Licenciado don Juan de Valcarzel of the town of Chiquinquira, where it was directed that each able-bodied Indian in this town pay a yearly *tributo* to the *encomendero* of four silver coins and four reales, but rather have it be two chickens, plus the *requinto* that belongs to his majesty. . . .

All of these aforesaid taxes each have the following clauses: that all able-bodied Indians shall pay *tributos* and *requintos* between the ages of seventeen and fifty-four, and so that all other Indians raise and breed chickens I order them to apply themselves to having them and breeding them for their own use and gain as well as for the sustenance of the Republic. Each Indian taxed at two chickens is obliged to have and raise in his house twelve chickens and one rooster, while those taxed at four chickens must have sixteen chickens and one rooster, by order and obligation of the *corregidor* of Indians. [End of folio torn.] . . .

And if the caciques, *gobernadores*, [or] captains of all Indian towns learn that some Indians have died, he has to make notice of this [by way of] the *corregidor*. . . . And for there to be proper accounting in collections, each *corregidor* must note with care and diligence any Indians that have died in their district at the end of each year, as well as those who will pay *tributos* once more, making a new list in order to know which able-bodied Indians are available each *tercio*, collecting from each their interests and *requinto* taxes, not as a group but by headcount. The collection is to be made clearly and without harm or grievance to the Indians, following the lists made for each *corregidor* regarding who will pay tribute, with the listed descriptions of Indians from each town carried out during this inspection, which include the ages of those who must pay taxes according to decree. Regarding Indians who have escaped or are absent, whose whereabouts are unknown and for whom interest in reales or *requintos* cannot be collected, payment cannot be required from the living on behalf of the dead, nor from those present for those who are absent, nor from widowed or unmarried women on behalf of their husbands, sons, brothers, and dead or absent relatives whose whereabouts are unknown and for whom [payment cannot be collected]. Regarding governing caciques and head captains, these cannot be charged interest nor charged the *requinto*. Given the care and work they must have in aforesaid collections and making delivery to *corregidores*, and given their *cedula real* [royal decree], they are relieved of the payments of taxes collected and owed until the present collection. . . .

The town of Nemocón de las Salinas of don Juan de Mayorga with fifty-two able-bodied Indians are each taxed at a yearly payment in interest of five silver coins and five Castillian reales, three chickens, and twenty-five pounds of salt. . . .

The towns of Soacha, Boza, Tuzos, Chipagachas and areas neighboring the *encomienda* of Captain don Francisco de Colmenares, with four hundred sixty-six able-bodied Indians, where each of the able-bodied Indians of the captaincies that are called rich [towns] of Boza and Soacha and their neighboring areas . . . shall give over in tax and pay tribute each year, subject to interest, four silver coins and six reales, one *quartillo,*[3] a cotton blanket of fine market cloth, and two chickens, to be paid to their *encomendero.* And all of the able-bodied Indians of the remaining *capitanias* of Baquira, Sueba, Basunga, and Tabita, which are called poor, are to give over in tax a yearly tribute, subject to interest, of four silver coins and six reales, one *quartillo* and two chickens, all of this to be paid to their *encomendero* in halves on the *tercios* of San Juan and Christmas, each year and also the *requinto* tax to the King. . . .

Encomiendas of Indians and the taxes and tributes of the latter in the Governorship of Antiochia . . .

The *encomienda* of Pique and Aqua de la Sal of Miguel Daza with twenty Indians.

The *encomienda* of Tahami y Vexicos of Diego Luis de la Camara with six able-bodied Indians.

The *encomienda* of Sirimoya y la Sal of Diego de Miranda with nine Indians.

The *encomienda* of Penderisco de Francisco de Guzman with nine Indians.

The *encomienda* Sisquiarco of Gaspar Gomes eight able-bodied Indians.

The *encomienda* [folio torn] and Aqua de la Sal with fourteen Indians. [End of folio torn.]

The *encomienda* of Uramaz y San Mateo of Francisco Alfarez with thirteen Indians. . . .

The *encomienda* of Guaracues of Captain Alonso de Rodas with seventeen Indians.

All the aforementioned are taxed each year in back payment two and a half pesos in twenty carat gold, as well as five and a half bushels of corn kernels and two chickens paid in halves on San Juan and Christmas, as taxed by the Licenciado don Francisco de Herrera Campuzano, Judge and Visitor, who performed his *visita* as per his deed and recorded in the city of Santa Fe de Antiochia on the date of December seventeen, sixteen hundred fifteen. . . .

There are two *repartimientos* belonging to the Royal Crown, of the Coyaymas of the Saldaña river and the Natagaymas of the great Magdalena River, whose number and *tributo* taxes are not recorded for the royal treasury and the *tribunal de cuentas*, as they have not been visited.

About the Government's *encomiendas* in San Juan de los Llanos and el Caguan, there is no information, as they have not been visited or taxed.

According to all the above as recorded in the decrees, inspections, and documents of those aforementioned in this document and that are in my offices I deliver this in a true and factual manner, excepting errors, and I certify this under the decree issued prior to this document by Don Francisco de Bustamante, bookkeeper for *corregidores*, quicksilver and tributes of this Kingdom of Santafe on the twenty-sixth of April of the year sixteen hundred and fifty-three. . . .

I, Rodrigo Çapata de Lobera, servant to the King and Lord and of the general [folio torn] of the New Kingdom, have signed, [folio torn].

Translated by Ana María Gómez López

Notes

All personal and place-names have been reproduced exactly as in the transcription of the original manuscript, including omissions of accent marks and inconsistent or dated spelling.

1. Juan Friede, "Demographic Changes in the Mining Community of Muzo after the Plague of 1629," *Hispanic American Historical Review* 47, no. 3 (August 1967): 338–43.

2. *Corregidor* was the title given to a Spanish official with administrative authority over a territorial subdivision termed a *corregimiento*, roughly comparable to a province.

3. A *quartillo* or *cuartillo* was one-quarter of a *real*, a denomination of silver coinage.

To Santafé! To Santafé!

Anonymous: Capitulaciones de Zipaquirá

"Los Comuneros" is the generic name, but observers used other names as well: "revolutionary movement," "communal movement," "insurrection." The hundred-day popular uprising that started in El Socorro province in March 1781 is remembered by its slogans, from "Viva Dios" and "Viva el rey" ("Long live God" and "Long live the king") to "Long live tobacco" and, famously, "Long live the king and Death to bad government." The people in the streets, in the towns of El Socorro province, including San Gil, Barichara, Simacota, Mogotes, Pinchote, Charalá, Guadalupe, Vélez, and El Socorro itself, were el común, hence "los Comuneros." Within a month, they had succeeded in organizing themselves into a force of four thousand men—badly armed but determined to see their demands met. With some disorder, the movement set up a junta, or governing body, and named as their leader Juan Francisco Berbeo, a Creole from the town of El Socorro, in present-day Santander.[1]

The movement expressed popular anger against tax hikes and against a prohibition limiting tobacco cultivation in a number of El Socorro districts. Taxes had been increasing since 1750 and had gone up again in 1779 due to a new war with England. Indeed, the viceroy, Manuel Antonio Flores, was absent from the capital because he was supervising defense works in Cartagena. His authority in Santa Fe (as the city of Bogotá was officially designated) had been delegated to the visitador *(official visitor), Joaquín Gutiérrez de Piñeres, who now wielded enormous effective and symbolic power but who was newly arrived from Spain. To locals, Gutiérrez seemed high-handed and overassiduous—he and other reformist bureaucrats patterned themselves on their well-known superior, the king's financial wizard, José de Gálves, who personified either enlightened absolutism or "bad government," depending on one's perspective. At a minimum, Gutiérrez lacked the tact to administer the ambitious and very unpopular tax restructuring he had been sent to implement in New Granada. Nor could he handle the Comuneros. When Gutiérrez sent a small troop of halberdiers to restore order, with an* oidor, *or royal judge, at their head, they were quickly taken prisoner. The Comuneros were not turned back; rather, they advanced in columns toward the city.*

The "Capitulations" that ended the revolt were signed on June 5, 1781, as the Co-

muneros camped near Zipaquirá, only a day's march from the capital. They were negotiated between Berbeo and Comunero captains, on the one hand, and the archbishop of Santa Fe, Antonio Caballero y Góngora, on the other, who pressured the Audiencia to approve his action and thus avoid the rebels' entry into Santa Fe. What contemporary Colombians understand as a starting point of national identity was in many ways a face-off between country and city.

Two clarifications are useful. First, although it began in El Socorro, it was not localist, as were so many other protests of the period. The Comuneros crossed provincial boundaries, and the revolt expanded beyond the traditional "kingdom" of New Granada (the Eastern Cordillera), reaching the Llanos and various Venezuelan provinces. Second, what began as a nucleus of mestizo cultivators, choking on a prohibition against growing tobacco, reached out to incorporate artisans, shopkeepers, and merchants; provincial whites; and indigenous people—all of whom resented the new tax regime or who hoped to see the reorganization of resguardos, a colonial system of communal landholding that did not allow administrative independence for indigenous communities. Some texts indicate that a few powerful white Creoles from Santa Fe itself secretly supported the Comunero movement, leading to more questions: Was this a traditionalist movement, playing out within the frame of the Austrian monarchy and the centralizing project of the Bourbon King, Charles III? Alternatively, do the clauses that call for naming American-born Creoles to public office express a nationalist idea that would later develop into the struggle for independence? Did the rebels' willingness to move against the city express a moral understanding that later generations might call revolutionary, as the ELN (Ejército de Liberación Nacional—see part V) did when they chose the Comunero town of Simacota to launch their own rebellion? Colombian historians have not resolved their debates about the Comuneros.

"Most Powerful Lord:

[I,] the Captain General and Commander of the cities, towns, parishes, and communities which make up most of this Kingdom [of New Granada], and on behalf of others to whom I lend my voice and assurance, because of the knowledge I have of their actions and so that we may do so unanimously and together as one voice, do hereby demand the suspension of the taxation and the reduction of the excesses that this miserable Kingdom has suffered so unbearably. No longer able to tolerate such an accumulation of these excesses, nor the rigorous means with which they are levied, the village of El Socorro was forced to shake itself free of them in the manner that is now notorious, an action joined by other parishes, cities, and towns having likewise suffered the same grievances; and having intervened, compelled by the agreement unanimously proposed by our leadership, I humbly appear before Your Highness on behalf of all those who elected me for this Command, and of the others who joined this same cause, present and absent, and by virtue of what the Commissioners have prepared for us, I declare and propose the following terms:

First, that the entire branch of the Royal Treasury of Barlovento shall cease to exist so completely that such a name is never heard again.

Second, that the commerce permits that have so disturbed the entire kingdom from the beginning of their establishment shall forever cease their annoyance.

Third, that the trade of playing cards shall also be abolished.

Fourth, that in view of [there being] such misery in this Kingdom, only half-real sheets of stamped paper shall be authorized for use by church officials, religious persons, Indians, and the poor; two-real sheets shall be authorized only for the deeds and lawsuits of persons of comfortable means, and no other paper is authorized. . . .

Sixth, that the newly imposed tax on tobacco be abolished completely. . . .

Seventh, that the misery of all the Indians is in a most deplorable state, one which I, who see it and am familiar with it, shall describe so that Your Highness may grasp it as well. I believe that looking upon them with all due compassion, there are few hermits more poorly dressed and fed. Because of their limited knowledge and tenuous faculties, they are entirely unable to fulfill the excessive tribute that is so insistently demanded of them, as well as of the oppressed mulattoes. The *corregidores* [Chief Magistrates] exact these tributes of them with unbelievable rigor and priests do so as well in order to profit above their stipends. Attentive to such misery, then, the total and annual contribution for the Indians shall remain at four pesos, and at two pesos for the mulattoes; priests shall not charge for rights or gratuities on baptisms, burials or weddings, nor require them to name an official for their holy days; if no participant requests them, the celebrations are to be paid for by the brotherhoods, a point that is in need of quick remedy. . . .

Eighth, that having established the tax on spirits with a provision for the sugar mills at eight pesos per vessel, and having increased this to what is now found in the Kingdom, the price shall be fixed at six pesos per large-mouthed jug and two reales per bottle; a fixed price for premium spirits shall be publicly announced and increased accordingly, should cities and villages so choose. . . .

Ninth, that the sales tax collected on all edible fruits shall henceforth cease; that only two percent shall be collected on the sale of Castilian grains, linens, blankets, cocoa, sugar, preserves, tobacco, horses, sales of land, houses, livestock and other trade; and that [the sale of] cotton shall be exempted from this tax, as it is a product sown and reaped only by the poor. We ask that this be established as a general point. . . .

Fourteenth, that salt, being such a principal, necessary, and indispensable item, neither the factory at Zipaquirá nor that at Chita shall charge more than two and a half reales per *arroba* for it, the price and purchase of which benefit this Kingdom. . . . The manufacture and profit [of salt] should remain with its original owners, the Indians; and if these, having moved elsewhere, enjoy the same amenities that they had before, then the inhabitants of the salt flats shall reap the benefit, giving Your Majesty one peso per each load, the price of which shall be publicly announced and sold at auction, if they wish, and guaranteed through their respective councils in order to avoid any despotic behavior by royal officials, who are intolerable. The ore shall never be worked or separated from the rock salt, for if this were to continue, those present would enjoy abundance but those to come after us would suffer scarcity. All the salt flats in the Kingdom shall be worked by the owners of the lands in which they are found, with an allowance of one peso per load for Your Majesty. . . .

Seventeenth, that the Community of El Socorro requests that in its villages there be a *corregidor* [Chief Magistrate] provided with a salary of a thousand pesos each year and that the capital of Tunja shall have no jurisdiction over this post, provided that those who hold it be Creoles born in this Kingdom; neither of these villages shall claim primacy, but the corregidor shall reside in one of the two [villages], those being San Gil and El Socorro.

Eighteenth, that all employees and officers in the present campaign appointed [to the rank of] General Commander, Captains General, Territorial Captains, Lieutenants, Sergeants, and Corporals shall keep their respective appointments. . . .

Nineteenth, that the scribes shall, by rights, take only half of the required fees, and that they shall declare the amount in silver and the purpose in the margins [of the documents they write]; and if it is determined that they have exceeded this fee for the third time, they shall be deposed from their offices for this reason alone; the same shall apply to ecclesiastical notaries. . . .

Twentieth, that under no circumstances, under any title nor cause, shall the breaking of laws and repeated orders for the interment, arrest, or identification of foreigners in any part of this kingdom continue. . . .

Twenty-first, that having constructed the gunpowder factory, by order of our Monarch and Lord, and having set the price at eight reales per pound, the arrival of the Regent caused the price to be raised to ten reales; and as the aforesaid gunpowder factory is beneficial to the Royal Treasury, it shall cost no more now than the eight reales per pound at which the price was first set.

Twenty-second, that the first, second, and third level jobs shall be reserved for the citizens [*nacionales*] of this America before Europeans, for every day [the Europeans] manifest the animosity they bear against the people from here—not even reciprocated sentiment serves to appease them—, and they ignorantly believe that they are the masters and that all Americans, without exception, are their inferior servants. . . .

Twenty-third, that the heaviest burden borne and suffered by everyone in nearly every city, parish, village, and town is the imposition of ecclesiastic fees, from which not even the most miserable being may escape because of the blind eyes of the Councils, the Synods, the laws, and legal documents; what we ask in this Capitulation is that the most costly services be entrusted to his Illustrious Lord, the Archbishop, so that, in fulfillment of his paternal office, he may find the solution.

Twenty-fourth, that the ecclesiastical *visitadores* shall arrange their undertakings according to the laws concerning provisions. . . . They shall only be provided with the food of the land during their visit, and all other expenses shall be borne by the Archbishop or the bishops who commissioned them when they do not pay personally, as their duty requires. . . .

Twenty-sixth, that the owners of lands that are crossed and bordered by royal roads for the traffic and trade of this Kingdom shall be obligated to allow free use of the ranchland for encampment and pastures for mules, for it has been noted that each private owner has installed fences around his lands, thus leaving the royal roads without territory open for encampments; in order to avoid this, it is ordered, as a general point, that the lands shall be opened

immediately and that, should the landowner fail to do so, the
traveler may destroy the fences.

Twenty-seventh, that the saltpeter found in the territories of Paipa, on
the hacienda of Don Agustín de Medina, shall be distributed to the
benefit of the public, at the price of two reales per load, weighed and
delivered by the administrators.

Twenty-eighth, that there being many passes and roads upon which
travelers are charged some sort of toll, benefitting private parties, we
demand that travelers be completely exempt from this toll, and that
they should pay only [those tolls] that benefit the villages and towns.

Twenty-ninth, that the Chiquinquirá bridge shall retain the toll of one
cuartillo [one-quarter of a *real*], so that the revenue may be used
to construct a bridge of masonry over that river; this contribution
and construction shall be overseen by the cabildo [town council]
of Tunja, and [the toll] existing today shall be reestablished by the
citizens and inhabitants of the county.

Thirtieth, that in remuneration for the poor results seen in the levies
unduly required by the local judges, we demand that they be
abolished forever, and that any citizen shall take his complaints to
the superior courts.

Thirty-first, that considering the poverty of many men and women
who, with very little earnings, establish a small shop, we ask that
they need pay no other tax than sales and personal taxes.

Thirty-second, that seeing how many men and women are sent to
prison, not so much for their offenses as for the profit of the jail
keepers or guards, we ask that only two reales be required for their
release, and if the sentence be long, that they pay nothing, just as it is
not permitted to turn the jail into a warehouse in order to bankrupt
the prisoners and start riots. . . .

Thirty-fifth, that as our primary objective has been to free ourselves
from the taxes for Barlovento and other tributes levied against us by
the *visitador* ([a burden] that has greatly exasperated our spirits and
moved them towards taking the resolution now so notorious to Your
Highness), and that because our desire has not been to forget our
loyalty as true and faithful vassals, we humbly beg Your Highness
to pardon us for all the laws that we have broken up to now; and so
that your royal word may remain entirely bound, we beg that it be
given, for greater solemnity, under oath on the four Gospels; and so
that its presence in the Royal Agreement may be verified, it shall be
referred to the commissioners and ratified again here in the presence

of the Illustrious Lord Archbishop, so that all of the *Comunes* may
know of your royal and inviolable word, by which these Agreements-
Capitulations are to remain firm and enduring, now and forever; we
ask that these be accepted and granted to us, and that their approval
be free of ambiguity.

[Signed at] the Battle Camp in the Zipaquirá Territory, 5 June, 1781
Most Powerful Lord,
At the feet of Your Highness, your most devoted vassal,

JUAN FRANCISCO BERBEO

Translated by Timothy F. Johnson

Note

1. In this context, "Creole" means a locally born subject of the Spanish king and is generally taken to refer to a person treated as white or close to white in terms of colonial racial
hierarchies.

Killing a Jaguar

Jorge Isaacs

*By the end of the nineteenth century, educated Spanish Americans seeking to un-
derstand the region and represent it to outsiders had access to a growing set of locally produced authors, even if their tastes were still shaped by European literature.
For multiple generations of lettered men and women in Mexico City, Buenos Aires,
Havana, or Santiago de Chile the writer who most represented Colombia was undoubtedly Jorge Isaacs (1837–95), whose novel* María *(1867) was not supplanted for
the hemisphere's readers until Gabriel García Márquez published* One Hundred
Years of Solitude *a century later. Isaacs's sentimentality and backward-looking
nostalgia for hacienda life stand out. In places his text is also notable for the way it
echoes white-supremacist assumptions about master-slave relations and evokes the
kind of patriarchal authority that likely appealed to readers uncertain about what
the future held for republics wracked by long bouts of political disorder.*

*The beautiful María of the novel's title is a tragic figure, marked by racial insta-
bility (she is the daughter of Jews, converted to Catholicism; Isaacs also had Jewish
heritage, on his father's side). She dies while the young man who loves her, Efraín,
is away studying medicine in London, where he has gone in obedience to his father.
There is an ambivalence at the heart of Isaacs's book: filial obedience is right yet
causes unhappiness. Isaacs's story centers on an idyllic hacienda called El Paraíso,
or Paradise, a place where slavery's violent side is erased. Efraín's parents are "good
masters." Yet the novel also recounts aspects of Ashanti history and contains a long
inset story about African lovers cruelly separated by enslavement. The racist descriptions that Isaacs includes, such as his sketch of the slave boy Juan Ángel, set
within the story of a hunting party excerpted below, are juxtaposed with sections
that critique the slave system. Isaacs is no less ambivalent about tropical nature.
In María the settings in which his characters find themselves are so lavishly described as to dwarf the action of the story itself. Readers move from sylvan glades
strewn with flowers to overwhelmingly powerful rivers and nighttime mountain
passes. One of the few characters presented in a wholly positive light is Braulio, who
flushes out the jaguar Efraín shoots. He is the white mountaineer whom generations
of Colombians after Isaacs would also take up as a symbol of the kind of pioneer*

spirit that could push Colombia away from the seemingly feudal structures of encomienda *and slavery.*

I went down to the precipitous bank of the river by the same path I had followed so many times six years before. The thunder of the current began to grow louder, and presently I discovered the waters eager to plunge over the falls; once over, they were changed into whirling foam, then became smooth and glassy in the quiet stretches of the river; always the same bed of rocks shaggy with moss, the same fringe on the bank of *iracales*, ferns, and reeds with yellow shoots, silky plumes, and purple flowers.

I paused in the middle of the bridge—a gigantic cedar flung there by a hurricane. Flowering parasitic plants grew out of the slime, and bluebells and heliotropes swung down in festoons beneath my feet to dip in the water. The luxuriant and towering vegetation at times arched the river completely, and the rays of the rising sun broke through it as if through the broken roof of an abandoned Indian temple. Mayo howled in cowardly fashion on the bank I had just left, but on my urging, at last made out to cross the fantastic bridge; then he was off at once ahead of me up the path which led to the cabin of old José, who was expecting my visit of greeting that day.

Passing along a dark and sloping ridge, and leaping over the heaps of dead trees thrown down by the last mountain-slides, I came out into the little plot planted with vegetables, from which I could see the smoke of the hut, situated in the midst of green hills; though, when I last saw it, it was in an unbroken forest. The cows, of fine shape and markings, were lowing for their calves at the gate of the corral. The poultry were noisily eating their morning meal. In the neighboring palm groves, which had been spared by the axe, the clamorous goldhammers quarreled in their hanging nests, and, in the midst of their pleasant chatter, one could hear now and then the shrill cry of the bird-catcher, who, from his moat and barbican, struck terror into the hungry macaws swooping down upon the cornfield.

The fierce dogs announced my arrival by their barking. Mayo was afraid of them, and kept by me whining. José came out to greet me, his axe in one hand, and hat in the other.

The little dwelling proclaimed industry, thrift, and neatness; everything was plain but convenient, and nothing was out of its place. The best room, which was scrupulously swept, had bamboo rush-bottomed seats scattered about, covered with bear-skins; some sheets of colored paper with pictures of saints on them were pinned with thorns to the unwhitened walls; on the right was José's bedroom, and on the left the girls'. The kitchen, built of strips of cane, and with a roof of the leaves of the same plant, was separated from the house by a little garden, where parsley, chamomile, pennyroyal, and basil mingled their odors.

The women were dressed with more than usual care. Lucía and Tránsito, the girls, wore petticoats of violet-colored chintz, and fine white chemises; their collars were of lace, tied with black ribbon, and under them their rosaries were partly visible; their necklaces were of opal-colored glass. Their thick, jet-black hair was arranged in braids, which danced upon their shoulders at every movement of their bare, agile feet. They addressed me with the greatest timidity; and their father, observing this, encouraged them, saying, "Do you think it isn't the same boy because he has come back from college such a wise young man?"

Then they became more smilingly at ease; we were drawn to each other in the most friendly manner by the remembrance of games together as children—a remembrance which has great power over the imagination of a poet, or of a woman.

With advancing age José's face had gained much; although he did not let his beard grow, his countenance had an appearance almost patriarchal—as has that of almost all old men of good habits in the land where he was born. Abundant gray hair shaded his broad and sunburnt forehead, and his smile bespoke the tranquility of his mind. Luisa, his wife, somewhat more fortunate than he in the contest with time, preserved in her manner of dress something of the city style, and her vivacity and pleasant ways made it clear that she was contented with her lot.

José led me to the river, and talked to me about his crops and his hunting while I was taking a plunge in the transparent pool whence the stream fell over a small cascade. On our return we found a tempting breakfast served upon the only table in the house. Maize appeared in many forms—in porridge served on plates of glazed clay, and in golden griddle-cakes. The only knife and fork of the establishment were crossed upon my plate, which was white, with a blue border. . . .

I placed in the good old man's belt the [knife] which I had brought for him; gave pretty rosaries to Tránsito and Lucía; and left in the hands of Luisa the reliquary which she had asked my mother to get for her. I then started down the mountain; it was precisely noon, so José said as he studied the sun.

The following morning at daybreak I took the mountain road, accompanied by Juan Ángel, who was loaded down with presents sent by my mother to Luisa and the girls. Mayo followed us; his faithfulness was too much for his prudence, for he had received many injuries in expeditions of this sort, and was far too old to go upon them.

Once across the bridge, we met José and his nephew Braulio, who were coming to find me. The former at once broached to me his plan for the hunt, which was to try for a shot at a famous jaguar of the neighborhood that had killed some of his lambs. He had followed the creature's trail, and had discovered one of his lairs at the head-waters of the river, more than half a league above his cabin.

Juan Ángel was in a cold sweat on hearing these details, and putting down on the fallen leaves the hamper which he was carrying; looked at us with staring eyes as if he were hearing of a plan to commit a murder.

José kept on talking of his scheme of attack: "You may cut off my ears if he gets away. Now we'll see if that boastful Lucas is only the braggart they say. Tiburcio I'll answer for. Have you got large bullets?"

"Yes," I replied, "and my long rifle."

"This will be a great day for Braulio. He wants very much to see you shoot, for I have told him that you and I consider shots very poor that do not hit a bear square between the eyes."

He laughed boisterously, clapping his nephew on the shoulder.

"Well, let's be off," he continued; "but let the boy carry this garden-stuff to the Señora, and I'll go back." He caught up Juan Ángel's hamper, saying, "Are these sweetmeats that María is sending for her cousin?"

"That's something my mother is sending Luisa."

"But what can be the matter with the girl? I saw her go by yesterday looking out of sorts. She was as white as a Castile rose-bud."

"She's well again."

"Here, you young nigger, what are you doing here?" said José to Juan Ángel. "Be off with that bag, and come back quickly, for it won't be safe for you to pass by here alone after a while. Not a word of this down at the house."

"Mind you come back!" I shouted to him, after he had crossed the bridge. He disappeared in the reeds like a frightened partridge.

Braulio was of about my age. Two months before he had come from Antioquia to live with his uncle, and was already madly in love with his cousin, Tránsito. The nephew's face had all of that nobility which made that of the older man so interesting; but the most striking thing in it was a beautiful mouth, not bearded as yet, whose feminine smile was in strong contrast with the manly energy expressed in the other features. Of a gentle and yielding nature, he was an indefatigable worker, a real treasure for José, and just the husband for Tránsito.

Luisa and the girls came out to welcome me at the door of the cabin, smiling and affectionate as ever. Frequent sight of me in the past few months had made the girls less timid with me. José himself in our hunting expeditions—that is, upon the field of battle—exercised a paternal authority over me, but this disappeared when he entered his house, as if our true and simple friendship were a secret. . . .

Once at sunset, years afterwards, journeying through the mountains of José's country, I saw happy laborers reach the cabin where I used to enjoy hospitability. After grace was said by the aged head of the family, they waited around the fireside for the supper which the dear old mother passed to them; one plate sufficed for every married couple; the children frisked about the room. And I could not bear to look upon the patriarchal scene, which reminded me of the last happy days of my youth.

The breakfast was hearty, as usual, seasoned with a conversation which revealed the eagerness of José and Braulio to begin the hunt. It must have been ten o'clock when all at last were ready, Lucas carrying the hamper which Luisa had made ready for us; and after José's repeated coming and going to collect and put in his great otter-skin pouch bunches of wadding and a variety of other things which had been forgotten, we set out.

There were five hunters—the mulatto Tiburcio, a peon from the Chagra hacienda, Lucas, José, Braulio, and I. We all had rifles; though those carried by Tiburcio and Lucas were flintlocks—most excellent, of course, according to their owners. José and Braulio carried lances also, with the blades very carefully set in the handles.

Not a single available dog stayed at home; leashed two and two, they swelled our expedition, whining with pleasure. Even the pet of Marta, the cook, Palomo, whom the very hares knew to be stone-blind, offered his neck to be counted among the able-bodied dogs; but José sent him away with a *"zumba!"* followed by some mortifying reproaches. . . .

Against my advice, we went back again to the river, and kept on up its course. In a little while Braulio found the tracks of the jaguar on the shingle, this time going down to the edge of the water. Braulio strapped his rifle to his back, and waded across the stream; he had attached a rope to his belt, and José held the end of it so as to prevent a false step from causing his nephew to plunge over the cascade just at hand. We maintained a profound silence, repressing the impatient whining of the dogs.

"Not a track here," said Braulio, after examining the sand and the thicket. Just then he stood up, about to return to us, and poising himself on the top of a rock, motioned us to be quiet. He seized his rifle, threw it to his shoulder, aimed as if to shoot at something among the rocks at our side, leaned lightly forward, cool and quiet, and fired.

The dogs seemed to understand what had happened. Scarcely had we loosed them when they disappeared in the gorges at our right, while José was helping Braulio across the river.

"Keep quiet!" said Braulio, as soon as he gained the bank; and while he was hurriedly loading his rifle he added, seeing me, "You come with me, young master."

The dogs were already close on the prey, and it seemed as if the brute were not finding it easy to get away, since the barking all came from one point. Braulio took a lance from José's hand, saying to us two: "You go above and below to guard this pass, for the jaguar will double on his trail if he gets away from us where he is. Tiburcio will stay with you."

Then he said to Lucas, "We two will go round and come out on top of the hill."

With his usual sweet smile, and with the coolest manner, he finished loading his rifle.

"It's a dear little cat, and I hit him." As he said this we separated. José, Tiburcio, and I climbed upon a convenient rock. Tiburcio kept looking at the priming of his rifle. José was all eyes. From where we were we could see all that was happening on the hill, and could guard the pass as requested, for there were but few trees intervening, though they were large ones.

Of the six dogs two were already *hors de combat*: one of them lying mangled at the feet of the fierce animal; the other, with entrails protruding between broken ribs, had come to find us, and giving forth the most heartrending cries, died at the foot of the rock upon which we had climbed. With his side turned to a clump of oaks, his tail playing about like a serpent, his back erect, his eyes flaming, and his teeth bared, the jaguar was uttering hoarse cries, and as he threw his enormous head about, his ears made a noise something like castanets. As he turned about, worried by the dogs, who were not much injured although not wholly unharmed, we could see that his left flank was bleeding; he tried to lick it from time to time, but this only gave the pack an advantage in rushing at him.

Braulio and Lucas appeared, emerging from the gorge and coming out upon the hill, though a little farther from the brute than we were; Lucas was livid. There was thus a triangle formed by the hunters and their game, so that both groups could fire at the same time without danger of injuring each other.

"Let's all fire together!" shouted José.

"No, no; we'll hit the dogs!" replied Braulio; then he left his companion and was lost to our sight.

Suddenly, Braulio's head appeared rising out of the gorge, a little behind the trees which protected the jaguar in the rear; his mouth was half-opened with his panting, his eyes were dilated, his hair was flying. In his right hand he carried the couched lance, and with his left he was pushing away the twigs which prevented him from seeing clearly.

We all stood silent; the very dogs appeared absorbed in the end of the adventure.

At last José shouted, "At him! Kill-lion, at him! Biter, Strangler, at him!"

It would not do to give the jaguar a breathing-spell; and setting on the dogs would make Braulio's risk smaller. The dogs renewed their attack all together. One more of them fell dead without a sound. The jaguar gave a horrible yell. Braulio was seen behind the clump of oaks, nearer to us, grasping the handle of the lance, from which the blade had been broken. The brute swung around in search of him. He shouted, "Fire, fire!" and leaped back at a single bound to the place where he had lost his lance-head. The jaguar followed him. Lucas had disappeared. Tiburcio turned olive color; he leveled, and pulled the trigger: his gun flashed in the pan.

José fired. The jaguar roared and bit at his flank again, and then sprang in pursuit of Braulio. The latter, turning his course behind the oaks, flung himself towards us to pick up the lance thrown to him by José.

The beast was square in front of us. My rifle alone was available. I fired. The jaguar sank backward, reeled, and fell. . . .

The Time of the Slaves Is Over

Candelario Obeso

Candelario Obeso was born the illegitimate son of a black washerwoman in the provincial town of Mompox; at age seventeen, he left for Bogotá to continue an education that had been funded in part by the efforts of his father, a Liberal Party lawyer. In 1877 Obeso published his best-known work, Cantos populares de mi tierra *(Popular Songs of My Land), which includes the two poems below, written in black Colombian vernacular. Strikingly, Obeso's book includes a poem that overlaps with Isaacs's earlier María (1867), as Isaacs had included a boga's song with lines very close to Obeso's "Canción del boga ausente." It is likely not that Obeso plagiarized but that both writers were inspired by the oral genres of river life.[1] Indeed, by dedicating, first, "Song of the Absent Rower" to Rufino José Cuervo and Miguel Antonio Caro, two of Colombia's foremost linguists and philologists, founders of the Academia Colombiana de la Lengua (Colombian Academy of Language), modeled on Spain's Real Academia de la Lengua, and, second, "Serenata," to their colleague Venancio González Manrique, also an academic and scholar, Obeso was explicitly affirming the legitimacy of black oral aesthetics to Colombia's creole academic and literary establishment. If "Song of the Absent Rower," about sex, love, and longing, is his most famous work, other poems allow us to hear a fiercer, more political voice. The oddly titled "Serenata," for example, is also from* Cantos populares *and speaks of a peasant man's intention to stay put, in his own riverside homestead. The poet suggests that war with the cachacos (as Bogotanos were and are still known) would misdirect black people's energies. Partisan conflict is figured against the freedom to work on one's own land. The poet puts it plainly: "The time of the slaves is over."*

Cantos populares de mi tierra *is Obeso's tribute to the black communities of the Magdalena River region, including the area near Mompox, the riverside city of Obeso's birth. In 1867, when he was eighteen years old, Obeso traveled to Bogotá after winning a scholarship to study at a military school founded by the Liberal war hero and former president Tomás Cipriano de Mosquera (see part II). His writing career was interspersed with periods of military and diplomatic service—he served as a soldier in the civil war of 1876, where his performance in the battlefield earned*

The *champan*, a long, partially covered rivercraft, dominated trade and passenger travel on the Magdalena for centuries, until its oarsmen were displaced by steamboats and their crews. The oarsmen, known as *bogas*, were often men of African descent, working in rowing teams of ten to fourteen men. Note that both a cook and a seated man are visible here. Watercolor and ink on paper by Joseph Brown, ca. 1840, 18.5 × 33.7 cm. Royal Geographical Society of London. In Malcolm Deas, Efraín Sánchez, and Aída Martínez, *Tipos y costumbres de la Nueva Granada / Types and Customs of New Granada* (Bogotá: Fondo Cultural Cafetero, 1989), 51.

him the title of sergeant. Fluent in French, English, Italian, and Spanish, he was also an official interpreter in Panama and briefly served as Colombian consul in Tours, France.

Despite his literary and public accomplishments, Obeso's final work, La lucha de mi vida *(My Life's Struggle), is laced with reflective disillusionment on his personal life, which was marked by poverty, scant critical recognition, and racial discrimination. Two years after his memoir was published, Obeso died in Bogotá from a gunshot wound to the gut. It remains unresolved whether his death was accidental (while cleaning a pistol) or a suicide.*

Song of the Absent Rower

To Mr. Rufino Cuervo and Mr. Miguel A. Caro

How sad the night is
Tonight, the night is so sad
A sky without a single star
Row on, row on!

For the black woman of my soul,
I soak in sweat
As I toil away at sea,
What will she do? What will she do?

Will she sigh in woe
For her beloved *zambo*
Will she even remember me . . .
Weep on, weep on!

Women are like everything
In this wretched land;
With art fish are hauled out
From the sea, out from the sea!

With art iron is molten,
The *mapaná* snake is tamed;
Sorrows faithful and firm
They are no more, they are no more!

How dark the night is tonight,
Tonight how dark is the night,
It is as dark as absence.
Row on, row on!

Translated by Stephanos Stephanides

Serenata

To My Friend, Señor V. Manrique

They say there is war
With the *cachacos*,
And the commotion*
Annoys me. . . .
When there were Conservatives
I was a soldier
Because I defended
My humble farm. . . .
If someone wants
To climb on high,
He should look for a ladder

Somewhere else; . . .
The time of the slaves
Is over;
Today we are as free
As the white. . . .
I for my part
When I work
I eat in my house, . . .
If not—I bear it. . . .
I know many,
Poor cripples
Who have died of hunger
Next to the handsome ones. . . .
. . . .
They want war
With the cachacos?
I do not move,
From here and my farm; . . .
If someone tries
To go to the top,
He should look for a ladder
Somewhere else! . . .

(*Trapisonda.) [Obeso's footnote defining *zamba-palo* for the reader]

Translated by Jason McGraw

Note

1. Obeso's version, however, is more metaphorical—many of his readers would have known that the *bogas* were not associated with work at sea. Another difference lies in Obeso's orthography, which emphasized the rhythms and song forms of the black poor. Isaacs's version can be found in Jorge Isaacs, *María, a South American Romance* (New York: Harper and Brothers, 1890), 271.

A Landowner's Rules

Ángel María Caballero

Throughout the twentieth century, Colombian coffee was produced by smallholder families and planters with medium-size enterprises—a fact established by census-takers in 1932 (see part VI). In a hemispheric context marked by latifundista *production for long-distance trade, Colombia stood out as unusual for the relatively equitable distribution of land dedicated to the principal export crop. Nevertheless, a significant percentage of the crop was produced on very large estates, and the symbolic and political meanings attached to large haciendas, many of which dated from the colonial period, remained important, especially from 1927 to 1934, when peasant activism reached a high point. No other coffee hacienda was as politically central to agrarian protest in Colombia as the estate known as "El Chocho," located in the immediate environs of Bogotá. Thus readers will want to note that "El Chocho" was an exception to the Colombian story of smallholder coffee production but a representative example of another Colombian story, that of feudal relations in the countryside. The excerpt below captures something of the extreme inequality that marked interactions between an* hacendado (hacienda owner) *and the people whose labor made the land valuable.*

The text is taken from a pamphlet of estate rules printed in Bogotá in 1896.[1] Decades later, labor relations at El Chocho became a cause célèbre among muckraking journalists in Bogotá. In the 1930s, a young politician named Carlos Lleras Restrepo prepared a report that described the internal stratification of tenants and workers on the hacienda. Later, as president in 1966–70, Lleras was associated with Colombia's only important experiment with land reform. In that early report Lleras found that El Chocho had 950 tenants, of whom 100 lived in the colder highland districts known as Subia and Noruega, and 850 in temperate parts of the property. The latter group occupied 5,500 hectares, producing coffee for export, sugar, and food crops. He wrote that tenants planted an average plot size of 6.5 hectares in the coffee-producing area of El Chocho and that each family produced an average of twenty-three bags of café pergamino (dried, harvested coffee still in its parchment husk). *That level of* production required a tenant family to use hired hands at harvest time, and, indeed, Lleras documented the fact that two thousand wage workers were brought onto the hacienda in this way, meaning that tenants acted as intermediaries and recruiters for landowners in need of hands.[2] Politically, Lleras's involvement, and the involvement of other urban radicals, including Jorge Eliécer Gaitán (see part V), derived its force from the fact that resident tenants had initiated union activity and undertaken a series of strikes. By the 1930s, impoverished tenant farmers were fighting back against the labor obligations laid out in texts such as this one.

Regulations for the Tenants of the Hacienda El Chocho (1896)

ARTICLE 1. The holder of the *Hacienda El Chocho* admits tenants on his lands; those leasing at present and those who are subsequently admitted are invariably subjected to the terms of these Regulations. As such, each of these by-laws are understood to be included in the partial lease contracts with each *colono*.

ARTICLE 2. The right to live and sow a specific plot of land rented by the owner of the hacienda to an individual is designated as a "stay."

ARTICLE 3. The hacienda considers as the direct or main leaseholder the individual whose name has been entered into the record book so that he will pay a standard rent in money and 18 days of mandatory labor a year.

ARTICLE 4. Aside from the direct leaseholders, all other individuals who share activities during the stay of the main tenant will be registered in a separate list, so that they will pay 6 days of mandatory labor required by the hacienda and which they will pay under the same conditions. These individuals thus inscribed will be referred to by the hacienda as *terrajeros* [sharecroppers]. . . .

ARTICLE 8. Every leaseholder is responsible for informing the hacienda about the *terrajeros* that work with him, so that these can be registered and the six [originally typeset as three, revised in handwriting to six] days of mandatory labor stipulated by this Regulation can be brought into effect. If this is not done, the tenant will pay this liability with twelve days instead of the six that the *terrajero* would have provided had he not incurred in this omission.

WITH REGARD TO ANIMALS

ARTICLE 11. Every leaseholder must pay 24 pesos [originally typeset as 40 centavos, revised in handwriting to 24 pesos] per month for each head of cattle six months and older, whether they are tied down or left loose.

Article 14. Each head of household can have as many pigs as they wish, so long as they are kept in pens or tied. If these conditions are not met, the holder of the hacienda and his dependents can have them killed, without any responsibility, whenever pigs are seen trailing their ropes.

Owners whose pigs cause damages for being left astray will pay compensation to the person affected whose amount will be set by two experts named by the hacienda.

WITH REGARD TO OBLIGATIONS

ARTICLE 18. The 12 days of mandatory labor will be paid by leaseholders on the day or week for which they are requested, for which they will be notified eight days in advance, along with which tools they need to bring and where they must present themselves.

ARTICLE 19. *Peónes* [day-laborers] younger than 18 and not suitable for work will not be admitted for mandatory labor. In addition, those who present themselves after six o'clock in the morning will not be admitted, as a full day of mandatory labor will run from 6 in the morning to 6 in the evening.

ARTICLE 20. All leaseholders who present themselves for mandatory labor will have lunch at 10 in the morning and eat supper at 2 in the afternoon, and will inform their households so that they can provide food during these times, as they will not be able to leave work for any reason before or after this time.

ARTICLE 21. The leaseholder that does not present himself on the day and time notified for mandatory labor despite being previously notified will pay double for his obligation, in addition to fees covering day(s) that the commissioner requires to make him meet his duty, which will be charged at 50 pesos [originally typeset as "diez reales," revised in handwriting to "50 pesos"] per day. Illness is not an excuse, and a *peón* needs to be sent in replacement. Outstanding fees to the commissioner will be paid in the same way as the lease.

ARTICLE 22. The leaseholders can take lumber, hay, rope, and firewood from the hacienda for their own use, yet it is absolutely prohibited to take these or any other objects outside for sale; whoever goes against this prohibition will be punished with strong fines, as well as termination of contract and a report to the relevant authority.

> *Signed in the hacienda El Chocho,*
> *on January 1st, 1896,*
> *Ángel María Caballero*

Translated by Ana María Gómez López

Notes

1. The editors thank Carlos Caballero Argáez and Rocío Londoño Botero for facilitating the inclusion of this text.

2. *Informe del Secretario de Gobierno al Sr. Gobernador del Departamento de Cundinamarca*, 1934 (Bogotá, 1934), 4–70.

Muleteers on the Road

Beatríz Helena Robledo

*Arre, in its dictionary meaning in Spanish, is "a voice used to move animals."
From it follows the verb* arrear, *which means "to drive draft animals, especially
mules," and related terms—from* arrieros *(muleteers) and* caminos de arriería
*(mulepaths) to folkloric expressions like "Arrieros somos, y en el camino nos en-
contraremos," meaning literally "We're muleteers, we'll see each other on the trail,"
but, more figuratively, "We're bound to meet again." Less vulnerable to the diseases
spread by biting insects and bats, more long-lived, proverbially stubborn and resis-
tant, and cheaper to feed, mules were Spanish America's beast of burden. Without
mules and muleteers the opening and settlement of the Andean and Mesoamerican
frontiers in the late colonial and early national periods would be simply inexpli-
cable. And prior to the Panama Canal, no other roadway in Spanish America was
as densely crisscrossed by mule caravans as the transoceanic route between Panama
City and Colón.*

*In Colombia, wherever paths were passable by mule, the driver and his pack
were key historical agents. In Antioquia the muleteer became a symbol of regional
identity—so much so that many Colombians equate mule-driving with the history of coffee cultivation and with Antioquia. Nevertheless, a reader can substitute "Santander," "Boyacá," "Cauca," or "Cundinamarca" for "Antioquia" in the
text excerpted here. Muleteers' historical influence extends throughout Colombia.
Across the Andean region especially, economic historians such as Frank Safford
have shown that transport costs posed obstacles for the development of regional and
subregional markets. Prices reflected trail conditions: merchants paid more or less
if the trail was* de subida *(going up) or* de bajada *(going down), a clue to the vertical axis of Colombian geography. For cultural historians, the* arrieros *prefigured
a set of rural rhythms that later generations would encounter in the form of trucks
and* el jeep willis *or the* yipao *(terms used for the military-style jeeps that became
popular in rural districts of Colombia in the 1950s and '60s, and which are still common today).*

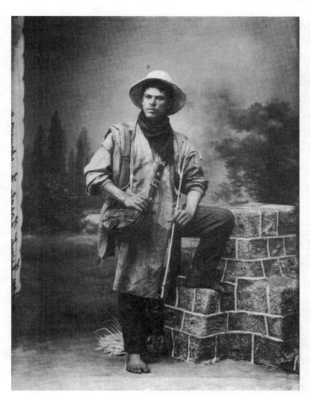

Studio portrait of a
muleteer, Medellín, ca.
1910. Photograph by
Benjamín de la Calle.
Biblioteca Pública
Piloto de Medellín. In
*El comercio en Medellín,
1900–1930* (Medellín:
Fenalco, 1982).

The bleeder was the first to wake up. That was not his given name nor was
it the nickname he went by, although it was very common for muleteers to
have clear, sonorous handles, easy to memorize, the better to keep track of
the merchandise. The daily journeys were very long, the roads were very
bad. If the merchandise did not arrive at its destination, there always needed
to be someone ready to give an explanation. A muleteer deposited his integrity and the quality of his work in the name he chose. The bleeder knew
this, but first he had to pass the test, learn all the tricks of the trade, and
perform his rite of initiation as an assistant, in order to reach the level of
independence, autonomy, and prestige possessed by good muleteers. . . .

When it rained all the drivers complained, "Man, I sure am stupid! Why
am I leading such a hard life? Noooo! There are so many other things one
can do!" And when we went out and it was dry we would laugh and say,
"Leave driving? Never! Driving has to leave me first! . . ."

Weather was a decisive factor. If paths were impassable, merchandise
had to be left in storehouses, which raised the cost of storage. If merchan-

Studio portrait of a muleteer, Medellín, ca. 1910. Photograph by Benjamín de la Calle. In Sociedad de Mejoras Públicas de Medellín, *Medellín el 20 de julio de 1910* (Medellín and Leipzig: E. V. Sperling, 1910).

dise was transported, the freight charges became almost impossible to pay. Mules stumbled easily, and there was always the risk that the load would get damaged.

The bleeder would get dressed, at least to start off the route, with a shirt, pants, and canvas sandals: later, it would be better to go barefoot in the marsh. He prepared the feed for the mules. The night before he had left lumps of *panela* (hard, molasses style brown sugar) soaking in water and now he would mix the sugar water with the bran. Grass, sugarcane, and molasses: these mules were pampered and had to be well taken care of, as success in a day's work largely depended on them.

This time there were twenty mules, all belonging to a merchant in Rionegro. It was the second trip for this bleeder. The first had been with contraband tobacco. What an adventure! But he had sworn not to do this again, holy Mother of God! Contraband was dangerous: one could go to jail and all, and he did not want to do anything risky. His dream was to be independent and own his own mules, so that no one would jerk him around.

While he fed the mules he remembered his first trip: it was with the mules of a man from Jericó, a wealthy man who owned many businesses. He placed the tobacco within hollow *guadua* trunks, capping off each end to keep them hidden. From the outside, the tobacco would appear like a regular load of merchandise. But of course not all of the tobacco was contraband! The rest of the mules were loaded the proper way, *como Dios manda*: round sacks, tightly wrapped in cowhide. It was a difficult load, and the sacks made the mules lose their balance. Also, the tobacco made some of the mules dizzy. The ones that didn't get lightheaded would make noise with their muzzles and turn into "tobacco mules," while the dizzy ones would stagger until they finally had to lay down. Their loads would have to be put on other mules, and they would have to follow along behind the pack.

Day was breaking. The clinking of pots and pans emerged from the kitchens, where the women prepared the food that their sons or husbands would take with them for their long stretches of work. It had to be food that would not spoil quickly. Rosalba Marín, daughter and granddaughter of muleteers, explains how to prepare the corn, their staple food:

> We prepared *estacas* for them, which were made first by cooking blanched corn, to make it last. After that, the corn would be milled, stirred with pork rinds, and made into patties that would be wrapped in plantain leaves and cooked in boiling water. That would be their meal because *arepas* would spoil. . . .
>
> We also prepared what's called a "muleteer cake," also made with corn. Others would call it a "tile cake," because it would curve like a brick roof tile. . . . That cake could last them a month or more without spoiling.

Aside from these foods, they took with them fatback, beans, brown sugar lumps, chocolate, arepas, and coffee to prepare on the road.

While the bleeder packed provisions on the horse, the muleteers gathered their cots, along with a daily ration of food, a blanket, and a fresh change of clothes, everything well-wrapped and tied with rope onto the horse.

Now to load the mules! They would take coffee beans to the storage house in Islitas [a town on the Nare river between Ríonegro and Medellín], both for export and to supply the towns along the way. The bleeder watches and learns from a veteran muleteer: "You blindfold the animal with a poncho while you load them on the right side. You secure the *enjalma* [the saddle pad] with the *retranca* [crupper] on the back and the *pretal* [a breast handle] on the front, to stop the saddle from sliding. Then you attach the *lía* [a thin leather rope] on the first sack, which you also use as a noseband. The first sack is hoisted with the *lía*, and then tied together to a second sack held by the bleeder. Then two sacks are tied over these to the saddle cinch with the *sobrecarga*, which is a longer rope made out of grass hemp. At the end of the cinch is the *garabato*, which is a fine wooden hook, generally from guava trees or *arrayán*. The *garabato* secures the *sobrecarga*, which is tied tightly with a slipknot called *nudo de encomienda*."

The bleeder asks the muleteer to show him how to make the knot again, for he knows full well that a muleteer that doesn't know how to tie a knot is not a true muleteer, and will never be one. . . .

It was six o'clock in the morning, and the beginning of a journey that could take days, maybe even months, since the goal was to make a "round trip," or rather, to travel and return with loads until the mules reached their limit and could not go on. The horse and the bleeder went first, followed by a pack of well-loaded mules and the muleteers on foot, ready for anything.

"On the road we'd meet up with other drivers, going from here to there and from over there to here, and that could immediately be a problem. If the kid on the horse saw a pack of mules approaching from far off, he would sound a horn—*ta, ta, ta!*—warning those who were coming and also those behind him so that the drivers would be alert because the paths were narrow. If one mule passed too close to another, a sack could hit another and a scuffle might start, there would be fights on the roads because of that. . . ."

The drivers would curse at the load and tighten it every time it got loose, always being careful so that the mules would not slip or fall into an abyss, and seeing that nothing got lost or damaged. The quality of their labor would determine if they would get more work in the future. They almost always drove large packs, *muladas* which they did not own, and it was there where they learned the trade, perfecting their skills until they were able to earn enough money to buy their own mules and become independent. They went from being a bleeder to a muleteer and then to a *caporal*.

The journey continues. The sun begins to set: the mules and the muleteers need to eat and rest. People at the inn know they are arriving because of the noise and the yelling. Juanita Cano smiles when she hears curse words in the distance. . . . mules do not move forward if you are not ready to badmouth them.

The overseer had chosen the inn, not so much for the delicious dishes Juanita Cano prepared, but because of the good pastures available for the mules. That was what was important: that the mules eat until they were full and thus get more out of them the rest of the way. It was good to go where the men could be comfortable, but often night would find them far from an inn. Then they would look for pastures and set up a tent. ". . . We would hang the tarp from a mango tree on the side of the road, and make a damn good sleeping place where we slept and cooked . . ."

Once at the inn, they unloaded the mules, and took them to graze, while they would eat and drink a bit over good conversation. It was a place to meet up with muleteers from other towns, a nocturnal spot for *tertulia*, or casual talk and the sharing of anecdotes. The oral tradition of the road was re-created on those nights of rest and leisure, where friends and enemies were made. ". . . We were all very good friends, we all knew each other, people from the mountain and the valley, muleteers, we'd get together and then go out with our cargo, travelling everywhere. Often we would go off and drink, and plenty of it—it took a lot to get us drunk. And then, all of a sudden, we would fight, even to the point of drawing blood, all because of some small drunken stupidity, and then the next morning, man, we would realize that the night before had been just a dumb thing, and we would say 'Oh, how stupid we are! No way! Come on, men, let's help each other work, let's go, whatever happened doesn't matter' . . ."

The bleeder could not stand how his feet hurt. He took out the lard candle that he carried in his *carriel*, melted some wax, and rubbed it on his feet along with some lemon juice. What a relief! He'd learned that this was the best way to take care of his feet so that the skin would not peel, especially during the rainy season.

It was a hard job, but fortunately the hardships were well known. The oldest muleteers carried a four-hundred-year-old tradition of traversing the roads of Antioquia in their blood. Before, there were other routes. Now, at the end of the nineteenth century and at the beginning of the twentieth, almost everyone headed south or southwest, because that was where "the money was," given the development of coffee production.

Translated by Ana María Gómez López

Campesino Life in the Boyacá Highlands

Orlando Fals Borda

The world of the hacienda, as glimpsed in the rulebook of the coffee-producing en-
terprise of "El Chocho" or in Phanor Eder's turn-of-the-century photographs of the
Manuelita sugar estate, developed in tension with the life of the rural towns that
border Colombia's large landholdings. By the mid-twentieth century, students of
rural Colombia were increasingly aware of the challenges faced by peasant families
struggling to hold on to land: lack of access to credit; inheritance systems that tended
to break up families' plots; and inadequate legal protection for titles that often ex-
isted as a patchwork of de facto and de jure land claims. A key voice in Colombian
discussions of el problema agrario *was that of Orlando Fals Borda (1925–2008).*

His first publications were marked by a language of "progress" and "rural devel-
opment" that the later Fals found deeply suspicious—a reader will find hints of the
sensitivity to place and to local voices that marks the work he did in the 1970s and
1980s, when he became a pioneer of participatory action research. There are also
hints of his practicality. As early as 1955 he warned that peasant cooperatives were
unlikely to gain any foothold in the Andes. Local people's fierce independence would
make any such project untenable. Nor did he romanticize peasant life. Women, he
noted, were often beaten by husbands intent on having "a real upper hand" (em-
phasis in the original). And he collected as testimony the following copla (a popular
four-verse form of song derived from Spanish musical tradition):

> Niñita de la mantilla
> Que te vas a cautivar:
> Cómpráte la mantequilla,
> Que harto cuero te han de dar.

> You, shawl-wearing girl,
> Who are about to be captured in matrimony:
> Purchase butter for yourself
> For the whipping you are going to get.

Hernán Díaz, *Peregrina de Chiquinquirá*, 1960. The photographer's understated title, *Chiquinquirá Pilgrim*, alludes to the layering of religious and nationalist imagery in an image that focuses on the face of an unnamed woman. The Virgin of Chiquinquirá became Colombia's patron saint in 1919 and continues to be worshipped by many in the country's Andean region. In Eduardo Serrano, *Historia de la fotografía en Colombia 1950–2000* (Bogotá: Editorial Planeta Colombiana, 2006), 4. Used by permission of Rafael Moure.

There are two indispensable items for breakfast, the *changua* soup and *chocolate de harina*, which may be served with rolls. *Changua* is made by heating a pot of water, adding a little milk if available, cibol, salt, and *cilantro*. In order to make *chocolate de harina*, the housewife mills on her stone mortar some corn, broad beans, and peas; she also melts one *panela* (a loaf of brown sugar) in a pot on the stove, then mixes the milled grains with the panela, adding some spice (*clavo* and *canela*) and finally one or two pieces of unsweetened chocolate. This mixture is kneaded into balls and stored for future use. Boiling one of these balls in water every day furnishes the second and last dish for breakfast. Coffee is not drunk except "black" served in demitasses (and this almost only in Chocontá restaurants), but it takes the place of chocolate as a drink for ill persons. It should be noted also that butter is not used as food but mainly as a liniment to give massages and reduce inflammations.

The usual dinner consists of two different soups, called *cuchuco* and *ajiaco,* served one after the other—for a farmer, dinner without at least one dishful of soup is incomplete. Cuchuco is a mixture of milled corn, barley, and wheat boiled in water to form a thick soup, adding certain herbs (*paico, guascas,* cilantro) for spice. Ajiaco is made of finely sliced potatoes and a mixture of peas, *arracachas,* yucca, and broad beans.

Tubers are the main dish for the supper, eaten between four and five in the afternoon. Boiled (very seldom fried) potatoes, *ibias,* and *rubas* are served in large quantities. And when they are available, corn, peas, broad beans, and string beans are served in the same dish with the tubers. For dessert, peasants may have a cup of a molasses drink called *guarapo,* perhaps a guava candy (*bocadillo*), or a piece of panela. Sometimes, before going to bed, they drink a cup of hot panela water.

For special occasions, beef, mutton, or chicken are prepared. These feasts have an accompanying dish of garlic cut in small pieces and mixed with pepper; each bite of mutton or beef is dipped in this garlic sauce. Corn is also prepared differently on festive occasions; these preparations are *arepas, envueltos,* tamales, and a sort of hominy, called *mute,* especially served in the Holy Week.

Farmers use two kinds of water according to its dirt content, one for cooking and the other for washing and sundry services (the many springs are classified according to the water they furnish—clear or muddy). Many farmers never drink water, believing it will make them ill—when a farmer is thirsty, he gulps guarapo, beer, or chicha. Perhaps local knowledge of polluted water from ponds and springs is the reason for this.

Chicha, the famous Indian corn drink which took the place of water, has been outlawed. The people of Saucío openly made and consumed this drink until December 31, 1948, the last day of its legal sale. Since that memorable evening, when peasants drank themselves into stupor, the farmers of Saucío have taken eagerly to beer. No one, as far as could be investigated, was making chicha in 1950. . . .

The two hamlet shops serve as local "country clubs," where farmers find a room dedicated to the sale of beverages and food. This area, which is not very large, is a part of the house where the owner family lives. While interior apartments are partly independent, this social room is open either to a yard or directly to the highway. A big wooden counter separates the clients from the manager; shelves occupy the whole wall behind the counter at one side.

The two owner families indulge in a division of labor for the management of their respective stores. The male head is the supervisor, who transports beer and foodstuff from Chocontá and who sees that there are no fights in the store; the adult females of the house are placed behind the counter, and they serve the customers, keep track of accounts, and receive the cash. (There is a folk-saying which forbids having male bartenders: "Ventera, que no ventero, porque ventero es la ruina—onde's ventero el que vende, ni siquer'el Diablo arrima." That is, not even the Devil would be a customer if there were a male attendant in the store.) Besides beer and cigarettes, which are the main trade articles, the stores sell bread, *panela,* candy, candles, and sundry items.

The stores also furnish tables and benches for the clients. Most farmers, however, prefer to stand by the counter for hours, exchanging information, joking, and gossiping. Otherwise, they organize a match of *tejo* for which the store supplies the necessary metal discs, and sometimes the gunpowder bags. It is also the responsibility of the store to keep these courts in good shape, to even the clay at both ends, and to moisten it in order to achieve the proper consistency. These courts are adjacent to the beer establishments— this is important because drinking is a part of the game.

It is the custom of the peasants to arrive on Saturdays and Sundays at about two o'clock in the afternoon. The climax of activity is four hours later, when tejo players come back into the tiendas to settle their accounts. Then, slightly inebriated, they start new and endless rounds of beer drinking.

The formality demanded in these beer bouts is as strict as that for the presentation of credentials by an ambassador. It follows the general pattern found in many areas of the Western world. When a person walks into a store and is acknowledged, those already in it will offer him a bottle of beer. After the newcomer gulps his first bottle, if he is a gentleman he is expected to offer a round of beer to all those in his conversation group. If this group is composed of six persons, the other five then feel the same social obligation to reciprocate for the group. It is easy to calculate the number of bottles of beer a man may drink in one night simply by counting the number of men in his conversation group. If more newcomers join, this geometric progression of beer buying and drinking becomes staggering. Needless to say, the men invariably return to their homes drunk and without much money left. Women also drink, but they do not frequent the stores with the assiduousness displayed by the men. But drinking is not looked upon as a vice. It is the normal outlet of sociability; it is expected of all adults. As declared by a peasant: "No person can have friends if he does not drink." . . .

The nonacceptance of alcoholic drinks means, in general terms, one of two things—either the abstainer considers himself superior and is thus insulting his fellows (who think they know him better), or, perhaps worse, he may be suspected of saving his money for some purpose other than drinking. . . . In the first case, social isolation of the snob is the result. In the second case, the miser is pointedly reminded with a common phrase: "En asuntos de tomata no se pierde la plata" (When it comes to drinking, money is not wasted).

One Lowland Town Becomes a World: Gabriel García Márquez Returning to Aracataca

Gabriel García Márquez

One indelible image of Colombian small-town life is that provided by Gabriel García Márquez in One Hundred Years of Solitude. *In Macondo, a fictionalized representation of the author's hometown of Aracataca in the hot Caribbean lowlands, townspeople's lives are tied to place in ways that evoke immediately recognizable aspects of Colombian rural life. They understand their history by reference to a few specific families; the fertility of their livestock indexes the town's fortunes; and their houses are vulnerable to rain and ants.*

In a letter to Gonzalo González, a fellow journalist from the Caribbean coast, García Márquez describes a visit to Aracataca and his plan to write a "long seven-hundred page novel," which he planned to call "La Casa." Fifteen years later, this novel would be presented to the public as One Hundred Years of Solitude. *We include this letter, along with an early sketch for the novel: both were published in March 1952 by* El Espectador, *one of several newspapers at which García Márquez worked as a journalist prior to his career as a fiction writer.*

My dear Gonzalo,

. . . I've just returned from Aracataca. It is still a dusty village, full of silence and the dead. Disquieting, perhaps overwhelmingly so, with its old colonels perishing in their back patios under the last standing banana tree, and an impressive number of sixty-year-old virgins, covered in rust, sweating out the last vestiges of sex under the drowsy hour of two in the afternoon. On this occasion I ventured to go, but I do not think I will travel back alone, much less after *Leaf Storm* is published and the old colonels decide to pull out their guns to wage a personal civil war solely against me.

I was also in the department of Valledupar. There it's different. I remain entirely convinced that people there remain anchored in the age of ancient romances. There are some tremendous fights about this in the *paseos*, which are sung by everyone. There is no question that God has to be there, hiding inside one of the water jugs in La Paz or Manaure. I had thought to write a chronicle about this trip, but I have now decided to save this material for "The House," a long seven-hundred-page novel I hope to finish in the next two years.

Un abrazo, from,
Gabriel García Márquez

The House of the Buendías
(Notes for a Novel)

The house is cool; moist during the nights, even in the summer. It is in the north, at the end of the only street in the town, raised on a tall and solid cement ledge. No stairs lead up to the tall doorframe; a long sitting room, noticeably unfurnished and with two full-length windows above the street, scarcely distinguishes this house from the others in the town. No one recalls having seen the doors closed during the day. No one recalls having seen the four rocking chairs made of *bejuco* in a different location or position; they are set in a square, in the center of the room, having seemingly lost any ability to provide rest and serving now only as simple and useless decoration. Now there is a gramophone in the corner, next to the invalid girl. But before, during the first years of the century, the house was silent, desolate; perhaps the most silent and desolate in the town, with its immense sitting room occupied only by the four rocking chairs (these days, the water jug's stone filter is covered with moss) in the corner opposite the girl.

On each side of the door that leads to the only bedroom, there are two ancient portraits laced with a funeral ribbon. The air inside the sitting room is harshly cold, yet elemental and wholesome, like the bundle of wedding clothes that hangs from the lintel over the bedroom door, or the dry spray of aloe leaves that decorates the inside of the door to the street.

When Aureliano Buendía returned to the town, the civil war had ended. Perhaps nothing remained of the bleak pilgrimage for the new colonel. All he had left was his military title and a vague unawareness of his disaster. But he also held within him half the death of the last Buendía, and a full ration of hunger. He still had the nostalgia of domesticity and the desire for a calm home, at peace, with no war, with a tall wall to block the sun and a hammock in the patio between the two forked trees.

In the town where the house of his ancestors once stood, the colonel and his wife found only the burnt roots of the forking trees and the elevated earthen floor, now swept away by the wind, day after day. No one would have recognized the place where the house had been. "Everything was so clear, so clean," said the colonel, reminiscing. Yet the almond tree grew green next to the small wooden outhouse, like a Christ figure among the wreckage, in the ashen remains of the back yard. On one side, the tree was the same one that had provided shade to the patio of the old Buendías. Yet on the other, the side that faced the house, its branches extended in mourning, scorched, as if half the almond tree was in autumn and the other was in spring. The colonel remembered the destroyed house. He remembered it because of its clarity, its muddled music, created from the waste of all the other noises that overflowed from the inside. But he also remembered the bitter and piercing smell of the latrine next to the almond tree, its small enclosure filled with deep silences that spread into crevices covered with plants. Among the rubble, brushing away the earth as she swept, doña Soledad found a Saint Rafael plaster figure with a broken wing and the vase of a lamp. There they built the house with its front facing the sunset, in the opposite direction of the original built by the Buendías killed in the war.

The construction began when it stopped raining, with no planning, without a preconceived order. In the hollow where the first tree had stood, they fastened the plaster Saint Rafael without ceremony. Perhaps it did not cross the colonel's mind as he traced an outline on the earth, but beside the almond tree where the outhouse had been, the air kept the same refreshing thickness as it did when the back patio was there. By the time they dug the four holes and said, "This is where the house will be, with a large sitting room for the children to play," the best part of the house was already finished. It was as if the men who had taken measurements for the house had marked off the limits of the air exactly where the silence of the patio trailed off. For when they raised the four pillars, the enclosed space was already clean and moist, just as the house is now. The coolness of the tree and the deep and mysterious silence of the latrine remained within. The town, with its heat and noise, was shut out. And three months later, when the roof was built, when the adobe walls were finished and the doors were put in place, the inside of the house continued to seem—even to this day—as something of a patio.

Translated by Ana María Gómez López

The Bricklayers: 1968 on Film

Jorge Rufinelli

In the 1960s and '70s, Colombian cities were remade by migrants from the coun-tryside—most of whom were looking for any kind of wage work. The rural poor became visible to urban Colombians in a new way during these decades, and young artists began to frontally engage the question of how to represent the reality they saw around them. Uruguayan-born film critic Jorge Rufinelli provides a sketch of Marta Rodríguez, one of Colombia's most acclaimed documentary filmmakers. Rodríguez came of age as an artist during the 1960s and produced her first documentaries alongside Jorge Silva, whose personal biography shaped the work they did together. Rufinelli emphasizes the larger context of Latin American documentary film; being a filmmaker in Colombia in the 1960s and '70s meant engaging with a medium that was introducing a generation to revolutionary ideas, both artistic and political. Rufinelli anchors his discussion of Rodríguez's life and work with references to Ca-milo Torres, Colombia's best-known leftist priest and a figure associated with the radicalism of that era (see part II).

Marta Rodríguez and Jorge Silva met in the sixties, and in finding one an-other they formed a duo of great creative coherence. These were the years of "militant film," as practitioners called it, when documentary filmmakers who followed this line set out not only to register social reality but also to denounce it and push for change. The sixties and seventies were long de-cades, marked by major works which seemed to light the way for others to follow. These included Solanas and Getino's *The Hour of the Furnaces*, in the sixties, and *The Battle of Chile*, directed by Patricio Guzmán, by the end of the seventies. If these were the "cathedrals" of documentary filmmaking, the "churches" were built by Brazilians, Colombians, Salvadorans, Argen-tines. . . . It's not going too far to call them "churches" and to expand it to "combative churches" when it comes to Rodríguez and Silva. Their films ran parallel to the commitment of third-world priests, and specifically to the activism of Father Camilo Torres.[1] . . .

A still from the documentary *Los Chircales*, by Marta Rodríguez and Jorge Silva, 1972. Used by permission of Marta Rodríguez.

Silva's social origins were humble. . . . Marta Rodríguez remembers him and synthesizes his biography eloquently and objectively:

[I met Jorge in '65.] Jorge was a person who had already made films—he had made a film called "Days of Paper." Jorge is from a very poor background, proletarian. Jorge was the child of an indigenous woman who migrated from Huila to a port town on the Magdalena River, Girardot. His father was a guy who had kids all along the river, one of those guys that . . . Well, Jorge never had a father. And his mother was a servant, a domestic, as that word is used here, so derogatory . . . It was him and his sister, and Jorge has his name taken away because the lady of the house has a son named Jorge. His mother's boss and a male servant given him the name José. He was sort of a messenger boy, the kid who took care of the pigeons. Until one day the señora says, "Two kids eat a lot! I can't put up with them!" And they're sent to the Orphanage. He's educated at the Orphanage until he's an adolescent. It was a very hard time. He wrote a screenplay; he wanted to make a film about the Orphanage. About the cold, the hunger, the fact that they gave them beans with beetles in them, about the loneliness, about missing his mother. When he left he went to work as a bricklayer to help his mother. But because he hadn't continued his education he spent his time at the Luis Ángel Arango library, he was an insatiable reader. . . .

Rodríguez and Silva filmed seven documentaries together, and the excellence of the first was immediately recognized (*Los Chircales*, "The Brickmakers," 1968–1972, 42 minutes, Golden Dove Award, Leipzig Film Festival). It is still one of the most eloquent Colombian documentaries in its description of social and political reality. Since it was first shown in Mérida, Venezuela, in 1968, it has been a model of committed filmmaking and of documentary work understood as a tool for creating consciousness and influence toward change. Singularly, *Chircales* had begun as a social research project of a group of students led by Camilo Torres, who shortly afterward joined the guerrillas. . . .

The film begins with images of the Plaza de Bolívar [in front of the Presidential Palace in Bogotá]: soldiers patrolling the plaza, triumphalist electoral speeches, an "official" voice informing us that Colombia does not have social inequality, the arrival of Rockefeller to the city. During the elections, an old voter tells us that he calls himself a "Liberal" because his father had been a Liberal but concludes, skeptically, that "nothing has come of politics, nothing has come of the Presidents." The real subject of the film is this "nothing": the absolute, pathetic poverty of the campesino brickmakers. They have come to the outskirts of the city where they are as exploited as in the past. "From an agrarian *latifundio* to an urban *latifundio*," says a narrator in a voiceover, explaining the social structure that is imposed on their productive labor. A landowner rents his land out to a boss who controls production; the wage workers lack access to "the means of production and to the final product of their labor." In a word, they live off a minuscule wage that only allows for survival.

Rodríguez and Silva chose to record the life of Alfredo and María Castañedo's family. Without a doubt, the film's most unforgettable images are those of the children brick-carriers. From the time they learn to walk they are used as beasts of burden to help the family's labor. Far from any ideal childhood, with protection or toys, these children suffer as slaves of a social regime crueler than what could be imagined. *Chircales* records daily life, and that recording is the film's commentary. Only a few scenes were staged: the ending, when the family is dismissed from the land, the eldest daughter's First Communion . . . in this last scene the film seems to leave its realist frame, very effectively, because it shows the "humanization" of the children, in the humble dreams and hopes of an adolescent girl.

In contrast to the typical documentary device ("giving voice to the voiceless"), as a film *Chircales* is not concerned so much with recording the "testimony" of its protagonists as with recording its own powerful and convincing images. But there are some stories recorded also: María's visit to a doctor who advises her, without additional information or help, to stop "churning out into the world so many beggars" (she has already eleven children). Or at the end, when after many years of working for the boss who rents the land, they are kicked off the land and again become declassed, marginal migrants. The film closes with the desolate image of the family on the road to another no man's land, but it is an image that is offset by a realist phrase from Camilo Torres, "the struggle is a long one, let's get started."

Translated by Ann Farnsworth-Alvear

Note

1. Rufinelli includes this note with the clarification that it is drawn from an unpublished interview with Marta Rodríguez: "In the fifties I lived in Spain for four years, my family went to live there and I was there in the post-war years. I arrived in fifty-three, and I was studying Sociology. It wasn't Sociology, it was Papal Encyclicals, that's what one studied in Spain. I took off for Paris because I couldn't stand it anymore and I met the worker-priests. . . . We had a welcome service at the bus station because many Spanish workers would go to Belgium to work in the coal mines. Camilo was there. He would meet them in Leuven, where he was studying Sociology. That was how I met Camilo. Then, in fifty-eight he came back to Colombia, and I came back at the same time. . . ."

Switchblades in the City

Arturo Álape, Interview with Jesús

Located in the mountainous southwestern region of the city and divided into thirty-five neighborhoods, the sprawling Bogotá neighborhoods that make up Ciudad Bolívar hold approximately seven hundred thousand people, almost 10 percent of the city's population. It was initially populated in the 1950s by people fleeing from "La Violencia" in the rural districts of Cundinamarca, Tolima, and Boyacá. In the early years of the twenty-first century, Ciudad Bolívar has absorbed a new influx of tens of thousands of internally displaced people from all parts of Colombia. Like those from previous decades, and as described in the piece below, newcomers today settle in through squatting invasions or "pirate" urbanization—the main means through which the new urban poor can obtain land. Gradually, peripheral settlements are legalized through the provision of basic services and urban infrastructure. Like other neighborhoods that receive desplazados *in Bogotá, such as Usme, Soacha, Tunjuelito, Bosa, or Kennedy, or Aguablanca in Cali and the* comunas *of Medellín, Ciudad Bolívar remains poorer than the rest of the city. In 2005, census takers categorized 76 percent of its households as living in poverty, and 25 percent as being in extreme poverty.*

In his book Ciudad Bolívar: La hoguera de las ilusiones, *writer and journalist Arturo Álape (1938–2006) collected oral histories of several young adults from Ciudad Bolívar. Among them was Jesús, a sixteen-year-old teenager who dropped out of school and joined an urban gang. The difficult conditions and lack of opportunities described by Jesús were sketched by Victor Gaviria in a 1990 film,* Rodrigo D: No Future, *about disenfranchised youth in Medellín (the first Colombian film to be chosen for the Cannes Film Festival). Like Gaviria's protagonists, Jesús describes young people pushed toward urban gangs or drug dealing. Another option is to join an armed group—FARC presence was strong in the corridor running from Ciudad Bolívar to the town of Sumapaz until paramilitaries arrived in the late 1990s. Then, during the hard-line years of the Uribe administration and even before, young men in Ciudad Bolívar like Jesús ran the risk of becoming* falsos positivos, *or "false positives," the term used for dead bodies that military commanders claimed as enemy casualties but that in reality were young people from Ciudad Bolívar, Soacha, and*

other locations who had been rounded up and killed in marginal urban neighbor-
hoods and then dressed as guerrillas.

The "false positives" phenomenon is connected to what paramilitary killers in
Colombia termed limpieza social, *or "social cleansing." Youngsters in Ciudad*
Bolívar and similar neighborhoods found themselves labeled as undesirables—
human beings whose deaths were unlikely to be investigated, such as drug addicts,
homeless individuals, transvestite prostitutes. The killings have continued. In
March 2009, principals from forty-two different public schools in Ciudad Bolívar
met with Bogotá district officials to discuss the targeting of young male students
by unidentified armed groups. Rudimentary photocopied pamphlets listing specific
names and imposing a 10 P.M. curfew on all male students were circulated, warn-
ing students, "Los niños buenos se acuestan a las 10, los niños malos los acostamos
nosotros." A rough translation: "Good boys are in bed by ten, bad boys are the ones
we'll put to sleep."

Approximately twelve years ago we arrived in Ciudad Bolívar. No, I'm
lying—it's been almost thirteen years since the invasion of Juan Pablo II
started. There were only open pasture fields everywhere, and the barrio
began with just four houses. People moved here on the down-low, because
people then weren't interested in settling the area from the hillsides on
down. This place used to be a mountainside—the only ones living here
were pine trees. There were *ranchitos*, covered in *paroi* [construction tarps],
and the roofs would be made out of zinc, with tarps on top.

We were from Simití, Bolívar. It is a little town farther down the coast.
They killed my father, and because of that we had to come here as a matter of life and death. When I say they killed him, it means that they also
wanted to finish off all his sons, finish the family off at the root. He had been
a lieutenant working for customs in Sopó and rumors started to circulate
about things he had done, deals he had broken with some people—I'm not
sure. He was punished with the law of revenge, a vengeance that was only
finished at the moment of his death, when he stopped breathing. That was
when my mother brought us to Ciudad Bolívar, in order to save us.

We came with four of my siblings, and four stayed behind, two men and
two women. There are eight of us altogether, four men and four women.
Of the four that live in Ciudad Bolívar, my sister is seventeen, I am sixteen,
my little sister is eleven, and my brother is thirteen. We first lived in a barrio
called Marco Fidel Suárez, which at the time was just a little pasture. Later
on, my grandfather had the idea that we should squat, so we invaded here in
Juan Pablo, and we've remained on this land up to today.

I was three at the time, or rather, four when we began to build our ran-

Family celebrating a child's baptism, 1985. Photograph by Gilberto Bustos. *Bautizo, Bogotá*, 1985 (MdB 1754), Álbum Familiar / *Museo de Bogotá*. Courtesy of Museo de Bogotá.

cho.[1] While I was growing up I spent my time helping my grandparents, even though you can't really do much when you're so little. There were no official plots when we built the house—you would look for a flat surface where the rancho could more or less stay up, building it where it would not tumble down. The house would grow. All of Juan Pablo II barrio was the result of invasion, as well as a large part of Compartir. When I was little I liked the barrio very much because we were in the company of friends and no one knew what it meant to kill a young man. Everyone was clean, and you could walk the barrio at ease.

. . . My house has been a *ranchito* for as long as I can remember, but it has always been a well-kept rancho. We lined the walls with paper, and my sisters liked having posters, decorations, and stuffed animals. They have always liked keeping the rancho clean. There were also my mother's porcelains: tigers, lions, elephants, and princess figures. We may have been poor, but the house was always warm. We always tried to keep everything clean so that there be no filth anywhere; as my mother would say, one has the right to be poor but not a slob. Cleanliness gives warmth to a small home. There was one room for everyone, and only two beds. My older sister and my brother slept in one, and I slept with my mother and my brother. We had chairs, a stove, a pressure cooker, everything. We cooked on a coal-burning stove, at a time when everyone used those large stoves. We had to bring water, and would go up to the tank many times. When there was no water tank, we kept hoses along the floor, connected to other black hoses. In other words, there would be several small hoses where one would make holes and cover them with large stones wrapped in plastic. Each time we needed water, we would remove a stone and gather some. No one would be left without water, as there were several of these hoses.

Electric light, back then? No way. Why would you need light when you are surrounded by mountains! We carried alcohol-lit torches to see in the darkness. For example, my mother had a flag hanger, a small rod she would use as a torch on one end. Every time she needed a light she would use it, and she would clear everything from the places where she would drop the lit rags, so that nothing would catch on fire. . . .

My mom worked as a seamstress making pants. When we first arrived, she worked in the kitchen of a restaurant. Later, she found a better job near Salitre, and she was able to get a street stand—a better arrangement. And so, little by little, she became more stable, until we were able to build the house.

The barrio was slowly building up when some men came, who at the time claimed to be *doctores* [meaning simply "professionals"] that sold squat-ted land. According to them, some business partners had bought up most of these lands, and were selling each plot for fifty thousand pesos apiece. This was more or less 1987, and fifty thousand pesos at that time was like half a million pesos today—fifty thousand pesos was definitely some money. You could set up parties with fifteen thousand pesos. Now there are more people coming, and all these families are mingling together. The barrio became crowded overnight. Many campesinos came, as many people here have been exiled from the countryside. For example, my grandparents came from Santa Rosa de Simití. There are people here from Tunja. There are people from Santander, and *paisas*.[2] Soon, one began to see supermarkets, and after a year, there were all kinds of things for sale. There were small stores and shacks, and people who knew the tradition of making *guarapo* [fresh sugar-cane juice]. I used to say, "Mom, give me fifty cents for a *guarapo*," and then would run out to the plaza and buy *guarapo*.

There was no drug addiction back then. Drug addiction began here in 1989 or 1990, when more than one *pelao* [a slang term for a child or young person; literally, *pelado*, or "hairless"] fell into the habit in Patricia's house. On December 8, 1990, almost one hundred thousand pesos were spent on drugs. That was when more than one *pelao* learned about drugs, and it took root. For example, my cousin, *el Chocho*, became addicted. Even I was "stung," and look, I'm okay now, but the others still have a lost look in their

Street kids in Bogotá, 1978. Photograph by Viki Ospina. In Eduardo Serrano, *Historia de la fotografía en Colombia 1950–2000* (Bogotá: Editorial Planeta Colombiana, 2006), 12. Used by permission of the photographer.

eyes. We used to call Patricia *la Cucha* [slang for "old lady"] . . . at that time, we were eleven or twelve, and started to come together as a *parche*. We would meet up and find our friends, and say "What's up, what is there to do? We have no money." Then we would say, "Well, let's go look for money then." Slowly more people were settling in the barrio, and San Francisco was becoming better off. And as children, we were drawn to taking what didn't belong to us. Sometimes we would come and unload on *la Cucha* and say, "Look, we brought this. Find us a client and sell him this. Find us some money." She would sell the merchandise we brought to her. We would tell her, "We brought this, will you buy it from us?" and she would say, "Let me look for a client and I'll have the money for you." At that time we would bring mostly clothes and pressure cookers—one could even find blenders in San Francisco then. And because these were makeshift ranchos, we would easily break open the *paroi* tarp with a knife. We tore the walls and opened holes to squeeze through the house from behind. The house would be closed while everyone was hard at work. When they arrived at night, they would find their houses broken open and we'd even have the nerve to say, "Oh! Robbers came into your house!" . . .

That is how brick walls started appearing. Brick! Everyone caught construction fever. You used to hear, "These ranchos made of *paroi* sure do fall over easy!" Then larger houses started being built as we grew older, when we were young adults. . . .

We formed the *parche* [corner gang] based on ideas people brought from outside the barrio. We were very poor then, and everyone around us wore designer clothes and had *presencia* [a stylish appearance]. There were many people that had nice clothes: they weren't clothes from the United States, or anything like that, but already it was good-quality clothing. *Manes* [a common slang term, from "man" in English] would come around from Las Acacias, from Marandú, from Villa Gloria. And yes, when they arrived, they would rob you if you just stood there. And I was no fool either: if I saw they were going to rob me, I would say something like, "What do you want?" "Take off your watch." "You want it? Well, come and get it then." We didn't know anything about knives then: we fought only with our bare hands, throwing punches! I don't like to admit it, but now I can't avoid using the *patecabra* [switchblade]. But back then we only had fistfights. . . .

The *patecabra* is a type of hand knife—the *patecabra* is our guardian angel. We started carrying it all the time. When another man would come to harass you, you'd usually threaten to fight back with punches. But then they might say, "Are we going to fight with metal?" "All right, we will fight with metal." So long as you had a jacket or sweater to carry the blessed *patecabra* everywhere, you could do anything! You were ready to gamble your life, to have both peace of mind and your temper ready at the same time. That is a way to pump up your spirit, with a machete. . . .

Then we started going into supermarkets. Often we would not pay at supermarkets or stores. And our *parche* grew when two friends were able to find *hechizos* [makeshift or handmade guns; literally the term means "spell" or "enchantment"], which could only fire one shot. Supermarket owners didn't know we were spreading out and that we were stealing from them. They would come out yelling angrily, "Hey, son-of-a-bitch *chino*, where do you think you are going?" "What do you mean, son of a bitch? Go back inside, bastard *cucho* [old man]." Because if you left without paying, they would run after you like crazy. I have to say, as a kid, I was never afraid of anybody. Fear is something you lose easily, like your shadow. You have to get rid of fear the first time you feel danger, or else fear becomes a deadweight for the rest of your life, and you will always feel stalked, cornered, terrified. If someone larger than me came around and said, "Faggot *chino* [slang for "a kid"]," I would retort, "What do you want?" "Well, what do you want?" It was as if God himself were in control of me. We've always said that we don't die on the day another person wants to kill us, but on the day when God [*mi Dios*] decides he needs us back.

We went several times to the northern part [of Bogotá], to watch those rich kids in disgust. Going downtown was like leaving a small rural village; we would go to the Parque Nacional, there were wealthy people around there. We started to steal leather jackets, shoes. We always went with two revolvers and two or three machetes. It was always five of us. Sometimes I would go with my machete. Other times I had to carry the *hechiza*: one feels safe with the *hechiza*, since the shot freezes the other person in their tracks. There was no discussion—when you had to rob a man, that was it. You didn't protest and say, "No, you rob him," or "No, you do it." The oldest would say calmly, "You rob him and I will watch your back." Then you mugged them. If one's teeth started chattering or your legs started shaking, then the group would mock you: "He is a *chirrete* [slang for "lowlife"], he shits his pants." *Chirrete* means you get scared, that you show no bravery, that you are a shitty coward. . . .

Back then it was only theft. As we got older, we discovered *el vicio* [vices, a common term to describe drug consumption]. Often we had money and would go headfirst into the *olla* [slang for a place to buy drugs; literally, "the cooking pot"], looking for *vicio*. . . .

And that is how we came across *basuco*[3] and more than one boy was lost for good, going through life with a lost look in their eyes, as if walking in another's shoes or having another person's thoughts. You carry a stranger inside your own body, and when you laugh it is another person's laughter. The feeling of *basuco* is really quite frightening, as if you're being chased in terror by the stalker of your soul. . . .

You never see the inside of *ollas*, only their owners. You go to the doorway and ask for what you want to buy. For example, six *titinas*, which cost five hundred pesos. In other words, marijuana. You will never be able to go inside, only if you are very close to the *jíbara* [dealer]. Then I would say, "How are you, doña?" "How are you, *mijo*, what are you up to? Come in." Then I would be served and leave as if all was normal. Normal—a average house, with a family and everything, normal. The *jíbara* has a husband and children. But they pay a tax. In other words, they give the police a cut. . . .

Policemen are dirty, and the toughest are the Vistahermosa police. When they catch you, they take your money from you. They say it's to buy wax, mops, cleaning services, gasoline. "If you give me enough to fill the motorcycle tank I will let you go." "I have no money." "Well, then you will have to be here for twenty-four hours. Goodbye, and keep your head down." And they would send you to the dungeon immediately. They have it ready for you. Even if you do settle with them, you will always be referred to as "that idiot who always gives us gasoline money," and they won't stop

Bodies dumped on the out-
skirts of Bogotá, ca. 1995,
part of a wave of so-called
social cleansing, in which
death squads kill those
they consider social un-
desirables. Photograph by
Tim Ross. In Roy Gutman
and David Rieff, *Crimes of
War: What the Public Should
Know* (New York: W. W.
Norton and Co., 1999), 93.
Used by permission of
The Image Works.

bothering you. And then they will start demanding other things. There are
some police in the barrio that are good, but many are purely wicked, pure
evil, human shit. I have a strong loathing for the police.

Violence began to happen because we started stealing too often from supermarkets. . . . So the owners came together and started paying someone,
perhaps another boy from the barrio or an elderly person, to take pictures
of your face and your home, as well as your corpse when you bid the world
farewell. Sometimes it was the *cuchos'* own daughters that brought information to their fathers—even your friends would squeal on you. . . .

Limpieza [social cleansing] happens at night: death disguises itself by
night, with people from the F-2 [police intelligence] and people from the
barrio. They know where you walk, where you hang out, and they will

Imported styles and urban cool in 1970s Cali. This photograph is a part of a series by photographer Fernell Franco, entitled *Galladas*, a colloquial expression that can refer to everything from a group of young friends to street gang alliances. More common terms in cities across Colombia today are *parceros* and *parche*. In María Iovino, *Fernell Franco* (Medellín: EAFIT, 2007). Courtesy of Fundación Fernell Franco.

search for you in those places until they find you, even in your sleep. They will kill whomever they find, even if you have nothing to do with it. Those who carry out *limpiezas* are usually masked and wear hoods so that no one can identify them. People look, but they are not able to recognize them. Only people from this barrio carry out the *limpiezas*. It's as if to say that "problems in the barrio stay in the barrio." It doesn't happen between barrios, but only with the young people from a particular barrio. And we are the ones that have to suffer death or wait for it. . . .

Death will always be something normal for me, because everyone was born to die. I don't deny that I would like to see my daughter be my age, turn sixteen. I would like to live to see that. That is if God allows me to. But if I die, it's not because another *man* comes and tells me "I'm going to kill you." I won't die when another man wants me to die. Death does not happen because of words alone. That has always been my goal: not to die when another person says, "I am going to kill you." "You can try to kill me if you want, but I will only die when God calls me back." . . .

I have many dreams for the future: I would like to do well one day, have good clothes, take care of my little girl and my *sardina* [slang for young woman, in this case referring to his girlfriend] in a good home, where all our needs are met. If my God provides, I would like to have another child, but with the same woman. I don't want to leave children all over the place. Now that I have my little girl nothing else matters, what I want is to get her ahead. That is the version of my life I have playing before my eyes.

Translated by Ana María Gómez López

Notes

1. In Colombian urban contexts, the term *rancho* generally refers to a precarious make-shift home built of a combination of found and purchased materials, including cardboard, wood, metal rods, and zinc sheets. Over time, as the owner acquires more materials, *ranchos* will be reinforced with brick and concrete, and additional floors may be added. However, the word *rancho* may also refer to rural homes, often with adobe walls and a thatched roof.
2. *Paisas* refers to people from Antioquia, as well as from Risaralda, Caldas, and Quindío, the central coffee-growing region of Colombia.
3. *Basuco*, a word that is derived from the Spanish *basura* or "trash," is low-grade, residual paste from intermediate stages of cocaine refining. It often contains high levels of toxic industrial chemicals, including gasoline, kerosene, and soda ash.

Desplazado: "Now I Am Here as an Outcast"

Anonymous

Estimates of how many individuals are displaced within Colombia's borders vary significantly according to source, but in 2015 something close to 5.3 million people were forced to flee their homes, putting the country at the top of a world list of countries suffering internal displacement. As high as such estimates are, they likely undercount the problem, as they fail to record multiple displacements, in which individuals or families (a majority of the displaced are women and children) are pushed by fear first from rural areas to towns and subsequently from towns to cities. Also, recent figures only consider at most those displaced during the last two decades, not accounting for the approximately 2 million Colombians who fled their homes between 1946 and 1966 during La Violencia.

As a displaced person I had to leave behind all of my things. I owned six hectares with cacao, animals, horses, pigs, chickens, and I lost everything. I used to go down to the wholesaler to sell my cacao. My son and I made a living that way. I sold my corn and timber other places.

Another son of mine had his cows taken away because supposedly they were stolen cattle. I had some cattle years before, which I purchased with credit from the Caja Agraria [Colombia's Farm Credit Bank]. It was a good time for the National Federation of Cacao Growers. But when business went down I had to sell the cattle to pay my debts to the bank.

Later, another son dropped out of school and told me that he wanted to work in the farm. We became partners, but he had to leave because of the fighting. Right now he's outside the department. I found out that he was sick, but I haven't had the resources to go visit him.

There's nothing here right now. In order to go out to the fields to harvest you need to ask the paramilitaries or the army for permission. When I came back four months ago they had taken all the animals, along with my son's 9 steers and about 70 head of cattle belonging to my wife—this was after the bombing in February [1997], and I had left behind 27 pigs, as well as 3 horses belonging to me and 3 belonging to my son.

Jesús Abad Colorado, *On the Path from La Unión to San José de Apartadó*. This photograph of a displaced family leaving their home was taken in Antioquia, northwestern Colombia, one of the country's most violent regions during the 1990s. In Carlos Alberto Giraldo, Jesús Abad Colorado, and Diego Pérez, *Relatos e imágenes: El desplazamiento en Colombia* (Bogotá: CINEP, 1997), 10. Courtesy of the photographer.

Also, I lost several hectares of fruit trees, and 23 sacks of corn that I had harvested were gone.

I had gone down to the municipality of Turbo to sell some cacao when, after my return, I found out about the bombing near Salaquí. My family was there. As soon as I could—eight days after the bombings happened—I went back to see what had been left of my family. My happiness was to find all of them safe.

The situation became more serious when the armed men sent word that everybody had to get out. On the one hand, the guerrillas picked many people up and took them away. On the other, paramilitaries sentenced all the campesinos who had collaborated [with the guerrillas] to death. Because of all the fear, people arrived to Riosucio as displaced.

I was able to go back to my land for a few days to harvest my crops. However, when the community of Salaquisito began to be displaced toward the town, I thought that staying alone would have meant I was writing my death sentence, and I also left.

My farm borders to the north with that of Mr. Arnoldo Gómez, a good man who was killed by the guerrillas. He owned between seventy and eighty-five hectares. My sons and I owned four houses, in addition to one being built by the young man who was disappeared before the bombings.

My family was very happy when I returned after the bombardments. They told me the story of what had happened: the guerrillas killed Mr. Arnoldo, took over his farm, and expropriated his belongings. Because the guerrillas were present and dominated the areas surrounding the river, the military decided to attack them with an air strike. Some of those displaced in Pavarandó and Turbo say that they were displaced because of abuses from the military, but that is not entirely true. The army did not come in committing abuses toward everyone. They came down hard on those who were guerrilla members or had connections to those people.

The truth is that the guerrillas were the ones who made the decision to pick many people up from several *veredas* [rural districts] near the Salaquí and Truandó Rivers, to get them to leave the department of Chocó. For instance, on the day we were displaced, there was a guerrilla commission that came to take over the community of Salaquisito, but fortunately we had already left for Riosucio.

For some time there were many people living in the encampment built by the guerrillas in don Arnoldo's farm: up to 600 and 700 guerrillas. Many had come here to take refuge, between January and February of 1996, after having been pursued by the army and the paramilitaries in other parts of Urabá. The guerrillas never abandoned that farm. They took turns holding camp there for several days. That is why in the towns around the Salaquí River the only law that was worth anything was theirs. In fact, when people had problems, they would go to the encampment so that the guerrillas would tell them what had to be done.

Almost all of us 285 inhabitants of Salaquisito are now displaced. I say this exact figure because I was the legal representative before the government for the community during the process of collective land titling under Law 70 of 1993, which protects the culture and territory of the Afro-Colombian population. Almost all of our people are in Riosucio, displaced, and have had to bear very strong hardships. There is no one left in the plots of land or the hamlets.

As campesinos, we have carried out agriculture to subsist and provide subsistence to others that have never struck the ground themselves—guerrillas, paramilitaries, and even many landowners. We produce for ourselves, for the municipality, for the department, and for the country. Products from here—particularly plantain—are sent to Cartagena and Barranquilla through the Atrato River and then through the Gulf of Urabá. That is, we work for our subsistence and that of many others who will never know what it's like to cultivate the land amid this violence and defenselessness. That will never know that we have had everything taken from us here without anyone ever finding out, or ever saying or doing something on our behalf.

We are currently in Riosucio as outcasts. We campesinos have a very strong sense of morality and pride: we do not like to steal or beg from anyone. That dignity means working for our food and sharing with other neighbors, providing them with a meal. If there is nothing to eat, we kill a chicken to give lunch to a friend. Rice is harvested, as is plantain, yucca. Nothing is lacking or left over.

This tragedy is making us come apart, and with this our culture of solidarity is destroyed; we are losing it. We lost possessions and goods. It seems incredible that with everything we have in this country we are in a state of misery, waiting every fifteen days or every month for foodstuffs from the government. . . .

I have not been back to the countryside since January (1997). It is very sad not to have the right to go to the place where I always was, where I lived with others, where I shed the sweat of my existence. I lived in that farm since I was seventeen until I was fifty-four years old. I raised eight sons, I put them through school with what the land gave me. When I had a toothache, I would be taken care of at my farm. Now I am here, as an outcast, waiting for foodstuffs or for a meal, without anything to do, without being able to go to the farm. Aside from all this—of feeling hungry and abandoned—there is an overbearing anger created by the humiliation one feels as an honest campesino, as a good person. I cannot find a name for that kind of humiliation.

Translated by Ana María Gómez López

An Agrarian Counterreform

Luis Bernardo Flórez Enciso

A paper produced in 2005 by Colombia's then deputy comptroller general, Luis Bernardo Flórez Enciso, titled "Forfeiture of Illicitly Owned Property: A Path toward Agrarian Reform?," allows for an economist's understanding of the problem of inequality in rural landholding. Flórez Enciso focuses on what is new about agrarian relations in the twenty-first century. "The purchase or unlawful appropriation of land by drug traffickers and illegal armed groups," he emphasizes, has created "a bona-fide agrarian counterreform." In economic terms, this new inequality was part of a decades-long process of consolidation within the cocaine trade, during the years when drugs became an important component of the country's GDP and its exports. Throughout the years of Plan Colombia, which was discussed as a US-funded plan to curtail drug trafficking, the country continued to be the largest cocaine exporter in the world.

Throughout the country, the physical space dedicated to growing and processing coca, poppy, and marijuana multiplied between about 1980 and 2006, as did Colombian exporters' sophistication and integration into international networks. Although the narco-economy involved a fluidity of systems and diversity on the ground, an order began to emerge as paramilitary and guerrilleros established themselves in the integrated spaces of drug production and export. By 2000, the drug economy had a spatial structure the general Colombian population began to accept as part of the country's reality. Certain tasks were performed in remote rural areas, of course, but it was in Colombian cities that traffickers worked out the details of financing, decided on trade routes to consumer countries, and laundered their money. When traffickers had a direct presence in the countryside, it was often marked by ostentatious display and illicit dominion over huge swaths of land.

It is worth noting that criminals' ability to control land in Colombia stems in part from the lack of an effective land registry. A public record of land titles, known as a catastro or cadastre, is used by the fiscal arm of the state to collect property taxes—it makes the legal status of a given piece of land transparent, and it serves as a guarantee to title holders. The fragility of Colombia's land registry contributed to the violence of the 1950s (La Violencia) and to that of 1990–2010. Especially in *departments far from the capital, such as Caquetá, Vichada, or Putumayo, and in the broad stretch of the middle Magdalena Valley, which includes municipalities from five different departments, legal instruments such as cadastres have long been almost wholly fictions, as is implied in the 2005 report excerpted here.*

Thank you to all the high-ranking officials and former members of the state, representatives of the agricultural sector, delegates of international organizations, as well as eminent researchers and academics who are with us today. . . . My role in this opening session is to lay out several affirmations which I consider essential, as well as some questions, in the hopes of interpreting the concerns and expectations of the citizenry on this matter. Without further ado, allow me to get started.

First affirmation: in the last twenty years, the most aberrant land concentration in this country has taken place through the purchase or unlawful appropriation of land by drug traffickers and illegal armed groups.

According to a document created by the Comptroller's Delegate for Defense, Justice, and Security, the purchase of land by narco-traffickers is around a million hectares—almost 3 percent of the national territory and 5 percent of all potentially exploitable land. Other estimates hold figures of 3 million hectares, such as in Roberto Steiner and Alejandra Corchuelo's study, carried out in 1999. Analysts such as Ricardo Rocha, in his 2000 investigation, indicate that narco-traffickers own almost 4.4 million hectares valued at $2,500 million. . . .

Land appropriation by narco-traffickers represents an enormous agrarian counterreform. This is evident in two ways. On the one hand, according to INCORA[1] estimates, narco-traffickers have appropriated almost 50 percent of the best lands in the country, while almost 70 percent of all landowners, particularly peasants, hold only 5 percent of that area, as stated in a study of illicit drugs led by UNDP (United Nations Program on Development) and the National Directorate for Narcotics. . . .

Thus there is a double logic: the first is the concentration, accrual, and profit-making through illicit investment in land, particularly cattle-breeding farms; and second, the amassment of suitable and strategically located land for coca cultivation and processing.

The means of acquisition are diverse, but fall into two categories: lucrative purchase through authentic money laundering; and appropriation through the use of arms, almost always at a lower price, in conflict areas. . . .

I must note that available statistics, and land concentration studies in general, do not fully reflect reality, as they are based in a nominal distribution of land property. An accurate calculation is more difficult, given that official land property records often present frontmen rather than real owners. Needless to say, narco-traffickers also use different and ingenious methods to not present themselves as legitimate owners of these lands. These circumstances, among others, have hampered seizure of land and property by the National Directorate for Narcotics.

Regardless, as a result of the aforementioned trend, our legal economy suffers from immense money laundering, as well as contraband, exchange rate revaluation, and job loss in the agricultural sector, with all of its repercussions on rural society, agricultural products, and export. And these problems will not be resolved, as believed in certain circles, by a free trade agreement with the United States. What should be a priority is an internal development agenda that promotes sustainable recovery for agriculture and redistribution of rural property, as well as revenue generation and productive employment for the peasantry.

Second affirmation: land concentrated with illicit resources or through violent means has contributed to a social and agricultural crisis in the countryside, and from a political viewpoint, worsened the manorial character of large-scale rural property tenure.

Aside from being one of the largest drug money laundering operations, perhaps more so than kidnapping and extortion, land concentration has had the following negative impacts on the rural sector, as well as Colombian economy and society as a whole, which I succinctly outline below:

> Wrong use of appropriated land, where often the most fertile and best located lands are made into large and unproductive haciendas, rather than used for agricultural activities. Thus, narco-trafficker properties do not contribute to food security, insofar as they are not efficient units of production, but rather illegal investments and amassment to legitimize their social and political insertion.
>
> Rural job creation has been restricted, leading to negative impacts in rural poverty levels and quality of life. Professor Alejandro Gaviria warned a few weeks ago that rural poverty increased from 66 percent to 69 percent between 2003 and 2004, while homelessness increased even more dramatically, from 24.9 percent to 28.3 percent. According to Gaviria, this problem is consistent with a worsening of unemployment in the countryside and an increase in the informal economy.
>
> Land prices have skyrocketed in several regions of the country, stimulating a speculative market that has negative impacts on production.

Land concentration by narco-traffickers, paramilitaries, and other illegal groups now define the guidelines for rural investment. This fact is further aggravated by land use patterns, such as extensive cattle breeding, in detriment to agriculture and environmental conservation. There is no doubt that this forceful transfer of land also brings violence and deteriorates agricultural production.

The political effect of having narco-traffickers seeming to engage in legal activity through rural land ownership often goes unmentioned despite its great importance. They attempt to appear as traditional landowners and inherit, if you allow me the expression, power inherent in manorial land tenure. The importance of this concept was highlighted a half-century ago by professor Antonio García, whom we should honor by bearing in mind the lessons he imparted.

From this perspective, narco-traffickers and other illicit armed groups, aside from being "war lords," become the holders of real power, both through legal and illegal means, particularly the latter, with the help of threats and private security applied through violent means. . . .

This is the most serious consequence of narco-trafficker land concentration in the country, as it attacks the heart of a democratic system. Unabated, this accelerated ownership increase will draw a political map of the country oriented toward authoritarian structures at the local and regional level, which sooner or later will reflect itself at the national level.

Third affirmation: the Colombian State has been completely inefficient in taking advantage of forfeiting rural assets acquired illegally, both to improve land distribution and to stimulate production.

The legal act of asset forfeiture, approved in the middle of the last decade as part of an antinarcotics policy, created great expectation. Nonetheless, the application of legislation regarding legal decisions, administration, and the final destination of seized properties has been complex and precarious.

Thus, INCODER [the government agency charged with rural development] has only received 5,300 hectares for agrarian reform. This derisory figure pales in comparison to the peasant population that lacks access to land and the enormous amount of land in the hands of narco-traffickers.

The current government's Development Plan sets the four-year objective of delivering 150 thousand hectares of land, of which 110 thousand come from asset forfeiture. However, in 2003 and 2004, only 5 thousand hectares were allocated from these seizures, less than 5 percent of the goal. It seems that these set objectives are far from being met. . . .

Fourth affirmation: agrarian reform continues to be a key element for national development. It is not, as some have suggested, an outdated subject.

It is obvious that there will be those for and against this affirmation at this forum. Allow me to provide some criteria for this discussion.

The country's growth cannot depend on external markets, as presented by passionate defenders of economic liberalization. It is necessary to expand the internal market, of which the rural sector is an essential component.

The Colombian food supply—that is, food security—cannot be conditioned to availability of external resources. Thus, it is necessary to strengthen internal production, obviously under adequate productivity conditions.

Given a basic principle of justice, embedded in the notion of rule of law, it is not possible to accept the current levels of poverty and not possible to leave unresolved the forced migration of thousands of peasants.

Many peasants are not granted credit due to the precariousness of their land titles or the size of their property, which closes their possibilities of production and income.

Natural resource exploitation and the destruction of fragile tropical ecosystems, particularly in the Andean region bordering on agricultural lands, is the main cause of periodic natural disasters in the country, both during the dry and rainy seasons. I hope that this is not in addition to the devastation of our natural parks as a result of massive fumigation.

Landowning power, both old and new, contributes little to our country's progress and peace.

In examining these problems and policies set out to improve them, I am obviously not referring to a simple redistribution of land, but to the need for implementing a new generation of innovative agricultural reforms. . . .

This is why I would like to end with an appeal so that the state and its institutions make the greatest attempt to accelerate asset forfeiture processes and dismantle, without weakness or waiver, the enormous territorial, political, and economic structure that illegally benefit these groups.

Translated by Ana María Gómez López

Note

1. INCORA is the Instituto Colombiano de la Reforma Agraria, or the Colombian Institute of Agrarian Reform. It dates from 1961 and was the product of political efforts that centered on inequality in the Colombian countryside. Political figures associated with INCORA in its early years included the radical priest Camilo Torres (see part II) and Carlos Lleras Restrepo (president in 1966–70, during the National Front years). Conflicts between Torres and Lleras are one indicator of the tension that characterized INCORA, which never adopted an effective policy of redistributing large amounts of land.

IV

Lived Inequalities

Racial inequality and a steep hierarchy of economic power have structured Colombian society for centuries. Despite a deep-seated tradition of radical republicanism, which in the nineteenth century meant that a language of "citizenship" and "equality before the law" pervaded political life, and despite the explicitly antiracist language of the 1991 Constitution, the ingrained rhythms of a colonial world divided between those who gave orders and those subjected to forced labor have been carried across long generations. Most writers take the Conquest as their starting point for understanding power relationships in Colombia: indigenous communities were decimated by war and by the imposition of a brutal system of tribute payments. Whole communities died in the emerald mines. Indigenous women had to navigate a world where community protections against rape and abuse suddenly disappeared and Spanish men held extraordinary power over their and their children's lives. Yet inequality in the Andes predated the Conquest. Archaeologists and historians have demonstrated that tribute systems and power hierarchies existed among indigenous people. During the early colonial period there was an indigenous nobility with a deep claim on power, as is clear in the life of don Diego de Torres, the cacique de Turmequé, who denounced Spanish abuses from the position of a nobleman to whom tribute was owed. In his famous petition to the king, excerpted here, he attempted to use the Spanish legal system against local Spaniards.

Throughout the seventeenth and eighteenth centuries, in fact, appealing to royal authority and taking grievances to court was common. North Americans are often surprised to learn that enslaved Africans, indigenous people, and others in disputes with those wealthier than they, used courts to their advantage across Spanish America and Brazil. Colombia was no exception, meaning that legal strategies for fighting inequality precede the 1991 Constitution by centuries.

One key to understanding hierarchies of race and class in Colombia is grasping their flexibility. In the distant past as well as in the present, the idea that improving one's station in life involves acquiescing to racial norms meant that "whitening" one's family was taken to be a good thing. Thus racism could permeate even intimate relationships. Nevertheless, oral history and popular music testify to a long tradition of "pushing back" against the white world and celebrating rebellious attitudes. Antiracism, too, has a long history in Colombia.

This part balances evidence of oppressive practices against documents that testify to the creativity of those on the lower rungs of the ladder measuring status and power. Some texts point to well-known figures, such as María Cano or Manuel Quintín Lame. Other texts speak to more diffuse cultural patterns, from the relationships between propertied women and domestic servants to the stylized practices by which technologies of beauty can reshape the life of a poor girl or a person marginalized for living a gay identity.

Rules Are Issued for Different Populations: Indians, Blacks, Non-Christians

Anonymous: Libro de acuerdos de la Audiencia
Real del Nuevo Reino de Granada

Spanish colonialism depended on explicit, juridical hierarchies that separated people into corporate groups, including Moors, Jews, conversos *(Jews forcibly converted to Catholicism), blacks, Indians, persons of mixed caste, and* vecinos.[1] *People were subject to the authority of the Crown in ways mediated by such classifications. Thus the colonial world based "citizenship" not on a body of laws but on a variable set of legal structures that applied or did not apply to different persons. Some aspects of this legal structure were imported from Castile; others reflected the slow accretion of ad hoc decisions made and unmade in the colonies. To suggest the way local officials' efforts repeatedly sought to impose their authority within what became Colombia, we excerpt three pronouncements. These were aimed, respectively, at Indians, blacks, and a catch-all category of Moors, Jews, and heretics. Recorded in a sixteenth-century "book of decisions"* (Libro de acuerdos de la Audiencia Real del Nuevo Reino de Granada) *that served as a record of governance in Bogotá, they remind us also of the textual specificity of the archives historians depend on, as well as interpretations of criminal incidents by local figures such as Juan Rodríguez Freyle, author of* El Carnero *(part V). The* Libro de acuerdos *begins on a prosaic note, explaining that it records only those governing decisions issued after 1551, "because the book holding the agreements made until that point, held by Alonso Téllez, scribe and señor to this* audiencia, *was burned in a fire at his house."*

Often historians take these kind of decrees issued by local governing bodies as evidence of the way people's behavior on the ground outpaced efforts at control. Did Indians continue to evade Spanish "masters," drink alcohol, and organize dances? Did conversos *and the children of those persecuted by the Inquisition continue to arrive in Colombia? Did black people continue to go visiting after dark? Most likely.*

In the city of Santafé, on the sixteenth of September of fifteen hundred fifty-five, the *señores* and *oidores* [magistrates], being the meeting Chamber of the Real Audiencia, stated that among *ladino*[2] and Christian Indians, and other natives of this Kingdom, as well as those outside of it, there is some disorderliness, as in being vagabonds and rendering service to no one, having no masters, gambling and committing other crimes, like infiltrating and residing among the Indians of non-Christian *repartimientos*,[3] spreading bad habits, games, and other vices which are of disservice to God Our Lord and His Majesty. In order to resolve this, the Judges said that the following order is effective now and shall remain regarding said male and female *ladino* and Christian Indians:

First, all said male and female *ladino* Indians shall serve Spaniards and have masters to which they serve. Each male Indian shall receive each year four blankets and four undershirts *de la tierra* [produced in the colony] and female Indians shall receive six blankets of local quality. Officials shall take special care to record and have an inventory of the names of said Indians and who they serve, so that they do not leave or become absent, and if they do, that they be sent for and brought back. For their first offense, they shall be placed in the *rollo y picota*[4] of the cities of this Kingdom, each city in its jurisdiction. They will be administered one hundred lashes, their clothes will be confiscated for the *alguacil* [sheriff], and they will be returned to serve their masters. For their second offense, their hair will be shorn, they will be administered fifty lashes, and returned to serve their masters again, and have their clothes be confiscated for the *alguacil*. . . .

Item, it was ordered that said Indians shall not engage in games, or drunkenness, or *areitos* [songs and dances, often of indigenous origin], or other rites and vices. Any male or female *ladino* and Christian Indian that is caught in said acts shall be punished by losing the blanket with which they are found and shall be administered fifty lashes, have their hair shorn, and have their offence announced publicly in accordance with the provisions made for the cities of this Kingdom. This was ordered.

I was present,
Diego de Robles

In the city of Santafé, on the twenty-first of January of fifteen hundred fifty-six, the *señores* and *oidores* of the meeting Chamber of the Real Audiencia stated that among the ordinances recently established by his Majesty for the House of Trade of Seville and for other issues concerning navigation and trade with the Indies, there is one, ordinance one hundred and twenty-two, which reads as follows:

Item, we order and decree that no Moor or Jew newly converted to our faith, nor any of their children, is allowed or can come to our said Indies without our express permission. Likewise, we defend and order that no *reconciliado* [an Inquisition term used for specific categories of heretics], nor the children or grandchildren of those who have publicly worn a *sambenito* [penitent's robe], nor the children nor grandchildren of those burned at the stake, nor anyone condemned as a heretic for the crime of heretic depravity passed down from the male or female line of descent, is allowed or can come to our said Indies, under the penalty of losing all their possessions, which shall go toward the Treasury of our Royal Majesties. These people shall be at our mercy and will be forever exiled from our Indies, and in the event that he should not have any possessions, he shall receive one hundred public lashes. . . .

It was ordered and mandated that the *fiscal* [appointed prosecutor] of said Audiencia take special care in the execution of what was aforesaid.

I was present,
Lope de Rioja

In Santafé, on the fifteenth of November of the year fifteen hundred and fifty-eight, the *señores* and *oidores* of his Majesty's Real Audiencia, having gathered in the meeting chamber, stated that it had come to their attention that within the city limits there had been and were still being committed serious and atrocious crimes and robberies and thefts and injuries and deaths and ill treatment of natives. Given that these have been and continue to be committed stealthily and at night, it is impossible to fully determine or confirm who are the people who carry out and commit these, aside from presumptions against black slaves, both from this city as well as against others who have escaped or left. In order to act and prevent these damages as much as is possible, the Judges ordered the public announcement that no black slave from this city, nor from outside of it, be allowed to walk after dark in this city, nor in its poor districts, nor its surrounding vicinity, after a set time at night. If a black slave is found alone or in the company of other Blacks, and not in the company of his master, he shall be taken to the royal prison of this Court or of this city, if he were to be arrested by its *alcalde* or *alguacil*. In any of the aforementioned prisons, the slave shall be administered fifty lashes and shall pay one peso as punishment, half for the *alguacil* who captures him and the other half for the poor of the prison. Likewise, if any of the aforementioned *alguaciles* find at night, past said hour, any *ladino* Indian or anyone who appears to be suspicious, he shall be brought to said prison and pay one peso, divided as stated, if a valid reason for him to be walking through the city at this time is not found. The *alguaciles* of this Audiencia Real and the city are required to patrol the city by night, under penalty contained in the laws and ordinances on the matter. . . .

In Santafé, on this day and on the aforementioned month and year, the fifteenth of November of fifteen hundred fifty-eight, in the presence of myself, the scribe, and the witnesses signed herein, in the voice of Juan, mulatto, town crier, this decree was announced in the public square of this city in front of numerous people that were there.

Witnesses, Diego Juárez and Melchor
de Guadalupe, and many other people.
—*Diego Suárez, scribe to Your Majesty*

Translated by Ana María Gómez López

Notes

1. *Vecino* was a status usually extended to nonindigenous residents and those having a racial status close to that of whites; the term implied a set of political privileges.
2. *Ladino* in this context includes Spanish-speaking Indians residing in towns.
3. *Repartimientos* were rural administrative units, applied to forcibly resettled Indians.
4. *Rollo y picota* refers to a wooden or stone column that served as a place of execution or lesser punishment that stood as a symbol and threat of royal justice in colonial urban settlements.

The Marqués and Marquesa of San Jorge

Joaquín Gutiérrez

When artist Joaquín Gutiérrez painted viceroys or nobles, he was careful to render goldwork, decorative embroidery, velvets, and brocades accurately. By law, specific fabrics were reserved for the nobility. Including them in a portrait conveyed information about the social position of the person portrayed. Several of Gutiérrez's detailed canvases survive, and they provide a visual index of the way Bogotanos aspired to the aristocratic protocols of the court in Madrid. Pictured here are the first marquis of Bogotá, don Jorge Miguel Lozano, one of the wealthiest residents of 1770s Bogotá, and his wife, doña María Thadea Gonzáles, a woman who bore nine children, among them Jorge Tadeo Lozano, a scientist, journalist, and Independence-era figure who is now a fixture of the Colombian curriculum.

The painted-in captions below their portraits allow glimpses of the elite world in which the couple moved. His reads: "El Señor D[o]n Jorge Miguel Lozano de Peralta, y Varaes, Maldonado de Mendoza, y Olaya, I[lustrísimo] Marqués de San Jorge de Bogotá. VIII. Poseedor del Mayorasgo de este nombre; Ha servido los Empleos de Sargento Mayor Alferes R[ea]l y otros varios de Republica en esta Corte de S[an]ta Fé, su Patria." (The accent marks and spellings are not modernized.) It is a listing of his full name and lineage, with an added note that he is the eighth heir, through his mother, to one of the largest landed estates in all of New Granada (a sign of the wealth this involved is the fact that he held monopoly rights to supply meat to the capital city), and that he has held various royal appointments. Hers reads: "La Señora D[oñ]a Maria Thadea Gonzales Manrrique del Frago Bonis, natural del Puerto de S[an]ta Maria, I[lustrísim]a Marquesa de S[a]n Jorge de Bogota." It not only gives her last names (her father had been president of the Real Audiencia in Bogotá) but also specifies her birthplace in Spain (near Cádiz). She seems to have died only a few years after sitting for this portrait.

Their clothing and the captions explaining who they are work together with the furniture, rich curtains, and coats of arms to cement an exalted impression of the family's social position. The date of the paintings was likewise part of the work of representing status, given that Jorge Miguel received his title of nobility only after being nominated by the viceroy in 1771. He had his new coat of arms installed over the

Joaquín Gutiérrez, *Marqués de San Jorge*, 1775. Oil on canvas, 143 × 101 cm.
Used by permission of Museo Colonial, Bogotá.

LA SEÑORA D.ᴬ MARÍA THADEA GONZALES MANRRIQUE
DEL FRAGO BONÍS, NATURAL DEL PUERTO DE Sᵀᴬ MARÍA.
I.ᴬ MARQUESA DE Sᴺ JORGE DE BOGOTA.

Joaquín Gutiérrez, *Marquesa de San Jorge*, 1775. Oil on canvas, 145 × 106 cm.
Used by permission of Museo Colonial, Bogotá.

entrance to his mansion and hosted a lavish party to celebrate his new title; within a few years he was also sitting for this formal portrait. Unambiguously proud to be a part of the aristocracy, the new marquis nevertheless had a complicated relationship with the Spanish Crown and, specifically, with local representatives of the king. He refused to pay the taxes he owed upon elevation to the nobility, and by 1777 he had been formally barred from using the title of marquis. He wrote a letter to the king using a language of resentment that was becoming common among criollos *or* creoles *(Spaniards born in the New World): "What value do we in this part of the world gain from all the services and merits that we have rendered Your Majesty? What advantage do we derive from the blood our ancestors gloriously shed in the service of God, our Lord, and Your Majesty? . . . What benefits do we receive from the viceroys here and their retainers who insult, mock, humiliate, and oppress us?"*

In 1781 the Comunero revolt (see part III) shook the viceroyalty to its core. When those who had risen in revolt reached the outskirts of the capital city, after marching south from El Socorro, in what is today the department of Santander, they were cognizant of being outsiders. Facing an opportunity to negotiate with the authorities, Comunero captain Juan Francisco Berbeo asked to have allies present: members of the capital city elite who supported the movement, including the marquis. Indeed, Lozano was suspected of having authored a broadside that had been read aloud to rally the crowds in El Socorro. Reprisals against him after the suppression of the revolt included his exile to Cartagena, where Lozano died in 1793.

An Indian Nobleman Petitions His King

Diego de Torres

In 1584 don Diego de Torres y Moyachoque traveled to Spain and presented to the king to issue a memorial de agravios, a formal complaint of twenty-two offenses committed by Spaniards against the naturales of Turmequé. Don Diego was the well-educated son of a conquistador and an indigenous noblewoman, Catalina de Moyachoque, and the language of his memoriam makes it clear he was part of a community that had been subjugated and incorporated into colonial society. Juan Rodríguez Freile (see part V) offers a telling description of don Diego: "A Mestizo, rich, a gallant man, and as such having many friends and many people who obeyed him, from among the naturales, added to this was that he was a great friend of the visitador [an appointed official charged with inspection] Juan Bautista Monzón." The mixed-race don Diego was embroiled in a racist political context. His father had another son, born in Spain to a Spanish woman, who challenged don Diego's right to the title of cacique and to lands he had inherited. The half-brother's challenge was upheld by the Real Audiencia in Bogotá, and by 1577, when don Diego sailed from Santo Domingo to Spain, he did so after having evaded a capture order issued in Bogotá. Despite that order, at least some well-placed Spaniards on the ground in Nueva Granada preferred him gone. "It would be most suitable," they wrote to the king, "if he did not return to this kingdom because he is good with words and good on horseback and skilled with arms and more loved by the Indians than is suitable and as he is the son of one of the first conquistadores perhaps your Royal Majesty can extend him favor there."[1]

By the 1580s the multiple languages of the Muisca region were in decline. Within indigenous communities nobles and commoners—both increasingly mestizo—were using Spanish, as in the memoriam excerpted here. Yet the memoriam is strikingly rich. It points to aspects of indigenous people's experiences in the aftermath of the Conquest that are only now being studied by academics, such as the domestic labor indigenous women performed in encomendero homes (point 6), and the effective existence of a local indigenous nobility in New Granada. As a well-situated mestizo cacique, able to press claims, don Diego felt himself equal to Spaniards and fully integrated into the symbolic and economic systems of the Catholic monarch of Spain.

Throughout the text, we feel his sense of political belonging. He speaks from the apex of a new native community, able to enumerate the oppressive conditions faced by those for whom he speaks and able to use effective comparisons to support his points, as in point 9. Today this educated, well-traveled spokesperson would be described as cosmopolitan.

Account that don Diego de Torres, Cacique, provided to his Majesty on the grievances that the Indian population of the New Kingdom hold towards people to whom they are entrusted to by his Majesty, and the manner in which matters that would best be remedied are consummated and come to pass, and the little fruit provided by their conversion.

Sacred Catholic, Royal Majesty:

ON HOW INDIANS WHO BELONG TO YOUR MAJESTY ARE MORE ILL-TREATED THAN OTHERS WHO DO NOT.

Your Majesty also commands through a new law and royal ordinance that the Indians and Indian towns that were passed or are placed under your royal crown, be provided better treatment and protection than others which are not, so that they understand that in coming to your royal crown they will grow and be protected, which is advisable for both spiritual and worldly matters. I certify to Your Majesty that it is true that there are no Indian towns more persecuted, humiliated, disturbed, or more poor than those placed under your royal crown, particularly those towns in the province of Tunja of which I am Cacique. They used to only be bothered by the *encomendero* and his servants, where they would finally recognize one as superior. Yet with regards to those who come on behalf of your royal crown, they do not know whom they must please, as the *gobernador* [governor] gives them orders, the *contador* [auditor] does the same, the *tesorero* [treasurer] does no less, as does the *corregidor* [administrative official] of said province, so that each of them when facing a town belonging to Your Majesty says "it is my duty to give orders," whereas another might consider themselves more suited to do so.

It is in this manner that each wants to send their servant or farmhands to make of use them in Your Majesty's towns, as some are sent as administrators while others receive taxes, and each of them takes an excessive amount of pay as civil officers, or deputy officers, or thousands of other thieves who steal and destroy Your Majesty's towns. As these are servants or close to the aforesaid persons, the miserable Indians do not know whom to seek out to remedy the grievances that are caused by them, and can only plead to heaven and weep their misfortunes, for the injuries done to them include taking advantage of their women and daughters. They apply a terrible cruelty toward Your Majesty's towns, and in order to secure their wages and have themselves be well paid, when they arrive on these commissions, they claim a certain amount of the taxes they gather to obey Your Majesty, and they say to the miserable Indians: "Brothers, I have spent [the equal of] so many salaried days on account of you, and you must pay for these costs when you provide the taxes you owe to his Majesty in full; the cost of my waged days will increase if you fail to obey, and the miserable Indians, seeing that part of the taxes they had for Your Majesty have been taken by them as their wages, must account for more than what they owe, and as their debt doubles they cannot comply in the time they have been given, and the civil officer, having completed the number of days for his commission, writes to his masters that the Indians have not paid their taxes because they are very sly and idle, and requests wages to pay for additional days to gather these, and having been given the days they request, they claim more than double the amount of money the miserable Indians have for Your Majesty, and they fall into the bad habit that if they are given one hundred for their wages, they will take out two hundred and ask that their days be extended, or might even connive into staying with all they have taken, as they do not only serve as civil officers on behalf of those that have sent them, but also eat the chickens that the poor Indians raise in their farms, who must provide for them and for their servants and the twenty horses that they take to fatten while they are in said towns. . . . And thus the miserable Indians faced with these evil deeds and thefts cannot comply, and the Officials of your royal treasury ask that the caciques be arrested for rebellion because they do not want to pay tribute to Your Majesty, and with this they are removed from their environment, over seventy leagues round trip to the city of Santafé, where they are taken as prisoners and are forced to pay for their stay at the royal prison, where they may spend more than five or six months suffering extreme [deprivation] until it pains to see such cruelty and they are left free, as they fall ill and die from such humiliation. . . .

ON HOW INDIANS ARE NOT TREATED AS FREE PEOPLE
AS YOUR MAJESTY COMMANDS

Through new laws and royal ordinances for the Indies Your Majesty has ordered and commanded that Indians from these parts be treated as the free people that they are and not receive any injury upon their person, proper-ties, women, and children. The city of Tunja uses bondage and diabolic cru-elty that goes against what Your Majesty has ordered and commands, where each wife of an *encomendero* of Indians has in their home many women that have been taken from towns belonging to this *encomienda* to spin thread, weave, garden, and do other services and farmwork that needs to be done inside their homes, and these women are often the daughters of the Indian nobles, which is something that affects the Indians greatly, to see their daughters, nieces, and kin in bondage for such long-lasting and thankless service, where they spend all their lives under lock and key, that they do not see the sun or the moon, and are forced to endure such a severe and miserable life, and are only taken into account for the sake of their labor. It is ignored that these women need to receive holy baptism and be educated in Christian teachings, and the reason they are kept under such cruelty and bondage is that if they were provided these sacraments which are so important to their salvation, they would escape and lose their lands, and so they are always kept imprisoned as described before, and if any manages to leave this perpetual confinement, they do not dare go back to their towns to be protected by their parents and kin so that these will not bear cruel punishment . . .

ON HOW THE UPBRINGING OF CHILDREN OF SPANIARDS
BRINGS HARM TO THE INDIANS

Yet there is a greater persecution and cruelty forced on these miserable women than those described before, which is that no Spanish women that has and possesses Indians from the *encomienda* will care to raise the children to which they give birth, for when giving birth, they will have many wet nurses chosen from the town, taking them against their will from their husbands and parents, and for this they pressure caciques and [principal] Indians in order to take the number they demand for the pregnant señora to choose the cleanest and those with the best milk, and it never fails that from this selection there will be three or four nurses whose breasts are taken away from their Indian children.

Translated by Ana María Gómez López

Note

1. Ulíses Rojas, *El Cacique de Turmequé y su época* (Tunja: Imprenta Departamental, 1965), 26. Cited by Jorge Orlando Melo, "Presentación: El Memorial de Agravios de don Diego de Torres, cacique de Turmeque, 1584," http://www.jorgeorlandomelo.com/bajar/turmeque .pdf, accessed January 31, 2014.

A Captured Maroon Faces His Interrogators

Francisco Angola

In the provinces that would later constitute Colombia, Africans and their descendants founded dozens of palenques, black-led settlements beyond the white authorities' reach. The palenques' history of resistance remains politically resonant in Colombia—a marker of the ways enslaved people transformed and preserved African ways and a long-lived symbol of black resistance.

The following text describes the Palenque del Limón, a settlement of escaped Africans near what is now Montes de María, in the department of Bolívar, that since the 1590s had sustained a peaceful and interdependent coexistence alongside white landowners. In the early 1630s, however, the area erupted in a maroon war. Francisco Angola was one of nineteen maroons captured by the Spaniards and forced to provide information. His tight-lipped declaration—in contrast to that of his companions—suggests his loyalty to the old guard, and a reluctance to reveal anything about the military-spiritual leadership of his community. The Palenque del Limón's highest-ranking leaders, Queen Leonor and Captain Francisco Criollo, both escaped the military raid and do not reappear in the historical record. But other palenques nearby did become permanent. In 1713 the free black town of San Basilio was formally recognized when fighters from the palenques successfully negotiated a truce with Spanish authorities. Today, people from Palenque de San Basilio (often rewritten as Palenke) understand themselves as descendants of cimarrones, people who won their freedom by escape. They express pride in that past, especially through the heroic symbol of Benkos Biohó, the most famous leader of the communities that later coalesced to become known as Palenke, where there is now a statue in his honor.

Colombia's palenques have parallels across the Americas. Often, maroon communities seem to have enjoyed moments of peaceful coexistence in which barter with neighbors was a strategy for survival, as in the early years of Palenque del Limón. At other times, maroons appear in archival records because white colonists accuse them of banditry or of raiding plantations for women, as was the charge in the Limón case.

Statement of Francisco Angola

In the Manga Castle[1] in the port of Cartagena de las Indias, on the 18th day of January, 1634, Señor Licenciado don Francisco de Llano Velasco, lieutenant general of the said city, and auditor general in this case, called before him one of the black maroons who had taken up arms in the Palenque del Limon, of those whom they brought as prisoners yesterday from the *palenque*, who said his name was Francisco Angola, from whom an oath was taken as required by law. And having so sworn and promised to tell the truth, his statement was taken in the following manner:

Asked if this declarant has been in the *palenque* of the black maroons of Limon, and how long he has been there, and what his responsibilities have been, and if he is free or a slave, he said that this declarant came as a small boy from Angola in the load of slaves that Captain Antonio Cutiño brought to Cartagena. And while in this city, Juan Angola, this declarant's friend, told him that the whites had them fooled. And pointing to the sun, he told him that that sun came from Guinea. "There is the road. Let's go." And the abovesaid and this declarant escaped into the forest and were there for some time; he does not know how long, except that one moon passed. And later, by walking, they ended up in the Palenque del Limon, where, after three years the said Juan Angola died in the said *palenque*. And they buried him in a hole in the forest, and they gave him a cross [on his grave]. And this declarant has served in the said *palenque* until the whites came and captured him. And that this declarant worked clearing and hoeing the blacks' fields and harvesting corn. And that is what he answered.

Asked how old he is, this declarant said that he does not know how old he is, except that as he has stated he went to the *palenque* as a boy. And by his appearance he seemed to be more than sixty years old.

Asked how many black men and women there were in the said *palenque*— including Creoles of the Palenque (i.e., those born in the New World), as well as maroons and blacks captured from the ranches—when the whites arrived at the said *palenque*, he said that the following Creoles were there: Francisco, the *palenque* captain, commander Simon, Gonzalo, Pablo, Juan, Cristobal, Sebastian Caribe, Gaspar, young Juanico, Luis, Manuel, young Cristobal. And Creole black women: Gracia, Felipa, Marta, Damiana and Isabel, Maria, and Queen Leonor, all people of the *palenque*, and the whole gang of boys and girls. And regarding maroons that have escaped to the *palenque*, there were the following: Juan de la Mar, Lorenzo who belongs to Alonso Martin, another Lazaro who belongs to Alonso Martin, Tumba, Barriga, el Morisco, and other blacks whose names he does not remember.

And he does not know how many black men and women they have captured from the ranches. And that is what he answered to what they have asked him. . . .

Asked to state and declare what people, either white or black, dealt and communicated with the said *palenque*, and who bartered with them, he said that all that he knows is that the blacks from Limon cleared Francisco Martin's fields and the aforesaid gave them knives and machetes and axes and head scarves and shirts. And this is what he answered.

Asked if the said blacks from Limon bartered with those belonging to don Juan de Sotomayor and went to his ranch for this purpose, he said that he does not know.

Asked if this declarant knows whether the said black Creoles and maroons have burned any ranch and killed any people therein and who were those who did it, this declarant said that as an old man whose feet and legs are injured, he did not go out with the said blacks [on the raids], but he heard el Morisco and Juan de la Mar say in the said *palenque* that the whites were worthless, that they already knew their tricks. And after this, he heard them say that they had burned Diego Marquez's ranch and had killed people. This declarant does not know who it was who carried out the said damage. And this is what he answered.

Asked which people from the said *palenque* went to burn the town of Chambacú and kill the Indians there, he said that he knows nothing about what is asked of him because, as he has said, he has always been infirm. And this is what he answered.

And everything that he has said and declared he said to be true, as charged by the oath that he has taken, in which he affirmed and ratified himself, it having been read to him. And he did not sign because he said he did not know how.

[Signed]
Licenciado don Francisco de Llano Velasco
Before me, Miguel Fernandez de Ortega,
Scribe

Translated by Katherine Joy McKnight

Notes

Personal names and place-names have been reproduced as they appear in the original manuscript, without the accent marks a modern reader would expect in Spanish.

1. Later named the Fuerte de San Sebastián de Pastellillo.

Carrasquilla's Characters: La Negra Narcisa, el Amito Martín, and Doña Bárbara

Tomás Carrasquilla

An improbable amalgam of iconoclasm, irony, and nostalgia distinguishes the best-known novel of Antioquia's Tomás Carrasquilla (1858–1940), La marquesa de Yolombó. *Published in 1926, the novel is set in the late eighteenth century and describes the rustic prosperity produced by the gold-mining economy of Carrasquilla's home region. Doña Bárbara Caballero, the protagonist, is a study in contrasts. She is a royalist and slaveholder but is sympathetic to emancipation. She glories in proper womanly attire and yet manages gold-mining operations in person. She is thrilled by the glitter of noble title, although her true nobility rests in a kind of homespun forthrightness. In creating his characters, Carrasquilla drew on childhood memories that included a rich reservoir of stories told by black servants, a debt he acknowledged and understood as part of an African legacy indelible in Antioquia's mountain towns. This was explicit in his depiction of townspeople's religiosity: "Half the town was African and no matter how much it was baptized and thrust into Catholicism, each black preserved inside and out, via transmission or ancestral belief, a good part of the savagism of their elders. These blacks, intermixed with the Spaniards of the time, who were more superstitious and fanatical than genuinely Christian, more about miracles than ethics, coincided and shared with Africans and Aborigines a common dogma of the devil and his legions of fearsome spirits. From this concatenation there arose a mixture and a jumble, in which no one knew what part was Catholic or Roman, what part Barbarian or Hottentot, and what part had come from local roots."*[1]

Carrasquilla's black characters are often used to express the fantasy that slaves loved their owners. The ironic side to this is that their loyalty signals a simplicity and moral transcendence that key "white" characters lack. Tellingly, doña Bárbara is tricked and robbed by a false nobleman, a Spaniard, but cared for lovingly by her slaves. To readers in the present this narrative also has a less palatable side—the nostalgia that pervades Carrasquilla's sketches of late colonial Antioquia has a racist undercurrent. In the excerpt below, the maid Narcisa does the work of "turning

A society girl in Pasto, celebrating the First Communion of a household dependent, ca. 1920. Photographer unknown. Private collection. Courtesy of Marco Palacios.

out" her mistress and doña Bárbara's young nephew. Narcisa makes certain that their clothes are perfect, and their superiority goes unquestioned: she is a "priestess" within the cult of slavery.

Doña Bárbara returns to her chair to rest. The contradictions of life: would she, the most noble, the wisest, and the wealthiest woman of Yolombó, the most elegant and harmonious in form, if not the most beautiful, be destined to live alone and melancholic among her poor blacks? Would she die without traveling to Spain, without meeting His Majesty? It was a disgrace. It was true that she was determined enough to go across land and sea alone, bravely facing all dangers and fly around the world, like the most resolute man; yet what could a woman do in faraway lands so distant from her own, without someone who would manage her interests and demand that she be respected? And who at home could accompany her? Who could oversee all of her duties during her absence?

Her father was in no condition for wanderings, and he was rooted to this land; her brothers, with their own obligations, foolish and boorish, were better hidden than shown off. And to think of a husband at this time was almost stupidity: twenty-nine years were not nothing, and she was already thirty. Her nieces, sisters, younger than her, were almost all married and mothers. . . . She had been left on the shelf: yet old and all, she could not settle with any ordinary-girthed man such as those around here. No chance! She had disdained too many since she was young to now stoop down so laughably. Well, no sir: Bárbara Caballero y Alzate would set herself up with a true Spaniard or clothe saints: well married or well put. There was no middle ground. With regard to the trip to Spain, there could be a solution, with or without tying the knot. Like she would a needle in a haystack, she would search for a staunchly honest man that could handle her wealth; and as soon as her nephew Martín was old enough, she would take off with him for Spain and even Jerusalem. Martín would be respectable and hold his nobility, no question. You could see it in him! God had not made a creature more exquisite, more *ladino* and gay, to end up a mere dabbler. And, anyways, where would the little devil be? She calls Feliciano for news:

—He left, my *Amita* [my mistress], for the fields, with three little blacks to get more corncobs. Is *su mercé*[2] feeling downhearted? I see you looking a bit annoyed.

—No, Feliciano. That is just your impression. I am very well and actually feel like singing.

—Should I bring you the guitar?

—Tonight, after dinner. Well: it seems that the plantings will give us more than we expected?

—Hold your tongue, *su mercé*! Here's where my God said: "Take corn and beans until you can't handle any more." This is such a land for food, it almost does not seem true. But *Amita*, we are being driven mad by the gulls, parrots, squirrels, and all such animals. Starting at dawn someone has to be in the plantings, throwing stones without mercy, because they'd be bringing in the harvest themselves before we could wake up. They pay no heed to ghost or scarecrow.

—They are probably hungry, Feliciano. My God gives to all. And, now that we are alone, I am going to tell you one thing: I believe that we might be able to marry the *negrito* Gabriel very soon. I have Chepa, Celedonio's *negrita*, reserved for him. They would make a handsome couple.

—Isn't he too young, *Amita*? He is only going to turn fifteen.

—The Church will take them at fourteen. We will ask the priest. In any case, the sooner the better.

Given that she does not do her hair for any man, she does it for her *negrería*. It would not be fit for them to see her appear in just any manner! What respect would she have as lady and mistress of thirty-seven blacks, not counting children, if she wore canvas sandals and a cotton skirt? Shoes and socks above all, regardless of state or place: like a sword to a knight's courage, this was the measure of a lady's nobility.

Shoes and socks were like a sacred ritual for her. She would only remove them when she had to cross flooded areas inside the mine, and then she would insert her bare foot into tall clogs. Polished and sculptural, she put the pride of her womanhood and race into those feet.

The *negra* Narcisa, her head waiting-maid, skilled at her job, had dressed her for this country excursion with embroidered socks and green morocco-leather clogs with cork soles, silver buckles, and heels styled after Louis XVI. She wore a midlength dress-skirt, cut from thick, dark wool grenadine, with blue threadings; a loose batiste shirt; and a light kerchief, worn as a shawl, and pinned with a coral brooch, over which hangs a gold rosary with a carved cross and an oval bearing Saint Bárbara on one side and Saint Dominic on the other. And Narcisa had not forgotten to include light straws for cleaning her nails and ears.

All her golden and curly tresses had been tied into a braid without hair parting, rolled on her crown and covered with a head scarf of reddish-black sheen, tied in biblical style. On its knot was placed the brightest-colored rose that was at hand. And, as the heat has sullied the color in her lady's face, she applies rouge to her cheeks with a brush of sachet paper and whitens her up with "queen's paste." What an artistic and resourceful *negra*!

She sees in her lady something of an idol, in whose worship she feels consecrated as if through divine ministry. And clearly, the idol lets herself be cared for as her priestess desires. This idolatry bonds the lady and the slave woman. . . .

Here comes the *negra*: she brings a silver burner holding incense, pine resin, and camphor, to perfume her *Amita*'s room. She closes the door so that the smoke penetrates everything. She herself makes an impression— tall and turned out: her feet tied into white canvas sandals; a dotted and red moreen skirt; a low-cut blouse with curled ruffles; a scarlet-dyed cap; and a short necklace made from red and blue glass beads.

Next she takes out the clothes for her *Amito* Martín. It would be unfit for the future lord, "as precious as a grain of gold," to look as slovenly and dirty as any beggar boy in front of his blacks. But the *Amito* is nowhere to be found. They call and yell for him, yet nothing. Finally, he is seen up above, with three little *negrillos* [pickaninnies]. He's got a sack with corn, beans, and a bunch of snails, which he has gathered in the plantings.

She washes his feet and cleans his face; the sapphire eyes and flushed lips stand out from such whiteness. Narcisa untangles his golden tresses and ties them into a ponytail, not ungracefully, and applies castor-oil cream. All for nothing: the kid cannot stay still for one second. Soon he snarls his plaid cloak going up the avocado tree; and his ankle-length pants and deep blue shirt become an indecency; and the ponytail comes undone. How meaningless is Aunt Barbareta's scolding!

He comes down from the tree to climb onto one horse, then another. From there he goes onto the backs of the three pickaninnies: he makes them go in circles around the house; later, they carry him, playing *silla de reina* back and forth across the patio. He has the makings of a cruel master—he strikes them with a cane, between cries of command, guffaws, singing, and horseplay. Fortunately, his whims do not make for long tyrannies: soon, he goes with his vassals to the mango tree, using his cane to disturb the cows from their nap, fighting them with a mantelet and, being unable to ride them, going astride their calves. *Amito* Martín is a devil on the loose.

The blacks wash the clothes, put up the awning for the night, set out the lassos and packsaddles, care for the bay gelding, and carry firewood. In the meantime, the *pacarana* is roasting and being seasoned on the spit.[3] The pot of beans boils, the kneading hand moves to and fro on the grinding stone, smoothing out the milky dough, more cornstarch than flour, while the corn pudding, a favorite of doña Bárbara, sets in the saucepan.

Soon each takes their hardshell gourd, their plate and their wooden spoon. They sit, lined up, along the hallway walls with the same discipline as in the mine. A black woman comes out with a tray full of bread baked in plantain leaves, and distributes one to each down the line. Other women bring out the saucepan and pot, holding them with rags. The smell of heaven spreads. A *zamba* uses a quartered hardshell gourd, the backwoodsman's ladle, to serve the beans; another uses Adam and Eve's fork [a stick] to place a slice of pacarana meat, some bacon, and a piece of that trembling corn pudding, custardy, like *natilla* and with a crisp crust. And now white teeth flash in black faces, "Why do I need you around?" There are second helpings; in the house of my Mistress Barbarita hunger has never shown itself.

She and the *infante* don Martín, at a small dressed table, rejoice in the perfumed chambers, with stews as simple as they are succulent, with steaming arepas made from tender corn, as well as sweet custards served for dessert after dinner, milked straight into *coyabrilla* fruits, smooth and red on the outside, yellow and rough on the inside. God bless the vines that serve as sweet shops for the campesino.

After a half hour break, the *negrería* gathers in the outside hallway; Narcisa spreads a mat from Pasto on the threshold, where the lady kneels down and everyone follows, kneeling in two lines, males on the one side, females on the other. Doña Bárbara's voice is heard deep, clear, and fervorous, like the original offerings made by [Saint] Dominic of Guzmán. Everything follows methodically and with devotion, where the solo does not upstage the chorus nor vice versa; yet that heretic Martín, with precocious wickedness, tries out his repertoire of gestures and pirouettes on the black women at the end of the hallway, where he has seated himself. The cunning boy well knows that Auntie Bárbara closes her eyes when she prays.

Night falls, and the entertainment begins with the last sign of the cross. There is almost a full moon, but the blacks, in one sweep, collect bracken and dead leaves and light a fire in the patio. Two stay behind to keep it going. Doña Bárbara organizes the acts for the soirée that her imagination has improvised. *"Perillero y sapa"* [a dance song], she orders, in way of a prologue. While each man calls out his partner, she tunes Feliciano's guitar. Five couples come out into the patio. Each of the ten holds in their hand a firebrand, in lieu of a torch. Whistles and *gaitas*,[4] small drums and bamboo maracas start to play, as does the guitar, kindled by those ringed and aristocratic little hands.

Translated by Ana María Gómez López and Ann Farnsworth-Alvear

Notes

1. Tomás Carrasquilla, *La marquesa de Yolombó: Novela del tiempo de la colonia* (Medellín: A. J. Cano, 1928), 79–80, cited in Helena Iriarte's online biography of Carrasquilla, hosted by the Biblioteca Luis Ángel Arango, http://www.banrepcultural.org/blaavirtual/biografias/carrtoma.htm. The editors thank an anonymous reader at Duke University Press for assistance with this text.
2. *Su mercé* is a form of colonial address derived from the Spanish *su merced*—an approximate translation is "your grace." The expression continues to be used colloquially in Colombia today.
3. A *pacarana* is a game animal, larger than a guinea pig.
4. *Gaitas* in this context refers to an indigenous musical instrument from the Caribbean lowlands of Colombia.

Carried through the Streets of Bogotá: Grandmother's Sedan Chair

Eduardo Caballero Calderón

Tipacoque, a small town located in the department of Boyacá, is the setting for several novels, essays, and articles by Eduardo Caballero Calderón (1910–93), who also describes for his readers the late nineteenth-century Bogotá of his childhood. A recognized Colombian journalist, writer, and diplomat, Caballero Calderón had upper-class credentials—his grandfather had been a minister in the administration of General Rafael Reyes Prieto, and his father, Lucas Caballero Barrera, was a general and the Liberals' commanding officer in Cauca and Panama. Nonetheless, his writing sketched interactions across class lines with sensitivity, a trait shared by his brother Lucas, a noted cartoonist who went under the nickname "Klim." In Memorias infantiles (1964), the writer provides vignettes of city life alongside descriptions of Boyacá's countryside; in both contexts he contrasts the lives of the privileged with those of the poor. In this excerpt, Caballero Calderón describes his grandmother's sedan chair, a windowed cabin on two long poles carried by several people. It was the way she traveled over nearly two hundred kilometers of unpaved, mountainous roads from Bogotá to Tipacoque, and she used it to navigate the colonial-era streets of Bogotá's then-wealthy downtown neighborhood of La Candelaria.

On only one occasion did my father agree to accompany my grandmother on her trips to Tipacoque, soon after he had married. The first part of the trip was to the valley of Duitama, where he had two haciendas managed by my uncle José Miguel Calderón. They traveled by mule-drawn carriage, with Salvador at the coachbox. Journeys would not last more than three hours, as the old woman tired quickly from the dust and the discomforts of the road. Travels would begin late in the day when the sun was already high: there were no stops to rest at *posadas*, only at a provisional camp. She would travel with a dinner table, a gilded bedstead, a table set, a chamber pot, and food provisions, surrounded by an army of servants and mules loaded up

Students at a rural school, turned out for a visiting photographer, ca. 1910. Photographer unknown. In Phanor James Eder, *Colombia* (New York: Charles Scribner's Sons, 1913), plate facing p. 250.

with canvas sacks. Father and the Calderón uncles escorted her on horseback, and lesser folk would ride on the same saddles as the peones.

They would stop for several days in Tunja at the house of my Uncle Arístides. She would spend some time in Duitama at the big old house my uncle José Miguel owned on the town square, which is now a school run by nuns. The carriage could make its way along the road without much trouble up to that point, or perhaps until the town of Santa Rosa de Viterbo, where she had been taken by general Reyes. But from the valley of Cerinza to the town of Soatá, where my grandmother made a stop at another one of her houses, the *tipacoques* would take turns to carry her in a sedan chair. My uncle Antonio María would give them special training in the hallways of Tipacoque in order to ease their rough manners and soften their pace. The seemingly endless climb to the *páramo* of Guantiva would begin at Belén de Cerinza and end in the village of Susacón, through mist and light rain on a road that was little more than a mule path. Long days would go by among those deserted marsh-covered plains, covered in the *frailejones, encenillo* trees, and digitalis plants that populated the *páramo* [high-altitude Andean tundra]. The caravan would spend the night in Soatá at a house my grandmother owned on the square, where she would be visited by the priest, town authorities, and poor relatives who had not yet migrated to the capital. From Soatá to Tipacoque, the royal road of Cucutá grew narrower, and twined rope had to be used to slither around steep crags barely covered with slate. After a month of this arduous trudge, my grandmother would arrive to Tipacoque, where she was greeted with celebrations like those received by her friend the bishop Maldonado y Calvo when he stopped by on episcopal visits. There were fireworks, traditional dances in the patio, and the constant ringing of the chapel bells.

The old woman would get bored after eight days in the hacienda, and would order to return as slow and cumbersomely as she had arrived. This was when she did not get bored along the way, and suddenly order the group to turn back and return to Bogotá before arriving to Tunja or Duitama. Given all of this, I take it as a given that my grandfather Calderón was a saint.

I never went on those trips to Tipacoque with my grandmother, since I was not born yet. But on the other hand I did ride with her several times in her sedan chair. One of my greatest pleasures—which happened rarely and was unpredictable, since my grandmother was as arbitrary and capricious as Divine Providence itself—was to accompany her to neighborhood mass. It was not because of the mass, even though I had already begun to prepare for my First Communion in the school of the Hermanas de la Caridad [Sisters of Charity]: it was the sedan chair. . . .

My grandmother would greet her neighborhood friends and have brief conversations with them (I would be teeming with impatience as the sedan chair swayed two steps behind with the door held open). I knew almost all of them, since neighborhood families were friends for ten blocks in any direction. My grandmother's contemporaries called her Ana Rosa, friends from younger generations would refer to her as doña Rosa, pious old maids and shame-faced women would say *misiá* Ana. My uncles would refer to her as *su merced*, or *mi madre*; mother and my aunts would call her *madrecita*, and her grandchildren would say *"mi madrecita."*

There were nuances in the language to express degrees of affection, kinship, or social differences. When my grandmother referred to Mama Toya and her third tier of servants, she would vary not only her grammar but also her vocabulary, whether voluntarily or unconsciously. She would address us with *"tú,"* and refer to people of respect as *"usted."* For Mama Toya, she used *"vos"*: *vos querés, vos tenés,* and *vos decís.* To us she would say *"tú quieres," "tú tienes,"* and *"tú dices."* And she would even imitate the incorrect language of Mama Toya and the servants, saying their strange words and locutions with a slight tinge of irony. Beautiful words (soothsay, shew, ardour, soothe, betimes . . .), that years later I would encounter in the classics, happily discovering that the inferior world of carriage men, gardeners, day laborers, and servant girls from Tipacoque expressed themselves in an archaic language miraculously trapped in colonial times. Mama Toya spoke of bodily humors (it was not that Damascus the gardener in Santa Ana smelled: it was that he had a "bad humor"). . . . The words that referred to animals, rural chores, and common handcrafts had a flavor one would have sought in vain in the deboned, algebraic, and schematic language used in so-called educated circles. There, language is not enrichened but crystallizes and becomes tarnished by foreign contact, which in a place as isolated and secluded as Bogotá meant books. We also had our own language with conventional expressions and invented code words, the better to isolate ourselves from the surrounding world. With my first girlfriend, the step of going from a dignified *"usted"* to a *"tú"* seemed to me as important as the first kiss. To say *"tú"* was an act violating the intimacy of another person, like a caress: when I said *"tú"* I felt a great voluptuousness, like that of mystics who in their highest degree of ecstasy begin to refer to the Lord as *"tú."*

At last, my grandmother would return to the sedan chair and signal the march to continue.

—Give yourself the sign of the cross!

—What for, *madrecita*?

—Father Astete[1] says to do so when you leave your home, enter the church, or before eating and sleeping . . .

—But he says nothing about the sedan chair, I thought to myself.

The strange vehicle would go fifty feet down Calle 11 before stopping in front of the convents of Santa Inés and Concepción, two old and large colonial houses standing on each side of the Archbishop's Palace. My grandmother sent weekly generous bundles of foodstuffs, as these old women lived off alms and were often starving to death. A muffled bell located in the interior patio of the convents would ring every other day, announcing to the pious that the nuns did not have a single piece of bread to eat. Servants would come out from the main houses of the Candelaria, carrying steaming soup tureens, freshly baked bread, and sacks of potatoes or corn.

—What do nuns do?

—Pray for us. What else would you have them do?

. . . After completing the family duty of visiting the nuns, my grandmother returned to her chair. She would head down the *calle de la Candelaria* to her home, which was located around the corner halfway down the next street. There was a narrow entrance that led to the *candelarios'* monastery, next to the tall, windowless wall of the church. She was a close friend of those old Spanish *chapetones*,[2] who in the afternoons would go two by two—Father Cándido and Father Alberto, Father Luciano and Father Manuel, Father Marcelino and Father Cirilo, Father Leonardo and Brother Jacinto—to visit her in the glass-paned room to drink chocolate. She would send for Father Alberto without leaving her sedan chair, and would hold long conversations about the canonization of Bishop Moreno, which she and the convent—although apparently not the pope's ambassador or the Vatican—were very interested in. The conversation would drag on as slowly as her sedan chair. Saint Bishop Moreno[3] was an apostolic prefect in Casanare: although dormant, the *candelarios* had a foundation there in order to justify their condition as missionaries. The bishop had died of throat cancer, and he was missing three accounts of miracles in order to be sanctified. My grandmother and the priest spent half their lives trying to find these in vain, yet would always have relics at hand with them in case such an occasion would arise. . . .

The sedan chair would swing gently along the cobblestoned street, which had a gully running down its middle. Past the corner and down Calle 12 was the house of my Aunt Amalía Pérez, widow of Clímaco Calderón, my grandfather's first-degree cousin on both sides of his family. Aunt Pérez was the daughter of don Santiago, a former president during the radical period. Her eldest son was fully consumed by his studies, until a tuberculosis in Paris really did consume him a few years later. Then there was the house of the Bermúdez Portocarrero family, who were regular visitors to the glass-paned room. Finally, there was my grandmother's house, where the entrance hallway was filled with clients of Papá Márquez, and with the poor that waited for food scraps from our cook. In front of the house, the stained-glass windows of the papal ambassador's residence shone in the sun like open windows to an imaginary sky.

The outing was over. My grandmother would sit at a small table in her dressing room before a spread with the aroma of *changua* [a savory milk-based soup], coffee with milk, and bread from María Mayorga. Mama Toya would untie grandmother's abundant silvery hair, combing and dividing it into braids as she ate. The old woman would give me a bite of toast that was still warm, and would then say goodbye to me, lowering her head slightly so that I could give her a kiss.

Translated by Ana María Gómez López

Notes

1. Father Gaspar de Astete (1537–1601) was a Spanish Jesuit priest and author of catechisms and popular guides to social behavior that included parenting and family life.
2. *Chapetón* or *gachupín* is a term used to refer to peninsular Spaniards who settled in the Americas.
3. Saint Ezequiel Moreno y Díaz (1848–1906) was a Spanish Augustinian Recollect friar associated with the slogan "Liberalism is a sin" (see part II). He was beatified by Pope Paul VI in 1975 and canonized by Pope John Paul II in 1992.

The Street-Car Bogotá of New Social Groups: Clerks, Switchboard Operators, Pharmacists

Augusto Morales Pino

Augusto Morales Pino (1912–2001) was a prolific writer and the son of Pedro Morales Pino, a well-known bandleader and musician who presented traditional Colombian rhythms to twentieth-century audiences. As a writer, the younger Morales Pino explored a wide variety of themes, from the biography of Independence heroine Policarpa Salvarrieta to Muisca life (in a romanticized form) to his father's music. One subject he returned to again and again was everyday life in his native Bogotá. In a series of novels published between 1938 and 1987 he sought to capture in characters and vignettes the life of "Los de en medio," or "Those in the Middle," as he titled the series. These were fully urban creatures—typists and workers at the telephone company, commuters who rode Bogotá's trolleys, and mujeres de oficina, or secretaries. Seen from the perspective of peasant cultivators, such city people seemed likely to have money and eat well—after all, they wore shoes and read newspapers. But Morales Pino sketched their lives in unsparing close-ups, focusing on their hardships during the 1920s and 1930s. Enrique, for example, at one point ends up laid off and finds himself forced to skip meals and to seek out poorer and poorer restaurants. Working girls give tips to a street vendor who sells secondhand records (early LPs made of shellac or vinyl), asking him to bring them cigarettes or candy, but they do not earn enough to rent private rooms. Morales Pino describes them sleeping on couches and sharing blankets in tenements. Families with a sick child or another sudden setback bring sewing machines, gold watches, or an inherited emerald to pawn shops to exchange exactly those objects that mark them as middle class for the possibility of surviving in their homes. His Bogotá is not glamorous. Nevertheless, life there is leavened by colorful city lights, the radio, the pride people take in having decent clothes and ordering in cafés. A political subtext pervades his prose as well. In the first of the three extracts included here, Enrique, the novel's protagonist, is disdained by his childhood sweetheart, Olga, whose better-off parents had prevented them from seeing one another. It's a moment marked by some bitterness but also a moment of self-recognition. In the second extract, a pharmacist's longtime assistant

Lisandro Serrano, *Busy*, 1940. Ink on paper, 11.7 × 13.5 cm. This sketch of a busy telephone operator provides one glimpse of the new pink-collar jobs that began to remake gender and class dynamics in Colombian cities in the early twentieth century. *Historia de la caricatura en Colombia* 5. 1988. Banco de la República. In Santiago Londoño Vélez and Benjamín Villegas, *Arte Colombiano: 3500 años de historia* (Bogotá: Villegas Editores, 2001), 220.

enjoys the satisfaction of keeping a neat shop and even the fact that her employer has gotten rich. In the third, an office worker's hidden heartbreaks are subordinated to the announced fact that she's late for work.

Morales Pino sets his quick sketches of the lower middle class in counterpoint to those "below." The protagonist, for example, repeatedly meets a destitute black man who wanders the city's streets haunted by the death of the woman he loved, long ago, in a shack built on a hot lowland riverbank. The office girls are set off from the prostitute Enrique visits one night in adolescent confusion. Morales Pino also shows his readers the way his "middling" characters look "up." They see films, listen to jazz and foxtrots on the radio, debate politics, and read (borrowed) books. High heels, cosmetics, and children's trips to carousels are a part of their world, however dear the cost of living. His Bogotanos would have been recognizable to contemporaries living in other world cities in the 1920s and '30s: New York, Mexico City, Buenos Aires, London, Cairo, Berlin.

Day of the Family, Bogotá, 1945. The Media Torta amphitheater was built in 1938 and is still an icon in the Colombian capital. In its first decade it was often used for public celebrations with didactic ends, as well as for cultural events and entertainment. (MdB 0959), Álbum Familiar / *Museo de Bogotá*. Courtesy of Museo de Bogotá.

I.

One day on his way home, feeling slightly fatigued from work, he spotted a slender blond girl walking in front of him, dressed in luxurious clothing, though he soon saw that it was a young woman walking with a little girl of about seven years old by her side. Enrique felt a strange curiosity that made him quicken his step. The memory of Olga entered his mind, but as he approached her he could tell that the young woman's hair was less blond, more lackluster, and not as curly or soft. Could it really be her? That seemed impossible.

He was on a busy street downtown, teeming with pedestrians blocking his way. The young woman and the little girl crossed the street and continued walking down the sidewalk on the opposite side of the street. At that moment a streetcar stopped right in front of him, making it impossible for Enrique to follow them.

Electric shop lights began to flicker on, and brightly illuminated signs cast their light playfully against the building walls. Newspaper vendors ran by calling out the latest news. Groups of men began to congregate on street corners and in café doorways.

Up ahead, Enrique caught a glimpse of them again, standing in front of a display window. He passed them, crossed the street, and waited for them on the corner. Filled with excitement, he could see the young woman's blond hair bobbing up and down over the shoulder of a man who was walking ahead of him. A couple of passersby nudged him out of the way. Suddenly he saw Olga's eyes, the same almond-shaped blue eyes, looking at him with indifference. How beautiful she looked! She was a sixteen-year-old girl with the body of a grown woman.

He experienced an uneasy feeling of inferiority. She kept looking at him as she walked toward him and at that moment he knew that she too had recognized him. As he approached her, he was unable to conceal his happiness.

Olga stopped. Her expression changed. With calculated coldness, she curled her lip in a gesture of disdain. She looked him up and down scornfully, beginning with his shoes and moving slowly all the way up to his hat. Then she continued on her way. Overcome by embarrassment, Enrique remained there, frozen, with his hand extended.

Passersby shoved him out of the way. He found himself in front of a café and walked in. He patted down the lapels of his jacket in robotic fashion and looked at his suit. He understood. In order to compose himself and lift his mood, he shrugged his shoulders and smiled at himself with a resigned look in a nearby mirror.

★ ★ ★

He remained seated at a table in the cafe, unable to bring himself to get up, and continued to smile stupidly, isolated from the murmur of conversations and cigarette smoke that surrounded him. As he sat quietly with his hat pulled far down over his eyes, he felt a nervous shiver run through his body.

Yes, it was the same sense of inferiority, of smallness, that he had experienced while at the house of a rich friend. He and his friend used to exchange books, and in his luxurious, comfortable house, he had felt the haughty gaze of his sisters, and the involuntary sense of embarrassment that washed over him, rendering his movements awkward. It was the same troubling feeling he'd sensed vaguely as a child when, while walking by Luis's house, he saw the proud little blond boy showing off his skates, riding them up and down the paved street.

So why didn't he look for other friends? He himself could have sought another way of life, one that kept these humiliations at bay.

Why didn't he just walk into a factory and begin to live the life of a worker?

But no: he understood that he couldn't do that, as much as he wanted to. The habits and ideas that had been instilled in him since childhood prevented this. He wanted to move up, not down.

There, in his childhood, remained a space filled with happiness in which social classes weren't so clearly marked, almost as if they didn't exist—or at least he couldn't discern them—among many other things he was now discovering.

The memory of Olga smiling at him from the front door of her house, unaware that he was poor, that he didn't belong to her world, not recognizing the differences in their clothing, now struck him as something unpleasant, a memory that he would never be able to separate from the insolent gesture of an elegant young woman.

Enrique looked up. In front of him, at a table next to his there sat an older man with glasses reading the newspaper while he slowly sipped a cup of coffee. His appearance was modest, and he dressed simply and smartly, though his clothes looked worn.

Yes—Enrique thought to himself—; now he understood. Right before his eyes he saw what would become of his life. One day he'd leave the archive where he'd been working, and bit by bit, slowly but surely, he'd move into a better office for an otherwise redundant job. His expertise would be in drafting memos or keeping ledgers; he'd probably earn about a hundred and twenty pesos per month. He'd have to wear glasses to defend his tired eyes. He'd work hunched over his desk for many years. Maybe he'd get married. One day he'd get fired. . . . And in the evening, after work, at the exact same time every day, he'd order a cup of coffee and read the newspaper. His life would be monotonous and unchanging, like a day at the office.

He was one of those stuck in the middle.

II.

Josefina competently wrapped the bottle exuding an odor of creosote and iodine.

—How much?

—Sixty cents.

The coins clicked cheerfully on the shiny glass counter. Before leaving the customer paused and looked at her kindly.

—You've been working here a long time—he said.

Josefina leaned forward on the counter with pride. She was still beautiful, though she had put on quite a bit of weight and the bags under her eyes revealed an unhealthy tinge.

—I've been working here for ten years.

—Yes, I remember . . . You started to work here when the pharmacy was still over by the church.

—Back then it was a small business. Now we have several branches. Doctor Aponte has gotten rich . . .

The customer looked around the clean and spacious pharmacy, reading the big colorful signs and clever advertisements urging customers to buy an assortment of excellent drugs with foreign names. He smiled as if thinking about days gone by.

—Good bye, Señora . . . —he said.

After he left, only the soft ticking of the clock could be heard in the silent establishment.

III.

A young woman quickly gets off the streetcar and walks past a church with a clock tower, the clock like a roulette wheel spinning a game of love, life, and death, measuring the passage of time with implacable slowness. She crosses the street at the next corner and enters an eight-story building.

She is tired, bored, and in a foul mood. She wishes she didn't have to work and could just remain in bed, waiting for something to happen— anything—even her own annihilation. He hasn't returned . . . , he'll never return. She enters the elevator and notices that everyone is looking at her with indifference. She hasn't had time to make herself look more put together or to wear her usual makeup, and her unpainted lips give her face a sickly pallor.

The elevator attendant opens the door with a clap to the floor of the company where she works. She exits quickly, removes her timecard from the board on the wall. Just then the clock strikes 8:32.

—Late—says the man monitoring the time cards.

—Late—responds employee number 125.

Translated by Brenda Werth

It Is a Norm among Us to Believe That a Woman Cannot Act on Her Own Criteria

María Cano

María Cano (1887–1967) was an anomaly in turn-of-the-century Medellín—a young woman who read widely, including writers frowned on by Colombia's Catholic hierarchy: Victor Hugo, Allan Kardec, Émile Zola. Her uncle Fidel Cano had founded El Espectador, *a daily paper that provided a home for Liberal Party intellectuals after their defeat in the War of the Thousand Days, and one of her nephews, Luis Tejada, was a well-known journalist. Her father had at one point directed Medellín's Escuela Normal (a secular institution), and in keeping with the family's freethinking principles María and her sisters had a lay education in a city famous for its strict Catholicism. She grew up in conversation with Spiritists and Radical Liberals, by her twenties was publishing emotionally focused short stories in a literary magazine, and by her thirties began to speak at political rallies.*

With lightning speed, María Cano became Colombia's most famous female orator. Medellín's left-leaning union movement had named her the city's "Flower of Labor" (other towns also named young women "Flowers of Labor"), and she used the title as a platform from which to organize opposition to the death penalty, support workers' rights, and mobilize opposition to the Conservative government. With Ignacio Torres Giraldo, her lifelong partner, and other founding members of Colombia's Revolutionary Socialist Party (PSR), including Raul Mahecha and Tomás Uribe Márquez, she spent 1926–28 on the road, supporting strikes and getting arrested. Her poise and aggressive rhetoric became legendary. A glimpse of that side of María Cano is visible in the description she offers below, of smashing a glass of champagne at the feet of a small-town politician whom she saw as a bourgeois opportunist looking to use her speech to burnish his own image.

Alongside her reputation as a fiery orator, whose contralto voice carried to crowds of working-class supporters and who was transfigured by revolutionary fervor when she spoke, however, another María Cano has long been a part of the Colombian feminist imagination. As a woman who fought not only for workers' rights but also for women's voices to be heard in political life, María Cano represented the struggle within the struggle. The PSR and the PCC (Colombia's pro-Soviet Communist Party, established in 1930 as an explicit rejection of the PSR) were organizations in which men made the important decisions. As an activist who was also a woman conscious of sexism, María Cano fought for respect from even those politically close to her—in ways that went beyond the normal factionalism that divided leftists from one another. Hence the importance of the letter reproduced here, written in 1930, in which she details her rejection of the charge of "putschism." She disagrees with the way the pro-Soviet faction has set out to accuse her and other PSR leaders of working too closely with disaffected Liberals in an attempt to overthrow the Conservatives. Beyond that, however, she explicitly insists that her ideas are her own—she is not following any man's ideas.

The letter is also important because she retreated into private life after it, maintaining a home with Ignacio Torres Giraldo and raising the boy he acknowledged as his son, Eddy Torres. Colombian feminists confront her legacy as a double-sided inheritance. She spoke out to defend her right to political activism and yet seems to have been effectively marginalized by men on the Left later in her life. By 1945, for example, when a group of Colombian suffragists set out to find her and bestow an honor upon her, she had effectively retired from politics. Nevertheless, she responded to them with an echo of her younger days: "We are part of the human current, a wave in an ocean that is impetuous or serene and that carries on its back the ship of the state. We cannot allow ourselves to be herded along narrow paths or confined to maudlin spheres, our fate removed from that of humanity. Being aware of our responsibilities should not mean that we lose the clear wisdom of our femininity.... Today as yesterday, I am a soldier of the world who offers her life for the liberty of all. This parchment, which I receive in earnestness, I place upon the mass of workers, embodying a milestone in the nation's evolution. I place it upon this flesh macerated by labor and upon its callused hands, as an advance on the recognition this nation will bestow upon them. Praise be to the workers of Colombia!"

A few clarifying notes: The "Heroic Law" she refers to is a 1928 law that cracked down on Colombia's union movement and resulted in the jailing of many labor leaders, even before the banana workers' massacre (see part VI). The CCCC refers to the Central Conspiracy Committee of Colombia, which she insists she did not participate in. Also, where María Cano uses the single letter c it is as an abbreviation for "comrade."

Compañero
Guillermo Hernández Rodríguez
Bogotá

Compañero:

I am writing in response to your letter, dated August 21. . . . You ask me to declare my position concerning the new political direction developed by the party. In this regard, I can say that given that it is the Comintern [Communist International, abbreviated by María Cano as IC] that has indicated this new shape [for the Party], one that wholly embodies the proletariat's hopes of emancipation, mine is the position of a Comintern soldier following on the true path.

You also ask for my position concerning the letter that the Comintern sent to the Party in February of this year, which criticizes and condemns "putschist" politics. According to you, I was "one of the elements that contributed to its development." If the Comintern is recognized as the leadership of the world revolutionary movement, it is because it possesses the difficult and marvelous science of being able to lead. I will always be content with what is generated from within the Comintern. It is just that on this occasion, the Comintern has had mistaken information regarding the movement developed by the C.C.C.C. (of which I was never a member), resulting from wrongful interpretation by its informants, or the malicious personalities of the same. I believe that, in judging these assertions as truthful, the Comintern has behaved soundly in condemning these actions. In reference to these assertions, I have stated that there have been distortions, either by coincidence or by malice, because that is clear. . . .

To justify the blame that today falls on two or three *compañeros*, they are given the hackneyed label of "chiefs," or, even more depressingly, "caudillos." Party leadership is called "caudillismo," when a position of responsibility is taken. Those who attain the trust of the masses and bring them together are condemned as "chiefs." Yet why should we be surprised by this, given that Lenin referred to this "extremism" in German communism, given that at the Party's Ninth Congress (April 1920) there was minority opposition to "chiefs"? Lenin called this "Communism's infantile disorder."

I have said that the Comintern has received wrongful information about the movement organized by the C.C.C.C., as it is claimed that this was a pact with the Liberal Party, a fusion, a handing over of the masses, when what existed was only a unified front of the entire Left, a transitory front, in which our Party ended up being absorbed when it itself believed itself able to absorb. There were tactical errors, to be sure, but the gap between tactical errors and being "Tools of Liberalism," or "Liberal-izers of the masses" is as wide as the gap between truth and falsehood.

The tactic of a unified front has its risks, as can be seen in the case of the front (ordered by the C.C.E.) formed in opposition to the Heroic Law, which had such terrible results. Or, more recently, the front formed in the protest held on [July] 17, where our *compañeros* were crushed by the enemy.

As I have stated several times, I was sympathetic to the movement, but not to its tactics. I devoted all my energies to it. And this, I realized later, was my mistake, when I understood the force of bourgeoisie habits in the masses, and the lack of a disciplined and well-organized Communist Party that could impose order on the Working-Class and Peasant Government. I knew all this was lacking, but my revolutionary faith in the Comintern led me to determine that it was enough to have a broad Commission in order to organize the Soviet State, impose a disciplinary line on our *compañeros*, and thus create the Communist Party.

I would have smiled when reading the manifestos published by the C.C.E. (prior to the Expansion Assembly), where we are branded as "Liberalism's collaborators," "Liberalizers of the masses," or, in other words, *traitors* to the proletariat, if these did not create erroneous and damaging obstacles to the tasks of the moment. This is not about the reputation of María Cano, Ignacio Torres Giraldo, or Tomás Uribe Márquez, but rather is about the disorienting effect of this on the masses, who see those they believed to be their most faithful defenders accused of treason, and who despite this remain in the Party, thus diminishing its credibility. And Lenin said it: "Without a Party that enjoys the trust of all honorable elements within that class, without a Party that understands the mood of the masses, struggle is impossible."

I believe that self-criticism is necessary, but not defamation. If there is factual evidence that we deserve those labels, then the proper sanction of condemnation should be applied. If there is just a mistake in tactics, it should be criticized and its risks shown so as to not come against this hurdle again, fostering a true Marxist education. The fact that current Party members have necessary knowledge does not imply the need for denigration of those who have erred due to ignorance, which exists up until today with few exceptions, you among them. Reading Marxism does not make one a Marxist, in the same way that one is not exempt from making mistakes for being a Marxist.

I said I would have smiled at the label of "liberalizer of the masses," as the proletariat of the entire country can attest that I lash out against Liberalism, unmasking it everywhere I go. For two years I traveled around the country together with c. Ignacio Torres Giraldo on a speaking tour, its events seeming more like "recordings" according to a *compañero* from the Montevideo Conference; however, they always included class struggle as the essence of our Communist doctrine, and an offensive against the privileged castes and against opportunism, one of the main factors of the evil corroding the masses and distancing them from their emancipation. The Liberal Party has been first in opportunism, which is why our darts were always aimed toward it. Those who listened to our lectures in Cartagena, Barrancabermeja, Magdalena, Southern Santander, Valle, and Tolima can attest to this. It was there, during the Third Congress of 1926, where I began working in the class struggle; I was at the time only a novice in socialism (it was still not referred to as communism) when I had to confront the Liberal Municipal Council who, meddling in the worker's cause, offered me a glass of champagne which I threw down at the feet of he who had given it to me, expressing my indignation in harsh and heated phrases. One of the most salient forms of *deliberalization* in the masses was electoral abstention, a strategy so criticized and resisted by our extremist Marxists that they labeled us as anarchists.

Nonetheless, it was a needed tactic at the time, when the masses only knew about traditional bourgeoisie parties. And it was then when in a short time the masses converged under the revolutionary flag of the working class, deserting the encampments of the bourgeoisie. Then those who succeeded in this campaign of attraction were called "caudillos," and so began a personalized campaign against us led by individuals who cannot, in principle, be called communists!

. . . I may have strayed from your questions, but this was necessary to clearly contest these charges. I recognize my mistake in hoping to create a movement without preparation of the masses and lacking a Communist Party, but I do not believe I deserve to be labeled a "putschist," nor any other term that follows from that. In recognizing I have made this prior-acknowledged error, I am not influenced by the fact that fellow comrades ["c.c." in original] such as Uribe Márquez and other good *compañeros* have committed the same. I have much appreciation for comrade Uribe Márquez, toward whom I profess profound affection, but this would not move me to own up to an error if I did not consider I had committed it. It does not surprise me that this is what you believe, it's an evil that goes with the territory. It is a norm among us to believe that a woman cannot act on her own criteria, and that she acts on reflex—following a priest, father, or friend. I believe I have educated myself sufficiently to act as my own guide.

You write that, under the current circumstances, one either stands with the Communist Party or one is on the side of fascism and imperialist reaction. You add that the committee does not doubt "I will turn toward the first path without hesitation." One cannot "turn toward" a path one has always walked on, loyally and unavoidably in revolutionary dignity, if somewhat lacking in capacity. Capitalism knows that I am its fiercest enemy. The proletariat knows that I have risen above everything, broken the chains of conventionality and been gripped by those that reactionaries persecute and hold shackled, in order to be with the workers on the ideological barricades of Marxism today and tomorrow. Violence is only destroyed with violence in the barricades of social revolution. And later—why not—be with them in the great work of revolution by the workers of the world. Everything is possible with the will and desire of revolutionary faith.

With communist greetings,
María Cano

Translated by Ana María Gómez López and Ann Farnsworth-Alvear

I Energetically Protest in Defense
of Truth and Justice

Manuel Quintín Lame

*Colombia's most important indigenous thinker, Manuel Quintín Lame (1880–1967),
also counts among the most prominent of the country's twentieth-century agrarian
militants. Born into a family of Nasa [previously referred to as Páez] terrajeros, or
sharecroppers, who worked plots owned by an hacienda near the city of Popayán,
Quintín Lame did not learn to read or write until military recruiters took him to
Panama during the War of the Thousand Days. After the war he continued as an
autodidact, aided by a copy of Colombia's published law codes, and he began a long
and combative career as a political organizer. From an emphasis on the abolition
of terraje, an old system by which Indian sharecroppers were required to perform
unpaid labor on an hacienda or in a landowner's house, he moved toward an insistence on ancestral land rights and the autonomy of the cabildo (local, Indian-
controlled government). The political path he followed took him from the National
Archives in Bogotá, where he pored over colonial court rulings, to repeated stints as
a leader of mobilizations, armed actions, and temporary takeovers of haciendas.
This activism, in turn, led to time in hiding, multiple arrests, and high-profile days
in court. Sometimes he was tortured and subject to vicious harassment; sometimes
a particular moment meant that opportunistic politicians sought his support. His
growing popularity meant that "white" opinion was divided and that Quintín
Lame's opponents sought, in turn, to divide the indigenous movement, often with
success.*

*Quintín Lame's longest and most infamous prison term lasted from 1917 to 1921.
After his release he spent time in the capital and in southern Tolima, where he was
sought out by new, younger organizers—from different ethnic groups and from
different political backgrounds—such as José Gonzalo Sánchez (1900–1950) and
Eutiquio Timoté (a presidential candidate for the PCC in 1934). These were leaders
who joined Colombia's newly founded Communist Party and dreamed of establishing
Indian Soviets—an idea entirely foreign to Quintín Lame's deep-seated Christianity
and traditionalism. Yet the older man continued his combative politics until his*

death, from his home in the municipality of Ortega, Tolima, and on two fronts. On the one hand, he pursued a legal strategy based in texts and judicial practice, and on the other, he refined a messianic, indigenista *discourse that imagined the possibility of a "little republic" of Indians, counterposed to the "big republic" of the whites.*

A few years after his death, indigenous activists founded the Consejo Regional Indígena del Cauca (Regional Indigenous Council of Cauca), and later, an indigenous armed guerrilla movement took Quintín Lame's name. Both groups took up his political goals, which became incorporated into the demands of indigenous organizations from all over Colombia and eventually gained an echo in the 1991 Constitution. Movements that claimed his legacy focused on recuperating and extending resguardo *lands, strengthening the autonomy of indigenous* cabildos, *defending cultural practices, educating the next generation in indigenous languages, and obtaining indigenous representation in the National Congress.*

Two texts are excerpted here. In the first, composed in 1939 but not published until 1971, Quintín Lame writes in a prophetic voice. His belief in divine justice, his deep Catholicism, and the pride he takes in being an indigenous intellectual are palpable. This is taken from a manuscript transcribed by Gonzalo Castillo-Cárdenas, a scholar of religion and an ethnographer, who presented Lame's writings as a "prophetic" source for those in the 1970s and 1980s who were seeking "Liberation Theology from below." Castillo-Cárdenas published Quintín Lame's writing in a Colombian edition, but he also translated it and ensured that the work circulated in the United States, where he held a professorship at the Pittsburgh Theological Seminary. For Castillo-Cárdenas, Quintín Lame's legacy had resonance throughout the Americas. The second text is different and suggests the variety of registers that Quintín Lame mastered. It is an unpublished letter in which we see a political militant still at work, on a very local level, decades after the trials and jailings that made him famous. With a group of cosigners, Quintín Lame denounces everyday abuses against "us, the Indigenous of the National Resguardo of Ortega and Chaparral."

This book will serve as a horizon in the midst of darkness for the Indian generations who are asleep in those immense fields of Divine Nature. Because the white man is the sworn enemy of the Indian who does not knock at the door of deceit, who does not want promises, who does not sell cheap; and the public functionary joins the capitalist landholder and the lawyer to cause the Indian to lose his plot of land, his cattle, etc.

It is not true that only those who have studied fifteen or twenty years, who have learned to think about thinking, are the ones who have a vocation, etc., having ascended from the Valley to the Mountain. Because I was born and reared in the mountain and from the mountain I have come down to the valley to write the present work.

Girls at a boarding school for indigenous children in Tierradentro (Cauca department, southern part of the central Colombian Andes), 1943. Photograph by Gregorio Hernández de Alba. In *Pioneros de la antropología: Memoria visual 1936–1950* (Bogotá: ICANH, 1994), 32. Courtesy of Carlos Hernández de Alba.

There was an oak tree, old and robust, cultivated by nature. I say "cultivated by nature" because a garden of flowers had grown on it, of the kind that civilized people call parasite flowers and which we Indians call *chitemas*, in the dialect of my Páez ancestors. Climbing on that tree at the age of six I was able to contemplate another treetop, even taller, proud and haughty, that crowned over the virgin forests which had witnessed my birth and that of my ancestors before and after October 12 of 1492. That tree was known as "the Oak of Lebanon" and it seemed to hail the two almighty natures, one human and the other divine, when the four winds of the earth passed by.

A thought came to me that as high as that tree would be placed my ideas in the Colombian nation, when I should come down from the Mountain to the Valley to take up the defense of my Indian race, proscribed, persecuted, despised, plundered, and murdered by non-Indians. Because this is what is shown by the deposit of actions, and confirmed by the witness of the past, witness that came together with today's announcement, that I should pre-

José Vicente Piñeros, *Portrait of Manuel Quintín Lame*, 1962. In Eduardo Serrano, *Historia de la fotografía en Colombia 1950–2000* (Bogotá: Editorial Planeta Colombiana, 2006), 21. Courtesy of Diego Piñeros.

pare myself for the defense of future generations of the Indian race of Colombia. . . .

I cannot take pride in sophisms saying that I spent a long time studying in a school or a college. My college was faith coupled with an untiring enthusiasm, because when I asked my father, Sr. Don Mariano Lame, to give me education, that is, to send me to school, he gave me instead a shovel, an ax, a machete, and a sickle, and sent me with my seven brothers to clear the forest. However, with that overpowering enthusiasm which I felt inside me, I thought that I should instead learn to write using a piece of wood, and a piece of coal, and with a needle on the leaf of a tree. The result was that knowingly I took a number of papers that belonged to my aged uncle, Leonardo Chantre. . . .

I studied ontology in the forests, and its immediate attributes when I studied the supreme reasons of God, of man, and of the world, and it taught me that the world, the human soul, and God are the three beings whose existence I wanted to discover. . . .

Likewise, the parents of an Indian family who bear a child endowed with intelligence must get this book [i.e., child] to be like a mirror that never loses its shine, in the midst of icy pyramids, or in the heat waves produced by the birds of prey of our enemies. But they will not prevail, provided that such a young man or young men rest their ideologies on God, through faith, because science accompanied by faith rests on God, the designer (*ordenador*) of the Universe and of Natural Law.

I have been and I am the man who sits with pride in the midst of my race, and in the midst of my enemies, who mocked me, who slandered me, who called me names; [in the midst] of the authorities who tortured me, tying me by the neck and the arms, as if I were a runaway murderer. This is what Dr. Alvarez Guzmán did, as mayor of Ortega, to make himself famous among his own kind. He set a post at the door of the dungeon of the Ortega jail, and had me tied to it by the neck, and arms, and around the waist, without movement for three days and three nights; and did not allow food to be handed out to me; he also opened the doors of the jail building and asked the people of Ortega, men and women, to visit and stare at me from the balcony, to show that he knew how to punish the Indian Quintín Lame: thus he displayed his greatness and demonstrated his courage, immortalized in the pages of history assigned to Nero.

We Indians ought to abandon and refuse the gifts of the whites, the bluffing mouthful (*pedantezco palabrerío*) that says: "I care for you as one of my family, as a true friend, and it is because of this love that I ask you to sell me your produce at a lower price, etc., etc."

The white lawyer says to the Indian (who has a legitimate complaint against a white man): "Your lawsuit does not look good at all, it is very difficult, but if you pay me 800 pesos, putting down half of it in advance, in a week your case shall be won." The Indian answers: "I have only 200 pesos with me." The white man says: "No, no, only if you give me 400!" The Indian answers: "In two weeks I'll bring them." Says the white man: "No! Bring them in a week" (and he promises and swears that the lawsuit will be won in favor of the Indian). The Indian brings the 400 pesos, and two months later comes back to ask: "How is my case going, Mr. Lawyer?" But the lawyer who is a loafer and a liar says: "I have done everything possible! The outcome lies almost entirely in my hands, but today I am broke. Give me 100 pesos, which I will appreciate as if it were a present." The Indian says: "Today I have nothing, but in a week I'll bring the 100 pesos, or at least fifty." Five months later, failing to hear from the lawyer again, the Indian asks the secretary of the Court about it, and she says: "It is already two months since your lawyer presented a brief, but he never came back again!" "But he told me that the case was practically won!" says the Indian. The secretary answers: "That man is really swindling you. Find yourself a good, honest lawyer, who at least shows up at the office!" But by this time the Indian's money has run out, he sinks in misery, and the lawsuit is won by the other side. The lawyer of the poor Indian is now happy because secretly he was in cahoots with the defendant! . . . .

In Popayán it was Doctor Miguel Arroyo Díez and Doctor Guillermo Valencia who infected the conscience of the judges against the accused Manuel Quintín Lame for having learned how to think. In Neiva it was Sr. Ricardo Perdomo C., and Doctor Luis Ignacio Andrade, and in Ibagué the director of the jail, Jesús Elías Quijano, and Doctor Marco A. Vidales, judge of the Superior Court.

It is said that Popayán is the cradle of sages, the cradle of poets, the cradle of philosophers, the cradle of the most famous jurists; but I did not consult with any one of them about my own defense in the years 1918 and 1919 when I was preparing it, like the chicks of the fowl when they flap their wings to challenge the infinite space on their own for the first time and to cross it; likewise I presented my bravest defense in the midst of all those learned men of the present age.

One of the prosecutors, together with the alternate prosecutor, came to the jail and called me apart to inquire how and in what way I was to begin my defense, so as to help me, saying that they owned no lands to protect, etc. But I immediately saw their ploy and answered them with a question about how were they going to begin their accusation against me. And they said: "We are not going to accuse you, but to defend you, etc., etc."

But when I looked at these young men with their lips bathed with smiles, suddenly the Queen appeared to me, the same who had consoled me out there in the forests, and in the dungeon, and in the jail when I was held incommunicado for one entire year, dragging around the dungeon of Popayán iron shackles weighing twenty-eight pounds by order of the aristocrats of Popayán mentioned before.

And who was this Queen? It was the very image of my thought which had been engendered in the deep and extensive Prairie of my body and my spiritual soul, within the sanctuary of my heart, which is the compass in a man's life, which compass oriented me when I had to cross two swollen rivers, one of tears, the other of blood; which compass pointed to me two paths, one of thistle, the other of thorns; but both of them to the right side, because on the left side was lying my non-Indian enemy, crouched like a tiger, ready to devour the Giant who was building the Palace of my thought, that is to say, the thought of the Indian who educated himself in the midst of the mother forest, so as to be able to confront and to fool those poets with ellipsis, when (one of them) who was running for president of the country asked me in several letters to tell the Indians that they should vote for him; to confront those minds which had been carved in the schools of Europe; to confront the pricking thorns of the rose gardens which had blossomed and were crowned with white flowers, or rather, what the poor little Indian today calls flowers, which covered the cemetery of illusions of those aged men, seventy or eighty years old, who ended their lives buried with their capes on. And today the eagle of my thought flies across those fields, transformed into logic and psychology according to the promise of that image that has not left me to this day, thanks to God's mercy, because God is above all things, and the man who rests on God's omnipotence is powerful, and is able to pass through files of two hundred thousand cannons and guns fired by slanderers, bribers, and perjurers against the Indian who attempts to assert his right before them. . . .

What shall I say of the great attempts against me, made by non-Indian men of Tolima, men of little minds, whose intelligence was clogged by cynicism, hate, envy, and deceit, to answer the Indian Manuel Quintín Lame, myself. But as God has said, "the gates of hell shall not prevail against the gates of heaven," because truth is a Queen whose throne is in heaven, and whose habitat is the bosom of God. . . .

I energetically protest in defense of truth and justice.

Mr. Criminal Investigation Judge: The lawyer, who defends the indigenous people that are slaves to arch-millionaire oligarchs in the town of Ortega, states the following with full respect for your authority:

I energetically protest against the refusal of justice toward us indigenous people, which violates in a distressing and unfortunate manner articles 156, 157, 158, and 159 of the Penal Code. We *indígenas* express this protest together with the small indigenous Cabildo of the Resguardos of Ortega and part of Chaparral from the Department of Tolima.

We protest against the refusal of the economy, industry, and commerce of indigenous people, who have been abused due to our ignorance and weakness, and regarded as lacking solemnity and as legal minors. We are the indigenous owners and absolute lords of the soil and subsoil, according to the objectives stated in the Deed numbered 162 and dated October 8, 1941, which was entirely violated by the Judicial Branch of Tolima, with backing from the Criminal Appeals Courtroom of the Supreme Court. We protest against the assault carried out by a gang of criminals, led by the Municipal *Personero* of Ortega Mr. José Galvis, who in 1946 stole all property belonging to the School of the Indigenous Tribe of Altolozano. Mr. Galvis stole this property, which was financed with funds from the *jefe* Quintín Lame, as Tolima's educational authorities denied schooling to indigenous people.

A case in point: during a ceremony held in 1957 in the *Población* of Ortega, schoolteachers asked a considerable number of young mestiza women what people had the conquistador Cristóbal Colón encountered on Guaraní land. The young women replied that there was a group of Indians, to which the school principal replied that the answer was mistaken, and asked them to sit down. I witnessed this event with other *indígenas* who were with me.

We protest against the burning of judicial documents ordered by Judge Ramón E. Rivera, to ensure that indigenous people could not defend themselves and could be sentenced without counsel. He did this in an unjust episode that was later verified by the Penal Judge of Guamo and later denied an appeal by the Tribunal.

The Police Inspector Jerónimo Alape de Ortega expropriated my one-room house, located in Tambillas . . . in the District of Ortega, and stole twelve loads of corn, all the kitchen utensils and work tools, and three new bedspreads and blankets. This theft was denounced to the National Office of the Inspector General, etc. . . .

The Municipal Treasury of Ortega stole the Maco finca, which consisted of thirty *plazas* [plots of eighty square meters] of land farmed with agro-industrial plantations, houses with several rooms, and equipment to hull coffee. This was all overseen by myself, Manuel Quintín Lame. This finca was auctioned by the Treasurer Eliseo Octavo.

The Municipal Treasurer of Ortega José Galvis auctioned the Cabral finca, property of Alisandro Pérez, which consisted of coffee and sugarcane crops for harvest, as well as plantain crops . . . houses with several rooms, etc., etc.

The Municipal Treasurer Eliseo Octavo auctioned the one-room house owned by Tobías Montiel in this town, and ordered it to be torn down with machetes, etc.

The Municipal Treasurer Eliseo Octavo ordered the burning of a one-room house belonging to the indigenous men Pastor Maseto and David Devia, located in Macule, now called Olaya Herrera.

The Municipal Mayor of Ortega, Mr. Antonio Álvarez Guzmán, ordered Abrahán Moreno to burn down the indigenous hamlet of Llano Grande. The flames destroyed the Indigenous *Cabildo* house, as well as the house used as the Tribe's indigenous school. . . .

I asked that the Notary office of Ortega be shut down because it has and continues to uphold a code of falsehood and not public good. This is because the Indigenous *Cabildo* has not given them nor the business owners of Ortega the land that belonged to our ancestors. The small Indigenous *Cabildo* are the owners and lords of the soil within the town limits of Ortega.

I protest together with others against the denial of Justice by the Supreme Court of Injustice and its Criminal Appeals Courtroom, which has filed 23 criminal reports within its offices. We will continue this position if there is any opposition to the defense of truth and justice, as well as cheating and judicial fraud against the Indigenous Race, which has been persecuted and murdered by nonindigenous civilization since October 12, 1492.

It is in this manner that we present our protest.

Mr. Judge and Mr. Lawyer, the defender of the indigenous people of the National *Resguardo* of Ortega and Chaparral, remains respectfully yours,

Ortega, September 1961

The foregoing is a true and accurate copy of its original.

> *Signed*
> *Alisandro Pérez*
> *Juan Evangelista Totena*
> *Misael Totena*
> *Rodolfo Totena*
> *Hermes Chilatra*
> *Custodio Vera*
> *Luís Timote*
> *Cornelio Yaima*
> *Responsible Signature*
> *Manuel Quintín Lame*

Translated by Ana María Gómez López

Note

All capitalization of nouns follows the original manuscript.

Bringing Presents from Abroad

Manuel Zapata Olivella

Manuel Zapata Olivella (1920–2004) enjoyed describing himself to colleagues and protégés as a vagabundo, *a tramp or wanderer—more than as a doctor, a folklorist, or prize-winning novelist. In his twenties, he interrupted his medical studies to walk and hitchhike through Central America and Mexico, alternately pitching up at consulates, getting hired at hospitals, looking up fellow students, and writing—anything to keep body and soul together while slaking his thirst for travel. He made his way across the US border and went by train to New York, where he sought out Langston Hughes. Later travels would take him to China; across Europe, where he and his folklorist sister, Delia Zapata Olivella, organized cultural tours; and to many of the places he would describe in his later work, including Senegal, Brazil, and the Caribbean. His earlier travel experiences are chronicled in* Pasión vagabunda *(1949),* He visto la noche *(1952), and* China: 6 A.M., *while his later experiences are palpable in his magnum opus,* Changó: El grán putas, *translated into English as* Chango: The Biggest Badass.

Zapata Olivella's intellectual legacy extends beyond his travel writing and novels and toward a generation that began to understand Latin America as fundamentally part of an African diaspora. Zapata Olivella wrote repeatedly about Colombia as a triethnic culture area, and he constantly emphasized the presence of African culture and African wisdom in the Americas. He organized conferences oriented toward diasporic studies and worked to bring together black intellectuals from Venezuela, Ecuador, Brazil, Cuba, Peru, and the United States. Politically a leftist and an antiracist, he defined himself by his passion for valorizing African legacies.

His fourth novel, Chambacú: Corral de Negros, *first published in Cuba in 1963, used a gritty social-realist style to hit hard at Colombians' collective desire to deny racism. A strong, moral black woman, La Cotena, has raised five children in a desperately poor, rat-infested community near Cartagena. Neither her strength nor her good faith is sufficient to protect her children from hunger and denigration. Her daughter, Clotilde, works as a maid in town. Her four sons include a boxer; a cockfighter; a revolutionary, Máximo; and a no-good whoring drunk, José Raquel. The mother would rather see her sons dead than drafted as soldiers and sent to kill*

people who have done no wrong to them, but José Raquel volunteers for the battalion
Colombia sent to the Korean War, even as Máximo is labeled a criminal by the same
government that rewards José Raquel's amoral behavior.

   Zapata Olivella's readers experience Chambacú through the eyes of Inge, a Swed-
ish woman who returns with José Raquel and then, abandoned by him, forms a
bond with his mother and Máximo. Yet even the despicable José Raquel has a hu-
man side—returning home with luxuries and gifts is his attempt to live out the
dreams of his childhood.

The swift motorcycle along the avenue. Dodging the buses and burro-drawn
carts. The red-print tee shirt inflated by the breeze. The glasses reflecting the
sun drew stares from the pedestrians. He was fulfilling the dreams he'd had
when he bought the motorcycle in Sweden. A triumphant ride through the
streets of Cartagena. The places where he had roamed barefoot and ragged
in his infancy. He greeted people first on one side and then the other. "It's La
Cotena's son." He crossed Heredia Bridge. From there, across the channel,
the heaped-up shanties of Chambacú. His brow dimmed. He had to return
to the dirty island. The rickety bridge of Chambacú. He braked the motorcycle in order not to get stuck in the mud. Monday. The men would not be
in the miserable corner store. He knew it. The women's derision. He never
imagined that the bike would cause him humiliation. In Europe he thought
only of the paved avenues and the masonry bridges of Cartagena. He did not
know the alleys of Chambacú. The bridge mudhole. It was no time to turn
back. He was in front of the puddle with his motorcycle and two suitcases
in the back seat. He had to cross it. He surveyed the terrain. There was no
other entrance to the island. At the opposite end other bogs surrounded
it, blocking the machine's way. He decided to take off his white shoes and
carry the motorcycle and the suitcases on his shoulders. He had untied the
ropes when Crazy Arturo approached him.

   "Pay me some loot and I'll carry the suitcases for you."

   He thought over the proposition. The demented fellow smiled, the hairs
of his beard sparse and snarled. He got drunk at José Raquel's expense and
now he demanded payment in advance for a favor.

   "Take these coins!"

   He thought he'd struck a bad deal. Crazy Arturo amidst the mire. The
suitcases threatened to tumble. He was about to throw himself into the
slime when his assistant reached the opposite shore. The inundated streets.
He had to grasp the bike by its handlebars and skirt the accumulated watch-
ers. The prying neighbors. He definitely had been a fool to bring the motorcycle to Chambacú.

On seeing the suitcases, Clotilde could not contain her glee. She had been awaiting them since the very moment her brother first mentioned them. . . .

Dominguito loosened the straps and cleaned the mud spatters with a rag. The open suitcases. A perfume of foreign merchandise spread through the room. It was not the familiar smell of trunks stuffed with old clothes, cigars, and pine soap. José Raquel looked with pride at the amazed faces. His hands held aloft a small transistor radio.

"What is that, my son?" asked his mother. Dominguito's eyes doubled in whiteness. Clotilde, expectant, held her breath. José Raquel turned the dials and the raucous music blared in his hands.

"A radio! A radio!" exclaimed Clotilde enthusiastically. The torment of having to listen to music on the only radio in the neighborhood would be over. La Cotena screwed up her face.

"Don't you like it, Mama?"

"Fine, my son, it's fine."

The mother knew what having a radio in the house meant.

"I see the transistor doesn't thrill you, but for you I've brought something good. Here!"

She accepted the package and began to untie it.

"A bolt of white cloth!"

"Yes, Mama. You can make yourself all the camisoles you want."

"It's a nice present, my son. I'm grateful to you for it."

"And what have you brought me, Uncle?" said Dominguito. José Raquel pressed his index finger to his lips.

"Close your eyes and wait."

The boy came over excitedly, his eyes shut tight. His uncle put a bat and a baseball glove in his hands. When he opened his eyes he was dumbstruck. He clung to his playthings and, after making his way through the tangle of legs, ran ardently toward the square.

"Where you going?" asked his mother and then said, displeased: "Goodbye school!"

The grandmother reinforced:

"He is such a poor student, he'll not only stop studying but also quit Miss Domitila's school."

José Raquel laughed. In that laughter dwelled a primal satisfaction that he had never had in his childhood. To play baseball, any fencepost pried free would do as a bat. He had to fashion clumsy mitts for himself with remnants of cloth from some decrepit set of sails. In his nephew's joy he belatedly lived an ancient illusion.

Cleaning for Other People

Anna Rubbo and Michael Taussig

Until very recently the statement that Colombian families either employ servants or send their daughters to work as live-in maids was taken as a truism for huge swaths of the country. In the 1983 essay excerpted below, two Australian researchers straightforwardly describe women's experiences working as maids in Cali. Both authors went on to long scholarly careers: Anna Rubbo as an architect and professor of participatory design, Michael Taussig as an anthropologist and writer with a string of well-known books to his credit.

In real terms, most Colombian households neither employ domestics nor include family members who work in other people's homes. On the one hand, a large middle class exists; on the other, a large percentage of people in poverty are unlikely to seek work as servants. Since the 1980s, census data has shown a steady decline in the number of homes that employ live-in maids, although many households hire women to perform domestic tasks during limited hours. Nevertheless, the cultural legacy of servanthood casts a long shadow in Colombia. Uniformed servants are a staple of television soap operas, and the lifestyles of middle-class and wealthy families alike depend on the labor of domestic workers. Almost always women, hired domestics do the work of ironing, cleaning, polishing, and preparing labor-intensive food. In theory, they earn at least the minimum wage and receive benefits, but in practice domestic workers face obstacles to gaining anything like fair treatment across the board.

T.R. is twenty-three and has been working as a servant since she was twelve. At first she hated it, but now has grown accustomed to taking orders "from people I can't respect." Her latest job lasted only four months, and she did all the housework, cooking, cleaning, and hand laundering for ten persons, for which she was paid the normal salary of 700 pesos per month and was allowed half a day off per week, otherwise bound to the house 24 hours a day. She emphasized how her mistress's orders would constantly change in accord with her fluctuations in mood, resulting in a stream of contradictory commands and constant confusion. *Caprichosa* (capricious) is what maids

A babysitter and her charge, Cartagena, 1948. *Con la niñera*, 1948 (MdB 1546), Álbum Familiar / *Museo de Bogotá*. Courtesy of Museo de Bogotá.

call this type of mistress, and it is an incessantly echoed complaint. She missed her young son and her husband, so she left and came home for a short respite.

She comes from a rural neighborhood near Puerto Tejada, and still re-members her peasant father saying: "I don't want any daughter of mine hu-miliated by the rich in Cali. We are peasants and we should live by working our land—not by serving others." But he died when she was eleven, and the one hectare of land they have retained from the expanding sugar planta-tions had to be divided when her mother died six years ago, one half being rented out to cover the costs of the funeral and wake, the other half being worked by the family. T.R. couldn't continue at school for lack of money and so became a servant-girl, "for necessity."

L.U. is from the same neighborhood, is forty-six and the mother of seven children. She and her husband live on a two-hectare farm, which is of a size generally considered just large enough to meet subsistence needs. In 1971 the government's agricultural extension agency, financed by USAID, began a rigorous campaign to convince the peasantry to modernize by adopting "green revolution" technology and uprooting their perennial crops of cocoa, coffee, and plantains. The bulk of the innovating peasants have been brought to ruin, or to the brink of it, as in the case of L.U.'s household, which owes 60,000 pesos to the government's Rural Bank. In a futile attempt to pay off debts, L.U. went to work as a live-in maid in Cali. Her husband worked the farm and in addition became a day laborer on the sugar plantations. Her eldest daughter and her mother ran the house, and she cooked and cleaned for a single elderly woman in Cali. The mistress treated her quite well, she says, paid her 700 pesos a month and allowed her half a day off a week. After six months she left, saying her children needed her.

G.C. was sent to work in Cali by her mother at the age of fourteen, her mistress being told to treat her "as a daughter." She was paid 200 pesos a month to do all household chores except cook lunch for the couple and their eight children. In the morning she began working at six, grinding the corn she had cooked the day before to make the family's *arepas* (corn cakes)—a very labor-intensive item particularly suited for families with domestic servants. After breakfast she washed, cleaned the house, and helped with lunch preparation. After lunch she washed up and finished the laundering (all by hand). After the evening meal she would iron the clothes. She became friendly with one of the daughters, and one day instead of washing clothes as instructed, she watched the soap opera on T.V. When her mistress caught her, became furious, and struck her, G.C. left and returned home.

Like her sister, M. entered domestic service at the age of twelve. Her father never lived at home and never supported her mother or the children financially. They lived on her mother's half-hectare farm, but when M. was nine years old they moved into the town and rented the farm. Her mother worked as a day laborer on the plantations, and when the daughters were barely old enough they were sent into service. M. was hired by a doctor's family to do all the household tasks at a rock-bottom salary. She stayed only a month because she was wakened one night by the master coming into her tiny cell, naked except for his underclothes. She screamed and the mistress came, telling her husband he had no right to abuse the maid. She was asked to stay on by the mistress, but she was too frightened and returned home. A short time later she found another job with a family of six, but again only stayed a short time as she had to wash thick bed covers once a week by hand, and her mother thought that was too heavy work for a young girl. So she returned home and worked as a day laborer on the plantations and as a contracted field hand on the large commercial farms for the following three years. When she became the de facto wife (*compañera*) of a young man and went to live in his mother's house, she gave up work at his request. She had two children there, but the relationship with her *compañero* was not very satisfactory. When she became pregnant a third time in 1975, she went to Cali to work as a maid in order to get some money for the future baby. Her mother-in-law looked after the two children, and M. found a job housekeeping for a woman who rented out rooms to seven medical students. As a live-in maid doing all the household work for eleven persons, she was paid a meager 500 pesos a month and given half a day off per week. The mistress did no housework and had no outside job; she lived off the rent, which provided her and her two children with a comfortable living.

M. got up at five in the morning to squeeze the orange juice for the *doctores*—the term she uses in common with all lower-class Colombians for one's school-educated superiors—then prepared and served their breakfast. Each morning she had to wash all the kitchenware because of the nocturnal cockroaches. Then she made the beds, arranged the furniture, washed the floors, began the laundering and prepared lunch. Sometimes the mistress's daughter would help her wash the plates. After lunch she would resume laundering until it was time to cook dinner, following which she would iron until 10 or 10:30 P.M. The mistress charged the boarders 250 pesos per month to have their clothes washed by M., keeping all the money to herself. Sheets were changed twice a week, amounting to a weekly washing of 44 sheets and 22 pillowcases—all by hand. The *doctores* wore clean clothes every day, sometimes wearing two shirts daily.

Comparing her life as a maid in Cali with that of her life as a field hand, M. says: "Sometimes you do better working for a labor contractor, but as a maid at least you work in the shade and have food and lodging. The worst part is having to leave the children behind. But what else can I do? If I stay here, I have to get a job as a field hand, and I don't feel strong enough for that. It's best if I send the kids to my mother-in-law on the farm and I go back to work as a maid . . ."

As an aid to analysis, we can very crudely divide Colombian households into two types: those that supply or are potential suppliers of female servants and those that employ servants.

Needless to say, servant-supply households are of the lower class (and usually rural). The servant per se can be seen as a bridge uniting the dominant classes with the dominated—at the level and through the medium of the domestic sphere.

Child care and household management in the servant-supplying-type households are heavily dependent on the work of children themselves, particularly that of girls. A chain of command and division of labor exist in which the elder children care for the younger and are responsible for household chores. Thus from their early years, girls in these households are rigorously socialized into servant-type roles, and women can leave such households to take up domestic service without completely disrupting the management of their homes and families.

On the other hand, in the servant-*employing*-type households, the opposite occurs. Instead of mother and children sharing household labor, the existence of the servant relieves them of that, and what the mother and children share is the power to command. From their earliest years these children are rigorously socialized into the use of a very personal type of power. Gross as this is, it is not without its subtleties, for, unlike a machine, a servant has feelings and a personality. Unlike a slave, she has some freedom to leave if conditions are too bad. The daily intimacies of common cohabitations as much as her role as a pseudo-family member demand that the servant be subtly manipulated as much as directly bullied—just as the servant herself has to rely on being manipulative.

A Feminist Writer Sketches the Interior Life and Death of an Upper-Class Woman

Marvel Moreno

The following short story by Marvel Moreno (1939–95), a writer from the Caribbean coastal city of Barranquilla, titled "Something So Ugly in the Life of a Well-Bred Wife" (Algo tan feo en la vida de una señora bien) evokes an interior world. In a gesture to Virginia Woolf, Moreno places her protagonist, Laura de Urueta, in a room of her own. Laura is alone with a set of watercolors she had done before her husband's disdain drained her of any will to paint. She is wealthy, a victim of psychic rather than physical violence. Published in 1980, when Moreno lived in Paris and had begun to distance herself from the kind of revolutionary politics that countenanced violence, "Something So Ugly" describes the multiple ways culturally sanctioned relationships can destroy women's struggles for self-realization, sexual fulfillment, and love. Moreno picks up themes explored by fellow Barranquilla writer Fanny Buitrago, whose 1963 debut novel, El hostigante verano de los dioses (The Harassing Summer of the Gods), scandalized Colombian audiences with its candid descriptions of sexual liberation and class dynamics in the country's Atlantic coast.

Laura de Urueta took the last Librium and reached over to turn on the air-conditioning.

The light in the room dimmed slightly, alluding to the threat of rain that would not materialize that afternoon; somewhere a fly was buzzing, and from below came the confused sounds of the new driver closing the garage door. Everyone had left. Eucaris the cook had gone. So she was all by herself.

For the first time in a very long while, Laura de Urueta began to remember, as she snuffed out a cigarette in a crystal ashtray. She found herself alone in that imposing house, where she had lived since her wedding day, without ever having the feeling that it was hers. The room—her room—was different; it belonged to her. She had decorated it according to her tastes, and the items she chose made Ernesto smile. In the room there was a divan designed with simple lines that she frequently used as a bed, in addition to her father's old desk, and some pillows. . . .

Laura de Urueta looked around her. Yes, the watercolor paintings were still there and the fly began to buzz again between the window and the curtain. The sleepiness and the peace that she had sought by taking the handful of tranquilizers were slow in arriving. She would wait another half hour before taking the sleeping pills. In any case, it was better to be awake when Ernesto called her from New York. He would call her without fail, as he had always done when he was away on business. One call every three days, from Miami, New York, Chicago, or wherever he was sent to negotiate patents, hire new technicians, or buy parts for the factory machines. He treated her very kindly and he always showed interest in her health and in her little problems. Luckily her mother would not be there to eavesdrop on her conversation. She couldn't tolerate her mother's attitude of indulgence, her platitudes. She couldn't stand the way she meddled in her life and reminded her constantly of how fortunate she was to have found Ernesto. Since her mother had come to live with her two years earlier, she had made an ongoing effort not to blow up in her presence. And in spite of everything, she still loved her. It was hard for her to see her mother so old and fatigued when she had never once known her to be tired or ill, and she had worked hard her whole life in order to maintain the social position her surname entitled her to, something her mother never ceased to repeat. There was no denying she had achieved this. And with great sacrifice her mother was able to uphold appearances so that she could go to a good high school, be a regular at the country club, and have a respectable house in which to entertain her friends, although she preferred not to remember anything about her old residence, the Olaya Herrera house. It would have been much better had they torn the house down and built a new building over the ruins. Ernesto was able to sell at a high price, and with the money from the house, her mother had given Lilian enough for a down payment on an apartment. That had been their wedding gift. She expected nothing less. Her mother adored Lilian. Seeing them together and noticing how much they resembled one another gave her the impression that she was no more than a link between two generations: someone who had existed solely in order for her mother to be able to recognize herself in her daughter, so that her mother's house could transform into her daughter's apartment, without mother or daughter having a particular need for either.

Now the sun began to shine. Suddenly a rose-tinted light inundated the room so intensely that it seemed to dilute the grays and mauves in the watercolors. The fly danced and flew against the glass pane of the window.

Not a sound came from the alert house. Laura de Urueta reflected on how difficult it was to be left totally alone. Achieving it had required an incredible amount of scheming and planning on her part; she gave the help all four days of Carnival off, she convinced her mother to spend a week with Lilian and her husband in Santa Marta. But who will keep you company? The help, mother, don't worry. Who will stay with you? Mother plans to return tomorrow, Eucaris, go and enjoy yourself. One would think she was an invalid, a newborn. People always tended to protect her, and it wasn't that her behavior invited this attitude; at least that is what she believed. It was just that her mother and Ernesto had considered her incapable and fragile her whole life; the servants, of course they did nothing but follow suit. In reality, she had never thought one way or the other about the weakness they attributed to her. And in fact, it allowed her to retreat and maintain a protective distance from them. If she didn't agree with them, she kept quiet and they were unfazed by her silence. If they wanted her to accompany them to one place or another, she could always say she wasn't able to or that she was indisposed. If she reached the point that she felt she simply could not stand them anymore, a migraine allowed her to lock herself in her room. What a good idea to have secured the room, as a place to isolate herself and make her own. The room allowed her to see two or more doctors at the same time without anyone knowing. That way she could buy all of the tranquilizers and sleeping pills she desired and die laughing at her depression. Because now she knew that this total lack of energy, the desire to remain still, to sleep, and to sink into an abyss, was called depression. And it was so intolerable. It was so intolerable to have to get out of bed and face the everyday routine, to find Ernesto and her mother discussing the news in the *Herald*, and to have to attend the meetings of the Pink Ladies, the Blue Ladies, the Catholic Ladies, etc. Thus it was an absolute relief to be able to end the day with four or five sleeping pills that promised to deliver her swiftly into the abyss—that white zone—where everything ceased to exist and sleep became dense, profound oblivion. What happiness, what pleasure to feel free, to respond to her own whims, not to have to listen to anybody. Remembering the boxes and pill bottles hidden in her room made her more tolerant, less vulnerable: a Librium, a Tranxene, a Valium. Taking them all at once with breakfast turned life into a party. It's a shame she hadn't discovered this earlier. . . .

The fly, whirring about in the curtain, blurred and seemed to double itself. Posters and watercolor paintings looked like smudges dissolving against a watery backdrop. How ridiculous. My God. Why was she crying? She looked for the box of Kleenex under the pillows. Because she was thinking foolish thoughts, that's why. It's a shame Maritza wasn't there. That afternoon, beside the pool, Maritza had made her feel better and she had agreed with her on everything. As always, she had to admit, Maritza had accepted her weakness. She knew her better than anyone, and so well, that (even though her mother would never believe it) Maritza had been opposed to her relationship with Horacio. You're going to get into trouble, she had told her on the very night that they met him. You're not prepared and you won't be able to resist him. Resist? Of course she would have resisted him. A sudden surge of strength made her feel capable of confronting and defying anything and everything. And no sooner had she arrived, she was forced to leave when her mother appeared with two policemen on the dock. Afterward, she had gone back to her same old self. She collapsed into her bed, disposed to die, she refused to eat, until one day, she took an entire bottle of sedatives for nerve pain. They had to rush her to the Prado Hospital where they gave her a transfusion. At least this, combined with the ambulance and the doctors' reproaches, had silenced her mother. Because from the moment her mother found her on the dock and dragged her home by force, beat her, yanked her hair and hit her head against the wall until she bled, she hadn't stopped insulting her. And she had continued to insult her even when she was in bed and refused to eat and her voice was barely audible, lost in a cottony white lethargy. Had Aunt Edith not arrived by chance on the exact day she took the sedatives, she might have died. That's what the doctors told her mother. She wasn't exaggerating when she said it would have been better that way. To have loved, to have known that feeling of fulfillment, to have discovered the beauty of the blue sky, the ocean scent of the air, the scurrying dance of crabs on the beach. To know all of this and then to lose it suddenly, never to find it again, made life pointless and absurd.

But had she really loved him? Had she loved that man whose face she barely remembered? She had never again thought of him, she told Maritza, and it was true. Since she awoke in the hospital connected to tubes and with a terrible pain in her arm, she had made the decision not to think about him anymore. Or maybe afterward, because the first thing she felt when she awoke was rage, an inexpressible rage at being yanked back to life. When only traces of her memory remained, she journeyed back dizzyingly into the earliest, most profound depths of her childhood, only to find herself returned abruptly to the smiles of the doctors and the contained hatred of her mother. Hatred? No, that was unfair to her mother. She had never understood her mother's feelings very well, but she shouldn't judge her that way. It was her disappointment that led her to react so harshly. For a woman who had lost both of her parents and had witnessed in five years of marriage how her husband squandered her inheritance setting up apartments for his mistresses, it was understandable that she would distrust men and consider sex a destructive and negative force. It was understandable that when she became a widow she would place all of her hopes in her daughter. And, in this case, the daughter had followed in her father's footsteps, abruptly throwing away all of her mother's years of hard work and last unfulfilled dreams. . . .

The church bells of the Inmaculada slowly struck six o'clock in the afternoon. Laura de Urueta stretched out over the pillows. Somewhere in the room the fly had ceased swirling about; perhaps it was pressed against the windowpane, trying to get into the garden. In general, she opened the window for them (let them be with the other flies) driven by a childhood impulse that made her gather objects together, fearing that they would suffer if kept apart. But that evening the fly would sleep with her. She felt incapable of getting up off of the floor. She felt incapable of doing anything other than allowing her mind to wander between memories and thoughts produced by the quiet drowsiness that was closing her eyelids. Very soon she would be sleeping, and not like everyday sleep, but rather the kind of sleep she had had the last time Ernesto was traveling. Twenty carefully chosen pills (she saw them lined up next to a pitcher of water) and once again, slowly, she would slip into a state that was: what was it? Happiness, though stated in such a way made it seem banal. But how else should she call the delightful sensation of floating amid the clouds? Twenty would liberate her, thirty would end it all. How foolish. She didn't have any reason to kill herself. She had no problems, no fears, and no feelings of guilt. Thank God she had learned to go about life without inconveniencing anyone. Her marriage to Ernesto was an open book. Her mother? To the extent she could, she had tried to make it up to her. There her mother was, living in her house, imposing her opinions (whether having her close or far away, neither helped her to understand what was going through her mind). She was more or less content, feeling that at the end of her days she had performed her duty, she said. Her anxieties had subsided when she met Ernesto, the right man for you, her mother had said immediately. And three years later she was married to that businessman with the calm eyes, who had calculated his marriage with the same perspicuity that had served him well in buying bankrupt businesses and turning them around in a year's time. Ernesto, she knew perfectly well, never erred. In twenty years of marriage he had never committed an error. His principal strength was his ability to detect the potential for success, precisely where others only saw failure. Who, for example, would have married her in that city? After such a scandal? Nobody. And in reality nobody knew the full truth because the doctors and Aunt Edith had kept as quiet as a tomb. And even if someone brought up the ambulance, the only thing that was known for sure was that she had tried to flee the city with a stranger. Luckily, knock on wood, even today the identity of that stranger remains a secret: both his identity and his profession, thank God. But people had a sixth sense for such things, and given that the hospital was involved, they assumed that she had lost her virginity. That was enough. No more friends, no more invitations, and the young men, who had behaved very properly toward her, began to treat her like she was a spectacle of some sort. She had to seclude herself in the Olaya Herrera house for four years, without leaving or going anywhere, even refraining from answering the telephone, fearing prank calls. Ernesto rescued her from her confinement. And in no time at all he had taken her to the country club and to his parents' house, where everyone could see them. And people changed, of course. In a blink of an eye her old girlfriends reappeared and planned more than twenty bachelorette parties for her. Radiant, and awestruck, her mother spoke of the miracle that had occurred. You were born with a lucky star, she said. She let herself get swept up in the excitement. She was surprised, actually, how happy she was to put her life back in order and become like the others again. Nonetheless, she was restless. It was a restlessness she did not want to face during her engagement, fearing that her unconscious (her self-destructive urges, she said) would undermine her. I already committed an error once, she thought, and it is incredible that he wants to marry me. And because of that, and because he had indulged her so patiently the day she told him about Horacio (portraying him in the worst possible light, just like her mother had instructed her to do), she didn't pay attention to the warning signs that her body alerted her to: her body, not her mind. She didn't have enough experience to know that people could be used for their weaknesses and shame. She was unable to imagine that. And after all, how could she reproach Ernesto? He was the best of fiancés: discreet and affable. He called her at twelve o'clock, and at eight o'clock he came to visit her. He was able to get her mother a loan at the bank, which he later paid off, in order to prepare her trousseau and the wedding. He was indeed the ideal fiancé, only that sometimes she found him to be a bit callous, a little evasive. She had already discovered that if he didn't agree with her ideas he became aggressive in such a way that chilled her soul. She shouldn't contradict him, or show herself to be too, what? excessive, in his words, as he extracted her gently from his arms. No drawn-out kisses or caresses in the dark interior of a car. You are not a fling, he had told her one afternoon on the beach. Not the long and deserted beach of Salgar, where she had gone so many times with Horacio, but another one, the Sabanilla? She didn't remember anymore.

What she did remember was that she was barefoot and that as she watched the sand suck up the sea foam from the waves, she had desired him for the first time. She had wanted him to take her and cover her with his body. And he had said, you are not a fling. It wasn't so much what he said, rather the way in which he looked at her. The disgust she saw in his eyes had left her cold. Nonetheless she had gotten married, maybe she was thinking that Ernesto would change once she was his wife, because she was young and she knew she was pretty and she still liked looking at herself naked in the bathroom mirror. But that was a lie, because really she was willing to pay whatever the price in order to get married. And Ernesto knew it. He knew better than anybody else that she would subjugate herself to his ideas, his way of life, his sexual indifference. Indifference? More accurate would be to call it egotism. Egotism and fear. That ancestral fear of the power of sex, to dominate and destroy, when manipulated by a woman. Ernesto had dispossessed her of everything, even that power she would use in spite of herself, by mere virtue of being a woman. And when he achieved his objective of turning her into a receptacle for his respectable masturbation, she had hated him. In a sense, she still hated him. She would never be able to forgive him for using her body in that way, ignoring and destroying her femininity. But for years, during all of those years in which he slept next to her, turned his back to her in bed, gave her innocent kisses on the cheek, and found pleasure on his own, she had refused to articulate the rage she felt. And it was almost like it didn't exist because she didn't give it a name. But it was there, beyond the silence, in the irritation she felt when she heard his footsteps in the bedroom, his voice in the darkness, in the way her body retracted from his touch. And above all, now that she thought about it, it was a look: the weapon of the weak. As she watched Ernesto dress, eat, speak and play the role of the person he thought made him feel secure and proud of himself, she was analyzing him implacably and without tenderness or compassion. And this he didn't know. . . .

She was surprised to feel no emotion. What she now remembered vaguely was not Horacio, not his face, or even herself, rather the silhouette of two teenagers holding hands, skipping over the rocks and running toward the sea. She remembered her white blouse billowing in the wind, a hand reaching for hers, a masculine scent mixed with brine and seaweed. Faint, imprecise images, like in a dreamscape or as if seen in slow motion; was she that girl holding her shoes in her hand? Seagulls sailing above the sea, Horacio's shadow as he carried her in his arms over the rusted railroad tracks that used to go to Puerto Colombia, because she was afraid of spiders hiding between the rails. She barely remembered anything, she told Maritza smiling. She couldn't even remember how Horacio was dressed, the color of his eyes, or if he was smiling or not. She could see his dark, wavy hair, his long hands, and that was it. No, she could also see his body, now eager, on top of hers. She loved his heat, the scent of his body. She pressed herself against him and they lost themselves on the sandy beach. There they made love a thousand times. Horacio always invented excuses in order to keep her there a little bit longer. They sought out secret hiding places, they had discovered a cave that the sea engulfed when the tide came in. There they would stay the whole afternoon. They were crazy, absurd even.

They loved one another, at least it seemed that way. She had loved him unconditionally, smitten since the first day when she had seen him emerge from the crowd of people applauding. He had chosen her by offering her a white rose he held in his hands. She felt weakened by the intensity of his gaze, surprised by his composure, and his ability to control the audience. Almost immediately he had sent her a ticket and asked to see her after the performance. You never know, Maritza had told her smiling, maybe he is the man of your dreams. But she hadn't wanted to, she thought it might seem improper. But when she turned around to leave, she had found him standing in front of her, staring at her with the same intense passion that had surprised her earlier. They had gone to the Heladería Americana, where she had ordered a Frozo malt that she left untouched. Maritza smiled teasingly and he couldn't stop looking at her. He was tender and thoughtful toward her. He offered her the cherry from his ice cream and as he held it up to her mouth, he caressed her cheek softly.

Laura de Urueta began to laugh. The cherry from his ice cream, how clichéd. But he had an extraordinary voice, and he talked about his life cavalierly but with harsh bitterness. He knew every corner of South America and boasted that he had worked every job. As a boy in Buenos Aires he had sold newspapers and later he had won a tango competition organized by Radio Belgrano. This had allowed him to become a radio host, but it made him realize that he was not cut out for the schedule. What can you do? He liked adventure, travel, and meeting different people. Occasionally when he was out of work he would sing tangos or work as a waiter in neighborhood bars. It was a hard life, but the less predictable the better. That is how he had learned how to become a man and get ahead by any means. She hardly dared to raise her eyes from the Frozo malt, thinking while he spoke with that crass yet sweet-sounding accent, how beautiful he was and what a formidable life he led. Beautiful, yes, despite having forgotten his face, she remembered that Horacio was the most handsome man she had ever met. What became of his life? Doing odd jobs here and there, his life had been reduced to that of a poor shiftless devil. But, who was talking? The woman? Or was it the girl who had listened to him, desiring to make him forget so much misery, trembling from the emotion of knowing that his leg was pressing against hers? . . .

She had been truly lucky to experience her first love with him. She still thought so, even knowing everything she knew. What was the insinuation behind his words on the night they were planning on escaping together, when he was shutting his suitcase? Luck, he had said, if you think about it, might actually be your misfortune. Much later, after she had met Ernesto and gotten married, after Lilian was born and gotten married, she had continued to think that maybe in saying those words Horacio had been referring to all of the hardship they would be forced to confront together: traveling economy class and staying in shoddy hotels. For years, each time she thought of that phrase, she had interpreted it in the same way, without bringing herself to admit that in speaking to her in that way, Horacio had been admonishing her by telling her how difficult it would be for her to find a man who had loved her the way he had. To accept that would have meant recognizing what her mother had revealed to her a week earlier, when she complained that Felipe had forgotten Lilian's birthday. Furious, her mother had confessed to her that it had been none other than Horacio who had called her to let her know of their intention to flee and where they were planning on meeting. But you, maybe you'd prefer that your daughter be miserable with someone like that man, she said. And her mother's eyes had been cold, not malevolent, but cold. On seeing her shock, she had stammered something like an apology. Laura, I am so sorry, I swore I would never tell you.

Faraway the sound of music could be heard and a drum beat interrupted the happy quarrel of the *gaitas*. Laura de Urueta remembered that it was the Saturday of Carnival. That music surprised her, however, because the festivities didn't usually reach the Prado and by that time they should have been on Bolívar Street accompanying the float with the Carnival queen. It didn't matter, after all, but it was so unusual that the drums could resonate so loudly, as though the festivities were approaching the house. Suddenly they stopped. Next to her the telephone rang. She heard Ernesto's voice asking her if she felt okay. Perfect, she answered as she lit a cigarette. Ernesto was happy, he wanted to know if she wanted him to bring her anything. Yes, she said, a charm made of coral. What? Was she crazy? It's for a gift I am making for Lilian's son, she explained. A couple more exchanges and she was able to hang up the phone. Finally she felt at peace. She poured some water into a glass, put the twenty pills she had prepared in her palm, and swallowed them in three gulps. Now she would sleep until the following day, peacefully, without worrying about anything else. She closed her eyes, seeking images to help her sleep. What happened to the drums? They could no longer be heard, but the fly had started to buzz again. Poor fly, maybe it was cold, it was cold in the room. She thought she should get up and look for the Mexican blanket on the divan. She also thought that she had never sat at her father's desk. It had been stored for years in the garage at the Olaya Herrera house accumulating spider webs and attracting termites. She had cleaned it and had it brought to her but she never used it. Her father, a disgraceful man. Once someone had told her a story. Who was it? Ah yes, that man who had spent his entire life reading Dante. My goodness, he knew the whole thing by heart. She and Maritza had found him at the bus stop and he had begun to tell them about how he used to hunt with her father when he was young. An excellent hunter, he said. One day he shot a monkey that was with her baby on a branch in a tree. He never figured out why. But he killed the baby monkey and the mother began to follow him, crying and showing him the dead monkey. After that, the man assured us, your father never hunted again. He sold everything, his gun, and his rifles. Still, he was disgraceful. He had mistresses, her mother repeated, who cheated on him and made a fool out of him. And to her? What had her father been to her? She took walks with him at sunset. He brought her to Washington Park and when she fell while running down the hill, he caught her in his arms. The hill, that feeling of vertigo, came over her again. As though if her father had released her she would have sunk to the bottom of the sea, the sea. Horacio, why didn't she remember his face? At the castle in Salgar there had been children, orphans, who had lollipops. I also lost my parents, Horacio told her. Yes, he certainly did pity himself. What a fraud. How many times had he probably repeated that same song and dance? He said he loved her madly, that it had never happened to him before, "Ché." He spoke of the stars and wore a coral charm around his neck. It would be better to try to sleep; where was the blanket? It was so cold. A crab appeared between the rocks. Crying again, Laura? You're walking backward, like the crab. Don't cry. I'm telling you that your father left for good. Her legs, she had lost them. She was going to remain paralyzed, no, just asleep. And if she took the last ten pills? Suicide is a form of revenge. Where had she read that? Revenge, but, what if she took them? She tried to open her eyes and after much effort was able to make out the glass of water and the bottle. There were some pills on the floor. She had taken the others. Now, oblivion, yes, but no more Ernesto and no more mother. Just sleep, ending it all. But what was that shape hovering outside the window? Someone was trying to get into the room. The window opened. She couldn't believe it. It was Horacio! Horacio was coming closer to her, indifferent to the laughter that accompanied him as he walked through the illuminated circus tent. The brass band began to play, boom da-da-da boom, crash, bang, boom, and in the pink haze of the spotlight she finally saw him. She saw his black satin shoes, his beautifully sequined suit, his calm, fixated eyes, looking at her intensely with that face that now came back to the surface from the depths of years gone by, slandered by forgetting and recovered at that very moment when everything started to become haze and silence, his sad, distant face that of a white clown.

Translated by Brenda Werth

Barranquilla's First Gay Carnival Queen

Gloria Triana, Interview with Lino Fernando

Gloria Triana is one of Colombia's pioneering film documentarians. She comes from an artistic family: her father was the noted Ibagué painter Jorge Elías Triana, and her brother, Jorge Alí Triana, is also a recognized film and theater director, screenwriter, and television producer. She has worked to produce images and narrations that challenge received understandings of indigenous people, peasant smallholders, folk musicians, and former guerrilleros. In a film titled Everyone Knows Their Own Secret (2007), Triana undertakes to allow gay artists to tell their own stories about their effort to make Barranquilla's Carnival tradition their own. In her words, the documentary aims to communicate the experience of being a gay or transgendered person in a city that "despite being open and cosmopolitan, accepts gays as divas during Carnival but the rest of the year discriminates against them as maricas [fags]."[1] Triana seeks to showcase gay artists' sheer talent and their push to turn the city's Carnival into a platform from which to claim respect and recognition.

"Gay men in Barranquilla are not all hairstylists, make-up artists, designers, and choreographers," she emphasizes, "but social exclusion, even in political circles, is such that we did not find professionals who would accept to be interviewed." Even those professionals who are "out" and openly live a gay identity, Triana says, were uncomfortable appearing on camera. In the documentary, she and coscriptwriters Esperanza Palau, also the film's director of photography, and Jaime Olivares, a scholar of Carnival, chose to stress the courage of those gay artists who participated in the film. They were intensely aware of the patterns of homophobic violence that mark Colombian culture. Tragically, Lino Fernando, who tells part of his personal story in the excerpt below, was murdered in his own home before the film's release.

While parades and political demonstrations in favor of people's right to marry whom they choose, to pursue careers and education without concealing their sexual identity, or raise children as gay parents are beginning to become a feature of life in the country's main cities, aggressive discrimination, rape, beatings, and murder remain part of the reality of being gay in Colombia.

Stamp commemorating the win of Vanessa A. Mendoza Bustos, Miss Colombia 2001. In her hometown of Quibdó, and elsewhere, black Colombians celebrated her election as a victory against racism.

LINO FERNANDO—STYLIST

In 1987, after returning to Barranquilla from working at a beauty pageant, I found out that I'd been asked to attend a meeting. And I went to the meeting and they told me: "We're here to tell you that we want you to be the Carnival queen."

The people were all there in the streets, looking at me—I was not rejected, not at all. Just the opposite: Everyone cheered me, everyone told me I looked *divina,* gorgeous. And that was, eighteen years ago, look—when I got off that little bus, Gloria, listen, my legs were shaking. And I put myself in God's hands. . . . I had a friend who called, and I told him, all right, I will go down in history for one thing or the other [voice breaking with emotion]. I'll be the first *loca* stoned in the streets or the first *loca* they cheer for.[2]

And it was the word on the street. They did a poll and they asked people, "Do you like the gay carnival?"—"Yes, they're divine, they're spectacular, why hadn't they been in it before, just divine, they should do it again, they live here, they're from here, they have their carnival queen"—everyone said it. And it turned into headline news in Barranquilla, nobody talked about anything else in the supermarket. "Did you see the *maricas* last night?" . . .

As I told you, people come for three reasons—some for admiration's sake, some because of their identity, others because of lasciviousness. . . .

I spoke to my mother. I told her, I said to her, "I need to tell you something. Something that I don't know how to tell you, and I know that you will be very disappointed in me. You will never have grandchildren from me, I will never marry a girl." She asked me, *"Mijo,* what's wrong? What's happening?" "All right, *Mami,* I am different. I prefer someone who's the same as me, my same sex. I'm gay, and I know that's going to be hard for you." And she said—"Yes, it's going to be very hard for me, but you won't stop being my son." It was terrible. . . .

Translated by Ana María Gómez López

Notes

1. Quotation from http://www.carnavaldebarranquilla.com/divascarnavaleras.html, accessed January 11, 2012. The editors thank Gloria Triana for her assistance with this text.
2. Literally, *loca* means "crazy woman," but it is also a derogatory term used in Colombia for effeminacy in gay men.

Passiflora incarnata.

Nicolás Cortés Alcocer, *Passiflora incarnata*. Botanical drawing produced for the Royal Botanical Expedition to the New Kingdom of Granada (1783–1816), directed by José Celestino Mutis. Passiflora incarnata (A.R.J.B 2023), Archivo Real del Jardín Botánico. Used by permission of Archivo Real del Jardín Botánico, CSIC, Madrid.

Pedro José Figueroa, Portrait of Simón Bolívar with allegorical figure of América, 1819. Oil on canvas, 97 × 75 cm. In Benjamín Villegas, *Once upon a Time There Was Colombia* (Bogotá: Villegas Editores, 2005), 160.

Françoise Désiré Roulin, *African-Inspired Funeral Rites in Lowland Colombia*, 1823. Watercolor on paper, 20 × 27 cm. The artist added a caption: "Bords de la Magdelaine. Le bal du petit ange" ("Banks of the Magdalena. The Little Angel's Dance"). Colección de Arte del Banco de la República, Bogotá.

A well-dressed woman sketched in Medellín in 1852 by British traveler Henry Price. By the time Colombia formally abolished slavery (1851), the vast majority of African-descendant people in the country had been free for generations, as this woman likely was. As part of a digital photography piece of her own, the artist Liliana Angulo photographed Price's watercolor sketch and displayed it in juxtaposition to her own portrait of a young woman in the current generation. Henry Price, *Retrato de una negra*, 1852. Watercolor for the Comisión Corográfica. Courtesy of Liliana Angulo.

Retrato de Lucy Rengifo, nacida en Medellín (*Portrait of Lucy Rengifo, Born in Medellín*), 2007. Photograph by Liliana Angulo. Angulo's piece is part of a series titled *Black Presence* and is explicitly an attempt to make visible the racial politics of the city of Medellín, often described as having a predominantly white population. Courtesy of the artist.

Frederic Edwin Church, *Tamaca Palms*, 1854. Oil on canvas, 68 × 91 cm. This painting was created in the artist's New York studio using sketches he had made along the Magdalena River the previous year, when he retraced part of Humboldt's travels. Note the *champan* in the foreground. Corcoran Collection, National Gallery of Art, Washington, DC, 2014.79.11.

José María Gutiérrez de Alba, *Cucambas*, 1874. Watercolor on paper. Spanish Liberal José María Gutiérrez de Alba traveled widely in Colombia in the 1870s and produced a set of watercolor sketches, including these two images of costumes worn for the religious celebration of Corpus Christi in Mariquita, Tolima, a town located in the central Colombian Andes along the Magdalena River. This image he titled *Cucambas*, a mythical figure that is still popular in carnivals across Colombia today. In Nina S. Friedemann and Jeremy Horner, *Fiestas: Celebrations and Rituals of Colombia* (Bogotá: Villegas Editores, 1995), 54–55.

José María Gutiérrez de Alba, *Matachines*, 1874. Watercolor on paper. In Nina S. Friedemann and Jeremy Horner, *Fiestas: Celebrations and Rituals of Colombia* (Bogotá: Villegas Editores, 1995), 54–55.

Débora Arango, *Masacre del 9 de abril*, 1948. Watercolor on paper, 77 × 57 cm. Arango's depiction is an intense montage combining multiple images of the riots that followed Gaitán's assassination (see parts II and V). A woman—perhaps a prostitute, given that Arango often visited bordellos and red light districts to sketch from life—rings church bells as custodians of the faith are visibly displaced. Soldiers run a victim through with their bayonets. "Viva Gaitán" appears on a placard above rioters who surround the leader's dead body, while, on the left, the assassin's corpse is dragged away. Used by permission of Museo de Arte Moderno, Medellín.

Andoque community resource map, drawn by indigenous anthropologist Levy Andoke. The Andoque community was one of many Amazonian groups, along with the Bora, Huitoto, Matapí, Miraña, Muinane, Nonuya, Okaina, and Yukunaí, that were subjected to forced labor and extraordinary violence during the rubber boom of the 1910s and 1920s, described in Jose Eustasio Rivera's *La Vorágine* (see part I). In Maria Clara van der Hammen, *The Indigenous Resguardos of Colombia: Their Contribution to Conservation and Sustainable Forest Use* (Amsterdam: NC IUCN, 2003). Courtesy of Levy Andoke.

Romance Tourism

Felicity Schaeffer-Grabiel

Colombians from many different kinds of backgrounds migrate to the United States, as well as to European countries, and they perform different kinds of labor on arrival. One unusual category of migrants comprises women who travel to the United States or to European countries as the fiancés of men who court them via the Internet, or who meet those who travel to Colombia on "romance tours." According to the anthropologist Felicity Schaeffer-Grabiel, these are women who perform emotional labor, who invest time in self-preparation, and who are exporters of a particular vision of femininity. She describes women's participation as "self-marketing," and she emphasizes that women who work in romance tourism understand plastic surgery and other technologies of beauty as tools to be used in the pursuit of multiple goals.

Schaeffer-Grabiel parallels women's ability to manipulate their appearance with their ability to interact with foreign men via the Internet—both, she says are strategies women use as they navigate their lives. Apart from economic gain, they are also seeking affirmation, pleasure, and the possibility of understanding themselves as modern people. Being modern, to them, is being a "go-getter," a person poised to take advantage of opportunities. They are taking initiative in their lives. Often, they are also fairly young: theirs are dreams of the future.

I followed various couples on dates during and after the tour and spent the evening with them as the translator. I accompanied an African American man, Seth (who is a taxicab driver in his mid-forties) and his Afro-Colombian date, Celia, to a restaurant that catered to tourists. During our meal together, Celia excitedly told us that she was going to have a liposuction procedure done, even though, as Seth reminded her, this was a dangerous surgery. Celia explained that she had saved up money for several months to afford the $1,300 for the liposuction (she would also use money that had been given to her by a previous U.S. boyfriend). She told us that her sister, who is now married to a man in the United States and has had a successful liposuction procedure, contributed to her decision. While Seth and I both told her that her body was perfect, she explained that while she liked her body, she wanted to improve it by thinning her stomach and fortifying her behind. She said, "If I have the opportunity to change something about my body, to improve myself, then I will. Just like Seth made the choice to come to Cali [to the Tour], I also decided to improve my life by choosing to do the surgery. It's an investment in myself."

Celia's desire, like that of many other women I interviewed, to invest in her body with the hopes of improving her chances of finding someone, indicates how women use beauty for their own aspirations and to willingly transform themselves into marketable products of exchange. Women described having to submit photos and physical descriptions with job applications. And women thirty or older complained they had a much harder time getting jobs and attracting foreign men who went after the young girls. These women thus participate in a well-worn development narrative, similar to the one for which many men congratulate themselves regarding their journey to Latin America: if you can change your life, you should, if you don't, you deserve the consequences that await you. Modern states encourage a citizenry organized around self-help, or what Foucault labels self-cultivation, because it shifts the gaze from larger social critique (revolution) and the state, to the self. Working on the body is equated with the embrace of an entrepreneurial spirit in which women's bodies become the object of self-improvement, self-help, and the promise of a democratic future. Hard work on oneself is equated with one's entrance into modern subjectivity and citizenship, where one can become transformed into the desired image and lifestyle. The shift in Cali from any reliance on the state—as a corrupt and violent force—has shifted to the arena of science, new technologies, the marketplace, consumption (rather than production), and individuals as the arena for change and mobility.

For Celia, her soft voice, graceful gestures (reminiscent of women groomed for beauty pageants), and desire for an enlarged behind articulate a complex desire for a more pliable construction of identity, ethnicity, and sexuality that has both local and global currency, that situates her subjectivity as both embodied and translatable in a broader context. Depending on the spaces and social situations Celia moves through, she feels that she can rework the meanings of her race and class. Because the tours are held at expensive hotels with men searching for "high quality" women (and the class implications that accompany their desire for quality), women must upgrade their bodies to blend into these tourist zones so they are not mistaken to be prostitutes or "green card sharks." Yet at the same time, these women garner currency in their local context and with foreign men for the embodied signs of authentic difference and hypersexuality. Perhaps influenced by beauty pageant culture, where women are groomed for respectable femininity, Celia alters her body in ways that confound the boundaries between sex work and marriage, increasing the visible markers of class, ethnic capital, and sexual appeal toward the goal of local mobility and/or movement across borders.

Women's sense of their bodies as pliable commodities is also a response to the foreign male's, and especially African American men's, erotic desire for large buttocks and a curvy body. . . . 20 percent of the men at the Cali Tour were African Americans (including two from Europe). For Afro-Colombian women, emphasizing their physique may be more complex than merely conformity to the demands of the tourist market and patriarchal desire; it is also a chance to pleasurably accentuate characteristics (such as large butts) that have been degraded by mainstream notions of ideal beauty in Colombia, characterized by whiteness, straight hair, and large breasts. Accustomed to being scrutinized on the grounds of physical beauty, these women capitalize on new cosmetic technologies and foreign configurations of desire to display their motivation and self-enterprising spirit in the face of limited opportunities for jobs, travel, and mobility at home. . . .

It is also apparent that a new language of privilege and modernity is being articulated through cosmetic alterations. It is through one's adherence to the norms of heterosexual femininity and male desire inscribed onto the body, rather than merely skin color, that one acquires a new language of global ascendancy. Cosmetic advances rearticulate long-enduring colonial legacies of racial difference as biologically based to create identities that are pliable, "democratically" available, and reliant on innovative technologies. Being civilized is equated with technologies of self-cultivation, with working hard, taking a risk, and jumping at opportunities that come your way. This is directly related to the role of U.S. state immigration in discouraging citizenship to those who may become a public charge, in other words, accepting only those whose enterprising spirit will contribute to the surplus labor of the nation.

They Are Using Me as Cannon Fodder

Flaco Flow and Melanina

Military service is mandatory for young Colombian men. However, active-duty soldiers are disproportionately from poor families. Draftees who have graduated from high school are rarely sent to combat, often serving only a year and benefiting from lighter assignments, while those recruited without a diploma serve for eighteen- to twenty-four-month periods, often in conflict areas. Given the lack of employment opportunities in rural Colombia, poor recruits regularly chose to continue beyond their draft time and accept postings in remote areas, where they face high levels of danger. The following song by rappers Flaco Flow and Melanina highlights issues of race and class while raising universal moral questions.

What hides behind the weeds
Shooting arrows of steel?
Until becoming a cat
More dangerous than Tony Montana
Remember *Mission Impossible* and Al Pacino
Kill or be killed

Enough with the bombs and explosions!
They counterattack with arrows and spears
He looks at his AK before letting it rip
His trigger finger in time with the drumbeat
Noises come from the swamp, a serenade
Straight ahead a straight file line marches
The sounds of rocks being crushed
Stock being packed and shipped off
Corruption, ambition, more than money
Hit you in the mouth and leave you bruised
It's the knight taking out
The tower, the queen and the pawn
With his spear

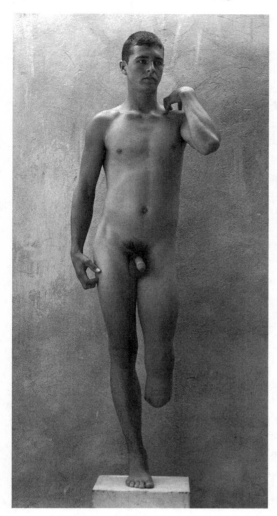

Miguel Ángel Rojas, *Quiebramales*, 2005. Large swaths of Colombia are covered by land mines, making the country one of the most mine-affected countries in the world. Soldiers such as José Antonio Ramos, posed here as Michelangelo's *David*, often bear the brunt of this invisible weapon. http://www.sicardi.com/artists/miguel-ngel-rojas/artists-artist-works#. Courtesy of the artist and Sicardi Gallery.

A lot of people try to talk to the jaguar dressed in a tiger suit
But you better shut your mouth or it all might blow
It's just that simple.

It's the weeds
It's the weeds that hide my face
That make me dirty
The reason for my pain
For my sorrow . . .

Some fight and others pray
Some hunt and others are prey
I'm a fighter, I no longer feel pain
Bitterness has healed my wounds
Fuck the government and the ruling class
Because my life ain't worth shit to them
The bullets shoot overhead
While my mother sits at home praying and praying
Crying for me every day
Eenie, meeny, miny, moe
Somebody got killed today
Thank God it wasn't me!
That's how this country works
That's how they treat me

Roses die in the countryside
The city weeps, terrified
Drowning out calls for justice
The noose choking it around its neck
Militia gangs poisoning it with hate
The cruelty of injustice everywhere
No more war, what is it good for?
Politicians get bodyguards
When there is a problem you can find them hiding in their dens
Like it's every man for himself
They don't know anything about how the people suffer
Pain runs so deep in my nation
Condemned to live life like this
Because of hypocrite politicians
Egotistical, oppressive traffickers
Soon enough, the truth will shame them all
Enough is enough! (Babylon!)

Fuck it!
They're using me for cannon fodder
I call my family and they got nothing to eat
They don't even pay me for this suicide mission
I go out with my military ID
And there ain't no jobs on the street
Fuck war, this motherfucking war!

You'll kill me and take my land
Some start it, others pay for it
The people supply the victims, and others supply the cure
The poor are the ones getting hurt
Paying for it with tears running down our face

That's how this country works
That's how they treat me

They have awakened my animal instinct
They have awakened my killer instinct
They made me fire the gun
What karma?
My soul has been stained
Oh my God!
I killed a man
Oh my God!
My hands are covered in blood
They congratulate me for killing a man
For leaving a child without a father or a name
A mother without a child
A church without a cross

That's how this country works
That's how they treat me

Who is Melanina?
He was the one singing this song
If anyone asks, tell them it was me
Who showed up? Me
Melanina spilled it
Who showed up? Everything I sing I sing for you
Who showed up? The messenger doesn't matter
It's that the message came across
The show is over
The monster is gone
Please, no more war!
Bang, bang!

Translated by Julián Roberts Espinel

V

Violence

Colombians wrestle with a painful past: here even more than elsewhere in Latin America, political life has been marked by successive waves of violence. Some have seen this as evidence of a deep savagery within Colombians themselves. That sentiment is often expressed in the voice of class snobbery, as if savagery were limited to the uneducated poor, whose ranks have yielded most of both perpetrators and victims. Such stereotypes can compound the scars of violence itself. Other kinds of observers have seen violence as a symptom of the uncontestable fact that the nation's political system has been oligarchic for centuries. On the latter view, public violence is one product of a sum of obstacles that prevent ordinary people from gaining access to economic and political structures that might improve their lives.

Whatever perspective they begin with, many ask what links the violence inherited from the early colonial period, or the Liberal-versus-Conservative wars of the nineteenth century, to everything that has followed. Those focused on the weakness of the Colombian state will find it significant that Gonzalo Jiménez de Quesada found it nearly impossible to bend other conquistadors to his will. Those concerned about the way memories of violence pass from generation to generation will note that a man conscripted by one side or the other in the War of the Thousand Days (1899–1902) might well have had parents who saw fighting in the wars of 1876 and 1885; a grandfather on either side of the so-called War of the Supremos in 1840–42 (or a grandmother who followed the troops); great-grandparents (*bisabuelos*) caught between Bolívar's army and the Royalists; and great-great-grandparents (*tatarabuelos*) who would have remembered the Comunero revolt of 1781 and its repressive aftermath. In Colombia, as in many national contexts, family histories include narrations of violence.

For the entirety of the country's history, military veterans have made political claims regardless of which side they served on in the multiple civil wars—the fact of having served gave them access to political actors wealthier than themselves. Party bosses and former comrades-in-arms had the prerogatives and responsibilities that went with a clientelist system, and aspects of this vertical chain survive in the present. A more recent phenomenon is civilian victims' ability to make demands on the state. In Colombia, the political category of "victims," which includes rural people forced to leave their homes, women who have suffered sexual attack, and the families of those killed, is horrifically large. Three points are worth emphasizing. First, public understandings of victims' lives is rooted in Colombians' knowledge of atrocities across generations. There have been countless massacres, with children and the elderly among the dead. Journalists' accounts, photographs, and person-to-person narrations of terror circulate in the national consciousness. Second, "victims" and "perpetrators" are political categories with particular and shifting histories. Capitalized, "La Violencia" still refers to the years 1946–64 (particularly the period between 1946 and 1953), when armed bands linked to the Conservative and Liberal parties attacked not so much one another as entire villages perceived to be political opponents. That violence intertwined with the Cold War years, which saw the formation of guerrilla armies. In the 1960s–1980s, and into the present, whole communities found that they could be taken as enemy targets. Into the 1990s, Cold War logics and Drug War logics increasingly overlapped, with both fueled by money and arms flowing primarily from the United States. Narco-traffickers and private armies teamed up with armed combatants of various stripes, including paramilitary units that had the direct or indirect support of the Colombian Armed Forces. Third, armed combatants from the 1990s to the 2010s have not competed for state power so much as for local dominance, negotiating power, and the ability to capture economic rents coming from the drug economy or landowning. Perhaps most importantly, atrocities have been committed across the spectrum. Massacres, attacks on civilians, land theft, and the use of child soldiers can be laid at the feet of guerrillas and paramilitary commanders alike. Other kinds of scandals have proliferated within the military itself, chief among them a set of documented overlaps between military and paramilitary in the spheres of logistics, intelligence, and personal connections. Colombians' hopes for peace are boundless and varied, but so too are their memories of violence.

Captains and Criminals

Juan Rodríguez Freile

For more than fifty years Colombian literary critics have described the extraordinary text known as "El Carnero" by Juan Rodríguez Freile (1566–ca. 1642) as a foundational text for understanding Colombian national identity. Although the original 1638 text disappeared, manuscript copies circulated for more than two centuries. Six of these have survived in the archives. "El Carnero" first appeared in print in 1859, and since then more than thirty editions have been produced, including the Instituto Caro y Cuervo version edited by Mario Germán Romero (Bogotá, 1997), from which the following short excerpt is taken. Transcriptions and titles can vary. As "Carnero" expert Darío Achury pointed out in the 1970s, "Nobody has rightfully explained why it is that instead of the extended and prolix original title that the author gave to his work, posterity knows it by the outlandish name of El Carnero." The original title, extended indeed, translates as follows (although given multiple extant copies that date from the colonial period with several "original" titles, determining the exact wording is probably impossible):

> *Conquest and Discovery of the New Kingdom of Granada of the West Indies of the Ocean Sea and the Founding of the City of Santa Fe de Bogotá, the First in this Kingdom, where was Established a Royal Court of Appeals and Chancellery, Being the Capital, It Became an Archbishopric: Recounting its Discovery and Some Civil Wars among its Natives; Its Customs and People and Whereof Came the Celebrated Name of El Dorado; The Generals, Captains, and Soldiers that Came to Conquer It, With all of the Presidents, Judges, and Inspectors that are part of the Royal Court of Appeals. The Archbishops, Prebends and Dignitaries of this Holy Church Cathedral, from the Year 1539, when it was Founded, until 1636, at this Writing; With Some Cases that have Happened in the Kingdom, Which are set Down in History as Examples, And not to be Imitated, in damage to Conscience.*

In this litany, why is conquest first and discovery second? And what links "Carnero" to the title inscription? Darío Achury has unearthed a range of possibilities: that "Carnero" is a reference to the leather bindings of the old copies that circulated in Bogotá, that it references the sexual scandals that pervade the text, or that "Carnero" was a word that meant a potters' field or common grave. This last possibility may be a way of emphasizing the violence in the text, as Rodríguez Freile traces a chain of adulteries, robberies, murders, lies, and conspiracies. In the following short extract Freile makes the conquistadors seem close to ungovernable, first because he mentions a murder in an almost offhand way and second because the possibility of an edict protecting Indians from encomendero *abuses causes a near-riot.*

Doctor Andrés Venero de Leiva governed the New Kingdom for ten years with great Christian piety. His indomitable wife, Doña María Dondegardo, greatly aided him with works of charity, such that no one left his presence without consolation. The president maintained peace and justice for everyone, putting great zeal into the conversion of the natives, having them to settle together in their villages, and encouraging the construction of churches for them. He sent a judge to visit the land and to encourage the native population and to settle their differences. His governorship was quite pleasant and they called it the Golden Age.

At this time in the city of Tunja, an *encomendero* from Chita, one Bravo de Rivera, had killed Don Jorge Soto and the president went there to see to it personally. Meanwhile, the edict that I mentioned earlier, regarding the personal service of these natives and how they should not be overburdened, offended, or mistreated, was proclaimed, charging all to see it through "under penalty of two hundred lashes."[1]

Several conquistador captains were gathered on the corner of the Calle Real when this was announced, and the first to speak out was Captain Zorro, who tossed his cape over his left shoulder and yelled, "By God, my captains, we're all as good as whipped! That damned thief got this land by luck! Follow me, gents, 'cause I'm going to cut him to pieces!" The gang set off for the administration buildings with their capes thrown back and their hands on their swords, shouting insults.

The Governor, Don Gonzalo Jiménez de Quesada, was under the portals of the plaza, speaking with Captain Alonso de Olaya, the cripple. Although he had heard the town crier, he didn't know what the proclamation was about; but he soon found out from the shouts of the first captains, leading the others in an uproar. He left Captain Olaya to join the others and, as fast as he could, ran up to the council chamber where he found the judge Melchor Pérez de Artiaga, held responsible for giving the order while the president was absent, as I mentioned. The Governor found him with a partisan[2] in his hands and yelled, "The staff! Get the King's staff of office! Now's not the time for partisans!"

It was said that the president's wife, Doña María, had entered the hall in hopes that her presence might avert some of the damage, and that he handed the staff to her. Some of the captains went to the window of the chamber with their swords drawn and raised, yelling, "Throw us the thief! Turn over that scoundrel!" and other insults. The other captains went up to the hall where they found Governor Jiménez de Quesada at the door. He told them, in the name of His Majesty, not to enter until they found out the truth. The captains angrily repeated the penalty in the edict. "I ordered no such thing!" the judge shouted back to them, which quieted the captains somewhat. The president's wife entered and summoned them to her quarters; those who were waiting at the window were told of what was happening, such that they all calmed down. They eventually blamed the secretary, the secretary blamed the scribe, and he blamed the quill, which brought an end to the hubbub.

Translated by Timothy F. Johnson

Notes

1. Rodríguez Freile had described a decree that Indians should not be used to carry merchandise long distances, in place of mules.
2. A partisan is a pole weapon similar to a halberd.

War to the Death

Simón Bolívar

On June 15, 1813, from his headquarters in Trujillo, Venezuela, Simón Bolívar (1783–1830) issued a statement to his fellow Venezuelans that became famous as a proclamation of "War to the Death." Opposing "Americans" to "Spaniards" radically simplified the emotional and political entanglements of real life, and sowing terror made Bolívar's lightning campaign more effective, allowing him to take Caracas in three months. But who the Americans were was unclear in geographic terms. The patriot armies would fight to create a nation officially called "Gran Colombia," including the present-day countries of Colombia, Venezuela, Ecuador, and Panama. Later the term "New Granada" was used for roughly the same region. When Bolívar speaks of "Colombian soil" in this text, it is not clear what exactly he means. Was it territory claimed by the Congress of Gran Colombia? The state of Cundinamarca? The Venezuelan Confederacy? Any definition would generate immediate dissent, as happened when Bolívar was victorious in Caracas, shortly after issuing the below decree.

The next year, 1814, dealt Bolívar a second defeat and was a year of massacres on both sides. The war's intensity began to lessen in 1816, but executions and arbitrary violence marked the war until 1820, when Bolívar and the Spanish general Pablo Murillo signed a treaty—later celebrated as having placed a limit on the cruelty—again in Trujillo, the same town where the original decree had been issued.

It is worth noting that firing squads were deployed against women as well as men. Patriot officers had both españoles and españolas killed, and, on the other side, more than forty women were executed on Spanish orders. Policarpa Salavarrieta, known as "La Pola," is the best-known and is a reference point for Colombians in the present; others are all but forgotten. The charge against Josefa Conde, an enslaved woman, was that of helping her owner supply rebel troops. Carlota Armero was killed for "refusing to marry a Spaniard and saying publicly that she would rather die than be married to tyrants."[1] Armero's language echoed the nativist sentiment articulated in Bolívar's 1813 decree.

Beyond its military purpose, "War to the Death" articulated a basis for legitimacy: Americans against Spaniards, the space of a continent, the power of a liberating army against political divisions. *In November 1819 Bolívar referred to this aspect of the decree in a letter to Francisco de Paula Santander: "You should remember the violent means I have had to employ to achieve the small success that has kept us alive. To bring together four armies—that have helped liberate us—it was necessary to declare war to the death." Within a few years, the Bolivarian idea that military legitimacy trumped political factionalism had taken on a new shape, and his allies hoped to see him named "president for life"—which did not elicit any more consensus among Creoles in 1826 than it would have in 1813. Bolívar died in Santa Marta in 1830, having seen the Union of Colombia, Venezuela, and Ecuador begin to come apart and having seen his political enemies come to power in Bogotá and Caracas.*

SIMON BOLIVAR, *Liberator of Venezuela, Brigadier of the Union, General in Chief of the Northern Army*

Venezuelans: An army of your brothers, sent by the Sovereign Congress of New Granada, has come to liberate you. Having expelled the oppressors from the provinces of Mérida and Trujillo, it is now among you.

We are sent to destroy the Spaniards, to protect the Americans, and to reestablish the republican governments that once formed the Confederation of Venezuela. The states defended by our arms are again governed by their former constitutions and tribunals, in full enjoyment of their liberty and independence, for our mission is designed only to break the chains of servitude which still shackle some of our towns, and not to impose laws or exercise acts of dominion to which the rules of war might entitle us.

Moved by your misfortunes, we have been unable to observe with indifference the afflictions you were forced to experience by the barbarous Spaniards, who have ravished you, plundered you, and brought you death and destruction. They have violated the sacred rights of nations. They have broken the most solemn agreements and treaties. In fact, they have committed every manner of crime, reducing the Republic of Venezuela to the most frightful desolation. Justice therefore demands vengeance, and necessity compels us to exact it. Let the monsters who infest Colombian soil, who have drenched it in blood, be cast out forever; may their punishment be equal to the enormity of their perfidy, so that we may eradicate the stain of our ignominy and demonstrate to the nations of the world that the sons of America cannot be offended with impunity.

Despite our just resentment toward the iniquitous Spaniards, our magnanimous heart still commands us to open to them for the last time a path to reconciliation and friendship; they are invited to live peacefully among us, if they will abjure their crimes, honestly change their ways, and cooperate with us in destroying the intruding Spanish government and in the reestablishment of the Republic of Venezuela.

Any Spaniard who does not, by every active and effective means, work against tyranny in behalf of this just cause, will be considered an enemy and punished; as a traitor to the nation, he will inevitably be shot by a firing squad. On the other hand, a general and absolute amnesty is granted to those who come over to our army with or without their arms, as well as to those who render aid to the good citizens who are endeavoring to throw off the yoke of tyranny. Army officers and civil magistrates who proclaim the government of Venezuela and join with us shall retain their posts and positions; in a word, those Spaniards who render outstanding service to the State shall be regarded and treated as Americans.

And you Americans who, by error or treachery, have been lured from the paths of justice, are informed that your brothers, deeply regretting the error of your ways, have pardoned you as we are profoundly convinced that you cannot be truly to blame, for only the blindness and ignorance in which you have been kept up to now by those responsible for your crimes could have induced you to commit them. Fear not the sword that comes to avenge you and to sever the ignoble ties with which your executioners have bound you to their own fate. You are hereby assured, with absolute impunity, of your honor, lives, and property. The single title, "Americans," shall be your safeguard and guarantee. Our arms have come to protect you, and they shall never be raised against a single one of you, our brothers.

This amnesty is extended even to the very traitors who most recently have committed felonious acts, and it shall be so religiously applied that no reason, cause, or pretext will be sufficient to oblige us to violate our offer, however extraordinary and extreme the occasion you may give to provoke our wrath.

Spaniards and Canary Islanders, you will die, though you be neutral, unless you actively espouse the cause of America's liberation. Americans, you will live, even if you have trespassed.

General Headquarters, Trujillo, June 15, 1813.

The 3rd [year].

Simón Bolívar

Note

1. Martha Lux, *Mujeres patriotas y realistas entre dos órdenes: Discursos, estrategias y tácticas en la guerra, la política y el comercio (Nueva Granada, 1790–1830)* (Bogotá: Universidad de la Andes, Facultad de Ciencias Sociales, 2014), 117.

A Girl's View of War in the Capital

Soledad Acosta de Samper

A young woman's diary provides a direct narration of what it was like to live in Bogotá during one of the many nineteenth-century wars that convulsed Colombia. Twenty-one-year-old Soledad Acosta (1833–1913) is well-read and passionate about politics—she copies poetry in both English and Spanish into her diary entries, reports on troop movements, and worries about the man she hopes to marry. Later in life, as Acosta de Samper, she became a prolific writer and publisher, producing novels and dramatic works, biographies, essays, and reportage. A feminist, she advocated women's education and personal freedom. The man she married publicly supported her writing career and supported women's education—that was José María Samper Agudelo, the intellectual and Liberal Party politician who is here described as one of the "brave and splendid" young upper-class men from Bogotá (cachacos) who joined forces with the Conservatives to defeat an insurrection led by General José María Melo. Melo supported career army men and the city's artisans, who favored protectionism against cheap imported goods, special privileges for militia men, and a rough egalitarianism in political life. For Acosta, daughter of an Independence-era general and an educated Scottish mother, an insurrection that promised to favor self-made military men and artisans over propertied families was a thing to be feared—although part of what comes through in the diary is how exciting it all was.

April 20

Finally, faithful diary, I find my way back to you. Oh! How many trials and tribulations have I suffered these last few days! Wars, agitation, sorrows, terror! I've even been locked up in the recesses of a monastery! My God, is this life? My God, why do you leave my wretched country at the hands of savage military men? Lord, is it to have us know the pains and misfortunes of life and not love our earthly dwelling so much? . . . .[1] How much can happen in four days, how much can change in our hearts, our lives. Woe is me! On Sunday the world smiled upon me, there was no cloud in my sky, what was yet to come in my life was sowed with flowers and pleasure—I thought my future was blessed! . . . . . . And now. . . . . . . Now [. . .]

331

Soldiers in the Cauca Valley, ca. 1862. Engraving by Alphonse de Neuville, from a sketch by traveler Charles Saffray. "Nothing could be more extravagant," wrote Saffray, "than those groups of men, of all colors and sizes, equipped in the most grotesque possible way." In Eduardo Acevedo Latorre, *Geografía pintoresca de Colombia: La Nueva Granada vista por dos viajeros franceses del siglo XIX* (Bogotá: Litografía Arco, 1968), 55.

April 21

Now that I find myself alone, if only for a moment, I will write everything that has happened in the past few days. . . . . . . Woe is me! How can I speak of this, my head is heavy with such terrible anguish and my spirit is a chaos that I barely comprehend [. . .]

On Monday, at what must have been five in the morning, I was jolted awake by cannon shots in the distance, and a terrible chill ran through my body because the image that came to mind was that of *** in the most terrible danger.[2] Barely dressed, I ran or rather I flew, to my room, and I rushed into the balcony window to see that the shots we had heard came from cannons I could see in the plaza. . . . . . . A dreadfully morbid despair seized my soul! What was happening? I saw people running and the cannons kept going off, and people were talking and rushing around and asking me questions, but I couldn't understand anything, I couldn't hear anything, it was as if I were in a horrible dream and I couldn't understand what was happening. The street emptied and the cannon stopped booming. General Barriga

Forced recruits in the Cauca Valley, ca. 1862. Engraving by Alphonse de Neuville, from a sketch by Charles Saffray. Describing this scene, Saffray remembered that the man who held the rope had assured him that it was only a precaution and that within a week the recruits would be "excellent soldiers, possessed of esprit de corps, and without desires to flee." In Eduardo Acevedo Latorre, *Geografía pintoresca de Colombia: La Nueva Granada vista por dos viajeros franceses del siglo XIX* (Bogotá: Litografía Arco, 1968), 35.

appeared at the window of the Palace. We asked him if this was a revolution. He answered, "I believe it is!" What a reply for a Government Minister [*Secretario del Gobierno*] to make! . . . . Hours passed. . . . . . . We finally learned what it was all about. General Melo, the troop commander, had revolted with all the armed forces and had proclaimed Obando Dictator, but when he refused that title, he was placed under arrest at the Palace with all his ministers and the *evil* Melo now commanded in the city, at the head of both the troops and the Democráticos. . . . . . We later learned that they had simultaneously entered the homes of all the Senators and Representatives to imprison them. . . . . . . Woe is me! What immense pain, my God, what fear took over my heart! I finally asked if they had gone to the home of Murillo (for there lived my beloved) . . . . The answer was for me a life sentence either of reprieve or of endless despair!. . . . . . . I was told the rebels had been there and had broken everything in the house; the doors had been torn down, the windows had been shot out, but they had found no one. . . . . . . I breathed again. . . . . . But I heard too that they were searching everywhere for *** and his friend. . . . . . .

[. . .]
Better sit . . . .
And think thee safe though far away
Than have thee near me in danger.[3]
[. . .]

Are you thinking of me? Yes, because you love me, yes, because you adore me. Without you everything is sorrowful, dark. Without you I live like a plant without leaves, like a bed without a stream, like a mountain without sweet birds to sing and comfort it. What is life without you, my beloved? What can I wish for, what can I think of if you are not with me, if I don't have the hope of seeing you? And now. . . . . . . now. . . . . . My God, what dismal affliction. In the street, I hear the Sentinel's rifle rattle as he moves, and it reminds me of the horrible unease I feel. How different were my thoughts eight days ago today, my God, on Holy Friday. I saw you before me, and filled with happiness I could gaze at you here! Eight days, and how much has my life's aspect changed. The clock strikes ten-thirty. I am very tired. Sadness weakens my body and agitates my soul. I will deliver myself to sleep's embrace. . . . . . . My ***, my poor beloved, what can he be doing now? . . . .

↳ what r the ⚹'s?

September 30
  All afternoon I have been embroidering ribbons with goldwork to send to La Mesa on behalf of the Ladies. They carry inscriptions such as "From the Ladies to their brave defenders," "To the young men of the Union," "Victory always protects the brave," "To our Patriot Liberators." To General López, París, Mendoza, and Julio Arboleda, I am also sending ribbons with different inscriptions, addressed to Justo. I purchased all of the materials with my own money, which I have saved in these last few months. Sofía was here and helped me. I called for María and she also came, so we will be able to send plenty if we work hard until the middle of next week. My secret hope is that *** gets one embroidered by my hand. [. . .]

November 25
  Days have passed and I haven't written. . . . . . . my consternation and anxiety have not allowed me to write down, until now, events in Bogotá.
  Everyone said that there would be a battle on the 22nd. At ten o'clock in the morning the Briceño girls arrived, and we took a spyglass to the house

we had gone to the day before to look out over the Savannah. We could make out Melo's troops on Chamisera road—they were heading to the bridge at Bosa, where the Constitutionalists were. Melo had gathered all his forces to attack and hold the bridge. He had four hundred men. The cavalry was well dressed and mounted—there were so many Melistas that we were filled with alarm, and we couldn't see the Constitutionalists because we couldn't see the Bosa bridge from that house. At noon we left and went to another house in Santa Barbara, very close to where the Briceños live. Although we did not know the owner, in times of war everything is allowed, and we went in to ask her for permission to look out over the plain. Our good-quality spyglass served as a passport, as she could also look through it. The poor Lady had her husband, her son, and a brother in the Constitutionalists' ranks. She welcomed us in and took us to the balcony window, from which we could see the bridge and the troops perfectly. Melo continued his advance and went into battle formation to attack our men. There seemed to us to be so few of them that we were filled with fear and dread. We returned home at one-thirty in the afternoon and organized ourselves to go back to witness the combat and learn what would be our fate, as we thought this would be the decisive battle.

At two o'clock we heard the first cannon shot. On the road to Santa Barbara we came across one of the Acevedos, who was very alarmed because she said our men could not hold out and defend the bridge. When we got to the house the balcony was full of people who had come to watch. On the bridge we could not make out who was fighting, there was so much smoke and the cannons went off relentlessly. . . . . . . I was seized by a grief and a despair so great that I could barely hold back tears. I looked again through the spyglass, and was reassured to see more Constitutionalists coming on the road from the town of Bosa, and entering into formation around the bridge. Nevertheless the cannon blasts were continuing, and the battle was hard-fought. The Melistas were almost at the bridge, and that was a terrible moment for all present. . . . . . . We all were in fear but nobody raised an alarm, we did not dare to *speak* our fear. . . . . . . I looked again. Some had binoculars. Then, a shout was heard . . . *run, run.* . . . . . . I saw a horse run through the middle of the fight, and then another, and another, and a whole squadron followed them up to Chamisera. *The Melistas were defeated! The Constitutionalists have triumphed!*[4] But what is this, cannon blasts are still being fired, the smoke envelops them. But our men are this side of the bridge, and the combat is happening in one of the small houses there. . . . . . . Those who ran came to a halt, reorganized themselves, some went into formation. But no one dared to come close. There was a ceasefire for a bit. . . . . . .

My God! The horror! *Who has died, who remains among the living?* was the call of my soul. The fighting began again, but this time it didn't last long. All of Melo's army began to retreat little by little, then they picked up the pace and ran. María sent for news of the battle from time to time, and I, my handwriting unsteady from my trembling hand, wrote to her what I saw. It was five o'clock when they retreated. At six o'clock, Luis Anzola escorted us home, convinced that the Constitutionalists had claimed a victory, which if not decisive was at least an important one. But what did we know about what might have happened? Who had perished there? Who knows how long it will be until we will be able to know. . . . . . . At seven I was in the balcony window when a group of Demócraticos, louts, and soldiers (I have forgotten to mention that we had seen them leave with Mercado, Posadas, Góngora, La Rosa, Chocontana, and others on the road to Bosa). These *devils* who came from Las Cruces started chanting *long live the Provisional Government and General Melo, down with López, Mosquera, and the Gólgotas,*[5] and they shot off fireworks and rang the bells. Despite having witnessed the battle, despite having seen the defeat of the evildoers, I was horrified and afraid, and I let myself be overcome by pain.

On the morning of the 23rd, we were going to go to the Briceños' house when we were told that our men were at Tres Esquinas. I received a slip of paper from Praxidis, who said that the Constitutionalists were at Las Cruces, and that [our troops] had gone up to her house shouting *Long live the Constitution!* The Melistas were in arms at the Plaza, on the balconies of the houses and the neighboring alleyways, patrolling the streets. Melo had sent his whole army to defend Bogotá. They said that at three o'clock there would be a battle in Egipto. [. . .][6]

Castro left with more than two thousand men to attack López, who was in Tres Esquinas. The Demócraticos insulted those that were at the Egipto Church, and from that block they fired their muskets and they shot back with their rifles. Bullets were coming down in the patios and fell on this house. They said that P. Gutiérrez, the leader of those in the hills, didn't have anything to give his soldiers and that the shopkeepers wouldn't sell him anything. The Ladies immediately sent them bread and food of all kinds. We sent the maids with provisions and tobacco. There they were told that very few of our men had died in combat at Bosa, and that most of Melo's people completely crumbled. They say that Ignacio Rovira, the only one we know, was killed there, and that Henao, José M. París, and others were wounded but not gravely.

At three o'clock we began to hear gunfire at Las Cruces. We went to the back patios, where we could hear better and see how some of our men up on some of the hills shot at the Melistas. The rooftops were filled with people watching [. . .] the shooting continued incessantly, and from time to time cannon blasts. Cheers shouted by the Constitutionalists could be heard across the hills [. . .] I could not stand it any longer and I went to my room, where I spent the bitterest hours and felt the most terrible anguish of my life. . . . . . .

Very early on the morning of the 24th, I wrote to the Briceño girls to ask if they knew the results from the battle the day before. They answered back that they did not know anything, and that although the fighting had taken place so close to them they had not been able to find out anything, and felt great dismay. I then wrote to Bolivia on a piece of paper, thinking that she would know everything and be right about things. I received a letter filled with lamentations, where she wrote that many people had died, that those who were wounded had no hope, and many exaggerations that not only filled me with fear but also were totally unfounded. But at least the name of he whom I felt such interest for was not among the list of the dead or wounded, and that gave me comfort. A thousand falsehoods ran through the streets, but I had hope. . . . . . . Finally Mercedes sent a letter with Justo for me to read, which filled us with happiness, since even though the Melistas had suffered defeat, there had been many who had been captured as prisoners the day before, and they didn't say that anyone we knew had been killed. In the afternoon a woman brought a paper from my ***! It was then that I was joyful. . . . . . . The words of *** were written on a page of *his* published poetry, and it read,

"Fucha, 24—I am safe and sound. Today I might have to fight, for I command half a squadron of brave and splendid cachacos. We have had two victories: the one on the 22nd at the Bosa bridge has been of great value, and more so the one yesterday. The results yesterday were as follows: the enemy is completely defeated and demoralized. It lost one hundred and three, including leaders, officials, and troops: many more are injured, one hundred and twenty-eight have been taken hostage, including one Leader, three cannons have been seized along with many weapons, and two hundred have defected this morning at dawn. Our loss has been two llanero commanders (H. Gutiérrez and Cisneros); three soldiers dead, and there seventeen injured, none of them in any grave danger. In Bosa José M. París was injured slightly, but he is better now and doesn't need any care. Victory is certain, and the courage of our soldiers is admirable! Farewell! Fear not and trust Providence, the just cause, and our revolution. —S."

All day long we had peace. Melo did not dare to attack López again. We sent thread and bandages for the wounded.

On the 25th we also had peace, but the Melistas can't stop. They are so despicable that they do not seem to belong to a civilized nation, and still I believe that these savages might be so horrified that they might cease committing such horrible actions. They have kept themselves busy only with trying to poison soldiers from the Constitutional camp, trading them aguardiente for tobacco, and have even sold them poisoned chocolate. We learned of this and sent word to Gutiérrez with the servants so that they would be careful. They say Góngora bought flour to poison it, making bread and biscuits to send to them! Their meals must be made from what the foodsellers bring. Never has such wickedness been seen before, and among brothers no less!

November 27

My *** wrote today. He says he is at the Quinta of Doña Teresa Rivas, and he says he can see the Coliseo Theater from there. . . . . . and I cannot see anything from here, not even the house where *he* is! He sent me a pansy[7] and a sprig of honeysuckle . . . Oh why, my God, do my tears run? Oh Lord, protect him!

Translated by Ana María Gómez López and Ann Farnsworth-Alvear

Notes

1. In this selection, suspension points are in the original. Our own ellipses points, to show abridgment, are in square brackets.

2. Here and elsewhere her future fiancé, José María Samper Agudelo, is concealed as ***.

3. English in original. Carolina Alzate notes that these are lines from Thomas Moore, *Lalla Rookh: An Oriental Romance* (1817). See *Diario íntimo y otros escritos de Soledad Acosta de Samper: Edición y notas de Carolina Alzate* (Bogotá: Alcaldía Mayor de Bogotá y Instituto Distrital Cultura y Turismo, 2003), 209n193.

4. Here and elsewhere, the emphasis is in the original.

5. "Gólgotas" refers in this context to the ideological Liberals, whose radical platform of top-down reforms (including free trade) was compared to the Calvary of Christ's death.

6. Egipto is a neighborhood in central Bogotá.

7. In Colombian Spanish, a pansy is called *un pensamiento*, or "a thought."

Let This Be Our Last War

José María Quijano Wallis

Writing in Paris in 1915, the memoirist José María Quijano Wallis (1847–1922) used an ironic tone reminiscent of Juan Rodríguez Freile to summarize Colombian history for the next generation: "The ambitions of our Independence caudillos gave rise to civil wars, which produced other heroes and caudillos, which could be called second-place caudillos, who in their turn were the instigators of new disturbances." When he attempted to explain why this happened he turned to political economy: "The lack of development of our national wealth and consequent impoverishment of our people has led the military caudillos, most of the time, to seek their livelihood and personal aggrandizement in the hazards of civil war, or in the intrigue and accommodations of politics. Thus, one can say that in Colombia, the first, if not the only industries of national, popular character, have been civil war and politics."[1]

Quijano Wallis wrote during a time of optimism. Knowing that many young Colombians felt a new era of peace had arrived, he sounded a warning. His own generation had been marked by what Colombians call the War of the Thousand Days (1899–1902) and by the memory of the successive conflicts that had preceded that war. His readers might celebrate their "thirteen years" of peace, but Quijano Wallis reminded them that the volcano of violence could return at any time.

Everything has been tested in Colombia: a central republic, a federal republic, a mixed regime; liberal constitutions such as those of 1832, 1853, and 1863; conservative constitutions such as those of 1842 and 1886; the temperate or moderate constitutions of 1830 and 1858; 2-, 4-, and 6-year presidential terms; universal and restricted suffrage; direct, indirect, and second term elections; *patronato* [see part II], a divorce from Rome, and a Concordat with the Vatican; industrial freedom and monopoly; the extension and the restriction of the principles of authority and freedom; the expansion and the limiting of social guarantees; a government organized (in 1863) such that a foreign diplomatic minister deemed it "organized anarchy" and one that was "organized despotism." In the end we have had Republic in all of its forms, and Democracy in all of its variations and derivations. Within the

Alfredo Greñas, *The Regeneration's Coat of Arms*, July 20, 1890. Printed in *El Zancudo*, a clandestine periodical known for its political satire and caricatures of current events in Bogotá. Available online at the Biblioteca Luis Ángel Arango website, www.banrepcultural .org/blaa. Courtesy of Banco de la República.

preserve of government, every faction took up its place, in the direction of the country, every faction led: Bolívar and Santander supporters, Ministerials, Conservatives, Liberals, Centralists, Federalists, Gólgotas, Draconian Liberals, Radicals, Doctrinaire Conservatives, pro-War Conservatives and pro-War Liberals, and Nationalists. And during the period referred to in this exposition, during the course of 80 years, neither constitutions, civilians, nor military officials could establish order, ensure liberty, guarantee property, or secure the well-being and progress of the Republic. . . .

An Italian historian relates that, soon after the terrible eruption of Vesuvius destroyed the beautiful cities of Pompeii and Herculaneum, a pillar was erected to indicate a limit beyond which for new houses and edifices should not be built, on pain of suffering the effects of another disaster. The following inscription was written on this pillar: *Posteri, posteri vestra rex agitur* ("Posterity, posterity, this is for your own good"). The people did not heed this, and we find that upon them came more eruptions and new catastrophes.

May it please God for all Colombians, young and old, military and civilian, ecclesiastical and lay, governors and governed, to not lose sight of and not to forget, as the settlers near Vesuvius forgot, the awful memory of our wars, so that the peace we have enjoyed during the last thirteen years might

Child soldiers in the War of the Thousand Days, from a photograph published in the Parisian magazine *L'Illustration* in July 1902. Photographer unknown. In Robert M. Levine, ed., *Windows on Latin America: Understanding Society through Photographs* (Coral Gables, FL: North-South Center, University of Miami for the South Eastern Council on Latin American Studies, 1987), 59.

be prolonged indefinitely. May it please Heaven that this period of tranquility, the first Colombia has enjoyed in a century, be indefinite, just as our glory and our progress shall be without end when called to reside in the bosom of Order, Harmony, and Peace.

Paris, 1915.

Translated by Ana María Gómez López and Ann Farnsworth-Alvear

Note

1. As cited by Charles Bergquist, *Coffee and Conflict in Colombia, 1886–1910* (Durham, NC: Duke University Press, 1978), 4.

The "Silent Demonstration" of February 7, 1948

Jorge Eliécer Gaitán

On February 7, 1948, Jorge Eliécer Gaitán (1898–1948) delivered his famous "Prayer for Peace" speech. Through the first few decades of the twentieth century, Colombian politicians from the upper classes had been proud of having maintained a formal peace, even if workers' protests and deep political splits characterized the nation as a whole. The Conservatives had won the War of the Thousand Days (1899–1902), and the Liberals found themselves in the political wilderness until 1930, when they returned in a ballot box victory. Radical personalities defined a new era. By the 1940s, Conservative caudillo Laureano Gómez Castro (1889–1965) and his follow-ers were inciting violence against Liberals, insisting that Liberalism was a sin (see part II). Among Liberal politicians, the magnetic personalities were Alfonso López Pumarejo (1886–1959) and Jorge Eliécer Gaitán (1903–48). López Pumarejo led a brief populist experiment he called "the revolution on the march." Gaitán then pushed further, setting off his political style against that of López Pumarejo, whom Gaitán painted as a representative of the elite, and against the Conservatives who opposed the populist reforms of the Liberals. Excerpted below is a famous speech he delivered in February 1948, only months before his assassination. That February rally was called the "Silent Demonstration," because no shouts were heard from the crowd. Gathered in front of the presidential palace, and dressed in black as a signal of their mourning for those already killed in La Violencia, Gaitán's followers were extraor-dinarily disciplined. No one could have anticipated that the violence would only increase and that his speech marked the end of the political theater of a caudillo raised before the crowd.

Gaitán had grown up in city neighborhoods shaped by different groups of work-ing people—independent artisans, storekeepers, taxi drivers, teachers, watchmen, laundresses, waiters, small proprietors, and renters. This was the fluid world that had produced his own class mobility and that fueled his politics. He knew that Co-lombia's electoral system was ballooning and that winning meant moving to its outer edge. Beyond the cities, he explicitly pitched himself to radicals in the countryside—

*banana workers who struck against the United Fruit Company, peasant settlers in
Sumapaz, sharecroppers in Cundinamarca already in contact with a diverse set of
leftists and Liberal Party activists in Bogotá. To win new voters he cultivated the
symbolism of opposition: other politicians were antinational plutocrats, whereas
he was an outsider, a man of "the people." He encouraged the sobriquet "el negro
Gaitán." But he was not a communist, and Gaitán positioned himself also as an
outsider to the pro-Soviet "club," which in Colombia was becoming a dogmatic and
closed-off sect (see part IV). When his platform is mapped onto the country's political spectrum, Gaitán was a fairly typical leftist Liberal—interested in widening
the scope of public schooling and public health, in building a competitive electoral
system, in distributing land to family farmers, and in the state taking an actively
pro-industrialization position. What was atypical was his fiery rhetoric. Gaitán
had cut his political teeth in Mussolini's Italy, where he had made a reputation as a
criminologist and studied with the famed positivist and socialist Enrico Ferri. Some
Colombian communists and even his erstwhile allies in the Liberal Party called him
a fascist, given phrasings that echoed the propaganda of Il Duce: "If I am advancing,
follow me. If I am going backward, push me forward. If I betray you, leave me behind.
If they kill me, avenge my death!"*

Mr. President Mariano Ospina Pérez:

I address you under the weight of deep emotion, interpreting the will
and desire of this immense multitude. Beneath its clamorous silence is
hidden a burning heart lacerated by injustice. They have gathered here
to ask that there be peace and mercy for the nation.

Your Excellency: all day today, the capital of Colombia has witnessed
a spectacle without precedent in its history. People coming from all
over the country, from all latitudes—from the scorching plains to the
cold plateaus—have congregated at this square, the birthplace of our
liberties, to express their irrevocable decision to defend their rights. It
has been two hours since the immense multitude began to flow into
the plaza, and yet not a single outcry has been heard, only the throb of
emotion resounding at the bottom of each heart. During terrible storms
there is a subterranean force, the force of the people, that has the power
to make peace when those who should make it, do not.

Mr. President: there is no sound of applause here, only the sight of
waving black flags!

Mr. President: you who are a man educated at a university should be
able to comprehend what the discipline of a party can bring about—how
it is able to defy the laws of collective psychology by repressing its emo-

Portrait of Jorge Eliécer Gaitán, ca. 1930. The ambiguity of Gaitán's self-presentation is suggested here. He is well dressed, but not ostentatiously so. He faces the camera not as an aristocrat but rather as a self-made man, with an expression that evokes both kindness and determination. Photographer unknown. Available at Biblioteca Luis Ángel Arango, Sala de Libros Raros y Manuscritos. FT1855, foto 10.

tion in silence, as is done by this immense crowd. You will understand that a party that can achieve this could very easily react if stimulated by a legitimate need to defend itself.

Nowhere in the world has a collectivity provided a better demonstration than this one. But if this rally is taking place, it is not for trivial reasons but because something serious has happened. There is a party committed to order, capable of carrying out this act, this demonstration to ensure that bloodshed is prevented and laws are obeyed because laws express our general conscience. I have not fooled myself in saying that I believed in the conscience of the people. This conception has been amply confirmed during this demonstration, where the hurrahs and the applause have ceased so that only the excited murmur of thousands of black flags can be heard, brought here in remembrance of our men who were so villainously murdered.

Mr. President: with calmness and serenity, with the emotion that

runs through the spirit of the citizens that fill this square, we ask that
you exercise your command, the same given onto you by the people,
to restore public tranquility to this country. Now, everything depends
on you! Those who flood the nation's territory with blood would cease
their blind treachery. Those who harbor ill intentions would fall silent
before the simple rule of your will.

We love this nation deeply and we do not want our vessel, always victorious, to have to navigate through rivers of blood as it moves toward
the harbor of its inexorable destiny.

Mr. President: on this occasion we do not call for economic or political theories. All we ask is that our nation not tread paths that bring us
shame in our own eyes and in those of others. We ask you for acts of
peace and civilization!

We, Mr. President, are not cowards. We are the descendants of brave
men who annihilated tyranny on this sacred soil. We are capable of
sacrificing our lives to save the peace and the liberty of Colombia!

Prevent violence. We seek the defense of human life, which is the
least a people can ask for. Instead of this blind and uncontained force,
we should make the most of the people's capability to work for the benefit of Colombia's progress.

Mr. President: Our flag is in mourning. This silent crowd and the
voiceless cry of our hearts ask only this of you: that you treat us, our
mothers, our wives, our children and our belongings, as you wish that
you, your mother, your wife, your children, and your belongings be
treated!

Your Excellency, we end by saying: good fortune to those who
understand that words of harmony and peace should not be used to
hide feelings of resentment and extermination. Misfortune to those in
government who hide their lack of mercy for their fellow men behind
kind words, for the finger of ignominy will point them out in the pages
of history!

Translated by Ana María Gómez López and Ann Farnsworth-Alvear

Dead Bodies Appear on the Streets

Gustavo Álvarez Gardeazábal

There are no exact figures for how many people were killed or displaced during La Violencia (The Violence), a fifteen-year period of extreme sectarian conflict that began slightly before (and then was fueled by) the 1948 assassination of Jorge Eliécer Gaitán, but estimates range from 250,000 to 300,000. Most were poor, rural civilians, and very few deaths were the result of crossfire between armed groups and official security forces. More often, killing rampages took place when partisans took control over a territory, purging those they saw as opponents. While violence was carried out by both Liberal- and Conservative-leaning groups, the emergence in the early 1950s of so-called pájaros *or* chulavitas, *gangs of assassins that were backed by the military and the Conservative Party, were especially significant in Boyacá, Cundinamarca, Antioquia, Valle del Cauca, Tolima, the coffee-growing areas of central Colombia, and the eastern plains regions. Many of these killings were brutal—carried out with machetes—and quartered or mutilated bodies were left on roads and in public spaces. Photographs of these atrocities were published in the influential book* La Violencia en Colombia, *published in 1962 by Monsignor Germán Guzmán Campos, Orlando Fals Borda, and Eduardo Umaña Luna, and images of that time remain etched in Colombians' collective memory.*

Prize-winning novelist Gustavo Álvarez Gardeazábal depicts the killing of Liberals by chulavitas *in a short story written about twenty years after this period of violence (Álvarez Gardeazábal himself was a small child when Gaitán was killed). He later went on to a political career, first as mayor of his home town of Tuluá, and then as governor of the department of Valle del Cauca. Through the years, he courted controversy: as a gay man in politics, as a public figure accused of collaborating with drug traffickers, and as a writer who continued to publish fictionalized denunciations of his detractors after a three-year stint in prison.*

That night the first dead bodies appeared on the streets.

Misiá[1] María Cardona and Josefina Jaramillo found two of them just outside the house of don Pacho Montalvo. At first they thought they were two drunkards because they did not see any signs of blood on the floor. They

El que esté sin pecado arroje la primera piedra.

An iconic photograph published in the book *Violence in Colombia*, published by Monseñor Germán Guzmán Campos, Orlando Fals Borda, and Eduardo Umaña Luna in 1962. The original caption reads: "Let he who is without sin cast the first stone." Together the image and the caption were an attempt to force Colombians to face the scale of La Violencia. The coeditors were activists determined to shame the nation into a collective effort to stop the killings. In German Guzmán Campos, Orlando Fals Borda, and Eduardo Umaña Luna, *La Violencia en Colombia* (Bogotá: Ediciones Tercer Mundo, 1962), 280–81. Courtesy of Brianda Cediel.

crossed the street to the opposite sidewalk, and even covered their eyes with their shawls. They continued walking straight to the church and greeted León María, yet during the entire mass they could not stop thinking about the strange manner in which the two drunk men were lying on the road. As they headed out, they mentioned this to Father Legui, who was coming in from the street. He only managed to answer them with a smile. Don Pacho Montalvo had called on him to give absolution to the two strangers thrown on his doorstep, each with a shot to the back of his neck. *Misiá* María looked at Josefina, shrugged, and went down the street of the Salesians until she reached the corner where doña Mercedes Sarmiento lived. There, they saw an enormous crowd of people gathered around the two strangers they had passed and thought were drunk. Don Pacho Montalvo took it upon himself

Luis Angel Rengifo, *Piel al sol*, 1963. Part of a series of thirteen engravings addressing La Violencia. Courtesy of the Museo de Arte Moderno de Bogotá.

to explain to them what was happening as they approached the crowd with curiosity and fear. They gave themselves the sign of the cross three times in a row and went quickly back home. They turned on the radio to see if they could find out more, but they heard only the unmelodious voice of Pedro Alvarado reporting damages caused by the overflow of the Tuluá River on the plots near the tuberculosis ward. The newspapers from Cali made no mention. Yet Luisita Lozano, who arrived just after both had said goodbye, told them that there had not only been two dead bodies at Pablo Montalvo's house. There were five—one had just been found in front of don Alfredo Garrido's house, another was down by the river, and Ercilia Rendón, who had come from the *galería* [local market], had seen two more being picked up in front of the butcher's stand.

Don Julio didn't want to say a word to anyone who approached him on the subject in the pharmacy that day. León María helped remove the two bodies at the market's entrance. He was intent on finding out their political affiliations, and so he searched through both of their pockets, only to face the devastating condition shared by all the dead bodies recovered in the last few months: none of them had any identification documents.

Pedro Alvarado gave a brief report on the noon news broadcast. Without further comment, he read the police commander's press release, stating that the causes of these five deaths were unknown, and that autopsies were being carried out on all of them to determine the cause of death, as allegedly none had any trace of wounds.

Those who heard the news and had seen the bodies immediately figured out what had happened. The cause was the governor's police. Since the names of the dead were unknown and no one was able to recognize them all morning at the morgue, people began to think that they had been killed elsewhere and had been dumped in Tuluá. There was no reason for violence here. Pedro Alvarado did not want to comment about what had happened on his news show, but he read the same police press release during each of his three broadcasts that day. *Misiá* María Cardona even came to believe that these men had been poisoned during some party in another municipality, and had been thrown on the streets of Tuluá by people trying to escape punishment. Luisita Lozano and Josefina Jaramillo also believed this, and in Mamá Margarita's sewing circle, doña Midita de Acosta shared the version told to her by the mayor's driver, who had remained silent all this time.

Neither *Misiá* María Cardona nor Josefina Jaramillo saw them, but four more bodies were left at the morgue the next day. Each had the same wound on the back of the neck, and had no identification papers and no chance of being recognized by the people lining up against the tiled tables where the bodies were placed before being buried amid the rows of NN—no names. León María went to inspect them and rummage through their pockets, as did the police. They did not bother to put out a press release that day, and Pedro Alvarado aired nothing more than another brief report: "Earlier this morning four more unidentified bodies appeared on the city's streets. Police are investigating the cause of death."

The mayor was not letting on that he was aware of the situation, but he forbade the radio station from transmitting any news that would cause alarm or commotion, or that strayed from the facts. By the third day there was only one newscast. This barely received any attention, not only because the residents of Tuluá were beginning to get used to the situation, but because rumors were beginning to circulate about León María, who was forced to send his daughters off to a boarding school in Manizales after he traveled to Cali and found scholarships for them at lightning speed. . . .

The day that León María and Agripina sent their daughters off, Father González went to give them his blessing. This was the beginning of the longest day of his earthly role as a confessor. At three in the afternoon, after he had just returned from seeing León María, a woman wrapped in shawls appeared, looking nervously from side to side. She had come to warn him that if he did not do something by that night, many dead bodies would appear strewn on the streets of Tuluá. The priest promised he would call the mayor to prevent this. However, he was not able to do so. For as soon as he said goodbye to the lady, who continued to look nervously around her as if she were being followed, Father Legui called him to listen to the radio. The coalition government had ended: there was a new cabinet, and, consequently, a new governor and new mayor. The Conservative Party was taking office after having won the elections.

Perhaps it was the news that caused the people of Tuluá the next day to think about everything other than who was responsible for causing its suffering. Father González began to realize this at nine o'clock that night, when he heard the first gunshots far off in the dark night. He remembered the words of the shawled woman, prayed a mea culpa, and closed the window. He had still not been able to go to sleep by midnight. It was a day that seemed to have no end. He continued to hear stray gunshots, sometimes close by, other times far away. He began to count the shots in order to fall asleep, but woke up with the sound of the first cars. There seemed to be trucks driving by speedily at a distance. They would stop at some point only to start up again. He kept looking out the window, and he could not make them out clearly, but he did confirm they were trucks. At four o'clock in the morning, the trucks stopped driving through and the gunshots ceased. Then the knocking started at the school window. Father González dressed hastily and began the longest series of funeral prayers he had given in all these years, even more than when the dead of the Frazadas massacre had been brought in. There was a corpse for him to bless on every block in Tuluá, except for those at the school where León María Lozano lived. Each had a wound at the back of the neck and each was stone-dead. None had identification papers, and no one recognized them when they were transferred to the morgue. Only one woman, the same one wearing shawls from the day before, came to the morgue and identified one of the bodies. Each had been placed naked on top of another. Those on the right were facing up, those on the left were facing down. A bedsheet had been drawn only over the first of the pile; the rest were shrouded only by flies. None had evidence of any other wound: aside from some traces of blood, only the humming of the flies and the smell of formaldehyde confirmed that there had been a massacre. Faces peered curiously through the screened windows, yet not one person came in, for no one in Tuluá had lost anyone.

When the shawl-covered woman arrived at around one and told the policeman at the morgue that she had come to claim a body, she was not allowed inside because it had been settled that those bodies were not from Tuluá. Those who overheard the policeman began to suspect that there was some plot to all this. Tuluá decided to blame the massacre of outsiders on the change in government: although none of the bodies had a single identification document, everyone in Tuluá knew that they were Liberals.

Pedro Alvarado reported this on the news during his last broadcast for the night. The mayor, a military official who had arrived that afternoon to replace his predecessor, fined him five hundred pesos and suspended him for three days. The shawled woman had told him about being refused entry to the morgue. She had gone back to Father González, who was escorting her. First, they went to Pedro Alvarado, who jotted down the facts. Then they went to the morgue again. The policeman saw the priest and let him in right away, believing he was there to bless the mound of jutting hands and feet and their increasing stench. Yet when he heard the screams of the woman who had come with Father González, he remembered that she was the one he had stopped at noon. Among the dead on the left, she recognized a hand. She grabbed it, and when she pulled it toward her trying to find a scar, all of the precariously balanced corpses came tumbling down on her, grasping at her shawls with the grip of death.

Father González tried to stop her, but despite the avalanche she did not move, clutching the hand that belonged to her husband, a worker at one of the dairy farms on the mountainside where she lived. The policeman came in and, failing to notice the priest's presence, saw the mess and said, "Goddammit, that woman . . ." The priest went in to find her. The woman was cleaning the corpse. She was cleaning the dried blood beneath his ears with one shawl, while trying to cover his naked body with another. She remained there until the priest came back with a coffin and Tarsicio Vidales, meagerly covered under his wife's shawl, was taken for burial.

The priest said mass for him right at the cemetery chapel. When he had finished, the city workers, who had already carted the other corpses to a mass grave they had dug next to the other NNs, helped the woman carry her husband's body. He was the only one identified among the thirty-three, but it was enough for Tuluá to relinquish any doubt that the dead were leaking in from the outside. Even now, Tuluá still believed in its far-fetched accounts: about the dead being pulled from the graves of nearby cemeteries, or people being poisoned at a party, or people swept away by a landslide. And María Luisa Sierra, who had once overheard León María talk about the horseman of the Apocalypse, claimed that people had gone to Father Ocampo to swear they had seen the horseman again, riding a mule. . . . Some went to León María to question him about this, to which he replied that he had nothing to say, since no corpses had appeared on his block. However, if he were to see the horseman—and who better than him to recognize what he had already set eyes on—he would send notice immediately. Despite this, Pedro Alvarado announced the following on his news broadcast, as if hiding the facts all the same: Liberals were being killed by the horseman of the Apocalypse.

He must have come back that night, as three more bodies appeared. No one knew them, yet they had identification documents and were only missing their voter's registration card. Three days later, after his suspension ended, Pedro Alvarado announced this once more: these deaths are political, and their voting cards are being removed. He said nothing else, and because he had not mentioned any party or the dead's political affiliation, they could not suspend him. He had learned to outsmart censorship, and while Tuluá took notice of this, the town did not pay any further attention. The far-fetched stories about sightings of the horseman of the Apocalypse continued, and the night of the dead was forgotten. Father Ocampo held a Corpus Christi procession in the town square, and Father González sprinkled holy water from a small aircraft belonging to Mario Gardeazábal, another of don Marcial's sons. But either heaven had forsaken them, or Tuluá already had been condemned beyond any prayer.

One week later, don Rosendo Zapata was killed. He had arrived to the bank on his usual schedule. From two o'clock onward, clients saw him working diligently on his large machine. He passed through one check after another, turning down overdrawn accounts and wiping clean his dark lenses. When the bank closed, his coworkers still saw him there. He did not leave his mechanized desk until six o'clock. He picked up his jacket, placing it over his shirt damp with sweat, and cleaned his glasses (which he used because his Fabiola had mixed up his eyedrops with a callus remedy— for two months no one knew if he would ever see again). Don Rosendo walked out with Ruca Gil, the savings cashier. They reached the corner of the Club Colonial, and she turned to walk up Calle 27 as he continued toward the Parque Bolívar. When he arrived at the bridge, the Puente Blanco, he stopped after Ester Castaño startled him with her voice, one so grating that she had once broken the vases in the home of doña Teresita de Peláez. She allegedly asked him about Fabiola, about his eyes, about the bank, and tried to find out information about León María's funds. She insists that he did not tell her anything. However, it is very possible Rosendo Zapata did answer her in great detail: ever since the night of Ospina Pérez's election, he had sworn to make Colombians understand the mistake they had made by every means possible. When they said goodbye, don Rosendo crossed the avenue and headed toward the river. He carefully walked up the stairs of the bridge and looked out at the stream. He must have listened to its sound with nostalgia, as he had never been able to forget the day he had been forced to leave his father's farm on the banks of the creek in La Rivera. He continued on his way, and as he went down the steps toward the corner where don Ignacio Kafure lived, he saw José Celín, León María's bodyguard, coming toward him. Elvita Gil also saw him, as she was crossing the street walking toward the bridge on the opposite sidewalk. The greeting was as instantaneous as the gunshots. Celín continued walking as if nothing had happened; Elvita Gil put her hands over her face. There, on the sidewalk by the Puente Blanco, lay Rosendo Zapata, head of checking accounts at the branch office for Banco de Colombia. He felt his eyes burn the same way they had on that August night, when he had told his Fabiola that the wind was stinging his eyes. He had asked her to squeeze some eyedrops for him from the green bottle, and she reached instead for Doctor Botero's corn removal remedy. Two drivers from the Gálviz bus lines picked him up. Don Ignacio Kafure threw a scapular from Our Lady of Mount Carmel on his body, and Elvita Gil went back to give the news to don Elcías. Tuluá had its first official death on its streets. It was October 22, 1949. Thirty-two minutes past six.

Translated by Ana María Gómez López

Note

1. *Misia* is a contraction of *mi señora* or "my lady." It is an expression of respect that is more colloquial than formal.

Cruelty Acted as a Stimulant

José Gutiérrez Rodríguez

In recent decades, the Colombian term autodefensas *(self-defense squads) has become a trademark of paramilitary groups that define themselves as combating leftist guerrillas and that are enmeshed in networks of narco-traffickers, cattle ranchers, and land barons. Ironically, however, Colombians' first use of the term* autodefensa *dates from the 1950s and early 1960s and was rooted in the tactics of the Colombian Communist Party—before the* FARC *abandoned "self-defense" in favor of a new strategy, that of creating a mobile guerrilla army.*

José Gutiérrez Rodríguez (1927–2008) was a writer, psychoanalyst, and activist of the Colombian Left. In the text excerpted below he recalls both the revolutionary mystique of Viotá, a peasant area of Cundinamarca less than one hundred kilometers from Bogotá, and the cruelty that was joined to the practice of "self-defense" in the area. Even before the FARC *coalesced, he offered an ethical and political criticism: if the guerrillas depended on cruelty, then they were armed groups that could not be a force for liberation.*

Remembering his early trips to Viotá as a young communist, Gutiérrez describes a heady time: "Here was the kingdom of comradeship in all of its splendor." Yet he also writes about the political realities of Viotá's so-called united front in a direct narration relatively free of the usual leftist propaganda about Viotá. The municipality had been converted into a nodal point for political refugees and guerrilla apprentices who imagined that they would study "the technique" of the autodefensas. *But Gutiérrez emphasizes the fact of cruelty and insists that neither the rebels' supposed strength nor the government's weakness inspired hope in the possibility of real revolution.*

It is interesting to pose a parallel comparison between the "self-defense" proclaimed by Colombian communism in peasant regions affected by the political crisis, and the situation of other regions influenced by the strategy of "resistance" proclaimed by Liberal leaders after their defeat in 1949.

This parallel explains why communism gained influence after the Liberal leadership began to call for remorse and forgetting (the main political characteristic of the currently governing Frente Nacional). When Liberal leaders abandoned yet again the sectors of the population previously welcomed by López and Gaitán, who had encouraged participation in general strikes, resistance, and guerrillas, communism not only failed to back down from its "peasant self-defense" thesis, but also maintained that this had led to political and military victories. To this day, [self-defense] has held a strong influence among bands that continue their armed struggle, either as Liberal guerrillas that oppose Conservative bandits or as Liberal bandits that flee and resist authorities.

The first time I visited the communist peasant region of Viotá, during a time of peace, I remember that I experienced some of the deepest feelings of joy and hope I had experienced in my entire life. The total absence of obstacles to having a direct relationship with the campesinos (who greeted visitors with no distrust whatsoever, no matter their social rank), brought me to feel faith in humanity. Here was the kingdom of comradeship in all its splendor.

Dedicated primarily to coffee cultivation, this region has for the past twenty years been home to agricultural workers organized by communists.

The old coffee haciendas that the campesinos took over by force in Viotá had been latifundia on which tenant farmers experienced cruel forms of exploitation. In a building that now serves as a union center, one can still see the old stocks with which the landowners tortured workers. . . .

The bear-hug with which any visitor is welcomed surprises Colombians that are far more used to social distance in personal interactions; we are victims of rigidity and inhibition. Coming from a dirty, barefoot campesino that lacks any social restraint, one finds that this same hug is repeated at every bend in the road, at every farm-stand and beside every campesino house one passes on the steep, climbing footpath. There are those among us who felt we were seeing the dawn of a new society.

Communist-endorsed "self-defense" was an abstract concept in the case of a region such as Viotá, given its prolonged isolation. Here, the main tactic for peasants was to remain alert and ready to fend off any attack, but abstain from taking actions against the government or against other peasants with different political affiliations. . . .

[At] the beginning of the Conservative regime [1949], Liberal guerrilla bands were formed by those who had to flee regions invaded by Conservatives or by those who could not tolerate the fear and insecurity created by this situation and who wanted to retaliate against the government. Had they acted in coordination, these bands could have even defeated the Conservative government.

But in Viotá none of this happened, since the incitements of the liberal press went unheeded and there had already existed, for many years, a structure of organization and training for "self-defense." In addition to being shielded by its topography, the region was protected by the inner strength of its inhabitants. . . .

Given these conditions, the communist militancy of this part of the countryside truly represented its cultural life. People felt a connection to to one another even when their work and family lives may have kept them isolated, or even when they lived many kilometers from their neighbors.

As a result of this lived cultural connection (which was taken up with religious assiduousness, above all else), when hiking through the Viotá mountains, one had the impression of being in a profoundly cultured place—where any chance encounter might yield an interesting conversation about world politics, about the economy, or about any of the intellectual topics that fall within the range of interests common to socialists and communists all over the world.

This was the most notable difference, compared to the mind-set of most campesinos in Colombia. In Viotá, one felt no difficulty in conversation, nor was there that fundamental distance of interests between the inhabitant of the city, the intellectual, and the campesino, which all over Latin America sometimes ends up being a burden for all parties. . . .

In contrast to the rest of the Colombian countryside, Viotá has its own history, its own epic ballads to sing, its own heroes (pioneers of the struggle for the land) . . . its own rituals and its own messianism, which adds up to a whole culture. . . .

The communists should have refrained from provoking the government, just as the campesinos advised. But instead they brought in a clandestine radio transmitter they received from the Liberals and installed it, even if they didn't dare operate it. . . . They also maintained military training schools and organized meetings with delegates from all over the country and with invited foreigners.

As a consequence of these provocations, the police tried to invade [Viotá] several times or at least enter to carry out searches. Then the military organization of the "self-defense" squads repelled the police in battles where the campesinos had the upper hand, given the topographic conditions and psychological circumstances of the attackers, who knew that they faced a shrewd, well-trained enemy which they feared like the devil himself.

Military victories were not the final measure for Viotá's "self-defense." In the end, a force composed of several hundred well-armed soldiers trained in guerrilla warfare (such as the battalion which fought in Korea at the time) would have been required to penetrate and hold military control in the region. Yet landowners who feared for their properties finally intervened so that the government would not send an expeditionary force.

Those landowners who now defended peasants were the same who years before had been their feudal masters. They probably knew that the feudal situation of twenty years prior could not be restored, and that they would likely lose what little they had left of their territories if there was a devastating open war with communist-led peasants.

War triumphs in Viotá acquired a legendary quality among guerrilla bands in regions weighed down by Conservative authoritarianism. Political refugees and guerrilla apprentices arrived there from all around the country to study the technique of "self-defense."

One of the battles mentioned had taken place a day before I arrived to the region, where I was on a fact-finding trip commissioned by the leadership of the [Communist] party. And I remember the cruelty painted on the faces of those combatants as they narrated the way in which they had surprised assailants at a bend in the road.

I can say, without exaggeration, that this cruelty was the main motivation that stirred the energies of peasants and rushed them to battle.

In effect, the battle produced a contagious excitement that spread through the region. And a people's vigil was known to take place that night.

Homes were abandoned, barricades were built, permanent watch rounds were arranged, and encampments appeared.

What was it that really moved these men to alter the rhythm of their daily lives, and spend nights singing and telling stories around bonfires? An objective answer to this question should consider, among many factors, the workers' desire for change, their yearning for fraternity, and their desire for adventure. But I would like to refer to that which particularly impressed me, and which constituted an effective drive that enthralled the people and readied them for combat: cruelty.

The military uniforms of dead police were considered trophies from recent battles. Those who claimed the glory of having been the killers wore their [victims'] caps and rifles: boots and cartridge belts were displayed by those who allegedly contributed to these deaths in a lesser degree. It was as if they had been symbolically quartered.

In speaking to some of these heroes, I found out that indeed a battle had not taken place, but that it had been a simple ambush in which the poor victims were made out to behave like frightened animals. One of the more "politically aware" comrades, a man described as affectionate, fraternal, and even kind-hearted, told me he shot a policeman and later finished him off despite his implorations. He proudly showed me a photograph that his "kill" had carried in his pocket, showing the victim, his wife, and their children. It was as if at the bottom of this cruelty was the practice common to the hunter who, after killing his prey, perpetuates its form through taxidermy.

During the last few years, we have developed in Colombia refined displays of cruelty that pale when compared to that comrade's feelings [toward his victim]. . . .

Perhaps [such] demonstrations of cruelty . . . [are] derived from the isolation and from hidden loneliness behind abstract ambitions of fraternity. At least that was what seemed to be the psychological significance in the symbolism of putting on a victim's boots, pulling on his hat, or saving his photos, all of which were acts accompanied by conscious feelings somewhere between childish pride, compassion, and sadism.

It should be noted, however, that the communists tried to combat this cruelty, establishing rules about "revolutionary justice" to control its occurrence. As a result of this, brutality was lessened in places where communist influence reached into the Colombian guerrillas.

Nevertheless, neither the communists nor any of Colombia's other political parties have dared to confront the issue of brutality that has developed in the countryside during the last fourteen years. It has become a problem of the gravest seriousness.

Translated by Ana María Gómez López and Ann Farnsworth-Alvear

Two Views of the National Front

Álvaro Gómez Hurtado and Ofelia Uribe de Acosta

*In December 1957, with the terrible violence of 1946–53 fresh in their memories, Co-
lombian voters overwhelmingly approved a plebiscite to establish a "civil front,"
later called el Frente Nacional. Designed to strengthen the Liberal and Conservative
Parties and disavow the military government of General Gustavo Rojas Pinilla, the
plebiscite had been drafted to reflect an agreement between Alberto Lleras Camargo,
head of the Liberals, and Laureano Gómez Castro, the Conservative firebrand who
had been deposed by Rojas Pinilla in June 1953. The outlines of their agreement had
been set out in what Colombians call the Benidorm Pact of 1956 and the Sitges Pact
of 1957, signed by the two party leaders in the Mediterranean coast of Spain. The
National Front established that the two primary parties would alternate the presidency and share power. Managed elections would lessen partisan passions and allow those with a stake in the political and economic system to do the administrative
work of governing the country as they saw fit.*

*The National Front had broad support, not least because loyal followers from
both parties fell into line behind their two leaders. Yet 1957 marked an important
shift, given that four years previously the military coup that installed Rojas Pinilla
had also enjoyed broad support—it, too, had been understood as a way to end the
violence. When Rojas imposed military law and ousted then-president Laureano
Gómez, wealthy families linked to the Liberal Party were behind him, as were the
majority of well-placed Conservatives and the country's Catholic hierarchy. Because
Gómez had profascist leanings and seemed poised to proclaim himself a dictator, the
coup against him was taken as "patriotism." But when Rojas Pinilla attempted to
extend his claim on power, using a populist rhetoric that echoed that of Argentina's
Juan Domingo Perón, he found himself without allies. The Church, the press, and
Colombia's political class as a whole rallied behind Lleras Camargo and the exiled
Gómez. Perhaps most importantly, the international context of the Cold War meant
that political instability was understood as likely to provide an opening for political
actors on the Left. Colombians knew that Washington would support a regime of
managed elections.*

Yet the National Front had its critics on both the Right and the Left. The views expressed by Álvaro Gómez Hurtado (1919–95), son of the Conservative leader, and Ofelia Uribe de Acosta (1900–1988), a left-leaning journalist and pioneering feminist, are particularly interesting as criticisms because both spoke from within the political system while implicitly recognizing the existence of political actors outside the National Front. The younger Gómez emphasizes the Front's inability to impose the rule of law across the national territory—in using the phrase "independent republics" he refers to armed groups linked to what emerged as guerrilla armies in the 1960s, with strongholds in areas of central and eastern Colombia such as Riochiquito, El Pato, Guayabero, Sumapaz, Alto Ariari, and Marquetalia.

Uribe de Acosta supported neither Rojas's coup nor the Benidorm Pact. Both, for her, silenced opposition voices. Further, she objects to the idea that the National Front should be credited with "civilizing" politics in Colombia. That, she says, ignores the possibility that women's sudden presence as voters may have been a more important change. Her position was rejected by the Liberals, who feared that women's votes would tend Conservative and who had refused to publish her prosuffrage opinions in the newspapers they controlled. Thus as a feminist she had a specific incentive to reject the National Front.

Álvaro Gómez's life in politics extended past his father's shadow. He was the Conservative Party candidate for president three times, was kidnapped by the M-19 guerrillas in 1988, and was assassinated in 1995 in a crime that has gone unsolved. He served as one of three presidents of the Constitutional Assembly of 1991, alongside former M-19 commander Antonio Navarro Wolff and Liberal Party leader Horacio Serpa Uribe, and played an important role in drafting the Constitution that emerged from that meeting.

Many of us, if we supported this first National Front Government, did so in good faith; we were moved by a decisive spirit of public service. Some of us can be proud of what was accomplished during this time, during the first two years, according to public opinion, the good years of this administration. What the National Front was based on was accomplished: to reconstitute the hope that had been lost. It was a time in which the parties worked together with common accord and civility, in a spirit of understanding. It was a time in which there wasn't yet talk of "bad Conservatives," there wasn't yet talk of past deaths and recriminations aimed at provoking revenge. . . . It should be acknowledged that the parties at that time behaved in an exemplary fashion. The initial years of the National Front were years that can be put forward as a model of good judgment in political leadership.

But in administrative terms we were not satisfied even then. . . . In the first instance there was the issue of justice. We had wanted to fulfill an old ambition held by Colombians, to fully reestablish the domain of justice in

Llanos guerrilla leader Guadalupe Salcedo greets General Gustavo Rojas Pinilla, October 1953. Salcedo commanded the Liberal guerrillas in Colombia's eastern plains between 1949 and 1953, organized to fight against attacks from Conservatives and the Colombian military during La Violencia. Shortly after General Rojas Pinilla took power in 1953, the Liberal guerrillas agreed to demobilize under an amnesty law, and a general pardon was given to Liberals and Conservatives alike who had committed atrocities during this period. However, peace attempts in the Llanos failed, as did most other political amnesties in Colombia during the twentieth century. Salcedo, like many other former Liberal guerrilla leaders, was assassinated years later under mysterious circumstances. Courtesy of Archivo Círculo de Lectores-ETCE.

such a way as to be able to say that in Colombia there would in fact be a deep rejection of impunity. That there would not be the kind of indifference that we see daily in the face of common crimes, political crimes, violent crimes, or even small breaches of trust. To be able to say that these were not the ways of our country but instead that in Colombia there reigned a decisive spirit in favor of combating impunity. But none of the important ideas addressing the issue of justice gained the support needed. We had to put up with ineffective justice ministers who were perfectly deaf to people's demands to combat impunity. . . .

   The political climate began to deteriorate, so much so that there was no longer agreement between the parties. Things were not being done as the outcome of a vigorous system designed to last but rather as a way to reap the electoral benefits of a set of constitutional rules. . . . We saw in today's session that there is no budget in place. Economic activity in the country is not shaped by an awareness of the rate of government spending. Budgets are simply a word used as a stenographic shorthand. . . . There is no real economic leadership. There is not even any elementary order to the way the government employs the rights we have so generously bestowed upon it. . . .

There is no economic policy right now. What about foreign policy? That truly has been an even greater mystery. I have genuinely tried to find out what the country's foreign policy consists of at present and I do not know. . . . A mystery policy, bandied about in banquets and trips and diplomatic niceties and even in a famous party with Fidel Castro in Cuba. And no one in the entire country knows what is the substance of this administration's foreign policy, absolutely no one. I would go so far as to say that not even the president of the Republic knows what his foreign policy consists of. Is it such a poor policy that it cannot even be outlined in general terms? I fear there simply is no policy, because reliable information one receives suggests that what Colombia lays out or proposes to manage the situation with Fidel Castro is changing every day.

And agrarian policy? What a disgrace! Four wasted years in which something could have been done. . . . Agricultural production is facing a tremendous crisis: production indices are down. They are down for potatoes, for panela,[1] for rice. . . . We are at a moment in which there is progress in agricultural techniques, in which extraordinary new methods of cultivation are being applied in various countries, along with innovative rational systems of warehousing products and amazingly efficient techniques for marketing and distribution. But here we are experiencing a tremendous agrarian crisis brought on by the government's incurable apathy on agrarian issues.

President Lleras will go down in history as one of the farmers' biggest enemies, because he had everything in his power and a great opportunity to help bring development, and he insisted instead on pushing an agrarian reform bill. On that pretext, the pretext that he would get an agrarian reform passed, he stymied any state action to develop Colombian agriculture.

Even though we have not seen effective action at the administrative level, if we were at the very least satisfied with the situation of public order and if this in turn had been the result of the National Front, maybe we could accept the situation. In exchange for everything else, at least we Colombians could live in peace. But no, not even that. Not at all. Here again arguments drawn from Colombia's past are of no use. The violence in this country initially developed out of what was understood to be political violence, at least in its basic features. There was an attempt to elevate the actions of bandits by calling them freedom fighters—the government minister used that phrase—and this was understandable to a certain extent because the fires of a declared civil war were raging within the nation-state. But that is precisely the issue: all this needed to change with the National Front. The need to ameliorate so much confusion, such as the confusion that was seen during the government of the armed forces when, in trying to defeat a group of bandits, found out that these bandits were covered by the flag of a political party. This was a disastrous mistake from years past but it was perhaps justified, or at least explicable, given a situation of civil war. But it cannot be justified in the same way at present, not under the National Front. No Colombian can legitimately invoke politics to reject the sovereignty of the Colombian state. This has not yet been understood. It has not been understood that in this country there are a series of independent republics that do not recognize the sovereignty of the Colombian state and within which the Colombian army cannot enter without it being said that the army's presence is an abomination, that it frightens the people, or that it scares away the inhabitants. A series of independent republics does in fact exist despite government denials of their existence. There are periodic false statements, mendacious statements—that all of the national territory is under state sovereignty. But it is not subject to Colombian sovereignty. There is the independent republic of Sumapaz, as well as the independent republic of Planadas and that of Riochiquito, that of a bandit called Richard, and now, we have the founding of a new independent republic announced here by the minister of government: the independent republic of Vichada. National sovereignty is shrinking like a handkerchief. That is one of the most painful outcomes of the National Front. That which should have served, precisely, to make all Colombians feel that they belong to one *patria* [homeland] is now justifying the most aberrant events, such as the existence of territories in the very heart of the country where people up in arms do not allow the authorities to enter. When there's a need to enforce that that government sovereignty does exist throughout the national territory and an official is sent out, and he has his hands tied. He is made subject to conditions and unable to perform his tasks or exercise his authority, and in many cases even force him to leave the area. In some regions, the only Colombian authorities that are tolerated are agents of the Caja Agraria [Colombia's Farm Credit Bank], who go out to lend money to the outlaws. That is the only governmental act performed by this, the first administration of the National Front.

President Lleras will go down in history as the founder of five republics, independent republics, because national sovereignty here has been shattered. This is stated easily enough, as though it were not of transcendent importance. These are separate territories; no one is going to go there. There are no senators who will risk going there. It's not good land; it's mountainous and there's no communication. The government doesn't spend money on anything. It doesn't spend money to build anything. It's not going to spend money to establish national sovereignty out on a mountain range. . . .

Before, the military went—regardless of whether they were well-prepared or badly prepared, well-armed or badly armed—without being afraid of losing communication, having what they needed or not having it. But they fought against those who did not recognize the sovereignty of the nation. Now, the first administration of the National Front doesn't do anything except tolerate the existence of independent republics. The army knows it constantly has to perform its actions balanced on a razor's edge, so as not to have the nation's sovereignty suffer more affronts and at the same time not invade the space of sovereignty of the independent republic. The tragedy of the Colombian army is that it has had to recognize foreign territories within its own nation.

ANABEL TORRES: Bled dry by violence, the country saw Gustavo Rojas Pinilla take power through a military coup in 1953. A strange event took place during his government. . . .

OFELIA URIBE DE ACOSTA: Yes, strange, or at least curious. Almost every Latin American country has granted women the right to vote during periods of military dictatorship. Colombia was not the exception. Legislative Act Number 3 of 1954 granted women the right to vote in the Constituent Assembly convened by General Rojas. He had previously ordered a commission to study the proposal, and said commission was once again set on denying it, when Rojas sent his minister Henao Henao to announce his irrevocable decision to grant the vote. . . .

AT: Ofelia, during Rojas's dictatorship your newspaper, *Verdad*, was the only one that dared publish, on the first page, photos of women demonstrating against the closure of *El Tiempo* newspaper. . . .

OU: . . . Our loyalty was to journalism, to free expression, and to politics. And in politics it is more important to defend principles—principles are above personalities, just as platforms should be above special interests and above the pettiness of power for its own sake. . . . As soon as the issue with the photos came out, a military officer who knew me well called me to say that I should get lost because they were going to raid the paper, which was published in my house. That was the end of *Verdad*. And the truth also is that with the financial problems we were going through and with the lack of support, even from women, I couldn't pay for everything anymore. The last edition came out August 18, 1955.

AT: Do you have an explicit position regarding the National Front, or reservations regarding this system of cohabitation that was put forward as a solution to the country's problems and as a return to democracy?

OU: My opinion of the Front was that it completely finished off our democracy. To begin with, it turned the country into so much booty to be distributed. Two-facedness and bossism existed before then, of course, but they were not a systematic, institutionalized form of government, nor did they happen nationwide, as was imposed. . . . after the Front, which imposed clientelism at every level. Political platforms and ideals were over. What each party cared about now was getting positions—they knew they had half of them for the taking. That's why I believe the Front put an end to democracy. The only sine qua non condition for democracy is that an opposition exists.

One of the most praised merits of the Front, according to its defenders, is that it ended violence during elections, and civilized politics. Instead, I believe that what civilized things was women's entering the field of elections. Before, elections were carried out with machetes, truncheons, sticks, and bottles. Men would brawl and shove each other in town plazas. Now, they had to vote with their wives, daughters, or sisters, and the presence of other women provided social restraint after long periods of violence. Everyone had to calm down. And elections turned into confrontations that involved flowers, music, and revelry.

Translated by Ann Farnsworth-Alvear and Ana María Gómez López

Note

1. *Panela* is a loaf of hard molasses or solid brown sugar sold domestically; it is a staple of many Colombian diets.

Starting Points for the FARC and the ELN

Fuerzas Armadas Revolucionarias de Colombia

and Ejército de Liberación Nacional

Although they are not the only guerrilla groups to have shaped recent Colombian history, the FARC (Fuerzas Armadas Revolucionarias de Colombia; the initials EP, for "Ejército Popular" or "People's Army," were added to the group's name in the early 1980s) and the ELN (Ejército de Liberación Nacional) are the two that have survived into the twenty-first century. To underscore their long trajectories we offer texts that speak to their origins. The Simacota Manifesto was read out on January 7, 1965, as part of the ELN assault on that storied town (symbolic of the Comunero rebellion of 1781). The other is circulated by the present-day FARC with the following title: "The Agrarian Program of the Guerrilleros *of the FARC-EP, Proclaimed July 20, 1964 in the Heat of Battle during the Armed Struggle of Marquetalia, Corrected and Expanded at the Eighth National Conference of the FARC-EP, April 2, 1993."*

In the leftist jargon of the 1960s, these are founding texts that correspond to two different "wars." The Simacota document represents the foquista *thinking of Régis Debray and Che Guevara, who held that a small group of ideologically committed fighters could create the "subjective conditions" that would lead to revolution. The ELN saw itself as such a group. The FARC document was instead a product of years of Colombian Communist Party (PCC) strategy, summarized by the slogan of "the combination of all forms of struggle." It reflected the thinking of fighters in retreat from the Colombian military's Marquetalia Operation of May 1964, many of them veterans of the 1950s Violencia in southern Tolima who had now joined the remnants of* autodefensas campesinas. *Significantly, however, two of the most famous and best-organized of what were called self-defense "republics," Viotá and Sumapaz, chose not to join the FARC—not in the 1960s and not afterward. Readers will want to note that although Manuel Marulanda Vélez, Jacobo Arenas, and the other signatories put their names to this document in 1964, the FARC as such was not announced until 1966. But FARC discourse was relatively consistent, and the way this text presents agrarian demands and positions armed campesinos as "victims" did not change over the years. The 1964 version of the text lists "four wars"; the 1993 version, "five wars."*

These texts date from a complicated context. In addition to the ELN and the FARC, the Marxist-Leninist faction of the PCC announced in late 1960s the creation of a "popular liberation army," the EPL, or Ejército Popular de Liberación (People's Army of Liberation), following the Chinese strategist Lin Biao's vision of "prolonged people's war." The EPL was like the ELN in that it was formed in the hothouse environment of universities and urban political struggle. As time passed, the political meanings attached to the different acronyms shifted. Within the ELN, for example, pro-Cuban leaders lost ground as the group found an unexpected source of militants in the new currents of Liberation Theology—especially after the death in combat of Camilo Torres (see part II). By 1973, however, the ELN was on the verge of disappearance—after a military disaster—and then had to reorganize itself almost completely.

New models were on the horizon by that point: Uruguay's Tupamaros, Argentina's Montoneros, and Nicaragua's Sandinistas. In Colombia, the April 19th Movement, or M-19, captured the imagination of many on the Left, when the older guerrilla groups seemed isolated and backward-looking, even if the FARC and the ELN later reemerged in the 1980s. The M-19 drew its leadership from the ANAPO (National Popular Alliance), which dated to 1961 and included many who opposed the National Front and retained affection for the brief dictatorship of General Rojas Pinilla, as well as from ex-FARC and ex-PCC militants. In a moment when the official political system was widely seen as illegitimate, the M-19 offered intrepid action—a kind of political incandescence, even if their popularity proved transient. They opened by stealing Bolívar's sword from the museum dedicated to the Liberator. The "Eme" (as the M-19 was referred to in Colombia) carried out theatrical terrorist actions: the mounting of "people's jails," into which they kidnapped businessmen and supposed collaborators of imperialism; the theft of six thousand rifles through a tunnel dug under an army installation in the north of Bogotá; or their spectacularly successful assault on the Dominican Embassy in March 1980, after which they held key diplomats hostage, including the US ambassador. Their theatricality alternately thrilled Colombians (as in the embassy takeover), or horrified them, as in a 1976 killing when the Eme kidnapped and executed José Raquel Mercado, a trade unionist they accused of collaborating with the CIA.

By 1982–86, when President Belisario Betancur declared a "democratic opening," a certain organizational rearrangement of the various guerrilla groups became clearer. The FARC signed a peace agreement in 1984, but also began to turn toward terrorist action. With a peace process on the table, and after the murder of several of their militants, the M-19 decided to launch an armed attack on the Palace of Justice in November 1985—with tragic results. Many questions have gone unanswered, and historians have work to do as they assess the M-19's action in taking over the Palace of Justice. To what extent did the guerrillas act to protect their own interests, and to *what extent did they act on behalf of drug traffickers? Was Pablo Escobar involved? What Colombians do know was the military responded with violence. Eleven of the Supreme Court justices were killed as part of a scorched-earth retaking of the building. Others in the building, such as cafeteria personnel and several students from Bogotá's Universidad Externado, were victims of forced disappearance. In December 2014, the Inter-American Court of the OAS (Organization of American States) ruled that eleven individuals had been disappeared by the Colombian military, including Supreme Court justice Carlos Horacio Urán Rojas. Judges found that the evidence demonstrated that Urán and the others had been taken to military battalions, tortured, and killed.*

Colombians also could not escape the conclusion that the Eme was politically irresponsible. Just a few months later, the depths to which the guerrillas had sunk was palpable: Hernando Pizarro Leongómez, brother of M-19 leader Carlos Pizarro Leongómez and member of the FARC until the 1980s, founded the Comando Ricardo Franco in southern Cauca with fellow FARC dissident José Fedor Rey Álvarez. Between November 1985 and January 1986, Pizarro and Rey allegedly killed over 160 of their own soldiers accused of collaborating with the CIA and the Colombian army. Members of the press were invited to witness the cruel execution of supposed infiltrators, and Colombians were now seeing the ugly, unvarnished face of so-called revolutionary war.

In trying to win over peasants and rural migrants, the guerrillas' methods have oscillated between that violent face of straight-out terror, on the one hand, and traditional clientelist strategies of co-optation, on the other. In securing material resources they have been more creative. Diverse modalities of extortion, kidnappings, and bank robberies had long been mainstays, but by 1985 the FARC had discovered something new. By connecting themselves to the drug economy, they gained access to a goose that laid golden eggs. At first the ELN hesitated; they lived off extortion money from Manessman Pipe and Steel, which was building an oil pipeline— perhaps they did not need the drug economy. Soon, however, they joined the FARC and, by then, the paramilitaries in tapping the cocaine trade. They got protection payments from coca growers and those who worked to produce the base paste; they worked trade routes and got involved in wholesaling the alkaloid. But in the production chain that added value to cocaine, the guerrillas were closer to poor, rural national producers than they were to global consumers. More professional trafficking groups, along with the paramilitaries, had an advantage. They could count on police protection where guerrillas could not, and they had better access to multilayered networks for trafficking and laundering money.

By the 1990s, the guerrillas had worn thin any cushion they might have had in public opinion. Attacks on oil pipelines, the country's electrical infrastructure, and bridges became increasingly common, while highways became the setting of mass kidnappings known as pescas milagrosas, *or "bounty fishing," a practice in which the guerrillas measured their luck by how many wealthy people they "caught" and managed to ransom. Yet it is worth noting here that their attempts to operate within formal politics had been disastrous. In 1984, militants from both the FARC and the Communist Party had supported a new party, the Unión Patriótica (UP) or Patriotic Union, which began to experience some electoral success but then was exterminated—literally, not figuratively. Dozens of candidates running for offices around the country were assassinated in a campaign of terror orchestrated by drug traffickers, paramilitaries, military officers, and police squads, and thousands of UP activists were killed.*

Peace negotiations in 1999–2002 led by the administration of Andrés Pastrana Arango raised the guerrillas' national political profile, but the process yielded little. By the early 2000s, Colombians' understandings of guerrilla violence had been shaped and reshaped by decades of brutality, including horrific massacres perpetrated by guerrilla commanders, such as in Machuca (1998) and Bojayá (2002). Because this kind of killing was not exceptional but rather had become the rule, it underscored the guerrillas' moral degradation and political failure. Even if the paramilitaries committed more human rights atrocities and more butchery, in most Colombians' minds nothing could justify massacres carried out by guerrillas who had taken up arms to pursue aims such as those expressed in these documents from the 1960s.

The Agrarian Program of the Guerrilleros *of the FARC-EP, Proclaimed July 20, 1964 in the Heat of Battle during the Armed Struggle of Marquetalia, Corrected and Expanded at the Eighth National Conference of the FARC-EP, April 2, 1993*

Fellow farmworkers, laborers, students, craftsmen, intellectuals, soldiers, police officers, patriotic officials, men and women of Colombia:

VICTIMS OF FIVE WARS

We are the nerve of a revolutionary movement that began in 1948. The collective power of large landowners, stockmen, big business, local political bosses, and merchants of violence has been set against us, farmers from south of Tolima, Huila, and Cauca. We have been victims of a "by blood or by fire" policy, endorsed and put into practice by the oligarchy that has seized power. Over the last 45 years, five wars have been unleashed upon us: one beginning in 1948, another in 1954, another in 1962, another on May 18, 1964—the day when senior officials formally announced the beginning of "Operation Marquetalia"—and the one we have faced since December 9,

Manuel Marulanda Vélez, having his feet washed by a woman identified as his wife, Sandra Ramírez, who was later part of the FARC negotiating team that traveled to Havana in 2012 for negotiations with the Colombian government (see part VII). Courtesy of *El Tiempo*.

1990, when the dictator Gaviria and high ranking military officers began the program of extermination against the FARC leadership in Casa Verde[1] and military aggression against the populist movement throughout the country.

We have been the victims of landowner and military fury because here, in this part of Colombia, the interests of the powerful lords of the land and those of the country's most reactionary sectors predominate. For this reason, we have had to bear, in flesh and in spirit, all of the brutalities of a rotting regime nourished by the domination of financial monopolies rooted in imperialism.

A DEAD END

For this reason [imperialism], North American planes, officials, and specialists participate in this war against us. For this reason, 16,000 men armed with weaponry of all kinds have marched against Marquetalia. For this reason, the tactics of economic blockade, of extermination areas, of air- and land-based attacks, and finally, of bacterial warfare, have been used against us.

Guerrilleros del hambre (Guerrilleros of Hunger), Chimichagua, Cesar. Photograph by Efraín
García, 1972. A group of campesinos from northeastern Colombia are seated in a circle
with implements of rural labor that at first glance resemble firearms. Those photographed here were part of an INCORA agrarian reform program. In Eduardo Serrano,
Historia de la fotografía en Colombia 1950–2000 (Bogotá: Editorial Planeta Colombiana,
2006), 51.

For this reason, the government, military officials, and Yankee imperialism
spend hundreds of millions on arms, supplies, spies, and informers. For this
reason, the government and senior officials buy off and corrupt consciences,
and kill, pursue, and imprison the Colombian people who rise up to fight in
solidarity with us, victims of a cruel and inhumane war of extermination.

We have knocked on all possible doors searching for help to avoid an anticommunist crusade, a crusade against our people, that would lead us into
a prolonged and bloody armed struggle.

We are revolutionaries fighting for regime change. We wanted and
fought for this change in the least harmful way for our people: the peaceful
way, the way of democracy. But this way was violently closed to us under
the official fascist pretext of combating supposed "independent republics,"
and since we are revolutionaries who, in one way or another, are playing the
historic role that corresponds to us, we have had to find another way: armed
revolution in the struggle for power.

The current regime has incorporated into its system of governing the clear mechanisms of fascism. The most confrontational and thoughtless figures are in command of the forces of repression. The official armed forces have put into practice the Theory of National Security, a philosophy of terror, of dirty war, of paramilitarism, and of death. They have the support and interests of the oligarchy and of a group of senior officials who claim for themselves the politics, the tactics, and the strategies of PREVENTATIVE WAR and of the INTERNAL ENEMY in order to maintain social discipline through monopolies, through the exploitation of our people and of our natural resources for the sake of imperialism, and through a predatory and reactionary dominant class such as that found in Colombia.

For this reason, the war has recently taken on a true national character that must broadly call upon all of our people to join the armed, revolutionary struggle against the military substructure of the regime. For this reason, the FARC-EP has established itself as a political-military organization that raises the Bolivarian banners and the libertarian traditions of our people in order to fight for power, lead Colombia to the fulfillment of its national sovereignty, and make popular sovereignty the rule. We fight to establish a democratic political regime that guarantees peace with social justice, respect for human rights, and economic growth with welfare for all of us who live in Colombia.

We fight for an agrarian policy that returns large, estate-owned lands to the farmers: for this reason, as of today, July 20, 1964, we are a guerrilla army fighting for the following Agrarian Program:

FIRST. In opposition to an agrarian policy of lies coming from the oligarchy, we endorse an efficient, revolutionary agrarian policy that will change the root of the social structure of the Colombian farmlands, freely handing over the land to those who work or wish to work on it, and based upon the confiscation of estate properties for the benefit of all working people.

The revolutionary agrarian policy will give farmworkers technical and infrastructural assistance, tools, and draft animals for proper economic exploitation of the land. The revolutionary agrarian policy is an indispensable condition for elevating the material and cultural quality of rural life, to rid it of unemployment, hunger, illiteracy, and the endemic illnesses that limit one's ability to work, to break the shackles of large landownership, and to promote the growth of our country's agricultural and industrial production. The revolutionary agrarian policy will confiscate lands occupied by imperialist North American companies, regardless of their titles and the activities to which they are dedicated.

SECOND. The settlers, occupants, tenants, sharecroppers, tenant farmers, and other workers on land owned by estate-holders and the government will receive the corresponding titles of ownership for the lands they work. All forms of latent land exploitation, sharecropping systems, and leasing in kind or cash will be eliminated.

Economic units will be created in rural areas according to the fertility and location of land, with a minimum of 10–20 hectares for lowlands and those neighboring towns and cities, and otherwise according to the fertility and communication networks there. All debt owed by farmworkers to usurers, speculators, and official and semi-official lending institutions will be annulled.

THIRD. The revolutionary government will respect the property of wealthy farmers who personally work their lands. Industrial methods of farmwork will continue. Large agricultural industries that, for reasons of social and economic order should be maintained, will be dedicated to the planned growth of the whole country.

FOURTH. The revolutionary government will establish a broad credit system with payment plans, seed distribution, technical assistance, tools, livestock, implements, machinery, etc., for individual farmers as well as for any production cooperatives that may emerge as part of the process. A planned irrigation and electric system, and a network of official centers for agro-technical research will be created. Sufficient public health services will be organized for undivided attention to public health problems in rural areas. The problem of rural education will be addressed, including the total elimination of illiteracy, and a system of scholarships will be created for the technical and higher education of children of farmworkers. A broad plan for rural housing and the construction of transportation routes from productive rural centers to markets will be completed.

FIFTH. Basic remunerative and sustainable prices will be guaranteed for agricultural products and livestock.

SIXTH. Indigenous communities will be protected, granting them sufficient lands for their development, returning to them the lands that were usurped by the landowners, and modernizing their systems of cultivation. Indigenous communities will enjoy all the benefits of this revolutionary agrarian policy. At the same time, the autonomous organization of the communities will be established, respecting their councils, life, culture, language, and internal organization.

SEVENTH. The success of this revolutionary agrarian program will depend on an alliance between workers and farmers and on a united front of all Colombians in the struggle for regime change, which are the only guarantee for the destruction of the old, landowning structure in Colombia. The success of this policy will rely upon the broadest multitudes of farmers, those who will unfalteringly contribute to the destruction of large land ownership. To such an end, powerful alliances of farmworkers, strong labor unions, consumer committees, and common councils will be organized. For this reason, this program is seen as a vital necessity, the struggle to forge the broadest front, unique among all of the country's democratic, progressive, and revolutionary forces, in order to wage a continual struggle until the oligarchic regime, in the service of Yankee imperialists who impede the fulfillment of the desires of the Colombian people, is thrown to the ground.

EIGHTH. The FARC-EP will enact the first Law of Revolutionary Agrarian Policy in due course. Because of this, we invite farmworkers, laborers, employees, students, craftsmen, small business owners, the national bourgeoisie willing to fight imperialism, democratic intellectuals and revolutionaries, and all Left and Center political parties who desire a change in the meaning of progress to join the great revolutionary and patriotic struggle for a Colombia for Colombians, for the triumph of the revolution, and for a democratic government of national liberation.

> *Marquetalia, July 20, 1964*
> *Manuel Marulanda Vélez, Jacobo Arenas,*
> *Rigoberto Losada, Isauro Yosa, Isaías Pardo,*
> *Luis Pardo, Jesús M. Medina, Darío Lozano,*
> *Tarcisio Guaracas, Parménides Cuenca,*
> *Roberto López, Miriam Narváez, Judith*
> *Grisales, Jesús Ortiz, Rogelio Díaz, Miguel*
> *Aldana, Hernando González Acosta, Gabriel*
> *Gualteros, Miguel Pascuas, Jaime Bustos,*
> *Alcides González and bros., David González,*
> *Andrés Lopez and bros., Luis Salgado, Pedro*
> *Ipús, Evaristo Losada, Vicente Torres, De-*
> *siderio García, Agustín Cifuentes, Abraham*
> *García, Ismael Valderrama, Miguel Garzón,*
> *Jaime García, José Domingo Rivera, Mariano*
> *Pérez Montes.*

The Simacota Manifesto of the National Liberation Army

Reactionary violence, unleashed by the many oligarchic governments and continued by the corrupt Valencia-Ruiz Novoa-Lleras regime, has been a powerful weapon of domination for the last 15 years.

Our education is in the hands of businessmen who get rich on the ignorance in which they keep our people; the land is worked by poor farmers who have nowhere to die and who exhaust their energy and that of their family for the sake of oligarchs who live like kings in the cities; laborers work for starvation wages, subjected to misery and humiliation by powerful foreign and domestic businessmen; young democratic professionals and intellectuals find themselves surrounded, facing the dilemma of whether to surrender to the dominant class or perish; in the countryside and the cities, small and medium producers watch as their economies are ruined by the cutthroat competition and monopolization by which nations are sold to foreign capital and its cronies; North American imperialists plunder the wealth that belongs to all Colombians.

Our people, however, who have felt the lash of exploitation, misery, and violence upon their backs, rise up and are ready to fight. Revolutionary struggle is the only way for our people to vanquish the current government of deception and violence.

We, who gathered the National Liberation Army, are fighting for the liberation of Colombia. The people, Liberal and Conservative, will stand together in a common front to overthrow the oligarchy in both parties.

Long live unity among farmers, workers, students, professionals, and honest people who wish to make Colombia a dignified homeland for true Colombians!

Liberation or death!

> *National Liberation Army*
> *José Antonio Galán Front*
> *Camilo Villareal [Fabio Vásquez Castaño]*
> *Andrés Sierra [Víctor Medina Morón]*
> *Simacota, January 7, 1965*

Both texts translated by Timothy F. Johnson

Note

1. *Casa Verde* refers to a December 1990 military operation against the FARC headquarters in La Uribe, Meta, during the administration of President César Gaviria Trujillo. Casa Verde had been established as a FARC encampment soon after Operation Marquetalia.

Where Is Omaira Montoya?

María Tila Uribe and Francisco J. Trujillo

In 1978, Colombian president Julio César Turbay Ayala (1978–82) issued his administration's National Security Statute. A measure to extend the powers of the military and police under the mantle of domestic security, the decree was a response to increased guerrilla activity from the FARC, the ELN, and the M-19. In practice, it drastically reduced the ability of Left-leaning Colombians to organize and protest. The timing of the National Security Statute was not coincidental: in September 1977, Colombian labor unions called a national general strike, which lasted almost a week. This was one of the largest strikes in the country's history, with support from workers, activists, and trade unionists nationwide. Colombian security officials carried out massive arrests and forceful interrogations, often using torture. Two of those captured by the military in the city of Barranquilla were Omaira Montoya Henao, who was pregnant, and her partner at the time, Mauricio Trujillo Uribe. Mauricio was tortured and held captive in a battalion; Omaira was never seen again. The following narrative of the disappearance is provided by María Tila Uribe, Mauricio's mother, herself a long-standing human rights activist. Tila Uribe is also the daughter of Tomás Uribe Márquez, a communist organizer famous for his involvement with the banana workers' strike of 1928.

Omaira's abduction took place prior to the implementation of the National Security Statute, but it points to the kind of repressive measures and military force authorized by Colombia's executive branch throughout the 1970s and 1980s. The country was repeatedly placed under martial law between the beginning of the National Front in 1958 and the 1991 Colombian Constitution—sometimes for periods of years. Turbay was not unique in granting extraordinary powers to security forces. Nevertheless, the institutionalized use of torture and the forced disappearance of political dissidents increased significantly during his administration.

The cruelest morning of my life was September 13 of that merciless year, 1977. As usual, when I woke up, I stretched out my hand to turn on the radio and listen to the news. I had gone to bed exhausted from overwork, and the night had been too short; I would have given anything to sleep a

Bernardo Salcedo,
Primera Lección, 1970.
Courtesy of Museo
de Arte Moderno de
Bogotá and Margarita
Salcedo.

little longer. At that very moment, the radio newscaster began presenting the first news of the day. . . . . . . "Attention! Attention! A guerrilla leader has been arrested in the city of Barranquilla. . . . . . . his name is Mauricio Trujillo Uribe!" I jumped up, dropping everything to the floor. I tried to leave, and then stayed put. Had I misheard this name and overstated libel? I changed to another radio station: the news was also being broadcast, and I could only hear the last segment of the announcement: ". . . . . . . dead or captured, alias 'Marcos,' the *guerrillero* Trujillo Uribe, leader of the subversive E.L. . . . ." By then I had no doubt and I ran to Marta in the next cell: "My son, Martica . . . my son!" She hugged me in silence, listening to the news. Seconds later, the cell filled with fellow *compañeras* [used here to refer both to female inmates and to women "in the struggle"], some half-dressed, barefoot, or in their underwear: more were crowding outside, and the whole prison heard the news. It was six o'clock in the morning, more or less. Some whispered among themselves as if at a funeral wake: they would not address me directly, only through the grieving looks on their faces, as the broadcasts had been misleading, saying he had been "killed in combat." Like me, they knew how to read between the lines—they figured out that he had been detained, not killed.

The situation was dramatic. That morning I learned what it means to grieve the death of one's child. The image that came to my mind was the hooded military interrogator who threatened to bring me my son's body. The interrogator. . . . . . dark unblinking eyes, gold-capped teeth, his sneering mouth, and a voice that I will never forget screaming at me, "Tell that son of a bitch to turn himself in!" I gave my tragedy the shape of that man, and I asked myself: "Does he have a mother? And if so, does she know that she brought a monster into the world?" In other more lucid moments I thought: "What is the difference? If not the hooded man, it would be anyone else on some payroll demanding a raise." A *compañera* brought me some water, leaning down and stating warmly as she handed it to me: "It's for his politics. The reason for his persecution was his ideals and commitment." She kept analyzing the reasons, and even though these were things I already understood, they were still useful for me to hear at that moment. The women tried to encourage me by talking and although nothing could fully console me in the depth of my pain, I had mixed feelings of pride knowing he was a revolutionary. [. . .] My eyes were clouded, my life passed in front of me as if it were a film. I saw him as a child, beautiful to me with his golden curls, playing with his sisters and little brother. But that was just for a moment, and then my tears, cries, and moans would begin again.

It was a terrible day, yet I feared the night all the more. María, who took care of me like a daughter, gave me sleeping pills that I swallowed all at once. The broadcasts continued the next day, and it was then that they named Omaira Montoya Henao. It had been the two of them! Both were in prison!

On September 14, the day of a nationwide general strike, my daughter Esperanza walked two kilometers from home in order to beg to see me. Her face revealed both grief and strength, and during the ten minutes of her visit, she consoled me, assuring me that her brother was alive. "I will search for him, Mother," she said, "that is what we have agreed with my uncles. We do not have money for the trip, but there will be solidarity. . . . . . ." She then made it plural: "I will search for both of them." I kissed her and as she was leaving said to her, "Bring me a piece of paper with your brother's handwriting," thinking that would be the only way I could be certain that he was still alive.

Those days of waiting for her to return felt like centuries. The radio only spoke of deaths and mass arrests throughout the country as a result of the enormous outpouring of this working-class protest. . . . . . . the death toll reaches 37 in the city of Bogotá. . . . . . . more than a thousand union members are in prison. . . . . . . arrest warrants issued for subversives. . . . . . . The minister is outraged. . . . . . . Democracy shall not be sullied. [. . .]

All of my *compañeras*, political or not, watched out for my daughter's return. When finally the guards called to announce I had a visit, there were exclamations of "It's her!" "Have faith!" as they walked me to the first door.

Our meeting was again a prolonged embrace, after which she pulled out a small piece of paper from her purse, and handed to me: "Mother, I am all right." I had an instant of horror when I saw it was not his handwriting, but she quickly told me: "He *dictated* it to me, they are his words [original emphasis]," and she recounted the main events of her trip. With time I learned how much she hid from me with what she said: She had made the trip almost penniless, with only a one-way ticket and not enough money to eat—totally broke. She stayed with a sympathetic family in a humble neighborhood, who treated her with enormous affection. Honest, selfless lawyers helped in the exhausting crusade of legal procedures. One in particular left his job to dedicate himself exclusively to the matter. In addition, residents of a squatter neighborhood collected money for Mauricio's case, and they protested in single file near the BIM [Brigada de Institutos Militares, a military intelligence office] with white handkerchiefs. When she went to the military brigade for the first time, they denied they had him. She was only able to see her brother because, after verifying the place where he was being held, she was determined to remain there despite attempts to mislead her or drive her away. When she managed to enter, as ordered by the military judge, he had already been transferred to Bogotá.

I only found out about the ordeal of his torture through a human rights publication, where it said Mauricio was a wreck: a cut on his forehead from a blow of a revolver's butt remained unstitched, his wrists no longer responded, and he was badly bruised and very weak. The next time my daughter came to see me, I asked her to tell me in her own words what she had seen, even if it had been cruel. She lifted my face tenderly: "You should be proud of him, mother, he was very brave and behaved with dignity. You have nothing to be ashamed of, and remember that your son is still ALIVE!"

I smiled at her, my face drenched in tears. After I gathered my strength, I asked: "And Omaira? How is she?"

"Omaira is not there . . . he is alone."

I do not know Omaira's mother, but I know of her infinite sadness [. . .]

My son made the circumstances of his torture and Omaira's disappearance known to military judges. He requested that the Minister [of Justice] and the Procurador [an office somewhat akin to that of the attorney general in the United States or Britain] investigate them and the facts of what had happened, and he wrote a public letter that was circulated by some of the media. *El Bogotano* elaborated on the information he provided, denouncing what had happened in a published article that provided the full names of those involved. The Committee in Solidarity with Political Prisoners (CSPP) and—later—the Committee of Political Prisoners' Relatives also denounced this case in their publications, as did the Permanent Committee for the Defense of Human Rights (CPDH) and Amnesty International, the latter making a record of this case in its Colombia report. I transcribe here excerpts from Mauricio's narration of the facts:

> . . . You felt it in the air: the news spread by word of mouth through working class neighborhoods, from Route 40 to downtown. The National Civil Strike was imminent. I traveled to Medellín, picked up Omaira, and arrived with her to Barranquilla. We received instructions to collaborate in tasks that would allow the Organization's presence to be felt on that historic day of the people. Then, as now, wages were not enough to make ends meet, monopolies did as they pleased, and the government's antinational policy regarding hydrocarbons was evident in the increase of gasoline prices. The "perpetual" state of siege and the approval of several repressive decrees created an environment of fear and oppression against union and labor organizations. In short, the people's discontent was clear. . . . . . . *Compañera* Omaira had some experience. She worked as a bacteriologist at the Hospital San Vicente de Paúl in Medellín. She was an outstanding activist and a woman of real strength. . . . . . . When they stopped us there were many passersby, given the place and time of day. A crowd formed to see what was happening. We screamed out our names and our condition of political activists at the top of our lungs. Weeks later, this was confirmed in a traffic officer's sworn testimony. . . . . . . As the first blows rained down on us we were dragged onto a truck. . . . . . . We headed toward the airport, and then the car made a turn toward Caracolí. At one point I addressed the lieutenant to warn him that Omaira had a heart condition, and not

to touch her. . . . . . . He laughed and said, "All the better, as nobody can make a complaint about a natural death." They left us out in a deserted place: Omaira was taken over to a vehicle, and I was led to a tree. At first a man with a kind demeanor interrogated me for a while, asking questions that I was unable to answer. . . . . . . They then proceeded to hang me from my arms and back, tying the belt from my pants underneath my handcuffs. I hung in the air like a pendulum, and then it was blow after blow, on my testicles, my head, and my stomach, with fists, boots, and clubs. They took turns. I was thrown to the ground. . . . . . . It was the good guy again: "Don't make them beat you, talk or they will kill you, spare me the trouble. . . . . . ." Again, I was strung up. Another go-round. Once more, I had the beating of my life and. . . . . . down again to the ground. . . . . . . And then the nice guy came back: "Look, come along, tell us what's up. . . . . . ." Third time up in the air. I started to get cramps all over. An old fat guy took me by the jaw, opened my mouth, and forced a handful of dirt down my throat, then another. . . . . . I began to choke, unable to breathe. Then all of sudden "HALT." Two men in uniform arrived: Colonel XX, head of the F-2, and a police major. They repeated the same questions I was asked before, only this time they guaranteed I would get a passport and a trip abroad. They left. It was all the same for them to have come and gone, but not for me. The lieutenant brought a gun to my forehead before my speechless face. I closed my eyes. . . . . . . The man slapped me in the face, and said that now it would be Omaira's turn because of my stubbornness, and that I should "prepare to die slowly. . . . . . very slowly. . . . . . ." I lost consciousness, and when I woke up Omaira was no longer with me. . . . . . . We were held in a military barracks. . . . . . . I experienced a strange kind of kidnapping. I was taken from one place to the next through uninhabited regions bordering the coast. . . . . . . By that time news of our capture was being covered by the press, which posed an obstacle for their sinister intentions, but I only learned that later. On the eleventh day, specialists from the BINCI [Batallón Único de Inteligencia y Contrainteligencia, or Military Battalion for Intelligence and Counterintelligence] and the Charry Solano Battalion came. . . . . . . Then it started all over again. . . . . . . about the dark history of the commanders of the National Liberation Army (ELN), and being told how mistaken we were. To top it off, they said they were also Leftists! They were, in their words, my "collaborators"! Then I had to go before a judge, "Doctor. . . . . . ." I began to feel dread: Omaira was not there. I spoke to him about her and our capture, providing information on how to find witnesses, as well as telling him to go to her apartment to collect witness testimony from the neighbors. Her clothes would still be there. He told me that he "was not going to waste his time." . . . . . . I do not blame him—we live in a nation where unemployment is rampant and it is not strange to find lawyers driving taxis. . . . . . . One would have to be a citizen of high personal integrity. Government officials are appointed and removed by the high military command. One doesn't need a lengthy explanation to understand the situation. . . . . . .

Mauricio is now in jail recovering from his torture, along with his father and other political *compañeros*. Knowing they are together brings me consolation. I have also learned from many others that, in public places throughout Colombia's cities, one can find flyers with Omaira's picture and the following caption: "Where is Omaira Montoya?"

Translated by Ana María Gómez López

Note

In this selection, suspension points are in the original. Our own ellipses points, to show abridgment, are in square brackets.

We Prefer a Grave in Colombia to a Cell in the United States

Los Extraditables

In 1979, as Colombians were beginning to export large quantities of cocaine, the national government signed an extradition treaty with the United States and set 1982 as the date by which extradition would become law. Few at the time imagined how deeply that decision would set Colombians against one another. Within a decade, hundreds of judges and two high-profile presidential candidates had been murdered, and the country was embroiled in a multifront war (among drug-funded guerrillas, paramilitaries, and complicit members of the country's security forces, as well as among competing drug cartels).

Pablo Escobar was the most visible opponent of extradition. He tried a political strategy, including a brief stint as a congressman, but by 1984 his approach to the extradition problem had become that of plata o plomo (money or bullets). Escobar's henchmen imposed that stark choice on Rodrigo Lara Bonilla, then minister of justice, who was murdered in Bogotá in April 1984, as well as on ordinary policemen, court officers at every level, and the Colombian Supreme Court. The capo also declared himself at war, initiating a spate of bombings in Bogotá, Cali, and Medellín that are remembered with terror by residents in those cities.

The pamphlet translated here, from December 1989, is representative of the populist language Escobar used to attack extradition. Traffickers emphasized their own "right to a nationality" and turned extradition into a referendum on governance. Had Colombians seen prosperity as a result of the status quo "oligarchic" regime? Traffickers' families had been targeted, now the families of the oligarchy would be held "hostage." The new rhetoric did not last, however. Within months, traffickers had returned to fighting among themselves, and extradition continued its zigzag history. The 1991 Constitution expressly disallowed it. By 1993 Escobar was dead and other traffickers had begun to view extradition differently. A 1997 constitutional amendment allowed it, and drug offenders in Colombia today seem to take the conditions of extradition as one more option to be broached in individual negotiations with the state.

LOS EXTRADITABLES

Preferimos una tumba en Colombia, A un calabozo en los Estados Unidos

LOS EXTRADITABLES
AL PUEBLO DE COLOMBIA:

1. Que hemos ordenado a líderes de los barrios populares la toma de rehenes de miembros de la oligarquía tradicional, especialmente de aquellos que no se han caracterizado nunca por realizar obras sociales en favor de la comunidad o de las personas desprotegidas.

2. Que los fondos obtenidos como fruto de estas acciones militares, serán utilizados en un cincuenta por ciento para la financiación de la guerra declarada por la oligarquía política y el otro cincuenta por ciento en la construcción de vivienda popular para los desamparados.

3. Que esta medida se toma como respuesta a la persecución oficial contra nuestras familias y organizaciones.

4. Que durante más de seis años, hemos estado llamando a la paz; pero sólo hemos obtenido como respuesta las antijurídicas y clandestinas extradiciones y los atropellos.

5. Que seguimos dispuestos al diálogo, como el pueblo de Colombia lo pide y lo desea.

6. Que no bajaremos la bandera y doblaremos nuestra lucha para sorpresa de un gobierno pro-imperialista y antipatriótico, que se autoproclama victorioso.

7. Que luchamos por nuestra familia, nuestra libertad, nuestra vida y nuestros derechos de nacionalidad y de patria.

LOS EXTRADITABLES

Press release that arrived by fax to Colombian news outlets in December 1989. It was from Los Extraditables, an organization run by Pablo Escobar and other leading Colombian druglords. In James Mollison, *The Memory of Pablo Escobar* (London: Chris Boot, 2007), 82.

· The Extraditables Inform the Colombian People:

> That we have ordered neighborhood leaders from *barrios populares* [working-class neighborhoods] to take hostages from among the members of the traditional oligarchy, especially those who have never been known for willingness to create social programs that benefit the community or for those who are most vulnerable.
>
> That funds obtained as the result from this military action will be used as follows: fifty percent for the financing of the war declared against us by the political oligarchy, and the remaining fifty percent for the construction of affordable housing for the poor.
>
> That this measure is taken in response to the official persecution faced by our families and our organizations.
>
> That we have been calling for peace for more than six years but that the only answer we have received has been illegal extraditions, carried out clandestinely, and attacks.
>
> That we are still willing to negotiate, following the demands and desires of the Colombian people.
>
> That we will not lower our flag. We will redouble our struggle, to the disbelief of this pro-imperialist, anti-patriotic government which self-proclaims itself as victorious.
>
> That we fight for our families, our freedom, our lives, and our right to nationality and country.

Translated by Ana María Gómez López

A Medic's Life within a Cocaine-Fueled Paramilitary Organization

Diego Viáfara Salinas

In 1982, the Procuraduría General de la Nación [Inspector General's Office] began investigating paramilitary organizations, such as Muerte a Secuestradores (Death to Kidnappers), or MAS. MAS was a death squad targeting guerrilla members, their families, and alleged supporters: by 1982 it was responsible for almost 240 assassinations. MAS was created by narco-traffickers Fabio Ochoa and Pablo Escobar and centered its activities in the Magdalena Medio region, with financial support from local landowners, cattle ranchers, and businessmen, and with regular collaboration from the army and police. While MAS actions were undoubtedly criminal, the alliance between paramilitaries, citizens, and security officials was legally permissible under Law 48 of 1968 (an outgrowth of Decree 3398 of 1965), which allowed civilians to use military weaponry and operate together with the Colombian army. This legislation, similar to that allowing civilian patrols in Guatemala, El Salvador, and Peru, was drafted on the recommendation of US military strategists, who favored using civilians in counterinsurgency campaigns.

What began as a questionable antiguerrilla tactic quickly provided a front for an illicit partnership between drug traffickers, the military, and police officers. The former helped fight guerrillas in a dirty war that served a common purpose, and the latter two gained access to money-laundering profits and lucrative drug-related activities. By the time President Virgilio Barco annulled Law 48 and ordered the arrest of paramilitary leaders in 1989, it was already too late: narco-paramilitaries were considered an international terrorist group by the US government and were implicated in attacks on Colombian judges, federal prosecutors, high-ranking government officials, and presidential candidates.

Testimony provided by a protected witness, a former guerrilla who then spent six years working for paramilitary commanders in the middle Magdalena (connected to MAS), offers a window on the trafficker-fueled violence of the mid-1980s.

MR. VIÁFARA: Good morning. I greet the authorities present here and the public in general.

My name is Diego Viáfara Salinas. I am a Colombian citizen and was born on January 1, 1955, in the municipality of Jamundí in the Department of Valle in a small town outside of Cali. I recently fled Colombia after defecting from a narco-paramilitary organization, of which I was a member for almost 6 years. I am currently under Federal protection, trying to learn English and start a new life in the United States.

During my high school years in Jamundí, I became involved with student activities in groups called "student welfare committees." The basic goal of these groups was to advocate political, social and agricultural reform. We marched, we had political rallies and even burned buses and threw rocks at policemen. At that time in Colombia, the subversive left was quite fashionable. We looked to the M-19 and other guerrilla groups as models to emulate. I later learned that these so-called social committees or student welfare committees were actually controlled by the insurgents, M-19.

In college I became involved with some subversive activities, to the extent that my studies were often interrupted by enforced periods of hiding. Nonetheless, I completed between 4 and 5 years of university studies in medicine, but I never received my degree, and consequently I was never licensed to practice as a physician.

In 1983, I was living in the city of Bucaramanga, Colombia. At that time, that was a stronghold of the members of the insurgency. We had information that there were armed civilian groups working in coordination with the military against guerrillas in the Middle Magdalena Valley in Colombia. I was instructed to infiltrate these armed groups so that our guerrillas, our Insurgency could better defend itself. I was following the orders of a physician, Dr. Carlos Toledo-Plata [M-19 commander].

The plan involved five people in two separate operations. My plan was for me and two colleagues to go to the Middle Magdalena and accept the amnesty offered to guerrillas at that time.

There were five of us, I repeat. Later on we had two separate operations. We had information that the Army was turning over amnestied guerrillas to these armed paramilitary groups. As it turned out, that was exactly what happened to me, although they decided to kill my two colleagues who had penetrated the group. I guess they thought that since I was a medic I could be more useful to them alive.

On December 29, 1983, I was taken by Army Captain Estanislao Caicedo from the Bárbula Battalion of Puerto Boyacá and turned over to members of a paramilitary group in the city of Puerto Boyacá. One of the first members I met was a man named Henry de Jesús Pérez. I ended up staying with this paramilitary organization for 6 years, working directly for Henry Pérez and his men. Henry is the son of Gonzalo Pérez, who is a very important person in the Middle Magdalena region.

I soon discovered that this group was made up of cattlemen, farmers and peasants in the region who have banded together because they were tired of being extorted and terrorized by guerrilla groups. Gonzalo Pérez had been a leader in the armed agrarian movement for years before it became allied with the narcotics traffickers, and he was committed to fighting the guerrillas with whatever means required.

I want to underscore that our group had nothing to do with narcotics traffickers in 1981, although there were plenty of estates owned by narcotics traffickers in the area. This was often misconstrued, because in December 1981, the narcotics traffickers, themselves, formed a paramilitary wing to fight the guerrillas and called it MAS, or death to kidnappers.

I learned that the armed civilians in Puerto Boyacá called themselves "the group," or "the organization," but never "MAS" at that time. I would estimate that the group—the paramilitary group—had something like 500 armed men at that time. In 1984, with my help, a front organization called the Association of Farmers and Ranchers of the Middle Magdalena was created. The acronym in Spanish is ACDEGAM.

Under this association the paramilitary organization was organized, operated and funded. The funds were provided by farmers and ranchers. The Association did have a legitimate side. I ran a pharmacy and offered general health care to the peasants in the Middle Magdalena region and other regions of Colombia. I worked as a paramedic, pharmacist and physician in the central office of ACDEGAM.

As far as I was aware, the unification of the narcotics traffickers and the cattlemen's association occurred in 1985. I personally became aware of it because of an incident which occurred involving a police detachment which detained a cargo vehicle carrying three men and a shipment of cocaine. The vehicle was traveling from the Hacienda Suiza, the Suiza farm owned by Jairo Correa and Francisco Barbosa, to Hacienda Nápoles, owned by Pablo Escobar.

The cattlemen's association was asked to get involved in the recapture of the men, vehicle, and cocaine, and I was summoned to Gonzalo Pérez's home to give medical attention to those wounded in the recapture. Twenty or 30 days after this incident, 30 men from the cattlemen's association were assigned to guard the cocaine laboratory at the Hacienda Suiza. Thus began the merger of the two groups. It later became routine for groups of patrolmen from our organization to be dispatched to various locations to protect a laboratory, a stash, clandestine airstrips or other interests of the organization.

By 1985, I was responsible for carrying out any order given to me by Henry Pérez, the leader of the paramilitary group in Colombia. Henry Pérez worked principally for José Gonzalo Rodríguez Gacha. At this point, the civilian paramilitary group was providing security to all the drug labs owned by traffickers in the region. I saw many of the labs because as a medic I was constantly traveling to those sites dispensing medicine, giving injections and attending to general sanitation to avoid epidemics. In traveling to those locations, I was often riding on or surrounded by bags containing tremendous amounts of dollars or cocaine.
. . .

Life in this organization could be, and usually was, quite brutal. I was present when many tortures and executions were carried out. I saw people sawed up, bit by bit, with a chain saw, and I saw women tortured, pregnant women, even. Other people were cut up into small pieces and dumped into the river after their execution so that no trace would be found of the bodies. On several occasions I took part in wholesale slaughters of supporters of leftist sympathizers, workers and peasants. This isn't something I am proud of, but in an organization it is a matter of survival, kill or be killed.

In addition to the killings carried out by the paramilitary groups, there are dozens of other independent assassin gangs. These assassins are simply hired guns who will kill for anyone who can pay the price. The gangs are typically made up of boys between the ages of 15 and 25, many of them already have 50 to 100 killings to their name. Each gang has its own name, such as Los Priscos, the Orphans, the Smurfs, the Magnificents, the Special Group, and the Nachos.

These were people that I often tended to as a medic, and I shared quite a bit of time with them. During this period I became pretty well acquainted with José Gonzalo Rodríguez Gacha, who we used to call Don Andrés. We never called him El Mejicano. I personally played soccer with him for recreation. Gacha was always very nice to me and he always gave me money, helping me out. He never carried a weapon.

He also advised me quite often to stop drinking, because I was drinking heavily at the time. However, I also saw the other side of him when ordering or planning assassinations. Gacha was fanatical about eliminating all left wing politicians and those belonging to subversive groups in Colombia. Henry Pérez followed Gacha's orders and carried out these assassinations, but Gacha always was the person who paid or who approved these assassinations. Gacha would frequently take more than passing interest in the assassinations and would specify exactly how he wanted a given person to be killed. From what I could see, Gacha was the top international drug trafficker in Colombia at the time. I even saw him give orders to Pablo Escobar once in a while. . . .

The second week in January of 1989, I was told to report to El Recreo farm. I was transported there by airplane. When I arrived, there was some kind of a summit meeting going on with Rodríguez Gacha, Fabio Ochoa, a representative for Pablo Escobar named John, Nelson Lesmes, Víctor Carranza and Leonidas Vargas, plus about 30 other powerful persons whom I did not know.

This meeting was to discuss the need for increased security at laboratories, as well as how to increase cocaine production. They also discussed plans to reactivate Tranquilandia, a major lab complex seized by the Government of Colombia in 1984.

A second meeting was held between Gacha and a smaller group of about five people in order to discuss the need to purge the organization of untrustworthy people. This caused me to worry about my own security, because I knew that I was being watched carefully because of my previous affiliation with the M-19 movement and because I allegedly had used drugs in a camp.

A short time later, they took away my weapon and gave me an older one, which was less serviceable. I had seen countless times that people were not allowed to retire from the organization, so I decided I had to escape. I managed to escape to Bogotá where I went to the offices of the newspaper *El Espectador*. I picked *El Espectador* because I knew that the organization had infiltrators in the other Bogotá newspapers like *La Prensa* and *El Tiempo*, and I also knew that *El Espectador* opposed drug trafficking.

The editors convinced me to tell my story for the Colombian security organization, which I did. Because of the information I gave them, laboratories were raided and several people were arrested, including, later on, Freddy Rodríguez, Gacha's son. Later the Administrative Security Department, known as the DAS, arranged my exit from Colombia and my entry into your country where I currently reside. I will gladly answer any questions you may have.

Thank you.

SENATOR NUNN. Thank you, Mr. Viáfara, I will turn to Senator Roth for the first questions.

SENATOR ROTH. Thank you, Mr. Chairman.

In your testimony, you discussed the camps at which the paramilitary forces were trained. Specifically what subjects were taught at these camps?

MR. VIÁFARA. At these camps they taught combat techniques, patrol techniques, martial arts, first-aid, general teaching on arms, explosives preparation, and techniques with different explosives. They had lectures, and, later on, practical exercises in the area.

They also had escort courses, raid courses and kidnapping courses. These were the fields covered, generally speaking, in these schools.

In the special courses, they included mapping courses, they taught people how to read a compass, and they also had intelligence and counter-intelligence courses.

SENATOR ROTH. What types of explosives were used?

MR. VIÁFARA. The explosives we used in training were TNT, dynamite, C-4 composition, ampho, and other home produced or home made explosives that we would make there. But the basic ones were TNT and C-4 composition. We would also use detonators.

SENATOR ROTH. Do you know of any instances in which the car bomb techniques were utilized by the paramilitary forces?

MR. VIÁFARA. Yes, of course. I learned how to make car bombs. . . . You could use remote control detonators or time devices, and just by merely pressing a button you could explode one of these bombs. Very often you would place a vehicle with a bomb near—or a vehicle that you targeted would go by and you would have, therefore, a time device to explode the bomb, or you would put a car in a certain place so that when the vehicle went by it would explode.

You would also use a clock device, so after some minutes or seconds the device would explode. The use of these charges was taught by mercenary instructors like the English and the Israelis. . . .

SENATOR ROTH. Well, I would like you to watch a videotape and then I will ask you some questions about it.

[Video presentation]

SENATOR ROTH. Were you present when the first part of this videotape, of the paramilitary training was made?

MR. VIÁFARA. Yes, sir.

SENATOR ROTH. Where was this videotape shot?

MR. VIÁFARA. The videotape at the beginning was filmed in a place called San Vito on the banks of the Magdalena River.

SENATOR ROTH. Why was this videotape shot?

MR. VIÁFARA. This video was filmed so that other patrolmen who were not able to attend the courses given by these instructors would have an opportunity to watch the film and learn something. This film was done by a colleague called Douglas Labrador, and he was instructed by Henry Pérez to do so. Douglas worked in the office where we had the computer—where the organization had the computer—to keep track of all the payments that were made for the patrol people.

SENATOR ROTH. Now, do you recognize any of the Israeli instructors shown in the first part of this videotape?

MR. VIÁFARA. Yes, of course. I lived with them. There is Klein and Teddy. I lived with them during the courses. . . .

SENATOR ROTH. Did the Colombian Army battalion which was located in the area near these training camps know about these foreign instructors? If so, did they say or do anything about this?

MR. VIÁFARA. The Bárbula Battalion, which is stationed in Boyacá, has been an accomplice of the organization for the 6 years that I was in the area. When the courses were given, for example, some rifles needed— FAL rifles or G-3s—for the course were provided by Bárbula Battalion. A mortar that was needed for practice during the course was also given to the organization by the Bárbula Battalion.

Ammunition, too, was provided by the Bárbula Battalion. I hope you will believe me, because what I am telling you is the truth; it is real. The commanders and some officers of the Bárbula Battalion worked with the organization for many years, perhaps back to 1983, from 1983 until late 1988 when I was there. I saw them. I was there shoulder to shoulder with them, and they were direct accomplices of the narco-military organization.

For example, they had radio communications directly with the organization. The Bárbula Battalion commander communicated directly via radio with anyone in the organization; Henry Pérez, any of them. And also, they carried out patrols working directly with the Bárbula Battalion members and members of our organization. . . . They receive favors or privileges from the organization and so they prefer to look the other way.

That is a reality; that is something that is real; I am not making it up. In my country, this is evident and it is obvious day by day. I personally witnessed this and I gave them, under orders of the organization, large amounts of money. I would turn over money to the commander of a police post or an Army command. This was money paid by the organization to them for them to look the other way in view of the unlawful activities of the organization.

SENATOR ROTH. You personally gave money to Army commanders.

MR. VIÁFARA. Just as I said, I personally, in 1988, went with Major Gavino, who has ties with the organization, and I distributed something like 23 million pesos in the area of Córdoba to the commander of police, and Pores Cordillo [unconfirmed name], the commander of the police in Careleta Córdoba, [unconfirmed name], the police commander in Montería, a member of the Army stationed in Montería, a member of DAS, stationed in Montería, also others in Caucasia and Planetarrica.

I personally accompanied Major Gavino and turned over to each of them money. This was something like a quota, a monthly quota or fee, paid by the organization to buy their silence in terms of their not reporting a secret airstrip in El Asio in Córdoba from where cocaine was flown to the United States. . . .

SENATOR ROTH. My time is up. Thank you, Mr. Chairman.

SENATOR NUNN. Thank you, Senator Roth. Mr. Viáfara, I just have a few questions.

You were originally a member of the M-19 organization, the leftist group, is that right?

MR. VIÁFARA. I was a sympathizer of M-19 and I engaged in penetration under the orders of Carlos Toledo-Plata.

. . . .

SENATOR NUNN. Why does the narco-military organization try to destroy M-19? What is the barrier between them?

MR. VIÁFARA. Historically, there is a conviction on the part of the drug kingpins that M-19 was the group that harmed its initial interest by kidnapping Marta Nieves Ochoa, the sister of Fabio Ochoa and Jorge Ochoa.

So from that time in 1981, it is known historically that the drug traffickers began to take reprisals against M-19 and the insurgent groups, guerrilla groups in Colombia, because the guerrillas went against the traffickers interests, either by kidnapping them or by making them pay protection monies, or through extortion.

So since that time, the traffickers publicly stated that they were creating a rightist organization to fight the M-19 and to fight the guerrillas, because they had kidnapped Marta Nieves and harmed their interest. And they said that since then they had only brought peace and progress to Colombia. This was said in a leaflet that they circulated in several cit-

Campaign car for Betty Camacho de Rangel, candidate for the Colombian House of Representatives, May 1986. Photograph by Lucio Lara, *Semanario Voz*. Camacho had connections to both the traditional Liberal Party and the Patriotic Union (UP), a party with ties to the FARC; the latter made her a target. She was killed in 1998 in a crime that went unsolved. Estimates of the number of people killed because they were members of the UP or had a less direct connection to the group, including presidential candidates, congresspeople, local officials, and sympathizers of all kinds, range from one thousand to four thousand. In Roberto Romero Ospina, *Unión Patriótica: Expedientes contra el olvido* (Bogotá: Centro de Memoria, Paz y Reconciliación, 2012), 110. Courtesy of Roberto Romero Ospina.

ies in 1981, giving rise to the creation of MAS, the Death to Kidnappers organization.

SENATOR NUNN. Is that rivalry still going on, is the killing still going on between those two groups today, or when you left Colombia, was it still going on?

MR. VIÁFARA. The rivalry between traffickers and the leftists of Colombia is evident from 1983 to the time I left. Their objective is to eradicate subversion in Colombia if possible. . . .

The war against the left in Colombia has been waged against the political arm of the FARC, the Patriotic Union. Thousands of members of the Patriotic Union have been killed in Colombia. I personally know that all of these killings have been carried out under the orders of the organization.

I witnessed very many killings of the leaders of the Patriotic Union. And this was done by the leaders of the organization that I belong to.

SENATOR NUNN. What about the killings of Government officials, police officials, judges and so forth?

Do you personally know who orders those killings? Did you have any direct contact with the people who were ordering the killing of Colombian governmental officials?

MR. VIÁFARA. Yes, of course, of course. For example, the killing of the political leader of the Patriotic Union, Dr. Pardo Leal, was carried out by our organization. It was master minded by Gonzalo Rodríguez Gacha, in coordination with Henry Pérez. The people that were instructed to kill the man were William Infantes and El Gato, the Cat, a brother of William Infantes.

There were three patrolmen that attended a course in the Galaxias school [a paramilitary training school in the town of Pacho, Cundinamarca, financed by José Gonzalo Rodríguez Gacha]. They had been trained also in the school of Magdalena Medio. They later on were picked up in the area where Dr. Pardo Leal was killed and they were taken by helicopter to the Yarí area where I was. I had an opportunity to chat with them, and we spoke of these things in our chat. And they told me how the assassination was carried out, how Pardo Leal was shot and how they had left the premises.

Note

Accent marks have been added to correct the spelling of Colombian names and places.

Carlos Castaño "Confesses"

Mauricio Arangurén Molina

In March 2000, Carlos Castaño Gil appeared in an interview broadcast on Colombian television. This was the first time the media had an interview with a commander of the United Self-Defense Forces of Colombia [Autodefensas Unidas de Colombia, or AUC], despite two decades of familiarity with paramilitary groups such as MAS (Death to Kidnappers), the group that Viáfara Salinas describes in the preceding text, and the AUC itself, which had begun as a MAS offshoot funded by drug traffickers operating near Puerto Boyacá. Around the time that MAS founders first began presenting themselves as vigilantes in a dirty war, Jesús Castaño, a dairy rancher in Antioquia, had been seized by the FARC and killed; his body was never found. His eldest son, Fidel, together with his younger sibling Carlos, vowed to avenge their father's death. By the late 1980s, the Castaños headed their own paramilitary group, the Peasant Self-Defense Forces of Córdoba and Urabá (Autodefensas Campesinas de Córdoba y Urabá, or ACCU); a few years later, it would be Carlos who would push to unify a loose network of paramilitary groups operating throughout the country. His was an umbrella organization that became known as the AUC.

When Carlos Castaño stepped forward as the AUC leader, all too many rural Colombians already knew this group firsthand, given their bloody campaigns targeting those they suspected of sympathizing with the guerrillas. For decades, paramilitaries murdered and disappeared trade unionists, peasant leaders, human rights defenders, and scores of unarmed civilians. Many had no ties with guerrillas whatsoever. Despite the growing death toll, with tens of thousands of deaths attributed to the paramilitaries by the 2010s, the AUC and other paramilitaries continued to enjoy considerable support, both from certain sectors of the military and the Colombian government, and from a swath of the general public. That support was what allowed "los paras" (as they are known in Colombia) to expand their illicit operations and consolidate themselves as a political force.

Yet Carlos Castaño sought a broader support base, seeking to influence Colombian public opinion and working to craft a narrative that positioned AUC commanders as "true patriots." In a set of interviews with journalist Mauricio Arangurén, who interjects his own voice throughout, Castaño presents himself alternately as an ur-

bane sophisticate and a gritty soldier. In places, Castaño works to portray himself as
a canny insider to power, elsewhere as an outsider on the run. In the excerpt below
his voice is played off against that of Diego Murillo Bejarano, also known as "don
Berna" (referred to in this text as Adolfo Paz, another alias), a well-known trafficker
and criminal from Tuluá, Valle who managed groups of hitmen and was a player
in the war between the Medellín Cartel and the Cali Cartel. After Pablo Escobar's
death, he merged cocaine trafficking with politically motivated killings, becoming a
key ally of the AUC and controlling the remnants of the Medellín Cartel to gain enor-
mous power in that city. "Don Berna" was extradited to the United States in 2008,
where he pled guilty to "conspiring to import multi-ton quantities of cocaine." That
guilty plea came three years after Berna turned himself in as part of a complicated
set of demobilization negotiations that the Colombian government began with the
AUC in 2003 under the Law of Justice and Peace. Berna confessed to his involvement
in the planning and execution of thousands of AUC-instigated murders. Along the
way, Berna may have taken part in the death and disappearance of Carlos Castaño,
his ally at the time of Arangurén's interviews. Carlos Castaño was reportedly killed
in 2004, although rumors that the death was faked continued to circulate for years
afterward.

The country has to recognize that finding Pablo Escobar was possible because we handed him over to the police after we had already brought him
down to his lowest level. He didn't have his bodyguards and he didn't have
the security of his most trusted men. The police were able to finish him off
in their own operation, without any intervention on our part, thanks to the
irregular war that we, as the PEPES, had launched to locate him.[1]

The first parastate group, in the strictest sense of the word, in the history
of Colombia was called: the PEPES.

Our existence was tolerated by the public prosecutor's office, the police,
the army, the DAS (Colombia's main intelligence agency), and the Attorney
General's Office. Even President César Gaviria Trujillo never ordered a
move against us. Journalists applauded in silence. And that was as it should
be!

When facing a monstrous threat such as Pablo Escobar, governments
have to be protected both from within the constitution and also from outside of it if need be. I have often asked myself why [that strategy] worked
against Pablo but not against the guerrilla.

Why was it that the guerrilla, the FARC, never denounced Escobar publicly? The ELN helped him! Terrible! With them there was an alliance!

Castaño took a quick sip of water. Visibly upset, he said: Excuse me, I'm a
bit agitated and I went off-topic, but there are some things that really bother

Fernando Botero Angulo, *Motosierra*, 2004. Dibujo (pencil and pastel on paper), 30 × 41 cm. In this drawing, titled *Chainsaw*, Fernando Botero depicts a paramilitary practice of using a chain saw to mutilate and dismember their victims. Colección Museo Nacional de Colombia, reg. 5814. Used by permission of Museo Nacional de Colombia and Samuel Monsalve Parra.

me. As I talk to you more, you'll have a clearer idea of what has been happening in this country for years.

I went on with my urban fight [against the guerrillas], which was also a fight against Pablo Escobar, since his friendship with all the guerrilla groups went beyond just political inclination. The M-19 kidnapped people for him and the holocaust of the Palace of Justice had already happened, financed by Pablo. He hid out several times in ELN-controlled zones; they protected him. He did business with the FARC, working through narco-traffickers like Carlos Lehder and "El Mejicano" [José González Rodríguez Gacha].

And what was more, Pablo always wanted me to help him in his war against the Cali Cartel and the Rodríguez Orejuela brothers. But I'm not helping anybody in a mercenary war! Not me!

Escobar knew that Fidel [Carlos's brother] was more likely to work with him, as long as I wasn't there. But for certain things he did need me. My contacts with the authorities and my friendship with various officials were very important for him. More than once I gave him information, to help avoid minor setbacks and to gain his confidence, while working toward my own ends.

"And how did you go about it?" I asked.

It was very simple. I had an extensive antisubversive network in Medellín, with a lot of contacts. Pablo knew that by sticking close to me he could find out what the army and the police thought about him. I've always had friends in the armed forces. One way or another it worked out. If they didn't talk to me they talked to my people, including a lot of ex-military and ex-police officers, who were now members of the *autodefensas*. And that's without counting the information I got from people who were still legal, whom Pablo didn't have access to anymore.

I'd give Pablo three or four accurate pieces of information, two false ones, and I'd keep quiet about a lot of important things. I knew what I was doing. It was a cold war against Pablo Escobar, and I had better be very careful. It wasn't a double-cross! It was betting on the government. If that makes me a traitor, then those who defend the *patria* [homeland] would have to be considered traitors. It makes me proud when people call me a traitor to Pablo Escobar. I was always at his side intentionally.

At that moment a loud noise distracted us. Two pickups came into the finca, and Castaño said:

"This must be Adolfo. Good. Now we can really begin with the history of los PEPES."

We left the little outbuilding to receive the famous "don Berna," who serenely got down from the pickup, and Castaño said:

"Adolfo limps, because he took seventeen bullet hits and lost his right leg in an attack. Despite that he goes everywhere and rides horses."

Berna approached slowly, since apart from the injury his considerable weight did not help him move around quickly.

"Good to have you here. Let me introduce you to the journalist I mentioned to you."

We went back to the little outbuilding and sat down. Castaño continued: "As those persecuted by Pablo Escobar we had already carried out some actions, but we still didn't have a name and we needed some way to identify ourselves. We were concerned about how the press and the search unit within the police would respond—we had to make it clear that ours were independent actions."

"One day I told Adolfo, 'Berna, I know what we're going to be called from now on: "los PEPES."'"

"He laughed and said, 'That's your thing man, PEPES is a brand of blue jeans.' So I said, 'Wait and see—sometimes a lot of imperfect roses have to come out of a bush before a really beautiful one blooms there.'" That day we put out a communiqué that was signed 'los PEPES,' but we'd already been acting as 'those persecuted by Pablo Escobar' for various months."

I asked: "On the 19th of June, Pablo Escobar had turned himself in, converting his jail, La Catedral, into a five-star hotel. He asked his friend and partner, Fernando Galeano, to visit him and Escobar killed him there. Was that the death that gave birth to 'those persecuted by Pablo Escobar'?"

"Yes sir, although the group, as such, came together months afterward," answered Berna. "I was Galeano's chief of security, and on July 3, 1992, almost a year after Pablo turned himself in, Pablo called him to La Catedral to talk about a serious sum of money that Pablo's men had stolen from Fernando. It was about twenty million dollars, that was the speculation. Before he left to go to the jail I told Fernando, 'Don't go up there Boss, let's send someone else, I don't trust Pablo.' But Fernando felt like Escobar never would hurt him, since he had only ever acted like his best friend.

"Fernando went up the hill to La Catedral, and I stayed behind worrying. The last words I heard from Fernando were, 'Don't worry, I'll be back early, I don't want to be up there when it gets dark.'

"Pablo had already taken a lot of money from a lot of people in the [drug trafficking] business, like Pablo Correa, Rodrigo Villa, Alfonso Cárdenas, and one of the nephews of the Ochoa brothers—he robbed them and then he killed them. . . . Pablo stooped that low because he lost his cousin Gustavo Gaviria, his right-hand man for finances. The police brought down the man who managed his narco-trafficking business for him. They weakened his economic situation, and no purse can sustain multiple wars.

"He was fighting the state. He placed eighteen car bombs. He financed a war against the Cali Cartel. He offered money to paid assassins, five million pesos for every police officer they killed. He ordered the death of two hundred police officers in Medellín, a horror that none of us wanted, but there was nothing to be done—the majority of the city were Pablo's friends, by force. He imposed a perverse principle: 'Either you're with me or you're against me.'

"Without exception, if you were in 'the business,' you had to pay out to help Escobar defray the cost of his fight against extradition. Fernando was giving him fifty thousand dollars a month.

"Arriving at La Catedral was strange. At least a hundred soldiers guarded it, but all of them were in Escobar's service, which meant that he didn't allow the police up there.

"Fernando got there for his appointment with Pablo, accompanied by a driver and a bodyguard, both of whom had to stay outside.

"I felt sure that something serious had happened, since Fernando had not wanted to spend the night there and now it was 10:00 A.M., Saturday morning. Right then I was told that Mario Galeano, one of Fernando's brothers, had been kidnapped. While we were confirming that it'd been Pablo's people, at 3:00 P.M., we found out that a group of armed men had tried to kidnap Rafael Galeano. He'd escaped, and now we were sure that it was Pablo's doing, and we started to get the Galeano family out of Medellín. We knew that what was starting was a confrontation with Pablo.

"Pablo called me the next day. With total calm, which filled me with terror, he said: 'This is an economic coup. I don't want publicity. If you want to work with me, I'll let you live.' And 'Hmm, one other thing, I need you to hand over Rafaelito Galeano, here's Rey.' Rey was the handle or nickname used by El Arete [Carlos Álzate Urquijo, one of Escobar's closest henchmen; the alias literally means "earring"]. Back then I was called 'Raúl.' I remember it like it was yesterday when El Arete, one of Escobar's bandits, got on the phone and told me, 'We're on foot, with holes in our shoes, and the money is rotting . . . What irony.' El Arete was talking about the almost twenty million dollars that they'd expropriated from Fernando. The one who stole that money worked for Pablo, he was called 'Tití' and his girlfriend was the daughter of the guy who guarded the hideout where the money was. 'Tití' and his girlfriend killed the old man and stole the money. They took it to Pablo and told him: 'This belonged to Fernando and El Negro Galeano and some of the dollars were rotting, because of the dampness in that place, Boss.'"

Immediately, I interrupted him to ask "Berna": "So Pablo decides to kill Fernando and he also ordered that his other partners, the Moncadas, would be killed and their money turned over to him?"

"Correct," Berna answered. "Kiko and William Moncada also died in La Catedral. . . In those few minutes I already knew that Pablo had killed Fernando and also Mario Galeano, so I took advantage right then to ask them: 'Make a good-will gesture and return the bodies.' I remember that El Arete asked about it and Escobar told him: 'Mario's body, maybe; Fernando's, that's impossible.'

"They weren't going to give me Fernando's body because they'd already thrown him in the Cauca River, after they had tortured him cruelly. They went through his hands with a drill, while they were asking him where the rest of his money was . . .

"The thing was, Pablo didn't only go against the Moncadas and the Galeanos. He went after everyone. The government decided to move him to a different jail and so they sent a commission to negotiate the transfer. That's how much they feared him! That ended up with Pablo holding onto the vice-minister of justice and the national director of prisons, and escaping from prison.

"Around that time I spoke to Rodolfo Ospina Baraya, who said to me, 'We have to get rid of that monster because he's going to kill us all.' 'Chapulín,' as he was called, was the grandson of ex-president Mariano Ospina Pérez, and he put us in touch with José Santacruz and with Miguel and Gilberto Rodríguez Orejuela [all leaders of the Cali Cartel].

"The help and support we got from the Cali Cartel made the difference, especially in terms of money and contacts. I met with the heads of the Cali Cartel, and when I got back I told the heads of los PEPES that we had support from that group."

"How much did the irregular war that you launched against Pablo cost?" I asked.

"It's hard to quantify the war against Pablo, over the fifteen months that it lasted we spent more than fifty million dollars. Most of that was put up by the Cali Cartel, specifically the Rodríguez Orejuela brothers."

"That much?" I asked to be sure.

"We got a lot of Pablo's people to turn on him and help eliminate him by paying informants. Information isn't free, and betraying Pablo was something people charged a lot for."

Castaño interjected . . . "Los PEPES never carried out an operation together with the police, and we were very careful about that. We did not want to cause problems for the institution—we were allies, but tacitly. Respectable people drew close to us and would tell us, 'It's important for the police search unit to know this.' We acted as a bridge and they trusted our information.

"Pablo had detonated a car bomb a few days before. After his terrorist action, we used the same strategy as Pablo used, but against his properties. We dynamited the Mónaco building and Las Colinas, and others he had in Medellín, also his finca, La Manuela, near El Peñol reservoir—the properties he cared about the most, and so he began to get worried.

"It wasn't only that he now had an irregular enemy with the same capacity that he had but also that this enemy began to gain adherents. As soon as we put out our first communiqué, many people in Colombia celebrated the group's appearance.

"While we were hitting Escobar," said Berna, "he killed a lot of people that gave us information. One of them was a kid nicknamed 'Penguin.' Escobar wanted to give us a lesson and he ordered a tremendous killing, a hundred bullets, for ratting him out. The war against Pablo was ten months of give and take. We also lost 'Big Head' and 'Cramps,' two important informants.

"Pablo had immense reserves of money and it was going to be a long fight. He still hadn't lost his important people.

"By the first semester of 1993, little by little, the balance began to tip in our favor and the information provided by los PEPES, and that we supplied via public figures, began to be more and more important to the police search unit, since the many false informants Escobar sent cost them time and trouble. The search unit didn't really understand Pablo's organizational framework of assassins, and that was our main advantage, apart from being irregular operatives. I think we got to where we had up to a hundred informants scattered across Medellín. We even paid up to a hundred or a hundred and fifty thousand million pesos for pieces of information, apart from what the Police paid their informants, which wasn't even thirty percent of what we paid.

"Operations that were exclusively police operations went off, but using our information: 'Poplar,' 'Tyson,' 'Tilton,' 'Plug,' 'Broadside,' 'Pigeon,' and lots of others.

"Overnight the pressure on Pablo increased and that's when his closest men began to turn themselves over. First 'Popeye' [Jhon Jair Velásquez], then 'Earring,' and 'Little Bear,' his brother [Roberto Escobar Gaviria], and then came two important captures that happened because of our information: 'Tití' and 'Cheesepuff.' This last one was very important because two hideouts were found with weapons and two thousand kilos of dynamite."

Just then, Castaño interrupted and said:

"Adolfo, don't forget that the help we gave to the police search unit grew because of an important intermediary. Don Alfonso Berrío lent around twenty houses and we got them about ten more, so they could install the triangulators for tracking telephone calls all over the city."

"The operation that led to Pablo Escobar's death was the one that marked the fall of El Chopo [Mario Castaño Molina], his second in command, who was called 'the street Pablo Escobar,'" continued don Berna. "He was a waiter at the Intercontinental Hotel and he ended up being the one in charge of Pablo's apparatus of terrorism and assassination. From hiding, Escobar would give the order and he would have the car bombs placed, he'd do the kidnappings and killings the 'capo' ordered him to do. 'El Chopo' was in charge of all the other gangsters, they felt respect and even terror for him—he was short and fat and he had a complex about his early baldness.

"We knew how important 'El Chopo' was and by going after his people we were able to track two of his gangsters going into Unicentro mall, in

Medellín. We captured them and we locked them up in one of los PEPES' houses. Without using violence to get them to give him up, Carlos told them who we were and what were their life chances. 'Guys, you're in the hands of los PEPES, and there's nothing left for you in this war. You can count the minutes you've got left.'

"Right away they came over to our side, like all of the rest, and they de-tailed for us where to find 'El Chopo.' 'I have an appointment with him at a place,' one of them said. Right away the Police search unit was informed, the guys got paid in dollars. Now the police had the information, but they couldn't identify 'El Chopo.' They never would have found him using the photo they were using to track him, he had really changed his looks. . . . In the final stages of the fight against Pablo, I made friends with one of the guys that worked the equipment that intercepted calls. I'd often show up at the headquarters of the search unit, near a parking lot by Atanasio Girardot stadium. The CIA was there, the DEA, and members of the United States Navy Special Forces. The ones I talked to the most were the men from the DEA.

"That December 2nd, one felt the demoralization, our exhaustion and fa-tigue were visible. Everyone went to eat lunch at the Carlos Holguín School and only a few of us were still at the parking lot. Carlos was in military action, which was news three hours before Pablo's death. He executed Gus-tavito Gaviria, the son of Gustavo Gaviria, one of the Cartel's big men. It was a terrible blow for Pablo. Gustavito was twenty-eight and he had al-ready become a little boss-man, a *capito* of capos. He was one of the few that Escobar had left.

"When the call triangulators were able to locate Pablo, an officer called more than four times over the radio telephone to say that they had him located between Carreras 70 and 80 and Calles 44 and 50. I heard it all on the radio telephone, since we had access to the search unit's frequencies. I remember hearing, 'He's talking and I think I know where he is.'

"I stayed in a parking lot near where Pablo was presumed to be, wait-ing for the news, which arrived with a huge amount of commotion. Pablo Escobar had just died, and to be honest I didn't feel either happy or sad. The people in the search unit shouted for joy and there were parties in Medellín, which means fireworks and maybe slaughtering a hog. Everyone hugged each other."

"It's very important to set one thing straight," Castaño responded ". . . The singleness of purpose that finished off Pablo Escobar came from Major Guerrero, of the National Police, who was the brains behind tracing him through frequency triangulators. The singular stubbornness of that man, without anyone giving him orders, was what made possible the location and death of Escobar. He spent months in a pickup truck with a parabolic antenna on the roof and, there, he was able to pinpoint the exact place where Pablo made his last phone calls. Escobar's end is owed in good measure to that major's tenacity and nothing has been said about him. . . . I [also] don't want to take anything away from the work of Hugo Martínez Poveda, the search unit's commander. That colonel didn't sleep to stay at work, he didn't think about anything else apart from finishing off Escobar. Pablo would send him cassettes where he would say: 'I'll kill your father, your mother, your kids, your siblings.' Escobar thought he could intimidate him, like he did others, like when he would say: 'Take my money or my lead.' But no. Martínez launched an unconditional, institutional war against Pablo, and there's no doubt in my mind that if he hadn't won that way, he'd have finished him off by extraconstitutional, irregular means. . . . I consider that the police who fought Escobar had a heroic attitude and, to me, they are true patriots. They were tigers! Really good people! I say this even though a lot of money flowed under the table from the Cali Cartel and from other places. It's normal for corruption to get its part, and it was so difficult to keep the group together. It was close to breaking apart only a few days before Escobar was eliminated. It was created so that it could act in a drastic manner and perform a surgery, but an operation can't be prolonged for years, because the surgeons will start getting sick. I'll tell you something, if los PEPES didn't get together the police would've invented a group like it. When a monster the size of Pablo Escobar is born, you need God and even the devil to fight against him."

"But Pablo dies and what about you two?" Berna's answer was just getting started, with excuses; Castaño's was short:

"Up to that point I was the army's favorite. I was taught by the army, trained by the army, supported and even protected by them. But I knew what was coming. They would start to search for me to capture me and shoot me down. That's the price that Colombians like me have had to pay in this war, not being able to come back to live in a city. . . . The move from legality to illegality was very hard. I stopped being a real person and became an outlaw. I couldn't come to get-togethers or to meetings with company presidents, I couldn't be part of the economic world.

"I had to leave behind my friends in the [Catholic] Church, whom I loved to have as friends. Having lunch with bishops and priests was over for me. So were conversations with good philosophers, water-skiing at El Peñol, hang-gliding on Matasanos Hill, cycling up to San Félix ridge. I started toward a different future, going into the bush."

"Berna" stood up from the table and said, *"Comandante,* I should go."

We walked him to the door and there he uttered the phrase with which we closed the Pablo Escobar episode.

"Mister Reporter, never forget this: Narcos only get together to kill or betray a friend."

Castaño smiled and said: "If anyone really knows them, it's Adolfo." He said good-bye: "Until next time, friend."

Translated by Ann Farnsworth-Alvear

Note

1. *PEPES* was an acronym used by Los Perseguidos por Pablo Escobar, or "those persecuted by Pablo Escobar."

The Song of the Flies

María Mercedes Carranza

It is impossible to sum up the human cost of massacres experienced by Colombians in the second half of the twentieth century and in the first decades of the twenty-first. The following poems by María Mercedes Carranza (1945–2003) represent one artist's struggle to represent the hundreds of collective homicides carried out by paramilitaries, guerrillas, and security forces alike. Carranza comes from a literary lineage: her great aunt was prose writer Elisa Mujíca, and her father, Eduardo Carranza, was a poet and diplomat who also directed the Biblioteca Nacional de Colombia. In 1997, the year Song of the Flies *was published, there were 187 massacres reported in Colombia, some involving a few people, some the deaths of many. The titles of Carranza's poems are locations in remote areas of the Colombian countryside, many largely ignored by urban Colombians before violent events gained them public attention. Some of the poems allude to a single event: Mapiripán, for example, refers to one of the most gruesome massacres committed by the United Self-Defense Forces of Colombia, where forty-nine peasants were killed with chain saws and machetes between July 15 and 20, 1997 (see part VII). Yet many of the place-names she uses as titles represent sites of repeated violence. Soacha made headlines well after Carranza's death as one of the main sites for* falsos positivos *(see the introduction to this volume and part III). Necoclí has also seen more recent violence, having found itself at the epicenter of paramilitarism and narco-trafficking in the 1990s. Former assassins led investigators to mass graves near this town, and the site was chosen for a peaceful march in 2012 demanding legislation to return land to peasants dispossessed by narco-traffickers and drug-funded paramilitaries, attended by President Juan Manuel Santos. Many of those who participated in this event later received threats from Los Urabeños, one of several groups known as the* Bacrim (bandas criminales emergentes, *or emergent criminal gangs) that formed after the demobilization of the AUC.*

Juan Manuel Echavarría, *Passiflora foetida*, 1997. Gelatin silver
print, 50 × 40 cm. In Juan Manuel Echavarría, *Mouths of Ash:
Bocas de Ceniza* (Milano: Charta, 2005), 60. Courtesy of the artist.

NECOCLÍ

Quizás	Maybe
el próximo instante	this next instant
de noche tarde o mañana	late at night or in the morning
en Necoclí	in Necoclí
se oirá nada más	only the song of the flies
el canto de las moscas	will be heard.

MAPIRIPÁN

Quieto el viento	Still wind
el tiempo	still time.
Mapiripán es ya	Mapiripán is now
una fecha.	a date.

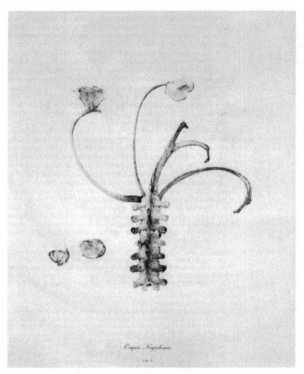

Juan Manuel Echavarría, *Orquis negrilensis*, 1997. Gelatin silver print, 50 × 40 cm. *Passiflora foetida* and *Orquis negrilensis* are part of a series of photographs of human bones arranged in the style of botanical prints, evoking the plates created by the Royal Botanical Expedition to New Granada under José Celestino Mutis. In Juan Manuel Echavarría, *Mouths of Ash: Bocas de Ceniza* (Milano: Charta, 2005), 54. Courtesy of the artist.

PORE

En Pore la muerte
pasa de mano en mano
    La muerte:
carne de la tierra.

In Pore death
moves from hand to hand.
    Death:
flesh of the earth.

ITUANGO

    El viento
ríe en las mandíbulas
    de los muertos.
    En Ituango,
el cadáver de la risa.

    The wind
laughs in the jaws
    of the dead.
    In Ituango,
the corpse of laughter.

VISTA HERMOSA

El alto tallo	The tall stalk,
espectral,	spectral,
quemada, yerta,	burned, rigid,
solitaria	lonesome
flor del páramo.	flower of the high plains.
Así	This is
Vista Hermosa.	Vista Hermosa.

SOACHA

Un pájaro	A black bird
negro husmea	pecks at
las sobras de	the remains of
la vida.	life.
Puede ser Dios	It could be God
o el asesino:	or the murderer:
da lo mismo ya.	it doesn't matter now.

Kidnapped

Major General Luis Mendieta Ovalle

For the better part of the last two decades, Colombia had one of the highest rates of kidnapping worldwide. Since the late 1970s, guerrilla groups regularly kidnapped Colombians and foreign nationals, both for political purposes and to obtain costly ransoms to finance their activities. While criminal gangs, drug traffickers, and the AUC also carry out kidnappings, the thousands of crimes attributed to the Revolutionary Armed Forces of Colombia (FARC), the National Liberation Army (ELN), and the April 19th Movement (M-19) have fueled strong sentiments among many Colombians. High-profile cases, such as that of Íngrid Betancourt Pulecio, a dual French Colombian citizen and former presidential candidate who was abducted with running mate Clara Rojas in 2002, have given kidnappings in Colombia notoriety abroad. While kidnappings had decreased by the 2000s, hundreds remained captive in Colombia's jungles into the first decades of the new century.

Kidnappings in Colombia have to be understood within a context marked by scale and intensity. There is a painful public memory of mass kidnappings, such as the ELN kidnapping of forty-six passengers and crew members from Avianca flight 9463 from Bucaramanga (1999); the ELN kidnapping of dozens of parishioners from La María church in Cali (1999); and the FARC abduction of twelve provincial legislators, also in Cali (2007). And there is an ongoing awareness that many of those still held captive by the FARC are army and police servicemen, used as human bargaining chips with the Colombian government. Many were kidnapped while posted to remote areas. Such was the case of Luis Herlindo Mendieta Ovalle: he was kidnapped in November 1998, when the FARC took over Mitú, the capital of the southwestern department of Vaupés. Almost 2,000 FARC soldiers were involved in this operation against 120 Colombian military and police personnel, who were either killed or taken hostage. The takeover of Mitú has been the FARC's only attack on a Colombian capital city, and marked the consolidation of FARC control over much of the country's southern Amazonian region. Over one hundred people were killed, and twice that number wounded. Three weeks after the attack at Mitú, the Colombian government provided a demilitarized zone for peace conversations with the FARC in

San Vicente del Caguán, a town in the neighboring department of Caquetá, as part of a peace process that was widely regarded as a failure.

Then a lieutenant colonel, Mendieta Ovalle was the highest-ranking official captured in Mitú and also the highest-ranking official kidnapped by the FARC up to that point. He was rescued on June 13, 2010, with Colonel Enrique Murillo Sánchez of the police force, also kidnapped in Mitú, and Colonel William Donato Gómez and Sergeant Mayor Arbey Delgado Argote of the army, both kidnapped during the 1998 attack by the FARC on Miraflores, Guaviare. Their rescue took place twelve years after their abduction and two years after the celebrated Operation Jaque, in which the Colombian military liberated Íngrid Betancourt Pulecio, three American military contractors, and eleven Colombian military police.

December 21, 2007

Mrs. María Teresa Paredes, José Luis, Jenny, Mr. Alfredo Mendieta, Mrs. María Agueda Ovalle, sisters, brothers, Mr. José Israel Paredes, Mrs. Aura Ardila, Olga, Hildo, Johanita, Alex, Carlos, José, Ricardo, Rossy Luz, William, Oscar, Flor, Alexandra, Hugo, Carmenza, Diana, José Alfredo, Vanessa, Cristian, Yolanda, Jonathan, Roberto, Pilar, Angie, Rover Jovany, and Diego:

Thank God that in this race against time, I am able to write these lines to you, as it is difficult to know when they will be coming around for the letters. This is the sixth letter in which I will tell you about myself. I will begin six and a half years ago, when we said goodbye to Marlen [Marleny Orejuela from ASFAMIPAZ, an association of families of kidnapped military and police personnel], who took the last written correspondence. At that time, twenty-eight members of public security forces were also in captivity. Alan Jara, ex-governor of Meta, arrived a few days later, as did Dr. Orlando Beltrán, senator, and House representative Consuelo González: we spent several months with them. Before I continue, I should thank everyone who wrote to me and sent letters and gifts with Marlen—I received everything, and answered all letters in the following days, but it was not possible to send them, and all remain deep in the jungle, along with many cards for birthdays, Valentine's Day, Mother's Day, etc. I thank María A. for the canned meat, which I ate last and saved until my birthday the following year—it was a special feast, which I enjoyed very much and savored slowly.

I continue: in December, Jorge Enrique Botero interviewed me for television for everyone to see and hear, yet they did not allow information of the three aforementioned politicians to be revealed. That weekend, thirty-one of us were able to spend time at the common site, playing games and enjoying the end-of-year holidays, despite fences and barbed wire.

In January, corporal Peña was taken away from the common site, because of incidents he initiated or his poor mental state. We were told he was being taken for psychiatric treatment, but we have known nothing about him since then, despite our constant questions about his condition. Dr. Gechem and Ms. Gloria de Lozada arrived to our captivity site that same month. We spent several months with them before we were separated. Twenty-seven of us security officers were left at a place nearby with Alan. Ten people were kept at another site, including the two ladies, the senator, and the congressman, as well as Íngrid, Clara, Senator Pérez and the three Americans, whom we also saw there. We found out Clara was pregnant, and a few months later she gave birth in the jungle amid subhuman conditions to her son, whom she named Emmanuel. A few days later, some of us were able to hold the boy in our arms on two or three occasions as he was taken to our site, where security officers specially trained in stitching made him small clothes, shoes, some toys, a backpack, and many other things. As the boy grew, they would bring him back so that they could take his measurements to make clothing, shoes, and different items. Buitrago, Durán, Durarte, Moreno, Amaón, Bermejo, Salcedo, Donato, and Beltrán excelled with their ingenuity and creativity, given their special abilities for these tasks. All handcrafts were made using recycled material each had, such as secondhand clothing or other items received.

Alan also stood out for his cooperation. We were drawn to him and his talks from the beginning, and he had countless stories to tell and share, given the academic experience he obtained in Russia, his trips to dozens of countries despite many odds and obstacles, and his political work in Meta. We always listened as he spoke about all those experiences, trials, problems, incidents that took place during his studies and travels, and the kind of jobs he had to take in order to explore and see the world without money, only with the desire to move forward. One of the anecdotes was that Alan had to go hungry in Russia—who would have thought!

His long stories about all these situations were discussed day and night. Alan had recently been in the United States learning English for three months: with the help of two small English handbooks that came along with what Marlen brought, and the pamphlet Johanita sent me, a few of us began to attend what resembled a class one hour a day. Yet a few days later, we had to begin walking through the jungle, chained and in small groups, because of security conditions. Occasionally, we saw the others during rest stops along the way. [. . .] As the days passed and the inclement travel on foot continued, some of us, such as Íngrid, Malagón, Guevara and myself, fell ill. We were transported in hammocks tied to a rod, which served as stretchers. In my case, I began feeling pain in my legs, bones, and joints. My feet got swollen from walking. At the beginning of my illness, I walked using a stick as a cane. My condition worsened as the marches continued: I limped, and then had to walk with the help of two forked branches that I used as crutches. Those treks were awful, given the difficulties posed by the jungle, the rain, and the insects. Finally, one day, after we arrived to a site at night, I could not get up to walk the following morning. As the march had to continue, they transported me and others in the conditions I described previously, which is how I was able to greet and talk briefly with Íngrid when we were ill and carried on "stretchers."

Time continued to pass, until one day all of us were separated and divided into small groups. There were ten of us in our group: Dr. Gechem, Ms. Gloria, Dr. Orlando Beltrán, Consuelo, Alan, Donato, Murillo, Clara, Delgado, and myself. (I began this letter yesterday, but there is no more sunlight, and the weather has gotten worse. This morning I began writing again, but it rains and there is not enough light. If God allows and conditions improve, I will be able to continue with this account.)

The ten of us continued to walk until we arrived to a site where we spent a few days and I could begin to recover. What happened to me? I believe some of my blood vessels were affected, as blood spread through all my legs and they acquired a dark color, almost black. . . . I feared the worst, but thank God I was a given an antitetanus shot. A few days later, I had ten penicillin injections, each with 5 million units, and slowly I began to recover. As was expected, they removed the locked chain from my neck when I became sick, but they claimed they had to transport my "personal items," all of which disappeared overnight. In other words, I was left with nothing except for the clothes on my back. Fortunately, at the beginning of this terrible ordeal, Delgado offered to help by carrying the small package where I keep my photographs. Thank God this remained safe. Later, I was given the blue sweatpants Maria A. sent me. I still have them with me to this day and use them as my pajamas. Delgado also helped by giving me two sets of underwear, a sheet, and a towel. Murillo gave me some shorts for the night, Donato lent me some pants, Consuelito a shirt, and Ms. Gloria a pair of socks. With all this, a new period of walking began, and days later they brought some clothes for all of us, so I could make do with those, and was able to return the loaned shirts and pants. Alan gave me toilet paper, Murillo gave me toothpaste during some days, but for three weeks I was brushing my teeth with only water, as I had no toothpaste after what happened, and my *compañeros* had too little, so I did not want to ask them for any.

How long did my illness last? I am unsure how much time passed, but I was not able to walk for approximately five weeks. The hammock trips were awful when crossing through rivers, difficult terrain, swamps, etc. When I was left on the ground, all sorts of insects would come—flies, mosquitoes, horseflies, ticks, ants of different colors and lengths, spiders, several types of bees, and wasps of various sizes—and I would have to shoo them with my hand. When I had to answer nature's call, I had to crawl through the mud on my arms, as I could not stand. At the beginning of my treatment, I had massages on my legs with Yodora deodorant cream. Like a child, I began to walk again, trying to take steps on my own, then using sticks, and later forked branches that looked like crutches. I could then start going to the bathroom, and then with the support of a cane I finally could walk slowly. Thank God we were near a creek, where I could do some therapeutic exercises, kicking my legs in the water as if swimming. I slowly began to restore my health. During that period of weakness, there was a misunderstanding within the group, and somebody demanded that I be tied to a tree with chains placed around my neck, right when I was beginning to recover. I believe that God is great, and that at that same time you were praying for me very much, because thanks to your devotion and who knows what other force I was able to make progress and recover to some extent. It was during those days that I heard through the grapevine a message from Carmenza, where she said that *Noticias 1* and *El Tiempo* had reported my death in an air raid. I believe you prayed for me even more then, and the result was my improvement. Unfortunately, a few days later, I was bitten by *el pito* [a blood vector for the Chagas parasite], and had seven sores on my body that left some scars.

I received thirty-eight glutamine injections during the following days, and I was able to overcome yet another parasitic illness. I would say that my physical strength held out for six years of my captivity, after which my health problems began and have persisted. In the following months, there were other treks that lasted days, not weeks. We have lived in different places, and there have been many inconveniences and incidents in each of them, as well as retribution from the guerrilla, who limit our access to provisions, space, resources, etc., making it difficult

to share each item that arrives or is given to us. I have had malaria twice
in the last few months, one lasting twenty days where I had to remain
lying down with a lot of medication. I finally recovered, but from then
after, perhaps as a result of the medicine, I have had pain in my chest
close to my heart, a sharp ache that hurts some days more than others.
Donato and Murillo have made suctions there using a candle, a coin,
and a jar, but this has not brought relief. The nurse kept on saying that
this was *frio y vientos* [a term used by Colombians to refer to chilled air
"inside" a body], which is why he and Consuelo have used newspaper
and toilet paper layers to suction my ear. Yet the pain returns: I have
asked for aspirin, and have taken almost 20, but I stopped using them
because the aching continues. I am currently trying to control the pain
with Voltaren cream, but also by doing breathing exercises and walking
around our campsite with Alan, sometimes for 20, 30, 40, or 50 minutes
or an hour, depending on the weather and other variables. This has
helped and I have kept this pain at bay. However, given the walks, I have
soreness in my bones and leg joints, particularly my knees, so at times I
stop walking, and the chest ache comes back. I still have a purple bruise
on my back that hurts occasionally, and I believe it is the result of a blow
I suffered when being carried on the hammock.

In the last four years, we have not had books to read, and I can count
with the fingers of one hand the issues of *Semana* and *Cambio* that we
have received and reread. The most important use of our time is when
Alan, Donato, Murillo, and I can occasionally study one hour of English
or one hour of Russian, depending on our spirits and other factors such
as the rain, etc. Alan is a good teacher, and this is how we spend our
time. However, the task of learning is made difficult because of our age,
brain cells lost due to sickness, captivity, lack of study materials such
as books, notebooks, pens, etc. Nonetheless, we continue doing this, as
it provides us with therapy and a way of passing the time. As José Luis
would say, we are still learning the verbs "to be" and "to have," not only
in English but also in Russian. We try to learn verbs, conjugations, and
expressions, as well as general English and Russian grammar. The four
of us, sometimes with Consuelito, spend the rest of the time playing
cards, Parcheesi, or dominoes. In due time, she will probably tell you
many of the details of what we have had to endure during the last few
years. Alan, Donato, and Murillo send their regards. I say goodbye again
to all of you, wishing you a Merry Christmas and a very good 2008. I
hope you go with God, and that the Virgin protects and cares for you.
Please take care of yourselves also, helping one another, old caring for

young, parents caring for children, children caring for parents, brothers and sisters, nieces and nephews, and families caring for one another. God and the Virgin be with you.

Luis

Translated by Ana María Gómez López and Ann Farnsworth-Alvear

Parapolitics

Claudia López and Óscar Sevillano

Colombia's investigative journalists have been at the forefront of efforts to denounce both garden-variety political corruption and the endemic problem of drug traffickers' influence. Strikingly, Colombian criminal networks gained a substantial degree of formal political power because they reinvented themselves using ideological language, as the allies and comrades-in-arms of rightist paramilitaries—a contrast to the leftist populism of Pablo Escobar's public rhetoric. Paradoxically, the consolidation of a narco-paramilitary political strategy happened just as the best-known paramilitary group, the Castaño brothers' AUC, publicly committed itself to demobilization. Between 2003 and 2006, the administration of President Álvaro Uribe Vélez oversaw the disarming of thirty thousand paramilitary members under the Law of Justice and Peace. Those demobilized were promised employment programs, welfare benefits, and monthly stipends, in exchange for which they pledged to cease criminal activity and reenter society.

The Law of Justice and Peace had its critics, both in Colombia and abroad. Many pointed to the continuation of paramilitary structures throughout the country, evident both in the immediate emergence of successor groups that went on committing human rights abuses and exporting cocaine, and in an emerging set of scandals that came to be known by the term "parapolitics." Investigative reports by a brave generation of journalists, such as the article below by Claudia López (later a senator for Colombia's Green Party) and Óscar Sevillano, revealed a new, entrenched form of mafia influence. Former and still-active paramilitary commanders could now rely on legislators they bought and sold, meaning that they could be more effective as legal actors than they had been as the heads of illegal armies. Through vote-buying and bribes, drug traffickers with roots in the paramilitaries of the 1990s became political brokers in the 2000s. In general, they threw their weight behind hard-liner Álvaro Uribe Vélez, a popular politician whose presidency marked an epochal shift in Colombian politics.

Uribe's supporters applaud his success in demobilizing the paramilitaries and strengthening the military's capacity against the guerrillas. They also tend to support his close alignment with the US military. His detractors, on the other hand, point to his vitriolic attacks on human rights monitors and his links to politicians suspected of links to paramilitary commanders—or to the 2016 arrest of his brother, Santiago Uribe, who was charged with first-degree murder and the creation of paramilitary groups in Antioquia. In their article, López and Sevillano gesture toward a middle-ground position, identifying Uribe's Democratic Security policy as having strengthened the government institutions and improved life for millions of Colombians, yet they lay out evidence connecting the ex-president to paramilitaries and kingpins. They also denounce the former president's rhetorical strategy, which included labeling reporters "señoritos" (city slickers) from Bogotá when they denounced vote-buying in the provinces.

At the time this article was prepared for publication [November 27, 2008], the national press reports that 34 of the 102 senators elected in 2006, or 33 percent, are being investigated for links with narco-paramilitarism, as are 25 of 168 House representatives, or 15 percent. These figures show that narco-paramilitarism has well surpassed the infiltration capacity of previous narco-traffickers. When Pablo Escobar got himself elected to the House of Representatives in 1982, his votes and those of his running mate amounted to less than 1 percent of the Senate vote. When the Cali Cartel's massive infiltration of the 1994 campaigns was discovered, those convicted afterward represented 8 percent of the Senate vote, or 12 percent, if taken together with others involved in the "Proceso 8,000." In 2006, those investigated for narco-paramilitarism represented 35 percent of congressional seats and 25 percent of the Senate vote. This steady growth indicates that narco-traffickers have progressively refined their methods for infiltrating themselves into political power and have increased their level of "success."

Aside from the 59 congressmen currently being prosecuted for "parapolitics," an additional 253 public servants throughout the national territory—elected officials, government employees, and servicemen combined—are also being investigated for links with narco-paramilitarism. Contrary to what has previously been acknowledged, "parapolitics" is a scandal not limited to congresspeople from the Atlantic Coast who sought paramilitary support for electoral advantage. Today it is an established fact that "parapolitics" is a national phenomenon involving the massive takeover of political representation and public power by narco-trafficking and paramilitarism, through politicians and other public servants at the local, regional, and national levels.

On the day following the congressional elections of March 2002, Salvatore Mancuso issued a press release in which he claimed: "We make recommendations for people regarding who they should vote for. In this regard, we can affirm with figures in hand that the original goal of 35 percent has been far surpassed, and that this constitutes a milestone in the history of the AUC. This support well exceeds our most optimistic expectations." On June 13, 2005, paramilitary leader Vicente Castaño [brother of Fidel and Carlos Castaño Gil] also made a statement along the same lines in an interview with *Semana* magazine: "I believe it is safe to say that we have more than 35 percent of friends in Congress. And by the next elections we will increase that percentage of friends."

Although these paramilitary commanders were careful not to reveal the names of their "friends," these were gradually discovered through investigative journalism and academic research. In September 2005, Semana.com published an investigation titled "Atypical Vote-Counts in the 2002 Congressional Elections," which released for the first time the names of twenty-three congressmen who had been supported by paramilitaries, insofar as this could be deduced from highly atypical electoral patterns registered in areas that had previously been through the blood and fire of paramilitary takeovers. This and other journalists' investigations thrust the topic of paramilitary infiltration in Congress into public debate. As a result of this media pressure, the Liberal and Conservative Parties, as well as Cambio Radical and La U [an abbreviation used for the political party of ex-president Álvaro Uribe], decided to exclude from their lists for the 2006 congressional elections several candidates allegedly linked to paramilitaries. However, those "expelled" were later received by other Uribe supporter parties, thus making the purge only lip service.

Following the 2006 congressional elections, Clara López Obregón, former candidate for the House of Representatives, requested that the Supreme Court of Justice investigate Mancuso's statements regarding paramilitary control of 35 percent of Congress. The court began an investigation in June 2006. At the same time, paramilitaries demobilized under the Law of Justice and Peace began to be prosecuted. Some middle-ranking paramilitaries have provided useful statements for "parapolitics" investigations. Of the top twenty paramilitary leaders, only Salvatore Mancuso and alias H. H. have provided useful information; the rest have denied or avoided altogether the subject of "parapolitics."

In an interview with the newspaper *El Tiempo* on November 25, 2006, Senator Miguel de la Espriella confirmed that in 2001 Carlos Castaño and Salvatore Mancuso summoned politicians from different political backgrounds and several regions of the country to a meeting. The meeting took place in the township of Ralito, in the department of Córdoba, and ended with the signing of a document disclosed to the country as the "Ralito Pact," in which paramilitaries and politicians from across the country pledged to "refound the nation." This pact was not unique: other verbal and written pacts among paramilitaries, politicians, and government officials make it clear that "parapolitics" had taken place before and after the 2002 congressional elections, and that their objective was not only to place "friendly" candidates into public office and governmental agencies, but also to perform lawmaking and state functions. . . .

The different pacts make it clear that imposing their candidates in all popular elections, whether for individual posts or as representatives to governing bodies, was not only done with the objective of gaining political representation, but rather to seize the governmental and state functions that candidates would have if elected. To begin with, by capturing local and regional positions, paramilitarism would have a smooth rise to do the same at the national level, as in fact happened in 2002 and 2006. They additionally gained the protection of impunity, as well as access to public and private business opportunities that allowed them to diversify their sources of income and, in some cases, more easily launder profits from illicit businesses.

The case of Salvatore Mancuso in Córdoba speaks to the seizure of political and state power by narco-paramilitarism. This former paramilitary leader has publicly admitted to backing at least three congressional candidates from Córdoba, as well as several candidates for mayoral office and city councils. He influenced appointments at the University of Córdoba, from the provost down to the administrative staff. He also had success with the governor's office, where he imposed at least two secretaries, including the secretary of health. He recognized having bribed members of the security forces, although he did not provide specific names. Additionally, Mancuso has broadly stated that for every kilogram of coca he would invest at least one million pesos in bribes. . . .

The testimony provided by Rafael García, former chief of information technology at the Departamento Administrativo de Seguridad [DAS, Colombia's main central intelligence agency], provided confirmation that paramilitaries used voter databases from the civil status registry to plan and execute a massive amount of electoral fraud in the 2002 elections. García's testimony and other evidence demonstrated that paramilitaries committed this breach through the DAS to erase the criminal records of narco-traffickers and paramilitary actors, plan coordinated actions, and create lists of citizens accused of being guerrilla allies whom they subsequently murdered. It also became public that Dieb Maloof, a senator at the time, diverted funds from the departments of Magdalena and Cesar to paramilitary groups in that area, and that these groups also intervened in important contracts such as the issuance of identity cards for Colombian citizens by the registry, presumably through Senator Álvaro Araujo.

Despite that demobilized individuals have mentioned some of their financial and economic backers in various informal statements, there have been no investigations that explain or demonstrate the ties between armed groups and business groups. The only definitive judicial case on this issue involves multinational corporations and banana companies such as Chiquita Brands. The extent of economic infiltration and seizure of the state by narco-paramilitarism still remains to be thoroughly determined and prosecuted.

In order to obtain a sense of the dimensions of this infiltration and seizure, it is enough to state that the General Attorney's Office is currently pursuing 334 investigations related to parapolitics throughout the entire country, involving politicians at the national, regional, and local levels, as well as contractors and members of official security forces. . . .

The president has never hidden his solidarity with politicians in his camp who are being investigated for parapolitics. In speeches, he has systematically presented paramilitarism as the offspring of FARC cruelty, presenting politicians linked to paramilitaries in some cases as "victims" of the absence of governmental authority and the lack of security in their regions. He has also systematically kept silent or kept to a minimum his statements about the evidence of complicity among paramilitaries, members of the armed forces, and politicians, who have colluded not only in electoral matters but also in perpetrating crimes against humanity, such as massacres, murders, forcing masses of people off their land. . . . The president has always taken sides in favor of members of his circle being investigated for links to paramilitarism. For example, he defended the ex-governor of Sucre, Salvador Arana, and made him his ambassador to Chile. He defended Jorge Noguera, the ex-director of the DAS, and named him consul in Milan. He also defended General Rito Alejo del Río and rendered him public homage. . . .

When parapolitics began to be uncovered in the mass media, the president launched himself against the journalists responsible and accused them of being "señoritos" from Bogotá who were trying to sully the name of politicians from the provinces. . . .

The president and other government functionaries constantly accuse the Supreme Court, the public prosecutor's office, and the judicial system of being "politicized," and of acting ruthlessly. They have even accused the Supreme Court of seeking out false witnesses and of participating in "plots" against the president of the Republic. . . .

Beatríz González, *Auras anónimas*, 2009. This art installation in Bogotá's Central Cemetery drew attention to unidentified victims in Colombia's conflict. Through the first decades of the twenty-first century the ongoing work of exhuming mass graves has meant that Colombians are increasingly aware of the number of clandestine cemeteries and mass graves throughout the country. Photograph by Laura Jiménez. Courtesy of Beatríz González and Banco de Archivos Digitales, Departamento de Arte, Universidad de los Andes.

Until only five years ago, political and judicial impunity in regard to paramilitarism and its effects was almost absolute. Significant progress has been made, thanks in part to elements of President Uribe's Democratic Security policy. These elements are the partial demobilization of paramilitary armies, the decision to regain territorial control and the state's monopoly on force, and the considerable tactical and strategic improvement of Colombian security forces. Colombia is a better and more viable country without 35,000 armed paramilitaries massively violating the human and political rights of millions of Colombians, and without an uncontrollable guerrilla force doing the same. Nonetheless, the vast, complex, and well-established structures of power that narco-paramilitarism has gained in Colombian social, economic, and political relations throughout the national territory, together with the fact that drug trafficking is a growing force, means that the capacity this kind of criminal organization has for resiliency, growth, and adaption is still very high.

Statistical categories and their descriptions have changed. Government figures never included paramilitaries, but rather self-defense groups. Presently, it is not self-defense groups that are mentioned, but emerging or criminal gangs. It is possible that the use of counterinsurgency as a justification for the tolerance that political and military authorities exhibit toward these private armies has now decreased, thanks to the policy of Democratic Security. However, [paramilitaries] are not nonexistent. Less than two years after the alleged end of paramilitarism, there are 10,200 men rearmed in criminal gangs, with the involvement of 4,500 paramilitaries who never reintegrated into society, or who did so and went back. All of them continue to organize themselves around the control of narco-trafficking and land. . . .

In order to overcome narco-paramilitarism and its effects, there needs to be a guarantee of reparation to victims and to all Colombians, and the assurance that such activity will not continue: that is the test the Colombian state faces. If it fails, its inability to meet this obligation will be judged not only within Colombia but also abroad. This is the challenge that parapolitics represents for our society.

Translated by Ana María Gómez López and Ann Farnsworth-Alvear

Turning Points in the Colombian Conflict, 1960s–1990s

Joseph Fabry, James Mollison, Robert Romero Ospina,

Daniel Jiménez, El Espectador, *and Ricardo Mazalán*

In 2012, negotiators announced a fourth round of peace talks between the FARC and the Colombian government in Havana, Cuba (see part VII). Many Colombians, particularly those in their late sixties or early seventies, listened to the announcement with some degree of war-weariness. They had been infants at the time of Gaitán's assassination in 1948. If they had been politically active as teenagers in the 1960s, they would likely remember hearing news broadcasts of the army's offensive against rebels in Marquetalia, municipality of Planadas, Tolima—which involved commandos parachuting into that remote and mountainous area to retake it from peasant guerrilla units that later coalesced into what became the FARC. Their entry into adulthood paralleled the country's descent into an armed conflict that was qualitatively different from both the civil wars of the nineteenth century and the partisan killing of the decades of La Violencia. This generation, those born in the late 1940s and early '50s, saw an inherited guerrilla war transform itself into something more frightening—the unpredictable violence of a multisided contest for power that was fueled by profits gained from cocaine. Memories of these years are intensely shaped by the visceral sense of fear that Colombians retain from the 1980s and 1990s. Specific signposts of collective memory, such as Pablo Escobar's face or the 1985 Palace of Justice takeover, are also markers of deep divisions among Colombians with direct memories of the late twentieth century.

The six images below chart a course through several decades of Colombians' conflicted sense of their shared past. Each is marked by sets of unanswered questions— even those who aspire to an "objective" assessment of what happened are very far from having the information they would need to arrive at preliminary conclusions. What really happened in Marquetalia and why? No consensus answer exists. Many know the town's name only because the FARC represents the confrontation there as a moment in which they launched a heroic struggle on behalf of the rural poor.

This is an exercise in storytelling that many Colombians find repellent. Similarly, few feel they have a definitive understanding of Pablo Escobar's relationships with politicians, which makes interpreting an image of him on the campaign trail difficult. Any attempt to tell a story about drug money and politics that Colombians (or others) will accept as a fair and accurate account is probably impossible. Pablo Escobar poured drug money into politicians' hands, so did his enemies, especially the antiguerrilla paramilitary units that steadily increased the clout they wielded within Colombia's political system through the 1990s and early 2000s. His name evokes terror for those who remember the targeted murders of the 1980s and 1990s, which included the systematic killing of police and judges, and the bombings of those years, in which bystanders died alongside those the traffickers had declared their enemies. Three of Escobar's acts of terrorism from late 1989 stand out as especially painful to Colombians: first, the September bombing of the El Espectador newspaper headquarters, which left dozens wounded and one dead; second, the bombing of Avianca flight 203 in November, which was an attempt to kill then presidential candidate César Gaviria but instead ended the lives of 107 passengers and crew; third, the early December bombing of the DAS, or Departamento Administrativo de Seguridad (Colombia's counterpart to the FBI), which left dozens dead and hundreds wounded in the center of the capital city.

By contrast to the secretive, internecine labyrinth of drugs and politics in recent years, this 1982 photograph of Escobar making a stump speech records a fleeting moment of relative openness, before many Colombians fully understood the national and international dimensions of the drug trade. Escobar began campaigning under the banner of Nuevo Liberalismo, headed by Luis Carlos Galán Sarmiento, but within months Galán expelled him from the party. Along with Rodrigo Lara Bonilla, assassinated by order of Pablo Escobar in 1984, Galán became a symbol of the way drug money held Colombian politics hostage. Like Lara Bonilla, Galán was assassinated in 1989 for supporting extradition to the United States for convicted drug traffickers and rejecting bribery.

Colombians use the term magnicidio, *or "magnicide," to describe the assassinations of Lara and Galán, and a list of the murdered political figures for whom that term is used suggests the intensity of the warfare that the cocaine kings declared on the country's political system in the late 1980s and early 1990s. In addition to Lara and Galán, those murdered include Jaime Pardo Leal, presidential candidate for the Patriotic Union, a leftist party allied with the FARC, killed in 1987; Carlos Pizarro Leongómez, presidential candidate for the M-19, assassinated in 1990; Bernardo Jaramillo Ossa, another presidential candidate for the Patriotic Union, also in 1990; and Álvaro Gómez Hurtado (see part V), presidential candidate for the Conservative Party, in 1995.*

By the late 1990s Colombians were deeply scarred by the level of bloodshed. The public at large took it for granted that all politicians were targeted by mafia figures for bribes, bullets, or both. People also took it for granted that historians would likely never know who had paid for the magnicidios. *In a few cases, it now seems more or less clear who might have given the orders—kingpin Rodríguez Gacha in the case of Pardo Leal, paramilitary commander and cocaine trafficker Carlos Castaño in the case of Carlos Pizarro and Bernardo Jaramillo (see above). But other cases remained unsolved and uninvestigated for decades afterward.*

The 1980s and 1990s saw the murder and persecution of organized alternatives to the two main Colombian political parties, Liberal and Conservative, especially as the party called the Patriotic Union (UP or Unión Patriótica) was systematically decimated. The group's posters, seen in a photograph here, made no secret of its connection to the FARC—in 1985 it seemed possible that the guerrillas might lay down their arms and enter electoral politics, taking "a step toward peace," as M-19 members in fact did in 1989. Between 1985 and about 1995 more than three thousand UP members were killed by paramilitaries and drug traffickers, foreclosing the UP's entry into electoral politics. Both the overlaps and the divergences between the Patriotic Union and the M-19 are significant. Both were targeted by paramilitary killers, but the M-19 became a civilian political force, while the Patriotic Union did not. One marker of the difference was that the M-19 succeeded in garnering a significant number of votes in the balloting that yielded delegates for Colombia's 1991 Constitutional Assembly (27 percent), even after Pizarro's death (he was replaced by Antonio Navarro Wolff, who went on to a long political career), and M-19 militants wielded influence as a new Constitution was being written. The Patriotic Union, with less than 3 percent of the vote, had no such influence.

For Colombians, the two most instantly recognizable images below are those of the tank at the door of the Palace of Justice in 1985 and Marulanda's empty chair in 1999. Within any given family these are likely to trigger interpretations that diverge along political fault lines. Events in the 2010s reopened the divisions that older Colombians remembered all too well. Military commander Alfonso Plazas Vega found himself facing charges of having violated civilians' human rights; he received a guilty sentence in a Bogotá court but then initiated a process of repeated appeals and sentencings, including a 2015 finding by Colombia's Corte Suprema de Justicia, declaring him innocent. The Inter-American Court of Human Rights, for its part, found the Colombian government culpable for disappearances and torture in the aftermath of the military assault on the building. Young people began to look at pictures taken during the 1985 siege in a new way, whether because they thought the army was being scapegoated or because they wanted to know the truth of what had happened to those arrested in the aftermath. Similarly, the photograph of Pastrana facing an empty chair means different things to different people. Those opposed to peace negotiations with the FARC see it as a sign of the guerrillas' bad

Colombian troops burn rural houses in the takeover of Marquetalia, in a confrontation that became a reference point for FARC militants. In the group's founding document, dated July 20, 1964, the army's Operation Marquetalia is listed as fourth in a series of wars against peasants in arms. Photograph by Joseph Fabry. Used by permission of Getty Images.

faith. Those sympathetic to the FARC see it as a calculated "photo op" on the part of President Pastrana, who, according to some, had been informed in advance that the guerrilla leader believed the possibility of paramilitary action made it unsafe for him to attend. In 2012, when Marulanda's comrades-in-arms did sit down at the negotiating table, the memory of this photograph's reception in the Colombian and international press was part of the political baggage carried by media advisers to both sides. As the country rewrites its history in coming decades, the visual record scholars, journalists, and teachers draw upon will include these politicized images.

Pablo Escobar during the 1982 campaign that gained him a seat in Colombia's House of Representatives. Photograph by Edgar Jiménez. In James Mollison, *The Memory of Pablo Escobar* (London: Chris Boot, 2007), 6. Courtesy of James Mollison.

Colombian army tanks entering the Palace of Justice in Bogotá. Photograph by Daniel Jiménez for *Revista Cromos*. On November 6, 1985, the
M-19 took Colombia's Supreme Court hostage in order to place the Betancur administration "on trial" for failing to meet peace treaty accords.
The Colombian military, under Colonel Alfonso Plazas Vega, responded
with a full-scale assault on the Palace of Justice. Over a hundred people
died, including twelve magistrates. In 2014, the Inter-American Court
found the armed forces guilty of assassinating magistrate Carlos Horacio
Urán Rojas, as well as of torturing and forcibly disappearing eleven other
people suspected of collaborating with the M-19. In Ana Carrigan, *The
Palace of Justice: A Colombian Tragedy* (New York: Four Walls Eight Windows Press, 1993), 144–45. Courtesy of *Revista Cromos*.

(*above*) The Patriotic Union (UP) was founded by the FARC and the Colombian Communist Party in 1985, during peace negotiations with the Betancur administration, following a 1982 amnesty. Many FARC members demobilized, joining civilian activists to form an alternative political platform. The posters in this image announce the first National Congress of the Patriotic Union, held in Bogotá on November 14–18, 1985. Beneath portraits of FARC leaders Manuel Marulanda Vélez, Jacobo Arenas, and Iván Márquez, the slogan reads "A step toward peace." Márquez, the only surviving member of the three, is a FARC representative in current peace talks with the Colombian government in Havana. Photograph by Lucio Lara, *Semanario Voz*. In Roberto Romero Ospina, *Unión Patriótica: Expedientes contra el olvido* (Bogotá: Centro de Memoria, Paz y Reconciliación, 2012), 297. Courtesy of Roberto Romero Ospina.

President Andrés Pastrana with an empty chair, in which Manuel Marulanda Vélez, or "Tirofijo," was to have been seated during peace talks in San Vicente del Caguán, Caquetá, 1999. The negotiations ended unsuccessfully in 2002. Photograph by Ricardo Mazalán. In Eduardo Serrano, *Historia de la fotografía en Colombia 1950–2000* (Bogotá: Editorial Planeta Colombiana, 2006), 226. Used by permission of the Associated Press.

(facing page) In 1985, President Belisario Betancur began meeting with M-19 guerrillas to work out the details for a cease-fire, something made impossible by the bloody events at the Palace of Justice in November of the same year. The M-19 would eventually demobilize in 1990, along with the Popular Liberation Army, the Partido Revolucionario de Trabajadores, and the Movimiento Indígena Quintín Lame. Under President Virgilio Barco, "Eme" leaders were pardoned, and former commander Carlos Pizarro Leongómez (center) became a presidential candidate. After he was assassinated in 1990, Antonio Navarro Wolff (right) became the public face of the M-19. That same year presidential candidates Luis Carlos Galán (Liberal Party) and Bernardo Jaramillo Ossa (UP) were similarly murdered. Used by permission of *El Espectador / Revista Cromos.*

VI

Change and Continuity in the Colombian Economy

As the second most populous Spanish-speaking country after Mexico, Colombia has a complex national economy. Its urban centers generate a huge demand for goods and services, and its 440,000 square miles of territory produce significant quantities of food and exports. Historically, Colombian exports have included both "boom" commodities (tobacco, quinine, ornamental feathers, rubber, coffee, cocaine) and minerals, particularly gold and fossil fuels. Although mining has moved through its own cycles of boom and bust, in Colombia it has provided a spine of continuity that connects the colonial era to the present.

Optimistic assessments of the historical arc of the Colombian economy point to its dynamism. When a new boom develops—as in the 1980s, when the national government contracted with a set of multinational firms and Colombia moved into the top ranks of coal exporters—local residents see new transport infrastructure and new residential patterns that flow from the expansion of exports. Economic indicators fuel the optimists' position that the export economy has helped create national wealth, as Colombia's historical growth rates compare favorably with those of many other economies. Pessimists emphasize the negative weight of inequality, measured across centuries. Colombians who pan for gold, tend plantings or harvest wild goods, grade coffee, trim roses, produce coca paste, work oil wells, or mine coal do gritty, often underpaid work. Pessimists ask questions about the long term, as they assess it: Given that indigenous people and enslaved Africans were treated ruthlessly in the colonial era, did they recoup their losses in the national period? Given that well-connected politicians and financiers in the twentieth century argued that foreign firms would facilitate a growth in overall national wealth, is there evidence that they were right? Scholars disagree about the answers to such questions, as well as about what policy should look like.

One thing Colombians generally agree about is that cocaine users north of the Mexican border create economic costs that can be tallied in Latin

American deaths and the destruction of hemispheric ecosystems. Another area of agreement centers on the existence of inequities. Rural dwellers' access to police protection, medical care, education, and other products of the urban service economy remains scarce. Some urbanites have a standard of living that many middle-class North Americans would envy, while others work as servants, hustle for petty earnings as peddlers, or beg on the streets. In the countryside, large holdings predominate in ways that can be traced to the actions of colonial-era *encomenderos* and *hacendados* (see part III), to the venality of politicians in the national era, and, most recently, to money-laundering by drug traffickers in the present. The economic effects of violence have played out along a steep slope of inequality—with Colombians at the bottom of the economic hierarchy suffering the most each time violence has flared in their nation.

El Dorado

Fray Pedro Simón

Alternately represented as a city of gold or as man covered in gold dust, the mythical lure of El Dorado is a deep-rooted part of Colombian and Latin American history. For foreigners, it symbolizes the conquistadors' dream of wealth. For Colombians, it conjures a specific image, that of a gilded prince who prepares to dive into Lake Guatavita: the gold that coats his body will be washed off and a sacred rite completed. One icon of the myth of El Dorado is the famous Muisca raft on display at the Gold Museum in Bogotá, which appears on Colombian currency and stamps and became a ubiquitous visual image almost immediately after being discovered in 1969.[1] Another is the text excerpted below, written by Fray Pedro Simón (1574–1628), a Franciscan friar who set himself the task of chronicling the conquest of New Granada, covering Venezuela, Colombia, and Ecuador. Fray Pedro emphasizes the conquistadors' disappointments and failures, including the mess that resulted when a vainglorious Spaniard undertook to drain the lake.

Along the banks of this river [the Orinoco], on the right, going upriver to the banks of the Papamene River, and down into the provinces of Caguán, which is behind this New Kingdom [of Granada], and entering the Orinoco again near its mouth, word arrives of El Dorado, in the pursuit of which great and costly journeys have been carried out, disturbing seas, rivers, and lakes, crossing over lands and provinces with terribly difficult paths, illnesses, shelters, and places to camp, and without offering any gain other than the loss of fortunes. The fame of El Dorado has rung out such that many think nothing of leaving their lands in the kingdoms of Spain to come and meet their absolute ruin. The pitiful end to which so many who risked these paths and expeditions have come serves as fitting testimony: not even one of the many who have tried has had anything but calamity befall him, without a day of rest; yet it does not cease to amaze to see how all those who attempt this meet the same sad fortune. . . .

The base of all the commotion that arose about El Dorado was this: After having settled the city of San Francisco of Quito—in the year that don Fran-

Votive raft worked in gold. Muisca, 1200–1500 AD. 19.5 × 10.1 × 10.2 cm. For Colombians, this is an instantly recognizable pre-Conquest object and the showpiece of Bogotá's Gold Museum. *Figura Votiva* 011373, Colección del Oro, Banco de la República. Courtesy of Museo del Oro, Banco de la República.

cisco Pizarro was the *adelantado* [frontier governor] of Peru—Captain Sebastián de Belalcázar, his lieutenant general, was carefully traveling all possible paths through all the lands and provinces, without omitting any that were known of, and making inquiries of the Indians. Having heard that there was a certain outsider in the city, he went and asked him about his land. [The outsider] replied that "it was called Muequetá, and its cacique, Bogotá." This was the New Kingdom of Granada, which the Spaniards called Bogotá. And asking if this land had the metal he was shown, which was gold, the Indian responded that it was plentiful, and that there were emeralds, which in his language he called green stones. He added that there was a lake in the land of his cacique, and that several times a year, his chief would ride out to the middle of it upon well-crafted rafts. He would be naked, but his entire body would be covered from head to foot with a very sticky sap and abundantly powdered with fine gold dust, such that when the gold set, it made a second skin of gold. When the sun shone upon him in the clear of the morning, which was when they made this sacrifice, he shimmered brightly as he went out into the middle of the lake and made his offering, throwing bits of gold and emeralds into the water as he spoke certain words. Then, his entire body would be rubbed over with certain herbs like soap, and all the gold that was on him would fall into the water, ending the sacrifice, and he would leave the water and get dressed in his robes.

This news was so much what was desired by Belalcázar and his soldiers, who were avid for larger discoveries than were being made in Peru, that they decided to discover the land the Indian had described. And in discussing among themselves what name they would give to set this province apart from their other conquests, they decided to call this the province of El Dorado, which was like saying: it will be called that province where the Gilded Man or the Cacique with the Golden Body goes to make his offerings. This is the root and the trunk from which the long branches of the fame of El Dorado have reached out to the world. . . .

Guided in this way by the Devil . . . they did not make these offerings in any waters but rather in those that seemed to have a particular reason for being extraordinary in their placement, provenance, or appearance . . . but of all the places the most frequented and famous place for this worship was the lake they call Guatavita which is about one league or a little more from the town of the same name. . . . Here, then, as a place accommodated for what the Devil demanded, they would make such offerings in the way he had ordered them to, and the Devil would appear in those same waters in the shape of a small dragon or large snake, and when he appeared certain elders, who because of this stayed in some huts along the water's edge, would offer him gold or emeralds. . . .

When word circulated that bearded men were coming who were searching carefully for gold among the Indians, they took much of what they had hidden and offered it at the lake. With this sacrifice, they pleaded for the *cacica* [a noblewoman said to live in the lake] to save them from these men who had come upon their lands like a plague.[2] They made this offering at their shrine rather than at their houses, where they risked the Spaniards taking it. Some of them did this with such quantities of gold that the cacique of Simijaca alone threw into this lake forty loads of gold carried from the village to the lake by forty Indians, as verified by these Indians and the nephew of this cacique, who had inherited the *cacicazgo* and [said that] at least forty *quintales* of fine gold had been thrown into the lake. Having an interest in verifying the truth of this, the *encomendero* of the town, Captain Gonzalo León de Venero, persuaded the cacique, Don Alonso, to show him some shrines, because it would be better to use the gold than to leave it offered up to the Devil without any benefit from it. The Indian responded in friendship and in confidence said that if he drained Guatavita Lake he would get infinite riches out of it, because his uncle alone had sent him with the referred-to loads of gold; and this was verified to be true, and that many others had done the same, some with more gold, some with less gold.

Moved by this news, many of the soldiers who had discovered this land tried to drain the lake, as did Captain Lázaro Fonte. . . . Antonio de Sepúlveda, a merchant from this city of Santa Fe, took it upon himself to do this, and returned to Spain in the 1580s, where he obtained from the council a document that gave certain conditions under which he and no other would have the power to drain the lake, and that the Royal Audiencia [in Bogotá] should give to him all that he would need and all the Indians he asked for to do the labor of draining. This he began to do upon his return from Spain, having houses built next to the lake and a boat from which its depth could be measured. . . . He then brought together many Indian dredgers, who began to open a channel from the height that the engineers thought would be sufficient, digging through rocks with great difficulty; soon they discovered that it was going to be much harder than they had thought. With huge outlays of tools, however, they did break through these cold mountains, *páramos* [high-altitude Andean tundra], and swamps, and as there was no other way but for the Indians to continue the work, they came out on the slopes of the two mountains where the lake drains. By cutting through here and there, and by using thick wood to brace it or force it, they began to open the drainage channel and thus it began emptying more than usual and the lake banks began to be uncovered. There in the clay and mud they began to find pieces of gold jewelry worked in a thousand ways: nose rings, breastplates, small serpents, eagles, emeralds. And the reason they found them was because not everyone had gone to the center of the lake to make offerings but, rather, when the offerings were low in value, they had been offered from the banks of the lake. In the end, the little amount they found there encouraged Sepúlveda to continue in the hope of getting back what he was spending and much more besides, as he surely would have done if the necessary labor had gone into building his drainage channel, and for every channel cut, they found larger and more valuable emeralds and pieces of gold, and even one that was about the size of an egg, as well as a few bishop's staffs, made of sheets of gold and covered in gold foil with gold piping and other jewels. All of this, worth some five or six thousand ducats, was taken to the Office of the Royal Treasury [Caja Real], as that was one of the conditions for having given the license; so that everything that was taken was divided between the merchant and the mint, with costs having been covered but without the King having to pay anything. In the end, as Sepúlveda's ambition exceeded his purse, it so happened that as the drainage channel was not well braced and many rains came, both sides of the channel collapsed, closing off the drainage again at a time when the merchant's fortune was not sufficient to clear out the earth again. Thus, he was forced to leave his outpost and his work and go off to die in a hospital without money for anything else; since then, no other has been bold enough to undertake such a risky proposition.

Translated by Ann Farnsworth-Alvear

Notes

1. A similar goldwork votive raft was found in the nineteenth century but was lost while en route to a European museum.
2. Fray Pedro recounts a legend associated with Lake Guatavita, involving this *cacica* and her husband's fury at having discovered her infidelity.

The Conquest Yields Other Treasures:
Potatoes, Yucca, Corn

Juan de Castellanos and Galeotto Cei

The gold and silver yielded by Spanish and Portuguese America transformed the world economy, but the way European, Asian, and African markets were changed by the arrival of new foods may have had a greater long-term impact. Europeans and others learned to eat potatoes, South Asians gained access to hot peppers, Africans began harvesting manioc: it is a long list. The Conquest-era passages included here describe potatoes, yucca, and corn (in the easily recognizable form of arepas). They are richly suggestive. An offhand note that war captains visiting comrades' homes in what later became Venezuela would bring their own bread and wine (which seems to have been arepas and manioc beer) allows a glimpse of social relations: "One Indian woman will make enough bread and wine for a single Spaniard." Similarly, readers of Juan de Castellanos's sixteenth-century description of Indian houses well-stocked with "truffles" (potatoes) can visualize the pre-Conquest economy of the Andes in a way that goes beyond the text itself.

Castellanos's long chronicle, parts of which were published in the 1580s, is titled Elegies about Illustrious Men of the Indies *and is one of the better-known narrations of the Spanish Conquest. The excerpts drawn from Galeotto Cei, a Florentine adventurer whose manuscript dates from the 1560s, are less familiar to Colombians. Together they provide some of the very earliest European descriptions of South American foodways.*

The houses [of the Indians] were all stocked with maize, beans, and truffles [potatoes], spherical roots which are sown and produce a stem with its branches and leaves, and some flowers, although few, of a soft purple color; and to the roots of this same plant, which is about 3 palms high, they are attached under the earth, and are the size of an egg more or less, some round and some elongated; they are white and purple and yellow, floury roots of good flavor, a delicacy to the Indians and a dainty dish even for the Spaniards.

Iucca [yucca] is a root from which you make bread and beverages in all of India [meaning the Indies] and of which there are two kinds. . . . The *caribe* is usually bigger than the *boniatta*, sending out knotted branches of a gray color, as tall as a man depending on the country, so that it is considered to be a shrub. It sends out long, thin leaves that are very green; the branches break easily. They plant it in this way: they take the smallest branches, the ones that are a thumb's width, and they make small sticks. . . . Both Christians and Indians have always made, and still do make, little mounds of earth, an arm's length in height and four or five arms' length around, not so far from each other that a man could not walk between them. They make these into the shape of pyramids, and put in 10 or 12 of those small sticks, the number depending on the size of the mound which they put up and the bearded roots grow there. They are fairly thin with a reddish brown peel and as white as milk inside with a large amount of juice. And in 22 months they have reached a state of perfection for making bread, but the *boniatta* does not take so long, and when they want to make bread from them, they unearth them and make it in this manner.

First they work the root with a cane or piece of wood used like a knife, removing that brown peel. Whoever eats that root raw and without squeezing out the juice will find that immediately his tongue swells, great amounts of viscous liquid will come out of his nose, he will suffer great confusion in his head, [and] a great thirst and fire in his stomach accompanied by a cruel swelling. We use as a remedy for whoever this befalls, when this happens on the mainland where this *caribe* yucca is rare and it is the local custom to eat the raw *boniatta*, and someone comes hungry to a place where it is growing and carelessly eats a few mouthfuls. As I was saying, we give the person oil to drink as a remedy or brine and other things that cause nausea. But if a great quantity has been consumed there is no remedy for the swelling that brings death. The other kind is often eaten raw, or cooked on a fire, or boiled, and does no harm. Returning to the method of making bread . . . after it is peeled they grate it either with a sharp stone, the bark of a tree, or a specially made grater until it resembles shavings of macaroni, and when they do this the Indians call it making *guarequitteri*. Then they take these shavings and put them in baskets called *zebuccan* made from reeds stretched out long and thin. [. . .] Then they hang a lid on the top and weights that pull it down, as it stretches it constricts serving them as a press to extract the juice that is its poison, and which if any man, bird, chicken, pig, or other animal were to drink from it they would die without a remedy. Once they have squeezed out the shavings, they remove them from the basket or *zebuccanes*, and it looks like sawdust. On stoves they have earthen dishes as large as a small wheel that the Indians call *arippos* or *burenes*, in which they put the shavings to a finger's depth depending on how thick they want the bread to be. If it is to be taken to sea or stored, or for slaves and their families, they make it thick and hard, but if it is to be eaten immediately and by Christians, they make it thinner and softer. Making it softer or harder is done by pressing more or less the hand over the dish where, since it is cooked only on one side, they turn it over and then place it to dry in the sun for one, two or three days according to the need so that it appears like a plank or sawdust made into a solid form. This is what they do for the bread that will be taken to sea or stored and it is so hard that you can hardly break it with your teeth. . . .

With nothing else, eaten on its own, it does not stay long in the stomach or in the belly so that, when nature calls, it is necessary to hold the reins tight or the trousers suffer damage. . . .

On the mainland there are more kinds of maize and one called *cariacco* is more tender and much better for bread but it bears less fruit. The ears are small, it grows in three months and some in 40 days, but the other kind is better for horses, for pigs and for storing. This grain is eaten in many different ways: in milk when it is fresh, by cooking or roasting the ears on a grill. . . . They soak it for a day or two and they grind it in stones . . . that are a little curved, and which they strike with the other stone that they hold in two hands, grinding the maize like painters do their colors. One Indian squats or kneels on one side of the stone putting a handful of the grain into the concave part with some water and with the stone in two hands they grind it over and over until it becomes a paste. Then they make little cakes like bars of soap and wrap them in the husk or in the leaves of the maize plant and cook them in a large earthen pot in which they can fit enough to give each Indian one or two. And sometimes they keep them for so long that they become vinegary and moldy and then they say that they are good. Often they leave the paste to become vinegary or strong for one or two days and this kind of bread is called *aiaccas*.

They make other sorts of bread in the manner of *stiacciatine* [pancake or flatbread], as high as a finger, round and more or less as big as a French plate. They cook them on a dish on the fire, greasing it with some fat so that it does not stick, turning it over on all sides until it is cooked, and they call this sort of bread *areppas*. . . .

One Indian woman will make enough bread and wine for a single Spaniard and because of this it is customary when a friend invites another man to his house, or hosts a celebration, or a wedding, that each person brings bread and wine for himself.

Translated by Meriel Tulante

Cauca's Slave Economy

Germán Colmenares

The historical work of Germán Colmenares (1938–90) emphasized the interweaving of economic and social life in the colonial era. When researching economic questions, such as the ups and downs of relative prices for different kinds of slaves, who appeared in his documents as "pieces," Colmenares also scrutinized demographics, the texture of family life, and profit margins for mercantile and agrarian interests in the region. Patiently, he combed through archives and found new ways to "read against the grain."

The text excerpted below explores the links between a world market in slaves and the local economic rhythms of Cauca province. Colmenares tries to take apart the conceptual frames his academic readers bring to the study of an "agrarian economy" or a "mining economy." These, he explains, foreclose understanding of what was above all a slave economy. Economic rationality and irrationality were indiscriminately mixed in a system that was feudal. Smugglers and slave merchants intervened in a market that had the hacienda at its center, and slave owners rotated "pieces" from mines to plantations and back, as they chose.

These were not the huge plantations of the French or British Caribbean in the early eighteenth century. That model of enormous tracts of land worked by large resident populations was never the Colombian pattern. Colmenares's work is part of an expanding effort by Colombian intellectuals to understand local cultural characteristics and the patterns of stratification that have shaped racial meanings over the centuries and are still palpable in the departaments of Cauca, Valle de Cauca, and the Chocó.

From among the first imports of the English company (between 1714 and 1718), the Spaniard Francisco de Ocasal purchased 29 *piezas* in Cartagena and resold some of them in Cali in about 1719. The price in Cartagena was then 215 *patacones* [silver peso coins] for an adult slave and 178 *patacones* for a child. In Cali they were sold for between 450 and 500 *patacones*, without distinguishing among them. Some fellow citizens became interested in this lucrative business. For instance, Francisco de la Flor Laguno, a Spaniard married to a *criolla* from a prestigious family and mayor of the city in 1720, acted on several occasions as an intermediary for merchant Alonso Gil, who purchased 12 *piezas* in Cartagena in April 1723, for 255 *patacones* each.

In 1724, we find the Spanish merchant, Captain Alonso Salgado, active in Cali. At the shipyard the previous year, together with buyers Francisco de Ocasal and Antonio Correa, he had purchased 108 black men for 221 *patacones* each, 26 black women for the same price, as well as 46 black girls and 20 black boys for 201 *patacones* apiece. Months later, he would purchase 27 black men, 23 black women, 4 black boys and 5 black girls on his own behalf. During two more years that he remained in Cali, he sold 91 slaves (35 percent of his purchases) for 38,740 *patacones*, (425 each, on average). On this occasion, the strongest buyer from Cali was the *alférez real*,[1] Nicolás de Caicedo Hinestroza, who acquired 33 *piezas* for 14,850 *patacones*. He was followed, in order of importance, though far behind, by doña Ana María de los Reyes, who owned land in Cañasgordas and mines along the Calima river, and who purchased ten *piezas* for 4,700 *patacones*.

The citizens of Cali were not satisfied for long with being mere intermediaries or solely buyers in a trade that could return profits of close to one hundred percent. Another Spanish citizen, Francisco Leonardo del Campo, also married to a *criolla* from a noble family, purchased 20 slaves in Cartagena during the first period of the *asiento*.[2] In 1726 (on June 26), this time together with merchant Francisco Garcés de Aguilar, he returned to acquire 74 slaves, old and young, for 17,620 *patacones*. The *piezas* were brought to Cali by the Spanish merchant Custodio Jerez (also a Cali *vecino*),[3] who registered 69 in Honda on August 11, claiming that three had escaped. . . .

In the second half of the 18th century, transactions of black *bozales* [recently arrived Africans], those who arrived to the city directly from Cartagena, practically disappear from Cali's market. While slaves were purchased and sold each year, these were almost always *"criollos,"* born on local *haciendas* and in *Caleño* households. Transactions of more than two slaves for *hacienda* work also began to taper off, unless the property was being sold. On the other hand, sales of *piezas* for domestic service, or for *cuadrillas* [work gangs] being sent to the mining centers, were increasingly frequent. In other words, the slave market sustained itself despite not being regularly supplied from the outside, although scarcity did limit the establishment of new haciendas.

It follows that work conditions allowed for the reproduction of "creole" slaves and for *mestizaje*. One should not lose sight of the fact that the system of production on *haciendas*, while slave-based, included patriarchal features that permitted and even encouraged slaves' reproduction—tasks were more or less routine and it does not seem that slaves were subjected to a work regime that was unusually harsh. In the shadow of the master's home, slaves generally tended their own plots, which enriched their basic diet of meat and plantain. Because of this, the frequent practice of withdrawing slaves from mines and sending them to an hacienda may not have been about employing them at tasks that were more productive in themselves, but rather about securing a return on investment that could bear fruit simply through the reproduction of slaves. . . .

The existence of a mining economy, alongside a region exceptionally suited for agriculture, favored this double character of landowners and mine operators. In the absence of any other labor for haciendas, the use of slave laborers became the rule, with their elevated cost being compensated by proximity to a flourishing market. Moreover, mining stimulated the creation of haciendas, and one of the incentives was precisely the possibility of transferring capital in the form of slave labor between both sectors.

As a whole, this system operated in such a way that landowners—and often those who did not own land—tended to channel their investments toward the purchase of black slaves, even if they were not in mining. Understanding this requires an acknowledgment that the conceptual frame of an "agricultural economy" or "mining economy" is too narrow, in hindsight, to explain a *slave economy*. Economic rationality and irrationality were mixed up together, within a type of feudalism.

Throughout, Cali's *vecinos* were eager to acquire slaves. Obviously, working mines, haciendas, and ranches necessarily required this kind of labor. But the demand for black slaves exceeded normal labor requirements or what would have been required to maintain productivity. The numbers of slaves occupied in domestic service and kept in urban areas is evidence of this.

Noblewomen's dowries always listed one or two slaves to remain exclusively in the bride's service, both to enhance her social standing and to extend the care her parents could provide her. There are also numerous letters of gift in which slave boys or girls are received by minors.

Social prestige could be tangibly measured by an abundance of idle slaves, who went from being a means to amass wealth to being the very symbol of opulence. Literally, they became an object. A person of status such as don Nicolás de Caicedo mentioned in his will no less than 31 slaves "in service." In 1777, his son held 77 such slaves, while nine municipal officers (*regidores* and *alcaldes*), had together 261, and still their household listings went on to include others: "servants," "free domestics" and "free blacks." In 1768, doña Barbara de Saa, widow of merchant and miner Juan Francisco Garcés de

Aguilar, who owned 151 slaves in the El Raposo mine, held 37 slaves in her home in Cali and just 20 at her Cañaveralejo ranch. Naturally, most of these slaves were women and children (17 and 13 respectively, in contrast to 7 adult men). This pattern also extended to convents, and even religious women, much as in the case of brides, were individually served by slaves.

Translated by Ana María Gómez López and Ann Farnsworth-Alvear

Notes

1. The *alférez real* was a royal standard-bearer, whose title indicated status. That status was often an inherited one; the Caicedo family in Cali held the *alferazgo* for over a century, and the last member of that family to hold the position, Manuel de Caicedo Tenorio, served as the inspiration for *El Alférez Real*, an 1889 novel written by Eustaquio Palacios.
2. The *asiento* was a concession granted by the Spanish Crown allowing monopoly privilege of supplying African slaves to the Spanish colonies in the Americas. In the period Colmenares describes it was held by the British.
3. *Vecino* was a status usually extended to nonindigenous residents and those having a racial status close to that of whites; the term implied a set of political privileges.

A Jesuit Writes to the King: Profits from Coca Leaf Could Surpass Tea

Antonio Julián

In 1787 the Catalonian Jesuit Father Antonio Julián published in Madrid a book-length survey of the environs of Santa Marta, titled La perla de América *(The Pearl of America). The book was the fruit of ten years' residence in Santa Marta, where he had arrived in 1749, and then of eight years' teaching at the Pontificia Universidad Javeriana in Bogotá. The Crown had expelled the Jesuits from the colonies in 1767, and Julián used his return to Europe as an opportunity to produce detailed descriptions for his book, including the excerpt below, a sketch of indigenous people near Riohacha and their cultivation of an "herb called* hayo." *The Pearl of America focused on the benefits that Spain would gain by developing the resources of Caribbean Colombia, not only the famous pearl fisheries of the region, but also the potential export of gold, gems, sugar, and brazilwood. His greatest optimism, however, he reserves for hayo, also known as coca leaf—an export product with the potential to surpass coffee, tea, and tobacco, in Julián's opinion. As the prolific historian Jorge Orlando Melo puts it in introducing Colombian readers to this text: "He did not lack for vision."[1]*

It is with singular pleasure that I begin my discussion of this plant, not so much to provide news to the curious, but to promote its cultivation and use in Europe, to the benefit of the Monarchy of Spain, and for the greater good and health of peoples and foreign nations. The latter have strived to introduce tea and coffee, and have tried to promote the virtues of these herbs. They have cleverly tried to make common their use, filling the cities with cafés as outlets for the fruits of their colonies and regions, with untold advantages for their states and commerce. We Spaniards, so easily swayed by foreign ideas and so quick to embrace their fashions as we are enthusiastic in giving up our own and not attaching importance to them, we allow the Indians to eat and find sustenance in an herb that could prove to be a very profitable new commercial endeavor for Spain while providing health to Europe, serving as a cure and tonic for so many ills, a replenisher of lost strength, and a prolonger of human life. It is the herb called *Hayo*, celebrated in the Province of Santa Marta, and throughout the New Kingdom. In Potosí, Kingdom of Perú, it is known as *Coca*.

Before stating its virtues, I want to refer to the manner in which it is used by Guajiro Indians. To date they alone use this herb in all of the New Kingdom. The manner in which they do so is curious, and seeing it provoked me no less admiration than laughter. I will tell what I saw, so as to make known the general custom of this nation. Finding myself in the *Rio de la Hacha* (now Riohacha), there appeared at our house a troop of Guajiros that came to see the Bishop who was there for a visit. Some of them were Christians from the mission of the Capuchin fathers; others were savages and gentiles, so innocent that when I asked one of them if he wished to become Christian, he furrowed his brow greatly, and in a deep voice answered with a firm "no." I went out, thus, to look at that troop of Indians. I was among tall youngsters, healthy, and well-built, with handsome faces and olive skin, whiter than that which other Indians in the Kingdom generally have. They carried folded over their right shoulder a cotton blanket, finely woven by their own hand (as they excel at such tasks), which covered most of their body, and hanging from their necks was a *mochila*, or a small shoulder bag, which fell underneath their left arm; and on their waist, like pious pilgrims, they carried a small gourd that held a tiny, rounded stick inside, which came out from a little opening. Inside that small bag they carried fresh green *Hayo* leaves, and inside the gourd was a finely powdered lime, which they make themselves from seashells, so white and well ground that it looks like starch, or like *manjar blanco*. As I was happily talking with them, I saw that every so often, each of them would reach into their bag and take out a fistful of herbs, place it in his mouth, and between chewing and talking they would be swallowing. When the dose was finished, they would put their hand on the little stick that protruded from the mouth of their gourd, which they call *Popóro* in their language, and they would stir the lime powder a little, and would take some out with the tip of the stick. Then with great skill they would apply it, using that brush to take away the green stain of the *Hayo* juice, leaving their lips painted white. The *Guajiros* were truly that refined. I asked one of them, who seemed more amiable and jovial, "Why do you eat the herb like this?" And the rascal Indian put his fingers to his nose, like a person taking snuff, and he answered me, "And white man, why do you do this?" and he did it exactly like a person taking

Tobacco. I confess the Indian left me red in the face, and I did not know how to respond, because when it comes to the ways and customs of diverse nations, it is difficult to be convincing about differences. . . .

The *Hayo* leaf is smooth, and ends in a single small point, and it is of a beautiful dark green hue. When the *Hayo* is in season, the Indians cut each of the leaves with their thumbnail at the leaf stem and place them in a cloth they have ready for this purpose. They gather the harvest, and later place it in clay vessels, while they wait to sell it to the pearl merchants that do business with the Guajiros, or to others for their own use.

Its commerce is constant, because the Guajiros use this herb continuously, chewing it day and night, at all times. And they are so fond and accustomed to it, that they would go without food rather than go without a secure supply of *Hayo*. As a person accustomed to tobacco snuff cannot be without his snuffbox, so to the Guajiro Indian cannot be without his *mochila* of this herb. So true is this, that their custom has become second nature. Knowing the Guajiro's passion for *Hayo*, the merchants travel to the towns of Molino and Villanueva, and they buy *Hayo* leaves with canvases, tools, and other small items the Indians have a liking for. They take the *Hayo* across the *Río de la Hacha*, or to other towns and *reducciones*[2] of Guajiros converted to Christianity, where savages also come and do their trading, with the Guajiros giving so many ounces of Pearls for so many bushels of *Hayo* leaves. In the past there was always a commerce for this herb in the interior of the New Kingdom, for aside from its use by savage nations, such as the Guajiros, the *Hayo* was widely sought after as food and sustenance for the Priests of their Idols, who were required to remain isolated, abstinent, chaste, and withdrawn, speaking and sleeping little.

I feel great disbelief that Europe does not make any use of the *Hayo*, given the great consumption of tea and coffee. I attribute this to three causes. The first is ignorance about the excellent qualities of *Hayo*, and there has not been a clever man to ascertain these for the public good. The second is that the Spanish nation has not been ambitious in introducing new fashions to other countries, even as we are willing to accept alien ones. The third is that foreign nations have more profit and advantages in promoting the use of tea and coffee, and not *Hayo*, fruit of the domains of the Spanish King. The fourth, which we can also add here, is that the news has not spread, and the time has not yet come to make taking *Hayo* a fashion. It may be that *Hayo*, like all things, will arrive in due time, and with the news that I provide of its admirable virtues and effects it would be introduced not as an idle, or useless, or destructive fashion to households and people, like others that arrive from overseas, but, rather, one that is healthy, useful, and beneficial to the well-being, vigor, and strength of the body, and that promotes long and prosperous maintenance of the individual.

Translated by Ana María Gómez López and Ann Farnsworth-Alvear

Notes

1. Jorge Orlando Melo, "La coca, planta del futuro: Un texto del siglo XVIII," *Revista Credencial Historia* 158 (2003): n.p., available at http://www.lablaa.org/blaavirtual/revistas/credencial/febrero2003/lacoca.htm.
2. *Reducciones* were settlements of forced relocation for indigenous people.

Bogotá's Market, ca. 1850

Agustín Codazzi

Opportunity is uppermost in the following prose sketch of products available in Bogotá's central market in the 1850s. Listing a bewildering span of fruits and vegetables, the Italian-born geographer Giovanni Batista Agostino Codazzi (1793–1859) —known to geographers and historians as Agustín Codazzi—emphasizes that Colombians could grow both temperate and tropical crops and that Bogotá was distinctly unusual in having access to such a range of produce.

What is not evident in his description is that moving this produce around was often prohibitively expensive. Some mountain passes, considered too dangerous for mules, were still traversed only by human porters. Their rates could be paid by passengers, riding on the porters' backs, but were generally too high to transport produce.

Codazzi wrote with authority—he had traveled widely in Europe and the Americas and had lived for a time in Istanbul, and his military career had taken him to the United States and the River Plate area between Argentina and Uruguay. In Venezuela he had held a governorship and had undertaken to map the nation for President José Antonio Páez. Given the civil war there, by the 1850s Codazzi was in Colombia, where General Tómas Cipriano de Mosquera recruited him to head the Chorographic Commission. With other members of the commission, including Manuel Ancízar (see part I), Codazzi drew the first full maps of Colombia's territory. In mid-nineteenth-century Bogotá few were able to so persuasively compare the Colombian capital to other cities in both the Old World and the New.

At the market one finds all the grains, vegetables, and fruits that high, temperate, and warm lands can produce, so that next to the strawberries, which grow wild high in the mountains are bananas and plantains from the lowlands [*de tierra caliente*] and cherries, peaches, and apples next to pineapples, mangoes, and melons; cucumbers from cool and hot climates, as well as the fruit of the *badea* vine, pomegranates, and *granadilla* fruit along with *treja de chila*, blackberries and *curubas*, borne from cool and hot climates; plums, guavas, and prickly pear, loquats, mamey fruit, *zapotes*, *anones*, and *uchu-*

Joseph Brown, *Mule Drivers in a Store in the Principal Street of Bogotá*, ca. 1840. Watercolor and ink, 22 × 31 cm, from a drawing by José Manuel Groot. Signs affixed to
the wall read "Today you can't buy on credit, maybe tomorrow" and "Gossip is bad
for you." Note military dress hats on top shelf. In Malcolm Deas, Efraín Sánchez,
and Aída Martínez, *Tipos y costumbres de la Nueva Granada / Types and Customs of New
Granada* (Bogotá: Fondo Cultural Cafetero, 1989), 130.

vas, paw paws, anise-berries, gooseberries, and papayas; the nut myrtle, and
mortiño with coconut, *guanabanas* and *chirimoyas*; oranges, citrons, lemons,
and limes, with dates, *granates*, star-apples and avocados, breadfruit, and
cachipay, as well as figs, wild figs, tree-strawberries, tree tomato; *mararay*
nuts, guava trees, calabashes, watermelons, *pitahayas*, *mamones*, tamarinds
and *guamas* of all kinds. With regard to vegetables, there are garlic, onions,
Spanish celery, asparagus, cabbages, Brussels sprouts, radishes, turnips, cilantro, squashes, cucumbers, sweet red and green peppers, cumin, toma-
toes, greens of several kinds, carrots, beets, cardoons, and globe artichokes.
With regard to the main foodstuffs, besides wheat, corn, and potatoes, there
are parsnips, yams, yucca, rice, peas, peanuts, garbanzos, beans, lentils, barley, broad beans, sugarcane, cacao, coffee, and sago, as well as tobacco, anise, flaxseed, butter, cheese, eggs, lard, wax, soap, twine and sacks made
of *fique* hemp, medicinal plants and an abundance of flowers. This assortment is available all year long, as the temperature allows for the flowering
of plants and [continual] ripening of fruits. Next to this garden are the delicate meats, domestic poultries, water birds, dry fish from the Magdalena,

Joseph Brown, *Carrying Poultry to Market in Andean Colombia*, ca. 1840. Watercolor and ink, 17 × 27 cm, from a drawing by José Manuel Groot. In Malcolm Deas, Efraín Sánchez, Aída Martínez, *Tipos y Costumbres de la Nueva Granada / Types and Customs of New Granada* (Bogotá: Fondo Cultural Cafetero, 1989), 87.

sardines, and captain fish, which is only caught at high altitudes. The sweet syrups with which the common people make their beverages are lined up next to *panela* [loaves of hardened molasses; see part V], white sugar, and the salt of Zipaquirá. Alongside are the piles of clay pottery made by the Indians, used for all household tasks, while the merchants lay out cloths, blankets, scarves and fabrics of all kinds from around the country and abroad, forming a great carpet before the cathedral steps. It would be difficult to find a market better provisioned with the fruits of every land, ranging from barley-growing areas to plantain regions.

Translated by Ana María Gómez López and Ann Farnsworth-Alvear

A Banker Invites Other Bankers to Make Money in Colombia

Phanor James Eder

Born in the Cauca Valley, Phanor James Eder (1880–1971) was the son of Santiago Eder, an Eastern European migrant who, with his children, built an industrialist dynasty that has endured more than a century. While his brothers managed family businesses in Colombia, Phanor spent most of his adult life in New York, where he developed a career as a legal adviser to banks and mining companies. Until 1922 he was a vice president at the Mercantile Bank of the Americas, the Bogotá division of which was run by future president of Colombia, Alfonso López Pumarejo. Eder's personal familiarity with Colombia ran through his professional life—as can be seen in the following text, chock-full of practical advice for bankers, and in his conclusion that Colombia was ripe for the arrival of international finance; he emphasized that the Germans were there already. The same year Eder published his overview, 1913, the Federal Reserve Act lifted restrictions on US banks, allowing them to enter foreign markets.

From a banker's perspective, Eder vividly describes the crippling inflation that followed the Thousand Days' War (1899–1902). He was well aware of the political backstory, played out during the years 1878–1900. During these years, defined by the centralizing drive of Rafael Núñez and his "scientific peace" slogan, the national government took on new costs: (1) a reorganized judiciary, (2) the financing of steam navigation and railroads, (3) indemnity payments to the Church (which were part of the 1887 Concordat with the Vatican), and (4) the refinancing of the external debt (negotiated in 1896). Above and beyond all of this was runaway military spending— Núñez depended on currency emissions to cover an expanded army, new equipment, and the direct costs of multiple civil wars: 1885–86, 1895, and 1899–1902.

In 1887, to bolster confidence, the government made a "solemn promise" not to exceed 12 million pesos in currency emissions. Within two years, however, Núñez and his protégé Miguel Antonio Caro faced bankruptcy, and they secretly approved further currency emissions. Then, during the War of the Thousand Days, the government used paper money to defeat Liberal insurgents. As Eder sketches it, a per-

son who had lent $1,000 in gold was by 1903 compelled to accept as full repayment paper money worth only $10. Real estate and food prices, especially, skyrocketed, and public employees' pay fell months behind. The government tried a return to the gold standard, fixing the peso to an intrinsic value similar to that of the US dollar, 1,672 grams of 22-carat gold, and recognizing devaluation by setting an exchange rate of 1:100 in converting old paper money to the new gold standard. Business confidence was largely restored and the interest rate fell, but the government did not have enough gold. One last time, the government used war powers to issue currency— and it was the need to do so that delayed President José Manuel Marroquín's signing of the decree ending the war until June 1903, months after the fighting had ended.

Meanwhile, older problems persisted, especially given fluctuations in the international price of coffee, the new wonder-export. Writing in 1913, Eder would have seemed overly optimistic to many—foreign investors were unlikely to see Colombia's credit crunch as an opportunity. But subsequent decades did prove him right: the coffee economy became a motor of growth.

Colombia's paper money[1] is a source of much amusement to the casual traveler who visits its ports for a few hours on one of those delightful Caribbean cruises so enticingly featured by the steamship companies. Upon his return home he will narrate with zest to a circle of friends or perchance readers— for he has been known to write an article or even a book from out the vast knowledge gleaned in those few hours—how he gave a ten-dollar bill or a five-pound note in payment of some small purchase and received hundreds of dollars in change; he will joke about the "high cost of living," how he paid five dollars for a few oranges, twenty dollars for a bottle of beer, a hundred dollars for a lunch! But to the business man in Colombia or the statesman grappling with its finances, the paper money is no subject for jest: it presents one of the most serious problems to be dealt with: because of it dire ruin has time and again stared the country in the face. Today, the monetary situation is somewhat brighter than it has been for years past, but the paper money at best is a grievous nuisance, a clog on the wheels of industry and commerce, and at worst, with its possibilities of violent fluctuations in value, a menace and a blight.

Till about 1881, Colombia had been on a bimetallic basis; the currency of the country was gold and silver and there was no paper. For some years previously prosperity had reigned, the exports were relatively large. But in 1883, notwithstanding the gold basis, foreign exchange was at a premium of 20 per cent. There was a financial crisis. One of the principal exports had been *cinchona* bark[2]—in 1875 over £2,000,000 of that article alone had been exported—but the enormous product from cultivation in Java and the Brit-

The Balcony at La Manuelita, Valle del Cauca, ca. 1910. Manuelita was long Colombia's top sugar producer. Before its ownership by the Eder family, the hacienda once belonged to George Henry Isaacs, father of Jorge Isaacs, and is named after Manuela Ferrer Escarpetta, Isaac's mother (see part III). Photograph originally published by Phanor Eder in *Colombia* (New York: Charles Scribner's Sons, 1913), plate facing p. 204.

ish East Indies reduced the price: whereas in 1879 the sulphate of quinine had reached the high price of 16s. 6d. an ounce, in 1883 it had dropped to 3s. 6d. The low price of coffee and tobacco, the other chief exports of Colombia, added to the gravity of the situation. The balance of trade was against Colombia. Already there had been a constant and progressive exportation of gold currency, as free coinage of both gold and silver was allowed, and the value of silver as prescribed by law and as legal tender was higher than its market value. Soon, little gold being left, the silver money, too, began to leave the country. It is said that during the crisis in 1883 the money in circulation in Bogotá, the capital, a city of 100,000 inhabitants, was reduced as low as $200,000. Private banks began to abuse the right which the law allowed them to issue notes, and still further contributed to the elimination of metallic currency.

After the triumph of Núñez in the revolution of 1885 and his defeat of the rebels, it was decreed that, dating from May 1, 1886, the monetary unit of the country should be the dollar (*peso*) bill of the National Bank. The Banco

The mill and outbuildings at La Manuelita, ca. 1910. Photograph originally published by Phanor Eder in *Colombia* (New York: Charles Scribner's Sons, 1913), plate facing p. 146.

Nacional was an institution founded with enormous privileges in 1880 by Núñez; its shares had been offered to the public, but none were taken: the Government became the sole shareholder, investing $1,047,009.30 out of an authorized capital of $2,500,000. It was given and availed itself of the right to issue bills, *redeemable in specie*. In 1886, however, it was granted the right to issue $4,000,000 in bills, without any obligation to so redeem them. This was the beginning of fiat money in Colombia. By a law of 1881 private banks were bound to accept the National Bank bills at their face value, under penalty of losing their own right to issue notes. Worst of all, it was prohibited by law to make contracts, either for cash or on credit, in any other money. . . .

When Caro went out of office in 1898, there was in circulation, in round numbers, $31,400,000 of the Banco Nacional bills. The next year, a revolution broke out in earnest. The Government needed money, lots of money, to carry on the war. The printing presses were at hand. Nothing could be simpler. Paper money was issued, not merely by the millions, but by the tens and hundreds of millions. The National Government issued it. The Departments issued it. Even some generals in the field issued it. The rate of exchange, which had been from 300 to 335 before the revolution (i.e., a paper dollar had been worth about 30 cents gold, almost on a parity with the silver dollar), began to go up, up, up. In 1900 the exchange rose above 1,000—the paper dollar was worth 10 cents gold; by the end of 1901 it had

Interior of Jorge Cristo y Cía, Cúcuta, 1915, with employees seated on burlap bags. This was a typical provincial import-export firm, sending coffee, hides, and rubber abroad and importing home furnishings, fabrics, and ready-made clothing. In Jorge Posada Callejas, *Libro azul de Colombia—Blue Book of Colombia* (New York: J. J. Little & Ives Company, 1918), 529.

Exterior of the Jorge Cristo y Cía building. In Jorge Posada Callejas, *Libro azul de Colombia—Blue Book of Colombia* (New York: J. J. Little & Ives Company, 1918), 529.

reached 5,000—the dirty sheet was then equivalent to two cents. The most violent fluctuations occurred, thousands of points a day, with the varying successes or rumors of defeat of the Government. In 1902 matters were even worse; exchange rose at one time as high as 26,000—the value of the paper dollar was a mere fraction of a cent! But the Government was triumphing— exchange began to drop. At the end of the war (1903) it was impossible to tell how much paper money was outstanding, what with the various issues and the mass of counterfeits, often better engraved than the genuine. The amount was certainly not less than a billion—the national issues alone, since 1885, amounted to $746,801,420 p/m! There was no pretense, no hope that this would be ever redeemable, but it was legal tender; old debts were paid off in this depreciated currency. The creditor who had loaned a thousand dollars gold, hard cash, had mockingly flung in his face and was by law compelled to receive a thousand *pesos* paper—worth ten dollars! . . .

A remedy for the more pressing evils had to be found. A law was passed in October 1903, at the first session of Congress after the revolution, prohibiting further issues of paper money, fixing a gold standard, permitting the circulation of foreign money, making paper money legal tender only at its market rate of exchange, permitting full freedom of contract to stipulate for payment either in gold or paper (*libre estipulación*), and finally, creating a Council or Junta of Amortización. This board was authorized to collect certain national revenues, some of which were payable in gold, and it was its duty to auction the gold so received and to burn the paper money received by it as the purchase price of the gold, as well as that received in payment of certain other revenues payable in paper.

By this law, too, customs duties could be paid either in gold or, most important privilege, in paper money at the current rate of exchange. Some tangible value was at last given. Solid land began to appear after the deluge in which all business was drowning. The Junta de Amortización performed its duties well: weekly, mountains of the fiat money were publicly burned. . . .

If [an] austere policy of puritanical economy could only be maintained Colombia's financial future would be not merely satisfactory, but brilliant. The national debt, which is less than $24,000,000 could be amply secured, and the paper money, which is less than $12,000,000 (in its equivalent in gold at the current rate of exchange), be amortized. The placing of a new loan, consolidating the various scattered items of indebtedness now outstanding, some of them at high rates of interest, would materially assist the problem.

The resources of the country are daily developing, its income daily increasing, yet its national debt *per capita* remains one of the smallest of any of the American nations. There is scarcely a country in the world, therefore,

which offers to the enterprising financier a better field for a large bank and loan venture, with a high and legitimate profit and a fair margin of safety.
. . .

The few banks now existing in the country are private institutions pure and simple. No Governmental supervision whatsoever is exercised, nor would it be practicable in the present state of the country's development. Not only are the quasi-public functions of banks unrecognized, but the people at large have not, except to a small degree in the largest cities, been educated up to their uses. Payments by cheque are very limited, thus throwing the entire burden for smaller ordinary transactions upon the currency of the country as sale medium of exchange; this, taken at its gold equivalent of ten or twelve million dollars, is utterly insufficient for the business needs of a nation of more than five million inhabitants widely scattered, especially when the shipment of currency from place to place is impeded both by its bulk and by the inadequacy of transportation facilities. In consequence, in larger transactions (for example, sales of real estate, herds of cattle, or wholesale quantities of merchandise), though in nowise partaking of an international character, settlements are commonly made by bills of exchange on Europe or the United States. Drafts not infrequently pass through a number of hands, serving as a medium of exchange for merchants and cattle-dealers at fairs or markets, go from town to town, and are in circulation for weeks, even months, before being finally transmitted for collection.

The smaller towns have no banks at all; even some of the important centres, like Santa Marta and Bucaramanga, have none. Where banking institutions do exist, a large share of the business is nevertheless absorbed by private mercantile houses, and some so-called banks are purely one-man, one-firm, or one-family institutions. . . .

The time would seem ripe for the establishment of foreign banks, or rather of banks with foreign backing. The Germans have already started, and with their usual commercial foresight they are doing it in the right way to gain public goodwill, that is, in co-operation with native capitalists. Conservative banking is badly needed in Colombia and will undoubtedly meet with large rewards.

Notes

1. Colombians used the abbreviation *p/m*, for *papel moneda* (paper money).
2. *Cinchona* is a large shrub indigenous to South America long used to produce quinine, an alkaloid with antimalarial properties.

How Many People Were Massacred in 1928?

Telegrams, American Legation in Bogotá and Consul in Santa Marta

In Gabriel García Márquez's famous novel One Hundred Years of Solitude *(1967), North Americans begin exporting bananas from the fictional town of Macondo, set near the novelist's hometown of Aracataca and near the larger town of Ciénaga, south of Santa Marta. García Márquez had sketched Macondo in a previous work, titled* La hojarasca, *or* Leaf Storm. *Readers interested in economic history will note the way the banana company blows into town and then out again, destroying local people's sense of order and their capacity for remembering their own past. García Márquez described his own work as indebted to that of his close friend Álvaro Cepeda Samudio, whose 1962 novel,* La casa grande, *poetically explored the difficulties locals faced in knowing what had actually happened, not only in the moment of the massacre but also in memory afterward. How many had died? Was it three thousand people, "all of the people who were at the station," as the character José Arcadio Segundo remembers it in* One Hundred Years of Solitude, *or was no one killed at all, as his fictional listeners tell themselves and as "the government" tells the citizenry?*

Historians offer inconclusive accounts. From a comprehensive 1979 study by Roberto Herrera Soto and Rafael Romero Castañeda to more recent work by Catherine Legrand and Eduardo Posada-Carbó, Colombians are left with a range of figures. Once it is established that banana workers across the Santa Marta region did in fact strike in 1928, and that strikers were massacred when General Carlos Cortés Vargas ordered soldiers to fire on a large crowd at Ciénaga on December 6, the question remains: "How many?" Labor organizer Raúl Mahecha reported a thousand deaths. Cortés Vargas himself said that forty-seven strikers were killed, which, as Posada-Carbó has pointed out, would have been an unprecedented number of deaths for a Colombian labor dispute. The nation had seen many bloody battles as part of its long history of internal war, but these striking workers were civilians. Their demands focused on forcing the United Fruit Company to comply with

Colombian labor law, especially regarding compensation for workplace accidents. Strikers also sought higher pay rates, subsidized housing, and controls on payments made in scrip. But the massacre is not understandable if one looks only at what the strikers sought to negotiate. More than specific demands, the strike was about the local politics of workers' resentments against the company. It is best understood in terms of the diffuse radicalism that fueled labor organizing across Colombia in the 1920s and '30s.

The following reports, from Washington's envoy and minister plenipotentiary in Bogotá and from the US consul at Santa Marta, show that State Department officials received conflicting accounts about the number of dead. These documents also point toward another question vital to Colombians' sense of the past. Did Cortés Vargas face a situation in which if he had not crushed the strike the US Navy might have landed troops? If so, did his action protect the nation's sovereignty? The US envoy at Bogotá, Jefferson Caffrey, thought that naval backup was unnecessary and that the US consul in Santa Marta, Lawrence Cotie, was overreacting when he cabled for a warship. Cotie insisted that American lives were in danger, but readers will interpret his terminology in multiple ways, as when he refers to "communists" with the caveat that military men used the term to characterize strikers. Caffrey's telegrams are more judicious: he is primarily concerned that Colombian Liberals will use the killings as "political ammunition" against the Colombian Conservatives allied to Washington.

Caffrey was right about this last point. Gaitán traveled to Ciénaga in July 1929, then returned to Bogotá having concluded an investigation that prompted him to denounce the Conservative government as bloodthirsty and illegitimate. His fiery rhetoric helped make the banana workers' deaths a political symbol in 1929–30 and even into the current century, especially after Chiquita Brands International, offspring of the United Fruit Company, admitted in 2007 to years of payments channeled toward paramilitary death squads, principally the AUC (see part V).

From Vice Consul in Charge, Lawrence F. Cotie.
Santa Marta, Colombia. November 15, 1928.

The labor organization in the so called "Banana Zone" in Santa Marta, presented a series of demands to the Manager of the United Fruit Company who rejected the demands and refused to receive the self-appointed delegates of the organization in his office because of their non-connection with either the company or the workers they were supposedly representing.

The petition, which is enclosed in triplicate as well as its English translation, is a clumsy piece of Soviet literature as can be seen by a cursory inspection of it. It should be noted that the labor disputants have incorporated demands within the petition that would force the responsibility for compliance directed at private planters upon the company.

. . .

From Vice Consul in Charge, Lawrence F. Cotie.
Santa Marta, Colombia. November 28, 1928.

The labor strike which began on November 12 is now entering its third week, and there is no indication of either side yielding . . .

TELEGRAM RECEIVED
FROM GRAY
Santa Marta
Dated December 6, 1928
Rec'd 3:50 P.M.

[To] Secretary of State
Washington
URGENT
December 6, 5 A.M.

Martial law in banana zone and Santa Marta province declared by Colombian Government last night. Demonstrations against the Government were held and broken up by the few soldiers in Santa Marta. Feeling against the Government by the proletariat which is shared by some of the soldiers is high and it is doubtful if we can depend upon the Colombian Government for protection. May I respectfully suggest that my request for the presence within calling distance of an American war ship be granted and that it stand off subject to my call and that the United Fruit Company wireless station in Santa Marta, call letters UJ, be used as we are without telegraphic communication and there is no other means of communication with Santa Marta. It is admitted that the character of the strike has changed and that the disturbance is a manifestation with a subversive tendency.

COTIE

TELEGRAM RECEIVED
From
Bogotá
Dated December 7, 1928
Received 9 P.M.

Secretary of State
Washington

. . .

Situation outside Santa Marta City unquestionably very serious: outside zone is in revolt; military who have orders "not to spare ammunition" have already killed and wounded about fifty strikers. However I have now before me original telegram sent today from Governor to the President saying "Santa Marta City completely quiet and railroad traffic restored as far as Ciénaga."

Government now talks of general offensive against strikers as soon as all troopships now on the way arrive next week. I am concerned about some 20 Americans still in outside zone and hope to learn they are in safety before any such offensive begins in view of danger otherwise of possible repercussions on them.

CAFFREY

TELEGRAM SENT
Department of State
Washington
To be transmitted via Tropical Radio
Washington, Dec. 8, 1928 (10 A.M.)

American Consul,
Santa Marta (Colombia)
Your December 6, 5 A.M.

The Legation at Bogotá reports that categorical orders have been given the ~~local~~ authorities at Santa Marta to protect all American interests [strikethrough in ink on original] . The Department does not (repeat not) desire to send a war ship to Santa Marta. Keep the Department informed of all developments by telegraph. [In handwriting: Teleg. cable, acknowledgement of receipt of this telegram]

[Signed]
Kellogg

AMERICAN CONSULATE
Santa Marta, Colombia. December 11, 1928
Subject: Labor Troubles and Social Revolution in the so-called
Banana Zone in Magdalena, Colombia.

The Honorable
The Secretary of State,
Washington.

Sir:

I have the honor to refer to the previous correspondence from this office upon the subject as given above and to enclose herewith confirmation copies of radiograms. . . .

I wish to say that during the entire time, from the beginning of the trouble to Sunday afternoon, I kept the Legation informed of the developments, as I knew of them for I realized that no information the Legation might receive from the War office in Bogotá could be anything but misleading. I was on the scene and in a better position to report upon developments so far as they affected our interest than the war office in Bogotá. It was natural to expect that Bogotá would make an effort to suppress the information and thereby allay the fears of those with intimate relations or interests in this district.

The troops are still vigorously pursuing the main bands of communists,—as the strikers are now called by the military—and excepting for occasional sniping by small groups throughout the entire zone, the situation is controlled by the army.

No information concerning the number of lives lost or value of the property destroyed is obtainable at this moment and I can only say that property belonging to the United Fruit Company, Colombian employees of the Company, and private planters, was destroyed. Looting and killing was carried on from the moment of the announcement of a state of Martial law was made and the fact that the American residents in the zone came out of it alive is due to the defense they put up for six hours when they held off the mob that was bent upon killing them. From Wednesday night to Saturday afternoon no information concerning those Americans was received in this city and there was no way to get in touch with them because the wires were down and the tracks were pulled up and between the place where they were last heard from and Santa Marta there was a stretch of territory that was under the control of mobs of armed men and women.

I was justified in calling for help and I shall welcome the opportunity to defend the position I took on the morning of the sixth and until the afternoon of the eighth. I placed my services at the disposal of the

American citizens and the United Fruit Company and did not during all that time relax for one moment the watchful attitude that the occasion demanded.

A more detailed report will be sent forward as soon as possible.

I have the honor to be, Sir,

Your obedient servant,

[Signed]

Lawrence F. Cotie

Vice Consul in Charge

LEGATION OF THE

UNITED STATES OF AMERICA

Bogotá, Colombia. December 14, 1928.

The Honorable

The Secretary of State,

Washington.

Sir:

Referring to my recent reports concerning the strike of the banana workers in the Santa Marta district . . . I have the honor to report that, according to the latest information made public, the number of strikers killed by the military forces during the recent disturbances was something over one hundred, while the wounded reached 238.

The opposition press, that is, the press of the Liberal party, is conducting a violent campaign against the Government for the methods used in breaking up the strike, and is bandying ugly words about, especially referring to the Minister of War and the military forces, words such as murderer and assassin are being used.

Although the thinking people of the country realize that it was only the Government's prompt action that averted a disaster, this insidious campaign of the Liberal press will undoubtedly work up a great deal of feeling against the Government and will tend to inculcate in the popular mind a belief that the Government was unduly hasty in protecting the interests of the United Fruit Company.

The Conservative journals are defending the Government's course but I doubt that their counter-fire will suffice to do away with the damage the Liberal journals are causing.

I have the honor to be, Sir,

Your obedient servant,

[Signed]

Jefferson Caffrey

LEGATION OF THE
UNITED STATES OF AMERICA
Bogotá, Colombia. January 16, 1929.

The Honorable
The Secretary of State,
Washington.

Sir:

With reference to my previous reports concerning the Santa Marta strike . . . I have the honor to report that the Bogotá representative of the United Fruit Company told me yesterday that the total number of strikers killed by the Colombian military exceeded one thousand.

I have the honor to be, Sir,
Your obedient servant,
[Signed]
Jefferson Caffrey

LEGATION OF THE
UNITED STATES OF AMERICA
Bogotá, Colombia. July 22, 1929.

The Honorable
The Secretary of State,
Washington.

Sir:

I have the honor to refer to my dispatch No. 189 of July 11 reporting that General Cortés Vargas, Military Commander of the Santa Marta district during the period of martial law, had terminated his report on the strike and events in the banana zone to be presented to Congress, and intimating that it was highly probable that the report would contain either open or veiled references to the possibility of American intervention.

The press of July 20 contained . . . excerpts of the report in question. A copy of this article as it appeared in EL TIEMPO of that date is enclosed. The pertinent part reads as follows in translation:

"'A person worthy of entire confidence informed us that he knew from a sure source that there were two ships lying to in the waters of Santa Marta; it was to be supposed that they were warships of the American Navy.' He (Cortés Vargas) called General Díaz, commanding the Córdoba regiment, to his office and said to him: 'Prepare your mind

to face the rebels and kill before foreign troops tread upon our soil.'—
——Now, reviewing matters calmly we still believe in the imminence
of that peril when we read in the New York Times of December 7 which
reads (in English): 'Secretary Kellogg said he understood the Colombian
Government is fully capable of maintaining order and that he does not
contemplate asking the Navy Department to LAND [emphasis in El
Tiempo] Marines to protect American lives and property. . . . The Secretary of State did not speak of sending but of disembarking, that is to say
that the marines were near, ready for such a manoeuvre upon receiving
the proper order.'"

It is of course impossible to foretell how Congress will treat Cortés Vargas' report or that which the president has prepared . . . but as
indicated in despatch No. 419 and despatch 450 of July 11 reporting the
visit of Eliécer Gaitán to Santa Marta to "collect material" for a "serious
interpellation" of the Government, and as becomes increasingly evident
from subsequent press reports, the events of the banana zone are going
to be the subject of much heated debate in Congress. . . .

The President made his report on the subject to Congress when it
convened on July 20. . . . His references to the United Fruit Company
are favorable: "on one side," he says "were seriously threatened foreign
interests which requested action from the Government before applying to their Government (tutela) to protect their rights, from which the
State would have suffered a kind of humiliation of its sovereignty with
all its lamentable consequences." A little further on he speaks of the
Nation being "exposed to a foreign intervention with impairment of
sovereignty, if the Government should not duly apply the remedy which
the circumstances required."

From all the foregoing the Department may judge the importance
now being attached here to the Santa Marta strike and the golden opportunities it contains as internal political ammunition at a time when
such ammunition is in great demand.

> *I have the honor to be, Sir,*
> *Your obedient servant,*
> *[Signed]*
> *Jefferson Caffrey*

Strikers or Revolutionaries?

Strikers and Revolutionaries?

Mauricio Archila Neira and Raúl Eduardo Mahecha

Legendary figures of the Colombian Left are indelibly linked to the 1928 banana workers' strike, whether or not they were present in Ciénaga. María Cano, already famous as an agitator and orator for her visibility in connection to strikes by railroad workers and stevedores, was arrested in her hometown of Medellín in the wave of repression after the massacre. Ignacio Torres Giraldo and Tomás Uribe Márquez were also imprisoned. Even beyond the repression, however, the 1928 strike marked an internal crisis for Colombian revolutionaries, who split into factions. In part, the infighting was fueled by the beginnings of Stalinist purges emanating from Moscow (which tore the PSR apart and which are palpable in texts written at the time by María Cano and Ignacio Torres Giraldo, included in part IV), but activists were also demoralized after the massacre. Historians, too, have had difficulty assessing the meaning of 1928. How should one interpret the language used by national officials of the PSR (Partido Socialista Revolucionario), who wrote from Bogotá to tell their person on the ground not to "confuse a strike with a revolution" but themselves seem to have begun talks with Liberal Party politicians to perhaps attempt an armed movement against the Conservative government? Did General Cortés Vargas overreact to a mass movement that was "only a strike," or was 1928 a moment when at least one region of Colombia came close to experiencing something like the Mexican Revolution?

A key person on the ground was Raúl Eduardo Mahecha Caycedo, a PSR militant who had organized oil workers' strikes in Barrancabermeja, starting a long tradition of labor radicalism there. The pieces below allow glimpses of Mahecha in action: showing oil workers an internationalist flag bearing three eights on a red background—representing a workerist dream of eight hours for labor, eight for rest, and eight for study—urging them to strike and reminding them that they could also use guns, and, later, excoriating his communist colleagues for having missed a chance at real revolution. The speech Mahecha made after leaving Colombia clandestinely, traveling to several Latin American countries, and arriving in

Buenos Aires in 1929 for what the South American Secretariat of the Communist International called the First Latin American Communist Conference is striking. The Comintern official running the conference, Swiss communist Jules Humbert-Droz, supported Mahecha and allowed conference delegates to hear a surprisingly open set of debates. The Colombians present disagreed with one another about what had happened in the banana workers' strike the previous December, and their opinions mattered to communist delegates from all over the Americas, who asked questions and took sides. (Historian Klaus Meschkat, after extensive research in former Soviet archives, points out that such sharp exchanges were increasingly impossible in Moscow, where Stalin was moving to eliminate debate; Humbert-Droz himself was purged and later jailed.)

Mahecha seemed to reject his former radicalism after 1930. Returning to Colombia after a stint in the Soviet Union, he settled down in Bogotá and stayed out of politics. Historian Mauricio Archila spoke with one person who recalled that he "didn't like to talk about Barranca." When Mahecha was asked if he would go back to the oil town, he is said to have responded, "What for?"

Raúl Eduardo Mahecha was a stutterer. He had difficulty talking when he was having a conversation with you, but when he got up on the stand to speak it would seem that he was completely transformed. He forgot his stuttering then. . . . When he spoke with the workers he expressed himself with natural warmth, he didn't use fancy words, he went directly to the point.

The language he used was so that everyone could understand him, even though he was a lawyer, he came here as a lawyer. His office was by the Pipatón Hotel, over where 4th Avenue is being built, there by the riverbank.—Rafael Núñez, interviewed by Mauricio Archila Neira

He arrived—Raúl E. Mahecha—in Barranca at the end of '22, beginning of '23, and he came looking to practice as a lawyer. He was from a Conservative background, he belonged to the same family as General Rafael Reyes. And so he had been in the army, but he had heard about the Russian Revolution in 1917, and he didn't really accept the Communist platform so much as the Socialist platform of Engels and Marx, and of Lenin, the inventor of Communism. And Raúl E. Mahecha had also heard about the work of Sacco and Vanzetti in the United States and the origin of the 1st of May, and with that the idea of eight hours for labor, eight hours for rest, and eight hours for personal learning, the three eights. Equally, the Red flag with the three eights was his idea, in

Strikers in Barrancabermeja, 1927. Photograph attributed to Floro Piedrahita. Note the flag emblazoned with three eights, an internationalist symbol that labor organizers celebrated with the slogan "Eight hours for work, eight hours for rest, eight hours for study." In María Tila Uribe, *Los años escondidos*, 3rd ed. (Bogotá: Opciones Gráficas Editores Ltd., 2010), 187.

El Centro, and that was the flag for his proletarian movements.—Manuel Hernández, interviewed by Mauricio Archila Neira

Mahecha (Colombia): I am going to intervene here to clarify some of the points in debate about the Colombian question and to provide information I believe is necessary. It is possible that my intervention may be a bit disorganized.

You will note that I did not bring notes with me, because soldiers never bring pieces of paper with them. While others debate, we act.

I believe it is important to give a bit of history about the Colombian movement, to make clear the changes that took place in my ideology—which in large part is the process that has taken place in the ideology of the working masses in Colombia—that from being a Christian Socialist I began to be transformed, little by little, to the point where I assimilated Communist ideology. Many of the current leaders of the Party, in the first place, me—we were "Catholic, Apostolic, and Roman," which is to say, we came out of the Catholic Workers' movement.

As I remember it, the Colombian labor movement goes back to 1911–12,

Ricardo Rendón, an accomplished caricaturist prominent in Colombian arts and letters in the 1910s and 1920s, here takes as his target the extralegal influence of North American money and arms. In Ricardo Rendón and Beatriz Álvarez Rincón, *Ricardo Rendón en el diario La República, 1921–1923: Donación Alfonso Villegas Restrepo* (Bogotá: Banco de la República, 2005), 14.

when the first strike broke out in a British Company, where the workers were paid .40 pesos a day, for workdays that were interminable. And in that first strike, despite our affiliation being that of "Catholic, Apostolic, and Roman," and that meaning the rejection of violence, that strike was resolved by kicking ass [*se resolvió a "chingazos"*]. There's no other way when you're fighting against foreign companies and even the national bourgeoisie, both deaf to the most basic demands of the working class! (Applause.)

We asked for wages to be raised to $1.00; the [oil] company refused; we demonstrated, we broke all the machines. All hell broke loose; and once we were in the dance we all had to dance—even the priest in charge of the organization was going all out with his machete [*anduvo a machetazo limpio*] . . . ! (Laughter) We "torched" the station, the company's money was confiscated and divided up among the strikers (Laughter). The company put pressure on the government; various strikers were jailed and others of us were still out, we continued the strike until the company was defeated. . . .

Labor organizers charged with sedition and under arrest at the Tunja Panopticon, March 1927. Left to right: Raúl Mahecha, Ricardo López, Floro Piedrahita, Julio Buriticá, and an unknown prisoner. This photograph appears in a published memoir by María Tila Uribe, and her description of it provides a glimpse of the complexity of class relationships and understandings of modernity that were at play in early twentieth-century Colombia. Floro Piedrahita was an accomplished photographer and had his camera with him at the time of his arrest. As the prisoners were being taken on foot to the jail in Tunja, one of the mounted guards became interested in the "machine" Piedrahita carried. From muleback, the guard asked to see it, and upon their arrival at the jail Piedrahita showed him how it worked and asked him to take this picture of him and his fellow organizers in the stocks. In María Tila Uribe, *Los años escondidos*, 3rd ed. (Bogotá: Opciones Gráficas Editores Ltd., 2010), 240.

In 1914 there was another strike, in Neiva [Huila] . . . and then came another series of strikes, but the government brutally repressed these movements, killing many people, which brought as a consequence more strikes in protest and more repression. This opened the workers' eyes, those who comprehended that they would only obtain improvements in their lives through revolutionary action. And so, now we weren't "Catholic, Apostolic, and Roman" Socialists any more but rather just plain Socialists!

The mutualist system created by [that] priest only filled the needs of those who were "virgins." The workers understood that direct action was necessary and they continued starting strikes, not listening to the priests.

That was what happened in Barrancabermeja [Santander] in 1924. . . . In 1926 another strike broke out in this region. In an attempt to break the movement, the company and the government offered to give $200,000 to the strike leaders. They would offer anything so long as they could get rid of the Socialist movement, but they failed to achieve their objective. We told them that if they didn't grant our petition we would "torch" their petroleum wells. So, in the face of that threat and because the situation was getting worse, they accepted our demands, which later they went back on. In 1927 another strike broke out so that they would comply with the signed agreement. We called on the solidarity of the Magdalena river workers, who add up to 270,000. The government sent 2,000 men to Girardot to massacre the striking workers, but the *compañeros* at the port refused to let them board. (All right.) These 2,000 men were surrounded in such a way that they couldn't go either forward or backward. 3,000 men arrived from Bogotá, but the *compañeros* wouldn't give them ships; they sent forces from Medellín and the *compañeros*, in solidarity with us, told them that there were no trains available to transport the slaughterers. Given the situation and taking into account that we did not let the region's produce get out either, the government declared a state of siege, looking to bring its troops in without the help of boats or trains. In part, they succeeded in their objective. General Velasco didn't have more than 60 men, but he got them good and drunk and then he surprised us by sending them against us. We were at a demonstration when the police fell upon us, drunk, and started shooting without us having time to react, and more than thirty of us were seriously wounded. Later, reinforcements arrived from Medellín on rafts and there was another shootout, with the police forces and the army not getting the better of us. . . . The strike ended with very little advantage for the workers, but during this time the company lost 80 million dollars that they found had "evaporated." (Laughter).

Compañeros: Why have I believed it necessary to give this history of Colombia's revolutionary and labor movement? Simply, because there are *compañeros* here who have affirmed that our movement does not have an organizing tradition. Is it that these strikes happened just like that, with God's blessing? No, *compañeros*. Before each strike we worked for its organization and right when we have organized the workers—and when we have had the financial means in hand—we launched ourselves in struggle. It is false, then, to say that Colombian workers don't want to organize themselves. It's possible that this happens in Bogotá, where there aren't large masses of workers, but not in other regions, and especially not in the Cauca Valley, where there is a large concentration of workers. What is true is that distrust exists among the workers, against people who live off the workers' movement. And there are a lot of those in Colombia, and especially in Bogotá. . . .

In the Colombian revolutionary movement there have been a lot of crooks who would call themselves anarchists and live off the unions. Many of these were foreigners and because of this the workers have a lot of distrust for those who are not from their country. Me too—and I'm a pure-blood Indian—I had to overcome huge difficulties to be able to do propaganda among the workers of the banana zone. . . .

And here I have to open a parenthesis to tell the *compañeros* from Bogotá that you don't organize workers from behind a desk in Bogotá. You have to be there, united with them, living with the working masses. And that is exactly what I did. The workers are extremely distrustful, after having suffered betrayal innumerable times by those who call themselves workers' leaders. When I got there and began to penetrate the mass of workers, I was kicked off of more than one hacienda by the workers themselves. . . .

To get an idea of how it was that once the strike was declared we were able to support so many workers from the plantations and do it in so organized a way, even more organized than the Colombian army, it has to be taken into account that for the Colombian native disciplining oneself for combat is a simple thing, because as I have already said, we are talking about workers who are violent and who have a spirit of sacrifice. And there is an important factor that should not be discounted: like almost all the illiterate or semiliterate peasants in Latin America, the Colombian will follow the caudillo with which he feels most in sympathy. In this case, after ample propaganda work, we put ourselves at the head of what was a real army, whose spirit of struggle was even stronger because [the workers were] enthusiastic and because they had an understanding of the demands being pursued. Once the list of demands to be presented to United Fruit had been written up and approved by the workers, we began preparing for a bloody struggle, since we knew in advance that the strike would not be resolved peacefully but rather that there would be open battles before the movement was won or lost. Thus immediately upon learning that the imperialist company had resolved to discard our demand for a raise, we began by sending a commission of *compañeros* to Barranquilla to find out how many ships were in the port, which came to 140 ships, and to ask the *compañero* maritime workers to be in solidarity with the strike. I personally formed part of this delegation. As we did not have sufficient time, we had to make use of a hydroplane. After revealing to them the first part of our plan, we tried to win the support of these workers, who, from the very beginning declared themselves ready to offer the most complete solidarity to the striking *compañeros* of the banana zone, and they told us they would wait for our call to organize themselves and join us to make our army bigger. After this we organized the work with troops stationed in the city, with the objective of getting them to fraternize with the strikers, and we achieved, *compañeros*, the frankest success. (Applause.)

As you can see, comrades, the movement was not improvised but rather was the fruit of a labor of agitation and organization, and when we began the struggle the lines were drawn, lines of attack as well as of defense. After finishing that task, I went to Cartagena, where there were fifteen *compañeros* capable of leading the local movement, headed by an intellectual—a sincere person, good in any struggle. It was my intention to communicate to these *compañeros* my plan of attack, which can be summarized in short: the plan was to start the movement in the [banana] zone; to take three *departamentos* of the Colombian State; and then to take the attack to the capital, Bogotá. This plan was shared with the *compañeros* in Cartagena.

Although my exposition is maybe a bit disorganized, it is necessary to go into some detail to clear up what happened before and after the strike broke out. I think these details are important for defining our general tactics in countries where the situation is similar to that in Colombia. As an interesting point, to better understand the struggle against imperialism, I should say that allies can be found in social categories that are not proletarian, and small merchants, who with the penetration of imperialism suffer equally with workers and peasants, showed throughout their adherence to the movement and contributed financially toward the strike's success.

Despite our being well organized and positively prepared, and also despite the financial situation—we had collected 40,000 dollars from the workers—neither the company nor the workers believed in the potential of our organization. . . .

I was leading the strike while other *compañeros* took on the job of infiltrating the army to make propaganda and to get the soldiers to fraternize with us. I communicated to the C.E. that everything was prepared and that there were 32,000 men on strike, and that I was waiting for orders to extend the movement, now that the plan was in place: we would take over the ships, etc. I sent this letter by hydroplane. The strike broke out on November 12th at 5 in the morning. A strike committee was named. As soon as the strike was declared the barracks were entered and the soldiers were asked to turn over their arms: machine guns, cannons, etc. Because if they did not, no one would be left alive. In part because of our propaganda and in part because of the panic of our invasion, the fact is that the soldiers declared that they were on our side and they were willing to give up their arms. This situation scared the zone's commander and also the Yankee company, who saw that the strike was taking on a revolutionary character and saw that the strikers maintained a military discipline. They told the government that this was a movement led by officers from the Russian army. . . . [Ellipsis in original.] *Compañeros*: among the strike leaders, I was the whitest one! As if you could say the leaders were Russians! (Laughter.)

That day the women that saw Cortés Vargas arrive grabbed him and made him swear on the red flag that he would not order the soldiers against the strikers. Full of fear, he promised not to kill anyone. In effect, prisoners were released and everything made it seem like the company would settle the conflict. But it was only a truce. In order to motivate the officers, the "United Fruit" gave banquets, and gave them money and goods, to incite them to massacre workers. In the meantime, on the 29th, we found out that the government was concentrating troops in the banana fields, ready to launch them against us. We went there in the thousands! The *compañeros* had already worked with the troops and the 900 that were stationed there fraternized with us and promised us that they would turn over their arms and they committed, also, to shooting their officers when we thought it would be necessary. At that moment I communicated to the C.E. that everything was ready. *Compañeros*: the soldiers shouted "Long live Social Revolution!" (All right.)

That's how things were, and we were waiting for a resolution from the C.E. to initiate the insurrection movement. Everything was ready for action. The workers, the peasants, and the soldiers were fully in brotherhood [*fraternizados*]. All that was needed was a word from us and the public buildings of the zone would have been taken. And so, everything was ready to explode like crazy. But nothing came from Bogotá. A letter from *compañero* Prieto came, telling me "not to confuse a strike with an insurrection." Of course I wasn't confusing the strike with the revolution, but what the devil did you have to wait for to start the insurrection? All right. (Applause.) . . .

We were disciplined and we didn't strike the first blow there because we thought the insurrection had to be the whole country. We contacted Bogotá again, for them to give the order for insurrection, and ten of us on the conspiracy committee signed the note. The workers were impatient for insurrection, but we waited for a note in response. And the days passed, *compañeros*.

The commander of the zone communicated to the government that he could not leave the zone because in reality he was our prisoner. The government answers him that if he did not declare a state of siege and if he did not repress the insurrection energetically, the United States would send troops and the national army would be in a bad position. On the 5th of December, 1928, in the city of Ciénaga, we learned that the national government, together with the powerful, imperialist company, was suspending constitutional guarantees and declaring all of Magdalena under a state of siege. In effect, in the first hours of the 6th, at one fourteen in the morning, after publishing the state of siege in the cities of Ciénaga and Santa Marta, the government sent a mass of soldiers out from the Ciénaga barracks, three hundred in number, toward the railway station of that city, and with machine guns. We did not see the importance of this because we thought they were soldiers that had promised to be in brotherhood with us. Instead, these were Antioqueño soldiers that our propaganda had not yet reached. But we found that out later. It was one twenty in the morning on the 6th when the mass of soldiers, coming out from 6 streets, positioned themselves in front of the masses of strikers, 4,000 in number, who had stayed there in the car area of the station. General Cortés Vargas, civil and military chief of these forces, in charge of the plaza, ordered a bugle sounded for the strikers to leave. The bugle had not finished when "Viva la huelga!" was the answer from the compact masses of strikers. Simultaneously, another bugle blast was heard and the soldiers were seen readying their weapons and pointing their machine guns at the workers, by order of their officer, Cortés Vargas. The workers are not intimidated; instead they answer with a thunderous "Viva la huelga!" "Down with traitors and Yankee imperialism!" A last bugle blast and a new shout of long live the strike was silenced by 300 soldiers firing point-blank and by machine guns aimed against the strikers. More than 600 of our *compañeros* fell, 200 of them dead. . . .

At dawn on the memorable 6th of December, the striking workers that had survived the murder at Ciénaga and were on the banana zone road to Retén, were pursued by more than 600 soldiers. From there, small battles were fought in the towns of Río Frío, Orihueca, and there was a battle with thousands of strikers in the town of Sevilla and the Company station with its warehouses and dependencies. This battle started at 10:30 in the morning between the government forces and the state police and also all the North American employees of the company, which added up to more than 700 perfectly armed men, hunkered down in the Company's armored cement buildings. It was a desperate and fearful fight, in which the strikers were short of arms, with only 107 "Bras" rifles and 100 shotguns without enough ammunition, and a few hundred machetes and some tools. The butchery added up to more than 340 wounded, most of them not serious, and 15 dead, among them the famous socialist revolutionary leader Erasmo Coronel. This battle finished at 5:30 P.M. because the strikers were cut off on both their flanks and battered by more than 300 reinforcements that arrived from Aracataca. The government lost around 100 men, between soldiers, police, and officials, the majority of whom were buried in the banana groves during the night of the 6th and dawn of the 7th. For our part, we didn't leave anything standing, we "torched" everything in sight. It was a cruel struggle. *Compañeros*, this is the tragic balance sheet of the banana strike: 1,004 deaths, counting men, women, and children; 3,068 wounded, more than 500 *compañeros* jailed and hundreds of comrades sentenced to many years in prison.

In this way, to satisfy the interests of a foreign company, Colombia's reactionary government has assassinated native workers who demanded living and working conditions that would be more human, in the hell of the banana groves.

This tragic balance sheet owes to the lack of decision by *compañeros* in Bogotá. They gave us neither solidarity for the strike nor the order to make the revolution. It doesn't matter if the fault was on the part of the c.c.c.c. or the c.e.; the fact is that we were left without help.

The South American Secretariat and the Communist International should intervene in the workings of our Party and put things in order. We need their help. The situation in Colombia is still revolutionary. The workers are preparing themselves for struggle and soon there will be more "bust-outs." Let's hope that this time we send the Yankees, the *godos* [colloquial term for Conservatives], and the Liberals off to the devil himself. (All right. Prolonged Applause.)

Translated by Ann Farnsworth-Alvear

Coffee and "Social Equilibrium"

Federación Nacional de Cafeteros

By 1932, Colombian optimists pointed to a new economic identity centered on coffee, an export product that carried connotations very different from petroleum or bananas, both of which were seen as serving foreign interests. A "coffee census" conducted and published by the Federación Nacional de Cafeteros (Colombian Coffeegrowers Federation) established a link between coffee and a domestically owned agricultural sector of small and medium-sized producers. Most coffee producers operated on a small scale. Only 645 coffee producers could be described as haciendas. Of these, 324 were middling size, having between 60,000 and 100,000 cafetos (coffee shrubs), and 321 were large, with more than 100,000 cafetos. Incidentally, the Hacienda El Chocho, with its tenant farming system, was in this latter group (see part III).

Francisco Mejía, *Escojedora*, Medellín, 1930. *Escojedoras* were women who hand-selected dried coffee beans prior to export. *Trilladora Don Carlos*, [1930], Francisco Mejía (1899–1979). Biblioteca Pública Piloto de Medellín / Archivo Fotográfico. In Malcom Deas and Patricia Pinzón de Lewin, eds., *Colombia a través de la fotografía, 1842–2010* (Madrid: Fundación Mapfre: Taurus, 2011), 78. Courtesy of Biblioteca Pública Piloto de Medellín.

According to data obtained through the census, there are 149,348 coffee-producing properties, of which 129,556, or 86.75%, have fewer than 5,000 trees. This shows that the vast majority of the country's coffee plantations are almost small orchards.

146,477 or 98.08%, contain fewer than 20,000 trees. That is, they constitute what we call small properties. There are only 32 coffee companies of more than 100,000 trees each; these comprise only 0.21% of the total number of coffee-producing properties.

All of this interesting and truly unexpected data shows how the coffee industry is not only the fundamental and decisive factor of our national economy, but at the same time is also an admirable element of social equilibrium. Given the very nature of its organization and its exceptionally favorable circumstance of providing adequate and almost permanent labor to women and children, it achieves property division in and of itself, in an automatic fashion, without the need for laws or expropriations.

Translated by Ann Farnsworth-Alvear and Ana María Gómez López

Two Views of a Foreign Mining Enclave: The Chocó Pacífico

Patrick O'Neill and Aquiles Escalante

Beginning in the 1880s, foreign firms pushed for exclusive mining contracts in Bogotá, telling Colombian legislators that the expensive equipment and technical know-how they imported would allow higher profits, resulting in returns to the Colombian state. Whether or not local people would benefit was not a primary concern in the mining agreements of the nineteenth and twentieth centuries, despite some legislation requiring that those resident on the land receive compensation in the case of damages caused by mining. In the twenty-first century, the paired questions of who benefits from extractive industries and who is left holding the bag of environmental destruction have become much more politically potent, and the 1991 Constitution established "prior consultation" with indigenous and Afro-Colombian representatives as a legal requirement for any government negotiations involving land occupied by ethnic communities (see part I).

From gold to petroleum to coal, and through a range of other minerals, the specific way different foreign mining investors have operated in Colombia has varied, and local people tell a variety of stories about the interaction between communities and outsiders. Some such stories are relatively well known, such as those that circulate about "La Troco," a nickname used for the Tropical Oil Company (owned by Standard Oil of New Jersey in the 1920s and '30s, but later nationalized as part of what is now Ecopetrol). La novia oscura (The Dark Bride), a 1999 novel by Laura Restrepo set in "La Troco's" Barrancabermeja (referred to by its earlier name, "Tora"),[1] describes the city as boasting mainly "putas, plata and petróleo"—whores, money, and oil. Others stories are more obscure, such as those told about "La Chocó Pacífico," a New York company that extracted gold and platinum along the San Juan River in northwestern Colombia for nearly a hundred years, from the 1880s to 1974. Two texts extracted below take readers into the world of South American Gold and Platinum (SAGAP), the name used by North American investors for the Chocó Pacífico operation. Together they allow a glimpse of some of the key issues Colombians debate in reference to the mining economy. The first is from a memoir by Patrick

O'Neill, a manager who had grown up in the hardscrabble mining world of early twentieth-century Alaska and who rose through the ranks to become the chairman of International Mining (a later incarnation of SAGAP). O'Neill speaks of the potential for positive change foreign firms could provide when they chose—in the shape of technical training, health care, schooling, and building materials. But he is also aware that foreign company employees often considered themselves better than local people, and he describes what happened when the Chocó Pacífico was nationalized in the 1970s. Wage workers lost everything—their pensions disappeared in corrupt dealings, jobs dried up, and local families faced hunger.

A second view offers a different perspective, that of Aquiles Escalante Polo, a left-wing anthropologist writing in the 1960s. He had trained in the United States but was loyal to a nascent Afro-Colombian struggle for visibility. Escalante's book La minería del hambre *(The Mining of Hunger) described the company's health services and antimalaria campaigns and recognized that wage workers benefited in many ways, but even in describing a clinic he offered a critical counterpoint: "The walls are of wood and the roof of zinc, as is the case with all the buildings put up in this country by the company, which is looking only at the short term." Escalante focused on the fact that local people's legal rights had been trampled on—their land had been taken away, they faced racial discrimination by company employees, and their longtime practice of panning the rivers along which they lived was criminalized whenever the company claimed its dredges had the right-of-way. In the present, artisanal miners are still engaged in attempts to stop the incursions of multinational firms—a cause championed by the Grammy Award-winning Colombian hip-hop group ChocQuibTown in a 2010 album titled* Oro *(Gold).*

When I started working in a mine in 1931 at the age of 15 the price of gold was $20.67 per ounce. In 1935, when I was working for the F.E. Co. in Fairbanks, the price was increased to $35 per ounce. . . . Costs had increased to the extent that operations were no longer profitable at $20.67 per ounce, but at $35 per ounce the operations were very profitable. However, by the time I left the company in 1953 to go to South America costs had again increased to the extent that the operations in Fairbanks were only marginally profitable. In Colombia the mines (except for the one I went to work for) were doing well with gold at $35, as the local currency, the peso, was devaluing regularly and faster than costs were increasing.

The Colombian company was called Compañía Minera Chocó Pacífico and was located in the Chocó region of Colombia. The headquarters camp was at Andagoya, at the junction of the San Juan and Condoto rivers, which emptied into the Pacific Ocean north of Buenaventura. It was a very hot, humid climate with an average of 270 inches of rain each year; temperatures varied between 80 and 92 degrees Fahrenheit. I had been told in New York that the company was losing money, but they believed that with technical help the company could be profitable. As I visited the operations and the camp I was appalled by the living and working conditions of the workers, and I soon realized that the basic social problems of illiteracy, poverty-level wages, inadequate housing, extremely poor medical attention, excess personnel, and so forth had to be resolved before the operations could be restored to a profitable level. The conditions had been badly misrepresented when I accepted the job in New York, and things were so deplorable that I would have left the first week if there had been a flight out. The weather was so bad that it was ten days before a plane came in. By then, however, I could see a real challenge, so I stayed.

Most of the men were working barefoot, and I was surprised to see that some of the welders had leather jackets and aprons but were welding without shoes. Many of the women were bare-breasted. There was a hospital but it was in poor condition. It had three doctors, as mandated by law, but lacked equipment such as an X-ray machine, a laboratory and proper equipment. The doctors were treating people with a variety of very expensive drugs, hoping that one of them would work. They had no conception of industrial medicine. Malaria and other tropical diseases were prevalent. Although most staff houses were well screened and had small electric burners and iceboxes, the workers' houses were in deplorable condition. . . .

I had been hired as chief engineer with the understanding that in a year I would be familiar enough with the language (Spanish) and the operations that I would take over as manager from the current manager, who had been there for many years and was ill and wanted to leave. In the meantime I was to do everything possible to make the company profitable. There was much that could be done to improve the efficiency and economy of the company, but it all depended on improving the health and living conditions of the workers and paying them enough so they could eat properly and then reducing the number of employees. All of these things required an infusion of capital, which the parent company in New York was not willing to provide. I wrote frequent reports to New York advising the actions that were necessary but every time they wrote back saying that when operations were profitable they would go ahead with my recommendations. This went on for a year and then I gave 30-day notice, as I could not see any hope of accomplishing the things that I thought essential for progress. . . .

The man who owned the controlling stock in South American Gold and Platinum Company, Sam Lewisohn, had recently died, and his widow had decided to sell the stock. Lew Harder, a broker in New York, placed the stock with business associates and family. Lew and two associates visited Andagoya shortly before I was to leave to see what they had bought. The manager asked me to show them around even though I could not help but be critical of the New York management. For three days I showed them around the operations while saying what I thought should be done. They went back to New York, had a proxy fight, and took control of the company. . . .

Orders were immediately placed for electric or kerosene stoves, refrigerators, and toilets for all the company houses that did not have them. Lumber, screening, paint, and the like were made available, along with help for the workers to make their homes secure against insects. Social workers were brought in, and many sewing machines were purchased to teach the women to sew clothes for their families. Boots or shoes were supplied to all workers. Wages were increased. . . . Shortly after the laboratory equipment and a technician arrived there was a noticeable reduction in drug costs, and as living conditions and medical treatment improved it became possible to start reducing the number of employees. Meantime, test work had commenced on the dredges to improve recovery of gold and platinum. Bucket line speeds were increased. . . . Morale of the employees was greatly improved when I issued an order to the effect that training of locals would commence to replace foreigners wherever possible. The gold-dredging operations in the Yukon, in Alaska, and in California had been training operators for many years, and it was relatively easy to obtain experienced men, but this became more difficult as those operations reduced their activities and dredges closed down. I could see the potential of many of the local workers while I was working there, and I thought it was a poor reflection on the companies that they had not trained local people. I put out an order that we would not hire any more foreigners. It was surprising how quickly local people could be trained and there was never any noticeable loss in production, but there was a very noticeable decrease in costs without all the expense of importing foreigners and sending them and their families on three-month vacations every third year. . . .

Not long after I instituted the policy of training and promoting local people I was on a visit to Andagoya when we received word that a new governor had been appointed for the Chocó department and that he was making an official visit to Andagoya. The company had not had good relations with the Chocó department governing group, and I was determined to improve the situation. The manager at Andagoya at the time was an engineer from Montana who had worked for many years at Andagoya and then at a smaller operation further south called Nariño. He was moved up to Andagoya to replace the sick manager at the time I went to New York. I discussed with him my interest in improving relations with the new governor and suggested that we have a big luncheon with all our staff and that at the luncheon he sit on one side of the governor and I sit on the other side. The manager said he would not sit down to eat with any black man, governor or not. I replied that the man's color should not make any difference; he was the governor and would be treated accordingly. The manager adamantly refused to sit with him. I said that I knew that the manager had had a local woman for many years and had children by her who were in school in Montana, so I could not understand his statement that he would not sit down to eat with a black person. He said that was right and that a man had to have some principles. I told him that I could not understand his so-called principles and that they were so far from any that I had that he should pack his bags and leave, as there was no way that he and I could work together. He left for good the next morning. . . .

At one time local politicians, many of whom were lawyers that the company had educated, petitioned the government to nationalize the Chocó Pacífico Company. The minister of mines and several aides visited the operations to hold public hearings on the proposal. After the local politicians had their say it seemed that the minister would side with them, but then one employee stood up and gave a very stirring speech about how well dressed and housed he and his family were. It was just a few years ago, he said, that all of them had been barely existing, living in rags in a grass shack along the river, and if the politicians had their way they would destroy the company with graft, corruption, and poor management and the employees would once again be barely existing in rags in a grass shack watching the river flow by. His speech carried the day and the government took no action on the proposal to nationalize the company so it continued operating. However, about 20 years later, after the nationalization of major mines in Chile and other countries, a proposal to nationalize all the mines in Colombia without compensation was presented to Congress. It seemed very probable that such a proposal would succeed in Congress, and I was worrying about what we could do when I happened, on a flight from Medellín to Bogotá, to sit beside an astute, well-connected lawyer who had been a minister and ambassador. I explained our problem to him and asked if he would be willing to help us. He thought that he could, so I put him on the payroll in Colombia and then we went to New York to negotiate a deal with Lew Harder and the board. We made a deal with the gentleman and agreed to pay him a percentage of any funds received in dollars in New York from a sale of the properties. He first arranged with the president and leaders of Congress to put the proposed law on hold to give us time to negotiate. Then he sought the support of ANDI [the National Association of Industrialists],[2] convincing them that if the government nationalized the mining industry it would be but a short step to doing the same to other industries in the country. He then got a group of businessmen and bankers together and convinced them to buy the mining companies, which they did, except for the Frontino company. A reasonable sale price was arrived at, and the funds were remitted to New York. The auditors at year's end were sure that we had paid off or bribed someone but were finally convinced that the deal with the negotiator was a legitimate business deal. I never knew whether or not he had paid someone, nor did I care, since he got the job done that we had contracted with him to do. It was interesting working with such a well-connected lawyer: it would normally take a week for me to get an appointment with the minister of mines and longer for one with the president. In the morning the lawyer would call the president or the minister of mines or any of the bankers we were negotiating with and invite them for lunch at his elegant home, and they would be there, so the negotiations moved right along.

The people in the Chocó operation did not fare as well, unfortunately. The Chocó operation was marginally profitable and could have continued operating for many years with the conservative management of International Mining. However, the group that took over the companies had a more extravagant lifestyle than we had ever dreamed of. We had had an older Oldsmobile in Bogotá with a chauffeur who was not badly dressed (usually because he wore my hand-me-downs). They, on the other hand, soon had three new Mercedes cars with liveried chauffeurs. Then they acquired a much newer and bigger airplane than we had had, as well as larger and better-furnished offices in both Bogotá and Medellín. They also increased the staff. Fortunately for them the price of gold went up dramatically, so they were able to absorb higher costs for awhile. In the Chocó they had problems with the local people and politicians, though, and soon the new group took out all the company's cash reserves and then turned the company over to the union. The union leaders were soon stealing the production, so there wasn't any money for wages and supplies, and the company soon closed down. It was an unnecessary but very real tragedy, as pensioners who had worked faithfully for many years lost their pensions. The employees, too, lost not only their jobs but their well-earned pensions. I received heart-breaking letters from some of the old pensioners and workers, and occasionally sent some of my own money to help the saddest cases. I tried to do what I could with the people to whom we had sold the company and the government to help the destitute pensioners. The government finally paid partial pensions for a brief time, but it was a very sad ending for a company that had treated their people well for many years and had done so much for the community.

———————

If one manages to spend time in Condoto and interact with the native population of impoverished miners, one of the first things one perceives is a set of conflicts over land, between the natives and the Chocó Pacífico Mining Company. This is most immediately apparent in the *corregimiento* [local administrative district] of Opogodó, where the Company's dredges devour the national wealth.

Who owns the geographic location contained within and symbolized by the political limits of the municipality of Condoto? . . . Rooted in the minds of many local people one finds the false idea that all of Condoto's land is the property of the Company. Psychosocial instruments deployed in a scientific way contribute to the distortion of local people's rational thinking. This situation is manifest when the dredges are going to initiate work in a new place. Before the machines arrive, lawyers for the foreign firm begin to circulate the rumor: "all of this land belongs to the Company." If someone thinks that they are the owner, or doubts the emissaries' words, they take their question to Condoto's mayor, whose automatic reply is: "this land belongs to the Company." We can say that this long practice has made our unfortunate countrymen lose any notion of what it means to own land. . . .

The case of residents of Opogodó . . . is an example of the coexistence of two distinct subcultures governing the behavior of subjects interacting about this. On the one hand, a local subculture teaches people that land possession is a patrimony passed on by those from whom one has received one's immediate genetic inheritance. They overlook the fact that the Company has recourse to a chain of legal statutes granting it usufruct rights, which emanated from Colombian legislators in order to guarantee rights to the soil and the subsoil needed for its operations.

It is an established fact that the land titles Chocó Pacífico displays are not always authentic or real. A petition signed by various natives of Opogodó and directed to the Director of INCORA [the Colombian Institute for Agrarian Reform][3] in Bogotá expresses the disagreement, resentment, sense of protest, and the viewpoint of Condoteños in connection to landholding. The document reads as follows:

Lower Opogodó River, October 16, 1963
Señor
Gerente del Instituto de Reforma Agraria
[General Manager of the Colombian Institute for Agrarian Reform]
INCORA
Bogotá

Señor Gerente,

We the undersigned to this letter address ourselves to you in the most respectful way to make known to you the following:

Since we were born, more than thirty years ago for some of us and more than forty for others, we have lived in the region of the "Lower Opogodó River," within the jurisdiction of the Municipality of Condoto, Chocó Department.

This is the same land where our great-grandparents, our grandparents, and our parents lived. Thus we have inherited the possession of this area, where there are not titles other than the peaceful possession of the land by our families for more than a century.

The Chocó Pacífico Mining Company, Inc. has acquired ownership rights over part of this extensive area, which it has obtained at giveaway prices from extremely poor residents. They have mercilessly taken over this land, because it is rich in gold and especially in platinum, and in five years of dredging they have taken out of it more than eighty million pesos. With the complicity of the authorities in Condoto and with the lawyers on their payroll, it is now the case that they want to dispossess us of our land [as well], to dredge it.

We claim the right of possession to what we consider to be ours, by right of peaceful inheritance for so many years, but the Mayor of Condoto has gone so far as to threaten us, backing up the Company in its pretention, to the point of charging some of us rent for our houses and for the land we've had for so many years.

The company tells us that this land is theirs, but it cannot show legal title because there are no titles in Chocó except that of possession and we have that since we were born, as we have already said, by inheritance from our ancestors, without anyone legitimately disturbing us.

Because of this, Señor Gerente, we ask with all due respect that you send a delegation of competent and trained persons as quickly as possible, so that they can come to verify that what we have stated and to stop the Chocó Pacífico Company from committing the abuses and outrages that up to today they have been committing, with the negligence and complicity of the authorities in Chocó.

We want your office to be personally convinced of the way this Company, which is insatiable in its voracity, has profited itself in this province, paying only a miserable amount of tax, and at the same rate today as twenty years ago. We want your own eyes to see the desolation and misery that has transformed very extensive territories. . . .

The anguished cry we make to you, Señor Gerente, is because Dredge no. 3 of the Company is very close to our land, and we do not want to sell. As we have said, they are threatening us to dispossess us without having any title.

We are ready to stop the Company's rapacity and to block the Dredge going through the land we think is ours, whatever it takes. . . .

Here on our land we will be better able to more fully and objectively state our claims, which we consider to be fully justified. INCORA should assess the titles the Company says it has, and their legality. INCORA should say who are the true owners and should stop the Company from forcing us into poverty, as it has done to so many over forty years.

It is worth noting that there is Avianca service from Bogotá to Condoto on Mondays, Thursdays, and Saturdays.

In the hopes that our petition is attended to and with feelings of great respect,

> *We remain faithfully yours,*
> *Delia Mosquera, Lucila Mosquera, Manuel*
> *Mosquera, Abraham Cranja, Celestino*
> *Moreno, Diógenes Moreno, Manuel Moreno,*
> *Feliciano Urrutia, Juan Urrutia, Luis José*
> *Urrutia, Ostancio Urrutia.*

Translated by Ann Farnsworth-Alvear

Notes

1. On the origins of the names Tora and Barrancabermeja, see Eugene Havens and Michel Romieux, *Barrancabermeja: Conflictos sociales en torno a un centro petrolero* (Bogotá: Tercer Mundo Editores, 1966), 22–23.

2. The Asociación Nacional de Industriales (ANDI) was founded in the 1940s as a political vehicle for Colombian industrialists. Currently the organization translates its name as "National Business Association of Colombia."

3. INCORA is the Instituto Colombiano de la Reforma Agraria, or Colombian Institute of Agrarian Reform, with headquarters in Bogotá. See note on page 241. INCORA was dissolved in 2002 and replaced by INCODER (Instituto Colombiano de Desarrollo Rural). Responsibilities previously understood as falling beneath the umbrella of INCORA are now distributed among a variety of Colombian government agencies.

Carlos Ardila Lülle: "How I Got Rich"

Patricia Lara Salive and Jesús Ortíz Nieves

In Colombia, biographies of individual businessmen often yield more information than published company histories, given the country's long tradition of entrepreneurship and the way the financial interests of specific individuals can cut across different economic sectors. The entrepreneurial career of Carlos Ardila Lülle is a case in point. His father, who was from the Comunero town of El Socorro (see part III), set up shop in Bucaramanga and by 1915 was known as a good businessman in that key town—a spot of economic dynamism in the Eastern Cordillera. Decades before, a small group of Germans had settled there, including Ardila's maternal grandfather—whose story overlaps with that of the German migrants profiled by Pedro Gómez Valderrama (see part VII).

The young bumangués (native of Bucaramanga) married into one of Medellín's wealthiest factory-owning families, then went to Cali to manage a bottling plant owned by his father-in-law—in a society and a business environment marked by distrust, family connections were key. But Ardila had ambitions that went beyond managing a subsidiary. With a new product based on the scent of apples he took over market share from Colombia's biggest soft drink firm, Postobón. The "soda wars" that ensued included everything from lawsuits to breaking rivals' bottles and bordered on the picaresque. Then Ardila Lülle moved on to more sophisticated stratagems: an all-out price war and buying up shares in the opponent company, which required that he create a financial intermediary (put together by the Bogotano Jaime Michelson Uribe, who later was undone by one of Colombia's first huge financial scandals). By this point he was the kind of businessman who knew how to mobilize political connections, in this case those of future president Belisario Betancur.

Later in Ardila's life, the organizational chart for his empire included soda, beer, textile, agro-industry, packaging, communication, and financial companies. His contemporary Julio Mario Santodomingo was behind a similarly diversified set of firms, and commenters often linked their names, as in a joke that circulated at about the time of the magazine piece excerpted below: "What do you get when you put together Colombia's two great captains of industry [Ardila, the soft-drink king, and Santodomingo, who owned the largest brewery]?" The answer: a refajo, the local term for a drink made by mixing sweet soda with beer. Ardila and Santodomingo had things in common. Both made their initial fortunes in a world that no longer exists, one marked by the amount of money and nationalistic spirit that went into empresas nacionales (national firms). Through most of the twentieth century, Colombian companies that produced for the domestic market could count on protectionist tariffs—meaning that their profits derived not only from the products made in their factories but also from "milling customs duties," in a phrase used by their critics. With the Colombian economy as a whole, Ardila and Santodomingo then moved into a new, more globalized business world. Two firms that had been taken as symbols of Colombia's nationhood in the twentieth century, Bavaria (beer) and Avianca (the national airline), were sold by Santodomingo to foreign investors. And although Ardila took over Coltejer, the Medellín-based textile producer that had long stood for national pride, textiles were no longer a protected industry, and multiple strategies to save Coltejer failed. It was bought by the Mexican textile giant Kaltex in 2008. The puff piece excerpted here captures something of the deference with which homegrown captains of industry are treated in Colombia and the nostalgia that infuses Colombian representations of the growth of familiar national brands. Journalists Patricia Lara Salive and Jesús Ortíz Nieves went on to long careers. In Lara's case, writing was combined with a 2006 turn as a vice-presidential candidate for the left-wing party Polo Demócratico Alternativo.

When Jean Martin Leloux, a Belgian passing through Cali in February 1954, handed him a small flask with apple essence to smell, the young man looked him in the eyes and asked, "And what is this used for?" The Belgian answered coldly, "To make desserts."

Carlos Ardila Lülle was 23 years old then. For three years, he had been manager of Lux, a [carbonated soft drink] business based in Medellín, having graduated as a civil engineer from the Escuela de Minas in Antioquia's capital two years previously. He arrived to Cali to set up a plant for Valle [Valle del Cauca] only a few months earlier, and his position as administrator was more about how he was labeled on the payroll than about his daily reality. In practice, he was a jack-of-all-trades and did not even have a secretary. The factory had no more than thirty employees.

The flask held by the Belgian gave off a scent that surpassed that of apples. Ardila thought an apple-flavored soda, which did not exist anywhere in the world, might be profitable. He supervised the blend himself, adjusted the sugar, and tested its effervescence. Lux was then a small company compared to Postobón, a massive soft drinks company at the time. Some close to him told him there was no point in taking this risk, that consumer habits in Cali were already set, that the competition would be very difficult. The risk proved worthwhile: in mid-July on 1954, at the National Athletic Games held in Cali, he introduced the soda—to complete success. A 12-pack of soda cost 80 cents at the time. But the response to the new *manzana* was such that in Medellín Ardila priced it at 1 peso and 20 cents. "Within three months we had seventy percent of the soda market in Cali," Lülle recalls, sitting at a table in the boardroom of the organization that carries his name. . . .

Postobón, the competition, was hard hit, and spent several years figuring out what to do. It was then that the first bottle war began. Postobón would purchase Lux bottles and subsequently break them. Later, in 1956, the price war broke out. Postobón increased the price of its beverages throughout the entire country, except in Cali and Medellín, where Lux was growing stronger. Ardila went to Bogotá and complained to Joaquín Vallejo Mejía, a cabinet minister in the junta that replaced the military government of Gustavo Rojas Pinilla. The official did not pay him much attention. By then, however, he had a good lawyer, Belisario Betancur, who would undertake litigation in Bogotá while Ardila Lülle tended to business in Cali and Medellín. He cut costs drastically to beat his competition, with his company's very survival at risk. He even reduced the amount of sugar in the bottled soda. It is with great emotion that Ardila Lülle recalls the faith with which his employees worked. The manager of one plant, he recounts, even asked to have his salary withheld during the crisis. The competition grew tired of losing money in these two cities, and they called him to settle an agreement: the crisis ended.

By the beginning of the sixties, he knew he had to open a plant in Bogotá. He began at a site on what is now Avenida de las Américas, diagonal to the Centro Nariño. The other part of his strategy was more ambitious: to avoid another war he had to purchase stock in Postobón. The rationale was something along the lines of "If you cannot handle your enemy, buy him out." And this required capital. He therefore founded Financiera Lux, a company that used funds from individuals and paid them interest. Ardila used the money to purchase stock at Postobón. "That's illegal now," he notes.

In addition, Jaime Michelsen, who directed the Grupo Grancolombiano, bought Postobón stock and then sold it to Carlos Ardila.

However, another fight was brewing over who would control Postobón. During this war, shareholders sold Postobón stock to Suramericana [a Medellín-based insurance company, one of the largest in Colombia]. Ardila and Michelsen started buying that company's shares. The struggle became so intense that Suramericana agreed to sell its shares of Postobón to Ardila and Michelsen, in exchange for the Suramericana shares they had purchased. "On March 22, 1968," says Ardila, without concealing his pride, "I became the majority shareholder of Postobón." . . .

To recap: Ardila owns the entire chain [of production]. He makes the bottles (Peldar), prepares the water (Postobón), produces the sugar (his sugar mills), manufactures the gas for effervescence (Líquido Carbónico), produces the bottle caps (Tapas La Libertad), makes the [packaging] boxes (Inverplast), has an enormous network of distribution and a transportation dealership (Los Coches), and airs his own publicity (RCN). It is no wonder that Fidel Castro once said to Alfonso López Michelsen, "Would you like me to tell you why Ardila Lülle is the most important businessman in Latin America? Because he has succeeded in halting the Coca-Cola invasion."

Translated by Ann Farnsworth-Alvear and Ana María Gómez López

The Arrow

David Sánchez Juliao

Seen from above, the Colombian economic landscape is marked by its history of mining enterprises, multinational firms, and dozens of medium or large-scale industrial experiments. Seen from below, however, it is a landscape of street sellers, live-in domestic servants, sweatshop day laborers, and ordinary people who depend on el rebusque, an umbrella term that encompasses street smarts, day-to-day hustling, and informal labor of all kinds. Official figures suggest that well over half of Colombia's workforce is in the informal economy. Through the voice of El Flecha (The Arrow), a failed boxer from the town of Lorica, in the department of Córdoba, writer David Sánchez Juliao provides a humorous listing that is nonetheless true-to-life in describing the many odd jobs Colombians do daily to survive. The narrator, whose nickname provides the title for this short story, jokingly suggests that being a writer should be included in his list of jobs people do when forced to hustle. It's a tongue-in-cheek remark for Sánchez Juliao, author and scriptwriter for several Colombian soap operas, a television genre that has regularly featured stories of underprivileged Colombians.

But *viejo* Deibi [Davy or David, written as it would be pronounced in Spanish], I was really out of it back then, because all I wanted was to become a boxer, *la madre*. Godamn'shit job for me to want, I wanted it so bad, more than wantin' food, no shit. Ever since I was livin' in this neighborhood where I still live, the coolest neighborhood in Lorica, 'cause it's the only one that's got a United States president's name—el Kenider [from Kennedy]. Well ever since I was livin' here, in this place where a black man has got no alternative aside from the ring and lookin' for fame—shit, man—yeah, because all the other jobs *viejo* Deibinson [Davidson], you know it man, are jobs for white people. *La madre.* That's right, not unless no shit man you're black and you get yourself in one of those jobs where you better be hustling man and wearing your little Holy Trinity charm (one-true-god-and-three-holy-persons). Yeah, because I don't have a damn clue how in this country a carpenter, a bodyshop welder, a bricklayer, water carrier, shoe shiner, Marlboro hawker, Kent cigarettes bit-seller, wheelbarrow pusher, sack hauler, brothel bouncer, busboy, old-whore's pimp, bus assistant, birdcage maker, snowcone seller, lottery ticket seller, writer (do not get mad at me, *viejo* Deibi, do not get mad, *please*), manager of a sidewalk stand, errand boy, peanut seller, accordion player, serenade singer, baptism photographer, gigolo for faded beauties, church sexton, newspaper hawker, coffee seller, tire repairman, car mechanic, or cable splicer, can survive. You barely make anything in those jobs, *viejo* Deibi, you know that, you cannot even make enough money to fool your hungry stomach, no shit. And take into account that a hungry stomach is like a little kid, huh!, you can fool it with a Colombiana [a soda made by Postobón], a lollipop, and that's it, until tomorrow, *chao.*

Over there in Kenider, I was living with my old lady [my mother]. And do you know how she made a living? Doing white people's laundry. That's how I got my first pair of boxing gloves—from the dirty underwear of the big bosses in Lorica. How ironic, huh? And with all that there are some sonofabitches who claim that boxing is a decent profession. They're sure kidding, huh?

Translated by Ann Farnsworth-Alvear, Ana María Gómez López, and Marisol Castillo

A Portrait of Drug "Mules" in the 1990s

Alfredo Molano

In recent decades, cocaine smuggled overseas from Colombia has generally been in the form of bulk shipments. Smugglers have used speedboats, submarines, and planes, with large quantities in any given transport. Nevertheless, Colombians are perhaps most familiar with the image of the "mule," a person who agrees to smuggle cocaine, often by swallowing small packages of cocaine prior to boarding a plane for Europe or the United States. Even as larger-scale smuggling became the bread and butter of trafficking organizations, the small-scale work of "mules" has continued to be important in the cultural landscape of the drug economy.

Writer Alfredo Molano sketches that landscape, using a fictionalized first-person narration to bring readers into a drug courier's world and pointing out that many different kinds of people ended up as "mules." Some, he says, did it for kicks; others, in desperation. To access the stories he includes, Molano interviewed people in Spanish and Latin American prisons, including the person he calls the "mule driver."

They kept coming in one by one until all the mules were there: two young women, a very well-dressed lady, and an older guy. All of them followed the instructions to the letter. I watched them carefully without their knowing it. They didn't even know why it was arranged for them to carry a magazine in their hand and drink a lemon soda. For us it was a test that allowed us to get to know their faces and study their defects. We had to reject the luke-warm, the nervous, the timid, the fearful. Over the course of a full hour I observed them down to the tiniest detail.

Three days later, and in the almost same order that they had arrived at the cafeteria, they got on the airplane. They were spread throughout the seats. None of them knew any of the others and, for sure, none of them knew me, the man who was going to be taking care of them. They didn't seem any more nervous than the other passengers, although each of them carried on average a kilo in their intestines.

When the stewardesses pull the doors shut and it quiets down inside, you feel as if you're halfway to a successful score because you've passed two

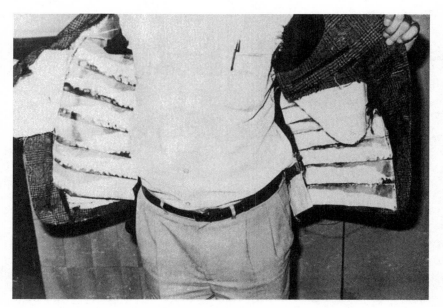

Early methods used by cocaine "mules" to conceal their consignments. Photograph by Colombian antinarcotics police, 1981. In James Mollison, *The Memory of Pablo Escobar: Archive of 350 Found Photographs* (London: Chris Boot, 2007), 49. Used by permission of *El Espectador*.

tests: you've stowed the luggage and been checked by DAS. You know that the police are looking at you and that at any moment they can walk up to a person and say "Come with me." The voyage stops right then and there. When the jet lifts off and you feel it shaking, you know that from that moment you're in another country, where other authorities hold sway, that our poor excuses for cops who can be bought for a thousand or ten thousand pesos are stuck back on the ground. But, in any case, you feel a lot more at ease when the plane picks up velocity and the past gets further behind you, although the cookies remind you who you are. Because you never stop feeling them in your stomach. Women who've had children say that they feel the same nausea at the third month of pregnancy.

There's no other way to do it because there are thirty, forty, or fifty little plastic bags, each of them about the size of a brownie, sitting in your intestines. For sure, the mules are forbidden to eat during the twenty-four hours before the trip, but, in any case, a kilo is a kilo. Some of them take the cookies with Coca-Cola, others with sugar water, and a few just with water. A few try to vomit and others simply can't swallow it at all. Those are the ones who miss the airplane. From early on the mules are checked out one by one with their suitcases, their papers, and their money, all of them ready to get the jump on the job. They pack and go out to the airport, where one person waits for them. In this journey one never flies alone; Madrid is a dangerous place and, for that reason, one person keeps a close eye on the rest.

When the overhead lights go out I take the time to look over their faces again, to figure out where they're all sitting and calm myself down. It was hard work not staring at Lucía, because she struck me as the kind I really like. But love on an airplane is a bad omen. Better, I thought, once we've unloaded I can tell her who I am and confess that I haven't stopped staring at her since the cafeteria. To be a mule driver you have to know how to control yourself and to take every step required. All the mule drivers, every one of them, has been a mule, and they've hit the jackpot more than once.

I made five trips before they gave me the responsibility of taking care of others. In fact, taking care of the merchandise they're carrying and that, in part, is one and the same thing. They pay you when he or she delivers the merchandise in good condition, or, to tell it like it is, when the mules take a crap and then clean the containers with soap and water so they don't smell bad. The hardest parts of the trip are the meals, because you've got to eat a little so that the stewardesses don't catch on to the trick. *Almost* all of them are spies, although plenty are mules too. Some are spies and mules at the same time, making them spymules. The difference is that they don't carry the merchandise the way we do in our stomachs but inside the walls of the cargo containers that carry their bags or in their powder compacts. They spy in order to gain the trust of the authorities, eliminate competitors, or shake off their bad dreams.

Among the mules there's one of every kind. There are sane people and corrupt people; people who make the journey because they have to and people who do it just for the thrill. I knew a mule from a good family, with a high-sounding last name, who made the trip solely so she could buy nice clothes in Madrid. She was from the coast, tall with big green eyes. Really wicked. She carried a good deal of coke, even for a mule, and traveled in first class. She was scandalous and flirted with whoever was close to her, big or small, old or young, man or woman. They seized her because she arrived on a three-day trip. From the moment she got into the airplane she began to attract attention. Well-dressed, wearing fur and high leather boots. Her boyfriend was very elegant as well, with an overcoat and an executive brief-case. They attracted attention from the time they showed their passports, both of them diplomatic. They drank champagne throughout the flight, and they made a loud, tacky party out of it. They slept for a while and when they woke up they started asking for champagne. It was a flight to Paris. In Martinique they went out to buy rum and almost didn't make it back. When the plane landed at Orly they had no idea where they had come from or where they had gone. Or where they woke up, because the police seized them for disorderly conduct, and, after going through their suitcases, discovered two kilos. The couple were forced to snap out of their drunkenness, handcuffed to a bed in the airport police station, and were later sent to the Rogny Marigni prison, one of fourteen prisons in Paris, where I ran into them again a year later. She was in the women's section and he in the men's. From a friend I was visiting I learned that they were both rich and they transported the coke just so they could party, dress in the finest clothes, and keep up appearances in their world. They gave the woman five years and the man one, because the merchandise was found in her suitcase.

I also got to know "troubled" mules who made the trip simply out of necessity. Women with five kids abandoned by their husbands. One of them, Doña Tila, was stuck in Carabanchel [a Madrid prison] on account of the "airport," that is to say, she had a kilo in her belly all because she was a widow with three kids. Her husband, a bus driver in Bogotá, was killed so they could get their hands on the day's proceeds. One night around nine he parked the bus in the lot as usual, got out, said goodnight to the watchman, and headed home. When he got to the corner the robbers jumped him, and they left him there spilling blood. She nearly went mad, but with three little kids it was her job to keep things together and look for a way out. She found it. She got involved with a con man who introduced her to the job. In one trip, if things go well, they pay between two and three thousand dollars, depending on the deal you've made. Because all of us aren't equal. Doña Tila paid her dues because she had to, and so they only promised her fifteen hundred. They gave her five hundred in the airport and another five in Madrid. The balance would be paid when she returned to Bogotá. The business is conducted that way so that the worker goes back, and since they aren't carrying money in their pockets there's no reason for them to get out of line because they're closely watched and observed. Very few mules make more than two trips.

They aren't allowed to find out much about the workings of the business because they'll get up to speed and take off to start their own line. For security reasons the individual mules don't know their companions on the trip or the rendezvous where they arrive. Security is security for the merchandise. The mules know all that they need to know in order to crap out the product in good condition and to come back for their money, which is waiting for them in cash.

Doña Tila was a woman from way out in the sticks. She ate everything they gave her on the plane and even asked for more. She'd never flown before and she thought that the plastic bags were tucked away who knows where. The result was, they asked her where she was going and, in spite of

A fully submersible seventy-four-foot-long Kevlar and carbon-fiber submarine built in the Ecuadorean lowlands near the Colombian border, designed to transport nine tons of cocaine. Photograph by the US Drug Enforcement Agency, 2011.

being told many times what her answers should be, she couldn't do it, she was too excited and didn't say a word. They asked her how much she was carrying, she took out her five hundred dollars—which for her was all the money she'd ever seen in her life and, definitely the guards were suspicious, they inspected her and forced her to get rid of the cookies. And then, what a sharpie she was, she told everything she knew; which was all they needed to put her behind bars on her own. In Carabanchel she threw herself into working in every part of the prison and from that she was able to support her kids in Bogotá. When her sentence was up she didn't want to leave the prison because she knew that in Colombia she wasn't going to find anything to help her finish raising her little sardines [from the Colombian colloquial term *sardinas*, which refers to young girls], who were already in college.

That time we arrived in Madrid without a hitch. There are two big steps, which are the heavy ones. The first is when you exit the plane and you walk down a long corridor, where they look everyone up and down and take in all the details: comportment, relaxation, uneasiness, your clothes, how you look. From there the candidates go to the second step, where they present their papers. This is the place where the guard comes up to one of the mules and says, "Come with me to be searched."

Luciano Romero: One among Thousands of Unionists Murdered in Colombia

European Center for Constitutional and Human Rights

and Peter Brabeck-Letmathe

Between 1986 and 2011, 2,863 union members were killed in Colombia, according to the Escuela Nacional Sindical, a think tank and labor rights organization based in Medellín. The International Labor Organization has received formal complaints of 1,580 murders, but only a very small percentage have been investigated by the Colombian authorities. Pinpointing why any given union leader or rank-and-file member was killed and whether or not their killing was motivated by their union activism is fraught with difficulty. Nevertheless, the staggering number of labor leaders murdered in Colombia is such that commenters from across the political spectrum regularly label it a situation of "impunity"—however much they disagree about who is to blame and whether or not trade agreements will benefit workers or harm them. Coca-Cola Company, Chiquita Brands International, and the Drummond Corporation are among the international firms accused of having benefited from violence against unionists. Who is responsible for creating a climate in which labor leaders know they are placing their lives in danger by publicly supporting a given union? Judge José Nirio Sánchez, who sentenced Romero's killers to prison, argued that Nestlé should be further investigated. He later left Colombia for exile in the United States, citing death threats. In 2009, he testified before the US Congressional Committee on Education and Labor at a hearing on violence against labor union leaders in Colombia. The following two texts, one circulated by internationally trained lawyers focused on human rights, and the other addressed to SINALTRAINAL chairman Luis Javier Sánchez Correa and signed by former Nestlé CEO Peter Brabeck-Letmathe, describe different positions.

On 10 September 2005 the Colombian trade unionist Luciano Romero was stabbed 50 times in a murder by paramilitaries in Valledupar, Cesar, in northeastern Colombia. Romero had for years previously worked for the Colombian Nestlé subsidiary company CICOLAC.

In connection with this crime, the European Center for Constitutional and Human Rights (ECCHR) and the Colombian trade union SINALTRAINAL (Sindicato Nacional de Trabajadores del Sistema Agroalimentario)—both represented by Zürich lawyers Marcel Bosonnet and Florian Wick—filed criminal complaints with the public prosecutor in Zug, Switzerland, against the Nestlé corporation and many of its senior management employees.

Those named in the complaint are accused of negligently contributing to the death of Romero through omission of a duty. As principals and guarantors of the company, they had a duty to act to prevent the crime. The murder took place in the context of an armed conflict in which trade unionists and other social groups are subjected to systematic persecution, primarily at the hands of paramilitaries and public authorities. In the years before his murder, Romero was repeatedly falsely branded as a guerrilla fighter by the local representatives of Nestlé. In Colombia, a defamation of this kind can effectively amount to a death sentence. Added to this is the fact that Nestlé's local agents were closely involved, on a number of levels, with paramilitary circles. It maintained supply relations with major landowners with connections to such circles; there is also evidence that the local subsidiary company made payments to paramilitary groups. The management of the Swiss company was aware of the risk-taking behaviour of their associates in Colombia and also knew of the resulting dangers for the lives of the affected trade unionists. It nevertheless chose not to act, saying that these matters were delegated to its Colombian subsidiary. The public prosecutor in Zug must now examine whether this conduct is legally relevant under criminal law. . . .

Luciano Romero campaigned for the rights of workers at CICOLAC and documented violations of the human rights of trade unionists. He suffered repression at the hands of the state, was subjected to repeated arbitrary detention by Colombian judicial police and received threats from paramilitaries (AUC).

Leading officials of Nestlé-CICOLAC also played a role: they repeatedly defamed him, falsely claiming he was a guerrilla fighter. He was accused, without grounds, of being responsible for a bombing on the factory premises in 1999.

When in 1999 the Inter-American Commission on Human Rights directed the Colombian state to adopt protective measures for Romero, all he received was a radio telephone. This did little to improve his level of safety.

A security programme with bodyguards and a bulletproof car was approved for him but never implemented. In 2002 Romero represented the workers as the trade union's chief negotiator in talks on a collective agreement in the CICOLAC factory. Months passed without any agreement. The management of the company spread accusations among the major landowners and milk suppliers that the demands of the trade unionists would push down the price of milk and threaten the company's Valledupar base. Claims like these are dangerous since Nestlé-CICOLAC had business dealings with milk suppliers who had links to paramilitaries. Figures such as Hernando Molina Araujo and Hugues Rodríguez were later handed down long prison sentences for paramilitary activities. As such, statements such as the one from the Nestlé-CICOLAC management could place the lives of trade unionists in danger.

Local Nestlé representatives were clearly aware of these risks, because as the labour dispute and the tensions reached their peak, they offered Romero help in obtaining a visa. He declined, explaining that his interest lay in continuing the work of the union in freedom and safety and that leaving the country would have been more counterproductive than helpful in this respect. When, in October 2002, the company parted ways with Luciano Romero in connection with the labour dispute, the threats continued. In 2004 he was forced to temporarily go into exile.

After his return he took a claim for reinstatement against his former employers. He also offered to act as a witness at the Permanent People's Tribunal to give testimony on Nestlé's corporate and trade union policies in Colombia. The Tribunal is an independent, internationally active institution which investigates complaints against corporations relating to human rights violations. Romero was unable to appear at the hearing in Bern in October 2005; he had been murdered just a few weeks before.

March 16, 2012
Vevey, Switzerland
Letter to Mr. Javier Correa, Chairman,
SINALTRAINAL trade union, Colombia
Mr. Correa,

We were extremely surprised to learn about the criminal complaint filed by SINALTRAINAL and the European Center for Constitutional and Human Rights (ECCHR) before the State Attorney of the Zug Canton in

Switzerland, accusing the undersigned, four colleagues and Nestlé s.a. of murdering Luciano Romero by negligence (*fahrlässige Tötung*).

As we have made clear to you and your organisation on many occasions, Nestlé condemns all forms of violence under any circumstances, has never used violence, nor has it associated with criminals. We therefore reiterate that Nestlé has absolutely no responsibility whatsoever, directly or indirectly, neither by action nor omission, for the murder of Luciano Romero. Members of Nestlé Colombia's top executive management have met you on numerous occasions to discuss the security of our employees. As you are aware, Nestlé provided security measures to SINALTRAINAL union leaders such as temporary relocation and increased security at their homes and at the union headquarters. These were not designed to replace the State's obligation to protect them, but your reaction to our offers was often negative, arguing that the protection of union leaders was the responsibility of the Colombian Government.

The murder of Mr. Luciano Romero was investigated and prosecuted by the courts of Colombia. Those who were found guilty were given long sentences of imprisonment. SINALTRAINAL has attempted to blame Nestlé for this homicide in other jurisdictions including a Federal Court in Florida. In all cases, neither Nestlé nor any of its executives were charged, indicted or convicted of any action or omission that could make any of them responsible for the murder.

We reject your double standards, on one hand denying during meetings with our executives and with me personally that your organization links Nestlé with violent acts against its employees and union leaders, while on the other hand initiating again a legal action against us based on terrible and false accusations, including the allegation that "our local subsidiaries made payments to paramilitary groups."

We reject all accusations of SINALTRAINAL against Nestlé and the five individuals included in the criminal complaint filed before the State Attorney of Zug and we reserve all our rights in any jurisdiction or court to seek protection of the name and reputation of the undersigned, the other four colleagues and Nestlé s.a., all falsely accused by you.

Sincerely,
[Signed]
Peter Brabeck-Letmathe
Nestlé Chairman

VII

Transnational Colombia

Whether it was discussed as a new "kingdom" dependent on Castile, a vice-royalty (after 1738), Gran Colombia (1819), the Republic of New Granada (1831), the Granadine Confederation (1858), or the United States of Colombia (1863), the Republic of Colombia (1886) has been part of an interconnected set of polities. Prior to the Conquest, too, trade networks and political projects connected those living in what is now Colombia to people far away from them. This chapter includes readings that offer glimpses of the multiple ways Colombia has been shaped by a transnational context—something immediately visible in one of the nation's founding documents, the self-defense offered by Antonio Nariño, translator of the French Revolution's Declaration of the Rights of Man and the Citizen.

Seen from the present, Colombians are transnational in another way—this is a nation of emigrants. Colombians look for one another in New York, Madrid, Tokyo, as well as in nearby Caracas, which has a large Colombian community. Colombia itself never experienced the levels of immigration that transformed Argentina, Uruguay, and Brazil—and attracted many fewer immigrants than even Mexico or Chile. Nevertheless, the national consciousness includes nineteenth-century Germans who settled in Santander and Arabs who moved their families and businesses to the Caribbean region at the turn of the twentieth century. Texts profiling these two groups stand in here for other immigrant groups as well. Similarly, texts that point to the hegemonic influence of the United States are not comprehensive but rather point to key moments: the separation of Panama, Kennedy's Alliance for Progress, and the military involvement linked to Plan Colombia. A final set of extracts suggests some of the realignments visible in the present. Transnational understandings now include the comparative thinking of a statesman such as former Brazilian president Fernando Henrique Cardoso, who has led the Global Commission on Drug Policy, as well as the creative networking of Afro-Colombians keen to connect with a larger diaspora, or indigenous activists such as Lorenzo Muelas, who addresses himself not only to others in Colombia but also to activists worldwide. Most strikingly, the peace negotiations of 2012–16 would not have been possible without involvement by the governments of Cuba, Norway, and Venezuela.

A Creole Reads the Declaration of the Rights of Man and the Citizen

Antonio Nariño

The upper-class Bogotano Antonio Nariño (1765–1824) was part of a specific group of late eighteenth-century American Creoles. These were women and men who believed in Enlightenment reason; followed the political news from Europe and the recently founded United States; and held varying opinions about the time-worn principles associated with the Spanish Empire. They read revolutionary authors (in French and English), and the subjects broached in their tertulias (conversation groups akin to the Parisian institution of salons) bordered on all that was prohibited by the Spanish Crown. Creoles and official censors moved together in a social and political world of ambiguities and casuistry, where it was not always clear what royal favor would allow and what it would not.

In 1794, when Nariño translated and then secretly published the French Assembly's Declaration of the Rights of Man and the Citizen, he misjudged his moment. The Spanish Crown had just joined an alliance of European monarchs against revolutionary France. Nariño may not have thought his translation involved a "crime," or may have calculated that the risks were limited, at least in Bogotá, but he was made into an example. Historians would later learn that of the hundred copies he produced, Nariño himself destroyed ninety-nine on being warned of the authorities' view—but to no avail. Despite his ambivalence and legal pleading, Nariño was sentenced to ten years in prison and to perpetual exile. After the trial, time in prison, deportation, and then an escape in Cádiz, Nariño was, as he put it when requesting a meeting with William Pitt the younger in London, "a Spanish American who was highly resentful."

Later, he returned to New Granada, involving himself in the patriot army and the whirlwind of independence politics. Colombian historians celebrate less his undistinguished military career and his ill-starred time as a politician than his vocation for journalism, particularly his writings in the prorepublican weekly La Bagatela, published in Bogotá in 1811–12. He is remembered, above all, for that 1794 translation and for associating himself with one of the most important political documents of the modern world. Any measure of Colombian democracy in the present requires discussion of the principles laid out by the French Assembly—what are now called human rights.

The following are extracts from the defense Nariño mounted, which angered the authorities perhaps more than his "crime," at least according to a biographer writing at the turn of the twentieth century, Soledad Acosta de Samper (see part V). The lawyer who signed for Nariño was arrested and imprisoned, so too the printer responsible for typesetting the original translation. The text of his defensa *was ordered burned.*[1]

I, Don Antonio Nariño, a prisoner in the cavalry barracks, in response to my detention as a result of the accusation of criminal authorship for the printing, without license, of a paper titled The Rights of Man, along with other charges resulting from the proceedings, do hereby appear before Your Honor with all due respect, in order to provide what is necessary and in the most lawful manner and form, and do hereby declare: that Your Honor must absolve me of the accusation made against me, declare me free of the crimes attributed to me, and order that I be restored my belongings and all my rights, my honor, my liberty, my sons, and my wife, my dear wife whose tears have been spilled so often at the feet of the altar; I hope these tears have persuaded Our Sovereign Tutor of my innocence, so that He might inspire benevolence in Your Honor today, worthy of the tribunal and in proportion to the zeal that I have constantly manifested, before Your Honor and the public, for my King and for my country. . . .

But before beginning my response to the charges against me, I beg Your Honor for permission to give thanks to Providence for my having been born in this capital city, where a sense of loyalty and love for the king is well established, where not only every citizen jealously guards this glorious characteristic of our city, but everyone, even the poor, feel personally offended by any slander made against our fellow citizens. The advantage of having been born in a city where public opinion, customs, and common ideas encourage the strong education I received from my parents, has allowed me to live and work such that now I can happily repeat what Demosthenes said in Athens, when he was accused of similar crimes: If you know me, just as Aeschines has described me, considering that I have lived nowhere other than here among you all, then silence me. Yes, Athenians: though my service may have been irreproachable, pronounce me guilty and condemn me. . . .

To address the issue with the clarity it deserves, I will divide it into all the points that I must discuss, according to what Your Honor has allowed me to draw from the paper for my defense. First: Even if the paper were

completely criminal, the manner in which it and its title were conceived ab-
solves me from the crime. Second: As the very same principles in this paper
are currently published in other books in the nation, it cannot be judged as
pernicious. Third: When compared to public national papers and to books
that circulate freely, the publication of this paper should not be a crime.
Fourth: The paper can only be seen as harmful as long as its true meaning
is ignored; but if one examines it under the light of sound reasoning, it does
not deserve the epithets that the prosecution gives it.

First, the paper is written as a series of precepts, has as its title The Rights
of Man, and was published by the National Assembly of France. Every man
capable of reading it knows that the National Assembly of France has no
right or ability to impose its precepts upon other nations. Therefore, anyone
who might read the paper and surmise that it is full of errors, sees nothing
more than the errors that the French National Assembly has prescribed to
the nation of France. Just as when we read a list of heresies, we see nothing more than the errors that men have committed, in different times and
different nations, in regard to religion, yet we remain the same Catholics
we were beforehand. Suppose for a moment that the paper truly expressed
what Carrasco claims, that the power of the monarchy was tyrannous. Such
a striking and repugnant claim, such a proposition so absolutely lacking
in adornment or disguise, one that displays the naked horror of its own
natural deformity: could this seduce even the most gullible? Among all who
know how to read, could there be anyone so stupid, so simple as to allow
himself to be completely persuaded by such a proposition, with no other
evidence or proof? If he does, will his stupidity be the rule for the rest of humanity? We must agree that a man so ingenuous as to be convinced by such
an offensive proposal would be seduced by any book. He might read, for
example, one of those respectable works in which the errors of the wicked
are repudiated, and would not able to separate the gold from the slag: he
would become wicked. He might read the Santafé newspaper, which circu-
lates freely in public hands, and would see the horrific snippets about the
French revolution, and would become a licentious zealot, unable to make a
decision and confusing truth with lies because he finds them together. He
would read the Spanish gazettes and the same thing would happen to him.
A book of mythology that glorifies the crimes of so many gods: shouldn't
this be prohibited so that some simpleton doesn't take things at face value
and turn polytheist? I could continue endlessly if I had to name all the ideas
that endanger simple people, not because of the nature inherent in those
things, but rather because of people's own blindness. If the Rights of Man
had been written in an attractive style, if it wasn't anything more than dry

and concise resolutions, if it was an eloquent discourse full of designs and deceits, graceful images, interesting scenarios . . . in that case it could easily seduce the unwary. But a monotonous and somber declaration, even if it were full of absurdities, can neither harm nor seduce anyone. If the reader is already corrupt, what he reads in no way harms him further; if he is not, then since there is nothing in the paper that might dazzle him, that might excite or persuade him, he will read it with the same indifference with which so many absurd proposals around the world are regarded. And truly, if a declaration of this nature could seduce unwary spirits and turn them away from one form of government because the National Assembly of France said so, we would be forced to agree that, humanly speaking, the many stupid declarations throughout the Koran could turn them away from the truths of our Holy Religion just because Mohammed said them. Therefore, one must admit that if the paper was written as it is and with the title it bears, even though it might be full of errors, including those noticed by Carrasco, and if neither its structure, nor its style, nor its title contain anything capable of seducing, then I am innocent of the crime.

Translated by Timothy F. Johnson

Note

1. Soledad Acosta de Samper, *Biografía del general Antonio Nariño* (Pasto: Imprenta Departamental, 1910), 33–34. Available online at the Biblioteca Luis Angel Arango, http://www.banrepcultural.org/blaavirtual/historia/bigan/bigan3.htm, accessed March 2015. The self-description attributed to Nariño in London is from the same volume: http://www.banrepcultural.org/blaavirtual/historia/bigan/bigan5.htm (p. 47 in print version).

Humboldt's Diary, May 1801

Alexander von Humboldt

A scientist and an explorer, humanist and philanthropist, courtier and politician, the Prussian aristocrat Friedrich Wilhelm Heinrich Alexander von Humboldt (1769–1859) personifies both the scientific spirit of the Enlightenment and the romanticism of the Age of Revolution. His vast self-published works are a font of interdisciplinarity and still provide points of reference for political scientists, bio-geographers, ecologists, and geologists alike. His critiques of slavery and inequality in the Americas continue to engage historians. Even later in life, as his fortune shrank and he became more and more a Court persona, he remained an advocate of social reform and scientific research. Humboldt maintained intense same-sex friendships, never married, and gave away what little remained of his fortune. After 1804 he did not return to Latin America, the place of his most famous fieldwork. Together with the French botanist Aimé Bonpland he had spent the years between 1799 and 1804 on foot, horseback, and canoe, in what still stands as one of the most fruitful scientific expeditions in the history of the Americas.

Part of Humboldt's fame derived from his impeccable timing. Because he traveled to what are now Cuba, Venezuela, Colombia, Ecuador, Peru, the Central American republics, and Mexico on the eve of the region's independence, and he began publishing his accounts just as the patriot armies were winning their wars, Humboldt was required reading for a generation. The trip through what is now Colombia, in 1801, was a diversion from the original plan, given Humboldt's interest in meeting the transplanted Spaniard friar José Celestino Mutis (1732–1808), whose long correspondence with scientists in Europe and leadership of New Granada's Royal Botanical Expedition (1783–1808) had gained him an international reputation as a leading botanist. Humboldt stayed a bit longer than he might have in Bogotá, giving Bonpland time to recover from malaria and himself time to study Mutis's extensive collection of catalogued specimens. He also worked on a chart of the Magdalena River, using the barometric readings he had taken from Cartagena to Honda. Importantly for the history of science in Colombia, he encouraged a young scientist from Popayán, Francisco José de Caldas, commenting on his meticulous astronomic observations

and incorporating Caldas's charting of the upper Magdalena into his own map—
published later in Paris, with credit given to Caldas.

Our extract is substantially incomplete for excluding the accompanying drawings
—in a record that married scientific observation with literary ambition and the
artistic effort of drawing and painting the landscape. As with the hundreds of color
plates produced by Mutis's expedition, Humboldt and Bonpland's work made the
New Granadan landscape available for the nationalist appropriations that grew
out of the Enlightenment. Yet Humboldt's representations of the landscape center on
overflowing diversity of nature and of human cultures—tropical America is marked
by its difference from Europe. More of an outsider than Mutis, who was fully Ameri-
canized, Humboldt included personal reflection, such as his description of the way
that this overwhelming vegetation could make him long for the tended European
countryside.

From Mompós to Honda

May 6th was the day we wanted to depart from Mompós. All rowers were
gathered. As soon as they saw that we were to mount the champan, a large
bargelike canoe, they remembered that they had not yet drunk away all of
their advance. Eight ran off and we spent the night in a brick hut a quarter
mile out of town. One of the most poisonous and most daring snakes, the
little coral, happened to find itself between our beds. It tried to hide under
the pillows. The noise made the snake anxious. It jumped up at those trying to chase it and only the skill of the Indians in tossing it about made for
them not being bitten. These sorts of experiences are unsettling but occur
frequently. That is why I seldom mentioned them in my journal about this
trip and the one to Río Negro. The antidotes are so well known and nature
is such a rich source of these antidotes [*Gegengifte*] that few, very few humans die of snakebites, only those who don't know to quickly use the cure
[*Heilmittel*]. So, for example, in the Chocó region (the warmest, most humid
and therefore the most heavily snake-infested region) one often finds traveling Indians and blacks at the wayside, bitten to death by a snake. Often
one can find the humans and snake, both dead, entangled while defending
themselves in their death struggle. Most snakebites, especially to the chest
(occurring when snakes drop down from trees), cause unconsciousness and
the snake then goes on to kill its enemy.

Upwards from Mompós, the view from the river is more varied, greener
and more pleasant. The riverbanks are less overgrown in long stretches
making the view less restricted. The land is more developed [*angebauter*], in
the manner of Spanish colonies or in comparison to the Orinoco extremely

CHUTE DE TEQUENDAMA. — VUE PRISE A LA PREMIÈRE TERRASSE.
Dessin de G. Vuillier, d'après une photographie communiquée par Madame S. Acosta de Samper.

Élisée Reclus, a French geographer famous for his left-wing anarchist politics, included this engraving of Tequendama Falls in his nineteen-volume atlas, *La Nouvelle Géographie universelle, la terre et les hommes* (completed between 1876 and 1894). The engraving is credited to Dessin de G. Vuillier and to Soledad Acosta de Samper (see part V), who had provided Reclus with a photograph.

cultivated. You see many, a great many single houses and plantings done by human hand on the riverbanks. En route to Badillo [see part II] there are for each day's trip (6–7 leagues), one village, and in between many free-standing houses, ranches and plots of cultivated land. The vegetation increases with every step passed the 9th degree latitude. Since passing Munchiques it is in fact quite beautiful. The river has lovely little islands, some covered with leafy trees resembling a floating forest, others covered with delicate willows, and others offering grasslands filled with swaying reeds. The willow islands [*Weideninseln*] are indeed of great beauty and an advantage of the Magdalene River is that [it has] tree types such as *Salix* willows that are missing in the Orinoco and the Río Negro. The willow tree has hanging branches resembling the *Salix babilonica*, but only the young branches hang down, the older branches do not. The leaf is small and of the lightest shade of green. They are gathered in small groups in wet areas, seldom reach higher than 12–15 feet and make a nice contrast to the thickly grown

A *sillero* or *carguero* was a porter, usually an indigenous or mestizo man paid to carry wealthy travelers and their belongings. The French botanist Édouard François André sketched a porter on a trail locals called "the Mount of Agony," and a Paris studio then reproduced it as an engraving. Engraving by Émile Maillard, 1879. From Édouard François André, "L'Amérique équinoxiale," included in Édouard Charton, *Le Tour du monde, nouveau journal des voyages*, vol. 38 (Paris: Hachette, 1879). In Benjamín Villegas, *Once upon a Time There Was Colombia* (Bogotá: Villegas Editores, 2005), 104.

riverbanks. These present a grand, celebratory and almost serious character because of their rich and beautiful vegetation, the mass of the thick cotton tree (*Bombax*), Caracoli tree (*Anacardium caracoli*), Indian fig (*Ficus Indica*). This character is representative of the land near the equator, from the 0–9th degree.

The thick growth of the vines and the loosely woven leaves of the Heliconias and Canagria plants cover the ground and fill in every space. Larger animals do not have enough space to move about because the thick plant growth covers everything. At the Río Casiquiare the tigers roar from the tree branches. This is also home to apelike creatures and birds that live permanently in the trees and never know the ground the trees are rooted in. Where there is space, organic matter will expand (Goethe, *Metamorphosis*) and always tempted by sunlight and warmth only internal forces such as fruiting and flowering put a limit to the extension. The ground is covered with a blanket of leaves from the mouth of the Orinoco, the cascades of the Río Caroní and all in between the Río Ventuari to the Río Guainía and the Río Marañon which is completely enclosed in woods.

Just as in the cold north, ice masses will form bridges over the massive ocean to connect distant lands, so too in the more friendly palmworld do the forest trees join their branches and seem to shake hands and build a second carpet, high up in the air, tightly woven of flowers and fruits. But it is this sight of plentitude, of gigantic shapes and the lack of light and airy spots and the spooky impenetrable darkness of the leaf cover that brings a sense of doom and dread to the soul.

The tropics are missing the friendly character of our German fields, our northern flora. We almost yearn for lighter thoughts and a less grandiose and less large and less rich natural world. So it is understandable how a riverbank of a grassy area with small flowers and individual palm trees or tamarind trees calms our soul. Especially the willows, a form of our fatherland, so familiar it could be from the banks of the Oder or Seine River.

Nature, which has given to humans an unquiet mind [*Gemüth*] and flexible fiber to restlessly wander from one place to the next, has also mixed its flowers so beautifully that no matter where one wanders there will always be a leaf, a blossom or fruit that will bring back one's own land of birth. How pleasant is this remembrance, how eagerly do humans listen to this voice of nature so that even the names of unknown plants in the southern zones are given to resemble those from the north.

In every corner of the world the Europeans have found plums, cherries, olives and apples. They have even detected the remotest semblance of tropical plants with those from the fatherland. The Dane sees birches, evergreens and willows as well as oaks everywhere, the Spaniard sees olive trees and Algarrobo (*Ceratonia Siliqua*); images of a homeland hover before everyone's mind.

Translated by Ingrid Schafroth and Elizabeth Millán

The Most Practical, Because the Most Brutal

José Asunción Silva

José Asunción Silva (1865–96) is perhaps Colombia's best-known poet, but his brilliant, biting novel, De sobremesa, *did not begin to gain the reputation it deserved until relatively recently, having been first published in 1925 with a small print run— only fifty copies. He had worked on it in the late 1880s and early 1890s only to have the manuscript lost in an 1895 shipwreck—a steamboat named L'Amérique traveling from Venezuela to Barranquilla— along with volumes of poems, short stories, prose works, and a second novel. Readers who love his poetry feel the loss as our own. Those who remember his "Nocturno III," for example, or who have seen it in Colombia's 5,000-peso bill, wonder what may have sunk that might have been comparable to its famous opening lines:*

> *Una noche,*
> *Una noche toda llena de murmullos, de perfumes*
>   *Y de músicas de alas*

> *One night*
> *a night full of whispers, of perfumes*
> *and of wing-songs*

A few years prior to the shipwreck, Asunción Silva had lost his sister Elvira (his grieving for her is palpable in "Nocturno III"), and he had begun to face the bankruptcy of the business ventures he had attempted after his father's death. In 1896 he pushed himself to rewrite De sobremesa, *which he left on his desk May 24. In translator Kelly Washbourne's words, the manuscript was "like a protracted suicide note for those who would read it as one."[1]*

   The book's protagonist, José Fernández de Sotomayor y Andrade, is a self-described decadent and sensation-seeker. We "hear" about his exploits and neuroses as he describes his time in Europe to friends who sit with him in their native Bogotá, and we read a fictional diary of his time abroad. Silva's novel is between genres, combining memoir, psychological sketch, personal diary, and so on. It also crosses states of mind and makes almost constant reference to European writers and artists, from Charles Baudelaire and Paul Verlaine to Dante Gabriel Rossetti and Wil-

liam Morris. In the excerpt below, Asunción Silva creates a dreamscape that aligns Fernández's unconvincing flights of fancy with a Nietzschean cult of willpower and echoes of Machiavelli. It's a satirical tour-de-force that skewers the pretensions of rich Colombians who imagine themselves "remaking" the nation while lining their pockets, but may in the end find they are unable to do either.

Wyhl, 5 July

I found a hiding place to hole up and think, a hovel built out of rough wood and inhabited by an old peasant couple. It is an inaccessible place where no tourists go, a wild woodland gorge, full of the sound of a torrent that turns to spray as it runs amidst enormous black boulders, and shaded by pines and the tallest chestnut trees. I have written to Paris asking them to send to me in Interlaken a host of things I need, and I will go tomorrow to climb up to the peak, bringing no other books than some studies of South American prehistory, written by a German, and some treatises on botany. I feel a strange emotion as I think of my hideout.

10 July

The old man and the old lady landlords have never been in a city, nor do they know how to read or write; they look at me like a strange animal, and only speak to me to say good morning or good night. Unable to eat their food, I feed myself with the milk of a few cows they have in a neighboring esplanade. My room, don José Fernández's room, the *richissime américain*'s room, has for furniture a bed the lowliest of my Paris servants would not lie in for any amount of money, a crude table on which I write, and an enormous wooden bowl, which in the morning they fill with ice water for me, collected from the torrent, in which to bathe. All that, luckily, cleaner than the best hotels in the world, probably. The thick sheets on the bed smell of the country, and the furniture shines as if just varnished. In these five days not one voluptuous image has passed through my mind, I have not felt any desires, and I have gotten drunk on air and ideas.

In the early hours I rise, and after a cold bath and milk still warm from the udder, I climb through the gray mist pierced by light, where the rugged mountain looks barely like bluish shadows, as far as a hill that towers over the landscape. It is a sea of white steam that slowly, slowly floods with light, until the sunbeams dissolve it and show the scene enshrouded in gentle mists, which float like shreds of a bridal veil over the blue of the faraway mountains, over the greens of the valleys, to come to rest on the silvery whiteness of a snowcapped mountain, on yonder horizon. . . . Then everything comes slowly into sharper focus, the sky grows bluer, the mist disperses, the colors sharpen, the greens intensify, the black or red of every bare rock is in evidence. All that is heard are the birdsongs and the muffled, dampened torrent that bellows in its riverbed of rock. The air has a vegetable smell and is thin, rarefied. . . . As I lie on the summit, on the blanket that is with me on all my journeys, I am overwhelmed by the penetrating and profound feeling of freshness that emanates from it all. I look around me and right in front of me I see by the yellowed, aureate verdure of a cluster of willows the old mill, whose great wheel, as it spins against the thick black wall moldy from the humidity, turns the current that moves it into thin streams and drops of transparent crystal and impalpable vapor, while the swallows that nest in the gable-ends and hollows of the ancient building crisscross over it with the wide-wheeling semicircles and hostile zigzags of their incessant nervous fluttering. The goat trail that leads up to the top passes by the foot of the mill, and with a sharp turn disappears behind one of the mountain's first spurs, which at that hour, seen from where I am, is a mass of silvered blackish mist, ridged by the green thickets that stand out above the second spur, whose tangled mass of contours the mist blurs in a hazy blanket. Further on in the distance lay the bluish darkness of the far-off peaks, with their silhouettes of pointy ridges and jagged rocks that cut dark rough bends against the pale diaphanous blue of the sky and the dazzling white of the morning clouds.

I turn my gaze downward and survey the valley with the green of its vegetal carpet, on which plays a bit of mist, with patches here and there of the dark masses of the brushwood and clusters of trees, intersected by the thin yellow lines of the trails, the narrow black line of the railroad, and the silver zigzag of the mountain stream crossing it; in a recess of the gully, at the foot of the mountain I can make out the roofs, the cupola of the church, and the village cemetery, half hidden by the green darkness of the foliage, and in front, on the horizon where the intruding mist once again erases the details, the undulations of the outline and the tangled bluish mass of another mountain range, which, opening in an irregular gap, shows in the distance the blinding immaculate whiteness of a snowfield.

Nature, but nature viewed thus, without a human voice interrupting the dialogue that it carries on with the pensive soul, with the voices of its waters, of its foliage, of its winds, with the eternal poetry of the lights and of the shadows! When isolated thus from all human ties, I hear it and I feel it, I am lost in it as in a divine nirvana. One night in the middle of the Atlantic, seated on the prow of the ship where the passengers were already sleeping peacefully, without the least worry, I succumbed, as I have done these mornings, to its mysterious spell and the captivating orgy it is for me to look upon it. There was no moon. The vessel was a black hulk escaping into shadow. The restful sea and the sky of a pure, pure dark blue blended together on the horizon; the constellations and the planets shone in the depths of the infinite blue; the bubbling spring of suns in the Milky Way was a path of pale light in the black immensity, and under the wake the ship left lay another Milky Way, where among the blue-green phosphorescence shone fine diamond dust. In the first hour of thoughtful quietude, scenes from the past came back to me, ghosts from dead years, memories of long-ago readings; then the particular gave way to the universal; some general ideas, like a theory of muses that carry in their hands the formulas of the universe, paraded through the field of my inner vision. Then four grandiose entities, Love, Art, Death, Science, loomed up in my mind's eye; they alone inhabited the shadows of the landscape, vast visions suspended between two infinities of water and sky; then those final expressions of the human fused in black vastness, and lost to myself, to life, to death, the sublime spectacle entered my being, as it were, and I scattered into the starry firmament, into the peaceful sea, as if fused in them in a pantheistic ecstasy of sublime worship. Unforgettable instants whose description resists the word's every effort to capture them! The light of dawn that fades the starshine and returned to the ocean its seasickening blue-green coloring brought me back to the realities of life.

Though not feeling these ecstasies at the grandiosity of the scene, I did feel at times a supreme peace descending over my spirit in the hours spent at the summit to which I climb. The plan that called for the only purpose to which to devote my life has appeared to me as clear and precise as a mathematical formula. To reach it I need to make an effort every minute for entire years, and to have an iron will that does not relent for an instant. More or less it will be this. I have to increase my fortune two- or threefold in order to begin. If the engineers' commission sent from London by Morrell and Blundell gives a favorable judgment of the gold mines I have almost negotiated with them and that in my father's will were evaluated at a paltry sum, the mines will provide me with several million francs when they are sold. The English should be cabling Paris any time now and the Mirandas will let me know by telegraph to Geneva, where I will go to spend the month of August. Once that transaction is complete I will transfer all my capital to New York and I will establish the firm with Carrillo for conducting the business he has planned out. After Carrillo are the Astors, the millionaires who have not made one wrong move since they began trading, and in his hands my gold will work for me, while I devote myself body and soul to traveling the United States, to studying the inner workings of American civilization, to looking into the wherefores of the fabulous development of that land of energy, and to seeing what may be made use of as a lesson, to test it later in my experience. From New York I will go for a spell to Panama to manage the pearl fisheries in person, the exploration of whose shoals will yield hitherto-unknown marvels like those produced when Pedrarias Dávila[2] sent the King and Queen of Spain the one pearl that adds the finishing touch to the royal crown. All the gold these explorations yield and what I possess today will be ready for the moment in which I return to my land, not to the capital but to the States, to the Provinces I will travel one by one, researching their needs, studying the best crops for the soil, the potential means of communication, the natural resources, the nature of the inhabitants, all this with a corps of engineers and experts that for all my compatriots know are probably Englishmen traveling in search of orchids. I will spend a few months among the savage tribes, unknown to everyone there and which appear to me to be exploitable members for civilization, given the awkward strength of some of them and the slovenly indolence of others. Afterwards I will settle in the capital and expend all my energy on intrigue, then push and shove my way into politics to gain any trifling office, of the sort that one receives in our South American nations by being friends with the president. In two years of devotion and incessant study I will have hatched a rational finance plan, which is the basis of all government, and I will learn administration down to its smallest detail. The country is rich, formidably rich, and has untapped resources; it is a matter of skill, of simple calculations, of pure science, to resolve the problems of the day. In a ministry, gained with my money and influence brought into the equation, I will be able to show something of what can be done when there is the will. Then I will be but a short step away from organizing a center where the civilized among all parties are recruited to form a new party, removed from all political or religious fanaticism, a party of civilized men who believe in science and place their efforts in the service of the great idea. Then to the presidency of the republic following the necessary campaigning, accomplished by ten newspapers that denounce previous abuses, after promises of contracts, brilliant jobs, big material improvements. . . . All that willingly. If the situation does not allow for those Platonic ideals, as hereafter I presume, I will have to resort to supreme measures to spur the country to war, to the means that the government with its false liberalism gives us in order to provoke a conservative reaction, to make use of the unlimited freedom of the press that the current Constitution grants, to report theft and general abuses committed by the government and by the States, I will have to draw on the influence of the clergy to rouse the fanatic masses, on the pride of the old conservative aristocracy hurt by the mob rule of recent years, on the selfishness of the rich, on the need that the country now feels for an order of stable things; then proceed to the South American situation, and after a war in which a few thousand wretched Indians succumb, one must attack the powers that be, sword at the ready, and establish a tyranny, in the early years supported by a formidable army and lacking any limits to power and that will transform in short order into a dictatorship with its new constitution flexible enough to allow Republican revolts to be stopped, naturally, for it is names that matter to nations, with their rival journalists thrown in jail every two weeks, its exilings of opposing bosses, its confiscations of enemy goods and stormy House sessions broken up with bayonet blows, the whole game.

This route seems the most practical to me, since it is the most brutal; it will require other studies, which I will do with pleasure, yielding to the attraction that the triumphs of force have always exercised over my spirit. How pleasurably I will study you, monstrous war machines, whose steel, whence the explosive mix bursts, spills out a shower of projectiles into enemy territory and sows death in the ruined rows; grenades of thundering picrates that upon exploding reduce stamping horses and the bodies of the riders to formless bloody remains; how I will inquire into the secrets of your strategy, the subtleties of your tactics, shadows of monsters whom degraded humanity reveres, legendary Molochs, Alexanders, Caesars, Hannibals, Bonapartes, at the foot of whose altars the human hecatomb reddens the soil and gives off the smoke of battle like incense!

Oh, how sumptuous to write, after installing a strong, large, benevolent government upon appointing the respective plenipotentiaries who will request their recognition before all the presidents of all the little republics like the Central or South American ones where things are done like that, and to think that by dint of a plan drawn up with the coolness with which one solves for x in an equation, one of them reached the post he strove for with the goal of changing a nation, raising it up, and running a vast test in experimental sociology on it. No effort will seem excessive to me for crowning the heights that the mere possibility of working on a wide scale represents.

In that far-off place the decisive years lie, in which all will be energy and action.

Budgets balanced through sound economic measures will bring down customs duties, which in the long term, facilitating enormous introductions of capital, will double the income; the removal of useless jobs, reorganization of taxes on scientific grounds, economies of all types; in a few years the country will be rich, and to solve its current economic problems, an effort to instill order suffices; the day will come in which the current deficit of the

businesses will be a surplus that is transformed into highways, indispensable railroads for the development of industry, bridges that cross torrential
rivers, and into all the means of communication we are lacking today, and
whose lack binds the country like a steel chain, condemning it to pitiable
inaction.

Those will be the years of trading on the studies I have done, put to the
test by the experts and engineers that traveled the country for years and
were paid with my gold. In those climates that run from the heat of Mada-
gascar in the deep equinoctial valleys, to the cold of Siberia, in the luminous
upland moors whitened by eternal snows, all the enriching crops, from the
plantain extolled by Bello in his divine ode to the lichens that cover the
polar ice caps, the husbandry of all work animals, from the ostriches that
populate the burning plains of Africa to the polar reindeer, will emerge, in-
cited by my employees and stimulated by the bounty of farming. Countless
sheep will graze in the fertile meadows, the branches of the coffee bushes
will bend under the weight of the purple clusters; in regular perspectives
where the eye is lost in the green twilight made by the shade of the protecting guama tree, the vanilla vine will climb nimbly through the misshapen
trunks of the rubber trees, hanging from its delicate Hanas its aromatic urn-
shaped sporangia, and in the steep mountainous terrain, the gold, silver,
and iridium will shine in the eyes of the miner after a tiring excavation and
the elaborate exploitation of the native mineral.

Doubtful of my own aptitudes, for however great my studies may have
been until that point, I will call economists renowned in Europe and consult the greatest statesmen in the world in order to proceed according to
their counsel as I arbitrate the measures that will crown the work.

These tasks having been devised and articulated, the new land will be
unveiled, bursting with wealth in the European markets, owing to treasury
agents who will cover them, and through the efforts of a wise diplomatic
corps, handsomely remunerated and selected from among the crème de la
crème of the national talents. The theretofore depreciated bonds will be an
investment as solid as the consolidated English ones; colossal loans advanced
by the Hutks and the Rothschilds, underwritten in favorable conditions,
will allow for the obtaining of the sought-for results with dutiful labor. The
immigration attracted by the minimal price at which the adjudication of
wastelands in territories now deserted will occur will flow like a river of
men, like an Amazon whose waves are human heads mixed with the indigenous races, with the old landowners that today are vegetating, sunk in a
wretched obscurity, with savage tribes, whose native fierceness and courage
will be a potent element of vitality; will populate down to the last barren

desert, will work the fields, exploit the mines, bring new industries, all the human industries. To attract that civilized immigration, colossal steamers from government-sponsored companies with sums that allow the cost of passage to be reduced to a minimum, practically eliminated, will cross the Atlantic and go pick up the crews, eager for a new life, in the ports of old Europe, where hunger casts them, and in those of Japan and China, countries overflowing with a hungry population, and in the wide roadsteads of the Indian peninsula, wherefrom the poor native, the disinherited pariah, the Bengali of almost feminine gentleness, all will emigrate longing for a new fatherland, to avoid the sting of the English lash on their backs.

Monstrous factories where those unhappy souls find work and bread will then cloud with the thick plumes of their smokestacks the deep blue skies that shelter our tropical countries; on the plains will quiver the metallic cry of the locomotives that go down the rails, tying together the cities and little villages that sprung up where fifteen years earlier were rough-hewn wood stations and where, as I write, amidst the tangled virgin jungle the colossal silk-cotton ceiba trees stretch their secular branches, interwoven with vines that snake among them and offer shade to the boggy jungle floor, the nest of reptiles and of fevers; like an aerial network of telegraph and telephone wires shaken by an idea they will run through the air; they will cleave the dormant current of the great arteries of the slow, mighty navigable rivers, on whose banks will grow the leafy cacao plantations, fast white steamships that overcome distances and carry the shipments of fruit to the sea; once these are turned to gold in the world's markets, their gigantic forces will return to the earth that produced them to multiply in geometric progression.

Light! More light! . . . The last words of the sublime poet of Faust will be the motto of the nation that thus embarks on the path of progress. Public education, overseen with special diligence and propaganda spread through all possible outlets—from kindergarten where the little children learn to spell among the roses, to the great universities in which the eighty-year-old men of learning, their hair grayed over their instruments of observation, give themselves over to the most audacious speculations they seek from human thought—will raise up the nation to an intellectual and moral level higher than the most advanced nations of Europe. Once the country is free of the dreadful problems that undermine the old European societies and erupt in them in nihilistic screams and exploding bombs, it will look calmly toward the future.

The capital transformed with pickax blows and with millions—as Baron Haussman transformed Paris—will welcome the foreigner bedecked in all the flowers of its gardens and all the greenness of its parks, it will offer in spacious hotels the creature comforts that let one forge the illusion he has not left his happy home, and will unfold a scene before him of wide avenues and small green squares, the statues of its great men, the pride of its marble palaces, the melancholy grandeur of the old buildings from the colonial age, the splendor of theaters, circuses, and the dazzling display windows of the shops; libraries and bookstores that bring European and American books together on their shelves will offer noble pleasures to his intellect, and as a flower of that material progress he could consider developing an art, a science, a novel with a clearly national flavor, and a poetry that sings of the old native legends, the glorious epic of the wars of emancipation, the natural beauties and the glorious future of the regenerated land.

It seems absurd at first blush to establish a conservative dictatorship like that of García Moreno in Ecuador or that of Cabrera in Guatemala, and to think that under that dark regime, with its dungeon gloom and inquisitorial evils, the miracle of the transformation I dream of will come to pass. It is not, if one thinks about it. The country is tired of windy demagogic speeches and false freedoms written in the constitution and violated every day in practice, and yearns for a clearer political model. It prefers the shout of a dictator whom one knows will follow through on his threats to platonic promises of respect for the law that are broken the next day. The success of the enormous enterprise depends on the skill with which, as the situation returns to normal after the victory, the modifications are launched that slowly will change the situation of the defeated party, and allow it to return to the political arena schooled in the harsh lesson of defeat, educated after the first years of running a tight ship in which its leaders learn the futility of armed combat. They will dream then of deals that will let them scale down subordinate positions, or they will raise their voices over abuses committed, but their speeches will have no impact, since the people will already sense the advantages of the new regime. Industrial development will absorb part of the forces that hitherto produced deep disruptions as they caused unrest in politics. Concessions, gradually granted, will steadily earn the administration the favor of the youth, who are disillusioned with the old ideals and the support of capitalists from all camps, who want security and well-being. To every advancement made in the material order, to every right respected, the opposing ranks will reply with a movement that draws them closer and allows new concessions. In the long term, their spirits soothed and the old caudillos with their overblown ideas gone from the scene, political bosses whose presence stood in the way of returning the necessary elasticity to the movement of the social body, a moderate, hardly viable opinion, since they will have no abuses to denounce or protests to raise like flags of war, an almost perfect balance will be struck between the demands of the most advanced and the foresightful prudence of the most backward.

O, slow apprenticeship in civilization by a fledgling nation, upon rendering you in my brain into a plastic, almost grotesquely reduced image, you remind me of the crawling tiny tot who babbles formless syllables; of the baby-walkers that keep him from falling as he ventures his first steps, of the upright toddling he does between chair and table, of the room he crosses, supporting himself on the furniture, of the thirty-foot walks that surprise the smiling mother, until the muscle hardened by exercise and the stamina of his nerves lets him walk clinging to the wet-nurse's hand. . . . The little legs that barely hold him will later have tendons and muscles and formidable bones with which he will dig spurs into the frisky horse on which he will cross the plain, and with his little rosy-dimpled hands, whose little fingers strain to hold a favorite toy, he will raise the hoe to work the soil of the country and the sword to defend it! . . .

I have a mental picture of the transformation of the country in the protagonists who will accompany me in every age and in every scene of the undertaking, from entering the capital in blood and fire, bursting bombs all around and the discharges of rifle fire of the vanquishing army, dispatched by the most select of the conservative aristocracy, my cousins the Monteverdes. Athletic, brutal, and fascinating, they will serve as makeshift generals on the battlefields, owing to their audacity of savages. I can see the old commanders gone gray in their duty, General Castro and the two Valderramas, for instance, until the day when these venerable old men who stand in the way of my plan are resting peacefully in their tombs with the civil leaders of the defeated party, men who, shaking in their sexagenarian boots, witnessed the bloody victory on the day the dictatorship was installed. Those who then were insipid little kids, some becoming potbellied ministers of state and others skinny opposition-party journalists, will realize, in that far-off age my imagination reaches, that the problems that seemed insoluble to their fathers practically solved themselves once the stable government was founded and the idlers were given something to do, once the land was cultivated and tracks were laid that would facilitate the growth of the country.

Then, shorn of the power that will wind up in good hands, retreating to a country estate surrounded by gardens and palm forests, wherefrom the blue of the sea can be spied in the distance, the cupola of some chapel shaded by dark foliage rising not far off, having had my fill of humanity and contemplating my work from afar, I will reread favorite philosophers and poets, write singular stanzas shrouded in hazes of mysticism and populated with apocalyptic visions that, contrasting strangely with the verses full of lust and fire I wrought at age twenty, will set the poets of the future to prolific dreaming. In them I will pour, as if into a sacred vase, the supreme elixir that the manifold experiences of men and life have deposited in the depths of my dark burning soul.

There I will live out the happiest disenchanted existence of a dethroned Dom Pedro II who read Renan in evening meditation. My being stripped down of all human feeling and inaccessible to all emotion that does not derive from some truth, unknown to men and glimpsed by me in the calming of old age and with the serenity that dreams-come-true can bring, just as I lie dying, on my still-warm corpse the legend will begin to form that makes me seem a monstrous problem of psychological complexity to future generations.

As long as even the first part of this plan is not brought to fruition I will not rest easy. For it is large. . . . Larger was that of Bolívar upon swearing the freedom of a continent on the Montepincio hillside, that of Napoleon, a poor unknown military man of no consequence when, enclosed at age twenty in a room at Dôle, he dreamt of changing the face of Europe and of passing out thrones to his brothers as if they were a fistful of coins.

"I was mad when I wrote this, wasn't I, Sáenz?" Fernández exclaimed, interrupting the reading, speaking to the doctor and smiling at him amiably.

"It's the only time you've been in your right mind," Sáenz replied coolly.

"I thought I had imagined all things possible and impossible with respect to you, except this, that you would get such poppycock into your head! You, president of the republic, how degrading to you," Rovira blurted with an indignant air. "You, president of the republic . . ."

"Tell me, the sale of the mines, the business in New York, and the pearl fisheries, did they produce for you the results you expected, José?" asked Luis Cordovez, deep in thought.

"Better than I expected," replied the poet.

"So then what stopped you, pray tell, what stopped you from doing what you could have been able to do, which was great, enormous?" asked Cordovez with his usual enthusiasm.

"Truffled goose liver pâté, dry champagne, tepid coffee, green-eyed women, japonaiserie, and wild literary schemes," answered Oscar Sáenz peevishly from his armchair somewhere in the shadows.

"You're a better psychologist than physiologist," responded Fernández.

"And you're a loon, for though you conceived that eight years ago, you are reading it to us now, instead of having carried it out by degrees. . . ."

The tea served by Francisco, the old manservant who was at the poet's side since he saw him being born, interrupted the reading for a few moments.

"You've had three cups of tea, three cups!" Sáenz shouted at Fernández, unable to contain himself upon seeing him fill for the third time his fragile little porcelain cup and stir the aromatic liquid with his teaspoon.

"Fernández, go on," said Cordovez, Sáenz, and Pérez as one, while Juan Rovira was rising to take his leave, saying:

"I'm an ignoramus. . . . No one loves you as I do. I am enchanted when I hear the adepts recite your verses and call you a great poet: suddenly I fancy hearing you read something like tonight; I'm paying all the attention God granted me, and I give my word of honor I'm in the dark about the better part of what I'm hearing. . . . What does all that you've read us have to do with the name of the estate, with the gallery painting or with the watermark on the white-leather-bound books? . . . I'm an ignoramus. . . . Tomorrow I'll send you the parasites that arrived today from the coffee plantation."

"The odontoglossum?" asked Fernández, using the technical name of the orchid out of habit, acquired from speaking of botany with the Englishman who tended the hothouse.

Notes

1. The stanza from "Nocturno III" included here is Kelly Washbourne's translation as well. See *After-Dinner Conversation: The Diary of a Decadent*, translated and with an introduction by Kelly Washbourne (Austin: University of Texas Press, 2010), 16.

2. The reference is to Pedro Arias Dávila, a late fifteenth-century conquistador and founder of Panama City, reputed to have been unusual for his ruthlessness and cruelty toward native people.

Grandfather Arrives from Bremen

Pedro Gómez Valderrama

In a novel that combined fact and fiction, titled La otra raya del tigre *(The Tiger's Other Stripe),* Pedro Gómez Valderrama *set out to describe the life and times of a legendary figure in the history of Santander, German engineer and businessman George Ernst Heinrich von Lengerke (1827–82), more commonly known as Geo von Lengerke. At age twenty-five, he had witnessed the defeat of the Liberal revolutionaries in Europe and was one among many in a generation of Germans who emigrated to the Americas. Gómez Valderrama positions von Lengerke as a grandfather to a fictional narrator, which is one strategy among several that allow him to describe the German presence in Santander from multiple perspectives. In the excerpts below, for example, the narrator's voice switches from that of the novelist to Lengerke himself to a fictional local viewing Lengerke's entry into Zapatoca, the town where the historical Lengerke built a lucrative quinine-export business, involved himself in politics, and pursued a dream of progress that centered on road building.*

It's worth noting that Lengerke arrived in Colombia in 1852, forty-plus years before Silva's fictional José Fernández de Andrade (see entry in this section) sought his hideout in Wyhl. The similarities and differences between the two are striking and point to the way European arrivals and upper-class Colombians shared a nineteenth-century mind-set—one that Asunción Silva distanced himself from but that Gómez Valderrama sketches with brio. Lengerke is legendary not only because he achieved wealth but also because the stories that circulate about him line up with cultural patterns in Santander—he is said to have been a great womanizer, a drinker, a man that drove hard bargains, and one always ready to mount violent raids against the local indigenous population. When Indian arrows killed the road workers and muleteers he hired, Lengerke attacked the "savages" as a way of removing an obstacle to progress.[1] In the excerpt below, Gómez Valderrama gives readers Lengerke before arriving in Santander. We meet him on the Magdalena River, dependent on local oarsmen, or bogas, following Humboldt's route to Honda but with very little of Humboldt's romanticism. The Magdalena River has also been a stage for other twentieth-century works of fiction, such as Gabriel García Márquez's 1985 novel El amor en los tiempos del cólera *(Love in the Time of Cholera)*

Joseph Brown, *A Magdalena River Steamer, the "Union," on Her First Trip Upriver in 1839.* Watercolor and ink on paper, 17 × 27 cm. In Malcolm Deas, Efraín Sánchez, and Aída Martínez, *Tipos y costumbres de la Nueva Granada / Types and Customs of New Granada* (Bogotá: Fondo Cultural Cafetero, 1989), 61.

and Álvaro Mutis's 1993 novella series Empresas y tribulaciones de Maqroll el Gaviero *(*The Adventures and Misadventures of Maqroll*), both of which have been translated into English by Edith Grossman.*

With the bow pointing south, the steamer wound slowly upriver through the muddy waters of the Río Grande de la Magdalena. Its large wheels turned rhythmically, propelled by the long, flat mass of "The Deep." Left behind were the straw-colored houses of Barranquilla, the dead hours of Santa Marta, the long days of the journey from Europe. The dense, distinctly green jungle on the riverbanks emanated a foul, hot stillness, interrupted only by the sound of the boat's boilers as it made its way upriver and the smack of the paddles of the wheels as they hit the yellow water, causing flocks of colorful birds to disband and inimical monkeys to shriek. Amid the hot, still air, the vessel made its way through the low river waters, carefully negotiating the partially hidden sandy banks. On the bridge near the helm, leaning on the rail and observing the banks, Geo von Lengerke—exiled citizen, ex-soldier, ex-German, ex-revolutionary—consummated his escape and entered what would be either promised or cursed lands.

He had been the only passenger to disembark in Santa Marta from the

English vessel, the *Mala Real*—the Royal Mail—which continued forth on her grueling journey. The days he spent in this first port town initiated a certain tropical disconcertment, which had only grown as he traveled along the coast toward Barranquilla, between mulatto settlements inhabited by the triumphant but malarial freed slaves. Luck was on his side when he found Hans, a mulatto with blue eyes, the child of one of the last adventures of a compatriot, who was now dead. Hans stammered out a kind of rudimentary German, and he served as translator while they waited for the boat. He took it upon himself to teach Lengerke his shaky Spanish, and this, combined with what Lengerke had taught himself on the journey across the ocean, allowed him to make himself understood.

Lengerke could make out hidden fields of crops embedded in the jungle flora as the coastal landscape slowly transformed. The Dutchman in command of the boat approached him on deck and invited him to come out of the sun and meet the passengers. Lengerke followed him and quickly was met by the smiles of young ladies, named Santa Cruz or from Santa Cruz, who were returning from France where they had completed their studies. After introducing him to their parents, the young women, speaking in French, arranged for him to be left in the hands of R. P. Jerónimo Alameda, who was on his way back from Rome and spoke German so poorly that it made Lengerke's Spanish seem admirable in comparison; an Englishman named Jeremy K. Arbuthnot, murmured an introduction as new British consul in Honda, and took advantage of a moment in which the girls from Santa Cruz were not present to introduce him to Michele Nodier, a Frenchwoman, still young and bountiful in form and spirit. With her arrogance, and because of their fear of contagion, she seemed to displace the rest of the female contingent.

The rest of the passengers arrived gradually: a married couple from Barranquilla on their way to Bogotá for the first time; a congressional deputy who told Lengerke over and over about the election of General José Hilario López, talked about the horrors of socialism, and reminded him that he was a man of great political merit in his province. With the help of señorita Amalia Santa Cruz, who translated what he said into French, the man, who paused at brief intervals to wipe the sweat from his brow, pondered the potential of the region and encouraged the foreigner to consider the benefits of settling there, especially, he maintained, since at that very moment his party's ascension to power was imminent. The contrary, he proclaimed to Lengerke, would mean war. . . .

The English consul always kept a double-barreled shotgun by his side, which he cleaned meticulously with a dust cloth. When flocks of birds flew by he shot them down and watched them fall with a howl of satisfaction. And if he saw caimans sunning themselves on the shore, he retrieved from his cabin a formidable Remington rifle, and after taking careful aim, he would pull the trigger and then peer far off in the distance to see if he had hit his target. So far he had yet to hit one, but he derived voluptuous pleasure from this sport.

At night, when the temperature cooled down and it was less disagreeable, when the tedium subsided and the sun started to set, they moored the boat on the shore until the next day. The sailors sang songs on the bow. Nobody could sleep, some sat on the deck, others walked around until fatigue overcame them. Occasionally, the roar of a tiger put the passengers on alert. Other times they thought they heard the silky slither of the snakes. Nodier dreamed that the snakes invaded the boat, enveloped and embraced her more tightly than anyone had ever embraced her before.

Nobody knew what Nodier was doing there. The rumor was that she was an opera singer who had been abandoned in Santa Marta for being unfaithful to the Director of the company, and that for months she had been working as a you-know-what in order to travel to Bogotá in hopes of finding a better life. She had nightmares that woke everyone with her screams. One night, while asleep in his cabin, Lengerke had to cover her mouth, in order to prevent their scandalous behavior from confirming what everyone already suspected about her, though the wooden walls of the boat betrayed willingly all of the effusiveness of the Frenchwoman. Her obsequious treatment of Lengerke made everything disastrously self-evident, but there was something about her that evoked goodwill, a hint of affection that showed through, like her lightly faded beauty becoming wilted by the heat.

Within this desperate party, beleaguered by the mosquitos' relentless pursuit, the infernal scorching heat, and the monotonous drone of paddle-wheels, the Frenchwoman proved strangely more notable than the Santa Cruz girls; she had a grander spirit, carrying with her the cool of Parisian *guinguettes*, the narrow streets of Marseille, the poison of the Mediterranean, the blue waves of the Atlantic, the sun over the sea, the bastions of Havana and Cartagena, and old outfits from Kingston, Point-à-Pître, Barbados, pouring all the sea-blue treacle from the Caribbean into this smooth-running river in the middle of the jungle.

It was still the Río Grande de la Magdalena when they reached Tenerife. Wide like death, it was the river of catfish, turtles, *bogas*, and the caiman. On its banks, seminaked villagers emerged from straw huts and tried to reach the boat, whose plume of smoke floated upward into the desperately blue sky. Sometimes the sun set over the water, and one almost expected to hear the hissing sound of the fire being consumed by water, while night descended and the jungle silenced the sounds of day. The mysterious night sounds started soon thereafter. Lengerke watched and became drunk from the colors, the astonishing mutations of the river, and the landscape, which, had they all been captured in a painting, would have been reduced to mere smudges of green. They entered the kingdom of the catfish. The colors of the fish at sunrise were blue, pink, and violet, but when the sun set over the water, bobbing up and down three times, that is when the green kingdom of the Caiman began. . . .

(We are in the middle of the journey, the grandfather continues at the bow, scrutinizing the waters, and suddenly an abrupt lurch, a surge in engine power, jarring movements, and then complete stillness. We have run aground.) The experienced *bogas* examined the situation. The hull was buried in an enormous sandbank. They would need more water to float it out, or the arrival of another boat—the next one would leave in eight days—to help tug the stranded boat out of the sand. Meanwhile, all other attempts were in vain. The only option was to wait it out (the heat intensifies, the sun beats down, there is no breeze, the armies of mosquitoes are like black clouds, two, three caimans; the grandfather sees four). The only thing that appeared the evening of the second day was a flotilla of *champans* that agreed to bring provisions. If the water level rose, they could leave, but this dry season was especially hard . . .

. . . Lengerke was hesitant, but finally became so impatient that he decided to risk it. He rented two *champans*, which would take him on the six-day journey to Honda. As they were lowering his luggage and provisions, he saw the Frenchwoman, who also commanded that they lower her belongings. The German was about to turn her away, but he caught the reproachful glance of Father Alameda and his defiant spirit held him back. He ordered all of Nodier's luggage to be brought down, and after shaking hands and bidding farewell, they boarded the boat, while the deputy shook his head fatalistically. They began to go upriver; the first day took them on a harrowing journey through Angostura. The aggressive waters demanded more strength from the arms of the *bogas*. At his side, Michele became upset by the heat and lamented her decision to leave the steamer. Lengerke looked at her calmly and moved to the other side of the boat.

(Far away, one could trace the outline of the Andes, magically turned golden by the evening sun. At the bow, the grandfather points out the depths of the jungle. At four o'clock, the sandy banks look like gold. We have to moor here, we can't go on at night. They start to cook the turtle they caught the day before over the fire. A *boga* tells them that in the morning they will see the tracks of the turtles that go to bury their eggs on the nocturnal river beaches. Mosquitoes busy themselves in attacking the Europeans. Night falls, and they observe the way the *bogas* carve out holes on the banks and cover themselves with the white, moist sand. They tell them it's because of the heat and a way of avoiding the mosquitoes, soon they are buried in the sand. Nodier wants to be buried too, and so a few meters away, she and Lengerke take off their clothes and submerge their bodies in the cool sand, buried up to their necks, until the next day. During the night, while they sleep, they feel the tiger's silence, but then the incredible violet and rose-colored dawn breaks and unleashes the perfumed timber of the jungle night, evoking aromas of flowers and decomposition. Water rinses off the sand and once again they are back in the ovenlike interior of the *champan* for five, seven days, stunned by heat and desperation, until the downpours of Honda, where they assist in the maneuvers to avoid a shipwreck. Finally, in the evening it clears, and they see Spanish houses and, both inviting and forlorn, the city where everything in the river begins and ends. This is where their first brush with the god ends, and the grandfather looks at them both and thinks that neither of them knows that this contact [with the god] marks a person forever). . . .

As of yesterday there is a foreigner in Zapatoca. It's not just someone from another area of the country. It's a foreigner. He is not from South America, but from Europe. Since its founding one hundred years ago, the town had only seen Spaniards, until they were kicked out by the patriots. They were the only foreigners. After that, nobody has recollection of any other, much less from Europe. People remember when Gran Colombia came to an end. A Venezuelan who married one of José de Jesús's aunts stayed here. And for two days there was an Italian priest who arrived convinced that we were all pagans. He marveled with surprise and wonder that we had a church, but nonetheless tried to preach to us and baptize us until all of the townspeople armed themselves with sticks and sent him running out of town all the way to the road leading to Barichara.

The man speaks Spanish with a strong accent and he pronounces his words patiently and deliberately. He has a stranger with him, but the stranger is one of ours, and must be from El Socorro. They are riding a pair of marvelous mules, and they bring four mounted *peones* and twenty mules with big packs and also six more mule-drivers. I had to talk to them in order to show them where don Ruperto's inn was and to let them know that he would give them the best rooms. At this point, nobody knows what they want to do, but it looks like they might be looking to establish a hat business. They have asked a lot about tobacco growing and about the regions where there are cinchona trees. The foreigner says he will stay a couple days; he seems to like the climate, the town appears to be clean, and he is not afraid of don Marcial—that pen-pusher—although he knows that the number of people that pettifogger has left in poverty is high, and that he wields more power than the mayor and the priest, old don Pastor Roldán, who has said many times over the last couple of days that he is not going to allow a heretic to settle in a Christian town, where we are the pride of the region, and where the radicals are nowhere to be found because we left them in El Socorro. He also has said that they want to go to Chucurí, and they must certainly have a reason, because these people can smell money from leagues away. Although, it makes me laugh to think about what they are going to find on the other side of the Sierra de la Paz; there's nothing there except tigers, iguanas, and guinea pigs; and now, with everything in an uproar, since the death of my General Santander, and, according to those who live in El Socorro, with everything heated and dangerous, maybe these people are trying to take advantage of the situation, despite the fact that here everything is so poor. It's hard to tell. People have to go places like Pamplona, Vélez, or El Socorro.

But it would seem that he sweet-talked the priest, because they paid him a visit and they say that the foreigner made a generous donation toward the completion of the church and that he promised to continue giving. He's a strange man and when he walks down the street, everyone looks at him. With his shiny gaiters, his broad-brimmed hat, his Smith and Wesson hanging from his belt, his knee-length riding jacket, and his silk handkerchief tied in a knot at his neck, he looks like a devil and even more so with his red hair, an unruly moustache, a thick neck, and a sure, measured step. He must possess impressive strength, or at least he seems to, now that he's procured a bay horse that prances on the rocks and is the same color as his owner's hair. He knows how to ride this horse that nobody else in the town has. One might think that Europeans don't know how to ride, but this one sits firmly in his saddle while he travels through the town. Now he's going down the hill of the cemetery, and he'll arrive at Zanjón. Each time he sees a pretty woman he looks at her as though she were naked. The women change their path and duck into the first alley they can find. He's walking around the plaza, it's four o'clock in the afternoon and there is nobody around. Over and over he paces back and forth in front of don Felipe Serrano's house, which has remained empty since he died. The house is full of furniture that he had brought from Bogotá and still has the velvet curtains that don Felipe put up for a dance, an occasion that, in the end, don Marcial prohibited, because don Felipe had refused to pay him for the lawsuit that he had won. He should be arriving at around four o'clock to eat at the inn; they say he brings bottles of French wine the likes of which no one here has ever tasted, but also yesterday he was spotted at the *guaraperia* outside of Chucurí, casually drinking two or three *guarapo*[2] drinks served in hollowed out calabash gourds with his friend, and then he slipped away without anyone noticing. Since they arrived and began appearing around town with their elegant frock coats, the life of the town has changed, without anyone being able to identify how, exactly, because outsiders have come and gone before and town life has continued to go on as usual. But now, in any case, the girls are already wondering if the man is single, and if his friend is, too. There are without a doubt already women sighing as they stand by the windows. It's not up to me to think or worry about these things. Rather, I must try to carry out my job, because, if not, the judge will fire me. But I also think sometimes of how good it would be to have a horse and some mules like he does, to look at that big house with an eye to buy it, to travel through the town like a prince, and to be the first one with hair the same reddish color as a bay horse to pass through the streets of Zapatoca as if he had paid for those very streets with his own money. That man must have something because the people who talk to him say that he is an educated, chosen man, who has a European air to him, from Germany, where he must be from, the same country Mr. Humboldt is from, whom my grandfather met when he passed through Magdalena and wrote some books about Colombia, and about Barrancabermeja, and Carare Opón, in which he talks about tigers, caimans, navigation, volcanoes and the snowy peaks, and even about trees and plants native to these areas in much greater detail than we who live here ever could. The priest said the foreigner was a heretic; nonetheless, the man gave him gold coins for the church and when he walks by the atrium he takes off his hat, and yesterday they told me that they also saw him take off his hat at the door to the Chapel of Santa Bárbara, right next to the house I want to buy some day when I have money and return from studying in Bogotá, if my father can send me, even if I have to travel by foot. . . .

But the truth is, it seems like this man has arrived with the idea of staying. Who knows what will happen to our town, which will not be calm again until he leaves for good. He has a lot of energy, he can't be that old, thirty at the most. But that imperial air of his is not reassuring. *No señor,* I don't like him here. His presence is unsettling; he's like a ghost from another world, different from the rest of us with his moppy red hair, his gold watch chain, his shiny gaiters and his meticulously tailored frock coat. Although maybe if he stays he will give people the opportunity to get out of poverty. *Sí señor,* out of poverty, because we don't know what kinds of

things these men are capable of inventing in order to make money, discover
mines, and uncover secrets that we don't know because the Spaniards left
without revealing them to us. The civil wars have dried out our brains. As
radical as I am and as much as I resemble my father, I don't know what we
are going to do in order to make people adapt to the idea of giving opportunities to everyone. Everything they say about Europe: the factories, the
railroads, the steamers, palaces and silks, women who resemble the Virgin
of the Church. All of this, everything, is so far removed from us. Yes, I wish
that a foreigner such as this one could teach us the way to obtain this and
then be on his merry way, *sí señor*. . . .

His arrival, like the coming of Alfinger and Federmann,[3] raised similar
suspicions. As time passed, people's reservations diminished and they became used to their different customs, though always present was the figure
of the conquistador, with his gleaming helmet, his broadsword, and his ancient shield, as he wandered through the wooded forest, crossing the rivers
with a despotic gesture from behind his armor. . . .

The Germans came. First Rafael Lorent, Lengerke's cousin, then Strauch,
Nortenios, Clausen, Goelkel, Hansen, and Hederich: a boisterous caravan
of peaceful conquistadors. The houses they built were different, and they
decorated them with nudes. They brought the latest fabrics from Europe
and made them into curtains, quilts, and luxurious sheets; they brought
porcelain, chests, and crystal. At first it seemed absurd to everyone that they
had to open a bottle of brandy in order to talk business, but it later became
the golden rule for merchants at the Club. On the outskirts there was a big
house, the *quinta* Dohsen, whose owner lived alone. There he established
a place of pleasure or a game preserve, where, according to rumors, late
at night and accompanied by lavish music, they practiced magical rites in
which naked women were invited to join the contented company of the
Germans. In those gatherings, it was known that they drank the imported
liqueurs and that "everyone made love to everyone," according to what was
said by devout followers in the church's atrium, who were both shocked and
possessed by the scandal.

The Germans continued arriving in the ongoing caravan. . . . They made
their way to Santander. Some were drawn there because of Lengerke, others
because of friends or relatives. In ten years the cavalcade filled the provinces
of de Soto and El Socorro with silent blond men who procreated tirelessly,
sowing their blue eyes and golden manes among the population. The Germans were in Santander like the drops of water that fall through a stone
filter. And ever more frequently, through relationships, children, and land,

they adhered themselves to the life of the region. Lengerke contemplated serenely the realization of a dream, the ongoing caravan, the cavalcade that was coming from Bremen.

Translated by Brenda Werth

Notes

1. See Álvaro Pablo Ortiz, *Geo von Lengerke: Constructor de Caminos* (Bucaramanga: Universidad Industrial de Santander, 2008), 132–33.
2. *Guarapo* in Santander refers to lightly fermented sugarcane juice; it is characteristically drunk in *totumas*, or the dried shells of calabash gourds.
3. Ambrosio Alfinger and Nicolás de Federmann were sixteenth-century German conquistadors who arrived to what is now Colombia and Venezuela in the service of the Spanish Crown; both led expeditions in search of gold.

We Were Called "Turks"

Elías Saer Kayata

Syrians and Lebanese together make up the most numerous group of immigrants to Colombia; their total number amounts to somewhere near ten thousand, with their peak migration years being 1880–1930. Those who arrived might as easily have ended up in Argentina, Brazil, or the United States—if they explicitly chose a less well-known destination such as Colombia (or Mexico, or Bolivia, or Peru, or Chile), it was generally only because they happened to have family there already. In an interview with the historian Eduardo Posada-Carbó, Elías Saer Kayata describes his own story onto the larger story of this community—one made familiar to many by the fame of Colombian singer Shakira Isabel Mebarak Ripoll, whose paternal grandparents emigrated to Barranquilla from Lebanon via New York City.

I was born in Damascus, capital of Syria, one of the most ancient cities in the world, in the first year of the century (1900), in the month of July. . . . From the end of the last century to the first years of the present, many people had emigrated to America, and several of them had returned. There were many stories about fabulous opportunities. At that time we only knew of three countries one could emigrate to: United States, Brazil, and Argentina. No one knew of the existence of other countries such as Colombia. But several of our relatives had already migrated there, and upon their return they talked about its appeal. For us, emigrating to the American continent meant finding abundance, riches, great opportunities—in other words, an earthly paradise. Many said, figuratively, that the roads of America were paved with gold. Nonetheless, it was still a matter of concern to set off on this exciting and attractive adventure. Encouraged by the enthusiasm of our relatives and friends who had emigrated before us, we trusted that our family in Colombia would help us get settled, and a small group of us decided to emigrate to Colombia in 1924. . . .

We were searching for a path toward a new life, new opportunities. And Colombia was our hope.

Those of us who arrived to Colombia—and the same thing must have happened in other countries—were called "Turks" instead of Arabs. There was a reason for this. Before the Turkish control [of Ottoman Syria] ended in 1920, all passports were issued by the Turkish authorities. Between 1920 and 1944, these were issued by the Syrian government under the French Mandate [for Syria and Lebanon]. It has been difficult to end this custom of referring to us as "Turks," and it continues to the present. . . .

After requesting an exit permit from the French and making arrangements with French ship companies, we traveled from . . . the port of Beirut in June 1924. I only carried with me a small suitcase with the most basic necessities. We set sail, casting nostalgic glances to the land we left behind, but with the exuberant excitement of hopeful youth searching for new horizons. There were many immigrants: Palestinian, Lebanese, and Syrian. Some of us had a set destination . . . but for many their final destination was unknown. They would emigrate not knowing what country they would travel to, which would only be assigned in France. After sailing for a week in the Mediterranean Sea, we arrived to Marseille. We spent four days at this port and then traveled by train to St. Nazareth, where we set sail again on a ship waving a French flag toward Colombia, on a trip that would last twenty-five days.

The ship, which should have left us in Cartagena, dropped us off in Puerto Colombia [department of Atlántico]. The port of Barranquilla had not yet been built. My cousins, Miguel and Abraham Saber, my friends José Bechara and Nicolás Char, and myself arrived [in Colombia] on August 1, 1924.

I remember that two things made an impression: the suffocating heat and the sandy, unpaved roads. In Barranquilla we immigrants could come in without a problem. It was fortunate that we had arrived first to this city. After going through customs, I left my travel companions and headed toward the city center to find a way to travel to Cartagena. As I did not speak the language, I requested help from a policeman who saw I was a newly arrived Arab and took me to the store of señor Elías Muvdi. Elías drove all of us to the Hotel Victory, which belonged to an Arab with the last name Chamie, were we rested and slept until the next day. We sent a telegram to the Chagüi family, in Cartagena, informing them of our arrival, and my relative, Mr. Bechara Saer, traveled to meet us in Calamar [a town in the department of Bolívar located on the Magdalena River]. We traveled from Barranquilla up the Magdalena River by boat, until we arrived at Calamar, six hours later. From there we took a train that left us in Cartagena at five o'clock in the afternoon. That train, which would continue working for twenty more years, ended its trip in the neighborhood of La Matuna, in front of the Torre del Reloj [Cartagena's city clock tower, a representative landmark of the city].

We stayed in Cartagena for two days. Later, we traveled by sea to the Sinú River, and from there we went to the town of Cereté [in the department of Córdoba]. We stayed there at an aunt's house, who received us warmly. Three months later, they helped us open a store for us in Ciénaga de Oro [Córdoba], and we began working on our own. A year later, in 1925, I received a surprise visit from my brother, Teófilo. The political situation of Damascus had gotten worse because of French presence. There were riots and protests against the foreign regime imposed on the Arabs. Teófilo had decided to emigrate, and here he was. This was a cause of great joy for me. But I did not stop thinking of our mother, Mariam, who little by little had seen her children travel to other continents, distant both in geography and in time. Four years before me, in 1920, my brother Michel, had traveled with his uncle Abdallah to New York when he was only sixteen years old. Now three of her sons had already left her.

In Colombia, Teófilo and I decided to further improve our economic circumstances, and we purchased a store in Cartagena, located in the public market of Getsemaní, which no longer exists today. At the same time, the economic situation in the United States had become unbearable. The country was in the midst of the 1929 Depression and its recovery would take more than ten years. Michel decided to come to Colombia, heeding our advice. In 1931, all three brothers were living in Cartagena. We founded Saer Brothers, which lasted until 1954. . . .

I have lived 62 of my 85 years in Cartagena. During all this time, I have only traveled back to my home country three times. . . . Today, in the autumn of my years, I do not regret having come to Colombia, which I love like my own country. In Colombia there are still frontiers to be explored, and I have reached complete happiness, with my children, my grandchildren, and all who surround me. And I trust with the hope and faith in God that understanding will grow between the Arabs who arrived here and the Colombians who graciously took us in, bringing together our two nations and our two peoples.

Translated by Ana María Gómez López

Two Presidents' Views: "I Took the Isthmus" and "I Was Dispossessed, Insulted, and Dishonored to No End"

Theodore Roosevelt and Marco Fidel Suárez

At the turn of the twentieth century, Colombia remained strikingly provincial, yet many people, even in rural areas, had come into contact with foreigners, and wealthy Colombians sometimes traveled abroad. Educated people understood that North Americans and Europeans were engaged in a set of struggles for world power, for example, and they were often divided about how best to navigate the global political whirlwind and reap benefits from it. In 1903, when Theodore Roosevelt instigated and openly supported a rebellion in Panama, many Panameños embraced the United States' tutelage. Some in the country's interior conspired with them. With Panama separated from Colombia, Roosevelt could more effectively ensure the defeat of French interests and guarantee absolute United States control over the planned interoceanic canal. As guarantor for Panama's rebel government, Washington set about negotiating a diplomatic agreement with the humiliated Colombian government. Quickly, it became clear that the North Americans were not limiting their negotiations to the Panama question. Big Oil was also at the table, and by the 1920s Colombia's political elite was divided over how to handle the intertwined diplomatic questions of sovereignty, Panama, and oil. Some politicians favored the North Americans, others the British. Some lined up with the big New York banks when these squared off against the petroleum companies after the 1929 crash; others supported oil interests. There were deep splits, too, over how to manage government revenues and what to do about the national debt, with the biggest argument being about how to negotiate an indemnity payment for Panama and how to spend that payment if and when the US Congress disbursed the funds. These disagreements are part of the context for the following excerpts: Roosevelt's erasure of Colombia in his phrase "I took the Isthmus," and President Marco Fidel Suárez's exasperated message, sent in code to his representative in Washington, who he hoped would value national honor more than indemnity payments. Needless to say, the payments were accepted. They flowed into the Colombian treasury in 1923–26.

In Europe I found that the two feats performed by Americans in the last decade which had really made a deep impression were the digging of the Panama Canal and the sending of the battleship fleet around the world. The Panama Canal I naturally take special interest in, because I started it. If I had acted strictly according to precedent, I should have turned the whole matter over to Congress; in which case, Congress would be ably debating it at this moment, and the canal would be fifty years in the future. Fortunately the crisis came at a period when I could act unhampered. Accordingly I took the Isthmus, started the canal, and then left Congress—not to debate the canal, but to debate me. And in portions of the public press the debate still goes on as to whether or not I acted properly in taking the canal. But while the debate goes on the canal does too; and they are welcome to debate me as long as they wish, provided that we can go on with the canal.

Now, I believe that I am telling the exact truth, that am speaking with scientific accuracy, when I say that the canal is the greatest feat of the kind by all odds that has ever been attempted by civilized mankind, and that our engineers and doctors under Colonel Goethals and Dr. Gorgas, have done their work there better than any corresponding men of any country have ever done any similar work before.

In the field of practical achievement, in statecraft, and in such material work as that of the Panama Canal, America has done its full part. It has done more than its full part. I am proud of this. If we could only have one species of achievement to our credit I believe it is better to have that species of achievement than the other. I have more sympathy for the Roman, the man of extraordinary administrative force, the man who could conquer and mold the world, the city-builder, the road-maker—I have more sympathy for him than I have for the more cultivated and less virile Greek; and I would rather see us produce statesmen of the type of Washington and Lincoln and master-builders like those who are building the Panama Canal than see us produce men of letters and men of art. But the two types of production ought not to be mutually exclusive. There is ample room for both, and no civilization is in any true sense complete that only produces one. . . .

And so here our work is worthless unless it stands comparison with the best kind of work that can be produced anywhere. We realize this very well in the field of applied science. In digging the Panama Canal, one reason we have been able to succeed has been that we had developed very much more efficient instruments—derricks, steam-shovels and the like—than our

HARPER'S WEEKLY

JOURNAL OF CIVILIZATION

Vol. XLVII.   New York, Saturday, November 21, 1903   No. 2448

Copyright, 1903, by HARPER & BROTHERS. All rights reserved

HELD UP THE WRONG MAN

"Held up the wrong man." Depicted here as strong and authoritative, Theodore Roosevelt confronts a barefoot, bewhiskered Colombia to maintain his control over the Panama Canal and the dollars used to pay for its construction. Turn-of-the-century Latin Americans routinely found themselves represented in demeaning ways in the US press. *Harper's Weekly*, New York, 1903, http://www.harpweek.com/Images/Source Images/CartoonOfTheDay/November/112103m.jpg. Used by permission of HarpWeek.

French predecessors had developed; we had developed the best machinery; we had developed the best kind of contractor, who could give us the best machinery; we had developed the kind of engineering and medical men who could grapple with the conditions better than any other men. It would not have helped us at all at Panama if we had failed and then had said that we had done "pretty well, considering we were a new country." In exactly similar fashion, our work in literature, art, and pure science must stand on its own merits, and must be the fruit of conscientious endeavor, and the very best of its kind.

February 28, 1920
Buga
Colombia
Washington
This cablegram must be deciphered by D. Urueta
LeColombia [Colombian Legation]
Washington

Fearing that each day diminishes Treaty approval possibilities, I think that perhaps Colombia will benefit by negotiating directly with Panama regarding limits, debt, and relations. This would allow important needs to be satisfied, although we would forget the 25 million, which are equivalent to far less today than in another time. I believe the boundary question will be difficult, given the United States' protectorate of Panama, and the tendencies Panamanians have to come to the Atrato. I also find it difficult to believe that the United States will allow the Panamanians to act independently. But if we succeed in having the Panamanians recognize limits, stipulations regarding the debt, and all the rest, it will not matter if we leave aside questions of money. Indeed, national honor will come out better. Colombia could then say: I was dispossessed, insulted, and dishonored to no end, and I do not want to continue in false hopes. This conduct, absolutely necessary, would constitute a fitting response and an unspoken sanction against one of the greatest injustices inflicted on a weak nation by an arrogant and unjust nation. Think about it, as I trust it to you only, only, only.

Marco Fidel Suárez

Translated by Ana María Gómez López and Ann Farnsworth-Alvear

Facing the Yankee Enemy

José María Vargas Vila

José María Vargas Vila (1860–1933) wrote more than one hundred books, including several huge best sellers. Throughout the Spanish-speaking world, readers thrilled to his erotic novels, flooded with tragic sentimentalism. Thousands of artisans, wage earners, university students, aspiring politicians, and women who dared to flout tradition bought his titles, especially Aura o las violetas *(1887) and* Ibis *(1900), which left a trail of suicides. Brisk sales allowed Vargas Vila to live opulently in New York, Paris, and Barcelona, but his fashionable life abroad had begun as an exile imposed by the Conservative government in Bogotá (1886–1930). Over a long life he befriended many Latin American anti-imperialists, notably Rubén Darío and José Martí, and Vargas Vila may have seen in them something of the Nietzschean ideal of manly strength romanticized in his novels.*

The 1902 essay excerpted below, "Ante los bárbaros. El Yanki: He ahí el enemigo" ("Facing the Barbarians. The Yankee: Behold Our Enemy") led to a second exile for Vargas Vila, who left New York for Europe (and republished the essay in Paris and Barcelona, in expanded versions). With Martí, who spoke of the United States as "the restless and brutal North that despises us," and Darío, whose poem "To Roosevelt" decried the "future invader," Vargas Vila sought a readership passionate about finding an identity for "tropical" America. Vargas Vila's sentiments are reflected in a 1926 silent film, Garras de oro *(translated as* The Dawn of Justice*), by Alfonso Martínez Velasco (working under the pseudonym P. P. Jambrina), which offered a scathing critique of Roosevelt's takeover of Panamá (see part VII).*

Among these peoples of America, who may not exist tomorrow, remaining merely as a vague nomenclature in the chronology of History, there is a degree of stupefying ignorance, which helps to explain, though not to justify, their abominable indolence toward the danger than surrounds them. . . . .

. . .

is it the ferment of the aboriginal race, lifeless and fatalistic, which submerges them into the unconscious sleep of Eternity, which comes so close to real death? . . . .

I myself do not know what takes place in the uncultured hearts of those jungles of men, upon whom words no longer bear power, and nothing, not even the memory of Death can awaken them to Life;

and yet, the only being there, the only great being there, is Death itself;

one could almost say it is the only thing alive.

all greatness has hidden itself in the Past. . . . .

only the dead are alive. . . . .

only they speak, making sounds that the living do not hear, but which in their eloquence eclipse the insignificant shrieks sent out from from the grandstands of Venality in the auction of the peoples. . . . .

America is only protected by the tombs of its heroes. . . . .

And oh how they wander, for their tombs are not unbound. . . . .

their tombs are hostages to the Conquest. . . . .

the tomb of Bolívar, lies in soil enslaved by the Yankees, sold, miserably sold by a savage cacique, by an illiterate Praetor, who cannot even spell out the name of his Crime;

the tomb of Santander, "Man of Laws," lies among lawless men, in a nation maimed by the Yankee; his tombstone cleaved by the sword of Treason, crowned in laurels;

the tomb of Morazán, lies in a country of entrenched Treason, which the Guatemalan hyena covers with its shadow, fetid and feral. . . . .

it is the Yankees' range; the tombs of Hidalgo and Morelos stand tall, "the tomb of eagles that have not yet been profaned. . . . .

groups of heroes, stand guard around them. . . . .

and the Yankee retreats, faced with tombs that are unconquerable. . . . .

that is a people [Mexico] that still remembers its Heroes, that still remembers their magnificent deeds, of Independence and Liberty; other peoples, in the epitome of their Degradation, do not want to defend their liberty but rather are satisfied to sell it;

will the hero come to us from Mexico, full of ideals and truth? A hero who bearing the ray of Damascus will set fire to the virginal foliage of our forests, and, in the light of that flame, a flame less bright than his own, descend upon our yoked and displaced peoples, and, like Bolívar, harness his conquering horse to the columns of even the farthest-flung Capitals of América, profaned by the yankee, or by the praetors that rule in his name?

will the Mexican people be our Liberators? . . . .

let me dream, in the shadow of my defeated flags. . . . .

[. . .]

the Orient was the land chosen by the pillaging race to begin their conquests over the weak and pillaged race, and the Islands of the Philippines were their first victim;

[...]

hordes of Barbarians from the North, ravaged, murdered, plundered the homes of an entire people which succumbed beneath the sheer numbers of the white volunteers and the semi-barbarous blacks, the drunken rabble of the *Model Republic.* . . . .

the silence of horror closed upon the burning Archipelago; a people drunken with greed, as if they had seen opened before them the cask that drove the centaurs mad, out-did the cruelty of the Tartars and the horror of the Syrian conquests; in the name of Civilization they sowed devastation and death, like the Goths of the Black Sea, determined to have only solitude as witness to their victory. . . . .

and Cuba?

it is still in the throes of being clutched in the eagles' talons!

no people remains there, only a shadow;

when a people loses their Independence, a void opens on the map;

with the horrific fascination of the abyss, our eyes are drawn to that somber opening, where the Great Antilles has been submerged.

Cuba is like a broken glass, thrown by the Prophet onto the path of the peoples of America;

it is an iron nail through our bowels;

its wounds are our wounds, its pain is our pain, and its descent will mark the beginning of our own disappearance;

Cuba cannot finish either its birth or its death, if all of us do not also feel alive through its life or perish in its death;

a neighboring people cannot ignore the funerals of a nationality, disappeared amid celebrations of force;

Oh Poland of the Tropics! Oh Martí!

The inanity of a dream of generosity! . . . .

[...]

Are we latinos, we americans of the South?

[...]

are we barbarians? no;

are we civilized? no;

we are as far from civilization as from barbarism;

we are peoples in gestation;

[...]

are we latinos?

no, not in the ethnic sense of the word;

we belong not to the Latin *race*, but to Latin *nations*;

race entails a unity of physical and ethnological traits, an anthropological homogeneity; while to be Latin or Latinized nations only suggests that we assimilated Latin temperament and culture, given by the predisposition of an ancestral seed;

it is true that we speak the language of the conquerors, but *language is not a feature of a race, but of a nationality*;

we lack the organic cohesion to be a purely Latin race, and we cannot become a Latin race, given the diversity of races that has formed us;

within the assembly of Europe's Latin nations, there is *one* race: all are white;

can we say the same about ourselves? no;

in America, there are white people, Indian people, black people, but there is not a sole white race, Indian race, or black race;

there is only race—our powerful tropical race—composed of all the human varieties that have led to its formation.

this is the reason for our amazing, yet hidden, organic potential for the future;

this is the reason why the stigmas of death and decadence which plague the Latin race do not concern us; such stigmas concern all the great races when they have reached culmination.

a race does not begin to decay until it has reached the apogee of civilization;

we have not yet reached that zenith;

we are, and will remain, barbarians;

the subtleties of false civilization have not finished our ethnic strength, with the archaism of our barbarity, almost as ancient as the World itself;

our health, the strength of our virgin peoples, is the assurance of our individuality;

a people that is born civilized is ill-born.

our strength is in having been born barbarians;

that which is weak and diseased in us comes from the refined races that gave us their blood;

our defects and our virtues, our weaknesses and our strengths, are the fruit of the mixture of our ethnicities with foreign infiltrations, and makes us stand alone as a mixed and mutable group, indescribable and limitless;

we are yellow and we are Berbers, Africans and Celts; we are connected to the Japanese and the Hottentots, the Iberians and the Iberian Celts, the

Chibchas [Muiscas] and the Aztecs; we carry the atavism from all of their religions, from all of their civilizations, from all of their barbarities;
  our history is there to be cried out. . . . .

Translated by Ana María Gómez López and Ann Farnsworth-Alvear

Note

In this selection, suspension points are in the original. Our own ellipses points, to show abridgment, are in square brackets. Vargas Vila's unusual punctuation and use of lower-case are also preserved in the translation.

Bogotá's Art Scene in 1957: "There Is No Room for Any of the Old Servilism"

Marta Traba

In 1983, President Belisario Betancur granted Colombian citizenship to Argentine-born Marta Traba as well as to her second husband, Uruguayan writer and literary critic Ángel Rama. A few months later, Traba, Rama, and several other Latin American intellectuals died in Spain in an airplane crash while traveling to Bogotá for a conference. She was deeply mourned in her adopted country.

The text below was prepared for an international audience in 1959, after Traba had been in Colombia five years. It communicates some of the intensity of her public speaking engagements and her television broadcasts, offering a taste of her passion for educating a broad public not only about Colombian art but also about the possibility of a political vision that would reject narrow nationalisms. Describing Traba's arrival to 1950s Bogotá, the Mexican intellectual Elena Poniatowska writes:

> *One night, while passing through Italy, president Eduardo Santos proposed to Alberto [Alberto Zalamea, Traba's first husband] to return to Colombia to work at the daily El Tiempo. He consults with Marta, and both accept. This began one of the most definitive stages in Marta's life. In Colombia, she comes into contact with an unknown reality: that of poverty in a continent where everything's still left to do. And Marta does. She enters television, organizes roundtables, talks, and conferences, and becomes a professor of art history at the Universidad de América, Universidad de los Andes, and the National University of Colombia, all in Bogotá. She is the founding director of the Museum of Modern Art of Bogotá (MAMBO), where she promoted young painters, undertook expositions inconceivable until then, and strove to remove art from the closed circle of the elite, so that the bourgeoisie would take down their seascapes, tourist scenes, and sunsets to hang a silkscreen by Myrna Báez, a drawing by Amelia Peláez.[1]*

Báez was a Puerto Rican artist, Peláez Cuban. Traba's sense of mission was fiercely pan-American and internationalist. It was also didactic, as Poniatowska's

description suggests. She hosted several weekly art education television shows, rang-
ing from European art history and Latin American avant-gardes to interviews with
Colombian artists, connecting Colombians to global art trends until 1966, when she
was expelled by President Carlos Lleras Restrepo for criticizing the military's re-
sponse to student protests at the National University.

    Several of the artists Traba mentions here went on to long careers, including
Fernando Botero (see images in part V), Enrique Grau, Alejandro Obregón, Eduardo
Ramírez Villamizar. Some of Colombia's best-known artists in the present, includ-
ing Doris Salcedo, are too young to have been a part of Traba's world. Nevertheless,
Traba shaped the art world Salcedo and others came to inhabit. In 2007, Salcedo
presented Shibboleth, *an installation in London's Tate Modern where the art-*
ist created an open crack running along the floor of the museum—a commentary
on racism, national boundaries, and the exclusion of marginalized communities.
Salcedo and other twenty-first-century Colombian artists are following in Traba's
footsteps in ways that echo the Argentine's call to denounce artists' long "subservi-
ence to themes imposed first by the Colony, later by the Republic, and finally by the
patria—the last a concept that is somewhat vague, but for that very reason all the
more sinister."

Painting is an art without a past in Colombia. During the Colony it was
nourished by trifling loans from Spain, and in the first century of the Republic it played the role of poor relation to French art. In colonial days painting was at the service of the Church and of the authorities, and its product
was restricted to a chronicling of the Indies; then in the nineteenth century,
the artists discovered the countryside and the moneyed middle class. The
nation started to produce genre painting in which attention was diverted
from Virgins to Indies, without producing the slightest disturbance in the
palette nor the least change in the documentary nature of the painting; the
middle class provided the subjects for portraits, with sufficient vanity to
demand not merely a good "likeness" but also a flattering presentation of
the model. . . .

Colombia adjusted to the common denominator of Latin America, the
product of artificial societies without the backing of a civilization in which
they could be properly minted. It is useless to seek an imaginary continuity between the pre-Columbian art, exterminated by the conquest, and the
European people or mixed bloods who entrenched themselves on the new
continent, not with any intention of civilizing it, but with the firm plan of
taming, evangelizing and exploiting it. The taming took the form of virtual slavery; the evangelism preached a religious spirit in search of catechu-
mens; the exploitation guaranteed the economic survival of the conquerors.

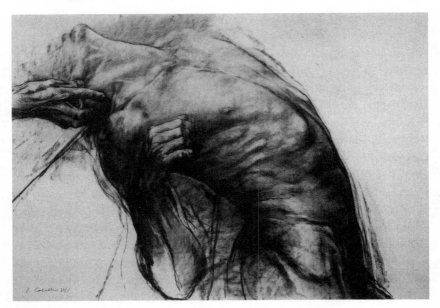

Luis Caballero, charcoal on paper, 70 × 100 cm, 1983. Son of Eduardo Caballero Calderón (see part III), Luis Caballero described his artistic work as autobiographical and lived as an openly gay man. He spent most of his adult life in Paris. His brother is renowned caricaturist and writer Antonio Caballero. Courtesy of Beatriz Caballero.

In such a program the forms of culture were nowhere to be found, nor was there provision for them in the work program adapted by the Republic. Therefore the painters were but able artisans who served God, the founding families and an incipient folklore.

. . . It is very difficult, if not impossible, to speak of "pictorial values" before the time of Alejandro Obregón. At present this man, a young forty years of age, is the most outstanding figure in Colombian painting, although others are catching up with him so impetuously that it is not impossible to foresee him soon obliged to share the crown which until now has been indisputably solely his. His painting started with the flaming, dizzy and chaotic exploitation of color, and ended in an individualistic organization of his canvas that restrained his coloristic excesses; but even then color is the orchestra conductor that compels all the other instruments to vibrate in unison. . . .

Every day it seems more necessary to convert the trio [of Obregón, Ramírez Villamizar, and Grau] into a quartet in order to make room for Fernando Botero. His work places before the art critic a maximum of tricks, violations and surprises. Up to the present his has been the performance of a magician, and we have never known what he would pull next out of his hat. . . .

We had begun to mistrust Botero's versatility, when the works exhibited at the Pan American Union in Washington in 1957, gave proof of a truly important change. A pictorial order, born neither of facile imitation nor of his fearsome passing enthusiasms, but arising from deeper convictions regarding the true values of painting, is to be seen in these works. A style which is truly his had been crystallizing during the past year or more and is making its appearance with strong originality. This had its first timid beginnings at the Tenth Salon of Plastic Arts of 1957 in Bogotá, where he exhibited a much-discussed and controversial *Festín de Baltasar* (*Belshazzar's Feast*), in which a monumental rounded form literally melts into a background and accessories painted with all the happy and unsubstantial floweriness of Marc Chagall.

Perhaps for the first time Botero meditated on how to consolidate an idea that he found seductive and original: the reduction of forms into masses that would express, not because of their size, but because of their very conception, a monumental idea. And so he succeeded in achieving unitary conceptions of heavy, rounded forms that are bound to plane or special backgrounds as heavy as they. But Botero's present art is not merely a matter of converting everyday forms into blocks; his color has lost the specious freedom of the Feast of Belshazzar and now accepts all the rules of the game, accompanying the forms with surprising seriousness and vigor. The imposition of the new forms of Botero (an imposition which takes place on the viewer almost against his will, because his first reaction is to reject such terribly enlarged coffee pots and such monstrous apples) is the test of his talent and also of his honesty. . . .

Unfortunately, in an exceedingly limited cultural environment such as that of Colombia, the lack of museums or of foreign art exhibitions, and the coercive insistence of the critics on the merits of the principal artists, concentrates attention on the influence of the latter to the neglect of other, international values, which would be a fairer and more desirable course.

The history of Colombian art is being written in these years, and rapidly, to make up for lost time. In spite of evident borrowing, Colombian art cannot be said to be continuing along the lines of the copyist of Colonial times, because—and I repeat—it has not imported merely techniques, but also the fundamentals wherewith to formulate its own, ambitious, personal plastic principles. . . . Colombia still is passing through a period of felicitous apprenticeship, in which there is no room for any of the old servilism. The results of this apprenticeship have not been delayed. Four painters and a sculptor [Édgar Negret] who can hold their own brilliantly in international circles is a very good record for a country just emerging from the typically republican stage of self-praise and the familiar panegyric, to seek cultural comparisons on a world level—a far less flattering and easy course, but the only valid one in our time.

Note

1. Elena Poniatowska, "Marta Traba o el salto al vacio," in *En cualquier lugar*, edited by Marta Traba (Madrid: Siglo XXI Editores, 1984), 12–13. Translation by the editors.

1969: The GAO Evaluates Money Spent in Colombia

US Senate Committee on Foreign Relations

Facing political transformation in Cuba, John F. Kennedy argued for drastic changes in US Latin America policy. Once elected, he positioned himself behind the view that Latin American societies were held back by what Kennedy's advisers called "semi-feudal regimes," which skewed land tenure and political processes in the region. The thinking was that two possibilities existed for change in Latin America: a reformist drive toward a "middle-class revolution," on the one hand, or a revolution of workers and peasants with communist or Peronist leadership, on the other. The Alliance for Progress (or Alianza para el Progreso) was an effort to guarantee the former. After the humiliating defeat of US-supported Cuban exiles at the Bay of Pigs in April 1961, Kennedy and his team accelerated their diplomatic efforts. Only a few months later, in August, when they presented the Alliance for Progress plan at the OAS meeting in Punta del Este, Uruguay, the only negative vote was from Che Guevara, Cuba's delegate. The plan was ambitious, calling for $20,000 million in aid over ten years, although perhaps only $500 million was disbursed. At Punta del Este, the Kennedy administration announced that the United States was in favor of economic reform, social change, the alleviation of poverty, and increased security in the region. It was an early statement of what became the binomial prodemocracy and counterinsurgency.

Colombia presented an almost perfect showcase, in the thinking of Alianza supporters, because it was one of only "a handful of nations which possess the preconditions for rapid economic and social advance and which are effectively using their own resources," as Kennedy's assistant Chester Bowles phrased it. The jargon of "preconditions" owed to the thinking of Walt W. Rostow, whose famous book The Stages of Economic Growth: A Non-communist Manifesto *(1960) articulated the notion that growth included a "take-off" period in which social conflict could easily become dangerous. Given that the Soviet Union had an expansionist strategy, US aid should target countries in their vulnerable "take-off" moment. With this as its premise, the Alianza emphasized the possibility of political modernization* to support a civil society with neighborhood associations, student organizations, and labor unions—all mobilized in favor of anticommunism. Alongside, the United States would push military aid for counterinsurgency.

How effective was the Alliance for Progress in Colombia? In an attempt to answer that question, congressional staffers and economists at the US General Accounting Office (GAO) prepared an unusually clear-eyed report, published in 1969. Using the language of economists but with a focus on the explicitly reformist goals of the Alianza, they signaled a gap between objectives and results, and they traced the various detours by which actions taken diverged from goals stated. Usefully, the report also helps answer another question: "Why was Colombia such a showplace for the Alianza?" In only two generations, Colombian politicians had somehow moved—in Washington's estimation—from being a useless bunch—"a corrupt pithecoid community" of "homicidal corruptionists," as Theodore Roosevelt had put it—to being an enlightened elite ready to act as a model for the region, which was what Kennedy found on his high-profile 1961 trip to Bogotá. Part of what lay behind this change in perception was the international prestige of Alberto Lleras (whom the report contrasts with Guillermo León Valencia, his successor in the presidency). Like Venezuela's Rómulo Betancourt, Lleras closed ranks with Kennedy against Cuba. In 1961–64, Colombia appeared a firmer ally than Argentina, Mexico, Chile, and Brazil—countries softer on Cuba.

Extracts below have been reordered for clarity.[1]

In mid-December 1961, the Lleras Camargo government asked the United States for $120 million [USD] in financial aid. The initial US response was that any large-scale assistance would be contingent upon monetary and fiscal reforms. Colombian officials argued that the development program required a higher rate of imports and that in any event both currency devaluation and import reduction were out of the question in the difficult political period prior to the elections. The United States did not then press the issue.

The National Front survived the congressional elections in March and its candidate, Conservative Guillermo León Valencia, handily won the presidential election in May. He took office in August.

Meanwhile, the loan agreement was signed in April 1962, in the amount of $30 million—drastically scaled down from the original Colombian request for $120 million. Terms were hard by 1962 standards—15 years at 3½ percent including a 5-year grace period on repayment of principal. Further, the loan was made as supporting assistance out of the foreign aid appropriation for the contingency fund, not the appropriation for development loans, which was supposed to be the source of Alliance for Progress money. This is an indication that its purposes were more political than developmental. The only provision written into the loan agreement designed to deal with the potentially inflationary situation in Colombia was a requirement that the pesos generated by the loan were to be frozen and not open to use by the Colombian Government "for any purpose." As will be related, this prohibition did not last. . . .

From the first program loan in April 1962, a primary objective has been political stability and maintenance of Colombia's democratic political institutions through support of the succession of National Front governments. This has been accomplished.

On the other hand, between 1961 and 1967, per capita gross national product increased only $276 to $295 a year, an annual average rate of 1.2 percent, compared to the Punta del Este goal of 2.5 percent. The peso has depreciated from 8.50 to the dollar in 1961 to 16.45 to the dollar in August 1968. The deficit in Colombia's balance of trade decreased from $142.6 million in 1961 to $64.5 million in 1967, but this improvement was more apparent than real, resulting from severe import controls imposed in early 1967 after a deficit of $290.2 million in 1966. An agrarian reform program, one of the earliest under the Alliance for Progress, was enacted in 1961, but through 1967 it had provided land titles to only 54,000 out of approximately 400,000 to 500,000 landless families, whose numbers, furthermore, are increasing by 10 percent a year. Although the agrarian reform has received some US assistance, the major emphasis of US aid policy to agriculture has been directed to increasing production for export. These efforts have achieved some success, but until recently they concentrated on providing credits and other assistance for large commercial farmers at the expense of rural social progress. The education policies of both the Colombian Government and the United States have vacillated from an emphasis on primary education to an emphasis on universities, with the result that little progress has been made in either. The literacy rate has remained relatively constant, but the absolute numbers of functional illiterates have increased from approximately 5 million to more than 6 million. Taxes have been increased, but not until 1967 were serious efforts made to improve collection. Colombia has barely begun to tackle the problems of more equitable income distribution, and the country's social structure remains essentially unchanged, with close to two-thirds of the population not participating in the economic and political decision-making process.

Thus, any evaluation of the aid program in Colombia must be subjective and will depend on the weight the evaluator assigns to the maintenance of political stability in a democratic framework. One of the factors which must be taken into account is the imponderable of what would have happened to Colombian politics if there had been no aid program or if different, or more rigorous, conditions had been attached to aid. At the time the various program loans were signed and their successive tranches released, officials of both the Colombian and United States Governments, as well as many independent observers, thought there was no acceptable alternative. In retrospect, this proposition seems less certain. Disbursement of program loans was chronically slow and was suspended more than once for periods of several months without bringing dire results.

Negotiations of the loan agreements and the joint review sessions which were held with Colombian officials prior to the release of each loan tranche concentrated heavily on the fiscal and monetary policies of the Colombian Government—international exchange rates, bank reserve requirements, prior deposit requirements for imports, budgetary deficits or surpluses, Government investment policies, import licensing policies, etc. Rarely did Colombian Government performance meet all of the previously agreed upon standards, though frequently it met many of them and occasionally exceeded some of them. These standards were aimed at economic stabilization—at controlling inflation and balancing the country's international accounts. They took into account considerations of economic development, but mainly from the point of view of maintaining an adequate level and appropriate distribution of imports to support industrial activity. Even less did the standards take account of the need for social reform. The basic problem, of course, was the difficulty of inducing economic growth while simultaneously applying the brakes to an inflationary economy. But in the process, the rhetoric of the Alliance for Progress was lost in the arcane world of international finance.

Further, it appears that although the aid program achieved some short-term successes with respect to economic stabilization and in influencing the Colombian Government's fiscal and monetary policies, the support which U.S. assistance provided at least contributed to making it possible for successive Colombian Governments, especially that of President Valencia, to postpone making more basic reforms in such fields as public administration, taxation, local government, education, and agriculture.

One of the difficulties which the United States encountered in trying to help Colombia resulted from a combination of two factors. First, the United States discovered that its influence was severely limited with respect to moving Colombia toward economic and social reform, especially in terms of the application of U.S. methods to institutional change. The lack of Colombian absorptive capacity in this area proved to be greater than had been anticipated. This was a measure of the cultural gap. Second, despite these difficulties, and at the same time, the United States wanted to establish a visible economic presence in Latin America in the early years of the Alliance in order to prove the sincerity of its intentions. This led initially to an emphasis on impact project loans. But the lack of well-prepared projects led in turn to reliance on program loans to deal with macroeconomic problems.

The aid in Colombia has bought time for Colombian political institutions to work out the changes which almost everybody in a position of responsibility in either country agrees must come. But Colombians have used this time at their leisure. The question which this study raises but cannot answer is: Would they have moved more expeditiously if they had had less time, or would the pressures have been so great that the whole structure of the country would have collapsed into anarchy or dictatorship?

The record, studied with the benefit of hindsight, indicates the former. But the record cannot fully capture the pressures of the moment in which U.S. decisions were made with respect to extremely complicated and subtle situations. Not the least of these pressures was the tendency to err, if at all, on the side of not taking a bigger gamble.

Note

1. The complete text is available online. See pdf.usaid.gov/pdf_docs/PCAAC189.pdf, accessed March 29, 2016.

Who Was Where during the Mapiripán Massacre?

Ignacio Gómez Gómez

Colombia's position in the world and its relationship with the United States changed dramatically in the thirty years after the Alliance for Progress. Cocaine replaced coffee in the country's international profile, and the image of Pablo Escobar displaced that of publicity icon Juan Valdez, with his mule and coffee sacks. Successive versions of the United States' War on Drugs took center stage through decades marked by the decline and then the recuperation of power by the Colombian state.

After 2002, however, the balance had definitively shifted. Guerrilla groups lost territory in campaigns launched against them not only by the armed forces but by paramilitary groups with shifting ties to army personnel and to the drug traffickers themselves. The "paras" were a product of the cocaine economy. They received direct funding from kingpins, controlled trade routes, and were themselves exporters (see part V).

The irony, of course, was that the Colombian state sought United States support to defeat guerrilla and paramilitary forces, both of which had money because of the drug trade to the United States. In Colombia, the War on Drugs has been a counterinsurgency war marked by free-flowing cash and human rights abuses. A piece published as part of an investigation by reporters at El Espectador newspaper provides a critical perspective on the US involvement in the 1990s. Ignacio Gómez Gómez describes one moment: the infamous Mapiripán massacre of July 1997, a gruesome five-day killing spree where AUC commanders used chain saws and machetes to torture, murder, mutilate, and behead their victims. Gómez pushes Colombians to question whether or not US military personnel are implicated by the fact that they were nearby. Gómez's starting point is an investigation ordered by US Senator Patrick Leahy, signaling a further layer of irony. The Colombian military was fighting a dirty war against narco-guerrillas enmeshed in the cocaine trade to the United States, in alliance with paramilitary commanders also enmeshed in that trade, but at the same time it faced the possibility of scrutiny by human rights investigators based in the United States and risked having its funding cut by senators sympathetic to Leahy's position.

This week, discussions over Plan Colombia will reach the Appropriations Committee of the United States Senate. Committee member Senator Patrick Leahy, author of an amendment that prohibits the U.S. military from training human rights violators. Together with Senator Edward Kennedy, Leahy requested rigorous scrutiny of military forces to be trained, in order to prevent the Pentagon from providing assistance to those who commit crimes against humanity, as occurred with the massacre in Mapiripán, Colombia on July 20, 1997, according to conclusions reached by the Investigative Journalism team of *El Espectador* (PIE).

Such scrutiny is made possible by three agreements that force the Colombian government to keep human rights records on military "trainees," while allowing the U.S. State Department to reject units with even one suspect in their ranks.

The first agreement was signed in July 1997, when relations between the two countries were at their lowest point.

Then ambassador Juan Carlos Esguerra and Assistant Secretary of State Barbara Larkin agreed on the final text in Washington on July 20, 1997. In Bogotá at the time and unable to obtain a visa to travel to the U.S., Ernesto Samper presided over an Independence Day military parade from his balcony, without the presence of any of his military commanders. General Commander Harold Bedoya Pizarro, an opponent of civilian oversight of human rights [violations] in the military, did not attend the parade. On July 22, he openly declared himself in rebellion and on July 25 he was replaced by Manuel José Bonnet. The General Inspector of the Armed Forces and other members of the high military command had celebrated Colombian Independence at the Army Special Forces School, built by U.S. Special Forces at Barrancón island on the Guaviare River.

Two hours upstream, Mapiripán was deserted, after the massacre of 49 of its one thousand inhabitants. The residents were still displaced on August 1, two weeks later, when it was officially announced that military aid from the U.S. for the Colombian Army was again made available .

The Green Berets had over three years of experience in Barrancón, and for two months leading up to the announcement of the agreement signed in Washington, they had been on the island conducting "military planning" exercises with troops under Colonel Lino Sánchez. Today, the Colombian General Attorney's Office [Fiscalía General de la Nación] has accused Sánchez of planning the Mapiripán massacre along with Carlos Castaño.

With support from the office of Senator Patrick Leahy, who requested and obtained information on this case, as well as from the International Consortium of Investigative Journalism (ICIJ) in Washington, the Investigative Journalism team of *El Espectador* (PIE) compiled and analyzed more than 4,500 pages of official documents in English and Spanish on the diplomatic, military, and humanitarian events that took place during that Colombian Independence Day commemoration in San José del Guaviare.

Based on this information, they concluded that the U.S. Army 7th Special Forces Group [Green Berets] conducted a "military planning" training session with soldiers under Colonel Lino Sánchez while Sánchez was planning the mass beheading of Mapiripán civilians. His objective was to eradicate the FARC and allow the United Self-Defense Forces of Colombia to take control of the black market in the south of Guaviare that, according to the State Department, was producing 30% of the world's coca leaf supply.

The United States Special Forces, under the command of the assistant secretary of defense on Special Operations and Low Intensity Conflict (SO-LIC), had trained in Colombia long before it was suggested that their operations should be examined in the light of human rights. Carlos Salinas, a specialist who works for Amnesty International in Washington, asserts that they have been [in the country] since 1962.

In 1996, when the Leahy Amendment (prohibiting assistance to military units implicated in human rights violations) went into effect, the State Department considered the majority of Colombian units "ineligible" for aid because of the record of human rights abuses carried out by military personnel.

SOLIC, however, continued to send trainers; according to its legal interpretation, Joint Combined Exchange Training program (JCET) was considered training for U.S. forces, rather than [military] aid for the country where it takes place.

These "exchanges" (or JCET programs), which take place in more than 123 countries every year, began to attract the attention of the press and the U.S. Congress in 1997, when the General Accounting Office (GAO) ordered an audit of their accounts and clarification of whether the programs counted as military aid. . . .

The official 1997 report submitted to the U.S. Congress in April 1998 included a list of six Special Forces deployments in Colombia. However, on December 22, 1999, SOLIC admitted in a letter to Senator Patrick Leahy that between just June and August of that year new deployments had been ordered, only one of which was included in the report. In total, more than fourteen deployments would have been ordered during that year, or 24% of the total number reported by the U.S. Southern Command for their jurisdiction.

With the exception of two, all of the visits were by the same team of instructors: the U.S. Army's Seventh Special Forces Group, permanently based in Fort Bragg, North Carolina. Members of this unit speak Spanish without accents and have been combat trained in the Amazon with a wide range of special skills, from organizing public opinion campaigns to night jungle combat, with or without technological support. . . .

For eight months beginning in May 1997, the Green Berets made the Army Special Forces School their base, five minutes away by boat or car from the Counternarcotics Base at San José del Guaviare, the "general headquarters" for the U.S. State Department's programs for the eradication of coca plantations. Barrancón is an island formed around a rock outcropping in the middle of the Guaviare [River]; from its heights one can see the river and Sabanas de la Fuga, a historic "sanctuary" for the FARC.

When Senator Leahy requested information about these activities, the director of SOLIC, Brian Sheridan, explained that the training course that began on May 14 in Barrancón dealt with "mission planning and military decision-making," as well as other material specific to a "light infantry."

Colombian reports indicate that the unit being trained was commanded by Colonel Lino Sánchez. Supervisors from the Counternarcotics Police Intelligence Office submitted a report to the State Department and the General Attorney's Office indicating that, at that time in San José, Sánchez was promoting a plan for introducing paramilitary units into fumigated areas within the framework of the U.S. programs, and announced that he had received aid that would enable him to "teach the guerrillas a lesson."

The General Attorney's Office discovered that on July 12, 1997, a group of fifteen men personally chosen by Carlos Castaño Gil flew in two planes from Urabá to the airport of San José del Guaviare, shared by the Counternarcotics Police and the garrison where Sánchez kept an office. On the road to Barrancón, Castaño's group joined the paramilitary forces of Casanare and Meta, and from there traveled by convoy to Charras, on the opposite bank of the Guaviare River across from Mapiripán.

The men crossed the river in boats without being noticed, near the Marine Infantry post in Barrancón, built by Americans for "river combat" training. More than 100 paramilitary soldiers remained in Mapiripán from July 15 to 20, unchallenged by civilian or military authorities.

These dates coincide with three Special Forces deployments mentioned in the report to the U.S. Congress, though none named by Sheridan occurred during the days of the massacre. Notwithstanding, the General Attorney's Office and other officials claim to have seen U.S. military personnel in San José while traveling to Mapiripán to assist survivors of the massacre and open their investigation. . . .

Five years before the massacre, the war in Guaviare had only begun to take on its current shape. In the early 1990s, Mapiripán had become one of the major coca "cities" due to its easy access from Villavicencio—by way of a cleared highway, an airport, and bridle paths. It was also accessible through southern tributaries of the river, connecting the jungle region to Miraflores and Calamar (department of Guaviare), by that time the world's largest zone of of coca cultivation.

In May 1992, the FARC's Fifth Front attacked Mapiripán and burned down the police station, which has never been rebuilt. Comandante Alex [a FARC leader] arrived to settle disputes between the *raspachines* (coca leaf farmers), the *chichipatos* (purchasers of basic cocaine paste), prostitutes, gasoline dealers, and traffickers, among others. In exchange for protection, [the guerrilla] established a 10% "tax" over the cost of the base or paste that circulated in the town, calculated according to the amount of gasoline sold to process it.

Antonio María Barrera Calle—[known as] Compadre Cotumare, one of the founders of the town four decades before—Sinaí Blanco, and other gasoline vendors were forced to become tax collectors for the guerrillas.

Two hours upstream, the Counternarcotics Police headquarters of San José del Guaviare had already become the main center for the U.S. State Department's programs against coca cultivation. First the fumigations, and later patrols by the U.S. Marines, dissuaded local farmers from cultivating coca close to the river. Family agricultural plots [*chagras*] went further into the jungle. Colonel Eduardo Ávila, assigned to this area, explained to the General Attorney's Office that "sometimes troops went (to Mapiripán), but since the guerrillas didn't show up, they got bored and were sent back."

For its part, the training camp of Barrancón was by then fully operational. "In an accord with the office annexed to the U.S. Embassy in Colombia, the Army Special Forces Training School was built in 1996 . . . [and] there is a small garrison of Marine Infantry at the base . . . apparently built by the Navy Seabees in 1994 as part of a training exercise," Sheridan explained to Leahy. In Bogotá, however, Colombia's Departamento Nacional de Planeación [National Planning Department] only became aware of the school in mid-1999, when for the first time it requested money from the Colombian government.

Months before the massacre, the director of the Municipal Advisory Unit for Technical Agriculture (UMATA), Anselmo Trigos, had begun collecting information on the farmers in order to implement a budget of $800 million pesos assigned by the National Plan for Alternative Development (PLANTE). Trigos received threats and was forced to leave after the FARC's 5th and 44th Fronts had subjected him to a "people's trial" on May 18, 1997.

In June, the paramilitary group led by René [Cárdenas] in Aguabonita (between San José and Barrancón) had begun operations, killing seven *chichipatos* for paying "taxes" to the FARC.

On May 14, according to Sheridan, the Green Berets had begun a JCET emphasizing "mission planning and military decision development" with "personnel assigned to the Special Forces School of Barrancón."

Colonel Sánchez told the General Attorney's Office that "at the end of May or the beginning of June an order to concentrate Mobile Brigade No. 2 in the area of Barrancón was received . . . and that at that time, Division Command decided to suspend all leaves of absence and turn all efforts toward retraining in Barrancón."

This officer (now awaiting trial as the mastermind of the massacre) stated that he spent his time between Barrancón and his office in the París Battalion at the southern part of the airport.

According to intelligence reports confirmed in a judicial hearing by Major Juan Carlos López and Colonel Arturo Beltrán (from the Counternarcotics headquarters at the northern part of the aiport), DEA agents, Marine Infantry, and Counternarcotics police visited Mobile Brigade commander (Sánchez) to request his collaboration in Operation Sapphire 2. Sánchez did not agree to collaborate because he had other plans.

On the night of June 21, the colonel himself went to the police, apologized for his absence and inquired about the results [of the Operation]. He then revealed his plan: "He declared"—states the report—"that in any case, the paramilitaries were fighting against a very strong enemy in the region, and that at that time he had support to teach the guerrillas a lesson, and even that his intention was to take advantage of the operation that developed by Counternarcotics to introduce self-defense [paramilitary] forces in the area, but that at the last moment certain problems had arisen." The police denied participating in the plan, as they later informed the General Attorney's Office and the U.S. State Department.

Two days later, on June 23, according to Sheridan, the training for Sánchez's troops concluded and on July 24 (four days after the massacre), the group of American instructors were sent back [to Barrancón]. In August, the group was joined by two more Special Forces units, the 4th Group of the Navy Seals, and the 8th Naval Unit for Special Warfare, to conduct an antidrug training with Sánchez's troops, the police, and Marine infantry.

On Saturday, July 12, at 3:05 and 3:20 in the afternoon, an Antonov and a DC-3 landed in San José from Necoclí and Los Cedros (Apartadó) respectively. According to the investigation by the General Attorney's Office [Fiscalía], fifteen men chosen by Castaño arrived in the Antonov under the command of "El Percherón," "Mochacabezas" [literally, the "beheader"], or "El Diablo" ["the Devil"]. Their only weapons were machetes and knives. Several tons of provisions were unloaded from the DC-3, along with the first edition of the magazine *Colombia Libre* [an AUC periodical] with a pamphlet titled "To the People of Guaviare." The pamphlet was signed by the recently created Guaviare Front of the United Self-Defense Forces of Colombia and threatened to kill anyone who paid "taxes" to the FARC.

According to the report sent to Senator Leahy by Assistant Secretary of State Barbara Larkin, "U.S. personnel involved in the counternarcotics programs in San José recall having seen an unusual number of Army personnel at the airport on the day in question." A paramilitary deserter states that Sánchez was in charge of flight coordination and arrivals.

Six months after the massacre, René Cárdenas was captured at a gas station in Aguabonita, where, according to prosecution witnesses, he met up with plane passengers and other paramilitaries and sent them by road on to Charras.

From there they had to cross the river to reach Mapiripán. René recruited two boatmen; one did not have a license and, since they had to pass through the Navy checkpoint in Barrancón (a site for other U.S. training), René spoke with the guards to arrange their crossing.

As afternoon fell on the 14th, an unidentified group attacked Charras; they forced all the townspeople out of their homes, gathered them in the central plaza, and handed out magazines and pamphlets. In the days preceding [this attack], the mayor of Mapiripán and his family had left for Villavicencio. The UMATA director, the registrar, the municipal spokesman, and the family of FARC Comandante Alex, who had begun to "work" for the Guaviare Front of the AUC, had also left, with their departure going largely unnoticed.

At dawn on July 15, more than 100 paramilitaries surrounded Mapiripán. The only authority in the town was Judge Leonardo Iván Cortés Novoa. The judge went to his office to report what was happening by telephone, but the paramilitaries did not allow him to enter.

The judge cautiously continued to search for a telephone. Around 2:30 in the afternoon he found one in service at the Hotel Monserrate. He called the commander of the Joaquín París Batallion, Colonel Hernán Orozco, reporting the situation in the town and the possible presence of Carlos Castaño in Mapiripán.

Colonel Orozco received the report and wrote an "urgent" memorandum to General Jaime Humberto Uscátegui, commander of the 7th Brigade in Villavicencio. He advised "quick and unannounced action in Mapiripán with personnel and equipment from the Mobile Brigade No. 2 (three battalions in Barrancón and three helicopters)." Uscátegui, also charged in this case, claims he did not receive this report.

According to the judge, 27 people were captured on the morning of the 15th. All of them were taken to Mochacabezas, who had occupied the killing floor of municipal slaughterhouse. Among the first [victims] was Cotumare. He was tortured all day long and his screams froze the jungle air that night. "Don't let me die in such a miserable way," witnesses recall him crying out.

These were the first victims of a total of 49 (4.9% of the estimated population of Mapiripán) whom Carlos Castaño admitted to murdering during the operation.

The paramilitary siege lasted until July 20, when the International Committee of the Red Cross, also alerted by the judge, sent a plane to Mapiripán to rescue him and other residents. Those fleeing to the airport received a parting gesture by Mochacabezas, who threw the dead body of a dog into the crowd. It had belonged to a local schoolteacher, and he had strangled it with his own hands.

On July 22, news of the incident reached the Colombian president's office. Just before, Harold Bedoya had declared his opposition [to civilian oversight] and called upon the military to join him. In this tense situation, the presidential adviser on human rights, Luis Manuel Lasso, arranged a trip from Bogotá to Mapiripán with the General Attorney's Office. Their plan was to fly in a police plane to San José and from there travel on a military helicopter to the [massacre] site.

The trip to San José went as planned but the military helicopter did not arrive. "The two available helicopters were engaged in activities in Barrancón, namely the closing ceremony for the Special Forces course and the visit by the Argentine Army's Chief of Staff," explained General Bonnet on July 24, the same day he replaced Bedoya.

Although Sheridan's letter does not mention any U.S. military presence in Barrancón during the dates of the massacre, the General Attorney's Office believes otherwise. According to the report by the prosecutor who directed the commission, military officials stated that the helicopters were used "during a social gathering with military personnel from the U.S. embassy." The incident escalated when, upon the request of the presidential adviser, the Army IV Division commander, General Agustín Ardila Duarte was summoned. "He made fools of the presidential delegation and paid more attention to the American guests than to the investigative mission."

. . .

As long as there is such secrecy concerning information on new military aid, the risk that this will be repeated grows, which is to say that without close scrutiny by the authorities and by public opinion, there may be another Mapiripán.

Translated by Timothy F. Johnson

A *Minga* of Voluntary Eradication

Asociación Popular de Negros Unidos del Rio Yurumanguí

(APONURY)

By the late 1990s the Pacific Coast rainforest region, along with other frontier zones, was transformed by Colombia's cocaine economy and by marauding bands of armed combatants. It was a transformation of shocking violence. By 2010, roughly half of Colombia's displaced were afrodescendientes from the Pacific region, and the place-names of certain riverside hamlets had become easily recognized symbols of atrocity. To give one signal example, on May 2, 2002, in Bojayá, 119 people were killed after having taken refuge in the town chapel during a firefight between FARC guerrillas and the paramilitary AUC (see part V). Before and after these recognizable moments are long years of shootings and scorched-earth campaigns up and down the rivers of the Pacific forestlands. The killings have happened alongside officially sanctioned fumigations—the story of the Plan Colombia years, not only for the Pacific Coast but also for many other parts of the country, including the southern department of Putumayo, the Montes de María highlands of Colombia's Caribbean region, and areas adjacent to and within the boundaries of La Macarena national park in the department of Meta.

Out of this sad panorama has come political creativity. Transnational, Internet-based organizing has become a means of survival, not only for the Afro-Colombian activists, but for grassroots organizing across the country. Networks in support of Afro-Colombian, indigenous, peasant, union, and human rights organizations in Colombia can result in local army commanders receiving calls from Sweden or New York. Grassroots leaders have taken their own protests across Europe and the United States in speaking tours, conferences, and presentations made to government officials.

One striking example is this very detailed press release from the Asociación Popular de Negros Unidos del Rio Yurumanguí (APONURY; Popular Association of United Black Residents from the Yurumanguí River), documenting a minga, an indigenous term that describes a community workday, that was convened for voluntary manual eradication. The contrast to the usual pattern of manual eradication *post–Plan Colombia, in which officials would descend on a coca crop, uproot it, and leave, is sharp. Activists from the Proceso de Comunidades Negras, a national-level organization committed to black visibility, joined local families mobilized by Law 70 (see part I). They engaged in an act of theater: to demonstrate that local people united by racial consciousness and by their right to control territory defined as "ancestral" could succeed where outsiders had failed and that working with local people, rather than against them, was the only way to limit coca cultivation.*

Explicitly, the Yurumanguí community expressed their opposition to "monoculture," meaning plantation agriculture focused on cash crops rather than subsistence. For planners in Bogotá and Washington, and for urban audiences sympathetic to a prodevelopment perspective, industrial oil palm cultivation appeared as a cash-crop substitute for coca and was presented as a positive good. But for activists intent on defending the collective land titles of black communities in the Pacific region, coca and oil palm plantations were both threats. Local residents experienced both as attacks on their persons, on their land rights, and on their structures of community. Beyond eradicating coca plantings, the symbolic action of a "Minga for Voluntary Communal Manual Eradication" was a claim to voice directed not only at the Colombian state but also at a transnational audience sensitive to the history of the African diaspora.

1. *"I am a respectable inhabitant of Yurumanguí, I do not consume or cultivate cocaine"*

In the year 2000, the general assembly of the Yurumanguí River Community Council, the highest community decision-making authority, concluded that "the entry of any type of illicit plantations (coca) or monoculture, such as oil palm, will not be permitted," in order to protect and preserve the territory as a space for life, happiness, and freedom. This task was entrusted to the Ethnic Territorial Organization APONURY (Popular Association of United Blacks from the Yurumanguí River), along with the Community Council and the Process of Black Communities, PCN.

We Yurumanguireños have decided to firmly oppose illicit monoculture plantations grown for illegal purposes, as well as oppose the expansion of oil palm monoculture, given the outcomes of both in our territory:

1. When coca plantations for illicit purposes increase, the government response is to fumigate, thus destroying subsistence crops and increasing problems among our population related to health, access to fresh water, environmental pollution, and food scarcity.
2. When coca plantations for illicit purposes increase, our territories be-

come more attractive [to outsiders] and more prone to an intensification of the armed conflict. The growing presence of paramilitaries, guerrillas, common criminals, and official security forces increases the risk of disappearances, massacres, and the displacement of the population.

3. When coca plantations for illicit purposes increase, there is also greater risk that these collective territories will be expropriated. It has been known for some time that the government has been preparing legislation that allows the confiscation of collective territories where these crops are planted.

4. When coca plantations for illicit purposes increase, settlers are encouraged to enter our territories. These are mainly *paisas*[1] who bring in these practices [of illicit crops and monoculture], which are later taken up by inhabitants of the territory.

5. When coca plantations for illicit purposes increase, brothels and prostitution proliferate, along with the risk of sexually transmitted diseases, such as AIDS. This fuels a loss of cultural values among the population.

6. When coca plantations for illicit purposes increase, our political and organizational strength is diminished, as is the possibility of building a new Colombia based on our dreams, aspirations, and ways of life. The cultural identity of our people is lost when life is destroyed.

7. When coca plantations for illicit purposes increase, the national government responds by imposing oil palm, presenting it as the only viable alternative in the substitution of illicit crops. And the government response will fail to comply with the terms of the agreements that have been made with the community regarding manual and voluntary eradication.

. . .

With resolve and logistical resources in place, a total of exactly 253 individuals from 13 rural districts that make up the Yurumanguí river basin gathered on November 8, [2007], in the community of Veneral del Carmen, in the lower section of the river. Men, women, young people, adults, and children attended to carry out the voluntary communal eradication, with the objective of protecting and ensuring the preservation of our space of life.

The Yurumanguí community, with political consciousness and empowered by the assembly's mandate, proceeded to manually destroy approximately 25 hectares of coca plantings cultivated in 4 different fields, located along creeks near the community of Barranco (in the lower section of the river).

Summary of successes gained through voluntary communal eradication

Area eradicated manually:	25 hectares
Number of participants in voluntary communal eradication:	253 people
Date of voluntary communal eradication:	Nov. 9–11, 2007

Translated by Ana María Gómez López, Alexia Temme, and Tivan Amour

Note

1. *Paisas* means Antioqueños, although people from the Pacific Coast sometimes use this term to refer to whites or mestizos from the interior of the country in general.

Latin American Ex-Presidents Push
to Reorient the War on Drugs
Latin American Commission on Drugs and Democracy

By the twenty-first century not only peasant cultivators and human rights activists but also former presidents and former ministers of defense around the Americas were questioning the militarization of drug policy. One former president of Brazil, Fernando Henrique Cardoso (in office 1995–2003), has been especially influential, pushing Latin Americans to shift their national policies away from interdiction and toward "harm reduction," in which drug use is approached as a public health problem rather than a criminal one. The following extracts from a 2008 statement by the Latin American Commission on Drugs and Democracy, a forum in which Cardoso was joined by César Gaviria (president of Colombia in 1990–94) and Ernesto Zedillo (president of Mexico in 1994–2000), highlight key aspects of an emerging Latin American perspective on drug policy. The report acknowledges, for example, that drug use in the context of violence and addiction is rising in Latin American cities and, conversely, that there are new pressures to protect access to coca leaf used for "ancestral purposes."

Violence and the organized crime associated with the narcotics trade are critical problems in Latin America today. Confronted with a situation that is growing worse by the day, it is imperative to rectify the "war on drugs" strategy pursued in the region over the past 30 years.

Prohibitionist policies based on the eradication of production and on the disruption of drug flows as well as on the criminalization of consumption have not yielded the expected results. We are farther than ever from the announced goal of eradicating drugs.

A realistic evaluation indicates that:

- Latin America remains the major global exporter of cocaine and cannabis, has become a growing producer of opium and heroin, and is developing the capacity to produce synthetic drugs;

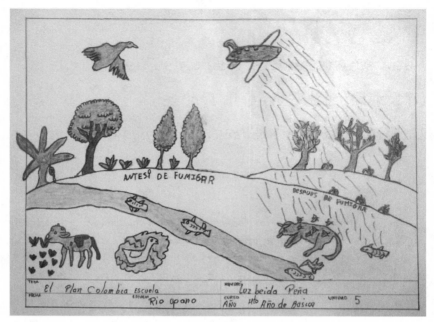

Luzbeida Peña, a child living on the Ecuador-Colombia border, produced this in-school drawing of "before and after fumigation." Between 2000 and 2015, US drug policy led to the aerial spraying of glyphosate-containing herbicides over land planted in coca. The Colombian government unilaterally ended such spraying in 2015. Courtesy of Luzbeida Peña Jimenez and Adolfo Maldonado.

- The levels of drug consumption continue to grow in Latin America while there is a tendency toward stabilization in North America and Europe.
- The in-depth revision of current drug policies is even more urgent in Latin America in light of their enormous human and social costs and threats to democratic institutions.

Over the past decades we have witnessed:

- A rise in organized crime caused both by the international narcotics trade and by the growing control exercised by criminal groups over domestic markets and territories;
- A growth in unacceptable levels of drug-related violence affecting the whole of society and, in particular, the poor and the young;
- The criminalization of politics and the politicization of crime, as well as the proliferation of the linkages between them, as reflected in the infiltration of democratic institutions by organized crime;

• The corruption of public servants, the judicial system, governments, the political system and, especially the police forces in charge of enforcing law and order. . . .

The challenge at hand is to drastically reduce the harm caused by illegal narcotics to people, societies and public institutions. To move in this direction, it is essential to differentiate between illicit substances according to the harm they inflict on people's health and the social fabric.

The search for more efficient policies, rooted in the respect for human rights, implies taking into account the diversity of national situations and emphasizing prevention and treatment. These policies do not deny the importance of repressive actions—including the participation of the Armed Forces in extreme situations, according to the decision of each country—to confront the threats posed by organized crime.

It is imperative to review critically the deficiencies of the prohibitionist strategy adopted by the United States and the benefits and drawbacks of the harm reduction strategy followed by the European Union. It is also important to question the low priority given to the drug problem by both industrialized and developing countries in other parts of the world.

Colombia is a clear example of the shortcomings of the repressive policies promoted at the global level by the United States. For decades, Colombia implemented all conceivable measures to fight the drug trade in a massive effort whose benefits were not proportional to the vast amount of resources invested and the human costs involved. Despite the country's significant achievements in fighting the drug cartels and lowering the levels of violence and crime, the areas of illegal cultivation are again expanding as well as the flow of drugs coming out of Colombia and the Andean region. . . .

Eradication efforts must be combined with the adoption of strongly financed alternative development programs adapted to local realities in terms of viable products and conditions for their competitive access to markets. It is important not only to speak of alternative cultivation but to envision a wide range of options, including the social development of alternative forms of work, democratic education and the search for solutions in a participatory context. Such initiatives must also take into account the legal uses of plants, such as the coca leaf, in countries with a long-standing tradition of ancestral use previous to the phenomenon of their exploitation as an input for drug production. Accordingly, measures must be taken to strictly adjust production to this kind of ancestral use. . . .

The deepening of the debate concerning the policies on drug consumption must be grounded on a rigorous evaluation of the impact of the diverse alternatives to the prohibitionist strategy that are being tested in different countries, focusing on the reduction of individual and social harm.

This construction of alternatives is a process that requires the participation of a plurality of social actors: law and order institutions, educators, health professionals, spiritual leaders, families, opinion makers, and media. Each country must face the challenge of opening up a large public debate about the seriousness of the problem and the search for policies consistent with its history and culture.

At the Inter-American level, Latin America must establish a dialogue with the United States government, legislators and civil society to jointly develop workable alternatives to the current "war on drugs" strategy. . . .

At the global level, we must move forward with the articulation of a voice and vision of Latin America to influence the international debate on illicit drugs, especially in the framework of the United Nations and the Inter-American Drug Abuse Control Commission. Latin America's active participation in the global debate would mark its transition from a problem region to a pioneering region in the implementation of innovative solutions for the drug problem.

A New Export Product: *Yo soy Betty, la fea* Goes Global

Yeidy Rivero

Colombian juxtapositions are as striking as any in the contemporary world. In the 1990s and into the 2010s, people who followed news stories about horrific massacres, deadly kidnappings, drug trafficking and its attendant violence, and ongoing human rights investigations often also followed Colombian telenovelas. Precisely during those awful decades of violence, audiences were treated to creative, professionally produced shows that circulated far beyond the nation's borders. The most famous such show was Yo soy Betty, la fea, *described in detail by media scholar Yeidy Rivero.* Ugly Betty, *as the show was retitled for North American audiences, became a global brand in a series of remakes that spanned the globe. The Colombian original, either with its Spanish soundtrack or in dubbed form, was rebroadcast in more than twenty countries, not only in Spain and Latin America but also in Japan and elsewhere in Asia. Latinos in the United States watched multiple versions, including reruns of the original as well as of a Mexican version. Other remakes and reimaginings followed. New versions of* Betty *were produced for television audiences in markets as diverse as Germany, Czechoslovakia, India, Turkey, and China, among others. But as Rivero points out, this was not simply a Colombian show that became an international magnet. Rather,* Betty *was transnational from the beginning, in that the scriptwriter and "showrunner" behind the show's success, Fernando Gaitán, understood his project as combining elements drawn from both United States and Latin American television genres.*

In Colombia, probably as a result of the high-culture, theatre and literary traditions that defined the television industry for many years, [soap opera] scriptwriters are seen as auteurs. "We do not sell stars, we sell stories," remarked media scholar Omar Rincón in reference to the centrality of the author in Colombian television. Nonetheless, while scriptwriters are at the top of Colombia's television hierarchical structure, only a few have the power to control different aspects of television production. In other words, just a handful of writers could be categorized as showrunners. Fernando Gaitán is one of those select few. As a scriptwriter who has spent most of his professional career working for RCN [a Colombian radio and TV network] and who has provided the company with various hits, Gaitán has the network's trust.

Highly protective of his creative work, Gaitán took over the executive and creative aspects of the *Yo soy Betty, la fea* production. As he responded when I asked about his involvement with Betty,

> I selected the director, the technical crew, the actors, and the editor. I did the budget, dealt with the press, selected my research team who, in addition to performing research for the telenovela, was in charge of the Bible. I took over the control of the filming of exteriors and interiors. I became involved in the selection of food and hotels, I also took the technical and artistic crew to *rumbear* [party] at my bar every 15 days. . . .

Gaitán's journalistic approach to creative writing, together with his interest in reenacting Bogotá's quotidianity, served as the starting point for *Yo soy Betty, la fea*.

> The idea came up at the channel RCN. I used to work a lot at the channel. There one can observe two drastically distinct worlds. One is the world of a typical industry and the other one is the world of the big divas of the country. These two worlds overlap. Naturally, I used to listen to the secretaries talking. These ladies used to go to their barrios and everybody used to ask them about the actors, how they behave, etc. . . . And there were a bunch of secretaries that were amazing. A very audacious cartel! On the other hand, there was a secretary of a big shot executive, who was *feíta* [ugly] and who was treated horribly by her boss. One day the secretary left and the boss did not know what to do with his life. He could not find anything. . . . On the other hand, here in Colombia, there is an obsession with plastic surgery . . . people take away ribs, they change their faces, have breast implants. . . . So, that is how all of Betty's themes began to develop.

The story of the ugly, clumsy, working-class, brilliant and hard-working Beatríz Pinzón Solano, a secretary at the high-fashion company EcoModa, was in fact the story of an unknown, hard-working, efficient and not very attractive RCN secretary. The seven "I do not give a damn about what you think of me" women of *El cuartel de las feas* originated from a group of apparently "kick-ass" secretaries at RCN. It is unclear who served as the muse for the other characters, but they might have been a collage of people, social actors who are part of Bogotá's world.

Trained in literature and a big admirer and follower of the *"gringo* sitcom," Gaitán is a self-taught television scriptwriter who learned the craft through books and instructional pamphlets. Today, after more than 20 years in the business, Gaitán is considered one of the best (and for some the best) Colombian television authors. According to several interviewees, Gaitán's winning scriptwriting formula comes from his character development, his vivid portrayal of aspects of Colombia's cultural and social environments and his mastership of comedy.

For Gaitán (as well as for several Colombian-media professionals I interviewed), humour is a key ingredient in the Colombian telenovela. "We are killing ourselves so much that we need to live the day-to-day with a good vibe," one interviewee satirically remarked in reference to the comedic elements in the Colombian television fiction. . . . Gaitán classified *Yo soy Betty, la fea* as a programme more attuned to the US sitcom than to the telenovela. "Schematically, in terms of script, set, filming, and episodic duration [in Colombia the original episodes were thirty minutes long], *Yo soy Betty, la fea* is very similar to a US situation comedy." This structural proximity to the situation comedy mentioned by Gaitán may have accounted for the migration of the *Yo soy Betty, la fea* format to places familiar with the sitcom genre but which, at the same time, were not conversant with the *telenovela* genre conventions. . . . Even when many global Betties are relatively loose adaptations of the Colombian version, those who transformed the concept in countries where audiences are not familiar with *telenovelas* probably diluted the melodramatic component of the format and exalted the comedic elements. . . .

In terms of the industry, Gaitán's use of the sitcom can also be seen as part of an industrial formula wherein all external influences are "devoured" and incorporated into the telenovela genre. This ongoing consumption and transfiguration of foreign influences has kept the Colombian *telenovela* and series fresh and original, a factor that has impacted the current popularity of Colombian formats. However, while the "devouring" of external ideas, formats and genres has helped sell Colombian television products, it was the international success of Betty that opened the global television market for Colombia. "Betty provided us the access to present other types of products on the market. . . . The market now demands the Colombian product," a Caracol network executive remarked. Today, and thanks to Gaitán's creation, Colombia is an active player in the global television world. . . .

When I asked Gaitán about the global Betties, his possible involvement as a creative consultant and, indirectly, his potential revenues, he simply replied, "I do not have any rights. RCN has all the rights." I also received a similar response when inquiring about the business arrangements for Gustavo Bolívar, the author of *Sin tetas no hay paraíso* (Without Tits There's No Paradise). In Bolívar's case, however, the situation was more complex, given that he had sold the rights of his book to publisher Oveja Negra y Quintero, who subsequently sold them to Caracol. The fact that Bolívar was hired to write the script for the television series was an "unexpected bonus," said another scriptwriter.

In Bogotá's television industry, the cases of Gaitán and Bolívar are not the exception but the norm. Colombia scriptwriters sell their scripts to television networks and, with this transaction, they give away all of their rights as authors. Certainly, someone such as Gaitán, who has had enormous commercial success and who has prestige locally and regionally, has been financially rewarded. But, as someone close to Gaitán expressed, "[The RCN network executives] have been very generous but they have not been just. In the case of Betty it has not been fair." . . .

Of course, Gaitán's control over the *Yo soy Betty, la fea* sales and format adaptations might be different today due to his managerial position at RCN. Then again, his situation is unique. He might be able to protect the spirit of future Betties and his other cultural creations, but other Colombian authors seem to be in a Catch-22 situation. Those I spoke to are fully aware of their lack of rights regarding their scripts and their limited financial remuneration, but at the same time they are also grateful for the employment opportunity that, while unstable, allows them to do what they love.

Today We Understand and Can Say No

Lorenzo Muelas

The U'wa, a small indigenous community living in the foothills and mountains of eastern Colombia, have resisted oil drilling and mineral resource exploitation in their ancestral lands for over two decades. In the early 1990s, Los Angeles–based Occidental Petroleum (Oxy) and other transnational corporations acquired exploration and drilling rights in the "Samoré Block," a potential oil field that stretches two thousand hectares between the department of Boyacá and Colombia's border with Venezuela. The U'wa told journalists they would commit collective suicide if drilling took place, making direct reference to a collective memory about resistance to Spanish colonization in the seventeenth century. Their public opposition to Oxy has garnered the U'wa numerous allies at home and abroad.

Lorenzo Muelas Hurtado, an indigenous leader from the Guambiano community in Cauca, has voiced strong support for the U'wa, describing their activist stance as part of a larger set of struggles against genetic prospecting, land grabs, and illegal actions by transnational firms. Muelas understood his political position as a transnational one. With U'wa leader Roberto "Berito" Cobaría, for example, Muelas met with activists from the Secoya community, a small indigenous group in Ecuador whose lands were being drilled by Occidental Petroleum and thus had good reasons to connect with the U'wa.

In his address to the Secoya, Muelas Hurtado urges them to uphold their legally recognized rights. His words carried particular weight, given that he had been a delegate to Colombia's National Constituent Assembly (Asamblea Nacional Constituyente) and had helped draft articles regarding indigenous and Afro-Colombian legal rights and collective landownership (see part I). Significantly, Muelas did not address himself only to the particular situation of the Secoya. Rather, he asked a transnational question. In the face of bribery, attacks on their immediate environment, and scientific attempt to "bank" indigenous people's genes, will ethnic minorities like the Guambianos, the U'wa, the Secoya and many others survive into the future?

Lorenzo Muelas
Message to the Secoya, August 1999

I am very happy to lay foot on Secoya soil. I would first like to say that we have come to speak to you truthfully about the consequences of oil. We have not come to help you negotiate a price to your advantage. Our only interest is that you continue to live on this land.

I am sure that Oxy (Occidental Petroleum), when they learn that the U'wa or myself have been here, will try to misrepresent why we have come: sometimes we are accused of being guerrillas or communists because we oppose the progress which they impose, which is why I want to warn you about the consequences.

I come here in recognition of our brotherhood. We Indian peoples across the entire continent have developed on our own. Our elders and our culture descend from 30,000 years of history, which is why we have our own rights. We Guambianos call this *derecho mayor*—higher law. The U'wa identify this as natural law, the Arhuacos name it law of origin, and the Koguis refer to it as our ancient right, granted after having lived for thousands of years.

I am outraged, and tears come to my eyes, when I see this colonization, when [outsiders] intrude into homes that do not belong to them, disrespecting the [Indian] peoples. They do not allow us to set foot in their homes, nor place our hands on the safe-deposit boxes they keep under lock and key. Why then do they have the right to violate our homes and cause us trouble?

Even so, today, there have been policy changes in every country. We no longer are as we were 500 years ago, when we did not even understand their language; today we understand and can say no. When I say that policies have changed, I mean, for example, that Ecuadorians have a new constitution, where both indigenous and Afro-Ecuadorian people have rights won by their *compañeros*.

I do not wish to let the legal instruments that the Constitution provides go to waste. In defending yourselves from transnational corporations this Constitution is but support to a higher law. It is not indigenous law, but it is the law recognized by your country, and as such, it is an instrument to be used.

We face many difficulties. The oil problem is only one of many issues that affect indigenous people. Throughout the world there are different problems and threats from corporations that are watching us. For example, there are biodiversity resources that they want to appropriate.

Lorenzo Muelas in his
capacity as a delegate
to Colombia's 1991
Constituent Consti-
tutional Assembly.
Photograph by Lope
Medina. Used by
permission of the art-
ist and Publicaciones
Semana, S.A.

There are even more outrageous issues, such as what they refer to as
"indigenous genes." In Colombia, Ecuador, and the rest of the continent, they are patenting our blood. They know that they are killing us
off, which is why they are capturing our blood in genetic banks, because
they want our courage and our spirit.

Where there is oil, the government and transnational corporations
set traps for us, as their interest is to explore and exploit. Oxy was present at our last [indigenous] congress, and one of them said to me, "We
will negotiate with the U'wa with checkbook in hand, and we will see if
they are able to say no. . . ." Up until now the U'wa have not negotiated;
they have upheld their principles and dignity, which is why I hold deep
love and respect for them.

I suffered greatly to think that the U'wa would yield, because Oxy buys people's consciences; but they said, "We were not born with money," and they did not sell their conscience for profit.

The U'wa have brought Oxy to a standstill. They have no need to discuss, or to read all of that paperwork: they simply say "No." They know that if they sit down to negotiate, they will be finished; they will grow tired and languish until they accept, and because of that, it is better to say no from the beginning. . . .

We invite you to say no, so that you can stay alive here on this land. You will never win at the negotiating table. I always say that we indigenous peoples are a nonrenewable natural resource. When the Secoya people disappear, they will never rise again.

Translated by Ana María Gómez López

Toward a Stable and Enduring Peace

Delegados del Gobierno de la República de Colombia (Gobierno Nacional) and Delegados de las Fuerzas Armadas Revolucionarias de Colombia–Ejército del Pueblo

On August 26, 2012, a group of negotiators who had been working in secret surprised Colombians by releasing what they called a "General Agreement for the Termination of the Conflict and the Building of a Stable and Enduring Peace." The General Agreement had resulted from months of confidential conversations held in Havana. Many found the choice of location unusual, given that the United States (which backed the Colombian government) had officially listed Cuba as a "State Sponsor of Terrorism" in 1982 and kept that designation in place until 2015. Yet there was a significant precedent for holding the talks in Havana, as President Álvaro Uribe Vélez, who preceded Santos in office and whose foreign policy was aggressively pro-Washington, had himself used Cuba as the location for a set of conversations with the ELN, precisely to seek a negotiated peace.

Santos had the cautious support of Colombia's political establishment and business elite, but few would have anticipated that the negotiations might drag on for so long. Although negotiators said publicly that they had begun their discussions in February 2012, there likely had been a set of contacts that preceded the Havana process, perhaps even beginning with a meeting between Santos and Venezuelan president Hugo Chávez that had taken place unexpectedly in August 2010, within three days of Santos's inauguration as president. Santos may have been laying the groundwork then for a reelection campaign in 2014 that would focus on giving his administration a chance at signing a "historic accord" with the FARC.

Such calculations aside, several specific aspects of the Havana process are worth noting. First, it produced texts marked by formality. Like official documents from the seventeenth and eighteenth centuries, each page of the General Agreement is signed in ink by each of the participants—including the official negotiators authorized by Santos, FARC delegates, and representatives of the Cuban and Norwegian governments, acting in their capacity as "guarantors" of the process. Second, the Havana process unfolded within carefully managed parameters of secrecy and discipline, which some observers saw as evidence of Venezuela's involvement as a "facilitator of logistics and support." Third, for the first time in its long history, the FARC accepted the possibility of laying down its weapons. Fourth, the council established by the General Agreement was quite pragmatic, accepting that "nothing is agreed until everything is agreed." This worked to shield the process, so that delegates could continue negotiating despite ongoing conflict and battles on the ground could continue despite ongoing negotiations. Fifth, and very significantly, the negotiation council was organized in such a way as to allow the FARC to rotate middle-ranking officers in and out of it. This slowed the process down, but it also pointed to the work that the FARC's high command had to do to maintain internal unity in the face of so huge an undertaking.

The high-profile and seemingly thorny issues of agrarian reform, reparations for victims, and the ongoing trafficking of illicit drugs did not in the end prove the most difficult to resolve. Rather, those who raised their voices in opposition to Santos's negotiations, as they progressed, asked whether or not FARC commanders would go to jail and whether or not they would be allowed to stand for elected office. When an accord did get signed, in late September 2016, it could not go forward without a plebiscite that asked Colombian voters to approve or reject the final agreement. In early October the "yes" campaign lost by a very narrow margin (see the introduction). Those who campaigned for a "no" vote, including former president Álvaro Uribe Vélez, could claim that hundreds of thousands of voters agreed that those who had given orders in the FARC should face prosecution and be barred from running for public office. But neither campaign could claim that or anything else as a mandate, given that most voters had stayed home. The historic plebiscite had not grabbed Colombians' imaginations enough to move more than 37 percent of eligible voters to the polls.

Immediately after the 2016 plebiscite, no one could say whether or not it would prove politically possible to hammer out a new agreement. If negotiators were asked to craft another deal, they might have to start again from this 2012 text. Even less clear was what effect the outcome of the 2016 plebiscite would have on the possibility of the government initiating a separate peace process with the ELN. How much could be salvaged from the 2012–16 process? A high-profile attempt to claim peace had failed, but the alternative option no longer seemed to be open war. There was room for optimism, not least because President Santos received the Nobel Prize for

Peace anyway, despite the "no" vote. Over a four-year period many young Colombi-
ans had become used to hearing the term "postconflict" used to describe the country
they lived in. For them, turning the page means moving into uncharted political
terrain.

The delegates of the Government of the Republic of Colombia and of the
Revolutionary Armed Forces of Colombia–Army of the People (FARC-EP),

As a result of the Exploratory Meeting that took place in Havana, Cuba,
from February 23 to August 26, 2012, and that included the participation of
the Government of the Republic of Cuba and the Government of Norway as
guarantors, and the support of the Government of the Bolivarian Republic
of Venezuela as facilitator of logistics and support,

Have come to a mutual decision to end the conflict, as an essential
condition for building a stable and lasting peace.

Heeding the public outcry for peace and recognizing that:

Peacebuilding is the responsibility of society as a whole and requires
the participation of all, without exception, including other guerrilla
organizations we invite to join this cause;

Respect for human rights throughout the national territory is an
objective of the State and must be promoted;

Economic development, with social justice and in harmony with the
environment, is a safeguard of peace and progress;

Social development, with equity and public welfare that includes the
great majority, enables our growth as a country;

A peaceful Colombia will play an active and sovereign role in peace and
development on a regional and global scale;

The expansion of democracy is essential for establishing strong
foundations for peace;

The Government of Colombia and the FARC-EP are fully committed to
reaching an agreement and invite all Colombian people, as well as organizations promoting regional integration, and the international community, to
support this process.

We have agreed to:

I. Begin direct and uninterrupted discussions of the points of the
Agenda herein established, with the aim of reaching a Final Agreement to end the conflict and contribute to the building of a stable
and lasting peace.

Antonio Caro, *La Gran Colombia*, placard, 150 × 100 cm, 2005. The artist uses a map of Ecuador, Panama, Colombia, and Venezuela together, to evoke both the short-lived republic (1819–31) that combined them and the seemingly utopian possibility of reuniting. Courtesy of the artist.

II. Establish a Deliberative Council that will meet publicly in Oslo, Norway, within the first 15 days of October, 2012, and maintain a central office in Havana, Cuba. The Council may meet in other countries.

III. Ensure the effectiveness of the process and to conclude the work on the points of the Agenda in an expeditious manner and in the shortest time possible, in order to meet public expectation of a timely agreement. In all circumstances, the time required will be subject to periodic evaluations of progress.

IV. Conduct discussions with the support of the governments of Cuba and Norway as guarantors and of the governments of Venezuela and Chile as facilitators. According to the requirements of the process, others may be invited by joint agreement.

V. The Agenda is as follows:

1. Program for Comprehensive Agricultural Development
   Comprehensive agricultural development is a determining factor in promoting regional integration and the country's equitable social and economic development.
   1. Access and use of land. Unproductive lands. Formalization of property ownership. Agricultural borders and the protection of natural reserves.
   2. Development programs with a regional approach.
   3. Infrastructure and land development.
   4. Social development: health, education, housing, and the eradication of poverty.

   5. Stimulus for agricultural and livestock production and for a supportive and cooperative economy. Technical assistance. Subsidies. Credit. Income generation. Trade. Formalization of labor.
   6. A system for food security.

2. Political participation
   1. Rights and guarantees for the exercise of political opposition in general, and specific rights for new movements that may arise after the signing of the Final Agreement. Access to mass media.
   2. Democratic mechanisms for civic participation, including direct participation at different levels and on diverse issues.
   3. Effective measures for promoting greater participation in national, regional, and local politics among all sectors, including the most vulnerable communities, with equal provisions and guarantees for safety.

3. Ending the conflict
   A comprehensive and simultaneous process, involving:
   1. A bilateral and definitive cease-fire and end to hostilities.
   2. The laying down of arms. The reintegration of the FARC-EP into civilian life—in its economic, social, and political aspects—according to their interests.
   3. The Government of Colombia will coordinate an investigation into the status of those persons imprisoned, prosecuted, or convicted for belonging to or collaborating with the FARC-EP.
   4. In a parallel fashion, the Government will intensify the battle to eradicate criminal organizations and their support networks, including the fight against corruption and impunity, particularly against any organization responsible for homicides and massacres or that attacks the defenders of human rights or social or political movements.
   5. The Government will review and make the institutional reforms and adjustments necessary to face the challenges of building peace.
   6. Guarantees for safety.
   7. Fact-finding around paramilitary activity, among other issues, will be addressed within the framework outlined in point 5 of this agreement (Victims).

The signing of the Final Agreement shall initiate this process, to be carried out within a reasonable time frame agreed upon by the participants.

4. Solution to the problem of illicit drugs
   1. Programs for the substitution of illicit crops. Comprehensive development plans, with community participation in the design, execution, and evaluation of the substitution programs and the environmental recovery of areas affected by such crops.
   2. Programs for the prevention of drug use and for public health.
   3. A solution to the production and commercialization of narcotics.

5. Victims
   Redress for victims is at the heart of the agreement between the Government of Colombia and the FARC-EP. Therefore, the following will be addressed:
   1. Victims' human rights
   2. Truth

6. Implementation, verification, and ratification
   Signing the Final Agreement initiates the implementation of all of the terms agreed upon.
   1. Mechanisms for implementation and verification.
      a. A system of implementation, giving particular attention to the regions.
      b. Commissions for follow-up and verification.
      c. Mechanisms for the resolution of disagreements.
      These mechanisms shall have capacity and power of execution, and will be comprised of representatives from each party and of the public, according to the case.
   2. Ongoing international accompaniment
   3. Timeline
   4. Budget
   5. Tools for dissemination and communication
   6. Mechanisms for the formal ratification of the agreements

VI. The following rules of operation:
   1. Up to ten persons per delegation will participate in the Council, of whom up to five can act as plenipotentiary spokespersons on behalf of the delegation. Each delegation will be composed of up to 30 representatives.
   2. In order to contribute to the advancement of the process, experts on issues in the Agenda may be consulted once an appropriate procedure has been established.

3. To guarantee the transparency of the process, the Council will produce periodic reports.

4. A mechanism will be created to communicate the Council's progress. The content of the discussions will not be made public.

5. An effective publicity strategy will be implemented.

6. To guarantee the broadest possible participation, a mechanism will be established for receiving, by physical or electronic means, proposals from citizens and organizations regarding the terms of the agenda. By mutual agreement and within a determined timeframe, the Council may make direct consultations and receive proposals regarding those points, or delegate a third party for organizing this public participation.

7. The Government will guarantee the resources necessary for the Council to function, to be administered in an efficient and transparent manner.

8. The Council will make use of any technology necessary to advance the process.

9. The discussions will begin with Point 1 regarding Programs for Comprehensive Agricultural Development, and will follow in the order agreed upon by the Council.

10. The discussions will proceed according to the principle that nothing is agreed until everything is agreed upon.

Signed on the 26th day of August of 2012, in Havana, Cuba.
On behalf of the Government of the Republic of Colombia:

> *Sergio Jaramillo, Delegate*
> *Frank Pearl, Delegate*

On behalf of the Revolutionary Armed Forces of Colombia–Army of the People:

> *Mauricio Jaramillo, Delegate*
> *Ricardo Téllez, Delegate*
> *Andrés París, Delegate*
> *Marco León Calarcá*
> *Hermes Aguilar*
> *Sandra Ramírez*

Witnesses:
On behalf of the Government of the Republic of Cuba:

> *Carlos Fernández de Cossío*
> *Abel García*

On behalf of the Government of Norway:

>*Dag Halvor Nylander*
>*Vegar S. Brynildsen*

On behalf of the Government of the Republic of Colombia:

>*Enrique Santos C.*
>*Álvaro Alejandro Eder*
>*Jaime F. Avendaño*
>*Lucía Jaramillo Ayerbe*
>*Elena Ambrosi*

Translated by Timothy F. Johnson

Suggestions for Further Reading

Part I. Human Geography

Ángel, Marta Herrera. *Ordenar para controlar: Ordenamiento espacial y control político en las Llanuras del Caribe y en los Andes Centrales Neogranadinos.* Bogotá: Academia Colombiana de Historia, Instituto Colombiano de Antropología y Historia, 2002.

Applebaum, Nancy P. *Mapping the Country of Regions: The Chorographic Commission of Nineteenth-Century Colombia.* Chapel Hill: University of North Carolina Press, 2016.

Bushnell, David. *The Making of Modern Colombia: A Nation in Spite of Itself.* Berkeley: University of California Press, 1993.

Fals Borda, Orlando. *Historia doble de la costa.* 4 vols. Bogotá: Carlos Valencia Editores, 1979–86.

Giraldo, Luz Mary. *Cuentos y relatos de la literatura colombiana.* 2 vols. Bogotá: Fondo de Cultura Económica, 2005.

———. *Ellas cuentan: Una antología de relatos de escritoras colombianas, de la colonia a nuestros días.* Bogotá: Editorial Seix Barral, 1998.

Gutiérrez de Pineda, Virginia. *La familia en Colombia.* Bogotá: Universidad Nacional de Colombia, 1962.

Jackson, Jean. *The Fish People: Linguistic Exogamy and Tukanoan Identity in Northwest Amazonia.* Cambridge: Cambridge University Press, 1983.

Jaramillo Uribe, Jaime. *Ensayos de historia social.* 2 vols. Bogotá: Tercer Mundo Editores, 1989.

MacPharlane, Anthony. *Colombia before Independence: Economy, Politics, and Society under Bourbon Rule.* Cambridge: Cambridge University Press, 1993.

Melo, Jorge Orlando, ed. *Historia de Antioquia.* Medellín: Suramericana de Seguros, 2001.

Millán de Benavides, Carmen, and Alejandra Quintana Martínez. *Mujeres en la música de Colombia: El género de los géneros.* Bogotá: Pontificia Universidad Javeriana, 2014.

Múnera, Alfonso. *El fracaso de la nación: Región, clase y raza en el caribe colombiano.* Bogotá: Banco de la República / El Áncora Editores, 1998.

Ochoa Gautier, Ana María. *Aurality: Listening and Knowledge in Nineteenth-Century Colombia.* Durham, NC: Duke University Press, 2014.

Pineda Camacho, Roberto. *En el país del río de la mar dulce: Un ensayo de historia colonial, 1540–1830.* Bogotá: Academia Colombiana de Historia, 2013.

Pomare-Myles, Lolia y Marcia Dittmann. *Birth, Life, and Death of a San Andrean.* Bogotá: Ministerio de Cultura de Colombia, 2000.

Posada Carbó, Eduardo. *The Colombian Caribbean: A Regional History, 1870–1950.* Oxford: Clarendon, 1996.

Rausch, Jane M. *Colombia: Territorial Rule and the Llanos Frontier.* Gainesville: University Press of Florida, 1999.

Safford, Frank, and Marco Palacios. *Colombia: Fragmented Land, Divided Society.* New York: Oxford University Press, 2002.

Tirado Mejía, Álvaro, Jorge Orlando Melo, Jesús Antonio Bejarano, and Jaime Jaramillo Uribe. *Nueva historia de Colombia.* 8 vols. Bogotá: Planeta, 1989.

Ulloa, Alejandro. *La salsa en Cali.* Cali: Ediciones Universidad del Valle, 1992.

Wade, Peter. *Blackness and Race Mixture.* Baltimore: Johns Hopkins University Press, 1995.

Waxer, Lise A. *The City of Musical Memory: Salsa, Record Grooves, and Popular Culture in Cali, Colombia.* Middletown, CT: Wesleyan University Press, 2010.

Williams, Raymond L., and Kevin G. Guerreri. *Culture and Customs of Colombia.* Westport, CT: Greenwood, 1999.

Part II. Religious Pluralities

Abel, Christopher. *Política, iglesia y partidos en Colombia: 1886–1953.* Bogotá: Fundación Antioqueña para los Estudios Sociales and Universidad Nacional de Colombia, 1987.

Árbelaez Camacho, Carlos, and Francisco Gil Tovar. *El arte colonial en Colombia: Arquitectura, escultura, pintura, mobiliario, orfebrería.* Bogotá: Ediciones Sol y Luna, 1968.

Arocha, Jaime. *Ombligados de Ananse: Hilos ancestrales y modernos en el Pacífico Colombiano.* Bogotá: Universidad Nacional de Colombia, 1999.

Bidegain de Uran, Ana María. *Iglesia, pueblo y política: Un estudio de conflicto de intereses: Colombia, 1930–1955.* Bogotá: Pontificia Universidad Javeriana, 1985.

Borja Gómez, Jaime Humberto. *Rostros y rastros del demonio en la Nueva Granada: Indios, negros, judíos, mujeres y otras huestes de Satanás.* Bogotá: Editorial Ariel, 1998.

Broderick, Joe. *Camilo Torres: A Biography of the Priest-Guerillero.* New York: Doubleday, 1975.

Butler Flora, Cornelia. *Pentecostalism in Colombia: Baptism by Fire and Spirit.* Cranbury, NJ: Associated University Presses, 1976.

González, Fernán E. *Iglesia y estado en Colombia durante el siglo XIX (1820–1860).* Bogotá: Centro de Investigación y Educación Popular, 1985.

Levine, Daniel H. *Religion and Politics in Latin America: The Catholic Church in Venezuela and Colombia.* Princeton, NJ: Princeton University Press, 1981.

Maya Restrepo, Luz Adriana. *Brujería y reconstrucción de identidades entre los africanos y sus descendientes en la Nueva Granada, siglo XVII.* Bogotá: Ministerio de Cultura de Colombia, 2005.

McKnight, Kathryn Joy. *The Mystic of Tunja: The Writings of Madre Castillo, 1671–1742.* Amherst: University of Massachusetts Press, 1997.

Ríos Oyola, Sandra Milena. *Religion, Social Memory and Conflict: The Massacre of Bojayá in Colombia.* New York: Palgrave Macmillan, 2015.

Tejeiro, Clemencia. *El pentecostalismo en Colombia: Prácticas religiosas, liderazgo y participación política.* Bogotá: Universidad Nacional de Colombia, 2010.

Part III. City and Country

Appelbaum, Nancy P. *Muddied Waters: Race, Region, and Local History in Colombia, 1846–1948.* Durham, NC: Duke University Press, 2003.

Arocha, Jaime. *Mi gente de Bogotá: Estudio socio-económico y cultural de los afrodescendientes que residen en Bogotá.* Bogotá: Alcaldía Mayor de Bogotá, 2002.

Asher, Kiran. *Black and Green: Afro-Colombians, Development, and Nature in the Pacific Lowlands.* Durham, NC: Duke University Press, 2009.

Cabellero Calderón, Eduardo. *Diario de Tipacoque.* Medellín: Editorial Bedout, 1982.

———. *El cristo de espaldas.* 2nd ed. Bogotá: Editorial Oveja Negra, 1988.

Cepeda Samudio, Álvaro. *La Casa Grande.* Translated by Seymour Menton. Austin: University of Texas Press, 1991.

García Márquez, Gabriel. *One Hundred Years of Solitude.* Translated by Gregory Rabassa. New York: Harper and Row, 1970.

González, Tomás. *In the Beginning Was the Sea.* Translated by Frank Wynne. London: Pushkin, 2015.

Laurent, Muriel. *Contrabando, poder, y color en los albores de la república, Nueva Granada, 1822–1824.* Bogotá: Ediciones Uniandes, 2014.

Leal, Claudia. *A la buena de Dios: Colonización en La Macarena, ríos Duda y Guayabero.* Bogotá: FESCOL/CEREC, 1995.

Leddy Phelan, John. *The People and the King: The Comunero Revolution in Colombia, 1781.* Madison: University of Wisconsin Press, 2011.

LeGrande, Catherine. *Frontier Expansion and Peasant Protest.* Albuquerque: University of New Mexico, 1986.

McGraw, Jason. *The Work of Recognition: Caribbean Colombia and Postemancipation Struggle for Citizenship.* Chapel Hill: University of North Carolina Press, 2014.

Mejía Vallejo, Manuel. *La casa de las dos palmas.* Bogotá: Editorial Planeta, 1988.

Molano, Alfredo. *The Dispossessed: Chronicles of the Desterrados of Colombia.* Translated by Daniel Bland. Chicago: Haymarket Books, 2005.

Mosquera Rosero, Claudia. *Estrategias de inserción de la población negra en Santafé de Bogotá: Acá en Bogotá antes no se veían negros.* Bogotá: Instituto Distrital de Cultura y Turismo, 1998.

Palacios, Marco. *¿De quién es la tierra? Propiedad, politización y protesta campesina en la década de 1930.* Bogotá: Fondo de Cultura Económica, 2011.

Reinhardt, Nola. *Our Daily Bread: The Peasant Question and Family Farming in the Colombian Andes.* Berkeley: University of California Press, 1988.

Riaño Alcalá, Pilar. *Dwellers of Memory: Youth and Violence in Medellín, Colombia.* New Brunswick, NJ: Transaction, 2006.

Sommer, Doris. "María's Disease: A National Novel (Con)Founded." In *The National Romances of Latin America,* edited by Doris Sommer, 172–203. Berkeley: University of California Press, 1991.

Tovar Pinzón, Hermes. *Que nos tengan en cuenta: Colonos, empresarios y aldeas, Colombia 1800–1900.* Bogotá: Tercer Mundo Editores / Colcultura, 1995.

Zamosc, Leon. *The Agrarian Question and the Peasant Movement in Colombia: Struggles of the National Peasant Association, 1967–1981.* Cambridge: Cambridge University Press, 2006.

Part IV. Lived Inequalities

Almario García, Óscar. *Castas y razas en la independencia neogranadina, 1810–1830.* Bogotá: Universidad Nacional de Colombia, 2013.

Baquero Melo, Jairo. *Layered Inequalities: Land Grabbing, Collective Land Rights, and Afro-Descendant Resistance in Colombia.* Berlin: Lit Verlag, 2014.

Buitrago Salazar, Evelio. *Zarpazo the Bandit: Memoirs of an Undercover Agent of the Colombian Army.* Translated by M. Murray Lasley. Edited by Russell W. Ramsey. Tuscaloosa: University of Alabama Press, 1977.

Caicedo, Andres. *Liveforever.* Translated by Frank Wynne. New York: Penguin Classics, 2014.

Colmenares, Germán. *Popayán: Una sociedad esclavista 1680–1880.* Medellín: La Carreta Editores, 1979.

Deas, Malcolm. *Del poder y la gramática: Y otros ensayos sobre historia, política y literatura colombianas.* Bogotá: Tercer Mundo Editores, 1993.

Dueñas Vargas, Guiomar. *Of Love and Other Passions: Elites, Politics, and Family in Bogotá, Colombia, 1778–1870.* Albuquerque: University of New Mexico Press, 2015.

Escalante, Aquiles. *El Negro en Colombia.* Bogotá: Universidad Nacional de Colombia, Facultad de Sociología, 1964.

Escobar, Arturo. *Territories of Difference: Place, Movements, Life, Redes.* Durham, NC: Duke University Press, 2008.

Farnsworth-Alvear, Ann. *Dulcinea in the Factory: Myths, Morals, and Women in Colombia's Industrial Experiment, 1905–1960.* Durham, NC: Duke University Press, 2000.

Friede, Juan. *El indio en lucha por la tierra.* Popayán: Editorial Universidad del Cauca, 2010.

Garrido, Margarita. *Reclamos y representaciones: Variaciones sobre la política en el Nuevo Reino de Granada, 1770–1815.* Bogotá: Banco de la República, 1993.

Jimeno, Myriam. *Juan Gregorio Palechor: The Story of My Life.* Translated by Andy Klatt. Durham, NC: Duke University Press, 2014.

Lasso, Marixa. *Myths of Harmony: Race and Republicanism during the Age of Revolution, Colombia, 1795–1831.* Pittsburgh: University of Pittsburgh Press, 2007.

Molina Echeverri, Hernán. *Documentos para la historia del movimiento indígena colombiano contemporáneo.* Bogotá: Ministerio de Cultura de Colombia, 2010.

Mosquera Rosero-Labbé, Claudia, Luiz Claudio Barcelos, and Óscar Almario García. *Afro-reparaciones: Memorias de la esclavitud y justicia reparativa para negros, afrocolombianos y raizales.* Bogotá: Universidad Nacional de Colombia, 2007.

Ordóñez, Montserrat. "One Hundred Years of Unread Writing: Soledad Acosta de Samper, Elisa Mújica and Marvel Moreno." In *Knives and Angels: Women Writers in Latin America*, edited by Susan Bassnett, 132–44. London: Zed Books, 1990.

Ordóñez, Montserrat, Carolina Alzate, Liliana Ramírez, and Beatriz Restrepo. *De voces y de amores: Ensayos de literatura latinoamericana y otras variaciones.* Bogotá: Grupo Editorial Norma, 2005.

Palacios, Arnoldo. *Las estrellas son negras.* Bogotá: Ministerio de Cultura de Colombia, 2010.

Rappaport, Joanne. *The Disappearing Mestizo: Configuring Difference in the Colonial Andes.* Durham, NC: Duke University Press, 2014.

————. *Intercultural Utopias: Public Intellectuals, Cultural Experimentation, and Ethnic Dialogue in Colombia*. Durham, NC: Duke University Press, 1998.

Salazar, Alonso. *Born to Die in Medellín*. Translated by Nick Caistor. London: Latin American Bureau, 1992.

Sánchez de Friedemann, Nina. *Criele criele son. Del Pacífico negro: Arte, religión y cultura en el litoral Pacífico*. Bogotá: Editorial Planeta, 1989.

Silva, Renán. *Universidad y sociedad en el Nuevo Reino de Granada*. Bogotá: Banco de la República, 1992.

Velásquez, Magdala, ed. *Las mujeres en la historia de Colombia*. 3 vols. Bogotá: Presidencia de la República de Colombia and Grupo Editorial Norma, 1995.

Zapata Olivella, Manuel. *Changó: The Biggest Badass*. Translated by Jonathan Tittler. Lubbock: Texas Tech University Press, 2010.

Part V. Violence

Abad Faciolince, Hector, *Oblivion: A Memoir*. Translated by Anne McLean. New York: Farrar, Straus and Giroux, 2013.

Álape, Arturo. *El Bogotazo: Memorias del Olvido*. Bogotá: Editorial Pluma, 1983.

Bergquist, Charles. *Coffee and Conflict in Colombia, 1886–1910*. Durham, NC: Duke University Press, 1978.

Betancourt, Ingrid. *Even Silence Has an End: My Six Years of Captivity in the Colombian Jungle*. New York: Penguin, 2010.

Braun, Herbert. *The Assassination of Gaitán: Public Life and Urban Violence in Colombia*. Madison: University of Wisconsin Press, 1985.

————. *Our Guerrilla, Our Sidewalks: A Journey into the Violence of Colombia*. Boulder: University of Colorado Press, 1994.

Campos Zornosa, Yezid. *El baile rojo: Relatos no contados del genocidio de la UP*. Bogotá: Random House Mondadori, 2008.

Carrigan, Ana. *The Palace of Justice: A Colombian Tragedy*. New York: Four Walls Eight Windows, 1993.

Carroll, Leah. *Violent Democratization: Social Movements, Elites, and Politics in Colombia's Rural War Zones*. Notre Dame: University of Notre Dame Press, 2011.

Comisión Nacional de Reparación y Reconciliación. Grupo de Memoria Histórica. *¡Basta ya! Colombia: Memorias de guerra y dignidad*. Bogotá: Centro Nacional de Memoria Histórica, Departamento para la Prosperidad Social, 2013.

Dudley, Stephen. *Walking Ghosts: Murder and Guerrilla Politics in Colombia*. New York: Routledge, 2003.

Duzán, María Jimena. *Death Beat: A Colombian Journalist's Life inside the Cocaine Wars*. Translated and edited by Peter Eisner. New York: HarperCollins, 1994.

Edwards, Jennifer Gabrielle. *The Flight of the Condor: Stories of Violence and War from Colombia*. Madison: University of Wisconsin Press, 2007.

Fals Borda, Orlando, Germán Guzmán Campos, and Eduardo Umaña Luna. *La violencia en Colombia*. Bogotá: Tercer Mundo Editores, 1962.

García Márquez, Gabriel. *News of a Kidnapping*. Translated by Edith Grossman. New York: Random House, 1997.

Henderson, James D. *Modernization in Colombia: The Laureano Gómez Years, 1889–1965.* Gainesville: University of Florida Press, 2001.

León, Juanita. *Country of Bullets: Chronicles of War.* Translated by Guillermo Bleichmar. Albuquerque: University of New Mexico Press, 2010.

López Hernández, Claudia, ed. *Y refundaron la patria . . . : De cómo mafiosos y políticos reconfiguraron el Estado colombiano.* Bogotá: Random House Mondadori, 2011.

Lux, Martha. *Mujeres patriotas y realistas entre dos órdenes: Discursos, estrategias, y tácticas en la Guerra, la política, y el comercio (Nueva Granada, 1790–1830).* Bogotá: Universidad de la Andes, Facultad de Ciencias Sociales, 2014.

Medina, Álvaro. *Arte y violencia en Colombia desde 1948.* Bogotá: Museo de Arte Moderno de Bogotá, 1999.

Osterling, Jorge Pablo. *Democracy in Colombia: Clientelistic Politics and Guerrilla Warfare.* New Brunswick, NJ: Transaction, 1988.

Palacios, Marco. *Between Legitimacy and Violence: A History of Colombia.* Translated by Richard Stoller. Durham, NC: Duke University Press, 2006.

Pécaut, Daniel. *Orden y violencia: Colombia 1930–1954.* Bogotá: Grupo Editorial Norma, 2001.

Pizarro Leongómez, Eduardo. *Las Farc: De la autodefensa a la combinación de todas las formas de lucha.* Bogotá: Universidad Nacional de Colombia, 1991.

Restrepo, Laura. *Delirium.* Translated by Natasha Wimmer. New York: Doubleday, 2007.

Rojas, Cristina. *Civilization and Violence: Regimes of Representation in Nineteenth-Century Colombia.* Minneapolis: University of Minnesota Press, 2001.

Roldán, Mary. *Blood and Fire: La Violencia in Antioquia, Colombia, 1946–1953.* Durham, NC: Duke University Press, 2002.

Rosero, Evelio. *The Armies.* Translated by Anne McLean. New York: New Directions, 2009.

Sánchez, Gonzálo, and Donny Meertens, *Bandits, Peasants, and Politics: The Case of "La Violencia" in Colombia.* Translated by Alan Hynds. Austin: University of Texas Press, 2001.

Sanders, James E. *Contentious Republicans: Popular Politics, Race, and Class in Nineteenth-Century Colombia.* Durham, NC: Duke University Press, 2004.

Tate, Winifred. *Counting the Dead: The Culture and Politics of Human Rights Activism in Colombia.* Berkeley: University of California Press, 2007.

Taussig, Michael. *Law in a Lawless Land: Diary of a Limpieza in Colombia.* Chicago: University of Chicago Press, 2005.

Uribe, María Tila. *Los años escondidos.* Bogotá: CESTRA/CEREC, 1994.

Vásquez Perdomo, María Eugenia. *My Life as a Colombian Revolutionary: Reflections of a Former Guerrillera.* Translated by Lorena Terando. Introduction by Arthur Schmidt. Philadelphia: Temple University Press, 2005.

Part VI. Change and Continuity in the Colombian Economy

Bejarano, Jesús Antonio. *El régimen agrario, de la economía exportadora a la economía industrial.* Bogotá: La Carreta Editores, 1979.

Betancourt, Dario, and Marta Luz García. *Contrabandistas, marimberos, y mafiosos: Historia social de la mafia colombiana (1965–1992)*. Bogotá: TM Editores, 1994.

Currie, Lauchlin. *The Basis of a Development Program for Colombia*. Baltimore: Johns Hopkins University Press, 1950.

de la Pedraja Tomán, René. *Historia de la energía en Colombia: 1537–1930*. Bogotá: El Áncora Editores, 1985.

Fluharty, Vernon Lee. *Dance of the Millions: Military Rule and the Social Revolution in Colombia, 1930–1956*. Westport, CT: Greenwood, 1975.

Gil, Leslie. *A Century of Violence in a Red City: Popular Struggle, Counterinsurgency, and Human Rights in Colombia*. Durham, NC: Duke University Press, 2016.

Kalmonovitz, Salomón. *Economia y nación: Una breve historia de Colombia*. Bogotá: Universidad Nacional de Colombia, 1985.

Lane, Kris. *Colour of Paradise: The Emerald in the Age of Gunpowder Empires*. New Haven, CT: Yale University Press, 2010.

Langebaek, Carl Henrik. *Mercados, poblamiento e integración étnica entre los Muiscas, siglo XVI*. Bogotá: Banco de la República, 1987.

Ocampo, Gloria Isabel. *La instauración de la ganadería en el Valle del Sinú: La hacienda Marta Magdalena, 1881–1956*. Medellín: Universidad de Antioquia, Instituto Colombiano de Antropología e Historia, 2007.

Ocampo, José Antonio. *Colombia y la economía mundial, 1830–1910*. 2nd ed. Bogotá: Ediciones Uniandes, 2013.

Palacios, Marco. *Coffee in Colombia: An Economic, Social, and Political History*. Cambridge: Cambridge University Press, 1980.

Restrepo, Laura. *The Dark Bride*. Translated by Stephen A. Lytle. New York: HarperCollins, 2003.

Sáenz Rovner, Eduardo. *Colombia años 50: Industriales, política y democracia*. Bogotá: Universidad Nacional de Colombia, 2002.

Safford, Frank. *The Ideal of the Practical: Colombia's Struggle to Form a Technical Elite*. Austin: University of Texas Press, 1976.

Taussig, Michael. *My Cocaine Museum*. Chicago: University of Chicago Press, 2009.

Tovar Zambrano, Bernardo. *La intervención económica del estado en Colombia: 1914–1936*. Bogotá: Biblioteca Banco Popular, 1984.

Twinam, Ann. *Miners, Merchants, and Farmers in Colonial Colombia*. Austin: University of Texas Press, 1982.

van Isschot, Luis. *The Social Origins of Human Rights: Protesting Political Violence in Colombia's Oil Capital, 1910–2010*. Madison: University of Wisconsin Press, 2015.

Vásquez, Juan Gabriel. *The Sound of Things Falling*. Translated by Anne McLean. New York: Riverhead, 2013.

Part VII. Transnational Colombia

Bal, Mieke. *Of What One Cannot Speak: Doris Salcedo's Political Art*. Chicago: University of Chicago Press, 2011.

Borda, Sandra, and Arlene B. Tickner. *Relaciones internacionales y política exterior de Colombia*. Bogotá: Universidad de los Andes, Facultad de Ciencias Sociales, Departamento de Ciencia Política–CESO, 2011.

Casement, Roger. *The Amazon Journal of Sir Roger Casement.* Introduction and additional notes by Angus Mitchell. London: Anaconda, 1997.

Cataño, Gonzalo. *La introducción del pensamiento moderno en Colombia: El caso de Luis E. Nieto Arteta.* Bogotá: Universidad Externado de Colombia, 2013.

Davis, Wade. *One River: Explorations and Discoveries in the Amazon Rainforest.* New York: Simon and Schuster, 1996.

Drake, Paul W. *The Money Doctor in the Andes: U.S. Advisors, Investors, and Economic Reform in Latin America from World War I to the Great Depression.* Durham, NC: Duke University Press, 1989.

Erlick, June Carolyn. *A Gringa in Bogotá: Living Colombia's Invisible War.* Austin: University of Texas Press, 2010.

Estrada Álvarez, Jairo, ed. *Plan Colombia: Ensayos críticos.* Bogotá: Universidad Nacional de Colombia, 2001.

Franco, Jorge. *Paradise Travel.* Translated by Katherine Silver. New York: Farrar, Straus and Giroux, 2006.

Helg, Aline. *La educación en Colombia: 1918–1957.* Bogotá: CEREC, 1987.

Holton, Isaac. *Twenty Months in the Andes.* New York: Harper and Brothers, 1857.

Jurado Valencia, Fabio, ed. *Mito: Cincuenta años después (1955–2005). Una selección de ensayos.* Bogotá: Editorial Lumen, Universidad Nacional de Colombia, 2005.

Meshkat, Klaus, and Jose María Rojas, eds. *Liquidando el pasado: La izquierda colombiana en los archivos de la Unión Soviética.* Bogotá: Taurus / FESCOL, 2009.

Murillo, Mario, and Jesús Rey Avirama. *Colombia and the United States: War, Unrest, and Destabilization.* New York: Seven Stories, 2011.

Mutis, Álvaro. *The Adventures and Misadventures of Maqroll.* Translated by Edith Grossman. New York: New York Review of Books Classics, 2002.

Paternostro, Silvana. *In the Land of God and Man: A Latin Woman's Journey.* New York: Penguin, 1999.

Ramírez, María Clemencia. *Between the Guerrillas and the State: The Cocalero Movement, Citizenship, and Identity in the Colombian Amazon.* Durham, NC: Duke University Press, 2011.

Reichel-Dolmatoff, Gerardo, and Richard Evans Schultes. *The Shaman and the Jaguar: A Study of Narcotic Drugs among the Indians of Colombia.* Philadelphia: Temple University Press, 1975.

Roca, José, and Sylvia Suárez. *Transpolítico: Arte en Colombia 1992–2012.* Barcelona: Lunwerg, 2012.

Rodrigues Widholm, Julie et al. *Doris Salcedo.* Chicago: University of Chicago Press, 2015.

Rodríguez-García, José María. *The City of Translation: Poetry and Literature in 19th Century Colombia.* London: Palgrave Macmillan, 2010.

Rosen, Jonathan D. *The Losing War: Plan Colombia and Beyond.* Albany: State University of New York Press, 2014.

Schneider Enriquez, Mary. *Doris Salcedo: The Materiality of Mourning.* Cambridge, MA: Harvard Art Museums, 2016.

Steiner Sampedro, Claudia, Carlos Páramo Bonilla, and Roberto Pineda Camacho. *El *paraíso del diablo: Roger Casement y el informe del Putumayo, un siglo después*. Bogotá: Universidad Nacional de Colombia, 2014.

Tate, Winifred. *Drugs, Thugs, and Diplomats: U.S. Policymaking in Colombia*. Stanford, CA: Stanford University Press, 2015.

Tokatlian, Juan. *Globalización, narcotráfico y violencia: Siete ensayos sobre Colombia*. Bogotá: Grupo Editorial Norma, 2000.

Ulloa, Astrid. *The Ecological Native: Indigenous Peoples' Movements and Eco-Governmentality in Colombia*. New York: Routledge, 2013.

Vargas, Ricardo. *Narcotráfico, guerra, y política antidrogas: Una perspectiva sobre las drogas en el conflicto armado colombiano*. Bogotá: Acción Andina, 2005.

Wylie, Leslie. *Colombia's Forgotten Frontier: A Literary Geography of the Putumayo*. Oxford: Oxford University Press, 2013.

Acknowledgment of Copyrights and Sources

Part I. Human Geography

"Ahpikondiá," by Gerardo Reichel-Dolmatoff, from "The Creation Myth" in *Amazonian Cosmos: The Sexual and Religious Symbolism of the Tukano Indians* (Chicago: University of Chicago Press, 1971), 24–28. Used by permission of the University of Chicago Press.

"'One after the Other, They All Fell under Your Majesty's Rule': Lands Loyal to the Bogotá Become New Granada," by Gonzalo Jiménez de Quesada, from "Epítome del Nuevo Reino de Granada," and by anonymous, from "Relación de Santa Marta," AGI (Archivo General de Indias) Patronato 27, R. 9, Folios 13v–16r, in Michael Francis, *Invading Colombia: Spanish Accounts of the Gonzalo Jiménez de Quesada Expedition of Conquest*, 38–44, 68–81, 104–10. Copyright © 2007 by The Pennsylvania State University Press. Reprinted by permission of the Pennsylvania State University Press.

"A City in the African Diaspora": (I) from "Factura de Venta," 1736. In *Caja Negros y Esclavos Cundinamarca*, Tomo 8, Folio 505R, Archivo General de la Nación, Bogotá, Colombia. Available at http://negrosyesclavos.archivogeneral.gov.co/portal/apps/php/documentation.kwe; (II) from "Rebelión," by Álvaro José Arroyo. Used by permission of Discos Fuentes Edimusica.

"Crossing to Nationhood across a *Cabuya* Bridge in the Eastern Andes," by Manuel Ancízar, from *Peregrinación del Alpha por las provincias del norte de la Nueva Granada* (Bogotá: Imprenta de Echavarría Hermanos, 1853), 132–40. Available at Biblioteca Luis Ángel Arango Virtual. http://www.lablaa.org/blaavirtual/historia/perealpha/indice.htm.

"A Gaping Mouth Swallowing Men," by José Eustasio Rivera, from *The Vortex*, translated by E. K. James (Bogotá: Panamericana Editorial, 2001), 155–56, 261–63, 272–75, 280–94.

"Frontier 'Incidents' Trouble Bogotá": (I) by Jane M. Rausch, from *The Llanos Frontier in Colombian History, 1830–1930* (Albuquerque: University of New Mexico Press, 1993), 269–74. Used by permission of University of New Mexico Press; (II) "Alfredo Villamil Fajardo to His Excellency the President of the Republic, Boca del Yavarí," by Alfredo Villamil Fajardo. In *Enrique Olaya Herrera*. Sección 2ª, Caja 28, Carpeta 30, Folios 30–60, Archivo General de la Nación.

"Crab Antics on San Andrés and Providencia," by Peter Wilson, from *Crab Antics: The*

Part II. Religious Pluralities

(Bogotá: Casa Editorial "El Liberal," 1912), 7, 113–16; (III) by Andrés Botero, from *Catecismo político y social* (Medellín: Tipografía San Antonio, 1915), as reproduced in Patricia Londoño Vega, *Religion, Culture, and Society: Medellín and Antioquia, 1850–1930* (Oxford: Oxford University Press, 2002), 51. Translation courtesy of Oxford University Press.

"Sabina, Bring Some Candles to Light to the Virgin," by Albalucía Ángel, from *Estaba la pájara pinta sentada en el verde limón,* edited by Martha Gómez Cardona (Medellín: Universidad de Antioquia, 2003), 161–83. Used by permission of Albalucía Ángel.

"We Were Not Able to Say That We Were Jewish," by Paula Douer, unpublished interview with Paul Hané (Bogotá, 1994). Courtesy of Paula Douer.

"As a Colombian, as a Sociologist, as a Christian, and as a Priest, I Am a Revolutionary," by Camilo Torres Restrepo, from "Message to the Christians," "Message to the Military," "Message to the Communists," and "Message to Students," translated by Robert Olsen and Linda Day, in *Revolutionary Writings* (New York: Herder and Herder, 1969), 172–75, 178–80, 196–98.

"Who Stole the Chalice from Badillo's Church?," by Rafael Escalona, from "La custodia de Badillo." Used by permission of Discos Fuentes Edimusica.

"Life Is a Birimbí," by Rodrigo Parra Sandoval, from *El álbum secreto del Sagrado Corazón de Jesús* (México: Editorial J. Mortiz, 1976), 19–21. Courtesy of Rodrigo Parra Sandoval.

"Our Lady of the Assassins," by Fernando Vallejo, from *Our Lady of the Assassins* (London: Serpent's Tail, 2001), 1–5, 10–12. Used by permission of Profile Books Limited.

"One Woman's Path to Pentecostal Conversion," from "Case History: Rosalinda," in *The Reformation of Machismo: Evangelical Conversion and Gender in Colombia,* by Elizabeth E. Brusco, 107–13, copyright © 1995. By permission of the author and the University of Texas Press.

"La Ombligada," by Sergio Antonio Mosquera, from *Antropofauna Afro-Chocoana: Un estudio cultural sobre la animalidad.* Serie Ma'Mawu, no. 11 (Quibdó: Universidad Tecnológica del Chocó, 2009), 44–64. Courtesy of Sergio Antonio Mosquera.

"A Witness to Impunity," by Javier Giraldo, SJ, from *Colombia: The Genocidal Democracy* (Monroe, ME: Common Courage Press, 1996), 26–31, 40–42. Spanish version courtesy of Centre d'estudis Cristianisme I Justícia (Barcelona). English translation used by permission of Common Courage Press.

Part III. City and Country

"Emptying the 'Storehouse' of Indian Labor and Goods," from "Encomiendas, encomenderos e indígenas tributarios del Nuevo Reino de Granada," *Anuario Colombiano de Historia Social y de la Cultura* 2 (1964): 425–27.

"To Santafé! To Santafé!," from *Capitulaciones,* held at Biblioteca Nacional de Colombia, *Documentos de los Comuneros,* Tomo III, Ms 371, Folio 13. Available as part of the series "Documentos que hicieron un país," at http://www.banrepcultural.org/blaavirtual/historia/docpais/indice.htm, accessed April 24, 2014 (URL no longer functional in May 2016).

"Killing a Jaguar," by Jorge Isaacs, from *María, a South American Romance*, translated by Rollo Ogden (New York: Harper and Brothers, 1890), 2–9, 21–25, 69–75, 84–89, 261–73, 279–88.

"The Time of the Slaves Is Over," by Candelario Obeso: (I) from "Canción del Boga Ausente," in *Cantos populares de mi tierra* (Bogotá: Instituto Distrital de Cultura y Turismo, 2004), 54–55; (II) from "Serenata," in *Cantos populares de mi tierra* (Bogotá: Imprenta de Borda, 1877), 30.

"A Landowner's Rules," by Ángel María Caballero, from *Reglamentos de la Hacienda El Chocho* (Bogotá: Tipografía El Globo, 1896), 1–8.

"Muleteers on the Road," by Beatríz Helena Robledo, from "Por Caminos de Arrieros," *Boletín Cultural y Bibliográfico* 23, no. 8 (1986): 43–56. Courtesy of Beatríz Helena Robledo.

"Campesino Life in the Boyacá Highlands," by Orlando Fals Borda, from *Peasant Society in the Colombian Andes: A Sociological Study of Saucio* (Gainesville: University of Florida Press, 1955), 147–49, 166–69. Reprinted with permission of University Press of Florida.

"One Lowland Town Becomes a World: Gabriel García Márquez Returning to Aracataca," by Gabriel García Márquez, fragment of "Auto-Crítica" and "La casa de los Buendía (apuntes para una novela)," in *Obra periodística: Textos costeños (1948–1952)*, Tomo II (Bogotá: Editorial La Oveja Negra), 580–81, 710–11. © Gabriel García Márquez, 1981 y Herederos de Gabriel García Márquez.

"The Bricklayers: 1968 on Film," by Jorge Rufinelli, from "Marta Rodríguez: El Documental vivo vuelve a vivir," *Secuencias. Revista de historia del cine*, no. 18 (2003): 84–101. Courtesy of Jorge Rufinelli and *Secuencias. Revista de historia del cine*.

"Switchblades in the City," by Arturo Álape, from *Ciudad Bolívar: La hoguera de las ilusiones* (Bogotá: Editorial Planeta, 1995), 203–41.

"Desplazado: 'Now I Am Here as an Outcast,'" by Carlos Alberto Giraldo, Jesús Abad Colorado, and Diego Pérez, from "Yo, Desplazado," in *Relatos e imágenes: El desplazamiento en Colombia* (Bogotá: CINEP, 1997), 127–31. Courtesy of CINEP.

"An Agrarian Counterreform," by Luis Bernardo Flórez Enciso, from "Extinción de dominio, reforma agraria, democracia y paz," paper presented at the conference *La extinción de la propiedad ilícita: ¿Una vía para la reforma agraria?*, Revista Economía Colombiana, no. 309 (Bogotá: Contraloría General de la Nación, 2005). Courtesy of Contraloría General de la Nación.

Part IV. Lived Inequalities

"Rules Are Issued for Different Populations: Indians, Blacks, Non-Christians": (I) from *Libro de acuerdos de la Audiencia Real del Nuevo Reino de Granada, 1551–1556*, edited by Enrique Ortega Ricaurte (Bogotá: Archivo Nacional de Colombia, 1947), 201–2, 235–36; (II) from *Libro de acuerdos de la Audiencia Real del Nuevo Reino de Granada, 1557–1558*, edited by Enrique Ortega Ricaurte (Bogotá: Archivo Nacional de Colombia, 1948), 108–9.

"An Indian Nobleman Petitions His King," by Diego de Torres, from "Agravios del

Cacique de Turmequé," in *Documentos inéditos para la historia de Boyacá y Colombia*, edited by Ulíses Rojas (Tunja: Biblioteca de la Academia Boyacense de Historia), 42–69.

"A Captured Maroon Faces His Interrogators," by Francisco Angola, from "Testimony of the Trials and Punishments Carried out by Field Marshall Francisco de Murga, Governor and Captain General of Cartagena, against the Rebel Black Maroons of the Palenques of Limon, Polin, and Zanaguare. Statement of Francisco Angola (1634)," in *Testimonio de los proçessos y castigos—qve se hiçieron—por el Maesttro de Campo Françisco de Murga gouernador y cappitan general de Cartagena—contra los negros çimarrones y alçados—de los palenqves—del Limon—Polin y Zanaguare, 1633–1644*. Housed at Archivo General de Indias, Seville, 550–51. Patronato 234, R. 7, no. 2.

"Carrasquilla's Characters: La Negra Narcisa, el Amito Martín, and Doña Bárbara," by Tomás Carrasquilla, from *La marquesa de Yolombó: Novela del tiempo de la colonia* (Medellín: A. J. Cano, 1928), 167–80. Courtesy of Mercedes Arango and Adolfo Arango (representatives for Carrasquilla's heir).

"Carried through the Streets of Bogotá: Grandmother's Sedan Chair," by Eduardo Caballero Calderón, from *Memorias infantiles* (Bogotá: Villegas Editores, [1964/1994]), 40–56. Courtesy of Beatríz Caballero and Villegas Editores.

"The Street-Car Bogotá of New Social Groups: Clerks, Switchboard Operators, Pharmacists," by Augusto Morales Pino, from *Los de en medio* (Bogotá: Editorial Kelly, 1967), 119–24, 234–35.

"It Is a Norm among Us to Believe That a Woman Cannot Act on Her Own Criteria," by María Cano, from "Letter to Guillermo Hernández Rodríguez, September 1930," in *María Cano, mujer rebelde*, by Ignacio Torres Giraldo (Bogotá: Editorial La Rosca, 1972), 149–58.

"I Energetically Protest in Defense of Truth and Justice," by Manuel Quintín Lame: (I) from "Las luchas del indio que bajo de la montaña al valle de la civilización, 1973," in *Liberation Theology from Below: The Life and Thought of Manuel Quintín Lame*, translated and edited by Gonzalo Castillo Cárdenas (Maryknoll, NY: Orbis Books, 1987), 98–100, 109–17; (II) from Archivo General de la Nación, *Ministerio del Interior. Despacho del Ministro*, Caja 25 / Carpeta 223, Folios 3r 4v.

"Bringing Presents from Abroad," by Manuel Zapata Olivella, from *Chambacú: Black Slum*, translated by Jonathan Tittler (Pittsburgh: Latin American Literary Review Press, 1989), 65–67. Used by permission of Latin American Literary Review Press.

"Cleaning for Other People," by Anna Rubbo and Michael Taussig, from "Up off Their Knees: Servanthood in Southwest Colombia," *Latin American Perspectives* 10, no. 4 (1984): 5–23. Copyright © 1983 by SAGE. Reprinted by permission of SAGE Publications.

"A Feminist Writer Sketches the Interior Life and Death of an Upper-Class Woman," by Marvel Moreno, from "Algo tan feo en la vida de una señora bien," in *Algo tan feo en la vida de una señora bien* (Bogotá: Editorial Pluma, 1980), 95–122. Courtesy of Camila Mendoza, the author's daughter.

"Barranquilla's First Gay Carnival Queen," by Gloria Triana, from *Cada uno sabe su secreto*, transcribed excerpt by Mariantonia Rojas Cabal and Andrés Castro Samayoa

(Colombia: Gloria Triana and Producciones El Sur Ltda., 2007). Documentary. Available at http://www.carnavaldebarranquilla.com/divascarnavaleras.html, accessed January 11, 2012. Courtesy of Gloria Triana.

"Romance Tourism," by Felicity Schaeffer-Grabiel, from "Flexible Technologies of Subjectivity and Mobility across the Americas," *American Quarterly* 58, no. 3 (2006): 891–914. © 2006 The American Studies Association. Reprinted with permission of Johns Hopkins University Press.

"They Are Using Me as Cannon Fodder," by Flaco Flow and Melanina, from "La jungla." Song lyrics. Courtesy of Benny Guevara, from Audio Lírica.

Part V. Violence

"Captains and Criminals," by Juan Rodríguez Freile, from *El carnero: Según el otro manuscrito de Yerbabuena*, edited and with an introduction and notes by Mario G. Romero (Santafé de Bogotá: Instituto Caro y Cuervo, 1997), 94–96.

"War to the Death," by Simón Bolívar, from "Decree of War to the Death," in *Selected Writings of Bolivar, Vol. 1, June 15, 1813*, translated by Lewis Bertrand, edited by Harold A. Bierk Jr. (New York: Colonial Press, 1951), 31–32.

"A Girl's View of War in the Capital," by Soledad Acosta de Samper, from *Diario íntimo y otros escritos de Soledad Acosta de Samper* (Bogotá: Alcaldía Mayor de Bogotá / Instituto Distrital de Cultura y Turismo, 2004), 201–2, 204–6, 206–9, 394, 428–34, 435, 439, 443–44, 459–60.

"Let This Be Our Last War," by José María Quijano Wallis, from *Memorias autobiográficas y de carácter social* (Rome: Grottaferrata, 1919), 519–51.

"The 'Silent Demonstration' of February 7, 1948," by Jorge Eliécer Gaitán, from "Oración por la Paz," in *Obras selectas, Part 1* (Bogotá: Imprenta Nacional, 1979), 317–18.

"Dead Bodies Appear on the Streets," by Gustavo Álvarez Gardeazábal, from *Cóndores no entierran todos los días* (Barcelona: Ediciones Destino, 1972), 63–66, 70–77. Courtesy of Gustavo Álvarez Gardeazábal.

"Cruelty Acted as a Stimulant," by José Gutiérrez Rodríguez, from *La rebeldía en Colombia: Observaciones psicológicas sobre actualidad política* (Bogotá: Ediciones Tercer Mundo, 1962), 85–93. Courtesy of Magdalena Restrepo de Gutiérrez.

"Two Views of the National Front": (I) by Álvaro Gómez Hurtado, from "Speech to the Colombian Senate. October 25, 1961," in *La paz, la violencia: Testigos de excepción,* by Arturo Álape (Bogotá: Planeta, 1985), 244–46. Courtesy of Enrique Gómez Hurtado; (II) by Ofelia Uribe de Acosta, "Una voz insurgente: Entrevista con Ofelia Uribe de Acosta," from *Voces Insurgentes,* edited by María Cristina Laverde Toscano and Luz Helena Sánchez Gómez (Bogotá: Universidad Central / SERCOLDES, 1986), 39–40. Courtesy of SERCOLDES and Universidad Central.

"Starting Points for the FARC and the ELN": (I) by FARC, from "Programa agrario de los guerrilleros de las FARC-EP," in *Las verdaderas intenciones de las FARC* (Intermedio Editores, una división de Circulo de Lectores S.A., 1999), 24–31; (II) by Ejército de Liberación Nacional, from "El manifiesto de Simacota," Enero 7, 1965. Available at Portal Voces de Colombia, http://www.eln-voces.com/index.php/voces-del-eln/comando-central/articulos/71manifiesto-de-simacota, accessed June 4, 2015. Courtesy of Ejército de Liberación Nacional.

"Where Is Omaira Montoya?," by María Tila Uribe and Francisco J. Trujillo, from *Desde Adentro* (Bogotá: Comité de Solidaridad con los Presos Políticos, 1984), 68–71, 74–76. Courtesy of María Tila Uribe.

"We Prefer a Grave in Colombia to a Cell in the United States," by Los Extraditables, from "The *Extraditables* Inform the Colombian People," press release, December 1989. Available at http://www.proyectopabloescobar.com/2011/04/comunicado-de-los-extraditables.html.

"A Medic's Life within a Cocaine-Fueled Paramilitary Organization," by Diego Viáfara Salinas, from "Statement by Diego Viáfara Salinas to the U.S. Congress, Senate Permanent Subcommittee on Governmental Affairs," in *Hearings on the Structure of International Trafficking Networks*, 101st Cong., 1st sess., September 12–13, 1989 (Washington, DC: U.S. Government Printing Office, 1989), 68–93.

"Carlos Castaño 'Confesses,'" by Mauricio Arangurén Molina, from *Mi confesión: Carlos Castaño revela sus secretos* (Bogotá: Editorial Oveja Negra, 2001), 142–55. Courtesy of Mauricio Arangurén Molina.

"The Song of the Flies," by María Mercedes Carranza, from "Necoclí," "Mapiripán," "Pore," "Ituango," "Vista Hermosa," and "Soacha," in *Song of the Flies (An Account of the Events)*, translated by Margarita Millar (San Francisco: Freedom Voices, 2009). Courtesy of Margarita Millar and Melibea Garavito Carranza.

"Kidnapped," by Luis Mendieta Ovalle, from "Letter from Coronel Luis Mendieta to His Family," December 21, 2007. Available at http://www.eltiempo.com/archivo/documento/CMS-3920866.

"Parapolitics," by Claudia López and Óscar Sevillano, from "Balance Político de la Parapolítica," *Revista Arcanos* 11, no. 14 (December 2008): 62–87. Courtesy of Claudia López and Óscar Sevillano.

Part VI. Change and Continuity in the Colombian Economy

"El Dorado," by Fray Pedro Simón, from *Noticias historiales de las conquistas de tierra firme. Segunda Parte* (Bogotá: Casa Editorial Medardo Rivas, 1891 [1620s]), 242–50. Available at http://archive.org/details/tierrafirmeindiaso2simbrich.

"The Conquest Yields Other Treasures: Potatoes, Yucca, Corn": (I) by Juan de Castellanos, from *Historia del Nuevo Reino de Granada, Canto Segundo*, 1886 (Antonio Paz y Meliá edition, 1601), 88. Translated by J. G. Hawkes in "The History of the Potato," Masters Memorial Lecture, *Journal of the Royal Horticultural Society* 219 (1966); (II) by Galeotto Cei, from *Viaggio e relazione delle Indie, 1539–1553*, edited by Francesco Surdich (Rome: Bulzoni, 1992), 13–15, 16–18.

"Cauca's Slave Economy," by Germán Colmenares, from *Historia económica y social de Colombia, 1537–1719* (Bogotá: Tercer Mundo Editores, 1973), 46–56.

"A Jesuit Writes to the King: Profits from Coca Leaf Could Surpass Tea," by Antonio Julián, from "De la celebrada planta llamada hayo, por otro nombre coca, pasto

Colombia," March 16, 2012. Available at http://www.nestle.com/media/statements/letter-to-colombian-trade-union, accessed February 1, 2013.

Part VII. Transnational Colombia

"A Creole Reads the Declaration of the Rights of Man and the Citizen," by Antonio Nariño, from "Defensa," in *Antonio Nariño: Escritos políticos*, edited by Javier Ocampo López (Bogotá: El Áncora Editores, Editorial Panamericana, 2002), 41–92.

"Humboldt's Diary, May 1801," by Alexander von Humboldt, from *Reise auf dem Rio Magdalena, durch die Anden und Mexiko* (Berlin: Akademie Verlag GmbH, 2003), 73–75.

"The Most Practical, Because the Most Brutal," by José Asunción Silva, from *After Dinner Conversation: The Diary of a Decadent*, translated by Kelly Washbourne, 85–97. Copyright © 2005. By permission of the University of Texas Press.

"Grandfather Arrives from Bremen," by Pedro Gómez Valderrama, from *La otra raya del tigre* (Bogotá: Siglo Veintiuno Editores, 1977), 11–19, 54–61. Courtesy of Pedro Alejo Gómez.

"We Were Called 'Turks,'" by Elías Saer Kayata, from "Breve historia del emigrante árabe Elías Saer Kayata," in "Appendix 1. Lorica, una colonia árabe a orillas del río Sinú," by Joaquín Viloria de la Hoz, from *Cuadernos de Historia Económica y Empresarial* no. 10, Banco de la República—Sucursal Cartagena (June 2003): 73–79. Available at http://www.banrep.gov.co/es/lorica-una-colonia-arabe-orillas-rio-sinu, accessed June 10, 2015. Courtesy of Joaquín Viloria de la Hoz.

"Two Presidents' Views: 'I Took the Isthmus' and 'I Was Dispossessed, Insulted, and Dishonored to No End'": (I) by Theodore Roosevelt, from "Speech at the University of California, Berkeley, March 23, 1911," *University of California Chronicle* 13, no. 2 (April 1911): 130–45; (II) by Marco Fidel Suárez, from "Cablegrama de indemnización por Panamá," in *Documentos que hicieron un país*, Archivo General de la Nación, Colombia. Available at www.lablaa.org/blaavirtual/historia/docpais/panama.doc.

"Facing the Yankee Enemy," by José María Vargas Vila, from *Ante los bárbaros (Los Estados Unidos y la guerra): El yanki: He ahí el enemigo* (Barcelona: Imprenta de José Anglada, 1918), 22–25, 47–49, 58–61, 116–23, 140–45, 191–210.

"Bogotá's Art Scene in 1957: 'There Is No Room for Any of the Old Servilism,'" by Marta Traba, from *Colombia* (Washington, DC: Pan-American Union, 1959), 1–18. Courtesy of Organization of American States and Fernando Zalamea.

"1969: The GAO Evaluates Money Spent in Colombia," by US Senate Committee on Foreign Relations, from *Survey of the Alliance for Progress Colombia: A Case of U.S. Aid: A Case Study Prepared by the Staff of the Committee on Foreign Relations, United States Senate, Together with a Report of the Comptroller General* (Washington, DC: US Government Printing Office, 1969), 667–76.

"Who Was Where during the Mapiripán Massacre?," by Ignacio Gómez Gómez, from "Los peligros de la ayuda militar," *El Espectador*, February 27, 2000. http://www.publicintegrity.org/2000/02/27/3308/risks-us-aid. Courtesy of Ignacio Gómez Gómez.

"A *Minga* of Voluntary Eradication," by Asociación Popular de Negros Unidos del Río

Yurumanguí (APONURY), from "Minga comunitaria de erradicación manual de cultivos con fines ilícitos en el territorio colectivo Ancestral del río Yurumanguí." Press release, November 2007. Available at http://prensarural.org/spip/IMG/pdf/MINGA_ERRADICACION_YURUMANGUI.pdf, accessed June 10, 2015.

"Latin American Ex-Presidents Push to Reorient the War on Drugs," by the Latin American Commission on Drugs and Democracy, from *Drugs and Democracy: Toward a Paradigm Shift,* 2008 Statement. Available at http://www.drogasedemo cracia.org/Arquivos/declaracao_ingles_site.pdf. Courtesy of the Global Commission on Drug Policy.

"A New Export Product: *Yo soy Betty, la fea* Goes Global," by Yeidy Rivero, from "Our Betty: The Legacy of *Yo soy Betty, la fea*'s Success in Colombia," in TV*'s Betty Goes Global: From Telenovela to International Brand,* edited by Janet McCabe and Kim Akass (London: I. B. Tauris, 2013), 51–61. Used by permission of I. B. Tauris.

"Today We Understand and Can Say No," by Lorenzo Muelas, from *Resistencia a la explotación petrolera: Mensaje de los U'wa a los Secoya* (Quito: Acción Ecológica, Oilwatch, 1999). Courtesy of Acción Ecológica and Lorenzo Muelas.

"Toward a Stable and Enduring Peace," by Delegados del Gobierno de la República de Colombia (Gobierno Nacional) and Delegados de las Fuerzas Armadas Revolucionarias de Colombia–Ejército del Pueblo, from "Acuerdo General para la terminación del conflicto y la construcción de una paz estable y duradera," August 26, 2012. Available at https://www.mesadeconversaciones.com.co/sites/default/files/AcuerdoGeneralTerminacionConflicto.pdf, accessed June 10, 2015.

Every reasonable effort has been made to obtain permission. We invite copyright holders to inform us of any oversights.

Index

Africans: arrival of enslaved, 22, 34–37, 62, 77–78, 97, 135, 447–49; Catholicism and, 34, 97, 105–9, 258, 260; cultural legacies from, 69–70, 73, 79, 135, 160, 257, 260, 293, 554; ethnicities among, 62, 77–78, 162; in fiction, 189, 260, 554; gender and, 22, 35–36, 189, 447–49; legal strategies of enslaved, 243; *palenques* and, 34, 257–59; in song, 36–39. *See also* Afro-Colombians; enslavement; racial patterns

Afro-Colombians, 13, 69–74, 293–94, 485–86; activism and, 13, 69–70, 511, 575–78; as *bogas*, 196–99, 534, 537–39; Caribbean island populations of, 62–68; collective land rights of, 13, 69–70, 587; in colonial era, 245, 247, 257–59, 447–49; as creoles ("criollos"), 258–59, 447; cultural practices of, 73–74, 98, 135, 162–65, 234, 577; curricular reform and, 69, 73–74; in fiction, 196–99, 260–65, 273, 293–95, 536; gender and, 36–38, 65–68, 135, 162–65, 262–65, 294–96, 315–17; intellectual work by, 293, 486, 575–78; as internally displaced people, 70, 232–35, 577; mining and, 77, 162, 260, 446–49, 485–94; musical traditions of, 34, 36–38, 77–79, 244, 295, 318–21; overt racism and, 88, 489; *palenques* and, 34, 62, 69, 135, 257–59; in photography, 71–72, 135–36, 206, 261, 313, 341; soccer and, 85–86. *See also* Africans; enslavement; Law 70 of 1993; racial patterns

agrarian reform, 200, 236–41, 344, 363, 373, 388, 563–64, 592. *See also* INCODER; INCORA

agriculture: Afro-Colombian communities' traditional practices of, 73, 576–77; in colonial era, 177–78, 448; development efforts and, 298, 563–64, 571, 594–97; for export,

174, 563, 576; internally displaced people and, 70, 232–35, 239; in left-wing rhetoric, 373–74, 388; among Muisca people, 27; in nineteenth century, 11, 40; in right-wing rhetoric, 363; subsistence and, 233–35; sustainability and, 238–40; tools of, 129, 372. *See also* agrarian reform; campesinos; landownership; *specific crops and products*

aguardiente, 59, 79, 83n4, 93–94, 338. *See also* alcohol; drunkenness

alcohol: beer, 150, 212–14, 458, 495–96; brandy, 49, 542; champagne, 131, 278, 282, 503–4, 532; *chicha*, 78–79, 83n3, 131; as lamp fuel, 225; manioc beer, 442, 445; *palma-chonta* wine, 49; within paramilitaries, 391; rum, 504; whisky, 66; wine, 442, 445, 541. See also *aguardiente*; drunkenness; *guarapo*

alférez real, 447, 449n1

Amazon region, 1–3, 9, 11–12, 18–19, 56, 60, 80; FARC strength in, 412; in fiction, 44–55; US combat training in, 569. *See also* Amazon River; War with Peru

Amazon River, 11; metaphorical reference to, 528; Peruvian border conflict along, 56, 59–61. *See also* Amazon region

Andean regions, 1, 11, 22–33, 40–43, 182–88, 253–56, 266–70, 454; campesinos in, 210–14, 355–59; in colonial era and before, 100–102, 243, 326–27, 437–43; in fiction, 266–71, 347–54, 538; indigenous people in, 243, 284–92. *See also specific departments, towns, and cities*

anticommunism, 4, 372, 465, 562, 588; Camilo Torres Restrepo's rejection of, 142. *See also* Communist Party of Colombia; paramilitaries

anti-imperialism, 142–43, 283, 368, 371–76, 474–76, 478–81, 551–55

170, 192, 411; of guerrilla militants, 368, 428; by guerrillas, 368–69, 412; homophobic, 312; of human rights advocates, 169; military associated with, 168, 469, 481; Pablo Escobar's responsibility for, 401–2, 404, 427; by paramilitaries, 391, 397–98, 420, 422–23, 566, 573; of Patriotic Union activists, 428; per capita rate of, 5; of Protestant pastors, 157; of Rafael Uribe Uribe, 123; Spanish Conquest described as, 292; of unionists, 506–9; used metaphorically, 114, 192, 286, 288, 292, 553. *See also* armed conflict; assassinations; *magnicidios*; Violencia, La

Murillo Bejarano, Diego ("don Berna"), 398, 400–407

music: *bailable* genre of, 81; commercialization of, 81, 173; cultural syncretism and, 75–81; "national" style of, 80; politicized, 34, 36–39, 82, 318–21; in provinces, 147–49, 174; punk genre and, 82; rap genre of, 318–21; religious, 78; salsa genre of, 36–29; Shakira Isabel Mebarak Ripoll and, 544; *vallenato* genre of, 81–82, 147. *See also* Afro-Colombians: musical traditions of; dance traditions; indigenous people: musical traditions and

Mutis, Álvaro, 535

Mutis, José Celestino, 177, 410, 517–18

narco-traffickers. *See* drug traffickers

Nare River, 207

Nasa (Paez) people, 168–69, 284–92

National Front (Frente Nacional), 4, 241, 494, 562, 563; criticism of, 360–66, 368; martial law and, 377

national identity, 1–3, 9, 12, 75, 530; biodiversity, 3; Catholicism and, 150; coffee and, 483; Constitution of 1991 and, 69, 98; emigration and, 75, 88–95, 511; in fiction, 522–43; geography and, 3, 9, 12, 494; historical writing and, 175, 325; in imagery, 211, 378, 494; islanders' alienation from, 62–64; "Latino" identity and, 551–55; music and, 75, 80–83, 147; names used for the nation, 328, 511; rurality and, 173–74, 183; soccer and, 9, 75, 84–87, 89; War with Peru and, 56. *See also* nationalism; racial patterns

nationalism: Comunero revolt as symbolic of, 40, 183; in drug traffickers' rhetoric, 384–86; Gaitanismo and, 343–46; in guer-

rilla rhetoric, 373–76; in Independence era, 79, 186, 328, 339–42; industrialists and, 496, 497; infrastructure and, 40–43; *llaneros* as symbolic of, 57; of Marco Fidel Suárez, 547–48, 550; in music, 81; natural beauty and, 3, 518; as sinister, 557. *See also* anti-imperialism

National University of Colombia, 141, 556; student protests at, 557

natural resources, 3, 40, 238–39, 450, 485, 576; Afro-Colombians and, 73, 164–65; as biodiversity, 12, 13, 416; collective landownership and, 73, 587–88; in fiction, 526; in guerrilla rhetoric, 373; indigenous people and, 588–89. *See also* coal; forests; gold; petroleum; platinum; rubber

Navarro Wolff, Antonio, 361, 428, 433. *See also* M-19

Neiva, 30–31, 289, 475

Nestlé, 63, 506–9

New Kingdom of Granada, as colonial-era name for Colombia, 23, 104, 176, 325, 438

Nicaragua, 63, 368

Norway, as guarantor of peace negotiations, 512, 593–94, 598

OAS (Organization of American States): drug reform and, 582; Inter-American Human Rights Commission of, 507; Inter-American Human Rights Court of, 369, 428–31; Pan-American Union as, 559; peace negotiations and, 428; Punta del Este meeting of, 561

Obeso, Candelario, 1, 173–74, 196–99

Obregón, Alejandro, 557–58

Ochoa Restrepo, Fabio and Jorge, 387, 391, 394, 401

oil. *See* petroleum

Opón region, 23, 141, 541

Orinoco River, 11, 44, 437, 518–19, 521

Ospina Pérez, Mariano, 129–30, 344, 353, 403

Pacific lowlands region, 1, 9, 12; cultural practices of, 162–65; drug trade and, 505; foreign mining firm in, 485–94; Law 70 of 1993 and, 69–74; music and, 77, 79; in photography, 71–72, 167; snakes in, as threat to indigenous people and black people, 518; violence in, 167, 232–35. *See also* Chocó; Panama